Advanced Qt Programming

Advanced Qt Programming

Creating Great Software with C++ and Qt 4

Mark Summerfield

♦♦ Addison-Wesley

Upper Saddle River, NJ · Boston · Indianapolis · San Francisco
New York · Toronto · Montreal · London · Munich · Paris · Madrid
Capetown · Sydney · Tokyo · Singapore · Mexico City

The publisher offers excellent discounts on this book when ordered in quantity for bulk purchases or special sales, which may include electronic versions and/or custom covers and content particular to your business, training goals, marketing focus, and branding interests. For more information, please contact:

> U.S. Corporate and Government Sales
> (800) 382-3419
> corpsales@pearsontechgroup.com

For sales outside the United States, please contact:

> International Sales
> international@pearsoned.com

Visit us on the Web: informit.com/aw

Library of Congress Cataloging-in-Publication Data

Summerfield, Mark.
    Advanced Qt programming : creating great software with C++ and Qt 4 / Mark Summerfield.
        p. cm.
    Includes bibliographical references and index.
    ISBN 978-0-321-63590-7 (hardcover : alk. paper)
1. Qt (Electronic resource) 2. Graphical user interfaces (Computer systems) 3. C++ (Computer program language) I. Title.

    QA76.9.U83S88 2010
    005.1'13—dc22

                                 2010019289

ISBN-13: 978-0-321-63590-7
ISBN-10:   0-321-63590-6

Text printed in the United States on recycled paper at Courier in Westford, Massachusetts.
First printing, July 2010

This book is dedicated to
Anna Rebecca Paterson

Contents at a Glance

www.qtrac.eu/aqpbook.html

Contents

List of Tables

Foreword

Way back in 1991, I sat on a park bench in Trondheim, Norway, together with Haavard Nord. We were doing our non-military service together at the regional hospital there, and needed to develop software for the storage and analysis of ultrasound images. The hospital used all sorts of computers and wanted the system to work on Unix, Mac, and Windows. This was a huge challenge and we scanned the market for available class libraries that could help us. We were appalled by the quality of what we found. On that park bench we decided to come up with our own solution to the challenge.

We were young, ambitious, and naïve. Sick and tired of wasting our time finding out how to use non-intuitive tools and libraries, we set our sights on improving the situation. We wanted to change the world of software development ever so slightly. Our goal was to make life easier for software developers. To make it possible to focus on what we all know is the fun side of developing software: being creative and turning out well-written code. So, we created the first crude versions of Qt, and incorporated Trolltech a few years later.

I think we achieved at least part of our goal. Qt has had tremendous success since it was first released in 1995.

In 2008 Trolltech was acquired by Nokia and in April 2009 it was time for me to move on. After 15 years and 27 days in the company I was no longer on the inside.

The product is in good hands, and the passion and hard work of the team are the same as ever. The Trolls at Nokia are making sure that Qt continues to be the rock solid framework you expect. Lars Knoll (of kHTML—WebKit—fame) today leads almost 150 dedicated Qt engineers. Nokia has also added the LGPL as a licensing option, making Qt accessible to even more developers.

This fall I was invited by Nokia as a guest of honor at the Qt Developer Days in Munich, Germany. This user conference—which also takes place in the U.S.—is a fantastic venue for Qt enthusiasts and has been increasing in size year by year. It was great feeling the buzz and talking to Qt users from all over Europe. I spoke to many developers who told me that Qt makes a real difference in their software work. That makes an old hacker feel good.

Qt as a good tool and class library is only half the story behind its success. You also need good documentation, tutorials, and books. After all, the goal was to make life easier for developers.

That is why I was never in doubt, back in 2003. I was President of Trolltech and Mark Summerfield, the head of documentation, came into my office. He wanted to write a book about Qt together with Jasmin Blanchette. A really good book, written by someone with intimate knowledge of the product and with a passion for explaining things clearly and intuitively. Who was better fit for the task than the head of Qt documentation, together with one of the best Qt developers?

The end result was a great book about Qt, which has since been updated and expanded.

Mark has now completed another important project.

A good book on advanced Qt programming has been missing in the arsenal of Qt programmers. I'm very happy that Mark has written one. He is a fantastic technical writer with all the necessary background to write authoritatively about Qt programming. His focus on detail and ability to express himself clearly and intuitively have always impressed me. In other words: You are in for a treat!

You are holding in your hands (or reading on-screen) an excellent opportunity to expand on your knowledge of all the cool stuff you can do with Qt.

Happy programming!

Eirik Chambe-Eng
The southern Alps, France
December 24, 2009

Introduction

For some time I have wanted to write a Qt book that covered topics that were too advanced for *C++ GUI Programming with Qt 4*,[*] even though that book itself has proved quite challenging for some readers. There is also some specialized material—not all of it difficult—that I wanted to cover that simply does not belong in a first book on Qt programming. Furthermore, in view of the sheer size of Qt, no one book can possibly do justice to all that it offers, so there was clearly room for the presentation of new material.

What I've done in this book is to take a selection of modules and classes from a variety of areas and shown how to make good use of them. The topics chosen reflect both my own interests and also those that seem to result in the most discussion on the qt-interest mailing list. Some of the topics are not covered in any other book, while other topics cover more familiar ground—for example, model/view programming. In all cases, I have tried to provide more comprehensive coverage than is available elsewhere.

So the purposes of this book are to help Qt programmers deepen and broaden their Qt knowledge and to increase the repertoire of what they can achieve using Qt. The "advanced" aspect often refers more to what you will be able to achieve than to the means of achieving it. This is because—as always—Qt insulates us as far as possible from irrelevant detail and underlying complexity to provide easy-to-use APIs that we can use simply and directly to great effect. For example, we will see how to create a music player without having to know anything about how things work under the hood; we will need to know only the high-level API that Qt provides. On the other hand, even using the high-level *QtConcurrent* module, the coverage of threading is necessarily challenging.

This book assumes that readers have a basic competence in C++ programming, and at least know how to create basic Qt applications—for example, having read a good Qt 4 book, and having had some practical experience. Readers are also assumed to be familiar with Qt's reference documentation, at least as far as being able to navigate it to look up the APIs of classes of interest. In addition, some chapters assume some basic topic-specific knowledge—for example, Chapter 1 assumes some knowledge of JavaScript and web programming, and the threading chapters assume a basic understanding of threading and Qt's threading classes. All these assumptions mean that this book can avoid ex-

---

[*] *C++ GUI Programming with Qt 4, Second Edition*, by Jasmin Blanchette and this author, ISBN 0132354160.

plaining many details and classes that are already familiar to Qt programmers, such as using layouts, creating actions, connecting signals and slots, and so on, leaving the book free to focus on the less familiar material.

Of course, no single volume book can realistically do justice to Qt's more than 700 public classes—almost 800 in Qt 4.6—and its much more than one million words of documentation, so no attempt is made to do so here. Instead this book provides explanations and examples of how to use some of Qt's most powerful features, complementing the reference documentation rather than duplicating it.

The book's chapters have been designed to be as self-contained as possible, so it is not necessary to read the book from beginning to end in chapter order. To support this, where particular techniques are used in more than one chapter, the explanation is given in just one place and cross-references are given elsewhere. Nonetheless, if you plan to read odd chapters out of order, I recommend that you at least do an initial skim read of the entire book, since chapters and sections devoted to one particular topic may of necessity have material relating to other topics. Also, I have tried to include lots of small details from Qt's API throughout, to make the book's content richer, and to show as many features as possible in context, so useful information appears throughout.

As with all my previous books, the quoted code snippets are of "live code", that is, the code was automatically extracted from the examples' source files and directly embedded in the PDF that went to the publisher—so there are no cut and paste errors, and the code works. The examples are available from www.qtrac.eu/aqpbook.html and are licensed under the GPL (GNU General Public License version 3). The book presents more than twenty-five examples spread over more than 150 .hpp and .cpp files, and amounting to well over 20 000 lines of code. Although all of the most important pieces of code are quoted and explained in the book, there are numerous small details that there isn't space to cover in the book itself, so I recommend downloading the examples and at least reading the source code of those examples that are in your areas of particular interest. In addition to the examples, some modules containing commonly used functionality are also provided. These all use the AQP namespace to make them easy to reuse, and they are all introduced in the first couple of chapters, and then used throughout the book.

All the examples—except for those in the last chapter which use Qt 4.6-specific features—have been tested with Qt 4.5 and Qt 4.6 on Linux, Mac OS X, and Windows. Applications built using Qt 4.5 will run unchanged with Qt 4.6, and later Qt 4.x versions, because Qt maintains backward compatibility between minor releases. However, where there are differences between the two Qt versions, the book shows and explains the Qt 4.6-specific approach, while the source code uses #if QT_VERSION so that the code compiles with either version with the best practices used for each. A few examples may work with earlier Qt 4.x versions, particularly Qt 4.4, and some examples could be backported to an earlier Qt version—however, the focus of this book is purely on Qt 4.5 and Qt 4.6, so there is no explicit coverage of backporting.

The book shows best Qt 4.6 practices, and despite Qt 4.6's numerous new features compared with Qt 4.5, this makes few differences to the code. One trivial difference is that Qt 4.6 has a shortcut for the "quit" action and Qt 4.5 hasn't; the source code uses the shortcut for Qt 4.6 and has equivalent code for Qt 4.5 by using #if QT_VERSION. A much more important difference is that Qt 4.6 introduced the QGraphicsObject class and also changed the behavior of graphics items when it comes to communicating geometry changes. We explain the differences in a sidebar and show the Qt 4.6 approach in the book's code snippets, but in the source code, #if QT_VERSION is used to show how to do the same things using Qt 4.6 and Qt 4.5 or earlier, and using the best approach for both. In the book's last chapter, Qt 4.6-specific features are shown, with two out of the three examples covered being conversions of examples presented earlier, and that make use of the Qt 4.6 animation and state machine frameworks. Modifying earlier examples makes it easier to see how to go from the traditional Qt approach to using the new frameworks.

The next version of Qt—Qt 4.7—will focus on stability, speed, and apart from the new Qt Quick technology (which provides a means of creating GUIs declaratively using a JavaScript-like language), will introduce fewer new features than in previous releases. Nonetheless, despite the huge ongoing development effort that is being put into Qt, and its ever increasing scope, this book should serve as a useful resource for learning about and using important Qt technologies in the Qt 4.*x* series, especially for Qt 4.5, Qt 4.6, and later versions, for some years to come.

Acknowledgements

My first acknowledgement is of my friend Trenton Schulz, an ex-senior software engineer at Nokia's Qt Development Frameworks (formerly Trolltech) who is now a research scientist at the Norwegian Computing Center. Trenton has proved to be a reliable, insightful, and challenging reviewer, whose careful reading, high standards, and numerous suggestions have considerably helped to improve this book.

My next acknowledgement is of another friend, Jasmin Blanchette, also an ex-senior software engineer at Qt Development Frameworks, coauthor with me of the *C++ GUI Programming with Qt 4* book, and now researching for a PhD at the Technische Universität München. We both came up with the idea for this book some time ago, and it is only due to pressure of work that he has been an excellent—and demanding—reviewer, rather than coauthor.

I would also like to thank many people who work for (or worked for) Qt Development Frameworks who read portions of the book and provided useful feedback, or who answered technical questions, or both. These include Andreas Aardal Hanssen (who gave particularly excellent feedback and suggestions regarding the graphics/view chapters, and who drafted the off-screen rendering sidebar for me), Andy Shaw, Bjørn Erik Nilsen, David Boddie, Henrik Hartz, Kavindra Devi Palaraja, Rainer Schmid (now at *froglogic*), Simon Hausmann, Thierry Bastian, and Volker Hilsheimer.

The Italian software company www.develer.com was kind enough to provide me with free repository hosting to aid my peace of mind over the long process of writing the book. And several of their developers gave me useful feedback, particularly on some of the examples in the early chapters. I'm especially thankful to Gianni Valdambrini, Giovanni Bajo, Lorenzo Mancini (who set up the repository for me), and Tommaso Massimi.

A special thank you to rough-cut reader Alexey Smirnov who spotted some errors and encouraged me to add support for network proxies to some of the networking examples.

I also want to thank *froglogic*'s founders, Reginald Stadlbauer and Harri Porten—the part-time consultancy work I do for them has helped fund the time to write this book, as well as introducing me to some programming technologies and ideas that were new to me. They've also turned me into a big fan of their GUI application testing tool, *Squish*.

My friend Ben Thompson also deserves thanks—for reminding me of certain mathematical concepts that I'd forgotten, and especially for his patience in explaining them to me until I understood them again.

This book (and some of my others) would not have been possible without Qt. So I'm very grateful to Eirik Chambe-Eng and Haavard Nord for creating Qt—and especially to Eirik for allowing me to write my first book as part of my daily work at Trolltech, and for taking the time and care to write the foreword to this book.

Special thanks to my editor, Debra Williams Cauley, both for quite independently suggesting that I write this book in the first place, and for her support and practical help as the work progressed. Also thanks to Jennifer Lindner who gave useful input on the book's structure as well as other feedback that I incorporated. Thanks also to Anna Popick, who managed the production process so well, and to the proofreader, Barbara Wood, who did such fine work.

I also want to thank my wife, Andrea, who experiences all the ups and downs of writing along with me, for her enduring love and support.

1

Hybrid Desktop/Internet Applications

The apparent ubiquity of the "computing cloud", the ready availability of web-enabled mobile phones and small form-factor netbook and smartbook computers—not to mention the Google Doc's file store—and the zero-deployment costs of web-based applications might lead us to believe that desktop applications are dinosaurs that don't yet know they're extinct.

But before we abandon C++ and Qt and switch to web programming and the subtle pleasures of JavaScript and HTML, it is worth reflecting on just some of the advantages that desktop applications can provide.

- *Availability*—outside of specialist mission-critical areas we can be sure that on rare (and always inconvenient) occasions the Internet will be unavailable—due to network failures, ISP errors, etc.—and web applications will be useless.*

- *Resource Access*—a desktop application has full access to the user's computer with none of the necessary security restrictions that limit the capabilities of web-based applications.

- *Look and Feel*—a desktop application doesn't have a redundant (and confusing) browser menu bar and toolbar in addition to its own menu bar and toolbars; it has its own keyboard shortcuts with no risk of conflict with those used by a browser; and it has exactly the look and feel it was programmed to have rather than one that varies from browser to browser.

- *Custom Widgets*—a desktop application can present the user with custom widgets specifically dedicated to the task at hand, and can provide a level of usability that web applications cannot match.

---

*See, for example, `opencloudcomputing.info/trends/cloud-computing-downtime` or the Cloud Computing Incidents Database.

Ideally we would like to have all the benefits of desktop applications, and at the same time enjoy all the advantages of Internet access when it is available. Thanks to Qt's *QtWebKit* module, introduced with Qt 4.4, this can be achieved, since *QtWebKit* allows us to create hybrid desktop/Internet applications that can work both offline and online.

The main disadvantage compared with web-based applications is in the area of deployment—the Qt application must be available on the user's computer. In cases where the deployment effort or bandwidth utilization must be minimized there are several approaches that can be taken. For example, we can put a lot of application functionality into relatively small plugins that can be updated independently. Or we could use application scripting to provide much of the application's functionality using the *QtScript* module for JavaScript (ECMAScript)—or a third-party module if we want to use a different scripting language—and just update or add individual scripts as necessary. Or we could put as much functionality as possible into the server and into web page scripts, thereby greatly reducing the number of times we need to update the client.

In this chapter we will focus on key aspects of Qt's support for hybrid applications. In the first section we will use the convenient QNetworkAccessManager class introduced in Qt 4.4, to create Internet-aware widgets. In the second section we will make use of the *QtWebKit* module, starting by developing a generic web browser component—a surprisingly easy task thanks to the functionality provided by the *QtWebKit* module. We will then make use of the generic web browser component—for example, to create a web site-specific application—and use the *QtWebKit* module to access the DOM (Document Object Model) of web pages downloaded behind the scenes so that we can extract information from them for further processing. And then we will see how to embed Qt widgets—including our own custom widgets—into web pages, to provide functionality that is not available using the standard HTML widgets.

Internet-Aware Widgets

Our definition of an Internet-aware widget is a widget that automatically retrieves data from the Internet, either as a one-off event when it is constructed, or at regular intervals.

The easiest way to create an Internet-aware widget is to create a widget subclass that makes use of a QNetworkAccessManager object. These objects are capable of performing HTTP (and HTTPS) HEAD, POST, GET, and PUT requests, and also of handling cookies (using QNetworkCookieJar) and authentication (using QAuthenticator).

In this section we will look at an example that uses one QNetworkAccessManager to read data from the Internet at timed intervals, and another QNetworkAccess-Manager that is used to download images on demand. This should be sufficient

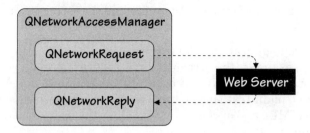

Figure 1.1 *A QNetworkAccessManager in communication with a web site*

to give a flavor of how QNetworkAccessManagers are used. Figure 1.1 illustrates the relationship between a QNetworkAccessManager and an external web site. Note that since QNetworkAccessManager is part of Qt's *QtNetwork* module, any application that uses it must include the line QT += network in its .pro file.

This section's example is a taskbar tray icon application. Such applications are typically used for frequently used controls such as volume controls, or to provide status information such as memory usage or the current date and time. In this section we will develop the Weather Tray Icon application (weathertrayicon). This application shows an icon corresponding to the current weather conditions at a specified U.S. airport with both the icon and the data retrieved from the U.S. National Weather Service (www.weather.gov).

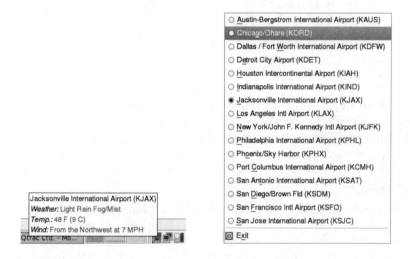

Figure 1.2 *The Weather Tray Icon application and its context menu*

Figure 1.2's left-hand screenshot shows the Weather Tray Icon application and a tooltip—the icon is under the bottom-right corner of the tooltip. The figure's right-hand screenshot shows the application's context menu. Once an hour the application downloads the weather data and the corresponding icon for the chosen airport's weather conditions and updates itself accordingly.

Taskbar tray icon applications like this work on all of Qt's supported desktop platforms. For example, the screenshots in Figure 1.2 were taken on Linux running Fedora with the GNOME desktop. On Windows and Mac OS X the tooltip would be plain text since Qt tooltips on those platforms don't support Qt rich text (HTML); and of course on Mac OS X the icon appears in the menu bar as we would expect.

When reviewing most of the book's examples we won't usually show the main() functions because they are almost all simple and standard. But in this case there are a couple of important deviations from the norm, so we will show the Weather Tray Icon application's main() function.

```
int main(int argc, char *argv[])
{
    QApplication app(argc, argv);
    app.setApplicationName(app.translate("main",
                                     "Weather Tray Icon"));
    app.setOrganizationName("Qtrac Ltd.");
    app.setOrganizationDomain("qtrac.eu");
    app.setQuitOnLastWindowClosed(false);
    if (int error = enableNetworkProxying())
        return error;

    WeatherTrayIcon weatherTrayIcon;
    weatherTrayIcon.show();
    return app.exec();
}
```

The function starts in the standard Qt way with the creation of a QApplication object. We set the application's name, which we can later use—for example, for dialog titles—accessing it with QApplication::applicationName(), and we also set the organization's name and domain which means that we can create QSettings objects whenever we want without having to bother giving them any arguments.

There are two unusual aspects to this function. The first is that we have told Qt not to close the application when the last window is closed. This is because normally a tray icon application has no window (it just has a tray icon), and any windows it does use are normally transient (e.g., a tooltip or a context menu), and their closure should not implicitly cause application termination.

The second unusual aspect is the call to a custom enableNetworkProxying() function. This function is discussed in the "Supporting Network Proxying" sidebar (➤ 9). If the function returns a nonzero error code it signifies that an error occurred in which case we return the error code and terminate the application.

Supporting Network Proxying

For machines that have direct connections to the Internet (e.g., using a broadband modem or router), the networking examples presented in this chapter should work as is. However, for machines that are on firewalled networks—typically corporate networks—the examples may fail to reach the Internet. Most firewalled networks provide some kind of proxy server through which Internet connections can be made. Qt provides support for such proxies, so we have added support for proxying to the browserwindow, nyrbviewer, rsspanel, and weathertrayicon examples, by having them call a custom enableNetworkProxying() function inside their main() function.

The enableNetworkProxying() function uses the AQP::OptionParser (supplied with the book's examples in directory option_parser and using the AQP namespace) to parse the command line arguments used to set up proxying. The command line options supported by the proxying-enabled applications are:

```
-h  --help              show this information and terminate
-H  --host=STRING       hostname, e.g., www.example.com
-P  --password=STRING   password
-p  --port=INTEGER      port number, e.g., 1080
-t  --type=STRING       (http, socks5; default socks5) proxy type
-u  --username=STRING   username
```

The proxying is set up in the enableNetworkProxying() function only if a hostname is specified. Here is the code; the parser is of type AQP::OptionParser.

```
if (parser.hasValue("host")) {
    QNetworkProxy proxy;
    proxy.setType(parser.string("type") == "socks5"
            ? QNetworkProxy::Socks5Proxy
            : QNetworkProxy::HttpProxy);
    proxy.setHostName(parser.string("host"));
    if (parser.hasValue("port"))
        proxy.setPort(parser.integer("port"));
    if (parser.hasValue("username"))
        proxy.setUser(parser.string("username"));
    if (parser.hasValue("password"))
        proxy.setPassword(parser.string("password"));
    QNetworkProxy::setApplicationProxy(proxy);
}
```

If a host is specified, proxying is set up using the given host, the default or given proxy type, and any other options the user has given. This sets up global proxying for the whole application. It is also possible to set up per-socket proxying using QAbstractSocket::setProxy().

The weather data is provided in various formats, but we have chosen to access it in XML format. The format itself is very simple, consisting essentially of a list of key–value pairs where the key is a tag name and the value is the text between the opening and closing tags. For example:

```
<weather>Fair</weather>
<temperature_string>49 F (9 C)</temperature_string>
<temp_f>49</temp_f>
<temp_c>9</temp_c>
<wind_string>From the Northeast at 5 MPH</wind_string>
<visibility_mi>9.00</visibility_mi>
<icon_url_base>http://weather.gov/weather/images/fcicons/</icon_url_base>
<icon_url_name>nskc.jpg</icon_url_name>
```

When the application first starts it sets its airport to the one that was last set by the user, or to a default airport the first time it is run. It then uses a QNetwork-AccessManager to retrieve the weather data. Two elements of the data are a URL and a filename for an icon that corresponds to the prevailing weather conditions at the airport. The application uses a second QNetworkAccessManager to retrieve the icon and sets this as the icon shown in the taskbar tray. In fact, the application caches icons to economize on bandwidth, as we will see shortly.

```
class WeatherTrayIcon : public QSystemTrayIcon
{
    Q_OBJECT

public:
    explicit WeatherTrayIcon();

private slots:
    void requestXml();
    void readXml(QNetworkReply *reply);
    void readIcon(QNetworkReply *reply);
    void setAirport(QAction *action);

private:
    ...
    QMenu menu;
    QNetworkAccessManager *networkXmlAccess;
    QNetworkAccessManager *networkIconAccess;
    QString airport;
    QCache<QUrl, QIcon> iconCache;
    int retryDelaySec;
};
```

We will show and explain all the methods in a moment—including the private ones not shown—but now we'll comment on some of the private member data.

The airport string holds the current airport, for example, "Chicago/Ohare (KORD)". The iconCache has QUrl keys and *pointers* to QIcon values. We will cover the others when we discuss the methods they are used in.

The QCache class caches items using a "cost" scheme. The cache's maximum cost defaults to 100—the sum of item costs is always less than or equal to the maximum. By default each item has a cost of 1, so unless we change the maximum or set our own item costs the cache will hold up to 100 items. When a new item is added, if the item's cost makes the sum of costs exceed the maximum cost, one or more of the least recently accessed items are removed until the sum of costs is less than or equal to the maximum.

Behind the scenes QCache uses a QHash to provide very fast lookup by key. However, out of the box, QHash cannot store QUrls as keys because Qt does not provide a qHash(QUrl) function.* This is easy to remedy with a one-liner:

```
inline uint qHash(const QUrl &url) { return qHash(url.toString()); }
```

Here we've simply passed the work on to the built-in qHash(QString) function.

We are now ready to review the methods, starting with the constructor.

```
WeatherTrayIcon::WeatherTrayIcon()
    : QSystemTrayIcon(), retryDelaySec(1)
{
    setIcon(QIcon(":/rss.png"));
    createContextMenu();

    networkXmlAccess = new QNetworkAccessManager(this);
    networkIconAccess = new QNetworkAccessManager(this);
    connect(networkXmlAccess, SIGNAL(finished(QNetworkReply*)),
            this, SLOT(readXml(QNetworkReply*)));
    connect(networkIconAccess, SIGNAL(finished(QNetworkReply*)),
            this, SLOT(readIcon(QNetworkReply*)));

    QTimer::singleShot(0, this, SLOT(requestXml()));
}
```

We give the application an initial icon to use while waiting for the first weather icon to be downloaded. Then we create a context menu with actions for changing the airport and for terminating the application.

Most of the constructor is devoted to setting up the Internet access by creating two QNetworkAccessManagers. One is used to fetch the weather data and the other to fetch the icon associated with the current weather conditions. We use separate network access managers so that they can work independently of

---

*Qt 4.7 is scheduled to provide a qHash(QUrl) function.

each other, and in both cases we create a single signal–slot connection since all we are interested in is when each download is finished.

Finally, we call the `requestXml()` slot using a single shot timer. This method makes use of the `networkXmlAccess` network access manager to fetch the weather data for the current airport.

We could have simply called `requestXml()` directly, but as a matter of style we prefer to restrict ourselves to calling "create" methods that contribute to the construction of an object in constructors, and to call any post-construction initializing method using a single shot timer. This ensures that by the time the initializing method is called, the object is fully constructed. This means that the initializing method can access any member variable or method— something that is not guaranteed to be safe during construction.

Before we look at the `requestXml()` slot, we'll briefly look at how the context menu is created, to see how the airport whose details must be downloaded can be set by the user.

```
void WeatherTrayIcon::createContextMenu()
{
    QStringList airports;
    airports << "Austin-Bergstrom International Airport (KAUS)"
                ...
             << "San Jose International Airport (KSJC)";
    QSettings settings;
    airport = settings.value("airport", QVariant(airports.at(0)))
                         .toString();

    QActionGroup *group = new QActionGroup(this);
    foreach (const QString &anAirport, airports) {
        QAction *action = menu.addAction(anAirport);
        group->addAction(action);
        action->setCheckable(true);
        action->setChecked(anAirport == airport);
        action->setData(anAirport);
    }
    connect(group, SIGNAL(triggered(QAction*)),
            this, SLOT(setAirport(QAction*)));
    menu.addSeparator();
    menu.addAction(QIcon(":/exit.png"), tr("E&xit"), qApp,
                SLOT(quit()));
    AQP::accelerateMenu(&menu);
    setContextMenu(&menu);
}
```

Here we have used a hard-coded list of airport names, but we could just as easily have read them from a file or resource. (If we wanted to list all the

U.S. airports we could easily group them—for example, by having states as top-level menu items, and airports as submenu items.) We use QSettings to set the current airport, defaulting to the first one in the list the first time the application is run.

For each airport we create a QAction and check the one that matches the current airport. Each airport action is added to a QActionGroup. By default a QActionGroup has its exclusive property set to true; this ensures that its actions have radio button rather than checkbox check marks and that only one airport is ever checked at any one time.

We also add an exit action and give it a specific keyboard accelerator. Then we call AQP::accelerateMenu() to provide keyboard accelerators for as many airports as possible, and then set the menu we have created as the application's context menu. If the application is being built on Mac OS X the call to AQP::accelerateMenu() normally has no effect, since Mac OS X doesn't support accelerators. See the "Keyboard Accelerators" sidebar for more about automatically setting keyboard accelerators (➤ 15).

We need to connect each action with the setAirport() slot and to parameterize each slot invocation in some way so that the slot knows which airport has been chosen. An easy way to do this is to call QObject::sender() inside the slot to see which action called it, and then to extract the action's text to determine the chosen airport. An alternative is to use a QSignalMapper. But in this case there is an even easier solution—instead of connecting each of the airport QActions we connect the QActionGroup instead. The QActionGroup::triggered() signal carries the relevant QAction as its parameter.

```
void WeatherTrayIcon::requestXml()
{
    QString airportId = airport.right(6);
    if (airportId.startsWith("(") && airportId.endsWith(")")) {
        QString url = QString("http://www.weather.gov/xml/"
                "current_obs/%1.xml").arg(airportId.mid(1, 4));
        networkXmlAccess->get(QNetworkRequest(QUrl(url)));
    }
}
```

The XML weather data for a given airport is in a file whose name matches the airport's four letter code. We have included this code in parentheses at the end of each airport's name, and use basic QString methods to extract it. Once we have the URL we need we use the XML network access manager to do a GET request on it. When a request is made a pointer to the QNetworkReply object that will receive the results is returned. These objects emit signals indicating progress, for example, downloadProgress() and uploadProgress(), and when the request finishes, the reply object issues a finished() signal.

The network manager that initiated the request also emits a finished() signal, and since we are not concerned with monitoring progress this is the only signal we connected to—and the reason why we ignored the QNetworkAccessManager::get() method's return value. Once the download is finished (successfully or not), the signal–slot connection shown earlier ensures that the readXml() method is called with a pointer to the reply object as its sole argument.

```cpp
void WeatherTrayIcon::readXml(QNetworkReply *reply)
{
    if (reply->error() != QNetworkReply::NoError) {
        setToolTip(tr("Failed to retrieve weather data:\n%1")
                    .arg(reply->errorString()));
        QTimer::singleShot(retryDelaySec * 1000,
                            this, SLOT(requestXml()));
        retryDelaySec <<= 1;
        if (retryDelaySec > 60 * 60)
            retryDelaySec = 1;
        return;
    }
    retryDelaySec = 1;
    QDomDocument document;
    if (document.setContent(reply))
        populateToolTip(&document);
    QTimer::singleShot(60 * 60 * 1000, this, SLOT(requestXml()));
}
```

If the request failed we put the error message in the tray icon's tooltip and try again later after a delay. The delay is held in the private retryDelaySec variable and is initialized to 1. (We must multiply by 1 000 because QTimer::singleShot() takes a timeout in milliseconds.) On each successive failure we double the delay interval—left shifting an integer by one bit doubles its value. So after a second failure we try again after two seconds, then after four seconds, and so on. At this rate, if we have a dozen failures the interval will be over an hour, in which case we reset it to start again at one second.

We vary the retry interval each time to avoid being mistaken for a denial of service attack and to avoid getting into an "unlucky" request/failure cycle.

As soon as the request succeeds and we have reset retryDelaySec back to 1, we parse the XML data. The QNetworkReply is a QIODevice subclass, so in addition to being able to emit network progress signals, it can also emit, for example, the readyRead() signal. And like any other QIODevice such as a file, we can read data from it, which by default is returned in a QByteArray. The QDomDocument::setContent() method can read XML from a QByteArray, a QString, or from a QIODevice, so we are able to directly pass it the QNetworkReply for parsing.

Keyboard Accelerators (for non-Mac OS X platforms)

Keyboard accelerators are important to users who are fast typists and to those who cannot—or don't want to—use the mouse. They are Alt+*x* key sequences (where *x* is usually a letter or digit) that the user can press to pull down a menu from the menu bar (e.g., Alt+F for the File menu). Once a menu appears, one of its menu options can be chosen by pressing its underlined letter or digit alone, so to create a new file the user would press Alt+F, N.

In dialogs accelerators are used to switch the keyboard focus to particular widgets—for example, a label that appears as Total: has a keyboard accelerator of Alt+T, and pressing this would be expected to move the keyboard focus to the label's buddy widget. Similarly, checkboxes and radio buttons often have accelerators and when pressed the accelerator toggles the checkbox's or radio button's state.

It is common to write accelerators using uppercase letters (e.g., Alt+E) both for display and in code. (Keyboard accelerators are distinct from keyboard shortcuts which are arbitrary key sequences associated with particular actions, for example, Ctrl+N to create a new file.)

For short menus and for dialogs that only contain a few widgets, setting accelerators manually (by including an & in the texts) is quite easy. But once we get to more than about fifteen menu items or widgets it becomes increasingly difficult to work out what the optimal accelerators should be. The ideal solution would be to get the computer to work out the accelerators for us, and that is the approach taken in this book.

In the aqp directory the alt_key.{hpp,cpp} module provides an API, and the kuhn_munkres.{hpp,cpp} module provides an algorithm that instantly computes optimal results, easily outperforming all the naïve algorithms. For example, to provide accelerators for a main window's menus we can write this line near the end of the main window's constructor:

```
AQP::accelerateMenu(menuBar());
```

That's all that is required. The Kuhn-Munkres algorithm is used to calculate optimal accelerators and respects any items that already have accelerators—for example, if we want certain menu options or labels to have particular accelerators no matter what. For dialogs we can use an equally simple approach, writing this line at the end of a dialog's constructor:

```
AQP::accelerateWidget(this);
```

The accelerator functions don't account for hidden widgets such as those on a tab page that isn't being shown. We can still handle such cases by using one or more calls to the AQP::accelerateWidgets() function, giving it a specific list of widgets to work on each time.

If the QDomDocument::setContent() method returns true, the parse succeeded, so we populate the tooltip with the new data—a process that might involve downloading a new icon too. If the parse failed, we leave the existing tooltip as is. And at the end we set a single shot timer to repeat the process one hour later.

The QDomDocument class is part of Qt's *QtXml* module, so to be able to use it we must add the line QT += xml to the application's .pro file.

The application's flow of control, from the initial GET request on the XML network access manager, to downloading the XML and icons, and then repeating the download every hour, is illustrated by Figure 1.3.

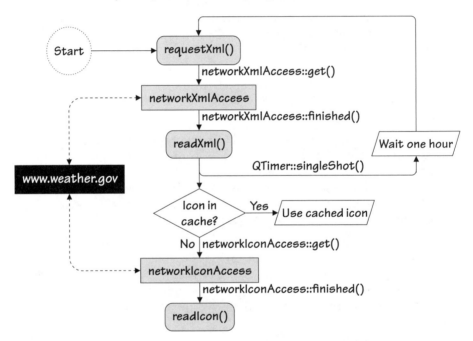

Figure 1.3 *The Weather Tray Icon application's flow of control*

For completeness, we will show the private populateToolTip() method, which we will review in three parts, followed by its two private helper methods.

```
void WeatherTrayIcon::populateToolTip(QDomDocument *document)
{
    QString toolTipText = tr("<font color=darkblue>%1</font><br>")
                             .arg(airport);
    QString weather = textForTag("weather", document);
    if (!weather.isEmpty())
        toolTipText += toolTipField("Weather", "green", weather);
    ...
```

Here we extract the text elements that we want to include in the tooltip, although we have omitted most of the code since each element follows the same (or very similar) pattern as the code shown for the "weather" element.

The private textForTag() helper method is used to retrieve the text for any given tag. This works because we know that for the weather data every tag is unique and does not contain any nested tags.

```
QString iconUrl = textForTag("icon_url_base", document);
if (!iconUrl.isEmpty()) {
    QString name = textForTag("icon_url_name", document);
    if (!name.isEmpty()) {
        iconUrl += name;
        QUrl url(iconUrl);
        QIcon *icon = iconCache.object(url);
        if (icon && !icon->isNull())
            setIcon(*icon);
        else
            networkIconAccess->get(QNetworkRequest(url));
    }
}
```

The icon that corresponds to the prevailing weather conditions is identified by two XML elements, the "icon_url_base" and the "icon_url_name". We attempt to extract both these elements' texts and to create a URL out of them. We then try to retrieve the icon from the cache using the URL as the key. The QCache::object() method returns 0 if there is no item in the cache with the corresponding key.

If we retrieved a QIcon pointer from the cache we use it—in fact we get a copy (which is cheap because Qt uses copy-on-write, and useful since QCache can delete items at any time). Otherwise we use the icon network access manager to download the icon. And if we initiate downloading an icon, the signal–slot connection set up earlier will ensure that the readIcon() slot (covered shortly) is called when the download has finished.

```
#ifndef Q_WS_X11
    toolTipText = QTextDocumentFragment::fromHtml(toolTipText)
                  .toPlainText();
#endif
    setToolTip(toolTipText);
}
```

Unfortunately, Qt rich text (HTML) tray icon tooltips are only supported on X11, so for Windows and Mac OS X systems we convert the HTML tooltip text to plain text. We do this by using the static QTextDocumentFragment::fromHtml() method to get a QTextDocumentFragment, and then using QTextDocumentFragment::

toPlainText(), to produce plain text. Using a QTextDocumentFragment is more convenient than doing the conversion by hand since not only does it convert HTML entities to the appropriate Unicode characters and strip out HTML tags, but it is also smart enough to convert
s into newlines.

```
QString WeatherTrayIcon::textForTag(const QString &tag,
                                    QDomDocument *document)
{
    QDomNodeList nodes = document->elementsByTagName(tag);
    if (!nodes.isEmpty()) {
        const QDomNode &node = nodes.item(0);
        if (!node.isNull() && node.hasChildNodes())
            return node.firstChild().nodeValue();
    }
    return QString();
}
```

Using QDomDocument is ideal for small XML files since it parses the entire file, holds all the data in memory, and provides a variety of convenient access methods.

Here, we begin by getting a list of all the QDomNodes that use the specified tag. If the list is nonempty, we retrieve the first node. In the weather data, every tag is unique, so there should only ever be one node for a given tag. In the DOM API, the text between tags is held in a child node, so it can be retrieved from a node by retrieving the node's first child, converting the child to a text node, and then retrieving its text data—for example, node.firstChild().toText().data(). Fortunately, Qt offers a shortcut—the QDomNode::nodeValue() method—which returns a node type-specific string, which in the case of text nodes is the text itself.

```
QString WeatherTrayIcon::toolTipField(const QString &name,
        const QString &htmlColor, const QString &value, bool appendBr)
{
    return QString("<i>%1:</i> <font color=\"%2\">%3</font>%4")
                    .arg(name).arg(htmlColor).arg(value)
                    .arg(appendBr ? "<br>" : "");
}
```

The private toolTipField() helper method allows us to factor out the formatting of each line of tooltip text. This slightly shortens and simplifies populateTool-Tip()'s code and also makes it easier to modify the formatting later on.

If an icon must be downloaded, once the QNetworkReply is ready, the signal–slot connection set up earlier ensures that the readIcon() slot is called. We will look at this slot in two parts.

```
void WeatherTrayIcon::readIcon(QNetworkReply *reply)
{
    QUrl redirect = reply->attribute(
            QNetworkRequest::RedirectionTargetAttribute).toUrl();
    if (redirect.isValid())
        networkIconAccess->get(QNetworkRequest(redirect));
```

This method is called when a request to download an icon has finished. We begin by checking to see if instead of the reply we are expecting we have received a redirect of some kind. If this is the case we initiate a new GET request to retrieve the icon data using the redirect's target URL. The QNetworkAccess-Manager doesn't perform redirects automatically for security reasons, but here we have chosen to trust the site. If security is a concern, we should really check the redirected URL—for example, that it is from the same domain and that it doesn't include some malicious JavaScript. In the common case, when there is no redirect in force, we will get an invalid redirect QUrl, and can proceed to read the reply's data.

```
    else {
        QByteArray ba(reply->readAll());
        QPixmap pixmap;
        if (pixmap.loadFromData(ba)) {
            QIcon *icon = new QIcon(pixmap);
            setIcon(*icon);
            iconCache.insert(reply->request().url(), icon);
        }
    }
}
```

If the reply is not a redirect then either we have the icon data or an error occurred. We read all the data that is available into a QByteArray and then feed the data to a QPixmap. If the QPixmap::loadFromData() method returns false then either the icon data was incomplete, corrupt, or in an unrecognized format, or there was a network error and no data was retrieved. In any of these cases we abandon the attempt to retrieve the icon, and the current icon remains unchanged.

If the download was successful, we convert the QPixmap into a QIcon and set the icon as the tray icon. Then we add the icon keyed by its URL to the icon cache safe in the knowledge that we will never cache more than 100 icons and that we will never needlessly download an icon that is already in the cache.

```
void WeatherTrayIcon::setAirport(QAction *action)
{
    airport = action->data().toString();
    QSettings settings;
    settings.setValue("airport", airport);
```

```
    requestXml();
}
```

This slot is called whenever the user chooses a new airport from the context menu. We retrieve the name of the airport, set this airport as the new default, and then call requestXml() to force the application to retrieve fresh weather data for the newly chosen airport.

Notice that we don't save any settings when the application terminates; instead we save the settings (in this case there is only one) whenever they are changed. This approach has the advantage that the settings are always up to date, even when the application is running or in the face of an unexpected crash, but the disadvantage that the code for saving settings could be spread all over the place, making maintenance more error-prone.

We have now finished reviewing a small application that uses the high-level and easy-to-use QNetworkAccessManager class to do basic Internet downloading. In addition to the Weather Tray Icon application, the book's examples also include the RssPanel application (rsspanel) shown in Figure 1.4.

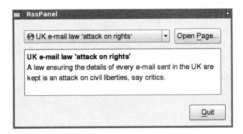

Figure 1.4 *The RssPanel application*

The RssPanel application features an Internet-aware RssComboBox that populates itself automatically from an RSS (Really Simple Syndication) feed—an XML file—given a suitable URL, and updates itself periodically. We won't review the code for this example because it is structurally very similar to the Weather Tray Icon example. However, it might provide an easier starting point for creating your own Internet-aware widgets. It also uses a QXmlStreamReader subclass to parse the RSS data it downloads, rather than the QDomDocument used by the weathertrayicon example.*

The rest of the chapter will continue the theme of retrieving data from the Internet, but using WebKit to display data (i.e., HTML pages), and to perform operations on downloaded data.

---

*Eventually, the *QtXml* module which provides Qt's DOM and SAX parsers may be phased out in favor of the much faster QXmlStreamReader and QXmlStreamWriter classes built into *QtCore*.

Using WebKit

WebKit is an open source web content rendering and editing engine that was originally created by KDE ('K' Desktop Environment) developers. WebKit is now used as the basis for many web browsers, including Google's Chrome, KDE's Konqueror, and Mac OS X's Safari, and is also used by most web-enabled mobile devices. WebKit aims to be standards compliant, and supports all the standard web technologies, including HTML5, SVG (Scalable Vector Graphics), CSS (Cascading Style Sheets—including CSS 3 Web Fonts), and JavaScript. Qt's *QtWebKit* module provides a Qt-style interface for WebKit and makes WebKit's functionality available to Qt programmers, and also provides considerable additional functionality of its own. To be able to use the module, it is essential to add the line QT += webkit to the application's .pro file.

Table 1.1 *The Main WebKit Classes*

Class	Description
QWebElement	A class for accessing and editing a QWebFrame's DOM elements with a jQuery-like API (Qt 4.6)
QWebFrame	A data object that represents a frame in a web page
QWebHistory	The history of visited links associated with a given QWebPage
QWebHistoryItem	An object that represents one visited link in a QWebHistory
QWebPage	A data object that represents a web page
QWebSettings	A data object that holds the settings used by a given QWebFrame or QWebPage
QWebView	A widget that visualizes a QWebPage

The most important *QtWebKit* classes are shown in Table 1.1, and the relationships between some of them are shown in Figure 1.5.

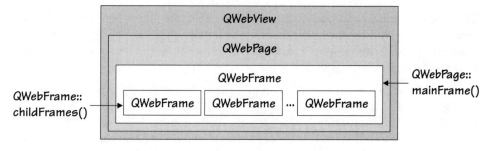

Figure 1.5 *Some QtWebKit classes in context*

Note that the only widget in *QtWebKit* is QWebView. For example, both QWebPage and the (one or more) QWebFrames it contains are data classes. Using QWebPage it is possible to download web content behind the scenes, process that content, and then reflect the results into the user interface in whatever way we choose —something we will see in this section's second subsection.

Now that we have an initial impression of what the *QtWebKit* module provides, we will look at some examples of its use. In the first subsection we will create a web browser window component. In the second subsection we will create a web site-specific application that makes use of the browser component and that reads and processes web pages behind the scenes. And in the third subsection we will show how to embed Qt widgets and custom widgets into a web page.

A Generic Web Browser Window Component

In the two following subsections we are going to use WebKit to help us develop two example hybrid desktop/Internet applications. In this subsection we will create the browser window component (browserwindow) shown in Figure 1.6 that the following examples make use of.

Figure 1.6 *The browser window component*

The browser window supports the standard browser features: forward, back, reload, cancel loading, zooming, open a given page, and the ability to return to a specific page in the browser's history. It also has a context menu and a toolbar (which can be hidden).

In addition, when a custom DEBUG symbol is defined (for example, by adding DEFINES += DEBUG in the .pro file), the browser window's context menu shows an additional option, Inspect, that when invoked launches the WebKit Web Inspector shown in Figure 1.7. This is a useful debugging tool that can provide a wide variety of information about a web page, including the page's DOM

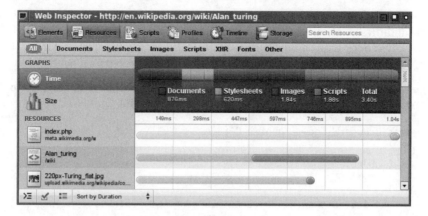

Figure 1.7 *The Web Inspector*

(Document Object Model), and the resources it uses (for example, style sheets, images, and JavaScript scripts), including their sizes and load times, and a lot more besides.

From Qt 4.6, the Web Inspector can be invoked in a more conventional way by creating a QWebInspector object, giving it a QWebPage, and then calling its show() method.

For the Web Inspector to be available (and for the Qt 4.6 QWebInspector class to work) we must switch on the QWebSettings::DeveloperExtrasEnabled web setting. We do this, and set various other settings, in the application's main() function, applying the changes to the global QWebSettings object, as this extract from main() shows.

```
    QWebSettings *webSettings = QWebSettings::globalSettings();
    webSettings->setAttribute(QWebSettings::AutoLoadImages, true);
    webSettings->setAttribute(QWebSettings::JavascriptEnabled, true);
    webSettings->setAttribute(QWebSettings::PluginsEnabled, true);
    webSettings->setAttribute(QWebSettings::ZoomTextOnly, true);
#ifdef DEBUG
    webSettings->setAttribute(QWebSettings::DeveloperExtrasEnabled,
                              true);
#endif
```

The global QWebSettings object's settings are inherited by all of the application's QWebPage and QWebView objects, although we can override them individually for every QWebPage and QWebView if we want to. The QWebSettings::ZoomTextOnly attribute was introduced in Qt 4.5, and affects the zoom factor. By setting the attribute to true we ensure that images are not zoomed (and therefore not distorted if they are pixmaps), so only the text is shrunk or enlarged when the user zooms.

At the time of this writing, the Qt documentation does not specify the web settings' defaults, so they may vary across platforms or minor Qt 4.*x* versions. We can always check what a particular setting's value is using QWebSettings::test-Attribute() which takes an attribute enum value and returns a bool.

To get an overview of the browser window's API we will look at the public and protected parts of the class definition in the header file.

```
class BrowserWindow : public QFrame
{
    Q_OBJECT

public:
    explicit BrowserWindow(const QString &url=QString(),
            QWebPage *webPage=0, QWidget *parent=0,
            Qt::WindowFlags flags=0);

    QString toHtml() const
        { return webView->page()->mainFrame()->toHtml(); }
    QString toPlainText() const
        { return webView->page()->mainFrame()->toPlainText(); }

signals:
    void loadFinished(bool ok);
    void urlChanged(const QUrl &url);

public slots:
    void load(const QString &url);
    void setHtml(const QString &html) { webView->setHtml(html); }
    void showToolBar(bool on) { toolBar->setVisible(on); }
    void enableActions(bool enable);

protected:
    void focusInEvent(QFocusEvent*) { webView->setFocus(); }
```

Most of the functionality, particularly the toolbar and context menu actions, is provided by private slots (not shown) which we will discuss as we encounter them in the following code snippets. The reimplementation of the QWidget::focusInEvent() is used to ensure that if the browser window is given the focus programmatically (by calling QWidget::setFocus() on it), the focus is passed on to the web view. The class also has some private variables (not shown) that provide access to its widgets.

Thanks to the considerable out of the box functionality provided by QWebView, the BrowserWindow class is quite small, with most of the code in the constructor and the create methods it calls. Here's the constructor.

```
BrowserWindow::BrowserWindow(const QString &url, QWebPage *webPage,
                    QWidget *parent, Qt::WindowFlags flags)
```

```
                : QFrame(parent, flags)
    {
        setFrameStyle(QFrame::Box|QFrame::Raised);

        webView = new QWebView;
        if (webPage)
            webView->setPage(webPage);
        load(url);

        createActions();
        createToolBar();
        createLayout();
        createConnections();
    }
```

We made the browser window a QFrame subclass so that we can give it a frame. This is helpful to users since web pages often contain widgets of their own (buttons, line editors, and so on), so by framing the browser window we make clear the boundary between the web page and the application in which it is embedded.

We allow the class's clients to pass in their own QWebPage if they prefer; otherwise QWebView creates a QWebPage for itself. This is useful if we want to use a QWebPage subclass—something we will see in the "Embedding Qt Widgets in Web Pages" subsection (➤ 44).

The createActions() method is slightly unusual because we only have to create a few of the actions ourselves. Here is an extract from the method which omits the creation of the zoomInAction, setUrlAction, and historyAction, since they are all created in the same way as the zoomOutAction that is shown.

```
    void BrowserWindow::createActions()
    {
        zoomOutAction = new QAction(QIcon(":/zoomout.png"),
                                    tr("Zoom Out"), this);
        zoomOutAction->setShortcuts(QKeySequence::ZoomOut);
        ...
        QList<QAction*> actions;
        actions << webView->pageAction(QWebPage::Back)
                << webView->pageAction(QWebPage::Forward)
                << webView->pageAction(QWebPage::Reload)
                << webView->pageAction(QWebPage::Stop)
                << zoomOutAction << zoomInAction << setUrlAction
                << historyAction;
#ifdef DEBUG
        actions << webView->pageAction(QWebPage::InspectElement);
#endif
        AQP::accelerateActions(actions);
```

```
        webView->addActions(actions);
        webView->setContextMenuPolicy(Qt::ActionsContextMenu);
}
```

We create a list of the actions we want the browser window to have, including the inspect action if DEBUG is set, and using QWebView's predefined actions where possible. We then use AQP::accelerateActions() to provide keyboard accelerators (i.e., underlined letters, not keyboard shortcuts such as Ctrl+X), on non-Mac OS X platforms (15 ◄). Then we simply add the actions to the QWebView and tell it to provide a context menu using these actions.

Note that we do not need to create signal–slot connections or provide slots for the actions provided by QWebView, since these are all built in.

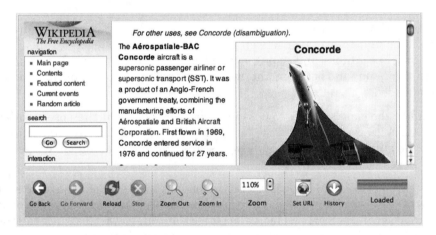

Figure 1.8 *The browser window component on Mac OS X*

We have not shown the createToolBar() method since it is mostly standard for C++/Qt applications. However, as Figure 1.8 shows—compared with Figure 1.6 (22 ◄)—the toolbar is laid out differently on Mac OS X than on other platforms. This is done because on Mac OS X it is common to have tool buttons display an icon with text beneath. And to make the entire toolbar layout consistent we put the labels for the zoom spinbox and for the progress bar beneath them rather than to their left as we did on other platforms. To achieve these differences we used #ifdefs in the code in browserwindow/browserwindow.cpp, making use of the fact that Q_WS_MAC is only defined on Mac OS X.★

The createLayout() method is small and standard, so we will skip it and move on to createConnections().

★As noted in the Introduction, all the source code is available from www.qtrac.eu/aqpbook.html.

```
void BrowserWindow::createConnections()
{
    connect(webView, SIGNAL(loadProgress(int)),
            progressBar, SLOT(setValue(int)));
    connect(webView, SIGNAL(urlChanged(const QUrl&)),
            this, SLOT(urlChange(const QUrl&)));
    connect(webView, SIGNAL(loadFinished(bool)),
            this, SLOT(loadFinish(bool)));
    connect(setUrlAction, SIGNAL(triggered()), this, SLOT(setUrl()));
    connect(historyAction, SIGNAL(triggered()),
            this, SLOT(popUpHistoryMenu()));
    connect(zoomOutAction, SIGNAL(triggered()),
            this, SLOT(zoomOut()));
    connect(zoomInAction, SIGNAL(triggered()), this, SLOT(zoomIn()));
    connect(zoomSpinBox, SIGNAL(valueChanged(int)),
            this, SLOT(setZoomFactor(int)));
}
```

We set up the first three signal–slot connections to allow us to keep track of loading progress and page changes so that we can keep the progress bar and progress label up to date. The remaining connections are for handling the actions we created ourselves, and to respond to the user interacting with the zoom spinbox.

Now that we have seen enough to have an overview of the browser window, we can review the methods used to provide its behavior.

```
void BrowserWindow::load(const QString &url)
{
    if (url.isEmpty())
        return;
    QString theUrl = url;
    if (!theUrl.contains("://"))
        theUrl.prepend("http://");
    webView->load(theUrl);
}
```

If the given URL string is empty we do nothing; otherwise we prepend "http://" as a courtesy if no scheme is specified, and tell the web view to perform the load. (We use QString rather than QUrl since it is easier to correctly add the scheme to a string than to a QUrl.)

```
void BrowserWindow::setUrl()
{
    load(QInputDialog::getText(this, tr("Set URL"), tr("&URL:")));
}
```

If the user invokes the set URL action, this method is called. If they cancel, an empty URL will be passed to the load() method which will then harmlessly do nothing.

```
void BrowserWindow::urlChange(const QUrl &url)
{
    emit urlChanged(url);
    progressLabel->setText(tr("Loading"));
}
```

Whenever the web page's URL changes (whether the user clicked a link, or used the set URL action, or used the history), this slot is called. We emit our own urlChanged() signal as a convenience to BrowserWindow users, and update the progress label to indicate that loading has commenced.

```
void BrowserWindow::loadFinish(bool ok)
{
    emit loadFinished(ok);
    progressLabel->setText(ok ? tr("Loaded") : tr("Canceled"));
}
```

When loading finishes, this slot is called with the bool ok signifying whether the load was successful. Again we emit a signal for the convenience of Browser-Window users, and again we update the progress label to reflect the current situation.

We don't have to worry about keeping the progress bar up to date since we connected the web view's loadProgress() signal to the progress bar's setValue() slot at the end of the constructor.

```
void BrowserWindow::setZoomFactor(int zoom)
{
    webView->setZoomFactor(zoom / 100.0);
}
```

If the user manipulates the zoom spinbox this slot is called and the web view's text is scaled accordingly. (If we want images to scale we must set the QWebSettings::ZoomTextOnly attribute to false.)

```
const int ZoomStepSize = 5;

void BrowserWindow::zoomOut()
{
    zoomSpinBox->setValue(zoomSpinBox->value() - ZoomStepSize);
}
```

The zoomOutAction is connected to this slot. A similar zoom-in action and slot are also present, although not shown. When these slots are invoked the setValue() calls result in the spinbox emitting a valueChanged() signal and that leads to the setZoomFactor() slot being invoked because of the signal–slot connection we saw earlier.

```
void BrowserWindow::enableActions(bool enable)
{
    foreach (QAction *action, webView->actions())
        action->setEnabled(enable);
    toolBar->setEnabled(enable);
    webView->setContextMenuPolicy(enable ? Qt::ActionsContextMenu
                                         : Qt::NoContextMenu);
}
```

In some use cases the application embedding the browser window does not want the user to be able to make use of the browser functionality beyond simply viewing and interacting with the page that is presented. This method makes it possible to disable or enable the browser window's actions.

```
const int MaxHistoryMenuItems = 20;
const int MaxMenuWidth = 300;

void BrowserWindow::popUpHistoryMenu()
{
    QFontMetrics fontMetrics(font());
    QMenu menu;
    QSet<QUrl> uniqueUrls;
    QListIterator<QWebHistoryItem> i(webView->history()->items());
    i.toBack();
    while (i.hasPrevious() &&
            uniqueUrls.count() < MaxHistoryMenuItems) {
        const QWebHistoryItem &item = i.previous();
        if (uniqueUrls.contains(item.url()))
            continue;
        uniqueUrls << item.url();
        QString title = fontMetrics.elidedText(item.title(),
                Qt::ElideRight, MaxMenuWidth);
        QAction *action = new QAction(item.icon(), title, &menu);
        action->setData(item.url());
        menu.addAction(action);
    }
    AQP::accelerateMenu(&menu);
    if (QAction *action = menu.exec(QCursor::pos()))
        webView->load(action->data().toUrl());
}
```

When this method is invoked it pops up a menu whose items correspond to the web pages the user has visited. The link data is retrieved from the QWebView's

QWebHistory. This holds a list of QWebHistoryItems, each of which has the web page's title, the page's URL, the page's icon—Qt provides a default icon if one isn't available from the web page's server—and a few other pieces of information.

The menu presents the links in reverse order, that is, from most recently visited at the top to least recently visited at the bottom. It also imposes a limit on the number of items shown, and eliminates duplicates—which means that the order of visiting is not strictly preserved. Some pages have very long titles, and in such cases we elide the title at the right-hand end (i.e., chop off the excess text and replace it with an ellipsis, "…"), using QFontMetrics::elidedText(). It is also possible to elide on the left or in the middle by passing Qt::ElideLeft or Qt::ElideMiddle as the second argument.

As we mentioned earlier, prior to Qt 4.7, Qt does not provide a qHash(QUrl) function, so we cannot store QUrls in a QSet out of the box. Since QSet is implemented in terms of a QHash, the solution is to add exactly the same qHash(QUrl) one-liner that we used for the Weather Tray Icon application we saw earlier (11◀).

If the user cancels the menu (e.g., by pressing Esc or by clicking elsewhere), QMenu::exec() will return 0; otherwise it will return the QAction corresponding to the menu option the user chose. If a QAction is returned we extract the URL that is held in its data. And once we have the URL, we ask the web view to load the corresponding page.

We have now completed our review of the browser window component. There are other standard browser features that we could add, some of which are easily done since WebKit already provides the necessary functionality. For example, we could add a search text function based on the QWebView::findText() method, and a print page function based on the QWebFrame::print() or QWebFrame::render() method.

In the following two subsections we will use the browser window as a fundamental part of two hybrid desktop/Internet applications. We will also learn how to download web content invisibly behind the scenes and how to inject JavaScript into web pages so that we can extract information from them. And we will learn how to enhance the browser window so that it can seamlessly display standard and custom Qt widgets that users can interact with.

Creating Web Site-Specific Applications

If people are using one particular web site a lot of the time then it should be possible to provide them with more convenience and functionality by creating a web site-specific application geared to their needs. The danger of such applications is that they can be vulnerable to changes in the web site, but this may be outweighed by the time savings achieved by the greater convenience of use—particularly if the site has a large number of users. Also, we might

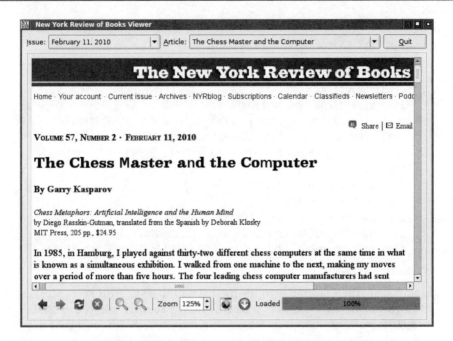

Figure 1.9 *The New York Review of Books Viewer*

be able to contain the effects of such changes so that they only affect the JavaScript we use behind the scenes without requiring source code changes at all.

Creating a custom site-specific application can also ensure that users can only access the site using a custom client application. Perhaps the best known example of this is Apple's iTunes Music Store, which (at the time of this writing) cannot be used with a standard web browser.

In this subsection we will look at the New York Review of Books Viewer application (`nyrbviewer`) shown in Figure 1.9. This application shows pages from the NYRB (*New York Review of Books*) using the browser window component from the previous subsection. What makes this application stand out as more convenient to use than viewing the site in a web browser is that it offers comboboxes listing the issues and the articles within a selected issue. This gives the user an easy way of seeing what issues and articles are available and a fast way of choosing an article to read.

Most of the functionality is already present in the browser window component, so we only need to concentrate on how we are going to populate the comboboxes with the correct data and how we are going to make them work. We will start by looking at the constructor.

```
const QString NYRBUrl("http://www.nybooks.com");
```

```
MainWindow::MainWindow(QWidget *parent)
    : QMainWindow(parent)
{
    createWidgets();
    createLayout();
    issueLinkFetcher = new LinkFetcher(NYRBUrl,
            scriptPathAndName("fetch_issue_links.js"), this);
    articleLinkFetcher = new LinkFetcher(NYRBUrl,
            scriptPathAndName("fetch_article_links.js"), this);
    createConnections();
    AQP::accelerateWidget(this);
    issueComboBox->setFocus();
    issueLinkFetcher->load(NYRBUrl);
    setWindowTitle(QApplication::applicationName());
    QTimer::singleShot(1000 * 60, this, SLOT(networkTimeout()));
}
```

We create the widgets and layouts in the usual way. The AQP::accelerate-
Widget() function uses QObject::findChildren() to find all the QLabels and
QAbstractButtons (and their subclasses, apart from QToolButtons) that are chil-
dren of the window and sets keyboard accelerators for them (15 ◄).

One novel aspect of the constructor is the creation of the two LinkFetcher
objects. These objects create QWebPage objects behind the scenes—recall that
QWebPages are data objects—and have their QWebPages download a specified page.
They then inject the JavaScript they are given when they are constructed into
the page, and this is used to extract relevant links. The web site URL they are
given is used to convert any relative links such as articles/22273 into absolute
links such as http://www.nybooks.com/articles/22273.

Once the link fetchers are created and connected, we start things off by telling
the issueLinkFetcher to download the NYRB web site's main page and to use
the fetch_issue_links.js script to extract the links to all the issues; these
can then be used to populate the issues combobox. And whenever an issue
is chosen, the articleLinkFetcher is told to download the current issue's page
and uses the fetch_article_links.js script to extract the links to all the issue's
articles; these can be used to populate the articles combobox. We will look at
the LinkFetcher class toward the end of this subsection.

We created the scriptPathAndName() method because we want to have some
flexibility regarding the scripts, as we will discuss in a moment.

One final aspect is that we have set up a single shot timer. This will time out
after a minute and call the networkTimeout() slot, so that we can provide an
error message if it transpires that the Internet is unreachable.

```
QString MainWindow::scriptPathAndName(const QString &filename)
{
```

```
            QString name = filename;
            QString path = AQP::applicationPathOf() + "/";
            if (QFile::exists(path + name))
                return path + name;
            return QString(":/%1").arg(name);
        }
```

This method looks for the script in the directory containing the application's executable and if it is found returns the full path and name for reading by the link checker. But if the script isn't in the filesystem then we fall back to using a script that has been embedded in the executable as a resource. This means that by default the application uses its own embedded scripts, but if we need to change the scripts—for example, if the web site undergoes changes—we can simply put updated scripts in the excecutable's directory and they will automatically be found and used in preference to the application's embedded scripts. (Of course those concerned with security might prefer to use a binary file format with a checksum or other measure to ensure that a locally installed script is legitimate, but such issues are beyond the scope of this book.)

The aqp.{hpp,cpp} module's AQP::applicationPathOf() function returns the path of the application (as a QString), or the path of the subdirectory inside the executable's directory, if a subdirectory is given as an argument. We cannot use QApplication::applicationDirPath() directly, since that does not account for the fact that the executable may be in a different directory depending on whether it is in its released form or is under development. (For example, during development on Windows the executable is normally in the debug or release subdirectory.)

```
        const QString InitialMessage(
                QObject::tr("Attempting to connect to the network..."));
        const QString FailMessage(
                QObject::tr("No issues or articles available"));

        void MainWindow::networkTimeout()
        {
            const QString text = browser->toPlainText().trimmed();
            if (text == InitialMessage || text == FailMessage)
                browser->setHtml("<h3><font color=red>Failed to connect "
                        "to the network</font></h3>Perhaps the proxy "
                        "settings are wrong, or maybe a proxy is needed. "
                        "Try:<br><tt>nyrbviewer --help</tt>");
        }
```

One minute after the application starts up this slot is called. If no Internet connection has been established, the browser's text will be the same as the InitialMessage or the FailMessage, so we try to provide some help to the user. (See the "Supporting Network Proxying" sidebar; 9 ◄.)

In the header file we have a private variable, `namesForUrlsForIssueCache`:

```
QHash<int, QMap<QString, QString> > namesForUrlsForIssueCache;
```

This cache's keys are the index positions of items in the issue combobox, and its values are maps whose keys are URLs and whose values are article names. We will see how it is used when we look at the main window's methods, but note for now that link fetchers can return a URL–name map for the links they have retrieved from the page they have downloaded. (We don't use a `QCache` because we don't ever want to get rid of the cached data.)

We won't show the `createWidgets()` and `createLayout()` methods since they are standard C++/Qt, but we will look at `createConnections()`.

```
void MainWindow::createConnections()
{
    connect(issueLinkFetcher, SIGNAL(finished(bool)),
            this, SLOT(populateIssueComboBox(bool)));
    connect(articleLinkFetcher, SIGNAL(finished(bool)),
            this, SLOT(populateCache(bool)));
    connect(issueComboBox, SIGNAL(currentIndexChanged(int)),
            this, SLOT(currentIssueIndexChanged(int)));
    connect(articleComboBox, SIGNAL(currentIndexChanged(int)),
            this, SLOT(currentArticleIndexChanged(int)));
    connect(quitButton, SIGNAL(clicked()), this, SLOT(close()));
}
```

Whenever a link fetcher finishes downloading a page and extracting the relevant links, it emits a `finished(bool)` signal with the Boolean indicating success or failure. For the issue link fetcher we connect directly to the `populateIssue-ComboBox()` slot, but for the article link fetcher we connect to the `populateCache()` slot, which in turn calls `populateArticleComboBox()` once the cache has been populated.

If the user chooses a different issue we must repopulate the article combobox, and if the user chooses an article we must load it into the browser window. These behaviors are set up by the third and fourth signal–slot connections. The application's overall flow of control is illustrated in Figure 1.10.

Now we will review the main window's methods, starting with those concerning the issue combobox and then looking at those that concern the article combobox.

```
void MainWindow::populateIssueComboBox(bool ok)
{
    if (ok)
        populateAComboBox(tr("- no issue selected -"),
                issueLinkFetcher->namesForUrls(), issueComboBox);
```

```
        else {
            issueComboBox->clear();
            issueComboBox->addItem(tr("- no issues available -"));
        }
    }
```

This slot is called only once, when the `LinkFetcher::load()` call made on the `issueLinkFetcher` in the main window's constructor eventually results in a `LinkFetcher::finished()` signal being emitted. The issue link fetcher retrieves the names and URLs of all the issues (since 2000). Once the retrieval is finished, the results are made available as a `QMap<QString, QString>` where the URLs are keys and the issue names are values. We send this map to the `populate-AComboBox()` method and ask it to populate the issues combobox using the map's data.

```
    void MainWindow::populateAComboBox(const QString &statusText,
            const QMap<QString, QString> &namesForUrls,
            QComboBox *comboBox)
    {
        comboBox->clear();
        comboBox->addItem(statusText);
        QMapIterator<QString, QString> i(namesForUrls);
        i.toBack();
        while (i.hasPrevious()) {
            i.previous();
            comboBox->addItem(i.value(), i.key());
        }
        if (comboBox->count() > 1)
            comboBox->setCurrentIndex(1);
    }
```

This method is called from both the `populateIssueComboBox()` slot and from the `populateArticleComboBox()` method.

We start by clearing the combobox's original contents and adding the status text as the first item. Then we iterate in reverse order over the URL–issue name map (or the URL–article name map, if it is being used to populate the articles combobox) that is passed in, and that was returned by a link fetcher. For the NYRB web site's issues and articles, the URLs encode the date, for example, `/contents/20090115`, so we are iterating in date order from most to least recent. For issues, the names are simply dates in U.S. format (e.g., "Jan 15, 2009"), and these are added as combobox item texts, with the URLs added as item data. For articles, the names are the actual article titles.

If there is more than one item, that is, there is at least one issue or article, we make the first (most recent) issue or article the current one, and this in turn

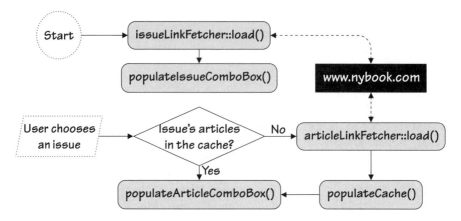

Figure 1.10 *The New York Review of Books Viewer's flow of control*

will cause the currentIssueIndexChanged() slot or the currentArticleIndex-Changed() slot to be called.

```
void MainWindow::currentIssueIndexChanged(int index)
{
    articleComboBox->clear();
    if (index == 0) {
        articleComboBox->addItem(tr("- no issue selected -"));
        return;
    }
    if (namesForUrlsForIssueCache.contains(index))
        populateArticleComboBox();
    else {
        articleComboBox->addItem(
                tr("+ fetching the list of articles +"));
        browser->setHtml(tr("<h3><font color=red>"
                "Fetching the list of articles...</font></h3>"));
        QString url = issueComboBox->itemData(index).toString();
        articleLinkFetcher->load(url);
    }
}
```

If a new issue is chosen we start by clearing the *article* combobox. If an issue is selected we check to see if we have already downloaded its URL–article name map; if we have, we can simply call populateArticleComboBox() which always retrieves its data from the cache.

If there is no cache entry for the newly chosen issue, we add status-indicating text to the article combobox and to the browser window. Then we retrieve the issue's URL (which is held in the issue combobox item's data), and tell the article link fetcher to download the issue's page and extract the article links from it. Once the download finishes the `populateCache()` slot is called thanks to the signal–slot connection we created earlier.

```cpp
void MainWindow::populateCache(bool ok)
{
    if (!ok || issueComboBox->count() == 1) {
        articleComboBox->setItemText(0,
                tr("- no articles available -"));
        browser->setHtml(tr("<h3><font color=red>%1</font></h3>")
                        .arg(FailMessage));
        return;
    }
    QTextDocument document;
    QMap<QString, QString> namesForUrls =
            articleLinkFetcher->namesForUrls();
    QMutableMapIterator<QString, QString> i(namesForUrls);
    while (i.hasNext()) {
        i.next();
        document.setHtml(i.value());
        i.setValue(document.toPlainText());
    }
    namesForUrlsForIssueCache[issueComboBox->currentIndex()] =
            namesForUrls;
    populateArticleComboBox();
}
```

If the download of URL–article names failed we inform the user via both the article combobox and by putting some text in the browser window. In the case of success we retrieve the URL–article name map from the article link fetcher. Then we add the now modified map to the cache and call `populateArticleCombo-Box()`.

We need the article names as plain text since they are going into a `QCombo-Box` (which cannot display rich text). Rather than creating and destroying a `QTextDocumentFragment` each time (i.e., `i.setValue(QTextDocumentFragment::from-Html(i.value()).toPlainText());`), we create a single `QTextDocument` and at each iteration set its HTML text and then call its `toPlainText()` method.

```cpp
void MainWindow::populateArticleComboBox()
{
    int index = issueComboBox->currentIndex();
    if (index > 0)
        populateAComboBox(tr("- no article selected -"),
                namesForUrlsForIssueCache[index], articleComboBox);
}
```

This method is only ever called if the cache has the required data, so we know that if an issue has been chosen then its links are in the cache. We populate the combobox using the populateAComboBox() method shown earlier (35 ◄), passing it a status text to add as the first item, the current issue's URL–article name map from the cache, and the combobox we want populated. If the user has chosen the first item in the issue combobox (the "no issue selected" item), we do nothing.

```
void MainWindow::currentArticleIndexChanged(int index)
{
    if (index == 0)
        return;
    QString url = articleComboBox->itemData(index).toString();
    browser->load(url);
    browser->setFocus();
}
```

When the user chooses a new item in the article combobox (apart from the first "no article selected" item), we retrieve the URL that is associated with the article title from the combobox item's data, and tell the browser window to load the corresponding page. We also give the browser window focus (which actually goes to the browser window's QWebView), so that the user can immediately begin scrolling with the keyboard up and down arrow keys.

We have now seen the complete implementation of the New York Review of Books Viewer application (except for the header, and the createWidgets() and createLayout() methods). We will now review the LinkFetcher class to see how that works behind the scenes to download pages and extract links. Here is its header:

```
class LinkFetcher : public QObject
{
    Q_OBJECT

public:
    explicit LinkFetcher(const QString &site_,
            const QString &scriptOrScriptName_, QObject *parent=0);

    void load(const QString &url);
    QMap<QString, QString> namesForUrls() const
        { return m_namesForUrls; }
    void clear() { m_namesForUrls.clear(); }

signals:
    void finished(bool);

public slots:
    void addUrlAndName(const QString &url, const QString &name);
```

```
private slots:
    void injectJavaScriptIntoWindowObject();
    void fetchLinks(bool ok);

private:
    QWebPage page;
    QMap<QString, QString> m_namesForUrls;
    const QString site;
    const QString scriptOrScriptName;
};
```

This class uses the `QWebPage` data class to load the URL it is given. It then uses the JavaScript script it was given to extract the relevant links from the page and populate the `m_namesForUrls` map with each link's URL and name.

We can make any `QObject` accessible to JavaScript. This means that the JavaScript that is injected into the pages that are downloaded can not only access the pages' elements (using the HTML Document Object Model), but can also access any `QObjects` we have made available. In particular, the JavaScript can do method calls on a `QObject`'s public slots and can access a `QObject`'s properties if it has any. In this case we will be passing a reference to the link fetcher instance, so the injected JavaScript script can communicate with our C++ code by calling the link fetcher's public slots.

```
LinkFetcher::LinkFetcher(const QString &site_,
        const QString &scriptOrScriptName_, QObject *parent)
    : QObject(parent), site(site_),
      scriptOrScriptName(scriptOrScriptName_)
{
    QWebSettings *webSettings = page.settings();
    webSettings->setAttribute(QWebSettings::AutoLoadImages, false);
    webSettings->setAttribute(QWebSettings::PluginsEnabled, false);
    webSettings->setAttribute(QWebSettings::JavaEnabled, false);
    webSettings->setAttribute(QWebSettings::JavascriptEnabled, true);
    webSettings->setAttribute(QWebSettings::PrivateBrowsingEnabled,
                              true);

    connect(page.mainFrame(), SIGNAL(javaScriptWindowObjectCleared()),
            this, SLOT(injectJavaScriptIntoWindowObject()));
    connect(&page, SIGNAL(loadFinished(bool)),
            this, SLOT(fetchLinks(bool)));
}
```

Since we are downloading the page behind the scenes and are only interested in its links, we change the `QWebPage`'s page settings. We switch off image downloading, plugins, and Java, and switch on JavaScript, and also `QWebSettings::PrivateBrowsingEnabled`, which prevents the `QWebPage` from recording

any history or storing any web page icons since neither is of any use to us and
would otherwise consume some memory and CPU time.

Whenever a page load is initiated, the JavaScript window objects for its
QWebFrames are cleared, ready for any new JavaScript that the new page's frame
or frames may contain. Since we need to inject our own JavaScript into the
main frame's window object for each page that is downloaded, we must ensure
that our JavaScript is re-injected whenever the JavaScript window object is
cleared. This is achieved by the first signal–slot connection shown here.

The second signal–slot connection ensures that as soon as the page has been
downloaded we try to extract its links.

```
void LinkFetcher::injectJavaScriptIntoWindowObject()
{
    page.mainFrame()->addToJavaScriptWindowObject("linkFetcher",
                                                  this);
}
```

The QWebFrame::addToJavaScriptWindowObject() method can add any QObject to a
QWebFrame's JavaScript window objects. The string first argument is the name
that the object will be accessible as in JavaScript (in this example, linkFetcher),
and the QObject second argument is a reference to the actual object—in this
case an instance of the LinkFetcher class itself.

```
void LinkFetcher::load(const QString &url)
{
    clear();
    page.mainFrame()->load(QUrl(url));
}
```

When the link fetcher is given a URL to load it starts by clearing the m_names-
ForUrls map and then tells the QWebPage's main frame to load the page. Once
loading is finished the fetchLinks() slot is called because of the signal–slot connection set up earlier.

```
void LinkFetcher::fetchLinks(bool ok)
{
    if (!ok) {
        emit finished(false);
        return;
    }
    QString javaScript = scriptOrScriptName;
    if (scriptOrScriptName.endsWith(".js")) {
        QFile file(scriptOrScriptName);
        if (!file.open(QIODevice::ReadOnly)) {
            emit finished(false);
            return;
```

```
        }
        javaScript = QString::fromUtf8(file.readAll());
    }
    QWebFrame *frame = page.mainFrame();
    frame->evaluateJavaScript(javaScript);
    emit finished(true);
}
```

If the load failed we notify any connected objects. Otherwise we check to see if the QString scriptOrScriptName private member variable holds an actual script or only the name of a script; and in the latter case we attempt to read in the script's text. Instead of creating a QTextStream, we open the file in binary mode and convert the QByteArray returned by the QFile::readAll() method into Unicode using the static QString::fromUtf8() method. Once the script is ready we tell the QWebPage's main frame to evaluate it, and then we notify any connected objects that we have successfully finished.

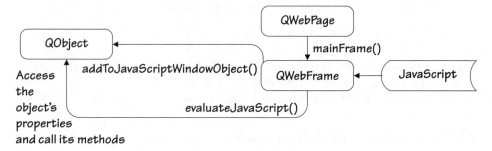

Figure 1.11 *Injecting JavaScript to access HTML elements and an application's QObjects*

The QWebFrame::evaluateJavaScript() method returns a QVariant that holds the value of the last JavaScript expression executed; we have ignored it because we have chosen a more versatile approach to JavaScript⇔C++ communication. Since we have set a reference to the link checker itself as an object accessible to the JavaScript script, that script can call any of the link checker's public slots and access its properties. In this case we have provided the addUrlAndName() slot expressly for the use of JavaScript scripts.

```
void LinkFetcher::addUrlAndName(const QString &url,
                                const QString &name)
{
    if (url.startsWith("http://"))
        m_namesForUrls[url] = name;
    else
        m_namesForUrls[site + url] = name;
}
```

Whenever the JavaScript script obtains the details of a link it calls this slot with the link's URL and name, and as a result the m_namesForUrls map is populated. Since the URLs might be relative or absolute, we prefix the relative ones with the site that was given to the link fetcher when it was constructed.

Figure 1.11 illustrates how by adding an application QObject to a web page, JavaScript executed in the context of the web page can access both the page's HTML elements (via the Document Object Model), and any application QObjects we give the page access to.

We have now completed our review of the LinkFetcher class, but to make sure we understand how things work we will show the fetch_article_links.js script (since it is by far the shorter of the two), just to see how it works and how it interacts with the link fetcher.

```
var links = document.getElementsByTagName("a");        Java-
for (var i = 0; i < links.length; ++i) {               Script
    if (links[i].href.search("/articles/") != -1) {
        linkFetcher.addUrlAndName(links[i].href, links[i].innerHTML);
    }
}
```

The JavaScript getElementsByTagName() method is used to retrieve all the "a" (anchor) tags—these are the ones that hold links, with the link itself held in the href property and the text between the <a> and </a> tags as the innerHTML property.

The key point to notice is the last statement, where we call LinkFetcher::add-UrlAndName() using the linkFetcher reference to the C++ link fetcher object.

The original fetch_issue_links.js script is very similar to the fetch_article_links.js script, but a bit longer (around 20 lines), since we read the issue links out of a combobox that appeared on the web site's home page.

About nine months into the writing of this book, the NYRB web site made considerable changes to its home page, and the issues combobox that the original fetch_issue_links.js script read the list of issues from has now gone. Nor do any other pages appear to provide such a combobox, or the list of issues in any other form. However, their web master pointed out that they have one page for each year that lists that year's issues. Armed with this information, we were easily able to write a new fetch_issue_links.js script—around 40 lines long—and simply put the new script in the same directory as the executable. And since we designed the application to use scripts it finds in the same directory as the executable in preference to the scripts embedded in its resources, without even needing to be recompiled, the program automatically uses the new fetch_issue_links.js script.

Since the new fetch_issue_links.js script must read one page per year of issues—we have set it to read the past five years—it runs slower than the original because it does a synchronous GET request for each page.* Nonetheless, the solution was easy to implement and works well. However, in the long term, we would want to avoid doing synchronous downloads in JavaScript, since they block the GUI application's event loop. So in this case the ideal solution would be to redesign the program so that it uses Qt's networking classes to do the GET requests to produce the list of issues, while keeping the fetch_article_links.js script for the articles. We leave this as an exercise, since it should be quite straightforward to do.

Before finishing this subsection's coverage of using JavaScript, it is worth discussing how to debug applications that use injected JavaScript like this—since it isn't easy! One simple way of dealing with the problem is to make sure that every script returns a value when evaluated, and to retrieve and test the value. In this example, we have taken a more versatile approach, and added a new public slot to the link fetcher's header file:

```
void debug(const QString &value)
    { qDebug("%s", qPrintable(value)); }
```

During development we called this slot from inside the JavaScript scripts (the debug() calls are still there in the source code, but commented out). For example, we have the following line inside the fetch_article_links.js script's for loop (although we didn't show it when we quoted the script earlier):

```
linkFetcher.debug(links[i].href + " * " + links[i].innerHTML);
```

Java-
Script

Adding debug() statements like this can be very useful. (Windows users must of course add CONFIG += console to their .pro file so that the debugging output will be visible.)

Unfortunately, using debug() statements doesn't work if the script has a syntax error, since the script won't run at all. One way to check a script for syntax errors is to pass its filename as the command line argument to Qt's qscript program (in Qt's examples directory). If the syntax is okay, qscript will attempt to run the script; otherwise it will provide an error message with the line number where the first error was found.

The New York Review of Books Viewer application covered in this subsection makes use of fairly basic JavaScript scripts (although the new fetch_issue_links.js script is more complex). Much more sophisticated scripts can be written, especially since scripts can access a downloaded page's DOM (Document Object Model). We can also use Qt 4.6's QWebElement class to access (and even modify) web pages via their DOM, which is very convenient for web sites that we know will remain stable or that we have control over. So, in each case, we must make the trade-off between the ease and convenience with which we can

---

* The new script uses the XMLHttpRequest object and is based on ideas from *JavaScript: The Definitive Guide* by David Flanagan, ISBN 9780596101992.

change our JavaScript scripts to keep up with web site changes, versus the power and asynchronicity of Qt's networking and web classes which make it easy to present a responsive user interface and allow us to do all our web programming in pure C++.

Embedding Qt Widgets in Web Pages

The range of widgets available in HTML is rather limited. Various solutions are possible, such as using proprietary content formats like Flash or using proprietary browser extensions such as those available for Internet Explorer, or by embedding a Java application. All these approaches require that the user's browser support them and this may not be possible in all cross-platform contexts. Another disadvantage of using proprietary formats or extensions is that we are limited to whatever functionality they provide.

Another solution is to embed Qt widgets. This has the advantages that we get complete control over the behavior and appearance of the widgets we embed, and it allows us complete freedom to build in whatever functionality we need. The disadvantage of this approach is that the browser must be able to support embedded Qt widgets.

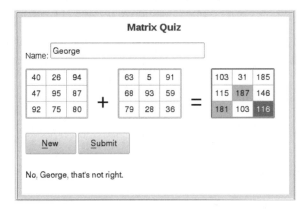

Figure 1.12 *The Matrix Quiz web page*

In this subsection we will review the Matrix Quiz web page shown in Figure 1.12. This web page is embedded in a browser window component and used in the Matrix Quiz application (matrixquiz).

The web page shows two randomly generated 3 × 3 matrices and invites the user to add them up by entering the appropriate values in the third matrix whose initial values are all zeros. If the user presses the New button a new pair of matrices is generated. If the user presses the Submit button the third matrix's values are compared to what they ought to be, and any incorrect values are highlighted in red—for example, cells containing the values 181 and 187 in

Figure 1.12. The cursor cell is shown in reverse video (e.g., white on black), and with a focus rectangle—here, for example, the cell containing value 116.

The web page is made up of a mixture of HTML elements and standard and custom Qt widgets. The title text, the "Name:" label, and the large "+" and "=" signs are all standard HTML elements. The name line edit, the buttons, and the result label could also have been HTML elements, but for the sake of the example we have used standard Qt widgets. The matrix widgets are custom widgets (a simple QTableWidget subclass)—something not possible in pure HTML.

As implemented, the browser window component we created earlier does not support embedded Qt widgets. We have added support simply by creating a custom QWebPage subclass that has the necessary support, and passing that in to the browser window rather than letting the browser window create its own standard QWebPage.

We will start reviewing the code by looking at a group of three tiny extracts from the Matrix Quiz application's main() function.

```
qsrand(static_cast<uint>(time(0)));

QWebSettings *webSettings = QWebSettings::globalSettings();
webSettings->setAttribute(QWebSettings::AutoLoadImages, true);
webSettings->setAttribute(QWebSettings::JavascriptEnabled, true);
webSettings->setAttribute(QWebSettings::PluginsEnabled, true);

QString url = QUrl::fromLocalFile(AQP::applicationPathOf() +
                                  "/matrixquiz.html").toString();
BrowserWindow *browser = new BrowserWindow(url, new WebPage);
browser->showToolBar(false);
browser->enableActions(false);
```

Qt's global qsrand() function is used to seed Qt's random number generator. Without this call, calls to qrand() would always return the same sequence of random numbers (since the seed defaults to 1 unless we explicitly set it). We prefer to use Qt's random functions since not all platforms (e.g., some embedded systems) support them, and although not relevant here, they are also thread-safe. (Qt's global functions, including qsrand(), are shown in Table 1.2.)

To make use of JavaScript we must enable it, and similarly to make use of embedded widgets we must enable plugins.

The QUrl class is normally used to create URLs for web pages on the Internet, but here we have used it to create a URL for a web page in the local filesystem using the file:// scheme.

When we create the BrowserWindow instance we not only pass it the URL of the web page we want it to use (as a string), but an instance of our custom WebPage class. We also hide the browser window's toolbar and switch off all its actions—

Table 1.2 *Qt's Global Utility Functions*

Function/Example	Description
`u = qAbs(n);`	Returns the absolute (positive) value of *n*
`x = qBound(min, n, max);`	Returns *n* if *min* <= *n* <= *max*; otherwise returns *min* if *n* < *min*; otherwise returns *max*

`qDebug("%d: %s",`
`    integer,`
`    qPrintable(string));`
	Prints C++ POD types to the console using `printf()` syntax; doesn't understand Qt types (Windows `.pro` files need `CONFIG += console`)

`qDebug() << number`
`    << string << hash`
`    << stringlist << map`
`    << variant << object;`
	Prints C++ POD types and any Qt `QObject`s to the console, including collections such as `QHash` and `QMap`; requires `#include <QtDebug>` (Windows `.pro` files need `CONFIG += console`)

`b = qFuzzyCompare(f, g);`	Returns `true` if floating-point numbers (or `QTransform`s in Qt 4.6) *f* and *g* can be considered to be equal
`x = qMax(n, m);`	Returns the larger of *n* and *m*
`x = qMin(n, m);`	Returns the smaller of *n* and *m*
`const char *s =` `    qPrintable(qstring);`	Returns a `char*` (using the local 8-bit encoding) from a `QString` suitable for `printf()` or `qDebug()`
`x = qRound(f);`	Returns *f* rounded to the nearest integer, as an `int`
`x = qRound64(f);`	Returns *f* rounded to the nearest integer, as a `qint64`
`x = qrand();`	Returns a pseudo-random number between 0 and `RAND_MAX` (as defined in `<cstdlib>`). This thread-safe function uses a default seed of 1; call `qsrand()` to set a different seed
`qsrand(u);`	Seeds the pseudo-random number generator with `uint` *u*
`s = qVersion();`	Returns a `const char*` that specifies the version of Qt the application is using (e.g., `"4.6.2"`)

now it cannot be used as a general browser but only to view and interact with the page we have specified.

For the rest of the code we will begin by reviewing the small `WebPage` class that provides support for embedded Qt widgets. Then we will look at the custom `MatrixWidget` class, and finally we will look at the `matrixquiz.html` page to see how the widgets are embedded and to see the JavaScript that is used to provide some of the page's functionality.

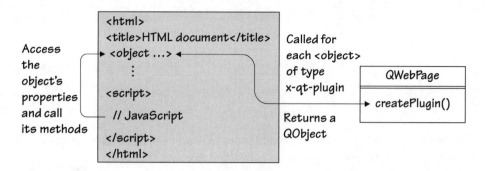

Figure 1.13 *Accessing QObjects embedded in an HTML document using JavaScript*

The WebPage class is a QWebPage subclass. The constructor (not shown) simply passes its optional parent argument to the base class; its body is empty. The only method that the subclass reimplements is the protected createPlugin() method, but before looking at that, let's look at an extract from matrixquiz.html showing how one of the buttons is created.

```
<object type="application/x-qt-plugin" classid="QPushButton"
    id="newButton" height="40" width="100">
Can't load QPushButton plugin!</object>
```

Whenever an HTML <object> tag with a type attribute of application/x-qt-plugin is encountered in a page held by a QWebPage, the createPlugin() method is called. This is illustrated in Figure 1.13.

```
QObject* WebPage::createPlugin(const QString &classId,
        const QUrl&, const QStringList &parameterNames,
        const QStringList &parameterValues)
{
    QWidget *widget = 0;
    if (classId == "MatrixWidget") {
        widget = new MatrixWidget(view());
        int index = parameterNames.indexOf("readonly");
        if (index > -1)
            static_cast<MatrixWidget*>(widget)->setReadOnly(
                    static_cast<bool>(parameterValues[index].toInt()));
    }
    else {
        QUiLoader loader;
        widget = loader.createWidget(classId, view());
    }
    if (widget) {
        int index = parameterNames.indexOf("width");
        if (index > -1)
```

```
            widget->setMinimumWidth(parameterValues[index].toInt());
        index = parameterNames.indexOf("height");
        if (index > -1)
            widget->setMinimumHeight(parameterValues[index].toInt());
    }
    return widget;
}
```

The default implementation returns 0, and in such cases the <object> tag's text (if any) is rendered rather than the intended object.

The classId argument is given the name of the object's class specified in the <object> tag as the classid attribute. Any other <object> tag attributes are passed in two parallel string lists, the first holding the attribute names and the second the corresponding attribute values. So, for the button <object> we saw earlier, the parameterNames list is ["id", "height", "width"], and the parameterValues list is ["newButton", "40", "100"].

The method starts by creating the requested widget as a child of the WebPage's QWebView. Any not-null widget returned by createPlugin() is rendered inside the HTML page by the QWebPage's associated QWebView.

If the requested widget class is MatrixWidget, we create a suitable instance and call MatrixWidget::readOnly() with a Boolean value if the parameterNames list has a "readonly" item. (In the HTML, we have made the first two matrices read-only, and the third one read-write.)

For any other kind of widget that is requested, that is, for any standard Qt widget, we could use the same technique as we use to create MatrixWidgets. But this would lead to a very long sequence of if ... else statements checking for classIds and would be tedious to maintain.

Fortunately, Qt already has a class that can create instances of standard Qt widgets based on their class name: QUiLoader. This class was originally designed to support the dynamic loading and rendering of *Qt Designer* .ui files, but here we have used its QUiLoader::createWidget() method to instantiate and return a pointer to the requested <object> widget. (Note that to use the QUiLoader class we must include the line CONFIG += uitools in the application's .pro file.)

Once the widget is created, we set its minimum width and height if these are given as <object> attributes. We don't use the id attribute in our C++ code, but we do use it in the JavaScript that provides the web page's behavior beyond that provided by the MatrixWidget and the other Qt classes.

We want the custom MatrixWidget class to be programmable using JavaScript in a web page. Just as with QtScript, a class's Q_PROPERTYs are available in JavaScript as JavaScript properties and a class's public slots are available as JavaScript methods. Here's the MatrixWidget's definition from its header file:

```
class MatrixWidget : public QTableWidget
{
    Q_OBJECT

public:
    explicit MatrixWidget(QWidget *parent=0);

public slots:
    void clearMatrix();
    void repopulateMatrix();
    QString valueAt(int row, int column) const
        { return item(row, column)->text(); }
    void setValueAt(int row, int column, const QString &value)
        { item(row, column)->setText(value); }
    void setHighlighted(int row, int column, bool highlight=true)
        { item(row, column)->setBackground(highlight ? Qt::red
                                                     : Qt::white); }
    void setReadOnly(bool read_only);
};
```

We defined some public slots—these will be accessible from JavaScript; but we
did not need to create any custom properties since the base class's rowCount and
columnCount properties are accessible to JavaScript and those are the only ones
needed. The setHighlighted() method sets a table item's background—this is
used to highlight cells that have incorrect values.

```
const int ColumnWidth = 40;

MatrixWidget::MatrixWidget(QWidget *parent)
    : QTableWidget(3, 3, parent)
{
    verticalHeader()->hide();
    horizontalHeader()->hide();
    for (int row = 0; row < rowCount(); ++row) {
        for (int column = 0; column < columnCount(); ++column) {
            QTableWidgetItem *item = new QTableWidgetItem("0");
            item->setTextAlignment(Qt::AlignCenter);
            setItem(row, column, item);
            if (row == 0)
                setColumnWidth(column, ColumnWidth);
        }
    }
}
```

We use the constructor to create a QTableWidget with a fixed number of rows
and columns and with a fixed column width. Every item is initialized to
contain the text "0" and to have centered alignment. Both the vertical and

horizontal headers are hidden, which is why the widget looks rather different from a standard `QTableWidget`.

```
void MatrixWidget::setReadOnly(bool read_only)
{
    setEditTriggers(read_only ? QAbstractItemView::NoEditTriggers
                              : QAbstractItemView::AllEditTriggers);
    setFocusPolicy(read_only ? Qt::NoFocus : Qt::WheelFocus);
}
```

If the widget is set to read-only we turn off all the edit triggers. We also change its focus policy so that it cannot accept keyboard focus; this means that when a keyboard user presses Tab in a widget preceding a read-only matrix widget the focus will bypass the read-only widget and go to the next focus-accepting widget.

In this example the focus starts in the "name" line edit; if the user presses Tab the focus will then go to the read-write matrix widget they must enter their answer in, skipping the two read-only matrix widgets in between.

```
void MatrixWidget::repopulateMatrix()
{
    for (int row = 0; row < rowCount(); ++row) {
        for (int column = 0; column < columnCount(); ++column)
            item(row, column)->setText(
                    QString::number(qrand() % 100));
    }
}
```

This method is used to populate the widget with random integers (as strings) between 0 and 99. The `clearMatrix()` method (not shown) is structurally very similar, only it sets every cell item's text to "0" and its background to white.

We have now seen all the relevant C++ code. The `matrixquiz.html` file contains the HTML for specifying the HTML elements and also an <object> tag for each of the Qt widgets and for each of the `MatrixWidgets`. These all follow the same pattern as we saw earlier, but just to demonstrate that there is no difference between using a standard Qt widget and a custom one, here is the <object> tag for the first of the `MatrixWidgets`:

```
<object type="application/x-qt-plugin" classid="MatrixWidget"
    id="leftMatrix" width="124" height="94" readonly="1">
Can't load MatrixWidget plugin!</object>
```

The `matrixquiz.html` file provides the web page's behavior using JavaScript. The <script> tag is at the end of the file since the JavaScript needs to access objects that are created earlier (i.e., the <object>s). Two functions are defined (which we will discuss in a moment), and these are followed by this final block of code:

```javascript
newButton.text = "&New";
submitButton.text = "&Submit";
resultLabel.text = "Enter the answer and click Submit";
repopulateMatrices();
newButton.clicked.connect(repopulateMatrices);
submitButton.clicked.connect(checkAnswer);
nameEdit.setFocus();
```

Java-Script

One interesting difference from C++/Qt is that in JavaScript and QtScript, signal–slot connections are set up using one of these syntaxes:

```javascript
object.signalName.connect(functionName)
object.signalName.connect(otherObject.methodName)
```

Java-Script

We won't show the `repopulateMatrices()` function since all it does is call `repopulateMatrix()` on each of the `MatrixWidget`s, but for completeness we will show the `checkAnswer()` function.

```javascript
function checkAnswer()
{
    var allCorrect = true;
    for (var row = 0; row < leftMatrix.rowCount; ++row) {
        for (var column = 0; column < leftMatrix.columnCount;
             ++column) {
            var highlight = false;
            if (Number(leftMatrix.valueAt(row, column)) +
                Number(rightMatrix.valueAt(row, column)) !=
                Number(answerMatrix.valueAt(row, column))) {
                highlight = true;
                allCorrect = false;
            }
            answerMatrix.setHighlighted(row, column, highlight);
        }
    }
    name = nameEdit.text == "" ? "mystery person" : nameEdit.text;
    if (allCorrect)
        resultLabel.text = "Yes, " + name + ", that's right!";
    else
        resultLabel.text = "No, " + name + ", that's not right.";
}
```

Java-Script

This function iterates over every cell in the three matrices. If the answer matrix cell's value is correct we clear its highlighting (i.e., set its background to white), otherwise we set its highlighting (i.e., set its background to red). If one or more values are incorrect we set allCorrect to false.

At the end we retrieve the user's name from the nameEdit QLineEdit and set the resultLabel QLabel with suitable text based on whether the user got the answer right or not.

We have now completed our review of the Matrix Quiz web page and the C++/Qt and JavaScript used to provide it with its appearance and behavior.

Embedding Qt widgets into a web page offers a powerful and sophisticated way of enhancing a web page's functionality, but it does rely on the user having a Qt-enabled web browser or using an application that provides a Qt-enabled web browser component such as the browserwindow developed in this chapter. There are many different ways of creating hybrid desktop/Internet applications, with a variety of trade-offs between them. These choices were enhanced by Qt 4.4, which introduced the *QtXmlPatterns* module that supports XQueries and the XPath language. And the choices have been further improved by Qt 4.6, which has introduced the QGraphicsWebView class (a QGraphicsItem version of the QWeb-View widget that is optimized for being shown in a QGraphicsView), and the QWeb-Element class that provides a nice jQuery-like API for accessing and editing a QWebFrame's DOM elements. Qt allows us to choose whichever approach is right in our particular circumstances which means that we don't have to sacrifice usability, functionality, or native look and feel for the sake of providing Internet functionality in our applications.

2

● Using QSound and QMovie

● The Phonon Multimedia Framework

Audio and Video

Qt 4 has always had the ability to play sounds from .wav files, and to show moving images from .gif and .mng files. Qt 4.4 introduced integration with the Phonon multimedia library. Phonon can play sound files (i.e., music), and video files (i.e., movies), so the integration considerably extends Qt's multimedia capabilities.

Short sounds can provide useful aural cues to users, although they cannot be relied upon exclusively since some users have hearing impairments and others have their sound systems muted or turned off or don't have sound output set up on their systems at all. Similarly, moving images can be used to provide reassurance that a process is still running and that the application has not frozen. Another use of moving images is to visually demonstrate what choosing a particular action or option will achieve. Moving images can be distracting—or even distressing—for some users, so they should be used with care, and users should be able to stop the motion if they want to.

In this chapter's first section we will see how to use the QSound and QMovie classes to add sounds and moving images to an application.

For multimedia applications, that is, applications whose purpose is to play music or videos, the Phonon multimedia framework offers far more power and flexibility than the basic QSound and QMovie classes. In this chapter's second section we will see how to create a music player and a video player, both using the Phonon framework.

Qt's multimedia support works on all Qt platforms with the same consistent APIs. However, the ability to play multimedia often relies on codecs and third-party libraries, and these may not always be installed—often as a result of the anti-competitive and strangulating effects of software patents.* There is

---

*For more on software patents, see the Patent Absurdity video, patentabsurdity.com, the League for Programming Freedom's patent page, progfree.org/Patents/patents.html, and Richard Stallman's "The Dangers of Software Patents" talk, www.ifso.ie/documents/rms-2004-05-24.html.

no nice answer to this problem at present, so audio and video files that will play on one platform might not play on another. The best way forward is to use open media formats such as the Ogg media container format (www.xiph.org/ogg), although, at the time of this writing, support for these is weaker on proprietary platforms like Windows than on open platforms like Linux and BSD.

Using QSound and QMovie

For playing short sounds and animated images (such as .gif and .mng files), the easiest approach is to use Qt's QSound and QMovie classes. Both classes offer simple play() (start() for QMovie) and stop() methods among others. In addition, QMovie emits a variety of signals including the stateChanged() signal (with an argument of QMovie::NotRunning, QMovie::Paused, or QMovie::Running), as well as frameChanged() and finished() signals.

To show how to use these classes in context, we will review the Movie Jingle application (moviejingle) shown in Figure 2.1. This application can load and display animated images, and can take snapshots which can be saved using any of the pixel-based image formats that Qt supports. In addition, the application plays a short sound (a "jingle") whenever an action is invoked, as well as providing the ability to switch the playing of jingles on or off.

Figure 2.1 *The Movie Jingle application*

We associate jingles with actions by creating a QAction subclass called Jingle-Action that extends the QAction API to provide for a jingle file and for a static bool to control whether jingles are played. The main advantage of subclassing QAction for this purpose is that it ensures that the jingle is played (if mute is off), no matter how the action is invoked (e.g., via keyboard shortcut, menu option, or toolbar button).

The `JingleAction` class provides the same constructors as `QAction`, and in addition a couple of constructors that take the name of a jingle file. Two methods are implemented in the `jingleaction.hpp` header:

```
QString jingleFile() const { return m_jingleFile; }
static void setMute(bool mute) { s_mute = mute; }
```

The private `m_jingleFile` variable is of type `QString`. The private `s_mute` static variable is of type `bool`, and is initialized to `false` in `jingleaction.cpp`.

The constructors that don't take a jingle file simply pass on their arguments to the base class and have empty bodies. On the other hand, the constructors that take a jingle file pass on their other arguments and have one method call in their body. Here is one example from `jingleaction.cpp`:

```
JingleAction::JingleAction(const QString &jingleFile,
        const QString &text, QObject *parent)
    : QAction(text, parent)
{
    setJingleFile(jingleFile);
}
```

Two other custom methods are implemented: setJingleFile(), and a private slot, play().

```
void JingleAction::setJingleFile(const QString &jingleFile)
{
    if (!m_jingleFile.isEmpty())
        disconnect(this, SIGNAL(triggered(bool)), this, SLOT(play()));
    m_jingleFile = jingleFile;
    if (!m_jingleFile.isEmpty())
        connect(this, SIGNAL(triggered(bool)), this, SLOT(play()));
}
```

Disconnecting and reconnecting the jingle action's `triggered()` signal are not strictly necessary, but we prefer to avoid emitting signals when there is no need to do so. No `clearJingle()` method is provided, since the call, setJingle-File(QString()), is sufficient.

```
void JingleAction::play()
{
    if (!s_mute && !m_jingleFile.isEmpty())
        QSound::play(m_jingleFile);
}
```

Here we play the sound if mute is off and if there is a jingle file to play. It is best to keep the duration of the sound very short—one second at most—to avoid the sound taking longer to play than the time it takes to perform the requested action.

Now that we have seen the key parts of the JingleAction implementation, we will look at some extracts from the Movie Jingle application's main window class to see how the jingle actions are used, and also to see how QMovies are used. We will start with a couple of enums defined in the main window class's header:

```
enum ReloadMode {DontReload, Reload};
enum MovieState {NoMovie, Stopped, Playing};
```

We will see how the enums are used in the following discussion of the main window's methods. Here is the main window's constructor:

```
const int StatusTimeout = AQP::MSecPerSecond * 5;

MainWindow::MainWindow(QWidget *parent)
    : QMainWindow(parent), movieState(NoMovie)
{
    movie = new QMovie(this);

    createActions();
    createMenusAndToolBar();
    createWidgets();
    createLayout();
    createConnections();

    AQP::accelerateMenu(menuBar());
    updateUi();
    statusBar()->showMessage(tr("Open a Movie file to start..."),
                             StatusTimeout);
    setWindowTitle(QApplication::applicationName());
}
```

The constructor begins by creating a single private QMovie object called movie that will be used to load and play animated images. We won't show the create-MenusAndToolBar(), createWidgets(), createLayouts(), and createConnections() methods since they are all standard C++/Qt. The actions that are created and the slots they are connected to will become apparent when we look at the application's methods—for example, the file open action is connected to a fileOpen() slot, and so on.

We will, however, review an extract from createActions() to discuss how it differs from similar methods used in other applications.

Once the widgets and connections have been created and set up, we automatically add keyboard accelerators to all the menus and menu items (15 ◀), and initialize the user interface ready for the user to interact with the application.

Although we don't show the layout code, we note that the main window has two labels side by side, the one on the left used to show movies, and the one on the right used to show snapshots of movies.

```
void MainWindow::createActions()
{
    jinglePath = AQP::applicationPathOf("jingles");
    imagePath = AQP::applicationPathOf("images");

    fileOpenAction = new JingleAction(
            jinglePath + "/fileopen.wav",
            QIcon(imagePath + "/fileopen.png"), tr("Open..."), this);
    fileOpenAction->setShortcuts(QKeySequence::Open);
    ...
}
```

We have only shown the creation of the first action since almost all of them follow the same pattern. The exception is the mute jingles action which is made checkable and initialized to be unchecked.

We begin by determining the directories where the jingles and images are to be found. And when we use the paths—which are kept as private instance variables for use in other methods—we use Unix-style path separators since these work on all platforms.

The jingle files must be in the filesystem—they cannot be Qt resources since at the time of this writing, the QSound class doesn't support resources. For this reason we have stored the application's jingles, and for consistency, its images too, in the filesystem rather than compiled them into a resource. (We discussed AQP::applicationPathOf() earlier; 33 ◄.) In view of this we must make sure that when the application is run it can find the jingles and images.

We will now look at the implementations of the methods the application provides to support its actions for opening, playing, and stopping a movie file, taking and saving a snapshot, and toggling the jingles' mute state.

```
void MainWindow::fileOpen()
{
    QString fileFormats = AQP::filenameFilter(tr("Movies"),
            QMovie::supportedFormats());
    QString path(movie && !movie->fileName().isEmpty()
            ? QFileInfo(movie->fileName()).absolutePath() : ".");
    QString filename = QFileDialog::getOpenFileName(this,
            tr("%1 - Choose a Movie File")
            .arg(QApplication::applicationName()), path, fileFormats);
    if (filename.isEmpty())
        return;

    movie->setFileName(filename);
```

```
        statusBar()->showMessage(tr("Loaded %1").arg(filename),
                                 StatusTimeout);
        movieState = Stopped;
        startOrStop(DontReload);
    }
```

The QMovie::supportedFormats() static method returns a QList<QByteArray> of
file suffixes—for example, ["gif", "mng"]. The aqp.{hpp,cpp} module's AQP::
filenameFilter() function returns a QString based on such a list—for example,
"Movies (*.gif *.mng)"—that is suitable for passing to the QFileDialog::get-
OpenFileName() function as a file filter.

If the user chooses a file we set the movie's filename to the given file and update
the status bar. Then we set the movie state, and call the startOrStop() slot to
immediately begin playing the movie. The startOrStop() method's parameter
has a default value of Reload, but here we have explicitly passed DontReload
since we have already loaded the movie.

```
    void MainWindow::startOrStop(ReloadMode reloadMode)
    {
        if (movieState == Stopped) {
            if (reloadMode == Reload)
                movie->setFileName(movie->fileName());
            movie->start();
            movieState = Playing;
        }
        else {
            movie->stop();
            movieState = Stopped;
        }
        updateUi();
    }
```

We must call QMovie::setFileName() if we want to replay a movie that has already been loaded and played, so we don't need to call it for a freshly loaded
movie. The movie is started or stopped depending on the value of the movie-
State, and the user interface is updated to reflect the current situation in the
updateUi() method.

```
    void MainWindow::updateUi()
    {
        if (movieState == Playing) {
            startOrStopAction->setText(tr("&Stop"));
            startOrStopAction->setIcon(QIcon(imagePath +
                                       "/editstop.png"));
            startOrStopAction->setJingleFile(jinglePath +
                                       "/editstop.wav");
```

```
    }
    else {
        startOrStopAction->setText(tr("&Start"));
        startOrStopAction->setIcon(QIcon(imagePath +
                                         "/editstart.png"));
        startOrStopAction->setJingleFile(jinglePath +
                                         "/editstart.wav");
    }
    startOrStopAction->setEnabled(movieState != NoMovie);
    takeSnapshotAction->setEnabled(movieState != NoMovie);
}
```

In this method we update the startOrStopAction jingle action's text, icon, and
jingle file to make it into a start action or into a stop action. If there is no
movie—for example, when the application starts up—then both the start or
stop action, and the take snapshot action, are disabled.

```
void MainWindow::takeSnapshot()
{
    snapshot = movie->currentPixmap();
    fileSaveAction->setEnabled(!snapshot.isNull());
    snapshotLabel->setPixmap(snapshot);
}
```

When a movie has been loaded (whether playing or stopped), the user can take
a snapshot of the current frame using the QMovie::currentPixmap() method. If
this results in a not-null pixmap (as it should), we enable the save action, and
in any case we set the snapshot label to show the pixmap.

```
void MainWindow::fileSave()
{
    if (snapshot.isNull())
        return;
    QString fileFormats = AQP::filenameFilter(tr("Images"),
            QImageWriter::supportedImageFormats());
    QString filename = QFileDialog::getSaveFileName(this,
            tr("%1 - Save Snapshot")
            .arg(QApplication::applicationName()),
            QFileInfo(movie->fileName()).absolutePath(), fileFormats);
    if (filename.isEmpty())
        return;

    if (!snapshot.save(filename))
        AQP::warning(this, tr("Error"),
                    tr("Failed to save snapshot image"));
    else
        statusBar()->showMessage(tr("Saved %1").arg(filename),
```

```
                              StatusTimeout);
    }
```

If there is a snapshot to save we pop up a suitable `QFileDialog` with a filter that shows the pixmap image formats that Qt can write to. If the user chooses a filename we attempt to save the snapshot under the given name, leaving `QPixmap::save()` to work out the file format to use based on the filename's suffix. If the save fails we pop up a message box; otherwise we note the successful save in the status bar. (See the "Avoiding Qt's Static Convenience QMessageBox Functions" sidebar, for why we use `AQP::warning()` and similar functions rather than Qt's standard static `QMessageBox` functions when presenting messages to the user; ➤ 61.) Another benefit of using the AQP convenience functions is that they put the application's name (using `QApplication::applicationName()`) in their title bars, so we only need to pass the rest of the title. (Compare the call to `QFileDialog::getSaveFileName()` and `AQP::warning()` to see the difference.)

```
    void MainWindow::muteJingles(bool mute)
    {
        JingleAction::setMute(mute);
    }
```

One of the actions created in the main window's constructor is the `fileMute-JinglesAction`, a toggle action whose initial state is unchecked. The action is added to the menu and to the toolbar and is connected to this slot to give the user control over whether jingles are played.

While `QSound` and `QMovie` are very useful for providing aural and visual cues, neither provides sophisticated multimedia capabilities. Fortunately, the Phonon multimedia library covered in the next section provides considerable multimedia functionality that we can step up to when we need it.

The Phonon Multimedia Framework

The Phonon multimedia library was created by KDE ('K' Desktop Environment) developers to make it easier to write multimedia applications for KDE. Phonon has two components—the front end which provides the generic multimedia API, and the backend which provides the actual multimedia services to the API. Qt's *Phonon* module provides a thin Qt-style wrapper around much of the Phonon APIs. To make the module available it is essential to add the line `QT += phonon` to the .pro file for any project that wants to use it.

One of the most important features of Phonon is that it can be used cross-platform thanks to its support for a variety of backends. On Linux it normally uses the GStreamer libraries, on Mac OS X it uses QuickTime, and on Windows it uses the DirectX and DirectShow libraries. Using other backend libraries is also possible—for example, the VLC and MPlayer backends

Avoiding Qt's Static Convenience QMessageBox Functions

The QMessageBox class provides several static convenience functions for popping up modal dialogs with the messages and buttons we want. However, Mac OS X users expect them to appear as *sheets*, not dialogs. A sheet is a modal dialog, but it comes into view by sliding down from its parent window's title bar and is shown centered at the top of the window (as if part of the window, and unmovable), rather than popping up as an independent dialog centered on top of the window and being movable and resizable.

To make our applications properly cross-platform, we have created our own message box convenience functions, AQP::information(), AQP::warning(), and AQP::question(). We have also created AQP::okToDelete(), a function that pops up a dialog with Delete and Do Not Delete buttons (➤ 101), and AQP::okToClearData(), a function that pops up a dialog with Save, Discard, and Cancel buttons (➤ 136). Both AQP::okToDelete() and AQP::okToClearData() return a bool, and in the case of AQP::okToClearData(), the function also calls the "save" method it is passed if the user asks to save. Here's the AQP::warning() function—all the others are similar.

```
void warning(QWidget *parent, const QString &title,
             const QString &text, const QString &detailedText)
{
    QScopedPointer<QMessageBox> messageBox(new QMessageBox(parent));
    if (parent)
        messageBox->setWindowModality(Qt::WindowModal);
    messageBox->setWindowTitle(QString("%1 - %2")
            .arg(QApplication::applicationName()).arg(title));
    messageBox->setText(text);
    if (!detailedText.isEmpty())
        messageBox->setInformativeText(detailedText);
    messageBox->setIcon(QMessageBox::Warning);
    messageBox->addButton(QMessageBox::Ok);
    messageBox->exec();
}
```

The message box only needs to exist for the duration of the function, since after the blocking exec() call finishes, it is closed. We hold the message box's pointer in a QScopedPointer (or in a QSharedPointer for Qt 4.5); this ensures that the pointer is deleted once it goes out of scope, which avoids the risk of a memory leak and saves us from having to explicitly delete it ourselves. (See the "Qt's Smart Pointers" sidebar; ➤ 62.)

Setting the window modality to Qt::WindowModal is essential to ensure that the window appears as a sheet on Mac OS X, although it will be a standard modal dialog on other platforms.

Qt's Smart Pointers

Qt 4.0 introduced the QPointer guarded pointer, Qt 4.5 introduced the QSharedPointer and QWeakPointer smart pointers, and Qt 4.6 introduced the QScopedPointer smart pointer. These pointer types wrap plain pointers, and they usually consume more memory and may be slower to access than plain pointers. Nonetheless, smart pointers are so useful and convenient—and can help avoid memory leaks—that they are well worth using.

In the context of Qt programming—thanks to Qt's parent–child ownership hierarchy—we rarely need smart pointers because we rarely need to call delete. However, any time that we do need to call delete, or have a pointer that may be set to 0 elsewhere, we should consider using a smart pointer.

The most commonly used and versatile smart pointer is QSharedPointer; this behaves much like the std::shared_ptr class that is available from Boost and that will be in the next C++ standard. Unfortunately, QSharedPointer's API is not quite the same as std::shared_ptr; in particular, to get the plain pointer held inside the smart pointer, the methods are QSharedPointer::data() and std::shared_ptr::get(). What makes QSharedPointer so smart is that it can be treated exactly like a normal pointer, it can be copied (so we can have two or more QSharedPointers pointing to the same object), but once the last (or only) QSharedPointer goes out of scope, it automatically deletes the plain pointer that it wraps.

If we don't use a smart pointer for an object allocated on the heap and that isn't part of a Qt parent–child hierarchy, then we are responsible for deleting the pointer once it is no longer needed. Putting a delete statement at the end of the code that uses the pointer is not sufficient, since an exception might occur that causes the function to be prematurely returned from, before the delete statement has been reached, and therefore causes a memory leak. One solution to this is to use a try ... catch construct, and to put the delete statement inside the catch block. This requires care to ensure that we catch all the exceptions that could occur; and we cannot use a catch-all exception handler since we don't want to accidentally—and silently—catch unexpected exceptions, thereby hiding bugs.

The best approach is to use RAII (Resource Acquisition Is Initialization)—which in practical terms means that we create our pointers inside scoped (or shared) pointer constructor calls. Now we don't have to worry about deleting the pointer ourselves, nor do we have to worry about exceptions causing the function to return early—because as soon as a scoped pointer (or the last shared pointer pointing to an object) goes out of scope for whatever reason, it will delete the object it points to.

Using Qt's parent–child object hierarchy, and also smart pointers, means that for some applications, calls to delete can be completely eliminated.

Table 2.1 *The Main Phonon Classes*

Class	Description
Phonon::AudioOutput	An audio sink media node that drives the sound card or headset
Phonon::Effect	A processor media node that can transform an audio stream
Phonon::EffectWidget	A widget for controlling an effect processor's parameters
Phonon::MediaNode	The base class for all media node types
Phonon::MediaObject	A media node that controls the playback of multimedia objects
Phonon::MediaSource	An object that provides media data to a media object source node
Phonon::Path	A data path from a media object source node to a media object sink node
Phonon::SeekSlider	A widget for showing and modifying a media object's playback position in time
Phonon::VideoPlayer	A widget that can load and play video media, and that automatically handles the creation of the media nodes and paths behind the scenes
Phonon::VideoWidget	A widget for playing video media
Phonon::VolumeSlider	A widget for showing and modifying a media object's volume

(code.google.com/p/phonon-vlc-mplayer). The platform-specific backend must be installed when building Qt—instructions are provided at qt.nokia.com/doc/phonon-overview.html.*

The Phonon framework in essence has three kinds of objects: media data sources, media nodes, and media devices. The classes representing these objects are listed in Table 2.1.

Media data sources are represented by Phonon::MediaSource objects, and these are given a file, URL, or QIODevice from which the media data is to be retrieved. These are not media nodes in their own right and can only be used if given to a media object source node.

Media nodes come in three varieties: source nodes (not to be confused with media data sources), processor nodes, and sink nodes. Source nodes are represented by Phonon::MediaObject objects and provide the media playback interface.

---

*At the time of this writing, building the Windows DirectShow backend is only supported when using a commercial compiler.

`Phonon::MediaObjects` have a current `Phonon::MediaSource` object, and can also have a queue of other media source objects ready to play one after the other as each one finishes.

The output from a `Phonon::MediaObject` must go to a sink via one or more paths. A path is represented by a `Phonon::Path` object, and must have a source node (a `Phonon::MediaObject`) and a sink node such as a `Phonon::AudioOutput` or `Phonon::VideoWidget`. The path may be direct, or can contain intermediate processor nodes to provide special effects.

The *Phonon* module does not support the direct manipulation of the data in media streams. It does, however, provide an indirect means of manipulating audio streams: effects processors. These processors, of class `Phonon::Effect`, can be added to the path between the source and sink where they transform the data flowing from one to the other. The available effects depend on the Phonon backend and are available from the `Phonon::BackendCapabilities::available-AudioEffects()` function. The effects might include amplification, positioning streams in the stereo panorama, equalizing, or resampling.

To apply an effect we create a new `Phonon::Effect` instance for the effect we want. Then, assuming that we kept the `Phonon::Path` pointer returned by the `Phonon::createPath()` function, we call `Phonon::Path::insertEffect()`, passing it the `Phonon::Effect` we have created.

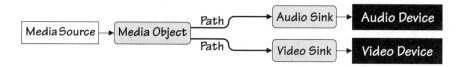

Figure 2.2 *The Phonon architecture*

The sink node is where the data is finally sent to the physical output device, such as the sound card, headset, or a video widget, represented by the `Phonon::AudioOutput` media node, or by the `Phonon::VideoPlayer` or `Phonon::VideoWidget` widgets which also serve as media nodes. The relationships are illustrated in Figure 2.2.

Now that we've got a feel for how the Phonon framework works in theory, we will see how to use it in practice. In the two subsections that follow we will review two examples, one that plays music and one that plays videos (including their sound track if they have one).

Playing Music

The Play Music example (`playmusic`) reviewed in this subsection and shown in Figure 2.3 shows how to create a music playing application. Such applications

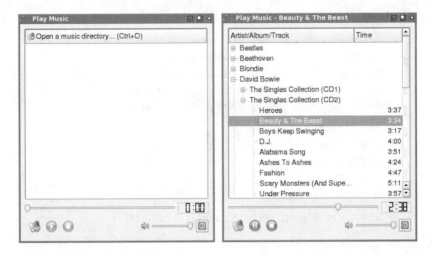

Figure 2.3 *The Play Music application at startup and with a music directory*

usually use playlists, a database, or the filesystem to organize tracks; in this example we have chosen to use the filesystem. When the program is started it has a blank central area and invites the user to choose a music directory. Once the directory is chosen, the program iterates over all the music files in the directory, recursing into any subdirectories, and populates a QTreeWidget with the artist, album, and track names, and with the duration of each track.

The user can navigate to a particular track using the mouse or keyboard, and play or pause the track using the Play/Pause toolbar button or by pressing the Spacebar thanks to the Space keyboard shortcut. Once the track has finished, the application automatically starts playing the next track, unless the user has clicked Stop.

The application's data is held in a QTreeWidget. For artists and albums just their names are held, but for tracks both the name and the corresponding filename are held—all in TreeWidgetItems, a simple QTreeWidgetItem subclass that we will discuss later. (The QTreeWidget is one of Qt's model/view convenience classes—a view that provides its own model. The model/view architecture, including the creation and use of custom models, is covered in Chapters 3 through 6.)

We will start by looking at the main window's constructor to get an overview of how the application is set up.

```
const int FilenameRole = Qt::UserRole;
const int OneSecond = AQP::MSecPerSecond;

MainWindow::MainWindow(QWidget *parent)
    : QMainWindow(parent), nextItem(0)
{
    playIcon = QIcon(":/play.png");
```

```
        pauseIcon = QIcon(":/pause.png");

        mediaObject = new Phonon::MediaObject(this);
        mediaObject->setTickInterval(OneSecond);
        audioOutput = new Phonon::AudioOutput(Phonon::MusicCategory,
                                              this);
        Phonon::createPath(mediaObject, audioOutput);

        createActions();
        createToolBar();
        createWidgets();
        createLayout();
        createConnections();

        setWindowTitle(QApplication::applicationName());
    }
```

The nextItem is a TreeWidgetItem that represents the next track to be played. It is set when the user chooses a track, and also automatically, when the current track comes to an end. Tree widget items can have multiple columns of data, and each column can hold a list of QVariants as user data. As we will see further on, we use this feature for tree widget items that represent tracks to store the track's filename in the first column's user data (i.e., in column 0), using the FilenameRole constant as an index into the item's user data.

The private mediaObject is used to play whichever track the user chooses, and the sound data is sent to the private audio output sink. For the audio output we must specify the category of sound that the audio is being used for. The category is used to identify where the audio output should go. For example, for a telephony application using VoIP (Voice over Internet Protocol) the sound will be sent to the user's headset, while a music player's sound will be sent to the sound card.

Once the media object and the output sink exist we can create a path to join them, and since we are not going to add any processors to the path for special effects, we don't keep a reference to the path we have created. In addition, we tell the media object to emit a tick() signal every second (1000 milliseconds) —we will use this to update the LCD number widget that shows the current position in time.

We won't look at the createActions(), createToolBar(), or createLayout() methods since they contain no surprises. But we will see how the Phonon widgets are created by looking at an extract from the createWidgets() method, and we will also look at createConnections().

```
    void MainWindow::createWidgets()
    {
        seekSlider = new Phonon::SeekSlider(this);
        seekSlider->setToolTip(tr("Playback Position"));
```

```
        seekSlider->setMediaObject(mediaObject);
        volumeSlider = new Phonon::VolumeSlider(this);
        volumeSlider->setToolTip(tr("Volume Control"));
        volumeSlider->setAudioOutput(audioOutput);
        volumeSlider->setSizePolicy(QSizePolicy::Maximum,
                                    QSizePolicy::Maximum);
        ...
    }
```

The seek slider is the top-most slider shown in Figure 2.3 (65 ◄). This slider
is used to show visually what proportion of the current track has been played,
and it is also possible for the user to manipulate it to skip forward or backward.
This slider is attached to the media object so that it can reflect or modify the
playing position. The volume slider (which also includes a mute button) is used
to set the volume. This slider is attached to the audio output sink.

We will look at the createConnections() method in two parts.

```
    void MainWindow::createConnections()
    {
        connect(mediaObject, SIGNAL(tick(qint64)),
                this, SLOT(tick(qint64)));
        connect(mediaObject,
                SIGNAL(stateChanged(Phonon::State, Phonon::State)),
                this, SLOT(stateChanged(Phonon::State)));
        connect(mediaObject, SIGNAL(aboutToFinish()),
                this, SLOT(aboutToFinish()));
        connect(mediaObject,
                SIGNAL(currentSourceChanged(const Phonon::MediaSource&)),
                this, SLOT(currentSourceChanged()));
```

The first four connections are from the media object to main window slots.
The tick() connection is used to update the LCD number widget that shows
the current track's position in time. The stateChanged() connection is used
to respond to state changes—for example, this allows us to enable/disable the
controls appropriately. The signal actually emits both the new (current) state
and the old (previous) state; but in this application we only care about the new
state. The aboutToFinish() connection is used to add the next track to be played
to the media object's queue to ensure a smooth transition from one track to
the next. When the media object's source changes, that is, when a new track
is loaded, the currentSourceChanged() signal is emitted, and we use it to update
the state of the user interface.

```
        connect(setMusicDirectoryAction, SIGNAL(triggered()),
                this, SLOT(setMusicDirectory()));
        connect(playOrPauseAction, SIGNAL(triggered()),
                this, SLOT(playOrPause()));
```

```
        connect(stopAction, SIGNAL(triggered()), this, SLOT(stop()));
        connect(treeWidget,
            SIGNAL(currentItemChanged(QTreeWidgetItem*,QTreeWidgetItem*)),
            this, SLOT(currentItemChanged(QTreeWidgetItem*)));
        connect(treeWidget,
            SIGNAL(itemDoubleClicked(QTreeWidgetItem*, int)),
            this, SLOT(playTrack(QTreeWidgetItem*)));
        connect(quitAction, SIGNAL(triggered()), this, SLOT(close()));
    }
```

The remaining connections are used to provide the general behavior of the
user interface, to set the music directory to be scanned in the first place, to play,
pause, or stop playing a track, and to choose a new track, or to quit the application.

We will now review all the slots, since they are all relevant to using the Phonon
framework. We will start with by far the most involved, setMusicDirectory(),
since this shows how the tree is populated and also how we can use a temporary
media object to retrieve information about a track. We will review the method
in three parts, and then look at the private helper methods it makes use of.

```
    void MainWindow::setMusicDirectory()
    {
        QString path = QFileDialog::getExistingDirectory(this,
                tr("Choose a Music Directory"),
                QDesktopServices::storageLocation(
                    QDesktopServices::MusicLocation));
        if (path.isEmpty())
            return;
```

We begin by asking the user to choose a music directory, defaulting to the directory provided by the static QDesktopServices::storageLocation() method.
For example, on Windows, the directory returned might be %HOMEPATH%\My
Documents\My Music or %USERPROFILE%\My Documents\My Music (with the environment variable replaced with the actual path).

```
        QApplication::setOverrideCursor(QCursor(Qt::WaitCursor));
        QSet<QString> validSuffixes = getSuffixes();
        treeWidget->clear();
        treeWidget->headerItem()->setIcon(0, QIcon());
        treeWidget->setHeaderLabels(QStringList()
                << tr("Artist/Album/Track") << tr("Time"));
        QHash<QString, TreeWidgetItem*> itemForArtist;
        QHash<QString, TreeWidgetItem*> itemForArtistAlbum;
        QDirIterator i(path, QDirIterator::Subdirectories);
        while (i.hasNext()) {
            const QString filename = i.next();
```

```
            if (!QFileInfo(filename).isFile() ||
                !validSuffixes.contains(QFileInfo(filename).suffix()))
                continue;
            addTrack(filename, &itemForArtist, &itemForArtistAlbum);
        }
```

We begin by obtaining a set of file suffixes that indicate those music files that the Phonon backend can play. We create two hashes, one to give the appropriate artist tree item for a given artist's name, and the other to give the appropriate album tree item for a given artist and album's name. (We must combine artist and album names for albums to avoid collisions in the rare case that two different artists have the same album name.)

To traverse all the music files we begin by creating a QDirIterator—such objects provide a very convenient way of iterating over all the files in a directory, automatically recursing into subdirectories, and providing the name of every file, directory, or other filesystem object that is encountered. For each name that refers to a file (rather than a directory, a link, or some other filesystem object), and has a suitable suffix, we call addTrack() to add the file's details to the tree widget.

The QFileInfo class has methods such as isFile() and isDir() to identify the kind of filesystem object a name refers to, as well as methods for returning components of the name, such as absolutePath(), fileName(), and suffix(). Other methods provide information on the permissions, such as isReadable() and isWritable(), and on aspects of state, such as the size(), and the created() date/time and lastModified() date/time.

```
        foreach (QTreeWidgetItem *item, itemForArtistAlbum)
            if (!item->childCount())
                delete item;
        foreach (QTreeWidgetItem *item, itemForArtist)
            if (!item->childCount())
                delete item;
        treeWidget->sortItems(0, Qt::AscendingOrder);
        treeWidget->resizeColumnToContents(0);
        stop();
        QApplication::restoreOverrideCursor();
    }
```

Toward the end we do some cleaning up. For example, if we have an album with no tracks we delete the album, and similarly if we have an artist with no albums we delete the artist. We then sort the items and resize the first column. We also stop any previous track from playing since the tree has been completely cleared and repopulated, which means that any track that was shown before may no longer be accessible through the user interface.

By default if we sort a tree widget's first column, the sorting is applied at each level of indentation, and uses a case-sensitive string comparison. We want to have the items sort differently, and for this reason we have populated the tree with custom `TreeWidgetItems` rather than with the `QTreeWidgetItems` they inherit. The `TreeWidgetItem` constructor (not shown) simply passes on its arguments to the base class and has an empty body. The only code we have added is a reimplementation of the inline `operator<()` member function:

```
bool operator<(const QTreeWidgetItem &other) const
{
    QString left = data(0, FilenameRole).toString();
    QString right;
    if (!left.isEmpty())
        right = other.data(0, FilenameRole).toString();
    else {
        left = text(0);
        right = other.text(0);
    }
    return QString::compare(left, right, Qt::CaseInsensitive) < 0;
}
```

The `operator<()` method *must* define a total ordering for the tree widget to work correctly. Yet at first glance, the code shown does not appear to provide such an ordering—but it does. The tree widget sorts each level of indentation independently under its parent item (and for top-level items under a notional invisible root item). So in this case artists are sorted together, and albums are sorted under their artist, and tracks are sorted under their album. When we have an artist or album there is no user data so the comparison is made between their texts, and when we have a track the comparison is made between their user data (filenames). This works nicely if the file naming scheme has names that start with track numbers, for example, `01-Space Oddity.ogg`, `02-Changes.ogg`, `03-Starman.ogg`, and ensures that at each level of the hierarchy we do have a total ordering.

Two other points to note on the subject of efficiency. We only check that one item's user data is empty, since if it is we are comparing either artists or albums so the other item's user data must be empty. And instead of doing the comparison like this: `return left.toLower() < right.toLower()`, we use the much faster `QString::compare()` function (which returns an `int`), and convert its result to a suitable `bool`.

We will now look at the two helper methods called by `setMusicDirectory()`.

```
QSet<QString> MainWindow::getSuffixes()
{
    QStringList mimeTypes;
    foreach (const QString &mimeType,
```

```
                    Phonon::BackendCapabilities::availableMimeTypes())
            if (mimeType.startsWith("audio/"))
                mimeTypes << mimeType;
        return AQP::suffixesForMimeTypes(mimeTypes);
    }
```

The Phonon framework identifies data using MIME types. The aqp.{hpp,cpp}
module's AQP::suffixesForMimeTypes() function accepts a list of MIME types
and returns a set of corresponding file suffixes. Although this looks clean and
simple, it isn't quite so straightforward under the hood, as the "MIME Types,
File Suffixes, and Magic Numbers" sidebar explains (➤ 72).

We will look at the addTrack() method in two parts.

```
    void MainWindow::addTrack(const QString &filename,
            QHash<QString, TreeWidgetItem*> *itemForArtist,
            QHash<QString, TreeWidgetItem*> *itemForArtistAlbum)
    {
        Phonon::MediaObject localMediaObject;
        Phonon::MediaSource source(filename);
        localMediaObject.setCurrentSource(source);
        if (!waitForMediaObjectToLoad(&localMediaObject, OneSecond))
            return;
        QString artist = localMediaObject.metaData(
                Phonon::ArtistMetaData).join("/").trimmed();
        QString album = localMediaObject.metaData(
                Phonon::AlbumMetaData).join("/").trimmed();
        QString artistAlbum = artist + "\t" + album;
        QString track = localMediaObject.metaData(
                Phonon::TitleMetaData).join("/").trimmed();
        qint64 msec = localMediaObject.totalTime();
```

The local media object, localMediaObject, is used purely to gather information
(meta-data) about each track. We begin by setting the media object's source
to the given filename. The media object will then begin loading the music file.
It can take a small but nonetheless nonzero time to load a music file to access
its meta-data, and in some cases the meta-data cannot be retrieved at all—for
example, if the file is corrupt. We have chosen to use a local event loop with a
timeout to handle this, as we will see when we cover the waitForMediaObjectTo-
Load() method further on.

We retrieve the music file's meta-data, joining the QStringList that each
QMediaObject::metaData() call returns into a single "/"-separated QString. The
QMediaObject::totalTime() method returns the duration of the track in mil-
liseconds. One item of meta-data we did not retrieve is Phonon::Tracknumber-
MetaData; this is sometimes empty, so we have preferred to order the tracks by
filename as we mentioned earlier.

MIME Types, File Suffixes, and Magic Numbers

There are three widely used methods for identifying the type of a file or of a "lump" of data received in an email or downloaded from the Internet. One method is to use a file suffix; for example, .png identifies Portable Network Graphics (PNG) files. Another method is to use magic numbers—these are typically a sequence of at least one byte usually at the start of a file—for example, PNG files begin with the eight bytes 0x89 0x50 0x4E 0x47 0x0D 0x0A 0x1A 0x0A.

Unfortunately, both file suffixes and magic numbers suffer from the same problem: there are no official standards, so it is possible for two or more file suffixes or magic numbers to refer to completely different types of files or data. Such duplication does occur in practice, particularly for file suffixes.

A third method of identifying files or data is to use a MIME type, for example, image/png for PNG data. MIME types have the advantage of being standardized by the IANA (Internet Assigned Numbers Authority), so each MIME type uniquely identifies the type of data it is associated with.

The *Phonon* module (and incidentally, Qt's clipboard and drag and drop system) uses MIME types to identify the kinds of files or data it can handle. This works well for data received by email or from the Internet. Unfortunately, using MIME types is not so convenient for handling files because we must somehow map MIME types to file suffixes or to magic numbers, and although MIME types are standardized, there is no official mapping between MIME types and file suffixes or magic numbers. On Linux systems a suitable—though often incomplete—mapping is usually supplied in the plain text file /etc/mime.types.

The aqp.{hpp,cpp} module provided with this book's examples contains a function with signature QSet<QString> suffixesForMimeTypes(const QString-List &mimeTypes) that uses the mime.types file if it is available (as well as its own data) to provide a suitable mapping from MIME types to file suffixes. The function works on all platforms, and it is easy to extend to include additional MIME types by adding to the mime.types resource file or by adapting the code.

Note: Apple Inc. has developed a fourth method of identifying item types (including files and lumps of data): Uniform Type Identifiers (UTIs). These are intended to avoid the problems that afflict the other identification methods, but at the time of this writing UTIs have not been widely adopted.

The code here has a slight fragility, in the case that the meta-data is incomplete or absent. One possible solution would be to set a missing artist and missing album to the filename, and to set the track to be a count number that is incremented for every track read.

```
        TreeWidgetItem *artistItem = itemForArtist->value(artist);
        if (!artistItem) {
            artistItem = new TreeWidgetItem(
                    treeWidget->invisibleRootItem(),
                    QStringList() << artist);
            itemForArtist->insert(artist, artistItem);
        }
        TreeWidgetItem *albumItem = itemForArtistAlbum->value(
                artistAlbum);
        if (!albumItem) {
            albumItem = new TreeWidgetItem(artistItem,
                                        QStringList() << album);
            itemForArtistAlbum->insert(artistAlbum, albumItem);
        }
        TreeWidgetItem *trackItem = new TreeWidgetItem(albumItem,
                QStringList() << track
                            << minutesSecondsAsStringForMSec(msec));
        trackItem->setData(0, FilenameRole, filename);
        trackItem->setTextAlignment(1, Qt::AlignVCenter|Qt::AlignRight);
    }
```

Each track must be placed in the tree as a child of an album, and each album in its turn must be the child of an artist. So we begin by looking in the item-ForArtist hash for the artist tree widget item that corresponds to the current track's artist. If this is the first track on the first album by the artist, there will be no such item, and QHash::value() will return a default-constructed Tree-WidgetItem value, that is, a null pointer. And in this case we create the item as a child of the tree's invisible root, that is, as a top-level item. Whether we create or retrieve the item, we end up with a tree widget item for the track's artist. And if we created the item, we add it to the itemForArtist hash so that it can be retrieved next time it is needed.

We apply a similar process to get the album item, only if we must create it (because this is the first track of the first album by the track's artist), we make the album item a child of the artist item. And so we end up with a tree widget item for the track's album. And if we created the item, we add it to the itemForArtistAlbum hash.

Finally, we create the track item, making it a child of the album item that itself is a child of the artist item. And we set the track item's first column to the track's name and its second column to the track's duration in minutes and seconds. We also set the track's first column's user data to its filename.

For completeness, and since we use it again later on, here is the minutesSeconds-AsStringForMSec() method:

```
QString MainWindow::minutesSecondsAsStringForMSec(qint64 msec)
{
    int minutes;
    int seconds;
    AQP::hoursMinutesSecondsForMSec(msec, 0, &minutes, &seconds);
    return QString("%1:%2").arg(minutes, 2, 10, QChar(' '))
                           .arg(seconds, 2, 10, QChar('0'));
}
```

The AQP::hoursMinutesSecondsForMSec() function takes a number of milliseconds and populates up to three integers passed by pointer with the hours, minutes, and seconds that the milliseconds represent. When QString::arg() is given an integer as first argument the other optional arguments are the field width, the base, and the padding character.

The addTrack() method uses the waitForMediaObjectToLoad() method to populate each music file's meta-data. One simple approach to doing this would be to have a while loop inside which we would keep checking to see if the meta-data is ready and to have a timer whose timeout we could use to break out of the loop if we have waited too long. Unfortunately such busy-waiting loops needlessly consume a lot of CPU cycles so we have taken a more efficient approach and have used a local event loop instead.

```
bool MainWindow::waitForMediaObjectToLoad(
        Phonon::MediaObject *mediaObject, int timeoutMSec)
{
    QEventLoop eventLoop;
    QTimer timer;
    timer.setSingleShot(true);
    timer.setInterval(timeoutMSec);
    connect(&timer, SIGNAL(timeout()), &eventLoop, SLOT(quit()));
    connect(mediaObject,
            SIGNAL(stateChanged(Phonon::State, Phonon::State)),
            &eventLoop, SLOT(quit()));
    timer.start();
    eventLoop.exec();
    return mediaObject->state() == Phonon::StoppedState;
}
```

We begin by creating an event loop and a single shot timer with the given timeout. The two signal–slot connections both stop the event loop, the first as the result of a timeout and the second as the result of a change of state. Once these are set up, we start off the timer and the event loop, and wait for the event loop to finish.

While the media object is loading it has the state Phonon::LoadingState. Once the media object's state changes we break out of the event loop. If the loading was successful the media object's state will be Phonon::StoppedState and we can confidently retrieve the media object's meta-data, so in this case we return true. If the event loop is stopped by the timeout signal we assume that the file is corrupt or for some other reason unreadable, and return false—in such cases the caller will skip the file and not add it to the tree.

We have now reached the point where we have scanned the music directory and have populated the tree with the details of every readable track we have found. The user can now navigate the tree, and whenever the current item changes, the currentItemChanged() slot is called.

```
void MainWindow::currentItemChanged(QTreeWidgetItem *item)
{
    if (!playOrPauseAction->isEnabled()) {
        QString filename = item->data(0, FilenameRole).toString();
        if (!filename.isEmpty())
            playOrPauseAction->setEnabled(true);
    }
}
```

If the playOrPauseAction QAction is disabled but the current item is now a track, we enable it so that the user can press the Play/Pause button. When this button is pressed the playOrPause() slot is called.

```
void MainWindow::playOrPause()
{
    switch (mediaObject->state()) {
        case Phonon::PlayingState:
            mediaObject->pause();
            playOrPauseAction->setIcon(playIcon);
            break;
        case Phonon::PausedState:
            mediaObject->play();
            playOrPauseAction->setIcon(pauseIcon);
            break;
        default:
            playTrack(treeWidget->currentItem());
            break;
    }
}
```

If a track is already playing, the Play/Pause button is being used as a Pause button, so we pause the media object and change the button's icon to indicate that it is now a Play button. If a track is paused, we do things the other way round, playing the media object and turning the button into a Pause button.

If the track is not being played and is not paused then the user must have pressed Play on a newly chosen item. In this case we call the playTrack() slot with the current item. This slot is also called if the user double-clicks an item.

```
void MainWindow::playTrack(QTreeWidgetItem *item)
{
    Q_ASSERT(item);
    QString filename = item->data(0, FilenameRole).toString();
    if (filename.isEmpty())
        return;
    if (!QFile::exists(filename)) {
        AQP::warning(this, tr("Error"),
                tr("File %1 appears to have been moved or deleted")
                .arg(filename));
        return;
    }
    nextItem = item;
    mediaObject->clearQueue();
    mediaObject->setCurrentSource(filename);
    mediaObject->play();
}
```

We begin by trying to retrieve the track's filename, and do nothing if the current item is an artist or album (and therefore has no filename), or if the file has been moved or deleted since the music directory was read—although in such cases we also pop up an error message. (See the sidebar for why we use AQP::warning() rather than QMessageBox::warning(); 61 ◄.) We set the nextItem to the current item, clear the media object's queue of media sources, set its current source to the track's filename, and start playing. As a result the currentSourceChanged() slot will be called.

```
const QString ZeroTime(" 0:00");

void MainWindow::currentSourceChanged()
{
    if (nextItem) {
        playOrPauseAction->setIcon(pauseIcon);
        timeLcd->display(ZeroTime);
        setWindowTitle(tr("%1 - %2")
                .arg(QApplication::applicationName())
                .arg(nextItem->text(0)));
        treeWidget->setCurrentItem(nextItem);
        nextItem = 0;
    }
}
```

If there is a next item (as there will be if this slot has been called as a result of the user pressing Play on a newly chosen track or double-clicking a track), we update the user interface, setting the LCD to 0:00 and showing the track's name in the title bar. We then set the next item to 0.

At any time while the track is playing the user can click Pause to pause playing, Play to resume playing, or Stop to stop playing. Every time the media object's state changes the stateChanged() slot is called, and at every time tick (each second in this case), the tick() slot is called. And if the user allows the track to play to the end, just before it finishes playing, the aboutToFinish() slot is called. We will now review these slots to see how they're implemented.

```
void MainWindow::stop()
{
    nextItem = 0;
    mediaObject->stop();
    mediaObject->clearQueue();
    playOrPauseAction->setIcon(playIcon);
    timeLcd->display(ZeroTime);
    setWindowTitle(QApplication::applicationName());
}
```

If the user clicks Stop we clear the next item to prevent the next track being played automatically if the current track is almost finished, and stop playing. We also clear the media object's queue, in case the next track has already been queued—we will see how tracks are queued when we look at the aboutTo-Finish() slot further on. Then we update the user interface to reflect the current situation.

```
void MainWindow::tick(qint64 msec)
{
    timeLcd->display(minutesSecondsAsStringForMSec(msec));
}
```

Every tick (in this example, every second), this slot is called and the LCD number widget's display is updated to reflect the track's position in time.

```
void MainWindow::stateChanged(Phonon::State newState)
{
    switch (newState) {
        case Phonon::ErrorState:
            AQP::warning(this, tr("Error"),
                         mediaObject->errorString());
            playOrPauseAction->setEnabled(false);
            stopAction->setEnabled(false);
            break;
        case Phonon::PlayingState:
```

```
                  playOrPauseAction->setEnabled(true);
                  playOrPauseAction->setIcon(pauseIcon);
                  stopAction->setEnabled(true);
                  break;
             case Phonon::PausedState:
                  playOrPauseAction->setEnabled(true);
                  playOrPauseAction->setIcon(playIcon);
                  stopAction->setEnabled(true);
                  break;
             case Phonon::StoppedState:
                  playOrPauseAction->setEnabled(true);
                  playOrPauseAction->setIcon(playIcon);
                  stopAction->setEnabled(false);
                  timeLcd->display(ZeroTime);
                  break;
             default:
                  playOrPauseAction->setEnabled(false);
                  break;
        }
    }
```

Whenever the media object's state changes we update the user interface to ensure that the appropriate actions are enabled or disabled, and in the case of an error we pop up a message box to explain the problem.

```
    void MainWindow::aboutToFinish()
    {
        QTreeWidgetItem *item = nextItem ? nextItem :
                                  treeWidget->currentItem();
        if (!item)
            return;
        item = treeWidget->itemBelow(item);
        if (!item) // Current track is the last track in the tree
            return;
        QString filename = item->data(0, FilenameRole).toString();
        if (filename.isEmpty()) { // item is an Artist or an Album
            item = item->child(0);
            if (!item)
                return;
            else {
                filename = item->data(0, FilenameRole).toString();
                if (filename.isEmpty()) // item is an Album
                    item = item->child(0);
                if (!item)
                    return;
                filename = item->data(0, FilenameRole).toString();
```

```
            if (filename.isEmpty())
                return;
        }
    }
    nextItem = item;
    Phonon::MediaSource source(filename);
    mediaObject->enqueue(source);
}
```

The purpose of the aboutToFinish() slot is to make the application play the
track following the currently playing track if the current track finishes without
having been stopped by the user. The code has to account for four cases. The
easiest case is where there is no item in the tree below the current track; this
means that the last track has been played and we do nothing and return. The
other cases all involve there being an item after the current one. If the following item is an artist, we must find the first track of the artist's first album. Similarly, if the following item is an album, we must find its first track. Otherwise
the following item must be a track. Once we have found the track to play we
set the next item to be the track's tree item, and add a media source based on
the item's filename to the media object's queue.

Providing the user does not click Stop, once the current track finishes, the media object will set its media source to the next queued track and will emit the
currentSourceChanged() signal. This signal is connected to the main window's
currentSourceChanged() slot we reviewed earlier (77 ◀), which updates the user
interface to reflect the fact that a new track has begun playing.

```
void MainWindow::closeEvent(QCloseEvent *event)
{
    nextItem = 0;
    mediaObject->stop();
    mediaObject->clearQueue();
    event->accept();
}
```

When the user terminates the application, it is important to stop the music
from playing—otherwise it will simply continue, even though the application's
window will no longer be visible.

We have now completed our review of the Play Music application. There are
two obvious improvements that could be made. The first is to have the application remember the music directory (e.g., using QSettings), and use it as the
default at startup. The second is to only read directories when first populating
the tree—this will make startup considerably faster if there are large numbers
(hundreds or thousands) of tracks—and only populate the details of each album when the user actually expands a branch. Both these enhancements are
left as exercises.

Although the application is fully functional, we did not make use of all the Phonon APIs available for playing music; nonetheless, we have covered all the most important aspects. Most of the rest concerns fine details. To take just one such detail as an example, it is possible to control how long to wait between finishing playing one track and starting to play the next one in the queue. This is governed by the `transitionTime` property. The default is 0, which means no gap. A negative gap can be used to crossfade the transition, and a positive gap creates a silent transition of the given number of milliseconds. In addition, it is also possible to programmatically seek to a particular position in time (if the media object's underlying media source supports this), and to connect to some of the other signals that media objects provide such as `finished()`, a connection we will see in the next subsection.

Playing Videos

Playing videos is very similar to playing music—at least in principle. The chief difference is that instead of just creating a path from the media object to an audio output, we also create a path from the media object to a video output. We will review the Play Video example (`playvideo`) shown in Figure 2.4 to see how this works in practice.

Figure 2.4 *The Play Video application playing a video (simulated)*

The Play Video example loads and plays a single video at a time, so instead of the user opening a directory as the preceding subsection's Play Music application required, they must open a video file instead. One consequence of this is that we do not create a queue of videos since there is only ever one in use at a time. Nonetheless, the Play Video application is very similar in structure to the Play Music example, so we will only focus on the Phonon-related aspects and especially the differences from the Play Music example. We will begin by looking at the main window's constructor.

```
const int OneSecond = AQP::MSecPerSecond;

MainWindow::MainWindow(QWidget *parent)
    : QMainWindow(parent)
{
    playIcon = QIcon(":/play.png");
    pauseIcon = QIcon(":/pause.png");

    mediaObject = new Phonon::MediaObject(this);
    mediaObject->setTickInterval(OneSecond);
    videoWidget = new Phonon::VideoWidget(this);
    Phonon::createPath(mediaObject, videoWidget);
    audioOutput = new Phonon::AudioOutput(Phonon::VideoCategory,
                                          this);
    Phonon::createPath(mediaObject, audioOutput);

    createActions();
    createToolBar();
    createWidgets();
    createLayout();
    createConnections();

    setWindowTitle(QApplication::applicationName());
}
```

Here we create a media object to manage the video, and create a path from it to a video widget (which is also a video output), and also to an audio output. Creating a path to an audio output is only useful for videos that have sound tracks, but since this application can play arbitrary videos we want to be able to play the sound track if there is one. One other point to notice is that we must specify that the audio's category is `Phonon::VideoCategory`, whereas for music we must use `Phonon::MusicCategory`.

We will skip `createActions()` and all the other create methods (apart from `createConnections()`), since they are all similar to what we have seen before. For example, the `createWidgets()` method is almost the same as the Play Music application's method of the same name, and is where the `Phonon::SeekSlider` and `Phonon::VolumeSlider` are created. Note, however, that we are not obliged to use the widgets provided by the Phonon framework, and could just as well create our own seek and volume controls, either by composing existing widgets or by creating our own custom widgets.

```
void MainWindow::createConnections()
{
    connect(mediaObject, SIGNAL(tick(qint64)),
```

```
                    this, SLOT(tick(qint64))));
        connect(mediaObject,
                SIGNAL(stateChanged(Phonon::State, Phonon::State)),
                this, SLOT(stateChanged(Phonon::State)));
        connect(mediaObject, SIGNAL(finished()), this, SLOT(stop()));
        connect(fullScreenAction, SIGNAL(triggered()),
                videoWidget, SLOT(enterFullScreen()));
        connect(stopAction, SIGNAL(triggered()), this, SLOT(stop()));
        connect(playOrPauseAction, SIGNAL(triggered()),
                this, SLOT(playOrPause()));
        connect(chooseVideoAction, SIGNAL(triggered()),
                this, SLOT(chooseVideo()));
        connect(quitAction, SIGNAL(triggered()), this, SLOT(close()));
    }
```

The first three connections are from the media object to main window slots. The tick() connection is used to update the LCD number widget that shows the current video's position in time. The stateChanged() connection is used to respond to state changes, and the finished() signal is used to detect when the video has finished playing.

The other connections are used to provide general application behavior: start or resume playing, pause, stop, choose a video to play, or quit the application.

One of the connections is from a toolbar button that when clicked switches the video widget to full screen mode. When this happens, only the video is visible, and the user no longer has access to the widgets for controlling the application. In view of this we must provide some means by which the user can return to non-full screen mode. We have achieved this by providing a keyboard shortcut (Esc) and by setting an event filter so that the user can simply click the video widget to return to non-full screen mode. Here are the lines from the createActions() method where the event filter and shortcut are set up:

```
    videoWidget->installEventFilter(this);
    (void) new QShortcut(QKeySequence("Escape"),
                         videoWidget, SLOT(exitFullScreen()));
```

And here is the code for the event filter:

```
    bool MainWindow::eventFilter(QObject *target, QEvent *event)
    {
        if (target == videoWidget &&
            event->type() == QEvent::MouseButtonPress &&
            videoWidget->isFullScreen())
            videoWidget->exitFullScreen();
        return QMainWindow::eventFilter(target, event);
    }
```

This event filter ensures that simply by clicking, the user can return to non-full screen mode.

We could have achieved the same effect by subclassing `Phonon::VideoWidget` and reimplementing its `mousePressEvent()` method. To provide small extensions to a widget's behavior using an event filter as we have done here can be a sensible choice. However, if more than one instance of the widget is required, or if more extensive behavior modification is required, then using a subclass is the best approach—especially since using large numbers of event filters can degrade performance.

We will now review those slots that differ from the ones with the same names in the Play Music application, starting with the longest, `chooseVideo()`, which we will review in three parts.

```
void MainWindow::chooseVideo()
{
    QString filename = QFileDialog::getOpenFileName(this,
            tr("Choose Video"), QDesktopServices::storageLocation(
                QDesktopServices::MoviesLocation), getFileFormats());
    if (filename.isEmpty())
        return;
```

The slot begins by prompting the user to choose a video, with the initial directory set to the user's "movies" directory (or to their home directory if they don't have a movies directory set). If the user cancels we do nothing and return.

```
    stop();
    playOrPauseAction->setEnabled(false);
    stopAction->setEnabled(false);
    mediaObject->setCurrentSource(filename);
    if (!mediaObject->hasVideo()) {
        QEventLoop eventLoop;
        QTimer timer;
        timer.setSingleShot(true);
        timer.setInterval(3 * OneSecond);
        connect(&timer, SIGNAL(timeout()), &eventLoop, SLOT(quit()));
        connect(mediaObject, SIGNAL(hasVideoChanged(bool)),
                &eventLoop, SLOT(quit()));
        timer.start();
        eventLoop.exec();
    }
```

Once a video has been chosen, any currently playing video is stopped and the relevant actions are disabled. As with music, there can be a noticeable time lag between loading a video with `Phonon::MediaObject::setCurrentSource()` and the video being available to play. If the media object's video data is not immediately available we use a local event loop with a time out, almost exactly as we did for the Play Music application. What is different here is that we stop the event loop once the video stream's status has changed, that is, video data has become available, or if we time out—using a longer timeout of three seconds in this case.

```
if (mediaObject->hasVideo()) {
    QString title(mediaObject->metaData(Phonon::TitleMetaData)
                  .join("/").trimmed());
    if (title.isEmpty())
        title = QFileInfo(filename).baseName();
    setWindowTitle(tr("%1 - %2")
            .arg(QApplication::applicationName()).arg(title));
    mediaObject->play();
}
else {
    setWindowTitle(QApplication::applicationName());
    AQP::warning(this, tr("Error"),
            tr("Cannot play video from %1").arg(filename));
}
}
```

Once the local event loop finishes, either video data is available, in which case we retrieve some meta-data and start playing the video, or we timed out, in which case we inform the user that we hit a problem. We do not explicitly enable the relevant actions—this is done in the stateChanged() slot, and the state will change as soon as playing begins.

```
QString MainWindow::getFileFormats()
{
    QStringList mimeTypes;
    foreach (const QString &mimeType,
            Phonon::BackendCapabilities::availableMimeTypes())
        if (mimeType.startsWith("video/"))
            mimeTypes << mimeType;
    return AQP::filenameFilter(tr("Video"), mimeTypes);
}
```

We only show this method for completeness. It creates a list of the video MIME types supported by the Phonon backend and then uses these to produce a list of file suffixes using the aqp.{hpp,cpp} module's AQP::filenameFilter() function. See the "MIME Types, File Suffixes, and Magic Numbers" sidebar (72 ◄) for more about mapping MIME types to file suffixes.

Apart from one small workaround, the stateChanged() slot is identical to the one used for the Play Music application, so we will only show the difference:

```
        case Phonon::PlayingState:
            videoWidget->setAspectRatio(
                    Phonon::VideoWidget::AspectRatioWidget);
            videoWidget->setAspectRatio(
                    Phonon::VideoWidget::AspectRatioAuto);

            playOrPauseAction->setEnabled(true);
            playOrPauseAction->setIcon(pauseIcon);
            stopAction->setEnabled(true);
            break;
```

When a video is first played it should be shown scaled to fit the video widget's area and respecting the video's aspect ratio. At the time of this writing, when playing certain videos on certain systems this does not always happen, so we manually make *two* different Phonon::VideoWidget::setAspectRatio() calls, to ensure that the video is scaled to fit and has the correct aspect ratio in all cases.

```
    void MainWindow::playOrPause()
    {
        switch (mediaObject->state()) {
            case Phonon::PlayingState:
                mediaObject->pause();
                playOrPauseAction->setIcon(playIcon);
                break;
            case Phonon::PausedState:  // Fallthrough
            case Phonon::StoppedState:
                mediaObject->play();
                playOrPauseAction->setIcon(pauseIcon);
                break;
            default:
                break;
        }
    }
```

The playOrPause() slot is much simpler than the one used in the Play Music application. We won't show the stop() and tick() slots, or the closeEvent(), because they are almost identical to the Play Music ones.

We have now completed our review of the Play Video application. An easier alternative to using a Phonon::VideoWidget is to use a Phonon::VideoPlayer. The video player widget provides convenience—no source, media object, path, or sink need be created—but at the price of lacking the finer control achievable using the video widget used in the example.

The *Phonon* module also includes the Phonon::MediaController class which is designed to provide control over the additional features that some multimedia provide, such as CD titles, DVD chapters, and DVD angles of viewpoint. At the time of this writing, no Qt Phonon backend supports these features.

This brings us to the end of our coverage of the *Phonon* module. At the time of this writing, the module does not support capturing multimedia—such as sound or video clips—or storing multimedia for later playback. Nor is there support for manipulating media streams, for example, for editing, or for mixing multiple input sources. All these gaps in functionality are likely to be filled in the future as Qt's *Phonon* module matures.

Qt 4.6 introduced a new low-level multimedia module: *QtMultimedia*. This module can read and play audio and video data much like the *Phonon* module, but has a lower-level interface that makes it more cumbersome to use than the *Phonon* module. For example, to play an audio file using *QtMultimedia*, we must create a QAudioFormat object with various technical details of the file's audio format—for example, its frequency, number of channels, sample size, and codec's MIME type—and then give the audio format object to a QAudioOutput object to play, along with a QFile object opened on the audio file in binary mode. In contrast, all these low-level details are handled automatically by the *Phonon* module which only requires that we give it a filename. It is best to start out using the *Phonon* module, and only use the *QtMultimedia* module if lower-level control than the *Phonon* module offers is required and is available using the *QtMultimedia* module.

3

- Qt's Model/View Architecture
- Using QStandardItemModels for Tables
- Creating Custom Table Models

Model/View Table Models

One of the big advances made when Qt 4.0 was released was the introduction of a model/view architecture for data items. Using this framework programmers were easily able to separate their data from its presentation—something only achieved with inconvenience in prior versions. As the Qt 4.*x* series has evolved, more functionality and features have been added to the architecture, making it more powerful, useful, and reliable than when it first appeared.*

This chapter is the first of four that explore different aspects of Qt's model/view architecture. In this chapter we will look at table models, and in the following chapters we will look at tree models, delegates, and views.

Every view provides a default delegate—which we can replace with a custom delegate—that is used to display each item, and for editable items, to provide a suitable editor. With regard to the built-in views, we will concern ourselves only with QComboBox and with the view widgets that require models to be supplied to them and that take full advantage of the power and flexibility of Qt's model/view architecture, such as QTableView and QTreeView. And we will, of course, cover custom views in the model/view views chapter.

Qt also supports list models, but we won't explicitly cover them here because they are in effect the same as table models that have a single column. (However, we will use a list model in Chapter 6, when we create a custom list model viewer.) We will cover tree models in the next chapter.

This chapter's first section presents a very brief introduction to the model/view architecture. Then, in the second section, we create a QStandardItemModel subclass that adds the ability to load and save its QStandardItems from and to a file. And in the chapter's third section we will create a custom table model as a drop-in replacement for the second section's custom standard item model subclass.

---

*In fact, a "new generation" model/view architecture is being developed for Qt—although when or even if it will mature and become part of Qt is a matter of conjecture. See labs.qt.nokia.com/page/ Projects/Itemview/ItemviewsNG to see how it is getting on.

87

In both the second and third sections we will see how to add rows (with in-place editing using a delegate), delete rows, and edit rows (again, using in-place editing). We will also create two QSortFilterProxyModel subclasses, one to filter in only those rows the user is interested in, and another to filter out duplicate rows. We will begin our coverage with a broad look at Qt's model/view architecture to provide some context.

Qt's Model/View Architecture

As we will see throughout this chapter and the next, models are used to store data items. Qt provides several widgets for viewing the data items held in models. There are pure view widgets: QListView, QTableView, QColumnView—a view that shows a tree hierarchy as a horizontal series of lists, an idiom used on Mac OS X—and QTreeView. All of these must be provided with a model—either our own custom model, or one of the predefined models provided with Qt. There are also convenience widgets—so named because they provide their own built-in model and can therefore be used directly; these are QListWidget, QTableWidget, and QTreeWidget. And there is QComboBox which can be used either as a convenience widget, that is, we can use it directly since it provides its own model, or as a model's view widget, in which case we provide it with the model we want it to use. View widgets are covered in Chapter 6.

All the standard views are provided with a default QStyledItemDelegate—this class presents items in a view, and for editable items also provides a suitable editor. Naturally, we can create our own delegates to achieve complete control over the presentation and editing of items in our views. Delegates are covered in Chapter 5.

The relationship between models, views, delegates, and the underlying data is illustrated by Figure 3.1.

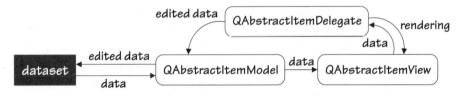

Figure 3.1 *Qt's model/view architecture*

In some contexts, using the convenience widgets makes sense—particularly for small datasets (hundreds or low thousands of items), providing the data they present will only ever be shown in a single widget at any one time. We have already used a couple of convenience views in earlier chapters—for example, QTableWidgets in the Matrix Quiz example from Chapter 1 (44 ◄), and a QTreeWidget in the Play Music example from Chapter 2 (64 ◄).

Probably the most important fact to understand about Qt's models is that although there is a single uniform API, there are two completely different kinds of model: table models that work in terms of rows and columns, and tree models that work in terms of parents and children. (List models are effectively the same as table models with a single column.) In this chapter we will cover table models and in Chapter 4 we will cover tree models.

In addition to considering the two *kinds* of model, there are three types of model we can use. One type is any of the predefined models that Qt provides, for example, the QStringListModel, the QDirModel, and its successor the QFileSystemModel—these can be used directly and require the least amount of work to use. Another type is the QStandardItemModel; this is a generic model that can be used as a list, table, or tree model, and that provides an item-based API rather like the APIs offered by the convenience widgets (such as QTableWidget). Using a QStandardItemModel is ideal for those cases where we have data that fits neatly into the idiom of a list, table, or tree of items, and can be used as is or usually with very little adaptation. And the last type is our own custom models derived from QAbstractItemModel (or from QAbstractListModel or QAbstractTableModel). These are ideal when we want to achieve the best possible performance, or where our model doesn't fit neatly into an item-based idiom. Some of Qt's model hierarchy is shown in Figure 3.2.

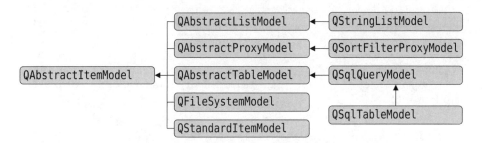

Figure 3.2 *Selected classes from Qt's model hierarchy*

Using a QStandardItemModel means that it is unnecessary to create a custom model, but at the time of this writing using QStandardItemModels has two potential disadvantages. First, it can be noticeably slower to load large datasets than from a custom model, and second, the API offered does not seem to allow as much functionality for tree models as can be achieved in custom models. Nonetheless, in most cases we can start out by using a QStandardItemModel, and later on, if the need arises, implement a custom model to replace it. A brief comparison of the QStandardItemModel and custom models is given in the "QStandardItemModels vs. Custom Models" sidebar (➤ 112).

Using QStandardItemModels for Tables

Table models work in terms of rows and columns, with every item having an invalid QModelIndex as its parent. There is no intrinsic difference between list and table models—list models are simply tables with a single column.

In this section we will see how to create a custom QStandardItemModel subclass that can load and save our custom data, and that holds each item of data in a QStandardItem. In the following section we will replace the QStandardItem-Model with a custom QAbstractTableModel subclass and use our own lightweight items to hold the data. The applications in both sections have exactly the same functionality, although on the machines we tested them on, the custom model-based one always loaded its data significantly faster than the QStandardItem-Model-based one.

Figure 3.3 *Editing a zipcode's state in the Zipcodes application*

Both examples use the custom ItemDelegate delegate for rendering and editing. This is covered in Chapter 5.

The Zipcodes applications—zipcodes1 and zipcodes2—load and save binary files that hold zipcode data—specifically, zipcode, post office, county, and state. There is no visual difference between the applications and they provide the same functionality. One of them is shown in Figure 3.3. The applications provide the standard behaviors we would expect—loading and saving, removing rows, and in-place adding and editing of rows, all of which we will cover. In addition, they also support the ability to select or filter the data in various ways, so as we review the applications, as well as learning about the models, we will learn how to create QSortFilterProxyModel subclasses, and how to manipulate a view's selection model.

The zipcodes1 application uses a simple QStandardItemModel subclass to load, edit, and save its data. The QTableView that displays the data accesses the data via a QSortFilterProxyModel subclass that filters according to the user's criteria. The comboboxes used to filter (or select) rows are populated using another QSortFilterProxyModel, one that filters out duplicates. The main window itself is dialog-style (using buttons rather than menus), but is otherwise quite conventional. As always, we will focus on the relevant details (in this case the model/view aspects), omitting much of the widget creation and layouts, and many of the methods.

Changing a Table Model through the User Interface

We will start out by looking at the main window—this will give us a high-level overview—and then we will look at the model subclasses the application relies on. But first we will look at the program's global constants.

```
const int MinZipcode = 0;
const int MaxZipcode = 99999;
const int InvalidZipcode = MinZipcode - 1;
enum Column {Zipcode, PostOffice, County, State};
```

The constants should be self-explanatory. Now let's look at the MainWindow class's definition in the header file, but omitting all the private methods, and omitting almost all the private data (i.e., most of the widgets).

```
class MainWindow : public QMainWindow
{
    Q_OBJECT

public:
    explicit MainWindow(QWidget *parent=0);

protected:
    void closeEvent(QCloseEvent *event);

private slots:
    void load();
    void load(const QString &filename);
    bool save();
    void addZipcode();
    void deleteZipcode();
    void setDirty() { setWindowModified(true); }
    void updateUi();
```

```
        void radioButtonClicked();
        void selectionChanged();

    private:
        ...
        QTableView *tableView;
        StandardTableModel *model;
        ProxyModel *proxyModel;
        bool loading;
    };
```

The load() and save() slots are used to load and save the application's data; we won't show them here, although we will show the custom StandardTableModel:: load() and StandardTableModel::save() methods they call when we cover the StandardTableModel subclass later on.

The addZipcode() and deleteZipcode() slots are used to add or delete a row of data; we will review both of these methods.

Most of the other private slots are invoked when the user interacts with the widgets used for filtering or selecting—for example, if they select a particular county in the county combobox. The private: block has several private methods and most of the widgets (most of which aren't shown because they are more concerned with the GUI than with model/view programming). When the user chooses to filter or select or interacts with the criteria widgets (e.g., by setting a minimum zipcode or choosing a particular state), this leads to the updateUi() slot being called, which in turn either calls restoreFilters() to apply filtering or performSelection() to select. All the other methods just show standard C++/Qt GUI programming.

The tableView is used as the application's view and the model is the application's model. However, the view does not communicate directly with the model, but via the proxyModel which filters in only those rows that match the user's filter criteria.

```
    const int StatusTimeout = AQP::MSecPerSecond * 10;

    MainWindow::MainWindow(QWidget *parent)
        : QMainWindow(parent), loading(false)
    {
        model = new StandardTableModel(this);
        proxyModel = new ProxyModel(this);
        proxyModel->setSourceModel(model);

        createWidgets();
        createComboBoxModels();
        createLayout();
        createConnections();

        AQP::accelerateWidget(this);
```

```
            setWindowTitle(tr("%1 (QStandardItemModel)[*]")
                    .arg(QApplication::applicationName()));
            statusBar()->showMessage(tr("Ready"), StatusTimeout);
}
```

The constructor begins by creating the model and the proxy model that the view will use. (Both these models are subclasses that we will review later on.) The rest of the constructor follows a familiar pattern. We will only look at a snippet from the end of the createWidgets() method, and we will skip the createLayout() method entirely. (We covered the AQP::accelerateWidget() function in an earlier chapter; 15 ◄.)

```
void MainWindow::createWidgets()
{
    ...
    tableView = new QTableView;
    tableView->setModel(proxyModel);
    tableView->setItemDelegate(new ItemDelegate(this));
    tableView->verticalHeader()->setDefaultAlignment(
            Qt::AlignVCenter|Qt::AlignRight);
}
```

Notice that the table view's model is the proxyModel, not the actual model that holds the data. The custom delegate is covered later (➤ 201). We set the alignment for the vertical header (the row numbers), so that they line up in the conventional way for numbers.

```
void MainWindow::createComboBoxModels()
{
    createComboBoxModel(countyComboBox, County);
    createComboBoxModel(stateComboBox, State);
}
```

```
void MainWindow::createComboBoxModel(QComboBox *comboBox, int column)
{
    delete comboBox->model();
    UniqueProxyModel *uniqueProxyModel = new UniqueProxyModel(column,
                                                            this);
    uniqueProxyModel->setSourceModel(model);
    uniqueProxyModel->sort(column, Qt::AscendingOrder);
    comboBox->setModel(uniqueProxyModel);
    comboBox->setModelColumn(column);
}
```

The two comboboxes that are used for filtering or selecting rows need to get their data from the underlying model. However, the same counties and the same states appear again and again for different zipcodes as the screenshot in

Figure 3.3 shows (90 ◄). So instead of having the comboboxes use the model, we have them use a custom proxy model that eliminates duplicates.

When we set out to create a combobox model we begin by deleting the old model. This is done because we call createComboBoxModels() whenever we load in a new file since we only want the user to be able to filter and select based on the values that are in the model that has been loaded. For example, we might load a file that only has Connecticut and Delaware zipcodes, in which case we don't want the user to be able to filter on Montana since that would have no matching rows.

The custom UniqueProxyModel uses the same columns as the underlying model, and when we create the proxy we must specify which column we want to filter for unique values. The proxy's source model is set to the underlying model and the combobox's model is set to the proxy—with the column the combobox should display specified using the QComboBox::setModelColumn() method. (We will review the unique proxy model later on; ➤ 107.)

The application uses about twenty signal–slot connections which are set up in the createConnections() method. We'll review them in four groups.

```
connect(model, SIGNAL(itemChanged(QStandardItem*)),
        this, SLOT(setDirty()));
connect(model, SIGNAL(rowsRemoved(const QModelIndex&,int,int)),
        this, SLOT(setDirty()));
connect(model, SIGNAL(modelReset()), this, SLOT(setDirty()));
```

These connections are all to the setDirty() method (which in turn calls set-WindowModified()). They are used to ensure that we know if there are unsaved changes, and to reflect this fact in the window title—with an "*" (asterisk) in the title bar or with a dot inside the close button on Mac OS X.

```
connect(countyGroupBox, SIGNAL(toggled(bool)),
        this, SLOT(updateUi()));
connect(countyComboBox,
        SIGNAL(currentIndexChanged(const QString&)),
        this, SLOT(updateUi()));
...
foreach (QRadioButton *radioButton, QList<QRadioButton*>()
            << dontFilterOrSelectRadioButton << filterRadioButton
            << selectByCriteriaRadioButton)
    connect(radioButton, SIGNAL(clicked()),
            this, SLOT(radioButtonClicked()));
```

If the user checks (or unchecks) the county group box's checkbox we need to know so that we can filter or select (or stop filtering or selecting) by county. If the group box is checked and the user changes the county we must re-filter or re-select accordingly. (There are also connections for the state group box and state combobox—these aren't shown because they are the same as the county ones.) There are also connections from the zipcode spinboxes' valueChanged() signals, again to the updateUi() slot, and again not shown.

The user can choose to filter or select—or to do neither, depending on which radio button they check. The radio button connections are used to ensure that we filter or select (or neither) appropriately.

```
connect(tableView, SIGNAL(clicked(const QModelIndex&)),
        this, SLOT(selectionChanged())));
connect(tableView->selectionModel(),
        SIGNAL(currentChanged(const QModelIndex&,
                              const QModelIndex&)),
        this, SLOT(selectionChanged())));

connect(tableView->horizontalHeader(),
        SIGNAL(sectionClicked(int)),
        tableView, SLOT(sortByColumn(int))));
```

The first two connections in this group are used to keep the user interface up to date if the user clicks or navigates to a particular item, and the third is used to provide sorting. (We will explain how the sorting works later on; ▶ 111.)

Note that views are actually associated with *two* models—the model that provides the data, and an internal model that is used to keep track of selections. The selection model is available from QAbstractItemView::selectionModel() and is of type QItemSelectionModel—this is a direct QObject subclass; it is not a QAbstractItemModel subclass.

```
connect(loadButton, SIGNAL(clicked()), this, SLOT(load()));
connect(saveButton, SIGNAL(clicked()), this, SLOT(save()));
connect(addButton, SIGNAL(clicked()), this, SLOT(addZipcode()));
connect(deleteButton, SIGNAL(clicked()),
        this, SLOT(deleteZipcode()));
connect(quitButton, SIGNAL(clicked()), this, SLOT(close()));
```

This last group of connections should be the most familiar. They provide the behaviors for when the user asks to load or save their data, or to add or delete rows, or to quit the application.

We have now seen the overall structure of the application and the connections used to provide its behavior. Most of the private slots and private methods are concerned with the user interface, so they are not relevant to model/view programming as such. Because of this, we will skip most of the user interaction-related slots and methods, but show all of those that are relevant to model/view programming.

```
void MainWindow::radioButtonClicked()
{
    if (dontFilterOrSelectRadioButton->isChecked()) {
        proxyModel->clearFilters();
        QItemSelectionModel *selectionModel =
                tableView->selectionModel();
        selectionModel->clearSelection();
    }
    else
        updateUi();
}
```

If the user clicks the Don't Filter or Select radio button, the filters and the
selection are cleared—so all the rows are shown. Otherwise the updateUi()
method is called to select or filter according to the user's criterion.

```
void MainWindow::updateUi()
{
    if (loading || dontFilterOrSelectRadioButton->isChecked())
        return;
    if (filterRadioButton->isChecked())
        restoreFilters();
    else
        performSelection();
}
```

Whenever the user changes the state of one of the checkboxes, comboboxes, or
spinboxes, this method is called. If the data is being loaded or if the user has
switched off filtering and selecting, we do nothing and return. Otherwise we
either filter or select according to the user's choice.

The performSelection() method is quite long so we will review it in two parts.

```
void MainWindow::performSelection()
{
    proxyModel->clearFilters();
    int minimumZipcode = minimumZipSpinBox->value();
    int maximumZipcode = maximumZipSpinBox->value();
    QString county = countyGroupBox->isChecked()
            ? countyComboBox->currentText() : QString();
    QString state = stateGroupBox->isChecked()
            ? stateComboBox->currentText() : QString();
```

We begin by clearing the filters so that no row is filtered away. Then we get
the minimum and maximum zipcode values and the user's choice of county and
state (or empty strings if they haven't set a preference).

```
        QItemSelection selection;
        int firstSelectedRow = -1;
        for (int row = 0; row < proxyModel->rowCount(); ++row) {
            QModelIndex index = proxyModel->index(row, Zipcode);
            int zipcode = proxyModel->data(index).toInt();
            if (zipcode < minimumZipcode || zipcode > maximumZipcode)
                continue;
            if (!matchingColumn(county, row, County))
                continue;
            if (!matchingColumn(state, row, State))
                continue;
            if (firstSelectedRow == -1)
                firstSelectedRow = row;
            QItemSelection rowSelection(index, index);
            selection.merge(rowSelection, QItemSelectionModel::Select);
        }
        QItemSelectionModel *selectionModel = tableView->selectionModel();
        selectionModel->clearSelection();
        selectionModel->select(selection, QItemSelectionModel::Rows|
                                          QItemSelectionModel::Select);
        if (firstSelectedRow != -1)
            tableView->scrollTo(proxyModel->index(firstSelectedRow, 0));
    }
```

The selection must be built up row by row. We start with an empty QItem-
Selection and then iterate over every row in the proxy model. (And this means
that we consider every row in the underlying model since we cleared the proxy
model's filters.) If a row matches the criteria we create a new QItemSelection
that just contains that row, and then we merge this into the selection of all the
selected rows that we are building up.

Once all the rows have been considered we clear any existing selection and
select all those rows (and there may be none of course) that match the user's
criteria. And finally, we scroll to the first selected row if there was one.

```
    bool MainWindow::matchingColumn(const QString &value, int row,
                                    int column)
    {
        if (value.isEmpty())
            return true;
        QModelIndex index = proxyModel->index(row, column);
        return value == proxyModel->data(index).toString();
    }
```

This helper method returns true if the given value matches the text at the given row and column—or if the value is empty. So if the user hasn't specified, say, a county, then this method will return true for any county.

```cpp
void MainWindow::restoreFilters()
{
    proxyModel->setMinimumZipcode(minimumZipSpinBox->value());
    proxyModel->setMaximumZipcode(maximumZipSpinBox->value());
    proxyModel->setCounty(countyGroupBox->isChecked()
            ? countyComboBox->currentText() : QString());
    proxyModel->setState(stateGroupBox->isChecked()
            ? stateComboBox->currentText() : QString());
    reportFilterEffect();
}
```

If the user checks the Filter radio button, or changes one of the comboboxes or spinboxes when the Filter radio button is checked, this method will be called. It simply uses the custom proxy model's custom methods to set the filter criteria to match the user's choices in the user interface, and this in turn will cause the view to update itself.

```cpp
void MainWindow::reportFilterEffect()
{
    if (loading)
        return;
    statusBar()->showMessage(tr("Filtered %L1 out of %Ln zipcode(s)",
            "", model->rowCount()).arg(proxyModel->rowCount()),
            StatusTimeout);
}
```

After the user has clicked the Filter radio button or changed a filter criterion, this method is called to show the results, that is, how many rows have been filtered out of the total number of rows in the dataset.

We use %L1, %L2, and so on, rather than plain %1, %2, and so on, to provide internationalized number grouping separators—for example, commas every three digits in a U.S. locale—to make the numbers more readable when there are a lot of rows. And in this case we want the translator to be able to translate an appropriate plural form (e.g., "… out of one zipcode" or "… out of %Ln zipcodes"), with a sensible fallback of "… out of %Ln zipcode(s)"; we discuss this in the "Using the Three-Argument Form of tr()" sidebar (➤ 276).

```cpp
void MainWindow::addZipcode()
{
    dontFilterOrSelectRadioButton->click();
    QList<QStandardItem*> items;
    QStandardItem *zipItem = new QStandardItem;
```

```
        zipItem->setData(MinZipcode, Qt::EditRole);
        items << zipItem;
        for (int i = 0; i < model->columnCount() - 1; ++i)
            items << new QStandardItem(tr("(Unknown)"));
        model->appendRow(items);
        tableView->scrollToBottom();
        tableView->setFocus();
        QModelIndex index = proxyModel->index(proxyModel->rowCount() - 1,
                                              Zipcode);
        tableView->setCurrentIndex(index);
        tableView->edit(index);
    }
```

If the user chooses to add a new zipcode we begin by switching off filtering and selecting. It is very important to switch off filtering, since if the new zipcode doesn't match the filter criteria it will immediately be filtered away, and the user won't get the chance to edit—or even see—the data they are adding.

Since we are using a simple QStandardItemModel subclass and holding the data in QStandardItems, adding a new zipcode in place is just a matter of appending a new row of suitably initialized QStandardItems. The new data is added to the underlying model—the proxy model used by the view will detect this and adapt itself accordingly. One subtle point to note is that for non-string data such as a zipcode, it is wise to explicitly specify the role under which the data is stored as Qt::EditRole, and leave Qt to produce a string representation when data for the Qt::DisplayRole is requested. (All the roles are listed in Table 3.2; ➤ 119.)

Once the data is added we scroll to the bottom of the table view (since we appended the new zipcode at the end), and initiate editing of the new zipcode's first column, so the user will immediately find themselves in a QSpinBox (actually a slightly customized QSpinBox subclass).

We do not call setDirty() and we have no connection from the QStandardItem-Model::rowsInserted() signal. This means that after adding to a freshly loaded or freshly saved dataset, the application does *not* consider itself to have any unsaved changes. However, if the user edits any of the newly added zipcode's cells—or any other cells—the itemChanged() signal will be emitted, and that is connected to setDirty().

The deleteZipcode() method is fairly long so we will review it in two parts.

```
    void MainWindow::deleteZipcode()
    {
        QItemSelectionModel *selectionModel = tableView->selectionModel();
        if (!selectionModel->hasSelection())
            return;
        QModelIndex index = proxyModel->mapToSource(
                selectionModel->currentIndex());
```

```
    if (!index.isValid())
        return;
    int zipcode = model->data(model->index(index.row(),
                             Zipcode)).toInt();
    if (!AQP::okToDelete(this, tr("Delete Zipcode"),
            tr("Delete Zipcode %1?").arg(zipcode, 5, 10, QChar('0'))))
        return;
```

If the user chooses to delete a row we begin by seeing if there is a selected cell, and if there is we convert the selection model's model index to the corresponding index in the underlying model using the QSortFilterProxyModel::mapTo-Source() method.

Once we know the row the user wants to delete (i.e., the selected cell's model index's row), we ask them for confirmation, and do nothing if they change their mind.

```
    bool filtered = filterRadioButton->isChecked();
    bool selected = selectByCriteriaRadioButton->isChecked();
    QString county = countyGroupBox->isChecked()
            ? countyComboBox->currentText() : QString();
    QString state = stateGroupBox->isChecked()
            ? stateComboBox->currentText() : QString();
    dontFilterOrSelectRadioButton->click();

    model->removeRow(index.row(), index.parent());

    createComboBoxModels();
    if (!county.isEmpty())
        countyComboBox->setCurrentIndex(
                countyComboBox->findText(county));
    if (!state.isEmpty())
        stateComboBox->setCurrentIndex(
                stateComboBox->findText(state));
    if (filtered)
        filterRadioButton->click();
    else if (selected)
        selectByCriteriaRadioButton->click();
}
```

Before deleting the row we remember the state of the Filter and Select by Criteria radio buttons and of the criteria comboboxes, and then switch off filtering and selecting by clicking the Don't Filter or Select radio button. We then remove the row, and then we restore any filtering or selecting that was in force before. Strictly speaking we don't need to save and restore the filtering/selecting state, but we do need to re-create the combobox models since they might contain one less row now—for example, if the user deleted a row that contained the only occurrence of a particular county or state.

Since it is common for applications to allow users to delete things, for convenience, we have created a custom AQP::okToDelete() function, which we show here for completeness.

```
bool okToDelete(QWidget *parent, const QString &title,
                const QString &text, const QString &detailedText)
{
    QScopedPointer<QMessageBox> messageBox(new QMessageBox(parent));
    if (parent)
        messageBox->setWindowModality(Qt::WindowModal);
    messageBox->setIcon(QMessageBox::Question);
    messageBox->setWindowTitle(QString("%1 - %2")
            .arg(QApplication::applicationName()).arg(title));
    messageBox->setText(text);
    if (!detailedText.isEmpty())
        messageBox->setInformativeText(detailedText);
    QAbstractButton *deleteButton = messageBox->addButton(
            QObject::tr("&Delete"), QMessageBox::AcceptRole);
    messageBox->addButton(QObject::tr("Do &Not Delete"),
                          QMessageBox::RejectRole);
    messageBox->setDefaultButton(
            qobject_cast<QPushButton*>(deleteButton));
    messageBox->exec();
    return messageBox->clickedButton() == deleteButton;
}
```

Apart from the return value, the signature is the same as for the AQP::information() and AQP::warning() functions, and the creation and setting up of the message box is very similar to what we did in those functions. The detailedText parameter has a default value of an empty string so can be omitted by callers. (See the "Avoiding Qt's Static Convenience QMessageBox Functions" sidebar, for why we use custom functions for message boxes; 61◄.) The qobject_cast<>() is necessary because the QMessageBox::setDefaultButton() method expects a QPushButton pointer, but we have used a QAbstractButton pointer for the delete-Button to make the comparison with QMessageBox::clickedButton() simpler, since this method returns a QAbstractButton pointer. (We introduced Qt 4.6's QScopedPointer class in the "Qt's Smart Pointers" sidebar; 62 ◄.*)

In theory we could have handled the dialog's deletion by calling QWidget::set-Attribute(Qt::WA_DeleteOnClose), but in practice we prefer to leave deletion to be handled by the smart pointer. This means that the message box is merely closed rather than deleted when a button is pressed, so after the QMessage-

---

*In the source code we have an #if QT_VERSION so that the code will compile with Qt 4.5 using QSharedPointer.

`Box::exec()` call finishes the message box still exists—which is essential if we want to check which button was pressed, as we do here.

Keep in mind that the `QDialog::exec()` method is going out of fashion, at least for larger projects. The problem is that although it is a blocking call from the user's point of view (i.e., it prevents interacting with the application's other windows), it does not block event processing. This means that it is possible for the application's state to change considerably between the call to `exec()` and the user accepting or rejecting the dialog. It is even possible that the dialog itself gets accidentally deleted. In view of this, it is safer to use `QDialog::open()` (or `QDialog::show()` for modeless dialogs), and use a signal–slot connection to respond if the user accepts the dialog. Nonetheless, while we accept that there are problems and risks with using `exec()`, none of the book's examples suffer from them, so we continue to use it, especially since it is convenient and needs less code than using `open()` and a connection.*

We have now seen all the relevant methods that are used to provide the behaviors in the user interface through which the user can manipulate the models used by the application. In the next subsection we will review the `QStandard-ItemModel` subclass that is used to load, edit, and save the application's data. And in the two following subsections we will review the `QSortFilterProxyModel` subclasses that are used for filtering the data and for ensuring that the comboboxes used for filtering and selecting always contain unique values.

A QStandardItemModel Subclass for Tables

The `QStandardItemModel` class provides all the functionality we need for manipulating tabular data and for interacting with views. The only additions that need to be made for handling real data are the ability to load and save the data from or to a file, and the ability to clear the data—to allow the user to create a new dataset.

We will start by looking at the constructor and the `clear()` method, and then we will see how the data is loaded and saved.

```
StandardTableModel::StandardTableModel(QObject *parent)
    : QStandardItemModel(parent)
{
    initialize();
}

void StandardTableModel::initialize()
{
    setHorizontalHeaderLabels(QStringList() << tr("Zipcode")
```

---

*See *Qt Quarterly* issue 30's "New Ways of Using Dialogs", qt.nokia.com/doc/qq/ for more details.

```
                        << tr("Post Office") << tr("County") << tr("State"));
    }
```

We have factored out the `initialize()` method since we need the same function-ality in the `clear()` method.

```
    void StandardTableModel::clear()
    {
        QStandardItemModel::clear();
        initialize();
    }
```

Notice that this method—and indeed the `StandardTableModel` class itself—neither knows nor cares if the model's data is dirty, so the handling of unsaved changes is a responsibility left to the class's clients—in this example, the main window class.

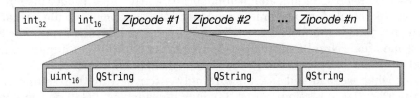

Figure 3.4 *The Zipcodes file format*

There are only two more methods in the subclass, `load()` and `save()`. The file format used to hold the zipcode data on disk is a binary format whose structure is illustrated in Figure 3.4. The file begins with a magic number and a file format version number, and then zero or more zipcode records each holding a zipcode, post office, county, and state.

```
    const qint32 MagicNumber = 0x5A697043;
    const qint16 FormatNumber = 100;

    void StandardTableModel::save(const QString &filename)
    {
        if (!filename.isEmpty())
            m_filename = filename;
        if (m_filename.isEmpty())
            throw AQP::Error(tr("no filename specified"));
        QFile file(m_filename);
        if (!file.open(QIODevice::WriteOnly))
            throw AQP::Error(file.errorString());

        QDataStream out(&file);
        out << MagicNumber << FormatNumber;
        out.setVersion(QDataStream::Qt_4_5);
```

```
    for (int row = 0; row < rowCount(); ++row) {
        out << static_cast<quint16>(
                    item(row, Zipcode)->data(Qt::EditRole).toUInt())
            << item(row, PostOffice)->text()
            << item(row, County)->text() << item(row, State)->text();
    }
}
```

Saving the data is quite straightforward. We begin by opening the file using
the filename that was used last time or the new filename if a new one is given;
the filename parameter defaults to an empty string. If there is no filename or
if we fail to open the file we throw an exception. If an exception is thrown the
MainWindow::save() method, which calls this method, catches the exception and
pops up a message box showing the error message.

Once the file is open we write our magic number and our file format number.
We use a (hopefully) unique magic number to identify our zipcodes file format,
and we use the file format number to identify the version of the file format we
are using. (Magic numbers are briefly described in the "MIME Types, File Suffixes, and Magic Numbers" sidebar; 72 ◄.) Having a file format number makes
it much easier to change the format later on since we can check the format
version when we load and adapt accordingly. After writing these numbers we
set the QDataStream version to Qt_4_5 (which is readable by Qt 4.5 or any later
Qt version), and then we write the data. Since our data is composed of just
numbers and strings we could just as easily have used an older Qt version (say,
Qt_4_0). The only advantage of using the most up-to-date data stream version
is that newer versions might support more Qt types than older ones or might
be faster to load or save or might store the data more compactly. Our policy is
to use the data stream version that matches the oldest version of Qt we want
our application to be buildable with.

Fundamental datatypes like integers always have the same format no matter
what version of QDataStream we use, so it is always safe to write such types before setting the version. However, Qt's own types and floating-point types may
differ in format between QDataStream versions, so we must always ensure that
for Qt and floating-point types we write and read using the same QDataStream
version.* Note also that for floating-point numbers we should *never* write or
read qreals since their size varies depending on the platform—we must always
explicitly use float or double.

For string data we can use each QStandardItem's text, but for non-string data
(such as a zipcode), we must use the data for the role it is stored under, usually
Qt::EditRole, as it is in this case. And when writing integers it is essential that

---

*Qt's representation of floats changed between Qt 4.5 and Qt 4.6. Providing we use QDataStream::
setVersion(), changes like this are no problem and will have no impact on our code or data.

we use exactly the right type—Qt provides them all, from `qint8` and `quint8` through to `qint64` and `quint64`.

Another way that we can save and load `QStandardItems` is to stream them since they support Qt's global `operator<<()` and `operator>>()` functions that take a `QDataStream` as first argument. And we can achieve finer control over what is written and read by creating a `QStandardItem` subclass and reimplementing the `QStandardItem::read()` and `QStandardItem::write()` methods that the streaming operators call. However, in this case we chose to use `QStandardItems` out of the box and to handle their reading and writing in our `QStandardItemModel` subclass.

The `Error` class that we use for throwing exceptions is from the aqp.{hpp,cpp} module; we will show it just for completeness.

```
class Error : public std::exception
{
public:
    explicit Error(const QString &message) throw()
        : message(message.toUtf8()) {}
    ~Error() throw() {}

    const char *what() const throw() { return message; }

private:
    const char *message;
};
```

There is nothing special about this class, but we prefer the convenience of passing a `QString` rather than a `char*` for the error message. To access the error message we must use `QString::fromUtf8(error.what())`.

The `load()` method is a bit longer than that needed for saving, so we will review it in four (short) parts.

```
void StandardTableModel::load(const QString &filename)
{
    ...
    QDataStream in(&file);
    qint32 magicNumber;
    in >> magicNumber;
    if (magicNumber != MagicNumber)
        throw AQP::Error(tr("unrecognized file type"));
    qint16 formatVersionNumber;
    in >> formatVersionNumber;
    if (formatVersionNumber > FormatNumber)
        throw AQP::Error(tr("file format version is too new"));
    in.setVersion(QDataStream::Qt_4_5);
    clear();
```

The method starts with almost the same code as the save() method for using
the existing filename or a new filename, so we have omitted those lines. Once
we have a filename and have opened the file—this time using a mode of
QIODevice::ReadOnly—we read in the magic number to check that we really
have got a zipcodes file, and then the file format version number. In this case
we only check the format version, but this is where we would handle different
formats appropriately if we needed to. Then we set the correct data stream
version and clear the model so that all its data is deleted.

```
quint16 zipcode;
QString postOffice;
QString county;
QString state;
QMap<quint16, QList<QStandardItem*> > itemsForZipcode;
```

Normally we would populate the model with each record as we read them
in. But we want to enforce an initial ordering on the data, so we have used a
local QMap ordered by zipcode to hold each record (as a QList of QStandardItem
pointers), and then at the end we will put the items into the model.

```
while (!in.atEnd()) {
    in >> zipcode >> postOffice >> county >> state;
    QList<QStandardItem*> items;
    QStandardItem *item = new QStandardItem;
    item->setData(zipcode, Qt::EditRole);
    items << item;
    foreach (const QString &text, QStringList() << postOffice
                                     << county << state)
        items << new QStandardItem(text);
    itemsForZipcode[zipcode] = items;
}
```

For each record we read in we create a corresponding QList<QStandardItem*>.
String data can simply be given to the QStandardItem constructor, but it is *essential* to set non-string data under a specific role, normally Qt::EditRole, and this
is what we do for the zipcodes. Once we have a list of items representing one
row of data we insert it into the QMap, using the zipcode as its key, so that we get
zipcode (smallest to largest) ordering.

```
    QMapIterator<quint16, QList<QStandardItem*> > i(itemsForZipcode);
    while (i.hasNext())
        appendRow(i.next().value());
}
```

Once all the records have been read we iterate over the QMap and append each
list of QStandardItems as a new row. We don't need to notify any associated

views that the model's data has changed, since the base class appendRow() takes care of this for us.

We noted earlier that loading into a QStandardItemModel was always slower than loading into a custom model on the machines we tested. This was also true when we loaded in the data directly (i.e., without using a QMap to provide ordering), so for our machines it appears that the time-consuming aspect of loading is the creation of each individual QStandardItem.

We have now completed our review of the StandardTableModel subclass. Since the only functionality it added to QStandardItemModel was loading, saving, and clearing the data, and since responsibility for errors and for handling unsaved changes was left to the class's clients, it was quite straightforward to implement. In the next section we will create a QAbstractTableModel subclass as a drop-in replacement so that we can compare the two approaches. But first we will look at the QSortFilterProxyModel subclasses that are used by the application's QTableView and by its QComboBoxes.

A QSortFilterProxyModel to Filter Out Duplicate Rows

The Zipcodes applications use two comboboxes to display counties and states that users can set to filter or select corresponding rows of data. Both these comboboxes need to get their data from the underlying model that holds all of the zipcodes data—but many different zipcodes may be in the same county and state, and we don't want any duplicates to appear in these comboboxes, so we cannot set them to use the underlying model directly.

The solution we have used is to create a custom QSortFilterProxyModel subclass that filters out all of a model's rows that have duplicates in a specified column. For filtering we must implement the protected filterAcceptsRow() method to filter rows, or the filterAcceptsColumn() method to filter columns. (For sorting we can implement the protected QSortFilterProxyModel::lessThan() method, although simply using a QSortFilterProxyModel provides sorting—and is what we rely on for the Zipcodes applications—as we will explain later.) In this particular case we also need to reimplement the setSourceModel() method as we will explain in a moment. But first let's see the definition in the header file.

```
class UniqueProxyModel : public QSortFilterProxyModel
{
    Q_OBJECT

public:
    explicit UniqueProxyModel(int column, QObject *parent=0)
        : QSortFilterProxyModel(parent), Column(column) {}

    void setSourceModel(QAbstractItemModel *sourceModel);

protected:
```

```
    bool filterAcceptsRow(int sourceRow,
                          const QModelIndex &sourceParent) const;

private slots:
    void clearCache() { cache.clear(); }

private:
    const int Column;
    mutable QSet<QString> cache;
};
```

We keep a mutable cache holding all the unique strings that the UniqueProxy-Model has seen in the specified column.

```
void UniqueProxyModel::setSourceModel(
        QAbstractItemModel *sourceModel)
{
    connect(sourceModel, SIGNAL(modelReset()),
            this, SLOT(clearCache()));
    QSortFilterProxyModel::setSourceModel(sourceModel);
}
```

If the source model resets we clear the cache since the data has radically altered. Should we also have created connections to clear the cache if rows are inserted or removed? For insertions, there is no need since new strings are automatically handled correctly because of the way we have implemented the filterAcceptsRow() method. For removed strings, whether we should delete them from the cache depends on whether we want the user to be able to access strings that might not be in the underlying data anymore, but in this case we have chosen to allow it.

```
bool UniqueProxyModel::filterAcceptsRow(int sourceRow,
        const QModelIndex &sourceParent) const
{
    QModelIndex index = sourceModel()->index(sourceRow, Column,
                                              sourceParent);
    const QString &text = sourceModel()->data(index).toString();
    if (cache.contains(text))
        return false;
    cache << text;
    return true;
}
```

Each of the comboboxes has its model set to its own UniqueProxyModel instance, with the column set to the relevant row (County or State); this was done in the createComboBoxModel() method (93 ◀). Whenever the combobox needs to access rows—for example, when the user drops down the combobox's list view—this method is used by the proxy model to filter out unwanted rows.

The algorithm is very simple: We get the underlying model's model index for the corresponding proxy row and retrieve the model's text for the column that was set when the proxy model was created. If the text is in the cache we have seen it before so we return `false`, which means that the row is filtered out. Otherwise we add the text to the cache (so any following rows that have the same text in the chosen column will be filtered out), and return `true` to allow the row to be used for the first and only time.

A QSortFilterProxyModel to Filter In Wanted Rows

The `UniqueProxyModel` shown in the preceding subsection is very useful, but specialized for one particular use case. For the Zipcodes applications we needed a much more sophisticated proxy model that would allow the user to filter based on a combination of criteria—a minimum and maximum zipcode, and optionally by county and state. The class we created to provide this functionality is `ProxyModel`, and as in the `UniqueProxyModel` the filtering is implemented in the `filterAcceptsRow()` method.

The `ProxyModel` subclass provides getters and setters for the filter criteria, an implementation of the `filterAcceptsRow()` method, and a `clearFilters()` method, in addition to the constructor. We will review all these except for the getters and setters; we will only look at one of each of them, because they are all structurally the same.

```
ProxyModel::ProxyModel(QObject *parent)
    : QSortFilterProxyModel(parent)
{
    m_minimumZipcode = m_maximumZipcode = InvalidZipcode;
}
```

We set the private minimum and maximum zipcode variables to an invalid zipcode value. The invalid value is used in `filterAcceptsRow()` to detect if it can skip comparing the zipcode.

```
QString state() const { return m_state; }
```

This getter is in the header file; there are similar methods for getting the county and the minimum and maximum zipcodes.

```
void ProxyModel::setState(const QString &state)
{
    if (m_state != state) {
        m_state = state;
        invalidateFilter();
```

```
        }
    }
```

All the setters follow the same pattern as this one: if the value has actually changed, first we set the given value, then we call invalidateFilter() to make the proxy model announce to any associated views that they need to refresh their visible data.

If an empty string is passed the effect is to switch off filtering by state. And the equivalent is true of the county setter.

```
void ProxyModel::clearFilters()
{
    m_minimumZipcode = m_maximumZipcode = InvalidZipcode;
    m_county.clear();
    m_state.clear();
    invalidateFilter();
}
```

No rows are filtered out if the minimum and maximum zipcodes are invalid and if the county and state strings are empty, so calling this method effectively switches off filtering.

```
bool ProxyModel::filterAcceptsRow(int sourceRow,
        const QModelIndex &sourceParent) const
{
    if (m_minimumZipcode != InvalidZipcode ||
        m_maximumZipcode != InvalidZipcode) {
        QModelIndex index = sourceModel()->index(sourceRow, Zipcode,
                                                  sourceParent);
        if (m_minimumZipcode != InvalidZipcode &&
            sourceModel()->data(index).toInt() < m_minimumZipcode)
            return false;
        if (m_maximumZipcode != InvalidZipcode &&
            sourceModel()->data(index).toInt() > m_maximumZipcode)
            return false;
    }
    if (!m_county.isEmpty()) {
        QModelIndex index = sourceModel()->index(sourceRow, County,
                                                  sourceParent);
        if (m_county != sourceModel()->data(index).toString())
            return false;
    }
    if (!m_state.isEmpty()) {
        QModelIndex index = sourceModel()->index(sourceRow, State,
                                                  sourceParent);
        if (m_state != sourceModel()->data(index).toString())
```

```
                return false;
        }
        return true;
}
```

The proxy filter returns true (keep the row) for every row when the minimum and maximum zipcodes are invalid and where the county and state are empty.

A zipcode is valid if it is greater than or equal to MinZipcode. If the minimum zipcode is valid and the row being considered has a smaller zipcode, we return false to filter out this row. Similarly, if the maximum zipcode is valid, and the row being considered has a zipcode that is greater than the maximum, we return false to filter it out. If the county is nonempty, we filter out rows that have a different county; and the same applies to states. And if control reaches the end of the method we return true (keep the row).

As this proxy filter and the one from the preceding subsection show, creating custom QSortFilterProxyModel subclasses to provide filtering is not difficult. And of course it is possible to chain filters—at some cost in performance.

Subclassing is not the only way we can use QSortFilterProxyModels. We can also instantiate them directly and use the setFilterKeyColumn() method to choose a column to filter by and the setFilterRegExp() method to set a regular expression such that those rows whose specified column's contents don't match the regular expression are filtered out. (We can also use fixed strings and wildcard patterns.)

For sorting, there are various approaches that can be taken. When a view is asked to sort it calls QAbstractItemModel::sort() behind the scenes, so one way to provide sorting is to reimplement this method since the base class implementation does nothing. For the Zipcodes applications the view calls QSortFilter-ProxyModel::sort()—since the view's model is the proxy model—and this has a default implementation that can sort integers and some basic Qt types such as QString and QDateTime. This is why all we needed to do to provide sorting for the Zipcodes model was to use a QSortFilterProxyModel and create a signal–slot connection between the view's horizontal header's sectionClicked() signal and the view's sortByColumn() slot.

We can also exercise finer control over proxy model sorting by calling setSort-CaseSensitivity() and setSortLocaleAware(); or we could subclass QSortFilter-ProxyModel and reimplement the lessThan() method.

Another way to provide sorting—for QStandardItemModel subclasses—is to use QStandardItemModel::setSortRole()—for example, to make the Qt::UserRole's data the data used for sorting. For this to work we must tell the view to support sorting by calling setSortingEnabled(true); and we must ensure that for every item, in addition to its usual data for the display or edit role, it also has data for the user role (or for whichever role we had set to be the sort role). Suppose,

QStandardItemModels vs. Custom Models

When we use a QStandardItemModel (or a QStandardItemModel subclass) to represent our data—whether as a list, table, or tree—all of the data items are held as QStandardItems (or as items of a custom QStandardItem subclass).

Conceptually, the QStandardItemModel stands in between the view widget plus model approach and the convenience widget with built-in model approach. Using a QStandardItemModel is easier than creating a custom model and more flexible than using a convenience widget since we can often use the QStandardItemModel directly, and even if we need to subclass it, we typically only do so to add a few methods such as methods for loading and saving. Another aspect of using a QStandardItemModel that some developers prefer is that it uses a more familiar item-based API rather than the model index-based API used by custom models.

The QStandardItem class offers a rich API that makes QStandardItems very easy and convenient to use out of the box. The most commonly used methods provide getters and setters for an item's background color, checkability, checked status, editability, font, foreground color, icon, status tip, text, text alignment, and tooltip. Additional data can be stored using roles not used by QStandardItem, for example, Qt::UserRole, Qt::UserRole + 1, and so on. And we can stream items to and from QDataStreams.

The price to be paid for all the convenience and power that QStandardItems offer—at least in theory—is memory, and perhaps speed of operation. A custom model might not need to store individual items at all, or might only need lightweight items such as strings or numbers.

In all cases it is usually easiest and quickest to use a QStandardItemModel and QStandardItems (or subclasses of them), at least at first. Using these classes allows us to quickly get a working prototype. If later on we find that memory consumption or speed of operation is unsatisfactory, we can then consider creating a custom model as a drop-in replacement.

The situations most likely to benefit from a custom model are where the items are flyweight, where we don't need most of the features offered by QStandardItems, and where the number of items is large (thousands or more). Also, in the case of tree models, the QStandardItemModel API does not appear to offer as much functionality as we can achieve using a custom model.

Creating custom list and table models is straightforward, so they are potentially an easy performance win where large datasets are involved. Custom tree models require rather more work and can be quite tricky to get right, but it may be necessary to create them simply to get the additional functionality they make possible—for example, the ability to move items (and their children, recursively) arbitrarily in the tree—assuming of course that this makes sense for the particular dataset we have created the model for.

for instance, that we had text items in English. We might store the actual texts in the Qt::DisplayRole, but for the Qt::UserRole we might store the same texts—but lowercased, and with any leading articles ("The", "An", and "A") removed, to provide a more natural ordering.

Creating Custom Table Models

Using a QStandardItemModel is usually the easiest and most convenient way to start out when it comes to representing our data in Qt. However, the QStandard-Items used by QStandardItemModel might be more heavyweight (e.g., consume more memory) than is necessary for our particular data since they must cater for the general case rather than for our specific case.

In this section we will replace the simple QStandardItemModel subclass used by the zipcodes1 application with a custom model, and in the process create the zipcodes2 application. Both applications have the same appearance and behavior, although zipcodes2 has always been faster at loading data on the machines we have used for testing.

The new application has just three new files: zipcodeitem.hpp, tablemodel.hpp, and tablemodel.cpp. All the other files are the same as those used by zipcodes1 (except for the standardtablemodel.{hpp,cpp} files which aren't needed of course). The zipcodes2.pro file also includes the line DEFINES += CUSTOM_MODEL, and the zipcodes1 files use #ifdefs where necessary to do things differently for zipcodes2.

Since most of the main window's methods are the same for both zipcodes1 and for zipcodes2, we will only cover those methods that differ—the constructor, createConnections(), and addZipcode(). We don't show the #ifdefs; instead we show the code as seen by the compiler for zipcodes2 when CUSTOM_MODEL is defined. (And in the previous section we did the same thing, showing the code as seen by the compiler when CUSTOM_MODEL was *not* defined.)

Changing a Table Model through the User Interface

The constructor is almost identical to the zipcodes1 constructor, but worth looking at again because we show an aspect that we did not show before.

```
MainWindow::MainWindow(QWidget *parent)
    : QMainWindow(parent), loading(false)
{
    model = new TableModel(this);
#ifdef MODEL_TEST
    (void) new ModelTest(model, this);
#endif
```

```
    proxyModel = new ProxyModel(this);
    proxyModel->setSourceModel(model);

    createWidgets();
    createComboBoxModels();
    createLayout();
    createConnections();

    AQP::accelerateWidget(this);
    setWindowTitle(tr("%1 (Custom Model)[*]")
            .arg(QApplication::applicationName()));
    statusBar()->showMessage(tr("Ready"), StatusTimeout);
}
```

The only differences from zipcodes1 are that we use a TableModel (a QAbstract-
TableModel subclass) rather than a QStandardItemModel subclass, and we set a
different initial window title.

For both applications we also create a ModelTest object (although we did not
show this before). This object is used to test models and is available from Qt
Development Frameworks at labs.qt.nokia.com/page/Projects/Itemview/Model-
test. It is very easy to use. Having downloaded it and, for example, put it in a
parallel directory, we must add it to our project's .pro file. Here are the relevant
lines from zipcodes2.pro (they are the same in zipcodes1.pro):

```
exists(../modeltest-0.2/modeltest.pri) {                          .pro
    DEFINES += MODEL_TEST                                         File
    include(../modeltest-0.2/modeltest.pri)
}
```

We use qmake's exists() function and only define MODEL_TEST and include the
.pri file if the file is actually available. Also in the .pro file we must add the
line CONFIG += debug, otherwise the Q_ASSERTs that the model test uses will be
removed by the C++ preprocessor.

We must also include the header file in the source file where we want to create
the ModelTest, in our case in mainwindow.cpp:

```
#ifdef MODEL_TEST
#include <modeltest.h>
#endif
```

We wrap all the model test-related lines in #ifdefs so that the application will
build even if the model test code isn't present.

The last step is to create a ModelTest instance and give it the model to be
tested—we did this in the main window's constructor. We don't need to do anything more, but if we use a custom model and make a mistake—of a kind that
the ModelTest can recognize—the ModelTest will assert to let us know that there

is a problem. For custom table models like the one we will create here, the work is fairly straightforward so the ModelTest might not really be needed—but for custom tree models such as the one we will create in the next chapter, using the ModelTest is really worthwhile.

There is only one difference between createConnections() in the two Zipcodes applications. Whereas in zipcodes1 we connected from the QStandardItemModel's itemChanged() signal to setDirty(), in zipcodes2 we replace this with a connection from the custom TableModel's dataChanged() signal to setDirty().

The only method that is significantly different between the two applications is addZipcode() which is somewhat simpler in zipcodes2. (The implementation used in zipcodes1 was shown earlier; 99 ◀.)

```
void MainWindow::addZipcode()
{
    dontFilterOrSelectRadioButton->click();
    if (!model->insertRow(model->rowCount()))
        return;
    tableView->scrollToBottom();
    tableView->setFocus();
    QModelIndex index = proxyModel->index(proxyModel->rowCount() - 1,
                                           Zipcode);
    tableView->setCurrentIndex(index);
    tableView->edit(index);
}
```

Unlike in the zipcodes1 version we don't have to create all the items in the new row here. Instead we simply call the QAbstractTableModel::insertRow() method, which in turn calls insertRows() with a count of 1. For custom models that allow insertions we must reimplement the insertRows() method anyway, so there is no extra work involved.

All the other classes and methods common to both applications are exactly the same, so there are no changes to the custom delegate or to the two custom proxy models (UniqueProxyModel and ProxyModel), and all the applications' behaviors are the same with no discernable difference between the use of the QStandardItemModel subclass and the QAbstractTableModel subclass. Of course, behind the scenes we must do rather more work to create a QAbstractTableModel subclass (since QStandardItemModel provides so much functionality out of the box), but we gain much finer control, and potentially more efficiency.

This ability to exchange one model for another—providing they handle the same data—without requiring any changes to the views or delegates, really highlights one of the key benefits of using Qt's model/view architecture.

A Custom QAbstractTableModel Subclass for Tables

In this subsection we will show how to create a QAbstractTableModel subclass. As for all QAbstractItemModel subclasses in Qt's model/view architecture, we must reimplement a particular set of functions so that our model subclass's API is compatible with the architecture and can be used in any context where such a model is required.

Table 3.1 (➤ 118) lists the methods that must be reimplemented in various cases. For example, all models must reimplement the methods that provide read-only support (flags(), data(), etc.), and editable models must reimplement both the read-only supporting methods *and* the editable supporting methods, and so on. (The methods that must be reimplemented to support drag and drop are not listed here—we will cover this topic in the next chapter; ➤ 159.)

For some resizable models it may make sense for them to be resized only in certain ways. For example, a table model might allow the insertion and removal of rows but not of columns. In such cases we must implement the insertRows() and removeRows() methods, but do not have to implement the insertColumns() or removeColumns() methods.

The TableModel discussed in this subsection is a QAbstractTableModel subclass that holds its data in a QList<ZipcodeItem>. We chose to use QList rather than QVector because in the general case it provides better performance than QVector, and this is particularly so for insertions and deletions in the middle. (Note that for really big lists, QLinkedList is a better choice if we need to do insertions and deletions in the middle.)

Items stored in a QList must be of an assignable datatype, that is, a type that provides a default constructor, a copy constructor, and an assignment operator. In addition, to use certain methods, it may be necessary to provide additional operators—for example, to use QList::contains(), QList::count() (for a specified value), QList::indexOf(), QList::lastIndexOf(), QList::removeAll(), QList:: removeOne(), or QList::operator!=(), the item class must provide operator==(). And to support sorting with the qSort() function the item class must provide operator<(). Here is the ZipcodeItem class which is completely defined in its header file:

```
struct ZipcodeItem
{
    explicit ZipcodeItem(int zipcode_=InvalidZipcode,
            const QString &postOffice_=QString(),
            const QString &county_=QString(),
            const QString &state_=QString())
        : zipcode(zipcode_), postOffice(postOffice_), county(county_),
          state(state_) {}
```

```
        bool operator<(const ZipcodeItem &other) const
            { return zipcode != other.zipcode ? zipcode < other.zipcode
                                        : postOffice < other.postOffice; }

        int zipcode;
        QString postOffice;
        QString county;
        QString state;
    };
```

The class has a default constructor—all the arguments can be omitted because defaults are provided for all of them. We have left C++ to supply the copy constructor and the assignment operator since the data members are values rather than pointers. There is no operator==() implementation so we cannot search for ZipcodeItems in the QList or do any of the other operations that depend on this operator. But operator<() is implemented—comparing zipcodes and using the post office as a tie-breaker—since we want to be able to sort the data by zipcode.

A more elaborate class would have used getters and setters and might have provided an isValid() method and operator==(), but none of these are necessary for the use made of the class by the TableModel so we haven't done them.

The TableModel class implements all the methods for supporting read-only access (flags(), data(), headerData(), rowCount(), columnCount()), both the methods for supporting editable access (setData() and setHeaderData()), but only two of the resizing methods (insertRows() and removeRows()); so the TableModel always has a fixed number of columns. In addition, the class has load() and save() methods and a filename() getter to provide support for loading and saving data from and to a file.

The TableModel has just two items of private data: zipcodes of type QList<Zip-codeItem>, and m_filename of type QString. The constructor simply calls the base class QAbstractTableModel constructor with the parent argument; its body is empty.

We will now review the TableModel's methods. Although the data they access is specific to the Zipcodes applications, the structure of their implementations can be generalized to any QAbstractTableModel or QAbstractItemModel, so although the code couldn't be cut and pasted as it is, it can serve as a general template for the implementation of these model/view methods for custom table models.

The QAbstractItemModel API Methods for Tables

We will begin by looking at the QAbstractItemModel methods that must be reimplemented to provide a custom table model whose items can be edited and that is resizable (in terms of rows, but not of columns).

Table 3.1 *The QAbstractItemModel API*

Method	Description
	All Models
data(*index*, *role*)	Returns the `QVariant` value for the given model *index* and *role* (of type `Qt::ItemDataRole`; ➤ 119)
flags(*index*)	Returns the bitwise OR of one or more `Qt::ItemFlag` values (➤ 119) to indicate if the item at the given *index* is enabled and if it can be checked, edited, selected, etc.
headerData(*sect*, *orient*, *role*)	Returns the `QVariant` header value for the section *sect*, orientation *orient*, and *role*
rowCount(*index*)	Returns the number of rows under the given parent *index*, i.e., the parent *index*'s child count
	Table and Tree Models
columnCount(*index*)	Returns the number of columns under the given parent *index*—often a constant for the whole model
	All Editable Models
setData(*index*, *value*, *role*)	Sets the *role*'s value for the given *index* to *value*, and if successful returns `true` and emits `dataChanged()`
setHeaderData(*sect*, *orient*, *value*, *role*)	Sets the header *role*'s value for the section *sect* and orientation *orient* to *value*, and if successful returns `true` and emits `headerDataChanged()`
	All Resizable Models
insertRows(*row*, *count*, *index*)	Inserts *count* rows at *row* under the parent *index* and returns `true` on success; reimplementations *must* call `beginInsertRows()` and `endInsertRows()`
removeRows(*row*, *count*, *index*)	Removes *count* rows from *row* under the parent *index* and returns `true` on success; reimplementations *must* call `beginRemoveRows()` and `endRemoveRows()`
	Resizable Table and Tree Models
insertColumns(*column*, *count*, *index*)	Inserts *count* columns at *column* under the parent *index* and returns `true` on success; reimplementations *must* call `beginInsertColumns()` and `endInsertColumns()`
removeColumns(*column*, *count*, *index*)	Removes *count* columns from *column* under the parent *index* and returns `true` on success; reimplementations *must* call `beginRemoveColumns()` and `endRemoveColumns()`
	Tree Models
index(*row*, *column*, *index*)	Returns the `QModelIndex` for the item with the given *row*, *column*, and parent *index*
parent(*index*)	Returns the `QModelIndex` of the given *index*'s parent

Table 3.2 *The Qt::ItemDataRole enum*

Flag	Description
Qt::Accessible-DescriptionRole	A description of the item to support accessibility
Qt::Accessible-TextRole	The text to be used by accessibility tools such as a screen reader
Qt::BackgroundRole	The background brush to use when rendering the data
Qt::CheckStateRole	The data item's checked state
Qt::DecorationRole	An icon for the data
Qt::DisplayRole	The text to display to represent the data
Qt::EditRole	The data in a form suitable for editing
Qt::FontRole	The font for rendering the data as text
Qt::ForegroundRole	The foreground brush to use when rendering the data
Qt::SizeHintRole	A size hint for the data
Qt::StatusTipRole	A status tip text for the data
Qt::TextAlignment-Role	The text alignment to use when rendering the data as text
Qt::ToolTipRole	A tooltip text for the data
Qt::UserRole	A role that can be used to hold custom data; additional data can be stored in Qt::UserRole + 1, etc.
Qt::WhatsThisRole	A What's This? text for the data

Table 3.3 *The Qt::ItemFlag enum*

Flag	Description
Qt::ItemIsDragEnabled	The item can be dragged
Qt::ItemIsDropEnabled	The item can be dropped onto
Qt::ItemIsEditable	The item can be edited
Qt::ItemIsEnabled	The user can interact with the item
Qt::ItemIsSelectable	The item can be selected
Qt::ItemIsTristate	The item has three check states (checked, unchecked, unchanged) rather than two
Qt::ItemIsUserCheckable	The item has a user-manipulatable checkbox
Qt::NoItemFlags	If this is the only flag, the item cannot be checked, selected, edited, etc.

```
Qt::ItemFlags TableModel::flags(const QModelIndex &index) const
{
    Qt::ItemFlags theFlags = QAbstractTableModel::flags(index);
    if (index.isValid())
        theFlags |= Qt::ItemIsSelectable|Qt::ItemIsEditable|
                    Qt::ItemIsEnabled;
    return theFlags;
}
```

If the model index we're given is valid we set the corresponding item's flags to allow it to be selected and edited—and to enable it of course. In fact, the base class implementation gives us `Qt::ItemIsSelectable|Qt::ItemIsEnabled`, so we only need to add `Qt::ItemIsEditable`; but we prefer to be explicit about our intentions. (The flags are listed in Table 3.3; 119 ◀.)

The `data()` method is the means by which all the data and meta-data concerning an item are accessed. Although the method isn't long we will look at it in four short parts for ease of explanation.

```
const int MaxColumns = 4;

QVariant TableModel::data(const QModelIndex &index, int role) const
{
    if (!index.isValid() ||
        index.row() < 0 || index.row() >= zipcodes.count() ||
        index.column() < 0 || index.column() >= MaxColumns)
        return QVariant();
    const ZipcodeItem &item = zipcodes.at(index.row());
```

The most unusual aspect of this method (and of the `headerData()` method) is that we do *not* call the base class method to handle our unhandled cases—instead we *must* return an invalid QVariant for those cases we don't handle ourselves. Returning anything other than an invalid QVariant for unhandled cases will not work!

Qt's model/view architecture expects the `QAbstractItemModel::data()` and `QAbstractItemModel::headerData()` methods to either return a valid QVariant which it then uses, or an invalid QVariant in which case Qt computes the value it needs as best it can. If we return a valid QVariant that isn't really the value we want—for example, if we return an empty string or 0 for an unhandled case instead of an invalid QVariant—Qt will use the value returned (since it is a valid QVariant) and confusion will reign.

We start by checking that the model index is valid and that its row and column are in range. If the checks pass we get a read-only reference to the relevant item in the `zipcodes` list ready for use further on.

We have chosen to handle two cases, requests for size hints (indicated by a role of Qt::SizeHintRole), and requests for item data (indicated by a role of Qt::DisplayRole or of Qt::EditRole—which in this example we treat as synonymous).

```
if (role == Qt::SizeHintRole) {
    QStyleOptionComboBox option;
    switch (index.column()) {
        case Zipcode: {
            option.currentText = QString::number(MaxZipcode);
            const QString header = headerData(Zipcode,
                    Qt::Horizontal, Qt::DisplayRole).toString();
            if (header.length() > option.currentText.length())
                option.currentText = header;
            break;
        }
        case PostOffice: option.currentText = item.postOffice;
                         break;
        case County: option.currentText = item.county; break;
        case State: option.currentText = item.state; break;
        default: Q_ASSERT(false);
    }
    QFontMetrics fontMetrics(data(index, Qt::FontRole)
                            .value<QFont>());
    option.fontMetrics = fontMetrics;
    QSize size(fontMetrics.width(option.currentText),
            fontMetrics.height());
    return qApp->style()->sizeFromContents(QStyle::CT_ComboBox,
                                        &option, size);
}
```

For each column we get the relevant text—except for the zipcode where we always use the largest allowed or the column's header text, whichever is longer. We then create a font metrics object and use it to calculate the size needed for the text. Notice that we use a recursive call to the data() method to obtain the font. We don't handle the Qt::FontRole ourselves so Qt will handle it for us because we return an invalid QVariant for our unhandled cases.

We need to allow extra room to account for the fact that when the user in-place edits a zipcode they will get a spinbox—which needs extra space for its spin buttons. Similarly, when the user changes the state they will get an in-place combobox which will need extra space for its drop down button. If we didn't provide the extra space, when the user started editing an item that had a spinbox or combobox editor, some of the item's text would probably be obscured. For the post office and county almost no extra space is needed since they are edited using a QLineEdit which just takes up a tiny bit of extra space for its frame, but giving them the extra space is harmless and makes our code a bit shorter since we can do the same computation for all the columns.

To obtain the actual size we need we use a QStyleOptionComboBox object, with its fontMetrics member set to the item's font's font metrics and its current-Text member set to the item's text. Then we pass this object, along with the size needed by the text (the contents size), to the QStyle::sizeFromContents() method (having obtained a pointer to the application's QStyle from the global QApplication object, qApp). We tell the method we want it to calculate the size needed to show the contents in a combobox (indicated by the CT_ComboBox first argument), and return the size it gives us. (There is no equivalent style that can be passed for a spinbox, and in any case a combobox needs more room than a spinbox and so can serve for both.)

```
    if (role == Qt::DisplayRole || role == Qt::EditRole) {
        switch (index.column()) {
            case Zipcode: return item.zipcode;
            case PostOffice: return item.postOffice;
            case County: return item.county;
            case State: return item.state;
            default: Q_ASSERT(false);
        }
    }
```

We treat display and edit data as the same (a fairly common but by no means mandatory practice). Although the ZipcodeItem member's datatypes vary (e.g., int and QString), a QVariant is always returned.

```
    return QVariant();
}
```

For all the unhandled cases (in this case, all the roles we chose not to handle), we return an invalid QVariant and leave Qt to handle those cases for us.

```
QVariant TableModel::headerData(int section,
        Qt::Orientation orientation, int role) const
{
    if (role != Qt::DisplayRole)
        return QVariant();
    if (orientation == Qt::Horizontal) {
        switch (section) {
            case Zipcode: return tr("Zipcode");
            case PostOffice: return tr("Post Office");
            case County: return tr("County");
            case State: return tr("State");
            default: Q_ASSERT(false);
        }
```

```
        }
        return section + 1;
    }
```

Table views normally have both horizontal and vertical headers so tabular models should provide header texts for both. We only handle the display role— we leave all requests for data for other roles to Qt by returning an invalid QVariant.

The section is the row if orientation is Qt::Vertical, or the column if orientation is Qt::Horizontal. For column headers we return suitable texts and for rows we return section + 1 to give the user 1-based row numbers.

```
    int TableModel::rowCount(const QModelIndex &index) const
    {
        return index.isValid() ? 0 : zipcodes.count();
    }
```

This method returns the number of rows (actually the child count) for the given model index. Table (and list) model items have an invalid model index as their parent, so if the index is invalid we return the total number of rows in the table (or list). If the number of rows was fixed (because we didn't implement insertRows() and removeRows()), we would be able to use a constant for the row count.

If the index is valid then we are being asked the row count (i.e., the child count) for an item—something that only makes sense for tree models—so when asked, for list and table models we must return 0.

```
    int TableModel::columnCount(const QModelIndex &index) const
    {
        return index.isValid() ? 0 : MaxColumns;
    }
```

This method returns the number of columns for the given model index. If the index is invalid we return the total number of columns in the table. (For list models we would inherit QAbstractListModel and not implement this method since the base class implementation is sufficient.) In this example, the number of columns is fixed (because we have not implemented insertColumns() and removeColumns()); but if we had implemented the appropriate resizing methods the number could vary.

If the index is valid then we are being asked the column count for an item (something that rarely makes sense), so in such cases we must return 0.

```
    bool TableModel::setData(const QModelIndex &index,
                             const QVariant &value, int role)
    {
```

```
    if (!index.isValid() || role != Qt::EditRole ||
        index.row() < 0 || index.row() >= zipcodes.count() ||
        index.column() < 0 || index.column() >= MaxColumns)
        return false;
    ZipcodeItem &item = zipcodes[index.row()];
    switch (index.column()) {
        case Zipcode: {
            bool ok;
            int zipcode = value.toInt(&ok);
            if (!ok || zipcode < MinZipcode || zipcode > MaxZipcode)
                return false;
            item.zipcode = zipcode;
            break;
        }
        case PostOffice: item.postOffice = value.toString(); break;
        case County: item.county = value.toString(); break;
        case State: item.state = value.toString(); break;
        default: Q_ASSERT(false);
    }
    emit dataChanged(index, index);
    return true;
}
```

This method starts with similar code to data() except that it returns a bool indicating whether the edit was successful or not. If the model index passes the tests we take a non-const (i.e., editable) reference to the corresponding ZipcodeItem, and set the relevant column's data to the data passed in.

We haven't implemented any validation for the string columns, although it would be easy to reject empty strings by adding an extra disjunct to the initial if statement—for example, || (index.column() != Zipcode && value.toString.isEmpty()). For the zipcode we only allow valid values.

If no change is made we *must* return false. Correspondingly, if the edit was successfully applied we *must* emit dataChanged() for the model indexes that were changed and return true.

It is possible that we might want one edit to have a cascading effect, and the model/view architecture supports this to some extent by allowing us to emit dataChanged() with a top-left and bottom-right model index to indicate a rectangular block of affected indexes. In the common case of only one index being affected we pass that same index for both arguments as we have done here.

```
bool setHeaderData(int, Qt::Orientation, const QVariant&,
                   int=Qt::EditRole) { return false; }
```

We have implemented this method in the header file. We have chosen to prevent the user from being able to edit the row and column headers. This is achieved by returning false regardless of the arguments.

If we allow header editing we *must* emit headerDataChanged() with the orientation and the first and last affected sections (rows or columns) and return true.

```
bool TableModel::insertRows(int row, int count, const QModelIndex&)
{
    beginInsertRows(QModelIndex(), row, row + count - 1);
    for (int i = 0; i < count; ++i)
        zipcodes.insert(row, ZipcodeItem());
    endInsertRows();
    return true;
}
```

For a model to be resizable it must implement insertRows() and removeRows() (or insertColumns() and removeColumns()—or all four methods). If the row is 0, the new rows will be inserted before any existing rows and if row == rowCount() the new rows will be appended.

Structurally, all reimplementations of insertRows() follow the same pattern: a call to beginInsertRows() *before* any changes are made to the model, then the code to perform the insertion, and finally a call to endInsertRows() *after* any changes have been applied to the model. The method must return true if any changes were made.

The calls to beginInsertRows() and endInsertRows() shown here can be used as is for any list or table model subclass. Tree models are slightly more complicated but we will see how to handle them in the next chapter.

In the Zipcodes case we insert one empty ZipcodeItem for each row that is to be inserted. In fact the zipcodes2 application never calls this method directly; but it does call insertRow() in addZipcode(), and that method (implemented in the base class) polymorphically calls insertRows() with the row and a count of 1.

```
bool TableModel::removeRows(int row, int count, const QModelIndex&)
{
    beginRemoveRows(QModelIndex(), row, row + count - 1);
    for (int i = 0; i < count; ++i)
        zipcodes.removeAt(row);
    endRemoveRows();
    return true;
}
```

This method is the analog of insertRows(), and has the same structure, only it calls beginRemoveRows() and endRemoveRows(). These calls, as shown here, can be used as is for any list or table model.

In this case we have used `QList::removeAt()` which removes and discards the value at the given row—this method *requires* that the row be in range. One subtle point to notice is that we always remove the "same" row—after deleting a row all the following rows are moved down one position so each subsequent `removeAt()` call removes what was the next row.

In a similar way to `insertRows()`, `removeRows()` is not directly called by the `zipcodes2` application; instead the `deleteZipcode()` method calls `removeRow()` for which the base class implementation calls `removeRows()` with the given row and a count of 1.

We have now finished reviewing the reimplementations of all the methods necessary to provide an editable table (or list) model that can also be resized (in terms of adding or removing rows).

Methods to Support Saving and Loading Table Items

In this subsubsection we will look at the `save()` and `load()` methods that provide the functionality for saving and loading table items to and from files. Both use exactly the same zipcodes file format that we discussed in the previous subsection, with the same magic number and file format version, and using the same `QDataStream` version (103 ◄).

```
void TableModel::save(const QString &filename)
{
    if (!filename.isEmpty())
        m_filename = filename;
    if (m_filename.isEmpty())
        throw AQP::Error(tr("no filename specified"));
    QFile file(m_filename);
    if (!file.open(QIODevice::WriteOnly))
        throw AQP::Error(file.errorString());

    QDataStream out(&file);
    out << MagicNumber << FormatNumber;
    out.setVersion(QDataStream::Qt_4_5);
    QListIterator<ZipcodeItem> i(zipcodes);
    while (i.hasNext())
        out << i.next();
}
```

This method starts out in a very similar way to the `StandardTableModel::save()` method we reviewed earlier, using the specified filename or falling back to the private `m_filename` if no new filename is specified. Just as before, the magic number and file format version are written out, then the data stream version is set. We then write all the items using a `QDataStream::operator<<()` overload.

```
QDataStream &operator<<(QDataStream &out, const ZipcodeItem &item)
{
    out << static_cast<quint16>(item.zipcode) << item.postOffice
        << item.county << item.state;
    return out;
}
```

As always when writing an integer to a QDataStream it is essential to specify the
signedness and number of bits we want to write.

```
void TableModel::load(const QString &filename)
{
    ...
    QDataStream in(&file);
    qint32 magicNumber;
    in >> magicNumber;
    if (magicNumber != MagicNumber)
        throw AQP::Error(tr("unrecognized file type"));
    qint16 formatVersionNumber;
    in >> formatVersionNumber;
    if (formatVersionNumber > FormatNumber)
        throw AQP::Error(tr("file format version is too new"));
    in.setVersion(QDataStream::Qt_4_5);
    zipcodes.clear();

    ZipcodeItem item;
    while (!in.atEnd()) {
        in >> item;
        zipcodes << item;
    }
    qSort(zipcodes);
    reset();
}
```

This method is similar to the corresponding StandardTableModel::load()
method. We have omitted the filename handling since it is similar to that used
in the save() method. The code used to read and check the magic number and
file format version, and to set the data stream version, is the same as that used
in StandardTableModel::load().

Once the data stream is set up ready to read, we clear the old data and stream
in every ZipcodeItem that is available—using a QDataStream::operator>>()
overload—adding each one to the zipcodes list. At the end we sort the list by
zipcode, and then call reset() to notify any associated views that the model's
data has radically changed.

```
QDataStream &operator>>(QDataStream &in, ZipcodeItem &item)
{
```

```
        quint16 zipcode;
        in >> zipcode >> item.postOffice >> item.county >> item.state;
        item.zipcode = static_cast<int>(zipcode);
        return in;
    }
```

Streaming in the ZipcodeItems using this operator, rather than reading the individual values and passing them to a ZipcodeItem constructor, creates a clear separation of responsibilities. We are able to stream most of the data directly into the ZipcodeItem&, but for the integer we must first read it into a variable of the correct signedness and size.

We have now completed our review of table models and seen how to create a custom QStandardItemModel to hold tabular data and how to create a custom QAbstractTableModel that provides the same QAbstractItemModel API as any other model. In the next chapter we will turn our attention to tree models, and in the two chapters after that we will look at delegates and views.

4

Model/View Tree Models

This chapter covers model/view tree models, and assumes a basic familiarity with Qt's model/view architecture, as described at the beginning of the previous chapter (88 ◀).

In this chapter we will look at tree models. In the first section we will cover using a QStandardItemModel subclass with its items held in a QStandardItem subclass. (In the previous chapter we used QStandardItems as is.) And in the second section we will replace the QStandardItemModel with a custom model. Just as with the table model examples in the previous chapter, we will see how to add and edit items in place, as well as how to delete items. And for the custom tree model we will implement drag and drop, cutting and pasting of items, moving items up and down among their siblings, and promoting and demoting items—in all cases with the moved items taking their child items along with them, recursively.

Tree models work in terms of parents and children, where an item's row is its position in its parent's list of children. (In theory, a tree model can be a recursive tree of tables, but none of Qt's views supports this.)

Many trees have a fixed structure or have items of different kinds—in such cases, moving items within the tree rarely makes sense. But for trees whose items (and child items) are all of the same kind, and where it makes sense for any item (and its children) in any position in the tree to be able to be moved anywhere else in the tree, we would want our users to be able to move their items freely. This can be done without too much difficulty using a custom QAbstractItemModel, as we will see. But we have not implemented moving items using a QStandardItemModel because, even though it is possible to insert rows anywhere in a tree's hierarchy using QStandardItemModel::insertRow(), the QStandardItemModel::takeRow() method only works with top-level rows since it does not accept a QModelIndex parent parameter. This means that if we wanted to move rows in a tree represented by a QStandardItemModel, we would end up having to do a lot of tedious copying.

In this chapter's first section we will see how to create a custom QStandard-
ItemModel subclass that can load and save our custom data. Each item is held
in a custom QStandardItem subclass. In the second section we will replace the
QStandardItemModel with a custom QAbstractItemModel subclass, and hold the
items in our own item class. The example in the second section also provides
significant additional functionality: the ability to move items and their children
to different positions within the tree, including support for drag and drop.

The Timelog applications—timelog1 and timelog2—load and save XML files
that hold "task" data. Each task has a name, a "done" state, and one or more
pairs of start–end date/times. Task names can have simple font style attributes applied to any of their characters—such as bold, italic, and coloring.
Tasks can be arbitrarily nested and the total time for a given task is the sum
of its own times and that of its children and their children and so on. Only one
task can be active (i.e., timed) at a time.

One important point to note about the Timelog applications' data is that the
individual start–end date/time pairs are *not* individually represented in the
user interface. Instead, each task is represented by its name, its done state,
and by two aggregates of the date/times—one of the task's total time for today,
and the other for the task's total time altogether. This means that each task is
represented by a single row in the tree.

In an analogous way to our earlier coverage of table models, we will show
similar things for trees: how to load and save all of a tree's items, how to remove
items (and their children, recursively), and how to add and edit items in place.
In addition, for the timelog2 application which uses a custom model, we will
also learn how to move tasks (with their children), and provide the user with
the means of using this functionality via the keyboard, menu options, toolbar
buttons, and using drag and drop. In addition we will see how to hide and show
tasks—for the Timelog examples this will be based on each item's done state.
But we will try to avoid covering application functionality that is not model/
view related—in particular we won't cover most of the code related to starting
and stopping timing and animating the timing icons.

Both examples use a custom "rich text" column delegate for rendering and
editing their task names. This is covered in Chapter 5 (➤ 193).

Using QStandardItemModels for Trees

The timelog1 application uses a QStandardItemModel subclass to load, edit, and
save its data, and uses a QTreeView with a custom delegate to display and edit
the data. The user interface is very conventional with a menu bar, menus, and
toolbar. As usual, we will focus on the model/view details, omitting most of the
widget creation and layouts, and many of the methods.

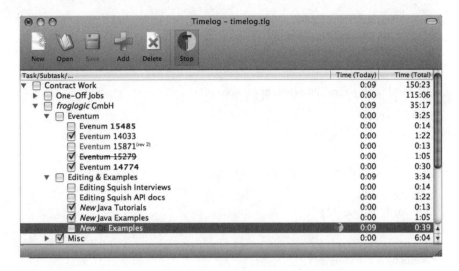

Figure 4.1 *The timelog1 application*

The application is shown in Figure 4.1, and it should be possible to discern from the screenshot that some task names use more than one font style and more than one color. In timelog1 the position of a task in the tree is fixed when it is added—in the next section's timelog2 example we will see how to support moving tasks to arbitrary positions (taking their child tasks with them).

The timelog1 application's user interface supports the conventional document-centric functionality—creating a new file, opening an existing file, and saving a file (where in this case the file holds a tree of tasks in a custom XML format), as well as adding new items and deleting existing items. In addition the user can start or stop timing a task (with the new amount of time added to the task's list of start–end date/times), and to hide or show "done" (checked) tasks.

Changing a Tree Model through the User Interface

In this subsection we will cover the bare bones of the application and its user interface so that we have enough context to understand the model-related discussion and code snippets presented in subsequent subsections. We will start by looking at an extract from the main window's class definition and then we will look at the main window's constructor, including the code for creating the tree model and tree widget and the most important signal–slot connections. The only other methods we will look at are those for adding and deleting tasks and for hiding (or showing) "done" (checked) tasks. (The methods used for manipulating the tree's structure, that is, for moving tasks, are only provided by the custom model version—these are covered in the next section.)

```
class MainWindow : public QMainWindow
{
    Q_OBJECT

public:
    explicit MainWindow(QWidget *parent=0);

public slots:
    void stopTiming();

protected:
    void closeEvent(QCloseEvent*);

private slots:
    void fileNew();
    void fileOpen();
    bool fileSave();
    bool fileSaveAs();
    void editAdd();
    void editDelete();
    void editHideOrShowDoneTasks(bool hide);
    void setDirty(bool dirty=true) { setWindowModified(dirty); }
    void load(const QString &filename,
              const QStringList &taskPath=QStringList());
private:
    ...
    QTreeView *treeView;
    StandardTreeModel *model;
};
```

The main window class should hold no surprises. There are several private
methods and some private data that we have omitted, but that will be covered
where necessary when describing the methods that we do cover. We won't show
the file handling methods—but we will discuss the load() method when we
discuss the following three extracts from the constructor.

```
const QString FilenameSetting("Filename");
const QString GeometrySetting("Geometry");
const QString CurrentTaskPathSetting("CurrentTaskPath");
const int FirstFrame = 0;
const int LastFrame = 4;

MainWindow::MainWindow(QWidget *parent)
    : QMainWindow(parent)
{
    createModelAndView();
    createActions();
    createMenusAndToolBar();
    createConnections();
```

```
AQP::accelerateMenu(menuBar());
setWindowTitle(tr("%1 (QStandardItemModel)[*]")
        .arg(QApplication::applicationName()));
```

The constructor starts out quite conventionally, creating the model and view, then creating the actions, menus, and toolbar, and then the signal–slot connections. We will skip the creation of the actions, menu, and toolbar, since it is all familiar and isn't relevant to the model/view programming that is our chief concern here.

```
timer.setInterval(333);
iconTimeLine.setDuration(5000);
iconTimeLine.setFrameRange(FirstFrame, LastFrame + 1);
iconTimeLine.setLoopCount(0);
iconTimeLine.setCurveShape(QTimeLine::LinearCurve);
```

This part of the constructor is shown for context. The application uses two timers, timer of type QTimer that is used to keep the display of item times up to date, and iconTimeLine of type QTimeLine that is used to produce an animated icon for the task being timed. The timer does an update every one-third of a second, and the iconTimeLine repeatedly loops (specified by a loop count of 0) over five frames (0–4) every 5 seconds. The curve shape determines the interval between frames: QTimeLine::LinearCurve ensures an equal gap. (Qt 4.6 has introduced a new animation framework that is higher-level and more sophisticated than using timers or QTimeLine; we cover this in Chapter 13.)

```
QSettings settings;
restoreGeometry(settings.value(GeometrySetting).toByteArray());
QString filename = settings.value(FilenameSetting).toString();
if (filename.isEmpty())
    QTimer::singleShot(0, this, SLOT(fileNew()));
else
    QMetaObject::invokeMethod(this, "load", Qt::QueuedConnection,
            Q_ARG(QString, filename),
            Q_ARG(QStringList, settings.value(
                CurrentTaskPathSetting).toStringList()));
}
```

At the end of the constructor we attempt to either load in the task file that was loaded the last time the application was run, or we create a new task file ready for the user to add tasks to. Our policy is to always do startup file loading after the main window has been constructed so that the main window appears as quickly as possible, even if the file or files being loaded are very large. (This also has the side benefit that files are only loaded when the main window is fully constructed.) We cannot use a single shot timer for loading because we need to parameterize the slot invocation.

The `QMetaObject::invokeMethod()` method is used when we want to invoke a slot via the event queue, that is, add the call to the queue so that the invocation takes place when the queue is empty, in this case, when the constructor has completed. The first argument is the receiving object, the second argument is the name of the slot to call, the third argument is the connection type to use, and the remaining arguments are the parameters. (In fact this method can be used to immediately invoke a slot by using a connection type of `Qt::Direct-Connection`—something that might be useful for calls that were the result of the user directly or indirectly selecting a method and its arguments via, say, a dialog. We will see a `Qt::DirectConnection` example in Chapter 12; ➤ 423.)

The two arguments passed to the `load()` slot are the task filename and the *task path*. The task path is a string list of task texts that identifies a particular task. For example, in Figure 4.1 (131 ◄), the task path of the highlighted item is `["Contract Work", "<i>froglogic</i> GmbH", "Editing &amp; Examples",` `"<i>New</i> <font color='#0000ff'>Qt</font> Examples"]`. The task texts use a simple HTML subset for font effects, something we will cover when we review the rich text delegate in Chapter 5 (➤ 193). Here's an extract from the `load()` method that shows the task path in use:

```
model->load(filename);
if (!taskPath.isEmpty()) {
    if (QStandardItem *item = model->itemForPath(taskPath))
        setCurrentIndex(item->index());
}
```

This block of code is inside a `try ... catch` block in case the loading fails. The `load()` method is used both by the constructor to restore the last used file, and also by the `fileOpen()` method—in which case the task path is an empty string list. The `QStandardItem::index()` method returns a standard item's model index. We will review the custom `StandardTreeModel::itemForPath()` method (and the corresponding `StandardTreeModel::pathForIndex()` method) later on (➤ 143).

```
void MainWindow::setCurrentIndex(const QModelIndex &index)
{
    if (index.isValid()) {
        treeView->scrollTo(index);
        treeView->setCurrentIndex(index);
    }
}
```

We created this tiny helper method as a convenience since its functionality is needed in more than one place. It makes sure that the item with the given model index is visible in the view and selected, scrolling the view and expanding items if necessary.

```
void MainWindow::createModelAndView()
{
    model = new StandardTreeModel(this);
    treeView->setAllColumnsShowFocus(true);
    treeView->setItemDelegateForColumn(0, new RichTextDelegate);
    treeView->setModel(model);
    setCentralWidget(treeView);
}
```

Here we create an instance of the StandardTreeModel (a QStandardItemModel subclass), and use a standard QTreeView to present the data.

The tree view shows three columns—task names, today's time, and total time. We leave the time columns to be displayed by the QTreeView's built-in delegate, but for the task column we must use a custom delegate so that the HTML is rendered properly rather than being displayed as plain text. One great benefit of using column delegates is that in most cases the same datatype is used for all the items in a particular column, so we can create datatype-specific column delegates which are much more likely to be reusable than model-specific delegates. (Delegates are covered in the next chapter.)

Although not shown, in the source code we have used an #ifdef to create a ModelTest object if the model test module is available, exactly the same as we did for the Zipcodes examples shown earlier (113 ◀). Although the model is a QStandardItemModel subclass that only adds functionality—loading and saving—and doesn't modify the behavior of the built-in functionality, it still causes the model test (version 0.2) to assert. There are actually two problems that the model test highlights. The first (line 106 of modeltest.cpp) looks like a harmless error in QStandardItemModel (the flags for an invalid model index are not 0).* The second appears to be due to over-zealousness rather than a real problem (and has a comment in the source above line 341 suggesting that the failing assert can be safely commented out). In both cases we commented out the problematic lines since both seemed to be false alarms.

```
void MainWindow::createConnections()
{
    connect(treeView->selectionModel(),
            SIGNAL(currentChanged(const QModelIndex&,
                                  const QModelIndex&)),
            this, SLOT(updateUi()));
    connect(model, SIGNAL(itemChanged(QStandardItem*)),
            this, SLOT(setDirty()));
    connect(model, SIGNAL(rowsRemoved(const QModelIndex&,int,int)),
            this, SLOT(setDirty()));
```

---

*The line numbers are correct at the time of this writing—for the subversion version which is different from the packaged version—but may be different for the model test you download.

```
connect(model, SIGNAL(modelReset()), this, SLOT(setDirty()));
```

We have shown only the first few connections. The updateUi() slot (not shown)
is used to keep the user interface up to date by enabling/disabling actions
depending on the application's state. The connections from the model all
(indirectly) set the windowModified property so that the user is given the chance
to save unsaved changes.

Most of the other connections simply connect an action's triggered signal to the
corresponding slot—for example, connecting the fileNewAction to the fileNew()
slot and the editAddAction() to the editAdd() slot. There are also a couple of
connections related to timers used for the timed item and to animate the timed
item's icon.

```
void MainWindow::closeEvent(QCloseEvent *event)
{
    stopTiming();
    if (okToClearData()) {
        QSettings settings;
        settings.setValue(GeometrySetting, saveGeometry());
        settings.setValue(FilenameSetting, model->filename());
        settings.setValue(CurrentTaskPathSetting,
                model->pathForIndex(treeView->currentIndex()));
        event->accept();
    }
    else
        event->ignore();
}
```

If the user quits the application this event handler is called. The stopTim-
ing() method (not shown) does what its name suggests. The setDirty() slot
is used to ensure that the window modified status reflects whether there are
unsaved changes, and this status is checked by the okToClearData() method.
If the okToClearData() method returns true, we save the user's settings—the
main window's geometry, the task file, the task path to the currently selected task—and then we accept the close event to allow the application to terminate. For completeness we will look at the okToClearData() method and the
AQP::okToClearData() function it relies on.

```
bool MainWindow::okToClearData()
{
    if (isWindowModified())
        return AQP::okToClearData(&MainWindow::fileSave, this,
                tr("Unsaved changes"), tr("Save unsaved changes?"));
    return true;
}
```

Since presenting the user with a "save unsaved changes" dialog is a common requirement, we have created a convenience function, AQP::okToClearData(), that provides the functionality we need. This function takes a pointer to the method it should call to perform the save if the user requests a save, a pointer to the window it should appear over (in this case the main window) and which is the instance on which the save method is called, the title it should have, the text it should display, and some optional extra text (which we don't pass in this case). The method pointer must be to a method of the window that is passed as the second argument, and that returns a bool indicating success or failure. The syntax for passing a method pointer is &*ClassName*::*MethodName*.

```
template<typename T>
bool okToClearData(bool (T::*saveData)(), T *parent,
        const QString &title, const QString &text,
        const QString &detailedText=QString())
{
    QScopedPointer<QMessageBox> messageBox(new QMessageBox(parent));
    messageBox->setWindowModality(Qt::WindowModal);
    messageBox->setIcon(QMessageBox::Question);
    messageBox->setWindowTitle(QString("%1 - %2")
            .arg(QApplication::applicationName()).arg(title));
    messageBox->setText(text);
    if (!detailedText.isEmpty())
        messageBox->setInformativeText(detailedText);
    messageBox->addButton(QMessageBox::Save);
    messageBox->addButton(QMessageBox::Discard);
    messageBox->addButton(QMessageBox::Cancel);
    messageBox->setDefaultButton(QMessageBox::Save);
    messageBox->exec();
    if (messageBox->clickedButton() ==
        messageBox->button(QMessageBox::Cancel))
        return false;
    if (messageBox->clickedButton() ==
        messageBox->button(QMessageBox::Save))
        return (parent->*saveData)();
    return true;
}
```

The syntax for specifying a member function parameter that takes no arguments is *returnType* (*Type*::*method*)(), where *returnType* is the type the method returns (which could be void), the *Type* is the class the method belongs to (for example, MainWindow), and *method* is the name we give to the method inside the function—this can be anything, and in particular it does not have to be the real name of the method. (However, when *calling* okToClearData(), the specific class and method must be passed—such as &MainWindow::fileSave, as we saw earlier.)

We have chosen to make okToClearData() a template function so that we don't
have to hard-code the class name. This means that we can use any class that
has a method that returns a bool, such as MyWindow::save(). Inside the function
the method is called saveData(), no matter what its real name is.

We discussed the setting up of a QMessageBox and the use of Qt 4.6's QScoped-
Pointer in the "Avoiding Qt's Static Convenience QMessageBox Functions"
sidebar (61◀) and the "Qt's Smart Pointers" sidebar (62 ◀).*

If the user chooses to save we return the result of calling the method that
was passed in. The syntax for calling a method passed as a pointer, and that
takes no arguments, is (*object->*method*)(). So in this example, what is actually called is MainWindow::fileSave(). If the file is unnamed and the user cancels
the save as dialog, the fileSaveAs() method (called from fileSave()) will return
false which in turn will be returned—in which case okToClearData() will return
false—so although no changes will have been saved, none will have been lost
either. The only way the user can avoid saving changes if they have an unnamed (i.e., new) file is if they explicitly choose to discard their changes.

For timelog1 the position of each task in the tree is fixed when the task is
created (a constraint that doesn't apply in timelog2, as we will see in the next
section). So when adding a new task we must give the user the opportunity
to specify where in the tree the new task should go. This is handled by the
editAdd() method which we will review in three parts.

```
void MainWindow::editAdd()
{
    QModelIndex index = treeView->currentIndex();
    StandardTreeModel::Insert insert = StandardTreeModel::AtTopLevel;
```

We retrieve the index of the current item (which may be invalid if there is no
current item—for example, if the user has just done File→New). We also make
an initial assumption that the new item must be inserted as a top-level item
using an enum from the StandardTreeModel—which is the only choice if there are
no existing items.

```
    if (index.isValid()) {
        QStandardItem *item = model->itemFromIndex(index);
        QScopedPointer<QMessageBox> messageBox(new QMessageBox(this));
        messageBox->setWindowModality(Qt::WindowModal);
        messageBox->setIcon(QMessageBox::Question);
        messageBox->setWindowTitle(tr("%1 - Add Task")
                .arg(QApplication::applicationName()));
        messageBox->setText(tr("<p>Add at the top level or as a "
```

---

*In the source code we have an #if QT_VERSION so that the code will compile with Qt 4.5 using
QSharedPointer.

```
                        "sibling or child of\n'%1'?").arg(item->text())));
        messageBox->addButton(tr("&Top Level"),
                              QMessageBox::AcceptRole);
        QAbstractButton *siblingButton = messageBox->addButton(
                tr("&Sibling"), QMessageBox::AcceptRole);
        QAbstractButton *childButton = messageBox->addButton(
                tr("C&hild"), QMessageBox::AcceptRole);
        messageBox->setDefaultButton(
                qobject_cast<QPushButton*>(childButton));
        messageBox->addButton(QMessageBox::Cancel);
        messageBox->exec();
        if (messageBox->clickedButton() ==
            messageBox->button(QMessageBox::Cancel))
            return;
        if (messageBox->clickedButton() == childButton)
            insert = StandardTreeModel::AsChild;
        else if (messageBox->clickedButton() == siblingButton)
            insert = StandardTreeModel::AsSibling;
    }
```

If there is a current item the user is given the choice of adding the new item as a top-level item, or as a sibling or child of the current item. If the user didn't cancel and didn't choose top-level we change the insert variable appropriately.

Notice that we begin the message box's message text with <p> (the HTML start of the paragraph tag). This ensures that the message text will be interpreted as HTML and displayed correctly. This matters because the message includes the name of the current task and the name might contain HTML markup.

```
    if (QStandardItem *item = model->insertNewTask(insert,
                tr("New Task"), index)) {
        QModelIndex index = item->index();
        setCurrentIndex(index);
        treeView->edit(index);
        setDirty();
        updateUi();
    }
}
```

We ask the model to insert a new task at the specified insertion position, with a default text, and with the given parent (which is ignored when inserting a top-level item). If the insertion succeeds (as it should), we retrieve the new item's model index, make the index current, and initiate editing so that the user can replace the default "New Task" name with the name of their choice.

```
void MainWindow::editDelete()
{
```

```
        QModelIndex index = treeView->currentIndex();
        if (!index.isValid())
            return;
        QStandardItem *item = model->itemFromIndex(index);
        if (item == timedItem)
            stopTiming();
        QString name = item->text();
        int rows = item->rowCount();
        QString message;
        if (rows == 0)
            message = tr("<p>Delete '%1'").arg(name);
        else if (rows == 1)
            message = tr("<p>Delete '%1' and its child (and "
                         "grandchildren etc.)").arg(name);
        else if (rows > 1)
            message = tr("<p>Delete '%1' and its %2 children (and "
                         "grandchildren etc.)").arg(name).arg(rows);
        if (!AQP::okToDelete(this, tr("Delete"), message))
            return;
        model->removeRow(index.row(), index.parent());
        setDirty();
        updateUi();
    }
```

If there is no selected item this method does nothing and returns. Otherwise it
asks the model for the item that corresponds to the selected model index and
retrieves its text and how many children it has. We use separate strings for
the three cases (no children, one child, many children), to make things easier
for translators.

The user is then asked to confirm the deletion, and if they click Delete, we
tell the model to perform the removal. (We reviewed the AQP::okToDelete()
function earlier; 101 ◄.) The removeRow() method in the ultimate base class,
QAbstractItemModel, does nothing and returns false, but the reimplementation
in our StandardTreeModel's immediate base class, QStandardItemModel, correctly
removes the given row—and all its children recursively—and returns true.

```
    void MainWindow::editHideOrShowDoneTasks(bool hide)
    {
        hideOrShowDoneTask(hide, model->invisibleRootItem());
    }

    void MainWindow::hideOrShowDoneTask(bool hide, QStandardItem *item)
    {
        QModelIndex index = item->parent() ? item->parent()->index()
                                           : QModelIndex();
        bool hideThisOne = hide && (item->checkState() == Qt::Checked);
```

```
        treeView->setRowHidden(item->row(), index, hideThisOne);
        if (!hideThisOne) {
            for (int row = 0; row < item->rowCount(); ++row)
                hideOrShowDoneTask(hide, item->child(row, 0));
        }
    }
}
```

The `editHideOrShowDoneTasksAction` is a toggle action connected to the `editHide-`
`OrShowDoneTasks()` slot. The slot is used to make the initial call to the recursive
`hideOrShowDoneTask()` method.

In `hideOrShowDoneTask()` we begin by determining if the current item should
be hidden, and then we call `QTreeView::setRowHidden()` to hide or show the
current item's row accordingly. If the row is hidden we don't have to worry
about any children since they are hidden automatically; but if the item's row
is not hidden we must check each of the item's children recursively, hiding (or
showing) them as appropriate.

We have now covered the essentials of the Timelog application's user interface
as it relates to using the tree model. This should give us sufficient context to
understand the custom `QStandardItem` subclass covered in the next subsection,
and the `QStandardItemModel` subclass covered in the subsection after that.

A QStandardItem Subclass for Tree Items

For `timelog1` we have chosen to use a custom `QStandardItem` subclass since we
want to add some custom data and methods relating to a task's start–end date/
times. Here is the entire class definition:

```
class StandardItem : public QStandardItem
{
public:
    explicit StandardItem(const QString &text, bool done);

    QStandardItem *todayItem() const { return m_today; }
    QStandardItem *totalItem() const { return m_total; }
    void addDateTime(const QDateTime &start, const QDateTime &end)
        { m_dateTimes << qMakePair(start, end); }
    QList<QPair<QDateTime, QDateTime> > dateTimes() const
        { return m_dateTimes; }
    void incrementLastEndTime(int msec);

    QString todaysTime() const;
    QString totalTime() const;

private:
    int minutesForTask(bool onlyForToday) const;
```

```
        QStandardItem *m_today;
        QStandardItem *m_total;
        QList<QPair<QDateTime, QDateTime> > m_dateTimes;
    };
```

One unusual aspect is that we keep pointers to the two QStandardItems that are
used to display the task's today's time and total time. This sacrifices a bit of
memory for the sake of convenience. The QList is used to hold all the start–end
date/times for the task, a list that is added to when the user starts timing
the task.

The only method we will cover is the constructor; the other non-inline methods
are used to increment the time if the task is being timed and to calculate the
times and return them in string or date/time form, so they are not relevant to
model/view programming—although they are in the book's source code.

```
    StandardItem::StandardItem(const QString &text, bool done)
        : QStandardItem(text)
    {
        setCheckable(true);
        setCheckState(done ? Qt::Checked : Qt::Unchecked);
        setFlags(Qt::ItemIsSelectable|Qt::ItemIsEnabled|
                 Qt::ItemIsEditable|Qt::ItemIsUserCheckable);
        m_today = new QStandardItem;
        m_today->setFlags(Qt::ItemIsSelectable|Qt::ItemIsEnabled);
        m_today->setTextAlignment(Qt::AlignVCenter|Qt::AlignRight);
        m_total = new QStandardItem;
        m_total->setFlags(Qt::ItemIsSelectable|Qt::ItemIsEnabled);
        m_total->setTextAlignment(Qt::AlignVCenter|Qt::AlignRight);
    }
```

We make the task item checkable (to reflect the "done" flag), and make it
enabled, selectable, editable, and user-checkable so that the user can check and
uncheck the task—typically by clicking it or by pressing the spacebar when the
task is selected.

In the StandardTreeModel subclass we only ever create StandardItems, one for
each task. Each of these in turn creates the QStandardItems used for the task's
times. For the time items we only allow them to be selectable and enabled
since we don't want the user to be able to edit them and we don't want them to
have checkboxes.

Now that we know what data a StandardItem holds and the methods it provides,
we are ready to look at the StandardTreeModel that holds all of the tasks.

A QStandardItemModel Subclass for Trees

The StandardTreeModel is a QStandardItemModel subclass used to represent a tree of tasks. In addition to providing file handling—load() and save()—the class provides the insertNewTask() method for adding a new task as we saw in the MainWindow::editAdd() method (139 ◄). It also has the pathForIndex() and itemForPath() methods for handling task paths that we discussed earlier (134 ◄; 136 ◄), which we will cover in this subsection. The class's only custom private data is a filename of type QString.

The application's data is held in an XML file format on disk. An extract from such a file is shown in Figure 4.2.

```
<TASK NAME="Editing &amp;amp; Examples" DONE="0">
    <WHEN START="2009-03-18T13:23:59" END="2009-03-18T13:25:15"/>
    <TASK NAME="Editing Squish Interviews" DONE="0">
        <WHEN START="2009-02-03T16:19:35" END="2009-02-03T16:34:02"/>
    </TASK>
    <TASK NAME="Editing Squish API docs" DONE="0">
        <WHEN START="2008-11-14T07:46:31" END="2008-11-14T08:25:55"/>
        <WHEN START="2008-11-14T09:55:26" END="2008-11-14T10:21:11"/>
        <WHEN START="2009-02-25T10:50:20" END="2009-02-25T10:51:29"/>
        <WHEN START="2009-02-25T10:52:02" END="2009-02-25T11:09:33"/>
    </TASK>
</TASK>
...
```

Figure 4.2 *An extract from a Timelog data file*

Each task's name and done status is stored in a TASK tag's attributes. Task names can contain HTML markup, and this markup must be properly escaped so that it doesn't conflict with the XML markup used to store the data. The done flag is stored using "0" for false and "1" for true. The start–end date/time pairs are stored as ISO 8601 date/time strings in attributes of WHEN tags inside the corresponding TASK tag. Hierarchies of tasks within tasks are achieved quite naturally by nesting TASK tags within each other to any level of depth.

In this subsection we will review all the StandardTreeModel methods since they are all relevant to model/view programming.

```
StandardTreeModel::StandardTreeModel(QObject *parent)
    : QStandardItemModel(parent)
{
    initialize();
}
```

```
void StandardTreeModel::initialize()
{
    setHorizontalHeaderLabels(QStringList() << tr("Task/Subtask/..."")
            << tr("Time (Today)") << tr("Time (Total)"));
    for (int column = 1; column < columnCount(); ++column)
        horizontalHeaderItem(column)->setTextAlignment(
                Qt::AlignVCenter|Qt::AlignRight);
}
```

We separated the initialization into its own method since we need to call it from
two different places.

```
void StandardTreeModel::clear()
{
    QStandardItemModel::clear();
    initialize();
}
```

The base class clear() method not only gets rid of all the model's items, but also
its headers. So after clearing we recreate the headers by calling initialize().

```
void StandardTreeModel::save(const QString &filename)
{
    if (!filename.isEmpty())
        m_filename = filename;
    if (m_filename.isEmpty())
        throw AQP::Error(tr("no filename specified"));
    QFile file(m_filename);
    if (!file.open(QIODevice::WriteOnly|QIODevice::Text))
        throw AQP::Error(file.errorString());

    QXmlStreamWriter writer(&file);
    writer.setAutoFormatting(true);
    writer.writeStartDocument();
    writer.writeStartElement("TIMELOG");
    writer.writeAttribute("VERSION", "2.0");
    writeTaskAndChildren(&writer, invisibleRootItem());
    writer.writeEndElement(); // TIMELOG
    writer.writeEndDocument();
}
```

The method starts with code like that used in the Zipcodes examples, using a
new filename if given or the existing filename otherwise. The caller is expected
to catch and handle any exceptions. The AQP::Error class is the same one we
saw before (105 ◄).

The QXmlStreamWriter class is capable of writing what we need without being subclassed. If the autoFormatting property is true, the XML is written out in a human-friendly format with indentation and newlines; otherwise it is written in as compact a format as possible without any unnecessary whitespace. The writeStartDocument() call writes the line <?xml version="1.0" encoding="UTF-8"?> at the beginning of the file—of course, the encoding attribute (and the encoding used)—will be different if we call QXmlStreamWriter::setCodec() to impose our own choice of encoding.

We have enclosed the hierarchy of TASK tags inside a TIMELOG tag (not shown) and given this tag a VERSION attribute to make it easier to change the file format in the future. The QXmlStreamWriter::writeAttribute() method takes an attribute name and a value—there is no need for us to do any XML escaping since the QXmlStreamWriter handles that automatically. We then call the write-TaskAndChildren() method to write all the tasks.

```cpp
const QString TaskTag("TASK");
const QString NameAttribute("NAME");
const QString DoneAttribute("DONE");
const QString WhenTag("WHEN");
const QString StartAttribute("START");
const QString EndAttribute("END");

void StandardTreeModel::writeTaskAndChildren(QXmlStreamWriter *writer,
                                             QStandardItem *root)
{
    if (root != invisibleRootItem()) {
        StandardItem *item = static_cast<StandardItem*>(root);
        writer->writeStartElement(TaskTag);
        writer->writeAttribute(NameAttribute, item->text());
        writer->writeAttribute(DoneAttribute,
                item->checkState() == Qt::Checked ? "1" : "0");
        QListIterator<
                QPair<QDateTime, QDateTime> > i(item->dateTimes());
        while (i.hasNext()) {
            const QPair<QDateTime, QDateTime> &dateTime = i.next();
            writer->writeStartElement(WhenTag);
            writer->writeAttribute(StartAttribute,
                    dateTime.first.toString(Qt::ISODate));
            writer->writeAttribute(EndAttribute,
                    dateTime.second.toString(Qt::ISODate));
            writer->writeEndElement(); // WHEN
        }
    }
    for (int row = 0; row < root->rowCount(); ++row)
        writeTaskAndChildren(writer, root->child(row, 0));
```

```
        if (root != invisibleRootItem())
            writer->writeEndElement(); // TASK
}
```

Notice that we do *not* use tr() for the tag and attribute names since they are part of the file format and not strictly speaking for human readers.

This method writes out a single task and all its child tasks recursively, but skipping the invisible root item. It begins by writing a TASK tag with the name and done attributes. It then iterates over all the task's pairs of start–end date/ times, writing a WHEN tag for each pair. And then it writes all of the task's child tasks (which in turn write *their* child tasks, and so on). The recursive structure is correctly preserved because each task's closing TASK tag is only written *after* its children (and their children, and so on) have been written.

Now that we have seen how the tasks are saved we can look at how they're load-ed. We will review the load() method in two parts for ease of explanation.

```
    void StandardTreeModel::load(const QString &filename)
    {
        ...
        clear();

        QStack<QStandardItem*> stack;
        stack.push(invisibleRootItem());
        QXmlStreamReader reader(&file);
        while (!reader.atEnd()) {
            reader.readNext();
            if (reader.isStartElement()) {
                if (reader.name() == TaskTag) {
                    const QString name = reader.attributes()
                            .value(NameAttribute).toString();
                    bool done = reader.attributes().value(DoneAttribute)
                            == "1";
                    StandardItem *nameItem = createNewTask(stack.top(),
                                                            name, done);
                    stack.push(nameItem);
                }
                else if (reader.name() == WhenTag) {
                    const QDateTime start = QDateTime::fromString(
                            reader.attributes().value(StartAttribute)
                                .toString(), Qt::ISODate);
                    const QDateTime end = QDateTime::fromString(
                            reader.attributes().value(EndAttribute)
                                .toString(), Qt::ISODate);
                    StandardItem *nameItem = static_cast<StandardItem*>(
                            stack.top());
```

```
                nameItem->addDateTime(start, end);
            }
        }
        else if (reader.isEndElement()) {
            if (reader.name() == TaskTag)
                stack.pop();
        }
    }
```

The load() method starts off with almost the same code as the save() method for handling the filename, so we have omitted it. The only difference is that we specified a mode of QIODevice::ReadOnly which causes the file to be opened in binary read-only mode. The QXmlStreamReader will read the <?xml?> tag to determine the correct encoding to use, defaulting to UTF-8 if none is specified.

Once the file is successfully opened we clear the existing items ready to populate the model with data read from the XML file.

We did not need to subclass QXmlStreamReader, since the functionality the class provides is sufficient for it to be used directly.

Whenever a new task is created it must be given a parent—either the task's immediate parent or the *invisible root item* provided by the base class to be used as the parent of top-level items. We use a QStack<QStandardItem*> to hold the parents, pushing tasks onto the stack and popping them off as necessary.

When we encounter a TASK start tag we create a new StandardItem to represent the task, giving it the parent from the top of the stack and the name and done flag retrieved from the tag's attributes. Once the new task is created we push it onto the top of the stack.

The QXmlStreamReader::attributes() method returns the current element's attributes as a QXmlStreamAttributes object. The QXmlStreamAttributes::value() method takes an attribute name and returns the corresponding value as a QStringRef, and with any XML escaping unescaped. For example, the task name "Editing & Examples" is stored in the XML file as "Editing &amp; Examples" but it is returned by value() in its original form.

Although we can sensibly compare QStrings and QStringRefs using the standard comparison operators, if we actually need the text of a QStringRef we must call its toString() method. For example, we extract the task's name into a QString using QStringRef::toString(), but for the "done" flag we simply compare the attribute's value to "1" to determine if the task is done.

Whenever we encounter a WHEN start tag we extract the start and end date/times and append them to the task at the top of the stack's list of date/times. And each time we meet a TASK end tag we pop the top of the stack.

```
    if (reader.hasError())
        throw AQP::Error(reader.errorString());
    if (stack.count() != 1 || stack.top() != invisibleRootItem())
        throw AQP::Error(tr("loading error: possibly corrupt file"));

    calculateTotalsFor(invisibleRootItem());
}
```

If an XML parse error occurs the `QXmlStreamReader::atEnd()` function will return `true` (causing the `while` loop to terminate), and `QXmlStreamReader::has-`
`Error()` will return `true` to inform us that an error occurred. If the stack does
not have exactly one item left at the end (the invisible root item), then something has gone wrong. If either kind of error occurs we throw an exception and
leave the caller to handle it.

If the load is successful, we call `calculateTotalsFor()` to make sure that every
task's time items show the correct times.

```
    StandardItem *StandardTreeModel::createNewTask(QStandardItem *root,
            const QString &name, bool done)
    {
        StandardItem *nameItem = new StandardItem(name, done);
        root->appendRow(QList<QStandardItem*>() << nameItem
                << nameItem->todayItem() << nameItem->totalItem());
        return nameItem;
    }
```

We saw earlier that when we create a `StandardItem`, inside the constructor two
`QStandardItem`s are also created to show the today's and total times (142 ◀). Once
we have created the new task we append the `StandardItem` that represents it,
along with its associated `QStandardItem`s for the times, as a new row under the
given root item (which will be the invisible root item if this is a new top-level
task). At this point the model takes ownership of all three items, so as is usually
the case with Qt, we don't have to worry about deleting them ourselves.

```
    void StandardTreeModel::calculateTotalsFor(QStandardItem *root)
    {
        if (root != invisibleRootItem()) {
            StandardItem *item = static_cast<StandardItem*>(root);
            item->todayItem()->setText(item->todaysTime());
            item->totalItem()->setText(item->totalTime());
        }
        for (int row = 0; row < root->rowCount(); ++row)
            calculateTotalsFor(root->child(row, 0));
    }
```

This recursive method is used to set the text for all the time items. We don't show the todaysTime() or the totalTime() methods since they are not relevant to model/view programming and in any case they are in the source code.

```
enum Insert {AtTopLevel, AsSibling, AsChild};

QStandardItem *StandardTreeModel::insertNewTask(Insert insert,
        const QString &name, const QModelIndex &index)
{
    QStandardItem *parent;
    if (insert == AtTopLevel)
        parent = invisibleRootItem();
    else {
        if (index.isValid()) {
            parent = itemFromIndex(index);
            if (!parent)
                return 0;
            if (insert == AsSibling)
                parent = parent->parent() ? parent->parent()
                                          : invisibleRootItem();
        }
        else
            return 0;
    }
    return createNewTask(parent, name, false);
}
```

This method is called by MainWindow::editAdd() to add a new task. It begins by using the Insert enum to determine what the new task's parent should be and then uses the same createNewTask() method used by the load() method to create a new task with the given task name ("New Task" is used in the editAdd() method), and with its done flag set to false (unchecked).

```
QStringList StandardTreeModel::pathForIndex(const QModelIndex &index)
    const
{
    QStringList path;
    if (index.isValid()) {
        QStandardItem *item = itemFromIndex(index);
        while (item) {
            path.prepend(item->text());
            item = item->parent();
        }
    }
    return path;
}
```

This method is used to return a task path, as shown earlier (134 ◄; 136 ◄). The method starts by adding the given item's text to the path QStringList and then prepends the item's parent's text to the list, and the parent's parent's text, and so on up to the top. Keep in mind that calling QStandardItem::parent() on a top-level item will return 0 (even though the QStandardItemModel has ownership of the item).

```
QStandardItem *StandardTreeModel::itemForPath(const QStringList &path)
    const
{
    return itemForPath(invisibleRootItem(), path);
}


QStandardItem *StandardTreeModel::itemForPath(QStandardItem *root,
        const QStringList &path) const
{
    Q_ASSERT(root);
    if (path.isEmpty())
        return 0;
    for (int row = 0; row < root->rowCount(); ++row) {
        QStandardItem *item = root->child(row, 0);
        if (item->text() == path.at(0)) {
            if (path.count() == 1)
                return item;
            if ((item = itemForPath(item, path.mid(1))))
                return item;
        }
    }
    return 0;
}
```

These methods do the opposite of pathForIndex()—they take a task path and return the corresponding item. The public method takes a task path argument and calls the private method with the invisible root item and the task path. The private method iterates over the children of the item it is given looking for one whose text is the same as the first text in the task path. If a match is found the method calls itself recursively with the found item as the new root item and with a task path that doesn't include the first (already matched) string. Eventually either all the strings in the task path will be matched and the corresponding item returned, or the matching will fail and 0 will be returned.

We have now completed our review of the timelog1 application and the QStandardItem and QStandardItemModel subclasses it uses. In the next section we will create a custom tree model as a drop-in replacement—one that has additional functionality.

Creating Custom Tree Models

As we noted when discussing QStandardItemModel in the context of tables, using this model is usually the easiest and quickest way to get an implementation up and running.

However, at the time of this writing, in the case of tree models, using a QStandardItemModel provides less functionality than it is possible to achieve using a custom tree model. Nonetheless, starting out using a QStandardItem-Model is almost always a good idea—we may not need the extra functionality a custom model can provide, and tree models are more complicated than list or table models, so using QStandardItemModel can save us a lot of work. But if we need to allow users to move items around arbitrarily in the tree—something that normally only makes sense for trees whose items are all of the same kind and can be nested arbitrarily (like our task items)—then there is currently no alternative but to use a custom tree model.

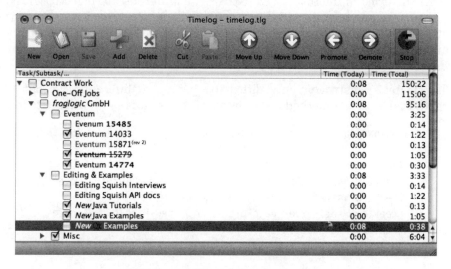

Figure 4.3 *The timelog2 application*

In this section we will create the timelog2 application shown in Figure 4.3. With this application we have followed a similar pattern to what we did with the previous chapter's Zipcodes applications, dropping some files and adding in some files and using #ifdefs to ensure that as much of the code is shared as possible. In this case we will replace the standarditem.{hpp,cpp} and standardtreemodel.{hpp,cpp} files with taskitem.{hpp,cpp} and treemodel.{hpp,cpp}, and add the line DEFINES += CUSTOM_MODEL to the timelog2.pro file.

Just as we did with the Zipcodes applications, we won't show the #ifdefs; instead we show the code as seen by the compiler for timelog2 when CUSTOM_MODEL is defined. (And in the previous section we did the same thing, showing the code as seen by the compiler when CUSTOM_MODEL was *not* defined.)

In the first subsection that follows we will review the model/view-relevant differences between timelog1 and timelog2—most of which are concerned with providing support in the user interface for moving items (and their children) about in the tree by cutting and pasting or dragging and dropping or by using one of the movement actions. In the second subsection we will cover the TaskItem class used to represent tasks and in the third subsection we will cover the TreeModel class which is a QAbstractItemModel subclass that holds all of the application's task data.

Changing a Tree Model through the User Interface

The only difference in member data between timelog1's and timelog2's main window is that timelog2 uses a custom TreeModel rather than a StandardTreeModel. In terms of methods, timelog2 uses a different hideOrShowDoneTask() method, and provides six additional methods to support moving items: edit-Cut(), editPaste(), editMoveUp(), editMoveDown(), editPromote(), and editDe-mote(). There are also corresponding actions in the user interface through which these methods are invoked.

The timelog2 constructor only differs by having a different title, but the createModelAndView() method has a couple of differences so we will quote it.

```
void MainWindow::createModelAndView()
{
    model = new TreeModel(this);
    treeView->setDragDropMode(QAbstractItemView::InternalMove);
    treeView->setAllColumnsShowFocus(true);
    treeView->setItemDelegateForColumn(0, new RichTextDelegate);
    treeView->setModel(model);
    setCentralWidget(treeView);
}
```

The most important difference is that we are using a TreeModel. Notice also that we have told the QTreeView to support drag and drop—but only for moving items within the tree. (Just as with timelog1, we haven't shown the #ifdef for using a ModelTest if that module is available, although it is in the source code.) The delegate is covered in Chapter 5.

The createActions() and createMenusAndToolBar() methods that are called from the constructor are only different from timelog1 in that they create and use the extra actions that timelog2 supports.

As for the signal–slot connections, the connection from the QStandardItemModel::itemChanged() signal to the setDirty() slot is replaced by one from QAbstractItemModel::dataChanged(). Also the new actions are connected to their corresponding slots—for example, the editCutAction's triggered() signal is connected to the editCut() slot.

The code snippet taken from the MainWindow::load() method shown earlier (134 ◄) is slightly simpler for timelog2:

```
model->load(filename);
if (!taskPath.isEmpty()) {
    setCurrentIndex(model->indexForPath(taskPath));
}
```

In timelog1 we had to retrieve an item using StandardTreeModel::itemForPath(), and then get the item's model index for the setCurrentIndex() call, but here we have a TreeModel::indexForPath() method that can be used directly.

Other methods that we reviewed earlier are also different: editAdd() is much shorter and simpler and hideOrShowDoneTask() is a bit different—we will show both of these. We won't show the editDelete() method since it is only different in that it can work with model indexes directly to get the name and child count of the item to be deleted rather than having to get those pieces of information from an item—the actual deleting using removeRow() is the same as before. We will also show a few of the new methods, although we will omit those that are almost identical to the ones that are shown.

```
void MainWindow::editAdd()
{
    QModelIndex index = treeView->currentIndex();
    if (model->insertRow(0, index)) {
        index = model->index(0, 0, index);
        setCurrentIndex(index);
        treeView->edit(index);
        setDirty();
        updateUi();
    }
}
```

For timelog1 we had to ask the user whether they wanted to add the new task at the top level or as a sibling or child of the selected task. But since timelog2 makes it easy to move a task around in the tree we can simply always add a new task as a child of the selected task and leave it up to the user to move it elsewhere if required.

Once the new task is created (by inserting a new row as the first child of the current task—or as a top-level item if the tree is empty), we get the model index of the new task's task name item and scroll to it. Then we initiate editing (to save the user having to press F2—Enter on Mac OS X—or to double-click), so that the user can immediately replace the default "New Task" text with their own text.

Another more subtle benefit of adding the item as a child of the current item is that it is created invisibly (unless it is a top-level task), so the view doesn't make any data() calls on it until we navigate to it. This doesn't really matter in this case, but in general it is usually best when applying changes to a tree to do so to invisible items (i.e., to child items of a collapsed parent), since this can avoid the view making data() calls on items that may have been moved or deleted.

```
void MainWindow::editHideOrShowDoneTasks(bool hide)
{
    hideOrShowDoneTask(hide, QModelIndex());
}

void MainWindow::hideOrShowDoneTask(bool hide,
                                    const QModelIndex &index)
{
    bool hideThisOne = hide && model->isChecked(index);
    if (index.isValid())
        treeView->setRowHidden(index.row(), index.parent(),
                               hideThisOne);
    if (!hideThisOne) {
        for (int row = 0; row < model->rowCount(index); ++row)
            hideOrShowDoneTask(hide, model->index(row, 0, index));
    }
}
```

These methods are very similar to the ones used for timelog1 and use the same logic. The key difference is that we work in terms of model indexes rather than items since we are using the QAbstractItemModel API (plus our own logical extensions such as the isChecked() method; ➤ 168), rather than the item-based QStandardItemModel API.

```
void MainWindow::editCut()
{
    QModelIndex index = treeView->currentIndex();
    if (model->isTimedItem(index))
        stopTiming();
    setCurrentIndex(model->cut(index));
    editPasteAction->setEnabled(model->hasCutItem());
}
```

This slot, like all the movement-related slots, devolves the bulk of the work to the model. This is necessary since when tasks are removed or moved the structure of the tree is changed and this must be reflected in all associated views.

If the cut task is being timed we stop timing since it doesn't make sense to time a task that won't be visible and that may be deleted (simply by not being pasted back). We then tell the model to cut the task with the given model index—and this includes all its children, and their children, recursively—and make the task whose model index is returned the selected task. We also update the paste action's enabled state so that the user will know that pasting is now possible.

```
void MainWindow::editPaste()
{
    setCurrentIndex(model->paste(treeView->currentIndex()));
    editHideOrShowDoneTasks(
            editHideOrShowDoneTasksAction->isChecked());
}
```

This slot is typical of almost all the movement slots provided by the timelog2 application: it tells the model to perform the work, then it scrolls to and selects the task with the model index that the model returns, and finally it hides or shows the done tasks to ensure that those shown (or hidden) are consistent with the editHideOrShowDoneTasksAction's state.

The task that is pasted back is inserted with all its children, and their children, recursively, but with the children (if any) collapsed and hence invisible until the user expands them.

The editMoveUp() slot is almost identical—the only difference is that we call TreeModel::moveUp() instead of TreeModel::paste(). The same applies to edit-MoveDown() where we call TreeModel::moveDown(). The editPromote() and editDe-mote() slots (which call TreeModel::promote() and TreeModel::demote()) are also very similar except that they begin by stopping timing if the selected item is the one being timed (just as we did in the editCut() slot). And in all cases, the method is applied to the selected task and its children, and their children, recursively.

We have now covered enough of the user interface-related methods and slots to give us the context we need to understand the TreeModel that is used to hold the task data. But before reviewing the TreeModel's implementation, we must first look at the TaskItems that the TreeModel uses internally to represent the tasks.

A Custom Item Class for Tree Items

We need an "item" class to represent each item in the tree. When we used QStandardItems we needed separate items for the task name and for the today's and total times. But since we will be using a custom model we can store all the data we need in a single TaskItem and have the model return the appropriate data for each column as required.

The `TaskItem` class has functionality of two kinds: methods for handling the
item data—the task's name and done state and its start–end date/times—and
methods for managing the item's children. As we will see in the next subsection, the entire tree is held by a single pointer to a root item (an unnamed `Task-`
`Item` that is the `TreeModel`'s equivalent to the `QStandardItemModel`'s invisible root
item), with every other task one of the root item's children, or one of their children, and so on.

Most of the `TaskItem`'s methods are in the header which we will look at in three
parts—two groups of methods, and the private member data—starting out of
order with the data, to provide context for the methods.

```
private:
    int minutesForTask(bool onlyForToday) const;

    QString m_name;
    bool m_done;
    QList<QPair<QDateTime, QDateTime> > m_dateTimes;

    TaskItem *m_parent;
    QList<TaskItem*> m_children;
};
```

We won't cover the method for calculating the task's minutes since it is irrelevant to model/view programming. Each task has data members that reflect
what is stored in the XML file: a name, a done flag, and a list of start–end
date/times. And in addition, to support the tree's hierarchy, each task item also
has a parent pointer and a list of children. The unnamed root item (which is
never saved or loaded and exists purely as a programmatic convenience) is the
only item with a parent of 0.

Contrast the data held in a `TaskItem` to the `StandardItem` and two `QStandard-`
`Items` needed for timelog1's `QStandardItemModel` version. While the custom data
held is the same in both cases (the task's name, done flag, and list of start–end
date/times), in terms of overhead, a `TaskItem` adds a pointer and a `QList` of
pointers, whereas the three `QStandardItems` needed by the `QStandardItemModel`
add a total overhead of nine pointers, nine ints, three `QVectors` of pointers, and
three `QVectors` of values (with each value holding an int and a `QVariant`)—this is
for Qt 4.5.0. Of course whether the extra memory matters is very dependent on
the application, and it remains the case that it is almost always better to start
with a `QStandardItemModel` and only implement a custom `QAbstractItemModel` if
performance or functionality requirements make it necessary to do so.

```
class TaskItem
{
public:
    explicit TaskItem(const QString &name=QString(), bool done=false,
                      TaskItem *parent=0);
```

```
~TaskItem() { qDeleteAll(m_children); }

QString name() const { return m_name; }
void setName(const QString &name) { m_name = name; }
bool isDone() const { return m_done; }
void setDone(bool done) { m_done = done; }
QList<QPair<QDateTime, QDateTime> > dateTimes() const
    { return m_dateTimes; }
void addDateTime(const QDateTime &start, const QDateTime &end)
    { m_dateTimes << qMakePair(start, end); }
QString todaysTime() const;
QString totalTime() const;
void incrementLastEndTime(int msec);
```

We will look at the constructor shortly; but we won't show the methods for calculating an item's today's and total times or for incrementing the last end time.

We must implement a destructor since `TaskItem` is not a QObject subclass and so we need to take ownership of the task items ourselves. When an item is deleted we delete all its children, and they in turn delete their children, and so on, recursively, so only the tree's root item needs to be deleted to delete all of the task items.

```
TaskItem *parent() const { return m_parent; }
TaskItem *childAt(int row) const { return m_children.value(row); }
int rowOfChild(TaskItem *child) const
    { return m_children.indexOf(child); }
int childCount() const { return m_children.count(); }
bool hasChildren() const { return !m_children.isEmpty(); }
QList<TaskItem*> children() const { return m_children; }

void insertChild(int row, TaskItem *item)
    { item->m_parent = this; m_children.insert(row, item); }
void addChild(TaskItem *item)
    { item->m_parent = this; m_children << item; }
void swapChildren(int oldRow, int newRow)
    { m_children.swap(oldRow, newRow); }
TaskItem* takeChild(int row);
```

The `childAt()` method is careful to use `QList::value()` rather than `QList::operator[]()`; this ensures that if an out-of-range row is given, a default-constructed value (i.e., 0) is returned instead of the program crashing.

When a child is inserted at a particular row or added at the end it is *essential* that we reparent it. This is because the `TaskItem` being passed may have been cut or moved from somewhere else in the tree and therefore already have a parent, which if not this item (and it normally isn't) is the wrong one.

There are only two methods that are in the `taskitem.cpp` file that are relevant to model/view programming: the constructor and the `takeChild()` method, both of which we will review.

```
TaskItem::TaskItem(const QString &name, bool done, TaskItem *parent)
        : m_name(name), m_done(done), m_parent(parent)
{
    if (m_parent)
        m_parent->addChild(this);
}
```

If a new task item is created with a not-null parent we make sure we add it to the end of the parent's list of children.

```
TaskItem* TaskItem::takeChild(int row)
{
    TaskItem *item = m_children.takeAt(row);
    Q_ASSERT(item);
    item->m_parent = 0;
    return item;
}
```

If a task item is taken out of the tree, that is, removed from its parent's list of children, we must set its parent to 0 to reflect the fact that no item owns it. This means that the returned pointer is our responsibility, so we should delete it or insert it back into the tree as soon as possible, to avoid the risk of it turning into a memory leak.

A Custom QAbstractItemModel Subclass for Trees

To implement a `QAbstractItemModel` subclass for trees that are both editable and resizable, we must normally reimplement all or almost all of the methods listed in Table 3.1 (118 ◄). However, for the Timelog application's task data—and quite often with trees generally—we don't need to reimplement `insertColumns()` or `removeColumns()` because the number of columns used is fixed.

To support moving items (with their children) using drag and drop we must also implement the drag and drop-related methods shown in Table 4.1. The drag and drop API requires us to serialize and deserialize model items, and as we will see, we can use the methods we use for loading and saving to help with this. We also want to provide the user with other means of moving items, and in support of this we have extended the `QAbstractItemModel` API with our own custom methods:

```
QModelIndex moveUp(const QModelIndex &index);
QModelIndex moveDown(const QModelIndex &index);
QModelIndex cut(const QModelIndex &index);
```

Table 4.1 *The QAbstractItemModel's Drag and Drop API*

Method	Description
dropMimeData(*mimeData*, *dropAction*, *row*, *column*, *parent*)	This method is called when a drop occurs; it must deserialize the *mimeData* and use it to perform the given *dropAction* on the item with the given *row*, *column*, and *parent*
mimeData(*indexes*)	Returns a QMimeData object that contains the serialized data corresponding to the given list of model *indexes*; this is used internally by the model to produce the data for a drop
mimeTypes()	Returns a QStringList of the MIME types that describe a list of the model's model indexes
supportedDragActions()	Returns the bitwise OR of one or more Qt::Drop-Actions (there is no drag actions enum)
supportedDropActions()	Returns the bitwise OR of one or more Qt::Drop-Actions (Qt::CopyAction, Qt::MoveAction, etc.)

```
QModelIndex paste(const QModelIndex &index);
QModelIndex promote(const QModelIndex &index);
QModelIndex demote(const QModelIndex &index);
```

Qt 4.6 introduced four new protected methods designed to simplify moving items in a model: beginMoveColumns(), endMoveColumns(), beginMoveRows(), and endMoveRows(). We don't use them so as to keep our code compatible with both Qt 4.5 and Qt 4.6. For projects whose minimum Qt version is Qt 4.6, the new protected methods are likely to be useful, but read their documentation carefully since they have some constraints.

In addition to the extra custom methods, the TreeModel class has methods and data related to timing items (which we won't cover), and the same methods (or equivalents) that we added to the QStandardItemModel: clear(), load(), save(), pathForIndex(), and indexForPath().

The TreeModel has various private methods that we will cover when the need arises as we discuss the public methods, and also some items of private data.

```
private:
    QString m_filename;
    QIcon m_icon;
    TaskItem *timedItem;
    TaskItem *rootItem;
    TaskItem *cutItem;
```

Of the TaskItems, the timedItem is a pointer to an item that has a parent—so we don't have to worry about deleting it. The rootItem is the root of the tree and must be deleted by us when appropriate. The cutItem is the item that has been cut but not pasted; if such an item exists it must be deleted at the appropriate time—for example, if a new file is opened or if the application is terminated.

All this means that the TreeModel can be used as a drop-in replacement for StandardTreeModel, but with additional functionality, in particular support for cutting and pasting items, dragging and dropping items, and moving items.

We will now review all of the TreeModel's model/view-related methods. We will start with the constructor and destructor, then look at the methods implementing the QAbstractItemModel API, then the isChecked() method (for completeness since we saw it used earlier), then the methods implementing the QAbstract-ItemModel's drag and drop API, then the movement methods, and finally, the file and task path handling methods.

```
explicit TreeModel(QObject *parent=0)
    : QAbstractItemModel(parent), timedItem(0), rootItem(0),
      cutItem(0) {}

~TreeModel() { delete rootItem; delete cutItem; }
```

The constructor only needs to initialize the member data pointers to 0 and pass its parent to the base class. The destructor must delete the root item and the cut item (which may be 0). We rely on the TaskItem destructor to delete each task item's children, and their children, recursively.

The QAbstractItemModel API for Trees

In this subsubsection we will review the QAbstractItemModel API methods that the TreeModel implements to provide an editable and resizable (in terms of rows, but not columns) tree. These methods are listed in Table 3.1 (118 ◄).

```
enum Column {Name, Today, Total};

Qt::ItemFlags TreeModel::flags(const QModelIndex &index) const
{
    Qt::ItemFlags theFlags = QAbstractItemModel::flags(index);
    if (index.isValid()) {
        theFlags |= Qt::ItemIsSelectable|Qt::ItemIsEnabled;
        if (index.column() == Name)
            theFlags |= Qt::ItemIsUserCheckable|Qt::ItemIsEditable|
                        Qt::ItemIsDragEnabled|Qt::ItemIsDropEnabled;
    }
    return theFlags;
}
```

This method's implementation is similar for all kinds of models. In this particular case we make all items selectable and enabled, but only allow task names to be checkable, editable, and to be dragged and dropped. As we will see shortly, we have implemented drag and drop such that if a task name is dragged the whole task including its times is dragged, as well as its children, but we prefer users to drag a name rather than a time since this makes it much clearer what is happening.

```cpp
const int ColumnCount = 3;

QVariant TreeModel::data(const QModelIndex &index, int role) const
{
    if (!rootItem || !index.isValid() || index.column() < 0 ||
        index.column() >= ColumnCount)
        return QVariant();
    if (TaskItem *item = itemForIndex(index)) {
        if (role == Qt::DisplayRole || role == Qt::EditRole) {
            switch (index.column()) {
                case Name: return item->name();
                case Today: return item->todaysTime();
                case Total: return item->totalTime();
                default: Q_ASSERT(false);
            }
        }
        if (role == Qt::CheckStateRole && index.column() == Name)
            return static_cast<int>(item->isDone() ? Qt::Checked
                                                    : Qt::Unchecked);
        if (role == Qt::TextAlignmentRole) {
            if (index.column() == Name)
                return static_cast<int>(Qt::AlignVCenter|
                                        Qt::AlignLeft);
            return static_cast<int>(Qt::AlignVCenter|Qt::AlignRight);
        }
        if (role == Qt::DecorationRole && index.column() == Today &&
            timedItem && item == timedItem && !m_icon.isNull())
            return m_icon;
    }
    return QVariant();
}
```

The data() method is key to Qt's model/view architecture, since it is through this method that all data and most meta-data are accessed. As we noted when discussing the TableModel (120 ◄) this method does not rely on us calling the base class implementation; instead we must *always* return an invalid QVariant for any cases that we don't handle ourselves.

The `itemForIndex()` method returns a `TaskItem` pointer from the tree, given a model index; we'll review this method in a moment.

We have chosen to treat `Qt::DisplayRole` and `Qt::EditRole` as synonymous, so if data for either role is requested we return it. Our data doesn't have columns as such, we just have a tree of task items, but we map columns to particular fields in our data, or in the case of the time columns to the appropriate calculated values. We also handle the `Qt::CheckStateRole`, returning the enum that corresponds to the task's done state.

For text alignment we have chosen to left-align the task name and right-align the times. We also supply an icon if data for the `Qt::DecorationRole` is requested—but only if the request is for the `Today` column and if the item is being timed. For all other cases, and for all other roles, we return an invalid `QVariant` and leave Qt to handle them for us.

```
TaskItem *TreeModel::itemForIndex(const QModelIndex &index) const
{
    if (index.isValid()) {
        if (TaskItem *item = static_cast<TaskItem*>(
                index.internalPointer()))
            return item;
    }
    return rootItem;
}
```

Whenever a `QModelIndex` is created (using the `QAbstractItemModel::create-Index()` method), in addition to supplying a row and column we can also provide a pointer (or a numeric ID). In the case of tree models it is very common to supply a pointer to the corresponding item in the tree—and as we will see, that is what we do in the `TreeModel` when we create model indexes. This makes it easy to get back a pointer to the item for a given model index—we can simply ask for the model index's internal pointer. If there is no pointer, or if the index is invalid, we return a pointer to the root item (which will be 0 if no items have been added to the tree).

```
QVariant TreeModel::headerData(int section,
        Qt::Orientation orientation, int role) const
{
    if (orientation == Qt::Horizontal && role == Qt::DisplayRole) {
        if (section == Name)
            return tr("Task/Subtask/...");
        else if (section == Today)
            return tr("Time (Today)");
        else if (section == Total)
            return tr("Time (Total)");
    }
}
```

```
        return QVariant();
    }
```

Qt's QTreeView only supports horizontal headers, so we provide the appropriate
name when one of these is asked for. And since headerData() uses the same
logic as data(), that is, relying on the return value rather than a base class call,
we return an invalid QVariant for any case that we don't handle ourselves.

```
    int TreeModel::rowCount(const QModelIndex &parent) const
    {
        if (parent.isValid() && parent.column() != 0)
            return 0;
        TaskItem *parentItem = itemForIndex(parent);
        return parentItem ? parentItem->childCount() : 0;
    }
```

The row count for an item in a tree is the number of children it has (but not
including their children, so the count does not work recursively). If the parent
is valid but the column isn't 0 we must return 0 since we only allow items in
the first column to have child rows. Otherwise we retrieve the parent index's
corresponding task item. If the parent index is invalid, itemForIndex() will
correctly return the root item (which could be 0 if the tree has no items).

```
    int TreeModel::columnCount(const QModelIndex &parent) const
    {
        return parent.isValid() && parent.column() != 0 ? 0 : ColumnCount;
    }
```

The custom TreeModel, in common with many other tree models, has a fixed
number of columns making this method simple to implement, and is similar
to the one we used for the custom Zipcodes table model (123 ◄). If the index is
valid and the column isn't the first (name) column, then we are being asked for
the column count of a time column; this doesn't make sense for this model, so
in such cases we return 0.

```
    QModelIndex TreeModel::index(int row, int column,
                                 const QModelIndex &parent) const
    {
        if (!rootItem || row < 0 || column < 0 || column >= ColumnCount
            || (parent.isValid() && parent.column() != 0))
            return QModelIndex();
        TaskItem *parentItem = itemForIndex(parent);
        Q_ASSERT(parentItem);
        if (TaskItem *item = parentItem->childAt(row))
            return createIndex(row, column, item);
        return QModelIndex();
    }
```

This method is used to provide model indexes to the model's users, and is also used by the model internally.

In addition to the obvious tests for validity, we also check the parent's column. We do not provide model indexes for items whose parent column is not 0 since we only allow items in column 0 to have child items.

A model index is made up of a row, a column, and a pointer (or numeric ID). For list and table models the pointer is normally 0, but for a tree model it is usually a pointer to (or the ID of) the corresponding item in the tree. Here we begin by retrieving the parent task item using itemForIndex() (162 ◀), and then retrieve the parent item's row-th child item. We then call QAbstractItemModel::create-Index() with the given row and column, and with a pointer to the task item, since this is the item that the model index being created actually refers to. It is this pointer to the task item that becomes the model index's internal pointer.

If we cannot create the index we must return an invalid QModelIndex. Note that there are only two public constructors for QModelIndex—a copy constructor and a constructor that takes no arguments and can therefore be used only to create invalid model indexes. So the only way to create a valid model index is to call createIndex(), or to use the copy constructor to copy an existing model index.

The structure of this method—and the structures of most of the other tree model methods shown here that implement the QAbstractItemModel API—can be used for any tree model that uses a tree of pointers to items that have the child manipulation methods provided by the item type (e.g., TaskItem and its methods or equivalent), and that has an itemForIndex() (or equivalent) method. So, the code shown here should be straightforward to adapt as needed.

```
QModelIndex TreeModel::parent(const QModelIndex &index) const
{
    if (!index.isValid())
        return QModelIndex();
    if (TaskItem *childItem = itemForIndex(index)) {
        if (TaskItem *parentItem = childItem->parent()) {
            if (parentItem == rootItem)
                return QModelIndex();
            if (TaskItem *grandParentItem = parentItem->parent()) {
                int row = grandParentItem->rowOfChild(parentItem);
                return createIndex(row, 0, parentItem);
            }
        }
    }
    return QModelIndex();
}
```

Returning the model index of an item's parent isn't quite as simple as it sounds, even though TaskItems have a pointer to their parent. This is because we cannot directly map from a TaskItem pointer to a model index. So what we must do is find the item's parent item, and then find what row that item occupies in *its* parent's list of children (i.e., the row of the item's parent in its grandparent's list of children). Once we know the row and have the parent pointer we use createIndex() to create the item's parent's model index.

Notice that if the parent item is the root item we return an invalid model index—Qt's model/view architecture uses the convention that the parent of a top-level item is an invalid model index (rather than the root item if the model has such an item), and so we ensure that our code respects this.

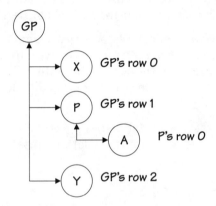

Figure 4.4 *An item's parent is its grandparent's row-th item*

Figure 4.4 illustrates the relationships between items, parents, and rows. In the figure, item A's parent is item P, that is, A is P's first (i.e., row 0) child, and item P's parent is item GP, that is, P is GP's second (i.e., row 1) child.

```
bool setHeaderData(int, Qt::Orientation, const QVariant&,
                   int=Qt::EditRole) { return false; }
```

We have chosen to make the headers read-only, for which this trivial implementation in the header file is sufficient.

```
bool TreeModel::setData(const QModelIndex &index,
                        const QVariant &value, int role)
{
    if (!index.isValid() || index.column() != Name)
        return false;
    if (TaskItem *item = itemForIndex(index)) {
        if (role == Qt::EditRole)
            item->setName(value.toString());
```

```
        else if (role == Qt::CheckStateRole)
            item->setDone(value.toBool());
        else
            return false;
        emit dataChanged(index, index);
        return true;
    }
    return false;
}
```

We use this method to support the editing of task items—in particular the task name and the done flag. We don't have to concern ourselves with the details of editing—the custom rich text delegate handles the editing of task names, and also the toggling of the done state using a checkbox (➤ 193).

If an edit is made we *must* emit the dataChanged() signal with the model indexes that were changed and return true; otherwise we must return false. The first model index is the top left and the second the bottom right of a rectangular region of model indexes. In this case we only ever edit one model index at a time so we use the same index for both.

```
bool TreeModel::insertRows(int row, int count,
                           const QModelIndex &parent)
{
    if (!rootItem)
        rootItem = new TaskItem;
    TaskItem *item = parent.isValid() ? itemForIndex(parent)
                                      : rootItem;
    beginInsertRows(parent, row, row + count - 1);
    for (int i = 0; i < count; ++i)
        (void) new TaskItem(tr("New Task"), false, item);
    endInsertRows();
    return true;
}
```

Qt's model/view API *requires* us to call QAbstractItemModel::beginInsertRows() before inserting any rows into a model, and QAbstractItemModel::endInsert-Rows() once the insertions are finished. The call to beginInsertRows() can be copied verbatim into other implementations—its arguments are the parent model index, the row where the new rows are to be inserted, and the row of the last of the new rows.

We begin by ensuring that there is a root item—there won't be one if the user has just done File→New, for example. Then we get the item that will be the parent item for all the inserted rows—this is either the given parent index's item (if the index is valid), or the root item (which means that the rows will all be top-level items). We then create count new task items, each with a default

text and done state, and each the child of the parent item. (Recall that in the
TaskItem constructor, if a not-null parent is given, the child adds itself to the
parent's list of children; 158 ◄.)

This method is called behind the scenes when a task (and its children) is
dragged and dropped to insert the dropped rows. Note also that there is an
insertRow() method (which we used in MainWindow::editAdd(); 153 ◄), but we
should not need to reimplement it since the base class implementation already
correctly calls insertRows() with a row count of 1.

```
bool TreeModel::removeRows(int row, int count,
                          const QModelIndex &parent)
{
    if (!rootItem)
        return false;
    TaskItem *item = parent.isValid() ? itemForIndex(parent)
                                      : rootItem;
    beginRemoveRows(parent, row, row + count - 1);
    for (int i = 0; i < count; ++i)
        delete item->takeChild(row);
    endRemoveRows();
    return true;
}
```

Qt's model/view API *requires* us to call QAbstractItemModel::beginRemoveRows()
before removing any rows from a model, and QAbstractItemModel::endRemove-
Rows() once the removals are finished. The call to beginRemoveRows() can be
copied verbatim into other implementations.

If there is no root item the tree is empty so there is nothing to delete—in this
case we do nothing and return false. Otherwise, to delete count rows starting
at the given row, we simply delete the item at the given row count times. The
first deletion deletes the row-th item, the second deletion deletes the row + 1-th
item (since that is now the row-th item due to the previous deletion), and so
on. Naturally, the children, their children, and so on, of any deleted item are
also deleted. Note that the TaskItem::takeChild() method (158 ◄) removes the
given item from its parent, sets the item's parent to 0, and returns the (now
parentless and ownerless) item—which we immediately delete.

This method is called behind the scenes when a task (and its children) is
dragged and dropped to delete the original dragged rows once they have been
dropped—the dropped rows are freshly inserted using insertRows().

We have now finished reviewing the reimplementations of all the methods
necessary to provide an editable tree model and that can also be resized (in
terms of adding or removing rows).

We will now look at one tiny method we added to extend the `QAbstractItemModel` API since it is a method whose use we saw earlier, and then we will look at groups of additional methods supporting drag and drop, moving items, and loading and saving items from and to disk.

```
bool TreeModel::isChecked(const QModelIndex &index) const
{
    if (!index.isValid())
        return false;
    return data(index, Qt::CheckStateRole).toInt() == Qt::Checked;
}
```

This is just a convenience method that we added to make the implementation of the `MainWindow::hideOrShowDoneTask()` method easier to read (154 ◄). Although we must implement the relevant parts of the `QAbstractItemModel` API, we are of course free to provide additional convenience methods such as this if we wish.

The QAbstractItemModel API for Drag and Drop

In this subsubsection we will review the `QAbstractItemModel` API methods that the `TreeModel` implements to provide drag and drop. These methods are listed in Table 4.1 (159 ◄). The way that Qt's drag and drop works is that we must serialize the dragged items, and then deserialize them when they are dropped.★

```
Qt::DropActions supportedDragActions() const
    { return Qt::MoveAction; }
Qt::DropActions supportedDropActions() const
    { return Qt::MoveAction; }
```

These two methods are trivially implemented in the header. Here we have specified that the only drag and drop action we support is moving. This makes perfect sense for the task data, but for other kinds of data it might make more sense to support copying, or both moving and copying (which can be achieved by returning `Qt::MoveAction|Qt::CopyAction`).

```
const QString MimeType = "application/vnd.qtrac.xml.task.z";

QStringList TreeModel::mimeTypes() const
{
    return QStringList() << MimeType;
}
```

★ Note that this code works for Qt 4.5 and later, but does not seem to work reliably for Qt 4.4 or earlier.

Qt's drag and drop system (and also its clipboard handling) uses MIME types to identify data. (We briefly discussed MIME types in an earlier chapter; 72 ◄.) We must reimplement the `mimeTypes()` method to return the MIME types our custom model supports. We have created a custom MIME type which we use to identify task data. As we will see in a moment, we have chosen to use the same XML format for dragging and dropping task data as we use for saving and loading it. This isn't as memory efficient as using a compact binary format but it does have the advantage that we can reuse the same code for serializing and deserializing task items as we do for saving and loading them.

```
const int MaxCompression = 9;

QMimeData *TreeModel::mimeData(const QModelIndexList &indexes) const
{
    Q_ASSERT(indexes.count());
    if (indexes.count() != 1)
        return 0;
    if (TaskItem *item = itemForIndex(indexes.at(0))) {
        QMimeData *mimeData = new QMimeData;
        QByteArray xmlData;
        QXmlStreamWriter writer(&xmlData);
        writeTaskAndChildren(&writer, item);
        mimeData->setData(MimeType, qCompress(xmlData,
                                              MaxCompression));
        return mimeData;
    }
    return 0;
}
```

This method is called automatically when a drag is initiated, and is passed the model indexes the user has started dragging. In the case of a tree model, if an item is dragged, that item's index will be in the list of indexes—but its children's indexes will *not* be in the list, although we are still responsible for dragging them (and their children, recursively) along with their parent.

The `mimeData()` method can be used to support the dragging of multiple items (since it can accept a list of model indexes). However, we have chosen to handle just one item being dragged (although this includes its children, and their children recursively of course). We retrieve a pointer to the item and create a `QByteArray` into which we write all the task data in the same XML format we use for storing the tasks on disk. We then use a `QXmlStreamWriter` to write the task and its children as XML data. (Figure 4.2 shows what the XML data looks like; 143 ◄.) Once the data is written, we compress it using maximum (i.e., slowest and most compact) compression—to reduce the memory needed because we have used a verbose XML format—and set the resultant data as the `QMimeData`'s data. The `QMimeData` returned by this method becomes Qt's responsibility so we don't have to worry about deleting it.

```
void TreeModel::writeTaskAndChildren(QXmlStreamWriter *writer,
                                     TaskItem *task) const
{
    if (task != rootItem) {
        writer->writeStartElement(TaskTag);
        writer->writeAttribute(NameAttribute, task->name());
        writer->writeAttribute(DoneAttribute, task->isDone() ? "1"
                                                             : "0");

        QListIterator<
                QPair<QDateTime, QDateTime> > i(task->dateTimes());
        while (i.hasNext()) {
            const QPair<QDateTime, QDateTime> &dateTime = i.next();
            writer->writeStartElement(WhenTag);
            writer->writeAttribute(StartAttribute,
                    dateTime.first.toString(Qt::ISODate));
            writer->writeAttribute(EndAttribute,
                    dateTime.second.toString(Qt::ISODate));
            writer->writeEndElement(); // WHEN
        }
    }
    foreach (TaskItem *child, task->children())
        writeTaskAndChildren(writer, child);
    if (task != rootItem)
        writer->writeEndElement(); // TASK
}
```

This method is used to write an item as XML data into the given QXmlStream-Writer. It is almost identical to the method of the same name that we created for the StandardTreeModel (146 ◄).

We never write the unnamed root item since it exists purely as a programming convenience and is not part of the data. Once the item's data has been written, we write all the item's children, and their children, recursively, so this method can be used to write the entire tree if called with the root item—although here it is always used to write a dragged item (and its children).

```
bool TreeModel::dropMimeData(const QMimeData *mimeData,
        Qt::DropAction action, int row, int column,
        const QModelIndex &parent)
{
    if (action == Qt::IgnoreAction)
        return true;
    if (action != Qt::MoveAction || column > 0 ||
        !mimeData || !mimeData->hasFormat(MimeType))
        return false;
    if (TaskItem *item = itemForIndex(parent)) {
```

```
            emit stopTiming();
            QByteArray xmlData = qUncompress(mimeData->data(MimeType));
            QXmlStreamReader reader(xmlData);
            if (row == -1)
                row = parent.isValid() ? parent.row()
                                       : rootItem->childCount();
            beginInsertRows(parent, row, row);
            readTasks(&reader, item);
            endInsertRows();
            return true;
        }
        return false;
    }
```

This method is automatically called when a drop occurs. If the action is acceptable—in this example, if it is a move—we begin by retrieving the item on which the data has been dropped. Drag and drop works by deleting the dragged items and creating a new set of dropped items that match those dragged. This means that any pointers to the dragged items are no longer valid after a drag and drop. To handle this we emit a custom stopTiming() signal which tells any connected QObjects (in this case the MainWindow) to stop updating the time of the timed item when a drop occurs. (It would, of course, be possible to check to see if the timed item was among those dragged and only emit the stopTiming() signal if it were, but our approach is faster and provides consistent behavior.)

Once we have the parent item under which the dropped items will go, we uncompress the QMimeData's data into our task XML format. Then we call the readTasks() method to recreate the dropped task (and its children, recursively) as a child of the parent item it was dropped on.

If the drop takes place we *must* return true; otherwise we must return false. In the case of moves, behind the scenes Qt uses removeRows() to delete the original dragged items.

We don't actually know how many rows we will be inserting since we don't know if the XML data describes an item with children. This doesn't matter since from the view's perspective, a drop either invisibly or visibly adds one child item (depending on whether the drop is onto a collapsed or expanded item), no matter how many children the item has, because any children are collapsed. If the given row is valid, we use it as the insertion row, otherwise we insert at the parent's row, or failing that as the last top-level item. The calls to beginInsertRows() and endInsertRows() are essential to prevent the view from becoming confused.

Note that the model test appears to be over-zealous when it comes to checking rows that are inserted as a result of a drop. We needed to comment out two lines (468 and 477) to prevent assertions that appear to be false alarms.

Unfortunately, drag and drop within tree views can be a bit fragile on some platforms. For example, when using Qt 4.5 on Linux it doesn't take too much effort to get a crash when doing drag and drop in a tree. And on Mac OS X (with both Qt 4.5 and Qt 4.6), although dragging and dropping works fine in most cases, it is sometimes not possible to drop onto any of the first few items. Fortunately, these problems do not appear to affect Qt on Windows, and in any case, moving items and promoting and demoting items using the toolbar buttons or using key presses give the user just as much freedom to move items as drag and drop provides.

```cpp
void TreeModel::readTasks(QXmlStreamReader *reader, TaskItem *task)
{
    while (!reader->atEnd()) {
        reader->readNext();
        if (reader->isStartElement()) {
            if (reader->name() == TaskTag) {
                const QString name = reader->attributes()
                        .value(NameAttribute).toString();
                bool done = reader->attributes().value(DoneAttribute)
                        == "1";
                task = new TaskItem(name, done, task);
            }
            else if (reader->name() == WhenTag) {
                const QDateTime start = QDateTime::fromString(
                        reader->attributes().value(StartAttribute)
                        .toString(), Qt::ISODate);
                const QDateTime end = QDateTime::fromString(
                        reader->attributes().value(EndAttribute)
                        .toString(), Qt::ISODate);
                Q_ASSERT(task);
                task->addDateTime(start, end);
            }
        }
        else if (reader->isEndElement()) {
            if (reader->name() == TaskTag) {
                Q_ASSERT(task);
                task = task->parent();
                Q_ASSERT(task);
            }
        }
    }
}
```

This method is used to read in a task from XML data, as a child of the given item. The method works recursively to account for the task's children, and their children, and so on. Structurally, the code is the same as that used in the StandardTreeModel::load() method we saw earlier (148 ◄).

This method can be used to load in an entire file of XML task data by calling it with the root item, but here it is used to recreate a dragged item (and its children) as a child of the given item.

We have now completed our review of the implementations of the QAbstract-ItemModel methods that support drag and drop. In fact, the implementations also work the same way for list and table models, since Qt uses the same approach to drag and drop in all three cases, so adapting the code to work for custom list and table models should be straightforward.

Methods for Moving Items in a Tree

For editable tree models that have items all of the same kind and that can be arbitrarily nested, it makes sense to provide more ways of moving the items than just drag and drop. Being able to move items using the keyboard is particularly welcome to those who cannot or don't wish to use the mouse, and of course because all the movement methods discussed here are invoked via QActions, they can also be used by mouse users by clicking the corresponding menu items or toolbar buttons.

We have provided three groups of methods: methods for moving an item up and down among its siblings, methods for cutting an item and pasting it back somewhere else in the tree, and methods for promoting and demoting items, that is, for making an item a sibling of its parent or a child of one of its siblings. Naturally, like the drag and drop implementations, these methods apply not just to the selected item, but also to that item's children, and their children, recursively.

```
QModelIndex TreeModel::moveUp(const QModelIndex &index)
{
    if (!index.isValid() || index.row() <= 0)
        return index;
    TaskItem *item = itemForIndex(index);
    Q_ASSERT(item);
    TaskItem *parent = item->parent();
    Q_ASSERT(parent);
    return moveItem(parent, index.row(), index.row() - 1);
}
```

An item can be moved up providing it has at least one sibling above it, that is, its row must be greater than 0. If this is the case we call the moveItem() helper method, passing it the item's parent, the item's current (old) row, and the new row—which for moving up is always one less than the old row.

The moveDown() method (not shown) is very similar except that there must be at least one sibling below the item to be moved and the new row is set to be one more than the item's current row.

```
QModelIndex TreeModel::moveItem(TaskItem *parent, int oldRow,
                                int newRow)
{
    Q_ASSERT(0 <= oldRow && oldRow < parent->childCount() &&
             0 <= newRow && newRow < parent->childCount());
    parent->swapChildren(oldRow, newRow);
    QModelIndex oldIndex = createIndex(oldRow, 0,
                                       parent->childAt(oldRow));
    QModelIndex newIndex = createIndex(newRow, 0,
                                       parent->childAt(newRow));
    emit dataChanged(oldIndex, oldIndex);
    emit dataChanged(newIndex, newIndex);
    return newIndex;
}
```

This method is called by moveUp() and by moveDown() to perform the move. The TaskItem::swapChildren() method uses QList::swap() to swap the two items in the task item's list of children. After performing the move the moveItem() method calls dataChanged() to notify any views that two items in the model have changed, and we return the model index of the moved item in its new position.

As always when calling createIndex(), we pass the item's row and column—the latter always 0 for this particular model—and a pointer to the TaskItem that represents the item.

Figure 4.5 illustrates moving an item—in fact the figure can be taken as an illustration of moving item A down or of moving item B up, since the effects of either move are the same. The items shown shaded on the right-hand side are those that have been affected by the move: items A and B because they have moved, and their parent, item P, because its list of child items has changed.

This method, like most of the movement-related methods, returns a model index to its caller. In most cases, including here, the model index is for the moved item. The model index is returned in the expectation that the caller will scroll to and select the item. This is especially convenient for users in the case of moving items up or down since they can select an item and then repeatedly invoke the Up action (or press Ctrl+Up or ⌘+Up on Mac OS X) to move the item above each of the siblings above it in turn until it becomes its parent's first child. And correspondingly the user could invoke the Down action (or press

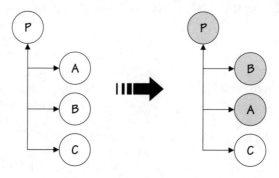

Figure 4.5 *Moving an item up or down by swapping it with its sibling*

Ctrl+Down or ⌘+Down) to move the item below each of the siblings below it until
it becomes its parent's last child.

```
QModelIndex TreeModel::cut(const QModelIndex &index)
{
    if (!index.isValid())
        return index;
    delete cutItem;
    cutItem = itemForIndex(index);
    Q_ASSERT(cutItem);
    TaskItem *parent = cutItem->parent();
    Q_ASSERT(parent);
    int row = parent->rowOfChild(cutItem);
    Q_ASSERT(row == index.row());
    beginRemoveRows(index.parent(), row, row);
    TaskItem *child = parent->takeChild(row);
    endRemoveRows();
    Q_ASSERT(child == cutItem);

    if (row > 0) {
        --row;
        return createIndex(row, 0, parent->childAt(row));
    }
    TaskItem *grandParent = parent->parent();
    Q_ASSERT(grandParent);
    return createIndex(grandParent->rowOfChild(parent), 0, parent);
}
```

This method follows a pattern that is common to most of the movement-related
methods: first we perform the action, then we create a model index to return to
the caller so that the view has an item to scroll to and select.

We begin by deleting the cutItem; this is harmless if the item is 0, and if it isn't then the item (and its children, recursively) is deleted since it cannot now be pasted anywhere. Next we get a pointer to the task item that is to be cut and store it in cutItem; we also get the item's parent and its row within its parent. Next we call beginRemoveRows() to notify the model/view architecture that an item is to be deleted, and then we remove the cut item from its parent's list of children. The cutItem is now parentless and it is our responsibility to delete it when appropriate. (In fact it is deleted in three methods: this one, clear(), and the TreeModel's destructor.) Once it is removed, we call endRemoveRows() to notify the model/view architecture that the removal is finished. (The Q_ASSERTs that compare the rows, and the child item with the cut item, are just sanity checks.)

When an item is cut from the tree, any associated views will automatically make the "nearest" item the current item. The views will choose the previous sibling if there is one, or failing that the next sibling if there is one, or failing that the parent. We prefer to always choose the previous sibling if there is one or failing that the parent, so we have made this method return the model index of the item we want to make current, expecting the caller to pass it to our custom setCurrentIndex() method. If we were happy with the default behavior we could make the method return void and simply finish it at the endRemove-Rows() call. We don't have this choice for the other movement-related methods though—they must always tell their associated views which item to select.

```cpp
QModelIndex TreeModel::paste(const QModelIndex &index)
{
    if (!index.isValid() || !cutItem)
        return index;
    TaskItem *sibling = itemForIndex(index);
    Q_ASSERT(sibling);
    TaskItem *parent = sibling->parent();
    Q_ASSERT(parent);
    int row = parent->rowOfChild(sibling) + 1;
    beginInsertRows(index.parent(), row, row);
    parent->insertChild(row, cutItem);
    TaskItem *child = cutItem;
    cutItem = 0;
    endInsertRows();
    return createIndex(row, 0, child);
}
```

This method is used to paste an item (and its children) back into the tree. We have chosen to always insert the pasted item as a new sibling of the selected item, and to occupy the row after its new sibling in their parent's list of children.

One consequence of this approach is that the user can never paste an item as a first child—to achieve that they must paste onto a first child (so that the pasted item becomes the second child) and then move the pasted item up. On the other hand we can paste an item as a last child simply by pasting onto a last child. Alternatively, if we had chosen to always insert the pasted item above the selected item then the user could paste an item as the first child (by pasting onto the first child), but not as a last child since pasting onto a last child would put the pasted item above the last child. Another alternative would be to pop up a menu—for example, with Paste Before Current Item and Paste After Current Item options.

We get the item—which will be the pasted item's sibling—that corresponds to the selected model index. We then retrieve the sibling's parent item and find out which row the sibling occupies in its parent's list of children. Then we call beginInsertRows() to notify the model/view architecture that a row is about to be inserted, and insert the cut item at the following row.

Once the paste is done we set cutItem to 0 since we must not paste an item that is already in the tree—we can only paste an item that has been cut out of the tree. Then we call endInsertRows() to notify the model/view architecture that the insertion is finished, and finally we return the model index of the newly pasted item so that the view can scroll to it and select it.

```cpp
QModelIndex TreeModel::promote(const QModelIndex &index)
{
    if (!index.isValid())
        return index;
    TaskItem *item = itemForIndex(index);
    Q_ASSERT(item);
    TaskItem *parent = item->parent();
    Q_ASSERT(parent);
    if (parent == rootItem)
        return index; // Already a top-level item

    int row = parent->rowOfChild(item);
    TaskItem *child = parent->takeChild(row);
    Q_ASSERT(child == item);
    TaskItem *grandParent = parent->parent();
    Q_ASSERT(grandParent);
    row = grandParent->rowOfChild(parent) + 1;
    grandParent->insertChild(row, child);
    QModelIndex newIndex = createIndex(row, 0, child);
    emit dataChanged(newIndex, newIndex);
    return newIndex;
}
```

Promoting an item means making it a child of its grandparent, occupying the row following its ex-parent. And, of course, all the promoted item's children and their children, recursively, come with it. Figure 4.6 illustrates the promotion of item B. The items shown shaded are the ones affected by the move: B's grandparent, GP, becomes its parent, and B's original parent's list of children no longer contains item B.

We begin by retrieving the task items for the model index of the item to be promoted and for its parent. If the item's parent is the root item it is already a top-level item and cannot be promoted further so we do nothing and simply return the item's model index. Otherwise, we find the item's row in its parent's list of children and remove it from its parent—at this point it is parentless and ownerless since the TaskItem::takeChild() method (158 ◀) removes the taken child from its parent's list of children and sets the item's parent to 0.

We do a sanity check Q_ASSERT to ensure that the child we have taken from its parent really is the item we are about to promote. Then we get the grandparent and find the row the parent occupies in the grandparent's list of children. Next, we insert the child in the row after its ex-parent; the TaskItem::insertChild() method (157 ◀) reparents the item it inserts, so afterwards, the item is safely back in the tree and has the correct parent.

At the end, we create a model index for the promoted item and emit data-Changed() to notify any associated views that the model has changed. Finally, we return the promoted item's model index to the caller.

```
QModelIndex TreeModel::demote(const QModelIndex &index)
{
    if (!index.isValid())
        return index;
    TaskItem *item = itemForIndex(index);
    Q_ASSERT(item);
    TaskItem *parent = item->parent();
    Q_ASSERT(parent);
    int row = parent->rowOfChild(item);
    if (row == 0)
        return index; // No preceding sibling to move this under
    TaskItem *child = parent->takeChild(row);
    Q_ASSERT(child == item);
    TaskItem *sibling = parent->childAt(row - 1);
    Q_ASSERT(sibling);
    sibling->addChild(child);
    QModelIndex newIndex = createIndex(sibling->childCount() - 1, 0,
                                        child);
    emit dataChanged(newIndex, newIndex);
    return newIndex;
}
```

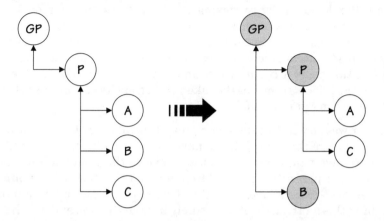

Figure 4.6 *Promoting an item by making it a child of its grandparent*

Demoting an item means moving the item such that it becomes a child of the sibling above it. And, of course, all the demoted item's children and their children, recursively, come with it. We could put the demoted item anywhere in its ex-sibling's (now its parent's) list of children, but we have chosen to always make the demoted item the last child of the sibling above it. Figure 4.7 illustrates the demotion of item B. The items shown shaded are the ones affected by the move: B's sibling above it, A, become's B's parent with B becoming A's last child and being removed from its original parent, P's, list of children.

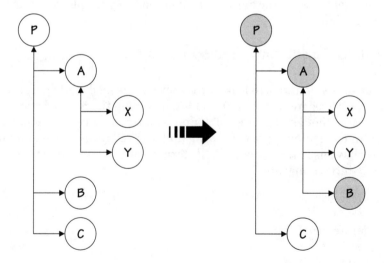

Figure 4.7 *Demoting an item by making it the last child of the sibling above it*

We begin the demotion by retrieving the task items for the model index of the item to be demoted and for its parent. If the item is its parent's first child then there is no sibling above it that we can move it to, so we do nothing and simply return the item's model index. Otherwise, we remove the item from its parent—at this point it is parentless and ownerless since the TaskItem::take-Child() method (158 ◀) removes the taken child from its parent's list of children and sets the item's parent to 0.

In a similar way to what we did when promoting an item, we do a sanity check Q_ASSERT to ensure that the child we have taken from its parent is indeed the item we are about to demote. Then we retrieve the item's sibling that preceded it in their parent's list of children and add the item as its sibling's last child. The TaskItem::addChild() method (157 ◀) reparents the item it adds, so after calling this method, the item is safely back in the tree and has the correct parent.

And at the end, just as we did for the promote() method, we create a model index for the demoted item and emit dataChanged() to notify any associated views that the model has changed. Finally, we return the demoted item's model index to the caller.

We have now covered all the methods that we added to extend the QAbstract-ItemModel's API to support moving items in the tree. Providing the item class uses a list of child items and has the methods used here (addChild(), insert-Child(), takeChild(), and so on—or equivalents), the implementations shown should be very easy to adapt for reuse in other custom tree models. This reusability is fortunate since as the clue of the littering of Q_ASSERTs might indicate, although most of the methods look deceptively simple, they can be quite tricky to get right.

Methods for Saving and Loading Tree Items

In this subsubsection we will look at the methods needed to support the saving and loading of tree items to and from files, including the methods for handling task paths. Although the timelog2 application has more functionality than timelog1 (in particular support for drag and drop, copy and paste, and moving items), we have used the same XML file format for both (143 ◀) so their files are completely interchangeable.

```
void TreeModel::clear()
{
    delete rootItem;
    rootItem = 0;
    delete cutItem;
    cutItem = 0;
    timedItem = 0;
```

```
        reset();
    }
```

This method is needed to support the fileNewAction. We must delete the root item and the cut item since we own these; but the timed item is an item in the tree so the root already owns it. (We won't say more about the timed item since its only importance is to do with timing a task—it has no significance in the context of the model/view programming we are considering here.) At the end we call QAbstractItemModel::reset() to notify any associated views that the model's data has changed radically so they must re-request any items that they want to show.

```
    void TreeModel::save(const QString &filename)
    {
        ...
        QXmlStreamWriter writer(&file);
        writer.setAutoFormatting(true);
        writer.writeStartDocument();
        writer.writeStartElement("TIMELOG");
        writer.writeAttribute("VERSION", "2.0");
        writeTaskAndChildren(&writer, rootItem);
        writer.writeEndElement(); // TIMELOG
        writer.writeEndDocument();
    }
```

This method starts out in the same way as the StandardTreeModel::save() method—so we have omitted that part of the code—using the existing filename or the one passed in as appropriate, and raising an exception if the file couldn't be opened (144 ◄). All the work is done by the writeTaskAndChildren() method that we saw earlier when we looked at implementing drag and drop and needed to serialize an item and its children in XML format (170 ◄).

```
    void TreeModel::load(const QString &filename)
    {
        ...
        clear();
        rootItem = new TaskItem;
        QXmlStreamReader reader(&file);
        readTasks(&reader, rootItem);
        if (reader.hasError())
            throw AQP::Error(reader.errorString());
        reset();
    }
```

This method starts in a similar way to the save() method regarding filename handling and raising an exception if the file couldn't be opened, so once again we have omitted the code. After clearing the existing tasks a new root item is created and the readTasks() method is used to populate the tree with the given root item and read its data from the given QXmlStreamReader. This is the same readTasks() method we used earlier to recreate dropped data under a particular parent item in the tree (173 ◄).

```
QStringList TreeModel::pathForIndex(const QModelIndex &index) const
{
    QStringList path;
    QModelIndex thisIndex = index;
    while (thisIndex.isValid()) {
        path.prepend(data(thisIndex).toString());
        thisIndex = thisIndex.parent();
    }
    return path;
}
```

This method provides a QStringList to represent a particular item in the tree and uses the same logic as the version we created for the StandardTreeModel.

It starts by adding the given item's text to the path QStringList and then prepends the item's parent's text to the list, and the parent's parent's text, and so on up to the top. Keep in mind that the parent model index of a top-level item's *model index* is *not* the root item (that's the parent of a top-level *item*), but rather an invalid model index.

The method is used by the main window's close event handler to save the currently selected item using QSettings when the application terminates.

```
QModelIndex TreeModel::indexForPath(const QStringList &path) const
{
    return indexForPath(QModelIndex(), path);
}


QModelIndex TreeModel::indexForPath(const QModelIndex &parent,
                                    const QStringList &path) const
{
    if (path.isEmpty())
        return QModelIndex();
    for (int row = 0; row < rowCount(parent); ++row) {
        QModelIndex thisIndex = index(row, 0, parent);
        if (data(thisIndex).toString() == path.at(0)) {
            if (path.count() == 1)
                return thisIndex;
            thisIndex = indexForPath(thisIndex, path.mid(1));
            if (thisIndex.isValid())
                return thisIndex;
        }
```

```
        }
        return QModelIndex();
    }
```

These methods do the opposite of pathForIndex()—they take a model index and a task path and return the corresponding model index. The public method takes a task path argument and calls the private method with an invalid model index (which in Qt's model/view architecture is used to signify the root) as the parent model index, and the task path it was given.

The private method iterates over the parent model index's children's model indexes looking for a child whose text is the same as the first text in the task path. If a match is found the method calls itself recursively with the child model index as the new parent and with a task path that doesn't include the first (already matched) string. Eventually either all the strings in the task path will be matched and the corresponding model index returned, or the matching will fail and an invalid model index will be returned.

When the Timelog application is started it uses QSettings to retrieve the path of the last file that was loaded and the task path of that file's selected item. If there was such a file this method is used to find the task path item's model index after the file has been loaded, so that the item can be scrolled to and selected to restore the tree to the same state as when the application was terminated.

In fact the state may not be completely restored since we only expand the tree enough to show the selected item, whereas the user may have had other parts of the tree expanded when they last terminated the application. It would be possible to restore all of the tree's state, but doing so might use a lot of storage in QSettings (e.g., in the Windows registry) if the user had lots of fully expanded top-level items with lots of children—so if this was required it would probably be better to record the state in the data itself (e.g., as an "expanded" or "visible" attribute), or use a separate file since, for example, the Windows registry has size limits.

We have now completed our review of tree models and seen how to create a custom QStandardItemModel to hold a tree of items. In addition we have seen how to create a custom QAbstractItemModel that provides the same QAbstractItemModel API as any other model, plus extensions to the API to support moving items in the tree and for saving and loading the tree to and from disk. In the next chapter we will turn our attention to custom delegates, and in the last of the four model/ view-related chapters we will look at custom views.

5

- Datatype-Specific Editors
- Datatype-Specific Delegates
- Model-Specific Delegates

Model/View Delegates

This chapter covers model/view delegates, and assumes a basic familiarity with Qt's model/view architecture, as described at the beginning of Chapter 3 (88 ◄).

All of Qt's standard view classes—QListView, QTableView, QColumnView, QTreeView, and QComboBox—provide a QStyledItemDelegate for the display and editing (in the case of editable models) of the data they access.*

In this chapter we will see how to set and use custom delegates that can be used to give us complete control over the appearance of items displayed in the view, or to allow us to provide our own editors for editable items, or both. Broadly speaking there are three approaches we can take, and this chapter covers all of them.

Qt's built-in delegates use particular widgets to edit particular datatypes. In this chapter's first section we will see how to change the widgets that Qt uses by default to our own choices of built-in or custom widgets. This is a very powerful approach—it affects all editable items of the relevant datatypes in all views—but for this reason it is also the least flexible approach, especially when compared to using custom delegates.

In the second section we will see how to create custom datatype-specific delegates that can be set for particular rows or columns. These delegates are very versatile and can be reused in model after model. Also, unlike simply changing the editor widget, creating a custom delegate allows us to control both the appearance and the editing of items. We will review two examples of this kind, the first being a simple read-only delegate that renders date/times in a custom way. The second is a more complex delegate for viewing and editing rich text items such as those that were used by the Timelog examples presented in the previous chapter.

---

*Qt also has a QItemDelegate class but this was superceded from Qt 4.4 by QStyledItemDelegate.

In some situations it is more convenient to create a model-specific delegate that handles all of the model's items than to use datatype-specific delegates for the model's rows or columns. In this chapter's last section we will look at how to implement model-specific delegates, taking as our example the delegate used by Chapter 3's Zipcodes examples.

Datatype-Specific Editors

If we want to provide a global editor based purely on an item's type, we can create a QItemEditorFactory and register a particular widget to use as the editor for a specified type (or for specified types). For example:

```
QItemEditorFactory *editorFactory = new QItemEditorFactory;
QItemEditorCreatorBase *numberEditorCreator = new
        QStandardItemEditorCreator<SpinBox>();
editorFactory->registerEditor(QVariant::Double,
                                numberEditorCreator);
editorFactory->registerEditor(QVariant::Int,
                                numberEditorCreator);
QItemEditorFactory::setDefaultFactory(editorFactory);
```

Here we have said that every editable item in every view that the application uses whose value is a double or an int will use the custom SpinBox as its editor.

```
explicit SpinBox(QWidget *parent=0)
    : QDoubleSpinBox(parent)
{
    setRange(-std::numeric_limits<double>::max(),
            std::numeric_limits<double>::max());
    setDecimals(3);
    setAlignment(Qt::AlignVCenter|Qt::AlignRight);
}
```

The only method we have reimplemented is the constructor. We have set the spinbox's range to go from the lowest negative to the highest positive double that the system supports, and to show three decimal digits and to align right.* The editor is shown in action in Figure 5.1. Having registered this spinbox we have ensured that all doubles and ints are presented and edited consistently for all the items in all the views used by the application.

Unfortunately, using a factory like this does not play nicely with QStandardItems for non-string data—at least not out of the box. This is because QStandard-

---

*We cannot use std::numeric_limits<T>::min(), since for floating-point types it returns the smallest value above 0 (some tiny fraction), rather than the most negative number (which is what is returned for integer types).

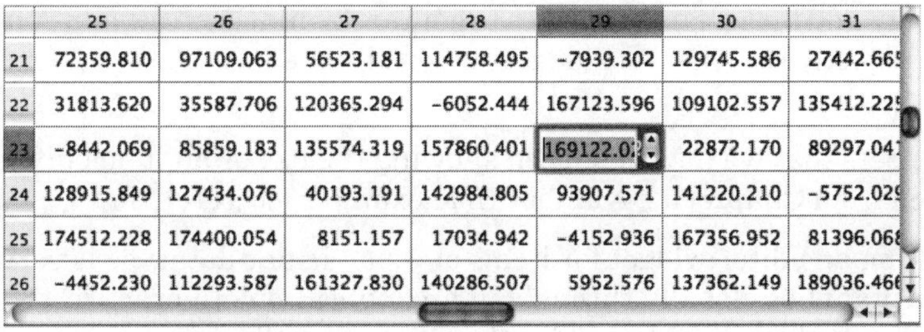

	25	26	27	28	29	30	31
21	72359.810	97109.063	56523.181	114758.495	−7939.302	129745.586	27442.665
22	31813.620	35587.706	120365.294	−6052.444	167123.596	109102.557	135412.225
23	−8442.069	85859.183	135574.319	157860.401	169122.0	22872.170	89297.041
24	128915.849	127434.076	40193.191	142984.805	93907.571	141220.210	−5752.029
25	174512.228	174400.054	8151.157	17034.942	−4152.936	167356.952	81396.068
26	−4452.230	112293.587	161327.830	140286.507	5952.576	137362.149	189036.466

Figure 5.1 *The factory registered SpinBox in action*

Items hold their data as QStrings, so when editing is initiated, a QString is presented for editing. But this does not cause our registered editor—SpinBox—to be used, since it is only registered for doubles and ints. The solution is quite easy though: we just ensure that we always store and retrieve our data from the QStandardItemModel using the Qt::EditRole, and we use a QStandardItem subclass to hold the data. Here's an example of such a subclass that holds double values:

```
class StandardItem : public QStandardItem
{
public:
    explicit StandardItem(const double value) : QStandardItem()
        { setData(value, Qt::EditRole); }

    QStandardItem *clone() const
        { return new StandardItem(data(Qt::EditRole).toDouble()); }

    QVariant data(int role=Qt::UserRole+1) const
    {
        if (role == Qt::DisplayRole)
            return QString("%1").arg(QStandardItem::data(Qt::EditRole)
                                     .toDouble(), 0, 'f', 3);
        if (role == Qt::TextAlignmentRole)
            return static_cast<int>(Qt::AlignVCenter|Qt::AlignRight);
        return QStandardItem::data(role);
    }
};
```

In the constructor we store the double using the Qt::EditRole. We also provide a clone() method to ensure that if the model duplicates an item it correctly creates a StandardItem instance rather than a plain QStandardItem.

The QStandardItem::data() method is *not* the same as QAbstractItemModel::data(); in particular it is a conventional C++ method that can make use of the base class version, so for unhandled cases it should always return the result of calling the base class—not an invalid QVariant. Here we only have to handle the display and text alignment roles to get the formatting we want—the double will be correctly returned (inside a QVariant) by the base class call for the Qt:: EditRole.

The snippets that we have just seen showing the use of an item editor factory are taken from Chapter 7's Number Grid example (numbergrid).

Registering an editor widget for items of a particular datatype is very powerful since it applies globally throughout an application. In practice, though, we rarely want to do this, and would rather customize the appearance and behavior of items on a model-by-model basis—something that is easily achieved using custom delegates as we will see in the next two sections.

Datatype-Specific Delegates

If we create a lot of custom models and usually create a custom delegate for each one, we may find that we end up duplicating a lot of code. For example, we may have several models, each with an associated custom delegate. The delegates will be different because the models have different datatypes in different columns, even though the code for handling each particular datatype—for example, using a customized date editor for date columns—is the same.

One way of avoiding the duplication and improving the reusability of our code —not just within an application, but across applications—is to create datatype-specific delegates that we set for particular rows or columns. For example, if we created a date-specific delegate, we could set it as the column delegate for every one of our models that has one or more date columns. This would eliminate a lot of duplicate code and make it trivial to use the delegate with new models that have one or more columns of dates. And we could also create other datatype-specific delegates, for example, for angles, colors, money, times, and so on, all of which would avoid code duplication and ensure consistency across our applications.

In this section we will look at two such delegates, both of which we will use for particular columns, although they could just as easily be used for particular rows. The first is a simple read-only delegate for showing date/times in a customized way, and the second is a delegate for presenting and editing "rich text"—text that uses a small subset of HTML markup for bold, italic, color, and so on—this was the delegate used by the Timelog applications we saw in the previous chapter.

A Read-Only Column or Row Delegate

Figure 5.2 shows the Folder View application (folderview) with its two QTree-Views. The right-hand QTreeView uses a custom DateTimeDelegate that shows

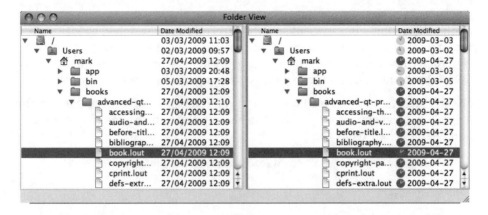

Figure 5.2 *The read-only DateTimeDelegate in action (right-hand view)*

the time data as a clock, and the date data as text using the ISO 8601 format. The model from which the data is taken is a `QFileSystemModel`, and to make the screenshots fit nicely on the page we have hidden a couple of columns.

The `DateTimeDelegate` shows the last modified time using an analog clock face, with a light background for AM times and a dark background for PM times—and with the background faded when the date is earlier than today.

Before we look at the delegate's code we will briefly review the code for creating the model, view, and delegate, to give us some context.

```
QFileSystemModel *model = new QFileSystemModel;
model->setRootPath(QDir::homePath());
QModelIndex index = model->index(QDir::homePath());
QTreeView *view = new QTreeView;
view->setItemDelegateForColumn(3, new DateTimeDelegate);
view->setModel(model);
view->setColumnHidden(1, true);
view->setColumnHidden(2, true);
view->scrollTo(index);
view->expand(index);
view->setCurrentIndex(index);
```

The static `QDir::homePath()` method returns the user's home directory. The `QDir` class has other similar methods, including `QDir::currentPath()`, `QDir::root-Path()`, and `QDir::tempPath()`, all of which return strings. It also has corresponding methods that return QDir objects (`QDir::home()`, and so on).

The `QFileSystemModel` is editable, so it is possible to use it as the basis for a file manager. Here we have simply used it to provide data to a `QTreeView` to which we have set a `DateTimeDelegate` for its fourth column—all the other columns will use the tree view's built-in `QStyledItemDelegate`. The call to `QFileSystemModel::`

setRootPath() does *not* set the currently selected item—the setCurrentIndex()
method does that—but instead sets the directory to be watched by a QFileSys-
temWatcher. If any changes occur to the watched directory's files or subdirectories, then these changes—such as a file being deleted or updated—are reflected
back into the model, and consequently show up in any associated views.

For the DateTimeDelegate we just need to reimplement the constructor and the
paint() method since we only want to change the appearance of the items it
handles, not their behavior.

```
class DateTimeDelegate : public QStyledItemDelegate
{
    Q_OBJECT

public:
    explicit DateTimeDelegate(QObject *parent=0)
        : QStyledItemDelegate(parent) {}

    void paint(QPainter *painter, const QStyleOptionViewItem &option,
               const QModelIndex &index) const;

private:
    ...
};
```

The constructor simply passes on the work to the base class. We will review
the paint() method and the private helper methods it uses to see how the item
is rendered.

```
void DateTimeDelegate::paint(QPainter *painter,
        const QStyleOptionViewItem &option,
        const QModelIndex &index) const
{
    const QFileSystemModel *model =
            qobject_cast<const QFileSystemModel*>(index.model());
    Q_ASSERT(model);
    const QDateTime &lastModified = model->lastModified(index);
    painter->save();
    painter->setRenderHints(QPainter::Antialiasing|
                            QPainter::TextAntialiasing);

    if (option.state & QStyle::State_Selected)
        painter->fillRect(option.rect, option.palette.highlight());
    const qreal diameter = qMin(option.rect.width(),
                                option.rect.height());
    const QRectF rect = clockRect(option.rect, diameter);
    drawClockFace(painter, rect, lastModified);
    drawClockHand(painter, rect.center(), diameter / 3.5,
                  ((lastModified.time().hour() +
```

```
                        (lastModified.time().minute() / 60.0))) * 30);
        drawClockHand(painter, rect.center(), diameter / 2.5,
                    lastModified.time().minute() * 6);
        drawDate(painter, option, diameter, lastModified);
        painter->restore();
    }
```

We begin by obtaining the last modified date/time for the item—that is, of the file, directory, or other filesystem object—whose details are to be painted. We then save the painter's state and switch on antialiasing.*

If the item is selected we paint the background using the appropriate background highlighting color taken from the palette. Then we compute the clock face's diameter which we need for various calculations further on, and also the rectangle to use for the clock's face.

With everything set up we draw the clock face, the minute hand, the hour hand, and then the date (as text), and finally we restore the painter to the state it had before we started painting, ready for it to be reused to paint the next item.

```
QRectF DateTimeDelegate::clockRect(const QRectF &rect,
                                    const qreal &diameter) const
{
    QRectF rectangle(rect);
    rectangle.setWidth(diameter);
    rectangle.setHeight(diameter);
    return rectangle.adjusted(1.5, 1.5, -1.5, -1.5);
}
```

This method returns a rectangle based on the given item's rectangle, with the same x- and y-coordinates, but reduced in size to be a square of the given diameter, and then slightly reduced again to allow some margin.

The QRect::adjusted() method (and the QRectF version) returns a new rectangle with the coordinates of its top-left corner and bottom-right corner adjusted by the given amounts. So in this case, the top-left has been moved right and down (since y-coordinates increase downward) by 1.5 pixels, and the bottom-right corner has been moved left and up by 1.5 pixels.

```
void DateTimeDelegate::drawClockFace(QPainter *painter,
        const QRectF &rect, const QDateTime &lastModified) const
{
    const int Light = 120;
    const int Dark = 220;
```

---

* At the time of this writing, Qt's QPainter documentation doesn't say which render hints—if any—are on by default, so we take a cautious approach and always specify the ones that we want.

```
    int shade = lastModified.date() == QDate::currentDate()
                ? Light : Dark;
    QColor background(shade, shade,
                lastModified.time().hour() < 12 ? 255 : 175);
    painter->setPen(background);
    painter->setBrush(background);
    painter->drawEllipse(rect);
    shade = shade == Light ? Dark : Light;
    painter->setPen(QColor(shade, shade,
                lastModified.time().hour() < 12 ? 175 : 255));
}
```

This method is used to draw the clock face—drawing an ellipse produces a circle if the rectangle is square as it is in this case. Most of the code is concerned with coloring using RGB (Red, Green, Blue) values which must be in the range 0–255, and which in this example depend on whether the time is AM or PM and whether the date is today or earlier. At the end we set the pen color to use for drawing the clock's hands since this depends on the colors used for the clock's face (to ensure a good contrast).

```
    void DateTimeDelegate::drawClockHand(QPainter *painter,
            const QPointF &center, const qreal &length,
            const qreal &degrees) const
{
    const qreal angle = AQP::radiansFromDegrees(
            (qRound(degrees) % 360) - 90);
    const qreal x = length * std::cos(angle);
    const qreal y = length * std::sin(angle);
    painter->drawLine(center, center + QPointF(x, y));
}
```

This method is called twice, once for the minute hand and once for the hour hand. The center point is the middle of the clock face, the length is a fraction of the diameter—shorter for the hour hand than for the minute hand—and the degrees is the angle proportional to the time the hand represents. We make sure that the angle is in range and subtract 90° from it to move the 0° position from the East used in geometry to the North used by analog clocks. We then compute the end point of the hand and draw a line from the center to the end point. (The qRound() function is described in Table 1.2; 46 ◄. The AQP:: radiansFromDegrees() function is in the book's aqp.{hpp,cpp} module.)

```
    void DateTimeDelegate::drawDate(QPainter *painter,
            const QStyleOptionViewItem &option, const qreal &diameter,
            const QDateTime &lastModified) const
{
    painter->setPen(option.state & QStyle::State_Selected
```

```
                          ? option.palette.highlightedText().color()
                          : option.palette.windowText().color());
        QString text = lastModified.date().toString(Qt::ISODate);
        painter->drawText(option.rect.adjusted(
                qRound(diameter * 1.2), 0, 0, 0), text,
                QTextOption(Qt::AlignVCenter|Qt::AlignLeft));
    }
```

We draw the date using the window text color—or the highlighted text color if the item is selected. And we use an item rectangle whose x-coordinate is shifted right to allow space for the clock face as well as some margin.

The QTextOption class is used to store the alignment, wrap mode, tab stops, and various formatting flags for an arbitrary piece of rich text. Its most common use when painting text is to provide the desired alignment, and for multi-line texts, the wrap mode.

Rendering date/times or other kinds of model data in a custom way can easily be done by creating a custom delegate and reimplementing its paint() method as we have done here. And, as with most painting in Qt, the work we must do is primarily concerned with using appropriate colors and with the mathematics of sizing and positioning. But when we have editable items, we may prefer to provide our own editing widgets, something that requires us to reimplement more methods, as we will see in the next subsection.

An Editable Column or Row Delegate

A custom delegate can be used for rendering items or for editing items, or for both. In the case of rendering we need to reimplement only the paint() method, but if we want to support editing we must implement some of the QStyledItemDelegate API shown in Table 5.1—at the least, the createEditor(), setEditorData(), and setModelData() methods.

The base class implementations of sizeHint() and updateEditorGeometry() are almost always sufficient, so we rarely need to reimplement them. Similarly, there is often no need to reimplement the paint() method, particularly if the data is simple plain text, dates, times, or numbers.

In the Timelog applications that we looked at in Chapter 4, we used "rich text"—a simple HTML subset that supports basic font effects such as bold, italic, and color. In addition, the rich text items (the tasks) were checkable. To provide support for this we created the RichTextDelegate which is shown displaying its context menu in Figure 5.3.

The RichTextDelegate provides both rendering and editing. The class implements most of the QStyledItemDelegate API—specifically, paint(), sizeHint(), createEditor(), setEditorData(), and setModelData(). In addition it has a private

Table 5.1 *The QStyledItemDelegate API*

Method	Description
createEditor(*parent*, *styleOption*, *index*)	Returns a widget suitable for editing the item at the given model *index*
paint(*painter*, *styleOption*, *index*)	Paints the item at the given model *index*—rarely needs to be reimplemented for plain text, dates, or numbers
setEditorData(*editor*, *index*)	Populates the *editor* with the data for the model's item at the given model *index*
setModelData(*editor*, *model*, *index*)	Sets the model's item at the given model *index* to have the data from the *editor*
sizeHint(*styleOption*, *index*)	Returns the size that the delegate needs to display or edit the item at the given model *index*
updateEditorGeometry(*editor*, *styleOption*, *index*)	Sets the *editor*'s size and position for in-place editing—rarely needs to be reimplemented

slot, closeAndCommitEditor(), and two items of private data—a QCheckBox pointer and a QLabel pointer. We will review all the methods, starting with the constructor.

```
RichTextDelegate::RichTextDelegate(QObject *parent)
    : QStyledItemDelegate(parent)
{
    checkbox = new QCheckBox;
    checkbox->setFixedSize(
            qRound(1.3 * checkbox->sizeHint().height()),
            checkbox->sizeHint().height());
    label = new QLabel;
    label->setTextFormat(Qt::RichText);
    label->setWordWrap(false);
}
```

There are three approaches we can use when it comes to rendering items in custom delegates. One is to paint everything ourselves—we did this in the DateTime delegate (188 ◄)—this has the disadvantage that we must account for platform differences ourselves. Another is to use Qt's QStyle class, for example, using QStyle::drawControl(), QStyle::drawComplexControl(), and so on—a powerful but rather low-level approach that requires a lot of care and quite a bit of code. Here we have taken the simpler and most high-level route: we will paint widgets, in this case the checkbox and label, leaving Qt to handle the platform differences and keeping our code as clean and simple as possible.

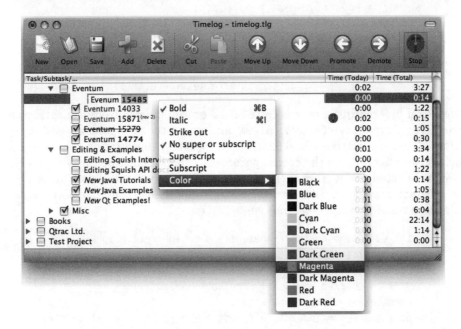

Figure 5.3 *The RichTextDelegate in action*

If we wanted to render only plain text we would only need a checkbox widget, since that shows a checkbox and an associated text. But since we want to show rich text we use the checkbox purely to show the checkbox (and give it no text to show), and use a label to show the rich text.

We make the checkbox occupy slightly more width than it actually needs, to provide some margin so that it doesn't abut the label. And we tell the label to treat any text it receives as rich text (HTML) and not to do any word wrapping.

```
~RichTextDelegate() { delete checkbox; delete label; }
```

When the delegate is destroyed we must delete the checkbox and the label— this is trivially achieved in the header file's inline destructor.

For ease of explanation we will review the paint() method in four short parts.

```
void RichTextDelegate::paint(QPainter *painter,
        const QStyleOptionViewItem &option,
        const QModelIndex &index) const
{
    bool selected = option.state & QStyle::State_Selected;
    QPalette palette(option.palette);
    palette.setColor(QPalette::Active, QPalette::Window,
                    selected ? option.palette.highlight().color()
```

```
                                : option.palette.base().color());
    palette.setColor(QPalette::Active, QPalette::WindowText,
                     selected
                     ? option.palette.highlightedText().color()
                     : option.palette.text().color());
```

We begin by creating a new palette based on the palette from the `option` parameter (of type `QStyleOptionViewItem`), and we set the new palette's `QPalette::Window` (background) color and `QPalette::WindowText` (foreground, i.e., text) color or to colors taken from the `option` parameter, and accounting for whether the item is selected or not. (We chose to use the `QPalette::base()` color rather than the `QPalette::window()` color for the background because this gave better cross-platform results on the machines we tested on.)

```
    int yOffset = checkbox->height() < option.rect.height()
            ? (option.rect.height() - checkbox->height()) / 2 : 0;
    QRect checkboxRect(option.rect.x(), option.rect.y() + yOffset,
            checkbox->width(), checkbox->height());
    checkbox->setPalette(palette);
    bool checked = index.model()->data(index, Qt::CheckStateRole)
                                        .toInt() == Qt::Checked;
    checkbox->setChecked(checked);
```

First, we set things up relating to the checkbox. We start by creating the check-boxRect rectangle which we will need later on when painting the checkbox. When we create the rectangle, we vertically center it in the available space if the `option` rectangle is taller than the checkbox. Then we set the checkbox's palette to the palette we created, and finally, we set the checkbox's check state to match that of the item.

```
    QRect labelRect(option.rect.x() + checkbox->width(),
            option.rect.y(), option.rect.width() - checkbox->width(),
            option.rect.height());
    label->setPalette(palette);
    label->setFixedSize(qMax(0, labelRect.width()),
                        labelRect.height());
    QString html = index.model()->data(index, Qt::DisplayRole)
                                        .toString();
    label->setText(html);
```

Although we set the checkbox to be a fixed size in the constructor and we never change this, for the label—even though we also set it to be a fixed size—we must set the size on a per-item basis. The labelRect rectangle that we create for the label is based on the rectangle given by the `option` parameter, but offset to the right (and reduced in width by the amount of the offset), to allow space for the checkbox. The reduction can lead to negative widths—for example, if the user has reduced the width of the containing window sufficiently—so we correct this using qMax(). Once the label has had its palette and size set, we retrieve the item's text (which is in HTML format) and set the label's text.

At this point, both the checkbox and label have the correct palette, size, and contents, and we have rectangles in which they can be drawn.

```
        QString checkboxKey = QString("CHECKBOX:%1.%2").arg(selected)
                                                       .arg(checked);
        paintWidget(painter, checkboxRect, checkboxKey, checkbox);
        QString labelKey = QString("LABEL:%1.%2.%3x%4").arg(selected)
                .arg(html).arg(labelRect.width()).arg(labelRect.height());
        paintWidget(painter, labelRect, labelKey, label);
    }
```

We have factored out the painting of the widgets into the private paintWidget() helper method. Also, we have used Qt's global QPixmapCache to save repainting identical pixmaps over and over again. The cache takes a string to identify each pixmap—we use both the selected state and the contents (the checkbox's checked state and the label's text) for this purpose. So, in the case of checkboxes, at most four pixmaps will be in the cache: (selected, unchecked), (selected, checked), (unselected, unchecked), and (unselected, checked). Once we have a key string for the cache we call paintWidget().

```
    void RichTextDelegate::paintWidget(QPainter *painter,
            const QRect &rect, const QString &cacheKey,
            QWidget *widget) const
    {
        QPixmap pixmap(widget->size());
        if (!QPixmapCache::find(cacheKey, &pixmap)) {
            widget->render(&pixmap);
            QPixmapCache::insert(cacheKey, pixmap);
        }
        painter->drawPixmap(rect, pixmap);
    }
```

We start by creating an empty pixmap of the correct size. The QPixmapCache:: find() method is used to retrieve a pixmap from the cache with the given key. The method returns true and populates the QPixmap it is passed by pointer—or by non-const reference (i.e., no &) for Qt 4.5 and earlier—if the key is found; otherwise it returns false. So, the first time we request a particular pixmap its key is not found and we render the given widget onto the empty pixmap and insert it into the cache. At the end we draw the pixmap in the given rectangle. (Another way to get a pixmap of a widget is to use QPixmap::grabWidget(), passing the widget as parameter.)

The main benefit of this approach is that it passes almost all the painting
and styling work on to Qt, and makes our code much simpler than it would
otherwise be—as well as more efficient thanks to the use of the pixmap cache.

```
QSize RichTextDelegate::sizeHint(const QStyleOptionViewItem &option,
                                 const QModelIndex &index) const
{
    QString html = index.model()->data(index, Qt::DisplayRole)
                                  .toString();
    document.setDefaultFont(option.font);
    document.setHtml(html);
    return QSize(document.idealWidth(), option.fontMetrics.height());
}
```

In most cases there is no need to reimplement the `QStyledItemDelegate::size-`
`Hint()` method, but here we have an unusual situation. Suppose, for example,
that we had the HTML text `The <b>bold</b> <font color='#0000ff'>blue</font>`
`bear`. This text contains 54 characters, but only 18 of them will be displayed.
The standard `sizeHint()` implementation would quite reasonably calculate the
necessary width based on the full 54 characters, so we must reimplement it to
produce a more accurate result.

The most obvious way of determining the width is to convert the text to plain
text and call `QFontMetrics::width()` on it. Unfortunately, such an approach
does not account for fine details such as characters that are super- or subscripts
(which almost always have a smaller font size), or for bold or italic characters
which are usually wider than normal characters, or for the use of a mixture of
different fonts. Fortunately, the precise calculations that are needed—and that
account for all the details we have mentioned and more—can already be done
by the `QTextDocument::idealWidth()` method that we use here.

On some platforms, creating and destroying a `QTextDocument` for every size hint
call is rather expensive, so in the class's private data we have a declaration of
`mutable QTextDocument document`; this means that we reuse the same `QTextDocu-`
ment each time.

```
QWidget *RichTextDelegate::createEditor(QWidget *parent,
        const QStyleOptionViewItem &option, const QModelIndex&) const
{
    RichTextLineEdit *editor = new RichTextLineEdit(parent);
    editor->viewport()->setFixedHeight(option.rect.height());
    connect(editor, SIGNAL(returnPressed()),
            this, SLOT(closeAndCommitEditor()));
    return editor;
}
```

This method is used to create a suitable editor for the item at the given model index. Since this delegate is being used as a column delegate for a column that holds rich text we don't need to know which particular item the editor is needed for. (Later on we will see a reimplementation of this method where the type of editor returned depends on an aspect of the item—for example, what its column is; ➤ 201.)

We have created a RichTextLineEdit widget (which is covered in Chapter 9; ➤ 342) to edit the HTML data the delegate is expecting to deal with. In this case it is *essential* that we set the editor's viewport's height to a fixed size—specifically to the option parameter's rectangle's height—to prevent the RichTextLineEdit from bobbing up and down as text is entered. (This arises because although the RichTextLineEdit is designed for editing a single line of text, it is actually a subclass of QTextEdit—which is designed to edit multiple lines.)

If the user presses Return (or Enter), we take this to be a confirmation of their edit, so we connect the RichTextLineEdit's returnPressed() signal (modeled on the QLineEdit's signal of the same name) to a private custom closeAndCommit-Editor() slot that we'll look at in a moment.

```
void RichTextDelegate::setEditorData(QWidget *editor,
        const QModelIndex &index) const
{
    QString html = index.model()->data(index, Qt::DisplayRole)
                                    .toString();
    RichTextLineEdit *lineEdit = qobject_cast<RichTextLineEdit*>(
                                                editor);
    Q_ASSERT(lineEdit);
    lineEdit->setHtml(html);
}
```

Once the editor has been created the delegate calls setEditorData() to initialize it with data from the model. Here, we retrieve the text (which is in HTML format), get a pointer to the RichTextLineEdit that was created by createEditor(), and set the editor's text to the item's text.

```
void RichTextDelegate::closeAndCommitEditor()
{
    RichTextLineEdit *lineEdit = qobject_cast<RichTextLineEdit*>(
                                                sender());
    Q_ASSERT(lineEdit);
    emit commitData(lineEdit);
    emit closeEditor(lineEdit);
}
```

Implementing a slot like this is often useful for editors that have a signal that indicates that editing has been successfully completed—such as QLineEdit's returnPressed() signal.

We use qobject_cast<>() in conjunction with the QObject::sender() method to get a pointer to the RichTextLineEdit and then we emit two signals, one to tell the delegate to commit the editor's data—that is, to copy the editor's data to the model—and another to tell the delegate to close the editor since it is no longer needed.

```
void RichTextDelegate::setModelData(QWidget *editor,
        QAbstractItemModel *model, const QModelIndex &index) const
{
    RichTextLineEdit *lineEdit = qobject_cast<RichTextLineEdit*>(
                                            editor);
    Q_ASSERT(lineEdit);
    model->setData(index, lineEdit->toSimpleHtml());
}
```

If the user confirms their edit—by clicking outside the editor, by tabbing to another item, or by pressing Return or Enter—this method is called. (The user can cancel an edit by pressing Esc.) Here, we retrieve a pointer to the RichTextLine-Edit and set the model's text to the editor's HTML. As we will see in Chapter 9 (➤ 342), the toSimpleHtml() method produces simpler and more compact HTML than, say, QTextEdit::toHtml(), with the limitation of being able to handle only a very limited HTML subset.

In the setEditorData(), closeAndCommitEditor(), and setModelData() methods we used a Q_ASSERT() to check that the qobject_cast<>()s succeeded. We tend to use assertions when the application's logic dictates that something *must* be true at a certain point (i.e., that if it isn't true we have a bug), and use conditionals (i.e., if statements) otherwise. (We will see many examples of both approaches throughout the book.)

This completes the implementation of the RichTextDelegate. Apart from the paint() method, all of the method implementations are straightforward. This is a direct consequence of the fact that this delegate is to be used as a datatype-specific—in this case rich text—column (or row) delegate, which means that it never needs to check the row or column of the item it is given to determine the datatype it is to handle, and always handles every item it is given in the same way.

Model-Specific Delegates

If we don't create lots of models it may be more convenient to create custom model-specific delegates as the need arises, rather than create a set of more generic column or row datatype-specific delegates. In this section we will look at a typical example of a model-specific delegate—it is the one used by the Zipcodes applications that we saw in Chapter 3 (90 ◀), and it is shown in action editing a state in Figure 3.3 (90 ◀).

We have called the custom delegate ItemDelegate, and made it a QStyledItem-Delegate subclass. The constructor—not shown—passes its parent argument to the base class and has an empty body. Out of the QStyledItemDelegate API (194 ◀) we have reimplemented the paint() method (purely to paint zipcodes—for the others we use the base class version), and the three methods for editing data, createEditor(), setEditorData(), and setModelData(). There was no need to reimplement any of the other methods, which is quite commonly the case. As usual, we will review each of the methods in turn.

```
    void ItemDelegate::paint(QPainter *painter,
            const QStyleOptionViewItem &option,
            const QModelIndex &index) const
{
    if (index.column() == Zipcode) {
        QStyleOptionViewItemV4 opt(option);
        initStyleOption(&opt, index);
        QString text = QString("%1").arg(opt.text.toInt(),
                                         5, 10, QChar('0'));
        painter->save();
        painter->setRenderHints(QPainter::Antialiasing|
                                QPainter::TextAntialiasing);
        if (opt.state & QStyle::State_Selected) {
            painter->fillRect(opt.rect, opt.palette.highlight());
            painter->setPen(opt.palette.highlightedText().color());
        }
        else
            painter->setPen(opt.palette.windowText().color());
        painter->drawText(opt.rect.adjusted(0, 0, -3, 0), text,
                QTextOption(Qt::AlignVCenter|Qt::AlignRight));
        painter->restore();
    }
    else
        QStyledItemDelegate::paint(painter, option, index);
}
```

We have chosen to paint zipcodes ourselves, but left the base class to paint all the other data. Notice that in this method, and the others that follow, we use `index.column()` to determine the column (and therefore the datatype) of the data we are handling—something that wasn't necessary for the column and row delegates we saw in the previous section, since they are set to apply to specific columns or rows in the models they are associated with.

The `QStyleOptionViewItem` class introduced in Qt 4.0 has been supplemented in subsequent Qt 4.*x* versions by `QStyleOptionViewItemV2`, `QStyleOptionViewItemV3`, and `QStyleOptionViewItemV4`, each of which has added new public members. In general, it is fine to use the `QStyleOptionViewItem` that is passed in as is, but in some situations we prefer to use a later version so that we can take advantage of the convenience of the extra members.

The correct way to get a later `QStyleOptionViewItem` version is to use the pattern shown here: create a `QStyleOptionViewItemV4` (or whatever version we need) with the one passed in as its argument, and then call `QStyledItemDelegate::initStyleOption()`, passing it the new style option and the model index of the item we are dealing with.

By getting a `QStyleOptionViewItemV4` we are able to access its `text` member (which contains the text of the item with the given model index), rather than having to use `index.model()->data(index).toString()` (although in this example we would have used `toInt()`).

Having obtained the zipcode, we convert it to an integer and then create a string to represent it that has the format we want—in this case, exactly five digits, padded with leading zeros if necessary.

For the painting, we begin by saving the painter's state. This is always necessary in delegates if we change the painter's state, since for the sake of efficiency, the same painter is reused for all of the view's items. We have switched on antialiasing, since as noted in a footnote earlier, we cannot be sure what the defaults are, so take the cautious approach of always specifying the render hints we want. We paint the background in the palette's highlight color if the item is selected, and set the pen (foreground) color appropriately. We then draw the text in the given rectangle, right-aligned and with a 3 pixel right margin (achieved by shrinking the rectangle slightly), so that the text does not abut the table cell's edge and so doesn't collide with the cell's outline. And at the end we restore the painter's previous state so that it is ready to paint the next item.

```
QWidget *ItemDelegate::createEditor(QWidget *parent,
        const QStyleOptionViewItem &option,
        const QModelIndex &index) const
{
    static QStringList usStates;
    if (usStates.isEmpty())
        usStates << "(Unknown)" << "Alabama" << "Alaska"
```

```
                              ...
                    << "West Virginia" << "Wisconsin" << "Wyoming";

    if (index.column() == Zipcode)
        return new ZipcodeSpinBox(parent);
    if (index.column() == State) {
        QComboBox *editor = new QComboBox(parent);
        editor->addItems(usStates);
        return editor;
    }
    return QStyledItemDelegate::createEditor(parent, option, index);
}
```

We use standard Qt widgets for editing most of the data, but use a tiny custom spinbox class for editing zipcodes. The createEditor() method must determine which editor is required (in this model, it depends on the column), and then create, set up, and return the editor, ready for it to be populated with the item being edited's data, and shown to the user. Note that it is essential that if we create an editor ourselves we give it the parent that was passed in—this ensures that Qt takes ownership of the editor, and deletes it at the right time.

For the state column we use a combobox and populate it with "(Unknown)" and with all the U.S. states. We store the states in a static QStringList so that the data is created only once.

In the case of the post office and county columns (which use plain text), we pass the work on to the base class which will return a QLineEdit—unless we have set a different editor using a QItemEditorFactory as we discussed earlier (186 ◀).

```
void ItemDelegate::setEditorData(QWidget *editor,
        const QModelIndex &index) const
{
    if (index.column() == Zipcode) {
        int value = index.model()->data(index).toInt();
        ZipcodeSpinBox *spinBox =
                qobject_cast<ZipcodeSpinBox*>(editor);
        Q_ASSERT(spinBox);
        spinBox->setValue(value);
    }
    else if (index.column() == State) {
        QString state = index.model()->data(index).toString();
        QComboBox *comboBox = qobject_cast<QComboBox*>(editor);
        Q_ASSERT(comboBox);
        comboBox->setCurrentIndex(comboBox->findText(state));
    }
    else
        QStyledItemDelegate::setEditorData(editor, index);
}
```

Once the editor has been created, Qt's model/view architecture calls setEditor-
Data() to give us the opportunity to populate the editor before it is shown to
the user. We must always handle the widgets we have created ourselves—and
pass on the work to the base class for those widgets the base class is responsible for.

The logic used here is almost always the same: retrieve the item for the given
model index, cast the QWidget pointer to be an editor widget of the correct type,
and populate the editor. In the case of the combobox, we take a slightly different approach since it already contains all the valid data, so we just have to
make its current text match the text for the corresponding item in the model.

```
void ItemDelegate::setModelData(QWidget *editor,
        QAbstractItemModel *model, const QModelIndex &index) const
{
    if (index.column() == Zipcode) {
        ZipcodeSpinBox *spinBox =
                qobject_cast<ZipcodeSpinBox*>(editor);
        Q_ASSERT(spinBox);
        spinBox->interpretText();
        model->setData(index, spinBox->value());
    }
    else if (index.column() == State) {
        QComboBox *comboBox = qobject_cast<QComboBox*>(editor);
        Q_ASSERT(comboBox);
        model->setData(index, comboBox->currentText());
    }
    else
        QStyledItemDelegate::setModelData(editor, model, index);
}
```

If the user confirms their edit, for the editor widgets we are responsible for, we
must retrieve the editor's value and set it to be the value for the item with the
given model index. For other widgets, we pass on the work to the base class.

For the spinbox, we take an ultra-cautious approach and call interpretText()
to make sure that if the user changed the value by entering or deleting digits
rather than by using the spin buttons, the value held by the spinbox accurately
reflects this. For the combobox, we take a more conventional approach and just
retrieve the current value.

For the sake of completeness, here is the complete ZipcodeSpinBox class:

```
class ZipcodeSpinBox : public QSpinBox
{
    Q_OBJECT

public:
```

```
        explicit ZipcodeSpinBox(QWidget *parent)
            : QSpinBox(parent)
        {
            setRange(MinZipcode, MaxZipcode);
            setAlignment(Qt::AlignVCenter|Qt::AlignRight);
        }
    protected:
        QString textFromValue(int value) const
            { return QString("%1").arg(value, 5, 10, QChar('0')); }
    };
```

If we only needed to set the spinbox's range and alignment, we could have used a standard QSpinBox and set them in the createEditor() method. We chose to set them in the constructor since we had to subclass QSpinBox anyway, so that we could override the textFromValue() method. We did this so that the spinbox's textual representation of the zipcode value is a five-digit number, padded with leading zeros if necessary—the same format used when painting zipcodes.

We have now completed our review of a typical model-specific custom delegate. Such delegates are not as versatile as generic datatype-specific row or column delegates which can be used for any arbitrary model, but they do keep all of the delegate code in one place and give us complete and direct control over the appearance and editing of items in our model. Also, as we saw here, we can often pass some of the work on to the base class.

Using custom delegates is the most common and convenient way to control the presentation and editing of a model's items. However, if we want to present items in a way that is very different from any of Qt's built-in views, or if we want to customize the appearance of multiple items in relation to each other (e.g., by presenting two or more items combined together in some way), then we will need to create a custom view. Creating custom views is the subject of the next chapter.

6

- QAbstractItemView Subclasses
- Model-Specific Visualizing Views

Model/View Views

This chapter covers model/view views, and is the last chapter covering Qt's model/view architecture. Just like the previous two chapters, this chapter assumes a basic familiarity with the model/view architecture, as described at the beginning of Chapter 3 (88 ◄).

Qt's standard model views, QListView, QTableView, QColumnView, and QTreeView, are sufficient for most purposes, most of the time. And like other Qt classes, they can be subclassed—or we can use custom delegates—to affect how they display the model's items. However, there are two situations where we need to create a custom view. One is where we want to present the data in a radically different way from how Qt's standard views present data, and the other is where we want to visualize two or more data items combined in some way.

Broadly speaking there are two approaches we can take to the creation of custom views. One approach is used when we want to create a view *component*—that is, a view that is potentially reusable with a number of different models and that must fit in with Qt's model/view architecture. In such cases we would normally subclass QAbstractItemView, and provide the standard view API so that any model could make use of our view. The other approach is useful when we want to visualize the data in a particular model in such a unique way that the visualization has little or no potential for reuse. In these cases we can simply create a custom model viewer that has exactly—and only—the functionality required. This usually involves subclassing QWidget and providing our own API, but including a setModel() method.

In this chapter we will look at two examples of custom views. The first is a generic QAbstractItemView subclass that provides the same API as Qt's built-in views, and that can be used with any model, although it is designed in particular for the presentation and editing of list models. The second is a visualizer view that is specific to a particular model and that provides its own API.

207

QAbstractItemView Subclasses

In this section we will show how to create a QAbstractItemView subclass that can be used as a drop-in replacement for Qt's standard views. In practice, of course, just as there are list, table, and tree models, there are corresponding views, and so here we will develop a custom list view, although the principles are the same for all QAbstractItemView subclasses.

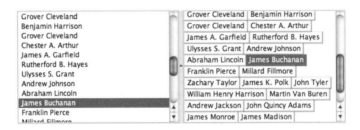

Figure 6.1 *A QListView and a TiledListView*

Figure 6.1 shows the central area of the Tiled List View application (tiled-listview). The area has two views that are using the same model: on the left a standard QListView, and on the right a TiledListView. Notice that although the widgets are the same size and use the same font, the TiledListView shows much more data. Also, as the figure illustrates, the TiledListView does not use multiple columns; rather, it shows as many items as it can fit in each row—for example, if it were resized to be a bit wider, it would fit four or more items on some rows.

One usability difference that makes keyboard navigation faster and easier—and more logical—in the TiledListView is that using the arrow keys does not simply go forward or backward in the list of items. When the user navigates through the items using the up (or down) arrow keys, the selected item is changed to the item visually above (or below) the current item. Similarly, when the user navigates using the left (or right) arrow keys, the selected item is changed to the item to the left (or right) as expected, unless the current item is at the left (or right) edge. For the edge cases, the selected item is changed to the item that is logically before (or after) the current item.

The QAbstractItemView API is large, and at the time of this writing, the Qt documentation does not explicitly specify which parts of the API must be reimplemented by subclasses and which base class implementations are sufficient. However, some of the methods are pure virtual and so must be reimplemented. Also, Qt comes with the examples/itemviews/chart example which serves as a useful guide for custom view implementations.

The API we have implemented for the TiledListView, and the one that we consider to be the minimum necessary for a custom QAbstractItemView subclass, is shown in Table 6.1. Qt's chart example reimplements all the methods listed in the table, and also the mouseReleaseEvent() and mouseMoveEvent() event handlers (to provide rubber band support—something not needed for the TiledListView). The chart example also implements the edit() method to initiate editing—again, something we don't need to do for the TiledListView even though it is editable, because the inherited base class's behavior is sufficient.

Before we look at the TiledListView class, here is how an instance is created and initialized.

```
TiledListView *tiledListView = new TiledListView;
tiledListView->setModel(model);
```

As these two lines make clear, the TiledListView is used in exactly the same way as any other view class.

Since the API that must be implemented is shown in Table 6.1, we won't show the class's definition in the header file, apart from the private data, all of which is specific to the TiledListView.

```
private:
    mutable int idealWidth;
    mutable int idealHeight;
    mutable QHash<int, QRectF> rectForRow;
    mutable bool hashIsDirty;
```

The idealWidth and idealHeight are the width and height needed to show all the items without the need for scrollbars. The rectForRow hash returns a QRectF of the correct position and size for the given row. (Note that since the TiledListView is designed for showing lists, a row corresponds to an item.) All these variables are concerned with behind-the-scenes bookkeeping, and since they are used in const methods we have been forced to make them mutable.

Rather than updating the rectForRow hash whenever a change takes place, we do lazy updates—that is, we simply set hashIsDirty to true when changes occur. Then, whenever we actually need to access the rectForRow hash, we recalculate it only if it is dirty.

We are now almost ready to review the TiledListView implementation, and will do so, starting with the constructor, and including the private supporting methods as necessary. But first we must mention an important conceptual point about QAbstractItemView subclasses.

The QAbstractItemView base class provides a scroll area for the data it displays. The only part of the widget that is a QAbstractItemView subclass that is visible is its viewport, that is, the part that is shown by the scroll area. This visible area is accessible using the viewport() method. It doesn't really matter what size the widget actually is; all that matters is what size the widget would need to be to show all of the model's data (even if that is far larger than the screen). We will

Table 6.1 *The QAbstractItemView API*

Method	Description
dataChanged(*topLeft*, *bottomRight*)	This slot is called when the items with model indexes in the rectangle from *topLeft* to *bottomRight* change
horizontalOffset()°	Returns the view's horizontal offset
indexAt(*point*)°	Returns the model index of the item at position *point* in the view's viewport
isIndexHidden(*index*)°	Returns true if the item at *index* is a hidden item (and therefore should not be shown)
mousePressEvent(*event*)	Typically used to set the current model index to the index of the clicked item
moveCursor(*how*, *modifiers*)°	Returns the model index of the item after navigating *how* (e.g., up, down, left, or right), and accounting for the keyboard *modifiers*
paintEvent(*event*)	Paints the view's contents on the viewport
resizeEvent(*event*)	Typically used to update the scrollbars
rowsAboutToBeRemoved(*parent*, *start*, *end*)	This slot is called when rows from *start* to *end* under *parent* are about to be removed
rowsInserted(*parent*, *start*, *end*)	This slot is called when rows from *start* to *end* are inserted under the *parent* model index
scrollContentsBy(*dx*, *dy*)	Scrolls the view's viewport by *dx* and *dy* pixels
scrollTo(*index*, *hint*)°	Scrolls the view to ensure that the item at the given model *index* is visible, and respecting the scroll *hint* as it scrolls
setModel(*model*)	Makes the view use the given *model*
setSelection(*rect*, *flags*)°	Applies the selection *flags* to all of the items in or touching the rectangle *rect*
updateGeometries()	Typically used to update the geometries of the view's child widgets, e.g., the scrollbars
verticalOffset()	Returns the view's vertical offset
visualRect(*index*)°	Returns the rectangle occupied by the item at the given model *index*
visualRegionForSelection(*selection*)°	Returns the viewport region for the items in the *selection*

°This method is pure virtual, so it *must* be reimplemented in subclasses.

see how this affects our code when we look at the `calculateRectsIfNecessary()` and `updateGeometries()` methods.

```
TiledListView::TiledListView(QWidget *parent)
    : QAbstractItemView(parent), idealWidth(0), idealHeight(0),
      hashIsDirty(false)
{
    setFocusPolicy(Qt::WheelFocus);
    setFont(QApplication::font("QListView"));
    horizontalScrollBar()->setRange(0, 0);
    verticalScrollBar()->setRange(0, 0);
}
```

The constructor calls the base class and initializes the private data. Initially the view's "ideal" size is 0×0 since it has no data to display.

Unusually, we call `setFont()` to set the widget's font rather than do what we normally do in custom widgets and just use the inherited font. The font returned by the `QApplication::font()` method, when given a class name, is the platform-specific font that is used for that class. This makes the `TiledListView` use the correct font even on those platforms (such as Mac OS X) that use a slightly different-sized font from the default `QWidget` font for `QListViews`.*

Since there is no data we set the scrollbars' ranges to (0, 0); this ensures that the scrollbars are hidden until they are needed, while leaving the responsibility for hiding and showing them to the base class.

```
void TiledListView::setModel(QAbstractItemModel *model)
{
    QAbstractItemView::setModel(model);
    hashIsDirty = true;
}
```

When a model is set we first call the base class implementation, and then set the private `hashIsDirty` flag to `true` to ensure that when the `calculateRectsIfNecessary()` method is called, it will update the `rectForRow` hash.

The `indexAt()`, `setSelection()`, and `viewportRectForRow()` methods all need to know the size and position of the items in the model. This is also true indirectly of the `mousePressEvent()`, `moveCursor()`, `paintEvent()`, and `visualRect()` methods, since all of them call the methods that need the sizes and positions. Rather than compute the rectangles dynamically every time they are needed, we have chosen to trade some memory for the sake of speed by caching them in the `rectForRow` hash. And rather than keeping the hash up to date by calling `calculateRectsIfNecessary()` whenever a change occurs, we simply keep track of whether

---

*For more about how Qt's font and palette propagation works, see `labs.qt.nokia.com/blogs/2008/11/16`.

the hash is dirty, and only recalculate the rectangles when we actually need to
access the hash.

```
const int ExtraHeight = 3;

void TiledListView::calculateRectsIfNecessary() const
{
    if (!hashIsDirty)
        return;
    const int ExtraWidth = 10;
    QFontMetrics fm(font());
    const int RowHeight = fm.height() + ExtraHeight;
    const int MaxWidth = viewport()->width();
    int minimumWidth = 0;
    int x = 0;
    int y = 0;
    for (int row = 0; row < model()->rowCount(rootIndex()); ++row) {
        QModelIndex index = model()->index(row, 0, rootIndex());
        QString text = model()->data(index).toString();
        int textWidth = fm.width(text);
        if (!(x == 0 || x + textWidth + ExtraWidth < MaxWidth)) {
            y += RowHeight;
            x = 0;
        }
        else if (x != 0)
            x += ExtraWidth;
        rectForRow[row] = QRectF(x, y, textWidth + ExtraWidth,
                                 RowHeight);
        if (textWidth > minimumWidth)
            minimumWidth = textWidth;
        x += textWidth;
    }
    idealWidth = minimumWidth + ExtraWidth;
    idealHeight = y + RowHeight;
    hashIsDirty = false;
    viewport()->update();
}
```

This method is the heart of the TiledListView, at least as far as its appearance
is concerned, since—as we will see shortly—all the painting is done using the
rectangles created in this method.

We begin by seeing if the rectangles need to be recalculated at all. If they do
we begin by calculating the height needed to display a row, and the maximum
width that is available to the viewport, that is, the available *visible* width.

In the method's main loop we iterate over every row (i.e., every item) in the model, and retrieve the item's text. We then compute the width needed by the item, and compute the x- and y-coordinates where the item should be displayed —these depend on whether the item can fit on the same *line* (i.e., the same visual row) as the previous item, or if it must start a new line. Once we know the item's size and position, we create a rectangle based on that information and add it to the rectForRow hash, with the item's row as the key.

Notice that during the calculations in the loop, we use the actual visible width, but assume that the available height is whatever is needed to show all the items given this width. Also, to retrieve the model index we want, we pass a parent index of QAbstractItemView::rootIndex() rather than an invalid model index (QModelIndex()). Both work equally well for list models, but it is better style to use the more generic rootIndex() in QAbstractItemView subclasses.

At the end we recompute the ideal width (the width of the widest item plus some margin), and the ideal height (the height necessary to show all the items at the viewport's current width, no matter what the viewport's actual height is) —at this point the y variable holds the total height of all the rows. The ideal width may be greater than the available width, for example, if the viewport is narrower than the width needed to display the longest item—in which case the horizontal scrollbar will automatically be shown. Once the computations are complete, we call update() on the *viewport* (since all painting is done on the viewport, not on the QAbstractItemView custom widget itself), so that the data will be repainted.

At no point do we refer to or care about the actual size of the QAbstractItemView custom widget itself—all the calculations are done in terms of the viewport and of the ideal width and height.

```
QRect TiledListView::visualRect(const QModelIndex &index) const
{
    QRect rect;
    if (index.isValid())
        rect = viewportRectForRow(index.row()).toRect();
    return rect;
}
```

This pure virtual method must return the rectangle occupied by the item with the given model index. Fortunately, its implementation is very easy because we pass the work on to our private viewportRectForRow() method that makes use of the rectForRow hash.

```
QRectF TiledListView::viewportRectForRow(int row) const
{
    calculateRectsIfNecessary();
    QRectF rect = rectForRow.value(row).toRect();
```

```
    if (!rect.isValid())
        return rect;
    return QRectF(rect.x() - horizontalScrollBar()->value(),
                  rect.y() - verticalScrollBar()->value(),
                  rect.width(), rect.height());
}
```

This method is used by the visualRect() method and by the moveCursor() and paintEvent() methods. It returns a QRectF for maximum accuracy (e.g., for the paintEvent() method); other callers convert the returned value to a plain integer-based QRect using the QRectF::toRect() method.

The calculateRectsIfNecessary() method *must* be called by methods that access the rectForRow hash, before the access takes place. If the rectForRow hash is up to date, the calculateRectsIfNecessary() method will do nothing; otherwise it will recompute the rectangles in the hash ready for use.

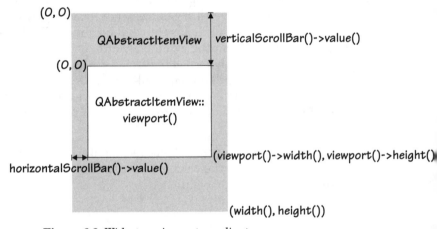

Figure 6.2 *Widget vs. viewport coordinates*

The rectangles in the rectForRow hash have the x- and y-coordinates of their rows (items) based on the ideal width (usually the visible width) and the ideal height (the height needed to display all the items at the current width). This means that the rectangles are effectively using widget coordinates based on the ideal size of the widget (the *actual* size of the widget is irrelevant). The viewportRectForRow() method must return a rectangle that is in viewport coordinates, so we adjust the coordinates to account for any scrolling. Figure 6.2 illustrates the difference between widget and viewport coordinates.

```
    bool isIndexHidden(const QModelIndex&) const { return false; }
```

We must reimplement this pure virtual method, and have done so in the header since it is so trivial. This method is designed for data that can have hidden items—for example, a table with hidden rows or columns. For this view, no items are hidden because we don't offer support for hiding them, so we always return false.

```
void TiledListView::scrollTo(const QModelIndex &index,
                             QAbstractItemView::ScrollHint)
{
    QRect viewRect = viewport()->rect();
    QRect itemRect = visualRect(index);

    if (itemRect.left() < viewRect.left())
        horizontalScrollBar()->setValue(horizontalScrollBar()->value()
                + itemRect.left() - viewRect.left());
    else if (itemRect.right() > viewRect.right())
        horizontalScrollBar()->setValue(horizontalScrollBar()->value()
                + qMin(itemRect.right() - viewRect.right(),
                       itemRect.left() - viewRect.left()));
    if (itemRect.top() < viewRect.top())
        verticalScrollBar()->setValue(verticalScrollBar()->value() +
                itemRect.top() - viewRect.top());
    else if (itemRect.bottom() > viewRect.bottom())
        verticalScrollBar()->setValue(verticalScrollBar()->value() +
                qMin(itemRect.bottom() - viewRect.bottom(),
                     itemRect.top() - viewRect.top()));
    viewport()->update();
}
```

This is another pure virtual method that we are obliged to implement. Fortunately, the implementation is straightforward (and is almost the same as that used in Qt's chart example).

If the item to be scrolled to has a rectangle that is left of the viewport's left edge, then the viewport must be scrolled. The scrolling is done by changing the horizontal scrollbar's value, adding to it the difference between the item rectangle's left edge and the viewport's left edge. All the other cases work in an analogous way.

Note that this method calls visualRect() which in turn calls viewportRectFor-Row() which in turn calls calculateRectsIfNecessary()—as already noted, this last method recalculates the rectangles in the rectForRow hash if the hash is dirty.

```
QModelIndex TiledListView::indexAt(const QPoint &point_) const
{
    QPoint point(point_);
    point.rx() += horizontalScrollBar()->value();
    point.ry() += verticalScrollBar()->value();
    calculateRectsIfNecessary();
```

```
    QHashIterator<int, QRectF> i(rectForRow);
    while (i.hasNext()) {
        i.next();
        if (i.value().contains(point))
            return model()->index(i.key(), 0, rootIndex());
    }
    return QModelIndex();
}
```

This pure virtual method must return the model index of the item at the given point. The point is in viewport coordinates, but the rectangles in rectForRow are in widget coordinates. Rather than convert each rectangle that we check to see if it contains the point, we do a one-off conversion of the point into widget coordinates.

The QPoint::rx() and QPoint::ry() methods return non-const references to the point's *x*- and *y*-coordinates, making it easy to change them. Without these methods we would have to do, for example, point.setX(horizontalScroll-Bar()->value() + point.x()).

We make sure that the rectForRow hash is up to date, and then we iterate over every row (item) in the hash—in an arbitrary order since hashes are unordered. If we find a value, that is, a rectangle, that contains the point, we immediately return the corresponding model index.

For models with large numbers of items (beyond the low thousands), this method might run slowly since in the worst case every item's rectangle must be checked, and even in the average case, half of the items must be checked. For the TiledListView this is unlikely to be a problem, since putting thousands of items in a list model of any kind is probably unhelpful to users—a tree model that grouped the items and made the top-level list of items a more manageable size would almost certainly be better.

```
    void TiledListView::dataChanged(const QModelIndex &topLeft,
                                    const QModelIndex &bottomRight)
    {
        hashIsDirty = true;
        QAbstractItemView::dataChanged(topLeft, bottomRight);
    }
```

This method is called whenever model data changes. We set hashIsDirty to true to make sure that when calculateRectsIfNecessary() is called it will update the rectForRow hash when the hash is next needed, and then we call the base class implementation. Notice that we do not call viewport->update() to schedule a repaint. The changed data might not be visible so a repaint might be unnecessary, and if it were necessary, the dataChanged() base class implementation would schedule the repaint for us.

```
void TiledListView::rowsInserted(const QModelIndex &parent, int start,
                                 int end)
{
    hashIsDirty = true;
    QAbstractItemView::rowsInserted(parent, start, end);
}

void TiledListView::rowsAboutToBeRemoved(const QModelIndex &parent,
                                         int start, int end)
{
    hashIsDirty = true;
    QAbstractItemView::rowsAboutToBeRemoved(parent, start, end);
}
```

If new rows are inserted into the model, or if rows are going to be removed, we must make sure that the view responds appropriately. These cases are easily handled by passing the work on to the base class; all that we must do is ensure that the rectForRow hash is marked as dirty so that it will be recalculated if necessary—for example, if the base class methods schedule a repaint.

```
QModelIndex TiledListView::moveCursor(
        QAbstractItemView::CursorAction cursorAction,
        Qt::KeyboardModifiers)
{
    QModelIndex index = currentIndex();
    if (index.isValid()) {
        if ((cursorAction == MoveLeft && index.row() > 0) ||
            (cursorAction == MoveRight &&
             index.row() + 1 < model()->rowCount())) {
            const int offset = (cursorAction == MoveLeft ? -1 : 1);
            index = model()->index(index.row() + offset,
                                   index.column(), index.parent());
        }
        else if ((cursorAction == MoveUp && index.row() > 0) ||
                 (cursorAction == MoveDown &&
                  index.row() + 1 < model()->rowCount())) {
            QFontMetrics fm(font());
            const int RowHeight = (fm.height() + ExtraHeight) *
                                  (cursorAction == MoveUp ? -1 : 1);
            QRect rect = viewportRectForRow(index.row()).toRect();
            QPoint point(rect.center().x(),
                         rect.center().y() + RowHeight);
            while (point.x() >= 0) {
                index = indexAt(point);
                if (index.isValid())
                    break;
```

```
            point.rx() -= fm.width("n");
        }
      }
   }
   return index;
}
```

Just as the `calculateRectsIfNecessary()` method is at the heart of the `Tiled-ListView`'s appearance, this method is at the heart of its behavior. The method must return the model index of the item that the requested move action should navigate to—or an invalid model index if no move should occur.

If the user presses the left (or right) arrow key we must return the model index of the previous (or next) item in the list—or of the current item if the previous (or next) item is the list model's first (or last) item. This is easily achieved by creating a new model index based on the current model index but using the previous (or next) row.

Handling the up and down arrow keys is slightly more subtle than handling the left and right arrow keys. In both cases we must compute a point above or below the current item. It doesn't matter if the computed point is outside the viewport, so long as it is within an item's rectangle.

If the user presses the up (or down) arrow key we must return the model index of the item that appears above (or below) the current item. We begin by getting the current item's rectangle in the viewport. We then create a point that is exactly one row above (or below) the current item vertically, and at the item's center horizontally. We then use the `indexAt()` method to retrieve the model index for the item at the given point. If we get a valid model index, there is an item above (or below) the current one, and we have its model index, so we are finished and can return that index.

But the model index might be invalid: this is possible because there may not be an item above (or below). Recall from the screenshot (208 ◄) that the items at the right-hand edge are ragged, because lines are of different lengths. If this is the case, we move the point left by the width of one "n" character and try again, repeatedly moving left until either we find an item (i.e., until we get a valid model index), or until we move beyond the left edge which means that there is no item above (or below). There will be no item above (or below) when the user presses the up (or down) arrow on an item that is in the first (or last) line.

If the `moveCursor()` method returns an invalid `QModelIndex`, the `QAbstractItem-View` base class harmlessly does nothing.

We have not written any code for handling selections—and we don't need to since we are using the `QAbstractItemView` API. If the user moves with the Shift key held down, the selection will be extended to create a selection of contiguous items. Similarly, while the user holds down the Ctrl key (⌘ key on Mac OS X), they can click arbitrary items and each one will be selected to create a selection that may include non-contiguous items.

We have left the implementation of support for the Home, End, PageUp, and PageDown keys as an exercise—they just require that the moveCursor() method be extended to handle more CursorActions (such as QAbstractItemView::MoveHome and QAbstractItemView::MovePageUp).

```
int TiledListView::horizontalOffset() const
{
    return horizontalScrollBar()->value();
}

int TiledListView::verticalOffset() const
{
    return verticalScrollBar()->value();
}
```

These pure virtual methods must be reimplemented. They must return the x- and y-offsets of the viewport within the (ideal-sized) widget. They are trivial to implement since the scrollbars' values are the offsets we need.

```
void TiledListView::scrollContentsBy(int dx, int dy)
{
    scrollDirtyRegion(dx, dy);
    viewport()->scroll(dx, dy);
}
```

This method is called when the scrollbars are moved; its responsibility is to ensure that the viewport is scrolled by the amounts given, and to schedule an appropriate repaint. Here we set up the repaint by calling the QAbstractItem-View::scrollDirtyRegion() method, *before* performing the scroll. Alternatively, instead of calling scrollDirtyRegion(), we could call viewport->update(), *after* performing the scroll.

The base class implementation simply calls viewport->update() and doesn't actually scroll. Note that if we want to scroll programmatically we should do so by calling QScrollBar::setValue() on the scrollbars, not by calling this method.

```
void TiledListView::setSelection(const QRect &rect,
        QFlags<QItemSelectionModel::SelectionFlag> flags)
{
    QRect rectangle = rect.translated(horizontalScrollBar()->value(),
            verticalScrollBar()->value()).normalized();
    calculateRectsIfNecessary();
    QHashIterator<int, QRectF> i(rectForRow);
    int firstRow = model()->rowCount();
```

```
            int lastRow = -1;
            while (i.hasNext()) {
                i.next();
                if (i.value().intersects(rectangle)) {
                    firstRow = firstRow < i.key() ? firstRow : i.key();
                    lastRow = lastRow > i.key() ? lastRow : i.key();
                }
            }
            if (firstRow != model()->rowCount() && lastRow != -1) {
                QItemSelection selection(
                        model()->index(firstRow, 0, rootIndex()),
                        model()->index(lastRow, 0, rootIndex()));
                selectionModel()->select(selection, flags);
            }
            else {
                QModelIndex invalid;
                QItemSelection selection(invalid, invalid);
                selectionModel()->select(selection, flags);
            }

        }
```

This pure virtual method is used to apply the given selection flags to all the items that are in or touching the specified rectangle. The actual selection must be made by calling QAbstractItemView::selectionModel()->select(). The implementation shown here is very similar to the one used by Qt's chart example.

The rectangle is passed using viewport coordinates, so we begin by creating a rectangle that uses widget coordinates since those are the ones used by the rectForRow hash. We then iterate over all the rows (items) in the hash—in arbitrary order—and if an item's rectangle intersects the given rectangle, we expand the first and last rows that the selection spans to include the item if it isn't already included.

If we have valid first and last selection rows, we create a QItemSelection that spans these rows (inclusively) and update the view's selection model. But if one or both rows are invalid, we create an invalid QModelIndex and update the selection model using it.

```
    QRegion TiledListView::visualRegionForSelection(
            const QItemSelection &selection) const
    {
        QRegion region;
        foreach (const QItemSelectionRange &range, selection) {
            for (int row = range.top(); row <= range.bottom(); ++row) {
                for (int column = range.left(); column < range.right();
                    ++column) {
```

```
                         QModelIndex index = model()->index(row, column,
                                                            rootIndex());
                         region += visualRect(index);
                }
            }
        }
        return region;
    }
```

This pure virtual method must be reimplemented to return the QRegion that encompasses all the view's selected items as shown in the viewport and using viewport coordinates. The implementation we have used is very similar to that used by Qt's chart example.

We start by creating an empty region. Then we iterate over all the selections— if there are any. For each selection we retrieve a model index for every item in the selection, and add each item's visual rectangle to the region.

Our visualRect() implementation calls viewportRectForRow() which in turn retrieves the rectangle from the rectForRow hash and returns it transformed into viewport coordinates (since rectForRow's rectangles use widget coordinates). In this particular case we could have bypassed the visualRect() call and made direct use of the rectForRow hash, but we preferred to do a more generic implementation that is easy to adapt for other custom views.

```cpp
void TiledListView::paintEvent(QPaintEvent*)
{
    QPainter painter(viewport());
    painter.setRenderHints(QPainter::Antialiasing|
                           QPainter::TextAntialiasing);
    for (int row = 0; row < model()->rowCount(rootIndex()); ++row) {
        QModelIndex index = model()->index(row, 0, rootIndex());
        QRectF rect = viewportRectForRow(row);
        if (!rect.isValid() || rect.bottom() < 0 ||
            rect.y() > viewport()->height())
            continue;
        QStyleOptionViewItem option = viewOptions();
        option.rect = rect.toRect();
        if (selectionModel()->isSelected(index))
            option.state |= QStyle::State_Selected;
        if (currentIndex() == index)
            option.state |= QStyle::State_HasFocus;
        itemDelegate()->paint(&painter, option, index);
        paintOutline(&painter, rect);
    }
}
```

Painting the view is surprisingly straightforward since every item's rectangle has already been computed and is available in the `rectForRow` hash. But notice that we paint on the widget's *viewport*, not on the widget itself. And as usual, we explicitly switch on antialiasing since we cannot assume what the default render hints are.

We iterate over every item and get each one's model index and its rectangle in viewport coordinates. If the rectangle is invalid (it shouldn't be), or if it is not visible in the viewport—that is, its bottom edge is above the viewport, or its *y*-coordinate is below the viewport—we don't bother to paint it.

For those items we do paint, we begin by retrieving the `QStyleOptionViewItem` supplied by the base class. We then set the option's rectangle to the item's rectangle—converting from QRectF to QRect using `QRectF::toRect()`—and update the option's state appropriately if the item is selected or is the current item.

Most importantly, we do *not* paint the item ourselves! Instead we ask the view's delegate—which could be the base class's built-in `QStyledItemDelegate`, or a custom delegate set by the class's client—to paint the item for us. This ensures that the view supports custom delegates.

The items are painted in lines, packing them in to make as much use of the available space as possible. But because each item's text could contain more than one word we need to help the user to be able to visually distinguish between different items. We do this by painting an outline around each item.

```
void TiledListView::paintOutline(QPainter *painter,
                                 const QRectF &rectangle)
{
    const QRectF rect = rectangle.adjusted(0, 0, -1, -1);
    painter->save();
    painter->setPen(QPen(palette().dark().color(), 0.5));
    painter->drawRect(rect);
    painter->setPen(QPen(Qt::black, 0.5));
    painter->drawLine(rect.bottomLeft(), rect.bottomRight());
    painter->drawLine(rect.bottomRight(), rect.topRight());
    painter->restore();
}
```

The outline is drawn by painting a rectangle, and then painting a couple of lines—one just below the bottom of the rectangle, and one just to the right of the rectangle—to provide a very subtle shadow effect.

```
void TiledListView::resizeEvent(QResizeEvent*)
{
    hashIsDirty = true;
    calculateRectsIfNecessary();
```

```
        updateGeometries();
    }
```

If the view is resized we must recalculate all the items' rectangles and update the scrollbars. We have already seen the calculateRectsIfNecessary() method (212 ◄), so we just need to review updateGeometries().

```
    void TiledListView::updateGeometries()
    {
        QFontMetrics fm(font());
        const int RowHeight = fm.height() + ExtraHeight;
        horizontalScrollBar()->setSingleStep(fm.width("n"));
        horizontalScrollBar()->setPageStep(viewport()->width());
        horizontalScrollBar()->setRange(0,
                qMax(0, idealWidth - viewport()->width()));
        verticalScrollBar()->setSingleStep(RowHeight);
        verticalScrollBar()->setPageStep(viewport()->height());
        verticalScrollBar()->setRange(0,
                qMax(0, idealHeight - viewport()->height()));
    }
```

This protected slot was introduced with Qt 4.4 and is used to update the view's child widgets—for example, the scrollbars.

The widget's ideal width and height are calculated in calculateRectsIf-Necessary(). The height is always sufficient to show *all* the model's data, and so is the width, if the viewport is wide enough to show the widest item. As mentioned earlier, it does not really matter what the view widget's actual size is, since the user only ever sees the viewport.

We make the horizontal scrollbar's single step size (i.e., how far it moves when the user clicks one of its arrows) the width of an "n", that is, one character. And we make its page step size (i.e., how far it moves when the user clicks left or right of the scrollbar's slider) the width of the viewport. We also set the horizontal scrollbar's range to span from 0 to the widget's ideal width, not counting the viewport's width (because that much can already be seen). The vertical scrollbar is set up in an analogous way.

```
    void TiledListView::mousePressEvent(QMouseEvent *event)
    {
        QAbstractItemView::mousePressEvent(event);
        setCurrentIndex(indexAt(event->pos()));
    }
```

This is the last event handler that we need to implement. We use it to make the item the user clicked the selected and current item. Because our view is a QAbstractItemView subclass, which itself is a QAbstractScrollArea subclass, the mouse event's position is in viewport coordinates. This isn't a problem since the `indexAt()` method expects the `QPoint` it is passed to be in viewport coordinates.

One final point to note about the `TiledListView` class is that it assumes that the user is using a left to right language, such as English. Arabic and Hebrew users will find the class confusing because they use right to left languages. We leave modifying the class to work both left to right and right to left as an exercise for the reader. (The widget's left to right or right to left status is available from `QWidget::layoutDirection()`; this is normally the same as `QApplication::layoutDirection()` but it is best to use the `QWidget` variant to be strictly correct.)

Like all of Qt's standard view classes, `TiledListView` has a one to one correspondence between data items and display items. But in some situations we might want to visualize two or more items combined together in some way—but this isn't supported by the `QAbstractItemView` API, nor can it be achieved by using custom delegates. Nonetheless, we can still produce a view that visualizes our data exactly as we want—as we will see in the next section—but in doing so we must eschew the `QAbstractItemView` API and provide our own API instead.

Model-Specific Visualizing Views

In this section we will create a view class from scratch as a `QWidget` subclass, and will provide our own API that is different from the `QAbstractItemView` API. It would have been possible to create a `QAbstractItemView` subclass, but since the view we want to create is specific to one particular model and shows some of its items combined, there seemed little point in making it comply with an API that wasn't needed or relevant.

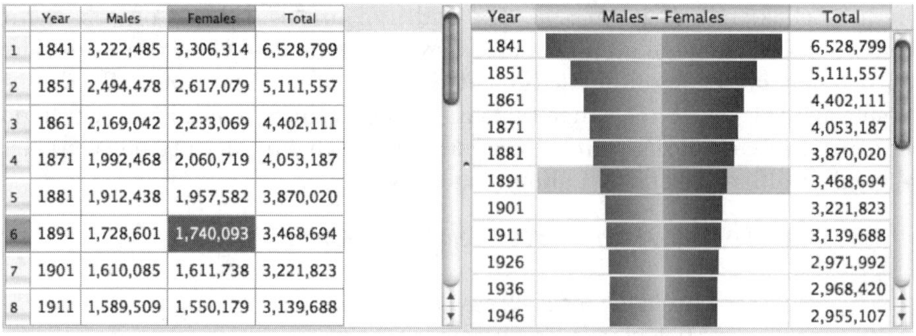

Figure 6.3 *A QTableView and a CensusVisualizer view*

The visualizer we will create is designed to present a table of census data. The model that holds the data is a table model, where each row holds a year, a count of the males, a count of the females, and the total of males and females. Fig-

ure 6.3 shows the central area of the Census Visualizer application (censusvisualizer). The area has two views of the data. On the left a standard QTableView
presents the data in the conventional way. On the right a CensusVisualizer view
is used to represent the data, and it does so by showing the males and females
as colored bars proportional to their numbers and using gradient fills.

We could not use Qt's QHeaderView to present the visualizer's headers because
we have combined two columns. Because of this we have created the Census-
Visualizer view as a QWidget that aggregates three other widgets inside itself: a
custom CensusVisualizerHeader to provide the horizontal header, a custom
CensusVisualizerView to visualize the data, and a QScrollArea to contain the
CensusVisualizerView and provide support for scrolling and resizing. The relationships between these classes are shown in Figure 6.4.

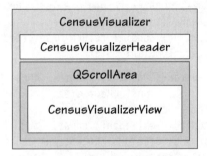

Figure 6.4 *The CensusVisualizer classes in relation to one another*

We will start by looking at the creation of the visualizer in the application's
main() function.

```
CensusVisualizer *censusVisualizer = new CensusVisualizer;
censusVisualizer->setModel(model);
```

This looks and works exactly like we'd expect—the visualizer is created and
we call CensusVisualizer::setModel() to give it the model. Later on in the
program's main() function, the QTableView is created, both views are laid out,
and various signal–slot connections are made to give the program its behavior.
We will ignore all of that and just focus our attention on the design and coding
of the visualizer class and its aggregated header and view classes.

The Visualizer Widget

The visualizer widget is the one that our clients will use directly, so we will
start by reviewing the CensusVisualizer class. This will give us the context
we need to then go on to look at the two custom classes that the visualizer
aggregates to provide its appearance. Here's the CensusVisualizer's definition
in the header file, but excluding its private data:

```
class CensusVisualizer : public QWidget
{
    Q_OBJECT

public:
    explicit CensusVisualizer(QWidget *parent=0);

    QAbstractItemModel *model() const { return m_model; }
    void setModel(QAbstractItemModel *model);
    QScrollArea *scrollArea() const { return m_scrollArea; }
    int maximumPopulation() const { return m_maximumPopulation; }
    int widthOfYearColumn() const { return m_widthOfYearColumn; }
    int widthOfMaleFemaleColumn() const;
    int widthOfTotalColumn() const { return m_widthOfTotalColumn; }
    int selectedRow() const { return m_selectedRow; }
    void setSelectedRow(int row);
    int selectedColumn() const { return m_selectedColumn; }
    void setSelectedColumn(int column);

    void paintItemBorder(QPainter *painter, const QPalette &palette,
                         const QRect &rect);
    QString maleFemaleHeaderText() const;
    int maleFemaleHeaderTextWidth() const;
    int xOffsetForMiddleOfColumn(int column) const;
    int yOffsetForRow(int row) const;

public slots:
    void setCurrentIndex(const QModelIndex &index);

signals:
    void clicked(const QModelIndex&);

private:
    ...
};
```

Although the data isn't shown, it is worth noting that the aggregated Census-VisualizerHeader is held in the header private member variable and the Census-VisualizerView is held in the view private member variable—both are pointers, of course. The class also holds a pointer to the model and to the QScrollArea that contains the CensusVisualizerView. The other private member data are all integers most of whose getters are implemented inline and shown here, and whose setters—for those that are writable—we will review shortly.

The maximum population is used by the view to compute the maximum widths of the male–female bars to make the best use of the available space, and is calculated whenever setModel() is called.

The width getters are used by both the header and the view when they are painting themselves. The selected row and column are kept track of and their values are used by the header to highlight the selected column, and by the view to highlight the selected item (or the selected male–female item pair).

The signal is included so that if the selected item is changed by the user clicking on the view, we emit a `clicked()` signal to notify any interested objects.

The non-inline parts of the `CensusVisualizer` class are the constructor and ten methods. The `paintItemBorder()`, `maleFemaleHeaderText()`, and `maleFemaleHeaderTextWidth()` methods are used by the aggregated header and view, so we will defer our review of them until we see them used, but we will review all the others here.

```
const int Invalid = -1;

CensusVisualizer::CensusVisualizer(QWidget *parent)
    : QWidget(parent), m_model(0), m_selectedRow(Invalid),
      m_selectedColumn(Invalid), m_maximumPopulation(Invalid)
{
    QFontMetrics fm(font());
    m_widthOfYearColumn = fm.width("W9999W");
    m_widthOfTotalColumn = fm.width("W9,999,999W");
    view = new CensusVisualizerView(this);
    header = new CensusVisualizerHeader(this);
    m_scrollArea = new QScrollArea;
    m_scrollArea->setBackgroundRole(QPalette::Light);
    m_scrollArea->setWidget(view);
    m_scrollArea->installEventFilter(view);
    QVBoxLayout *layout = new QVBoxLayout;
    layout->addWidget(header);
    layout->addWidget(m_scrollArea);
    layout->setContentsMargins(0, 0, 0, 0);
    layout->setSpacing(0);
    setLayout(layout);
    connect(view, SIGNAL(clicked(const QModelIndex&)),
            this, SIGNAL(clicked(const QModelIndex&)));
}
```

We begin by setting fixed widths for the year and total columns based on the largest numbers we expect them to handle, plus some margin.* The width of the total column set here is just an initial default; the actual width is recalculated in the `setModel()` method and depends on the model's maximum population. We then create the aggregated view and header widgets. Although we pass `this` as their parent, because we use a `QScrollArea` to contain the view, the view will be reparented to the `QScrollArea`.

---

*In this book the practice is to use "W"s when we want horizontal padding, and "n"s when we want a single character's width, for example, for horizontal scrolling.

The QScrollArea class is unusual for Qt in that it is *not* designed to be sub-classed. Instead the usage pattern is to aggregate the QScrollArea inside another widget as we have done here. Although this approach is by far the easiest to use, if we want to use inheritance, we can derive our subclass from QAbstract-ScrollArea as some of Qt's built-in classes do.

We install the view as an event filter for the scroll area—this means that every event that goes to the scroll area will first be sent to the view's event-Filter() method. We will see why this is necessary when we review the Census-VisualizerView class further on.

The layout is quite conventional except that we set the layout's margins and spacing to 0; this makes the CensusVisualizer have the same look as other widgets, with no extraneous border area, and with no gap between the Census-VisualizerHeader and the CensusVisualizerView (contained in the QScrollArea).

The connection is slightly unusual since it is a signal–signal connection. These set up a relationship whereby when the first signal is emitted the second signal is emitted as a consequence. So in this case, when the user clicks the view (i.e., to select an item), the view's clicked() signal goes to the CensusVisualizer, and this in turn emits a matching clicked() signal with the same QModelIndex parameter. This means that CensusVisualizer clients can connect to the CensusVisualizer's clicked() signal without having to know or care about the internals. This makes the CensusVisualizer much more of a self-contained component than it would be if, for example, it exposed the widgets it aggregates.

```
enum {Year, Males, Females, Total};

void CensusVisualizer::setModel(QAbstractItemModel *model)
{
    if (model) {
        QLocale locale;
        for (int row = 0; row < model->rowCount(); ++row) {
            int total = locale.toInt(model->data(
                                model->index(row, Total)).toString());
            if (total > m_maximumPopulation)
                m_maximumPopulation = total;
        }
        QString population = QString::number(m_maximumPopulation);
        population = QString("%1%2")
                .arg(population.left(1).toInt() + 1)
                .arg(QString(population.length() - 1, QChar('0')));
        m_maximumPopulation = population.toInt();
        QFontMetrics fm(font());
        m_widthOfTotalColumn = fm.width(QString("W%1%2W")
                .arg(population)
                .arg(QString(population.length() / 3, ',')));
```

```
    }
    m_model = model;
    header->update();
    view->update();
}
```

When a new model is set we must tell the header and view to update themselves. But first we must calculate a suitable maximum population. We do this by finding the biggest total population in the data, and then rounding it up to the smallest number with a most significant digit that is one larger. For example, if the biggest total is 8 392 174, the maximum becomes 9 000 000.

The algorithm used is very crude, but effective: we create a string that starts with the number's first digit plus one, followed by one less than as many zeros as there are digits in the number, and convert this string to an `int`. For the zeros we used one of `QString`'s two-argument constructors that takes a count and a character and returns a string that contains exactly count occurrences of the character.

Notice that we cannot retrieve the totals using `model->data(model->index(row, Total).toInt()`, because the model happens to hold the values as localized strings (e.g., "8,392,174" in the U.S. and UK, and "8.392.174" in Germany), rather than as integers. The solution is to use `toString()` to extract the data and then to use `QLocale::toInt()`—which takes an integer in the form of a localized string and returns the integer value.

The `QLocale` class also has corresponding `toFloat()` and `toDouble()` methods, as well as methods for other integral types—such as `toUInt()`—and also methods for extracting dates and times from localized strings. When a `QLocale` is constructed it defaults to using the application's current locale, but this can be overridden by using the one-argument constructor and a locale name that has the ISO 639 language code and ISO 3166 country code, or the two-argument constructor using Qt's language and country `enum`s.

In the constructor we set an initial width for the total column, but here we can set one that is appropriate for the actual total. The width is set to be the number of pixels needed to show the maximum number, plus space for a couple of "W"s for padding, plus space for a comma (or other grouping marker) for every three digits.

```
const int ExtraWidth = 5;

int CensusVisualizer::widthOfMaleFemaleColumn() const
{
    return width() - (m_widthOfYearColumn +
            m_widthOfTotalColumn + ExtraWidth +
            m_scrollArea->verticalScrollBar()->sizeHint().width());
}
```

This method returns a suitable width for the male–female column. It calculates the width as the maximum available width given the width of the Census-Visualizer itself, the widths of the other two columns, the width of the scroll area's vertical scrollbar, and a little bit of margin. This ensures that when the CensusVisualizer is resized, any extra width is always given to the male–female column.

```
void CensusVisualizer::setSelectedRow(int row)
{
    m_selectedRow = row;
    view->update();
}

void CensusVisualizer::setSelectedColumn(int column)
{
    m_selectedColumn = column;
    header->update();
}
```

If the selected row is changed programmatically, the view must update itself to show the correct highlighted item. Similarly, if the selected column is changed, the header must highlight the title of the selected column.

```
void CensusVisualizer::setCurrentIndex(const QModelIndex &index)
{
    setSelectedRow(index.row());
    setSelectedColumn(index.column());
    int x = xOffsetForMiddleOfColumn(index.column());
    int y = yOffsetForRow(index.row());
    m_scrollArea->ensureVisible(x, y, 10, 20);
}
```

This slot is provided as a service to clients, so that they can change the Census-Visualizer's selected item by using a signal–slot connection.

Once the row and column are set, we make sure that they are visible in the scroll area. The QScrollArea::ensureVisible() method takes x- and y-coordinates, and optionally some horizontal and vertical margin (which defaults to 50 pixels each). We've reduced the margins so as to avoid unwanted scrolling when the user clicks the top or bottom visible row.

There is actually a trade-off to be made here. If the vertical margin is too large, clicking the top or bottom item will cause unnecessary scrolling. And if the margin is too small, if the user Tabs to the widget and uses the down arrow to reach the bottom item, the item won't be shown fully.

```
int CensusVisualizer::xOffsetForMiddleOfColumn(int column) const
{
    switch (column) {
        case Year: return widthOfYearColumn() / 2;
        case Males: return widthOfYearColumn() +
                            (widthOfMaleFemaleColumn() / 4);
        case Females: return widthOfYearColumn() +
                              ((widthOfMaleFemaleColumn() * 4) / 3);
        default: return widthOfYearColumn() +
                        widthOfMaleFemaleColumn() +
                        (widthOfTotalColumn() / 2);
    }
}
```

This method is used to get a suitable *x*-offset for the current column. It does this by computing the given column's horizontal midpoint based on the column widths.

```
const int ExtraHeight = 5;

int CensusVisualizer::yOffsetForRow(int row) const
{
    return static_cast<int>((QFontMetricsF(font()).height()
                            + ExtraHeight) * row);
}
```

This method is used to get the *y*-offset for the given row, which it calculates by multiplying the height of one row by the given row index.

The *x*- and *y*-offsets returned by the xOffsetForMiddleOfColumn() and yOffsetForRow() methods assume that the CensusVisualizerView is exactly the size needed to show all the data. This assumption is valid because the CensusVisualizerView enforces it—as we will see when we look at the CensusVisualizerView::eventFilter() method. This means that even though only a portion of the view might be displayed, we don't have to do any scrolling-related computations because the QScrollArea that contains the CensusVisualizerView takes care of them for us.

We have now finished reviewing the CensusVisualizer class. Apart from the constructor and the setModel() method, it has very little code. This is because all of the widget's appearance, and most of its behavior, are handled by the instances of the CensusVisualizerHeader and CensusVisualizerView classes that the CensusVisualizer creates and lays out in its constructor. We will now review each of these aggregated classes in turn, starting with the header.

The Visualizer's Aggregated Header Widget

The CensusVisualizerHeader widget provides the column headers for the Census-Visualizer, as Figure 6.3 illustrates (224 ◄). Since we are painting it ourselves we have taken the opportunity to give it a stronger three-dimensional look than QHeaderView normally provides by using a different gradient fill. (If we had wanted to exactly match QHeaderView, we could have done the painting using QStyle methods.)

The class's definition in the header file is quite simple; here is its complete public API:

```
class CensusVisualizerHeader : public QWidget
{
    Q_OBJECT

public:
    explicit CensusVisualizerHeader(QWidget *parent)
        : QWidget(parent) {}

    QSize minimumSizeHint() const;
    QSize sizeHint() const { return minimumSizeHint(); }

protected:
    void paintEvent(QPaintEvent *event);
    ...
};
```

The constructor has an empty body. The only methods that are implemented are the minimumSizeHint(), the sizeHint(), the paintEvent(), and a couple of private helper methods (covered later) that paintEvent() calls.

```
QSize CensusVisualizerHeader::minimumSizeHint() const
{
    CensusVisualizer *visualizer = qobject_cast<CensusVisualizer*>(
                                        parent());
    Q_ASSERT(visualizer);
    return QSize(visualizer->widthOfYearColumn() +
                 visualizer->maleFemaleHeaderTextWidth() +
                 visualizer->widthOfTotalColumn(),
                 QFontMetrics(font()).height() + ExtraHeight);
}
```

The column widths are available from the parent CensusVisualizer, so we must cast—using qobject_cast<>() as here, or dynamic_cast<>()—to get a pointer to the parent that we can use to access the data we require. (If dynamic_cast<>() is used the compiler must have RTTI—Run Time Type Information—turned on, which most do by default nowadays.) The minimum width we need is the sum of the widths of all the columns, and the minimum height is the height of a character in the widget's font plus some margin.

The `maleFemaleHeaderTextWidth()` method, and the method it depends on, are provided by the `CensusVisualizer` class since they are used by both of the aggregated custom widgets. We show them here for completeness.

```
int CensusVisualizer::maleFemaleHeaderTextWidth() const
{
    return QFontMetrics(font()).width(maleFemaleHeaderText());
}


QString CensusVisualizer::maleFemaleHeaderText() const
{
    if (!m_model)
        return " - ";
    return QString("%1 - %2")
            .arg(m_model->headerData(Males, Qt::Horizontal).toString())
            .arg(m_model->headerData(Females, Qt::Horizontal)
                .toString());
}
```

The `maleFemaleHeaderTextWidth()` method returns the width needed by the male–female column to show its title, and the `maleFemaleHeaderText()` method returns the title itself.

```
void CensusVisualizerHeader::paintEvent(QPaintEvent*)
{
    QPainter painter(this);
    painter.setRenderHints(QPainter::Antialiasing|
                           QPainter::TextAntialiasing);
    paintHeader(&painter, height());
    painter.setPen(QPen(palette().button().color().darker(), 0.5));
    painter.drawRect(0, 0, width(), height());
}
```

The `paintEvent()` sets up the painter, passes most of the work on to the `paint-Header()` method, and finishes off by drawing a rectangle around the entire header.

```
void CensusVisualizerHeader::paintHeader(QPainter *painter,
                                         const int RowHeight)
{
    const int Padding = 2;

    CensusVisualizer *visualizer = qobject_cast<CensusVisualizer*>(
                                                parent());
    Q_ASSERT(visualizer);
```

```
        paintHeaderItem(painter,
                QRect(0, 0, visualizer->widthOfYearColumn() + Padding,
                    RowHeight),
                visualizer->model()->headerData(Year, Qt::Horizontal)
                                                .toString(),
                visualizer->selectedColumn() == Year);

        paintHeaderItem(painter,
                QRect(visualizer->widthOfYearColumn() + Padding, 0,
                    visualizer->widthOfMaleFemaleColumn(), RowHeight),
                visualizer->maleFemaleHeaderText(),
                visualizer->selectedColumn() == Males ||
                visualizer->selectedColumn() == Females);
        ...
    }
```

This method paints each column header in turn. For each one it calls paint-
HeaderItem(), passing it the painter, the rectangle in which to do the painting,
the text to paint, and whether this item (i.e., this column) is selected. We have
omitted the code for the total column since it is very similar to that used for the
year column.

```
    void CensusVisualizerHeader::paintHeaderItem(QPainter *painter,
            const QRect &rect, const QString &text, bool selected)
    {
        CensusVisualizer *visualizer = qobject_cast<CensusVisualizer*>(
                                                    parent());
        Q_ASSERT(visualizer);
        int x = rect.center().x();
        QLinearGradient gradient(x, rect.top(), x, rect.bottom());
        QColor color = selected ? palette().highlight().color()
                                : palette().button().color();
        gradient.setColorAt(0, color.darker(125));
        gradient.setColorAt(0.5, color.lighter(125));
        gradient.setColorAt(1, color.darker(125));
        painter->fillRect(rect, gradient);
        visualizer->paintItemBorder(painter, palette(), rect);
        painter->setPen(selected ? palette().highlightedText().color()
                                : palette().buttonText().color());
        painter->drawText(rect, text, QTextOption(Qt::AlignCenter));
    }
```

This is the method that actually paints each header item. We begin by getting
a pointer to the CensusVisualizer since we use one of its methods. Then we create a linear gradient whose coloring depends on whether this item is selected.
The gradient goes from a lighter color in the middle to a darker color at the top
and bottom, using lighter and darker colors than the ones used by QHeaderView,

to produce a stronger three-dimensional effect. Once the gradient is set up we use it to paint the item's background. Next we draw an outline around the item—actually we draw just two lines, one along the bottom, and the other on the right edge. And finally, we draw the text centered in the middle.

For completeness, here is the `paintItemBorder()` method:

```
void CensusVisualizer::paintItemBorder(QPainter *painter,
        const QPalette &palette, const QRect &rect)
{
    painter->setPen(QPen(palette.button().color().darker(), 0.33));
    painter->drawLine(rect.bottomLeft(), rect.bottomRight());
    painter->drawLine(rect.bottomRight(), rect.topRight());
}
```

We chose to draw the "outline" using just two lines because in this example it produces a better effect than drawing a rectangle.

This completes our review of the `CensusVisualizerHeader` class. The class is surprisingly straightforward, with most of the work simply a matter of setting up the painter and gradient and doing some simple drawing. This is quite a contrast with the `CensusVisualizerView` class where we must implement both its appearance and its behavior, as we will see in the next subsection.

The Visualizer's Aggregated View Widget

The custom `CensusVisualizerView` widget is used to display the model's data. It doesn't matter as such what size the widget is since it is embedded in a `QScrollArea` which provides scrollbars when necessary and generally takes care of all scrolling-related matters for us. This leaves us free to concentrate on the widget's appearance and behavior. Here is the public part of the widget's definition from the header file:

```
class CensusVisualizerView : public QWidget
{
    Q_OBJECT

public:
    explicit CensusVisualizerView(QWidget *parent);

    QSize minimumSizeHint() const;
    QSize sizeHint() const;

signals:
    void clicked(const QModelIndex&);

protected:
    bool eventFilter(QObject *target, QEvent *event);
```

```
    void mousePressEvent(QMouseEvent *event);
    void keyPressEvent(QKeyEvent *event);
    void paintEvent(QPaintEvent *event);
    ...
};
```

The class also has several private methods, all of which are used to support
painting the data—and which we will review later—and one private data
member, a pointer to the parent CensusVisualizer. We will briefly look at the
public methods and the slot, and then work our way through the protected
event handlers to see what they do and how they do it—but first we will look
at the constructor.

```
CensusVisualizerView::CensusVisualizerView(QWidget *parent)
    : QWidget(parent)
{
    visualizer = qobject_cast<CensusVisualizer*>(parent);
    Q_ASSERT(visualizer);
    setFocusPolicy(Qt::WheelFocus);
    setMinimumSize(minimumSizeHint());
}
```

The CensusVisualizerView is created inside the CensusVisualizer constructor
and passed as parent the CensusVisualizer itself (227 ◄). Nonetheless we have
chosen to keep a private CensusVisualizer pointer member (visualizer), to give
us access to the CensusVisualizer, because after the view has been constructed
it is given to a QScrollArea—and this takes ownership of the view and becomes
the view's parent. (Alternatively we could avoid keeping a member variable
and access the visualizer by calling qobject_cast<CensusVisualizer*>(parent()
->parent()) instead.)

Qt provides several different focus policies: Qt::NoFocus (useful for labels and
other read-only widgets), Qt::TabFocus (the widget accepts focus when tabbed
to), Qt::ClickFocus (the widget accepts focus when clicked), Qt::StrongFocus
(this combines tab and click focus), and Qt::WheelFocus (this is strong focus plus
accepting the focus when the mouse wheel is used). Here we have used Qt::
WheelFocus which is the usual choice for editable widgets.

We have omitted the minimumSizeHint() method's implementation since it is
almost identical to CensusVisualizerHeader::minimumSizeHint() (232 ◄), the
only difference being that here we have the visualizer member built into the
class. (The CensusVisualizerHeader's parent is the CensusVisualizer and it isn't
reparented, so it doesn't need a separate visualizer member variable.)

```
QSize CensusVisualizerView::sizeHint() const
{
    int rows = visualizer->model()
            ? visualizer->model()->rowCount() : 1;
```

```
        return QSize(visualizer->widthOfYearColumn() +
                qMax(100, visualizer->maleFemaleHeaderTextWidth()) +
                visualizer->widthOfTotalColumn(),
                visualizer->yOffsetForRow(rows));
    }
```

If a model has been set we allow enough room for all its rows; otherwise we allow room for a single row. The y-offset returned by the `CensusVisualizer::yOffsetForRow()` method is the height we need since we pass it a row that is equal to the number of rows in the model. For the columns we use the fixed widths calculated when the `CensusVisualizer` was constructed, plus the computed width of the male–female column (or 100 pixels, whichever is greater).

```
    bool CensusVisualizerView::eventFilter(QObject *target, QEvent *event)
    {
        if (QScrollArea *scrollArea = visualizer->scrollArea()) {
            if (target == scrollArea && event->type() == QEvent::Resize) {
                if (QResizeEvent *resizeEvent =
                        static_cast<QResizeEvent*>(event)) {
                    QSize size = resizeEvent->size();
                    size.setHeight(sizeHint().height());
                    int width = size.width() - (ExtraWidth +
                            scrollArea->verticalScrollBar()->sizeHint()
                            .width());
                    size.setWidth(width);
                    resize(size);
                }
            }
        }
        return QWidget::eventFilter(target, event);
    }
```

The `CensusVisualizerView` was made an event filter for the `QScrollArea` that contains it (227 ◀). This means that every event that is sent to the `QScrollArea` goes to this method first.

The only event we are interested in is `QEvent::Resize`. When this event occurs, that is, when the scroll area is resized, we also resize the `CensusVisualizerView` widget. We always make the view the height needed to show all of its data, and we set its width to the available width while allowing for the width of the vertical scrollbar. This means that if the user has scrolled the view and, for example, clicks a row, we can work as if the entire widget is visible without having to account for the scrolling to compute which row was clicked.

Inside an `eventFilter()` reimplementation we are free, at least in principle, to do what we like with the event: we can change it, replace it, delete it, or ignore it. To stop an event from going further (whether or not we do anything with it), or if we delete an event, we must return true to indicate that it has been handled; otherwise we must return false. Here we make use of the event, but don't want to interfere with its behavior, so we leave the arguments unchanged and call the base class implementation at the end.

```
void CensusVisualizerView::mousePressEvent(QMouseEvent *event)
{
    int row = static_cast<int>(event->y() /
            (QFontMetricsF(font()).height() + ExtraHeight));
    int column;
    if (event->x() < visualizer->widthOfYearColumn())
        column = Year;
    else if (event->x() < (visualizer->widthOfYearColumn() +
                           visualizer->widthOfMaleFemaleColumn() / 2))
        column = Males;
    else if (event->x() < (visualizer->widthOfYearColumn() +
                           visualizer->widthOfMaleFemaleColumn()))
        column = Females;
    else
        column = Total;
    visualizer->setSelectedRow(row);
    visualizer->setSelectedColumn(column);
    emit clicked(visualizer->model()->index(row, column));
}
```

The QMouseEvent::y() method returns the mouse click's y-offset relative to the top of the widget. Thanks to the CensusVisualizerView being embedded in a QScrollArea, and thanks to it always being exactly high enough to hold all the data—something we ensure in the eventFilter()—we can work directly with the y-offset no matter whether the widget has been scrolled. So here, we determine the row by dividing the y-offset by the height of one row.

To work out the column, we compare the x-offset: if it is less than the width of the year column then the year column was clicked; if it is less than the width of the year column plus half the width of the male–female column then the male column was clicked; and so on.

Once the row and column are known we tell the CensusVisualizer to select them, safe in the knowledge that doing this will also result in update() being called both on this view and on the header so that the correct row and column are properly highlighted. And finally, we emit the clicked() signal with the model index—as computed by the model—of the selected item, which in turn will cause the CensusVisualizer to emit its own clicked() signal with the same model index for the benefit of any connected objects.

```
void CensusVisualizerView::keyPressEvent(QKeyEvent *event)
{
```

```
    if (visualizer->model()) {
        int row = Invalid;
        int column = Invalid;
        if (event->key() == Qt::Key_Left) {
            column = visualizer->selectedColumn();
            if (column == Males || column == Total)
                --column;
            else if (column == Females)
                column = Year;
        }
        ...
        else if (event->key() == Qt::Key_Up)
            row = qMax(0, visualizer->selectedRow() - 1);
        else if (event->key() == Qt::Key_Down)
            row = qMin(visualizer->selectedRow() + 1,
                        visualizer->model()->rowCount() - 1);
        row = row == Invalid ? visualizer->selectedRow() : row;
        column = column == Invalid ? visualizer->selectedColumn()
                                    : column;
        if (row != visualizer->selectedRow() ||
            column != visualizer->selectedColumn()) {
            QModelIndex index = visualizer->model()->index(row,
                                                        column);
            visualizer->setCurrentIndex(index);
            emit clicked(index);
            return;
        }
    }
    QWidget::keyPressEvent(event);
}
```

This event handler is used to provide navigation inside the view by the use of the keyboard arrow keys.

Inside the CensusVisualizer we keep track of the selected row and column, but in the case of the male and female columns they are visually—and therefore from the user's perspective—a single column. To account for this, if the user presses the left arrow and the current column is either the male or the female column, we set the column to be the year column. If the current column is the year column, we do nothing, and if the current column is the total column we set the column to be the female column. The handling of right arrow presses is very similar (so we have omitted the code): if the current column is either the male or the female column, we set the column to be the total column. And if the current column is the year column we set it to be the male column, and if the current column is the total column we do nothing.

If the user presses the up arrow, we set the current row to be one less than the current row—or do nothing if they are already on the first row. And similarly, if the user presses the down arrow, we set the current row to be one more than the current row—or do nothing if they are already on the last row.

If the new selected row or column or both are different from the currently selected ones, we set the selected row and column. This will cause update() to be called on the view and the header, and will also ensure that the selected item is visible. We also emit a clicked() signal with the selected item's model index.

At the end, if we selected a new item, we must *not* call the base class implementation, since we have handled the key press ourselves and don't want it to go to the scroll area. This is because the scroll area handles the arrow keys itself, interpreting them as requests to scroll, which we don't want—or need—since we handle the scrolling ourselves. And conversely, if we didn't handle the key press, we call the base class implementation to handle it for us.

Compare this method with the mouse event handler where we set the row and column without having to ensure that the selected item is visible—since the user must have clicked it. But here, the user could be pressing, say, the down arrow, on the last visible row, so we must call QScrollArea::ensureVisible() (which is done by CensusVisualizer::setCurrentIndex(); 230 ◄) so that the view is scrolled appropriately.

Adding support for the Home, End, PageUp, and PageDown keys follows the same principles as the code used for the arrow keys, and is left as an exercise. (When implementing PageUp and PageDown, it is conventional to move up or down by the widget's visible height minus one line or row so that the user has one line of context by which they can orient themselves.)

The eventFilter(), mousePressEvent(), and keyPressEvent() methods that we have just reviewed provide the view's behavior. Now we will look at the paintEvent() and the private helper methods it uses to see how the view's appearance is rendered.

```
void CensusVisualizerView::paintEvent(QPaintEvent *event)
{
    if (!visualizer->model())
        return;
    QFontMetricsF fm(font());
    const int RowHeight = fm.height() + ExtraHeight;
    const int MinY = qMax(0, event->rect().y() - RowHeight);
    const int MaxY = MinY + event->rect().height() + RowHeight;

    QPainter painter(this);
    painter.setRenderHints(QPainter::Antialiasing|
                           QPainter::TextAntialiasing);

    int row = MinY / RowHeight;
    int y = row * RowHeight;
    for (; row < visualizer->model()->rowCount(); ++row) {
```

```
            paintRow(&painter, row, y, RowHeight);
            y += RowHeight;
            if (y > MaxY)
                break;
        }
    }
```

This method begins by computing some constants, in particular, the height to allow for each row, and the paint event's minimum and maximum *y*-coordinates, minus or plus one row's height to ensure that even if only a portion of a row is visible, it is still painted.

Since the widget is inside a QScrollArea and its height is always precisely that needed to show all the items, we do not *need* to compute any offsets or work out for ourselves what is visible and what isn't. However, for the sake of efficiency, we should paint only visible items.

The paint event that is passed in has a QRect that specifies the rectangle that needs repainting. For small widgets we often ignore this rectangle and just repaint the whole thing, but for a model-visualizing widget that could have large amounts of data we want to be more efficient and only paint what needs painting. So with the constants in place, we set up the painter and calculate the first row that needs painting, and that row's *y*-coordinate. (It may be tempting to initialize y with y = MinY; but MinY is not usually the same as row * RowHeight because of the—desired—integer truncation that occurs in the MinY / RowHeight expression.)

With everything in place, we iterate through the model's rows, starting at the first one that is visible, and painting each one until the *y*-coordinate takes us beyond the rectangle that needs repainting, at which point we stop. This ensures that we retrieve and paint at most the rows that are visible plus two extra rows, which could be a considerable savings if the model has thousands or tens of thousands of rows or more.

```
    void CensusVisualizerView::paintRow(QPainter *painter, int row,
                                        int y, const int RowHeight)
    {
        paintYear(painter, row,
                QRect(0, y, visualizer->widthOfYearColumn(), RowHeight));
        paintMaleFemale(painter, row,
                QRect(visualizer->widthOfYearColumn(), y,
                    visualizer->widthOfMaleFemaleColumn(), RowHeight));
        paintTotal(painter, row,
                QRect(visualizer->widthOfYearColumn() +
                    visualizer->widthOfMaleFemaleColumn(), y,
                    visualizer->widthOfTotalColumn(), RowHeight));
    }
```

This method is used simply to create a suitable rectangle and call a column-specific paint method for each column.

```
void CensusVisualizerView::paintYear(QPainter *painter, int row,
                                     const QRect &rect)
{
    paintItemBackground(painter, rect,
                        row == visualizer->selectedRow() &&
                        visualizer->selectedColumn() == Year);
    painter->drawText(rect,
            visualizer->model()->data(
                visualizer->model()->index(row, Year)).toString(),
            QTextOption(Qt::AlignCenter));
}
```

Once the background is painted, all that remains is for the item's text to be drawn. The text is retrieved from the model and painted centered in its column.

The CensusVisualizerView::paintTotal() method is very similar to this one (so we don't show it), with the only difference being that we right-align the total.

```
void CensusVisualizerView::paintItemBackground(QPainter *painter,
        const QRect &rect, bool selected)
{
    painter->fillRect(rect, selected ? palette().highlight()
                                     : palette().base());
    visualizer->paintItemBorder(painter, palette(), rect);
    painter->setPen(selected ? palette().highlightedText().color()
                             : palette().windowText().color());
}
```

Which background and foreground colors to use depends on whether the item is selected. This method paints the background and the border and sets the pen color ready for the caller to paint its text.

The paintMaleFemale() method is slightly longer so we will review it in three parts.

```
void CensusVisualizerView::paintMaleFemale(QPainter *painter,
        int row, const QRect &rect)
{
    QRect rectangle(rect);
    QLocale locale;
    int males = locale.toInt(visualizer->model()->data(
            visualizer->model()->index(row, Males)).toString());
    int females = locale.toInt(visualizer->model()->data(
```

```
                visualizer->model()->index(row, Females)).toString());
        qreal total = males + females;
        int offset = qRound(
                ((1 - (total / visualizer->maximumPopulation())) / 2) *
                rectangle.width());
```

We begin by finding out how many males and females there are and the total
they sum to. (We discussed the use of QLocale to get numbers from localized
strings earlier; 229 ◄.) Then we compute how much width the complete colored
bar should occupy and use that to work out the offset by which the bar must be
indented from the left and from the right to make the bar the right size within
the available rectangle.

```
        painter->fillRect(rectangle,
                (row == visualizer->selectedRow() &&
                (visualizer->selectedColumn() == Females ||
                  visualizer->selectedColumn() == Males))
                ? palette().highlight() : palette().base());
```

The first thing we paint is the background, with the color determined by
whether the males or females column is selected.

```
        visualizer->paintItemBorder(painter, palette(), rectangle);
        rectangle.setLeft(rectangle.left() + offset);
        rectangle.setRight(rectangle.right() - offset);
        int rectY = rectangle.center().y();
        painter->fillRect(rectangle.adjusted(0, 1, 0, -1),
                maleFemaleGradient(rectangle.left(), rectY,
                        rectangle.right(), rectY, males / total));
    }
```

Toward the end, we paint the item's border and then resize the available
rectangle—potentially making it smaller—so that it has the correct size and
position to serve as the rectangle for drawing the colored bar. Finally, we draw
the bar—with a tiny reduction in height—using a gradient fill which goes from
dark green to light green (left to right) for the male part, and from light red to
dark red (left to right) for the female part.

```
QLinearGradient CensusVisualizerView::maleFemaleGradient(
        qreal x1, qreal y1, qreal x2, qreal y2, qreal crossOver)
{
    QLinearGradient gradient(x1, y1, x2, y2);
    QColor maleColor = Qt::green;
    QColor femaleColor = Qt::red;
    gradient.setColorAt(0, maleColor.darker());
    gradient.setColorAt(crossOver - 0.001, maleColor.lighter());
    gradient.setColorAt(crossOver + 0.001, femaleColor.lighter());
```

```
        gradient.setColorAt(1, femaleColor.darker());
        return gradient;
    }
```

This method is shown for completeness. It creates a linear gradient that goes from dark to light in one color and then from light to dark in another color with a crossover between the colors at the specified position. The crossover point is computed by the caller as males / total; this ensures that the widths of the male and female parts are in correct proportion to their populations.

Qt also has QConicalGradient and QRadialGradient classes with similar APIs.

We have now finished the CensusVisualizer class and its aggregated Census-VisualizerHeader and CensusVisualizerView classes that do so much of the work. Creating custom classes like this is ideal when we have a model that we want to visualize in a unique way and where items are shown combined in some way so that using a custom delegate or a custom view based on the QAbstractItemView API is not sufficient.

We have now completed our review of the TiledListView class, and of the CensusVisualizer class. The TiledListView is much shorter because it didn't have to show any column captions and because it could rely on the base class for some of its functionality. If we want to present model data in unique ways, for example, graphically, or if we want to present some model items combined, then a custom delegate is insufficient and we must use a custom view. If we take the approach used for the CensusVisualizer class, we get complete control, and only have to implement the features that we actually need. However, if we choose to create a QAbstractItemView subclass, we still get complete control, we get some functionality for free, and we get much more potential for reuse—but we are obliged to reimplement all the pure virtual methods, and in general at least those methods listed in Table 6.1 (210 ◀).

This chapter is the last of the four chapters dedicated to Qt's model/view architecture. In general, it is easiest to start by using a QStandardItemModel, subclassing it (or QStandardItem) to make the data serializable and deserializable. Later on, if the need arises, a custom model can always be used as a drop-in replacement. Similarly, using one of Qt's standard views is the best way to start viewing model data, and if the need for customizing the appearance or editing of items is required, it is best—and easiest—to use custom delegates. However, if no combination of standard view and custom delegate can visualize the data in the desired way, then we must create a custom view using one of the approaches shown in this chapter.

7

- Executing Functions in Threads
- Filtering and Mapping in Threads

Threading with QtConcurrent

Threading is very popular, and sometimes very useful. However, because it is fashionable, some programmers seem to use it unnecessarily, and end up creating needlessly complicated applications. (See "The Threading Controversy" sidebar; ➤ 246.) Note that this chapter assumes a basic knowledge of Qt threading—it is designed to show how to use Qt's threading support, not as a tutorial on threading itself.*

Before we dive into threading it is worth pausing for thought about some of the issues threading raises. Most often we want to use threading to improve performance, but to achieve this sometimes requires us to approach things rather differently than when we are writing single-threaded applications.

In fact, we cannot be certain that using multiple threads will actually deliver better performance at all. For example, if we increase the number of threads we use in proportion to the number of cores the system has available, we might end up degrading performance because the gains are outweighed by the increased contention. And sometimes the most efficient algorithm in a single-threaded context may turn out not to be the most efficient when multiple threads are used. So, if we want to be confident that we really are delivering better performance, ideally, we should produce different implementations and profile them to compare their performance—using the same hardware and software configurations as our users.

Caveats aside, if threading is the right solution, Qt provides plenty of support for it. In particular, Qt 4.4 introduced the QRunnable class and the Qt-Concurrent namespace, both designed to provide high-level APIs to support threading without the need for programmers to use the low-level API offered by QThread and its related classes. These high-level APIs relieve us of many of

---

*Those readers familiar with threading in general, but not with Qt threading, might benefit from reading Qt's threading documentation, qt.nokia.com/doc/threads.html, or the "Multithreading" chapter of *C++ GUI Programming with Qt 4, Second Edition.*

245

The Threading Controversy

Thanks in large part to Java's built-in support for threading, and more recently the advent of multi-core processors, the interest in writing threaded programs has grown considerably in recent years.

Yet despite its popularity, threading is controversial. It can add significant complexity to programs and can make debugging and maintenance much harder than for single-threaded programs. And it isn't always possible to split up processing to make using threads worthwhile. Also, performance benefits are not always achieved due to the overhead of threading itself, or simply because it is much easier to make mistakes in threaded programs.

Leading Sun developer Tim Bray said, "Now that the best and the brightest have spent a decade building and debugging threading frameworks in Java and .NET, it's increasingly starting to look like threading is a bad idea; don't go there" (Tim Bray's weblog, "Processors" paragraph, www.tbray.org/ongoing/When/200x/2008/04/24/Inflection). Nor is his an isolated voice. One of the fathers of computer science, Donald Knuth, said, "I won't be surprised at all if the whole threading idea turns out to be a flop" (interview with Donald Knuth, www.informit.com/articles/article.aspx?p=1193856).

There seem to be two main problems. One is that using threading often requires programmers to add a significant amount of code to support threading that is actually tangential to solving the problems at hand. And worse, this code can be very subtle and difficult to get right, and can be very hard to debug. Another problem is that at a hardware level there are many different solutions to parallelism, each of which requires that compiler writers use different techniques, and which may be superceded by new hardware approaches as progress is made.

The news isn't entirely bad. One technique that might allow threading to be used in a higher-level way without burdening programmers with a lot of low-level bookkeeping (i.e., locking and unlocking) is software transactional memory. Libraries for this are under development for C++. And Qt itself provides the QtConcurrent functions—introduced in this chapter—which are designed to provide high-level access to threading, and that take care of all the low-level details. Other possible solutions include the Erlang and Go programming languages, and Apple's Grand Central Dispatch.

And, of course, there is another approach altogether, which can take advantage of multiple cores without most of the disadvantages of threading—but without some of its advantages, and with its own set of burdens: multi-processing. This involves handing off work to separate processes, for example, using Qt's QProcess class. While this approach can relieve us of some of the subtle risks and extra code required to support concurrency, it leaves us responsible for handling all the inter-process communication ourselves.

the responsibilities normally associated with threading (although some care is still needed).

The `QRunnable` class and the `QtConcurrent::run()` function are well suited to situations where we want to perform some background processing in one or more secondary threads without needing the full power and flexibility provided by `QThread`. These are covered in this chapter's first section.

The `QtConcurrent` namespace also provides functions for filtering, mapping, and reducing—concepts that we will explain when we cover these functions in this chapter's second section. These functions are ideal for situations where there are lots of items that need to be processed. Unfortunately, we cannot use these functions to process the items in a `QAbstractItemModel` or a `QGraphicsScene`, because Qt does not support the locking of models, scenes, or of the items they contain; however, we will see how to work around this problem at some cost in memory and processing overhead.

Sometimes, using the low-level API is the right approach. The next chapter shows the use of `QThread`. Using `QThread` is potentially one of the most challenging ways of doing threading in Qt—but the dividend we get is very fine control.

In both this chapter's sections and in the next chapter, we try to minimize the risks and complexities of threading. This is done primarily by avoiding the need to lock at all—for example, by giving each thread its own unique processing to do. And where locking is necessary, we try to minimize it, or try to make it transparent—for example, by creating classes that handle their own locks so that clients don't have to do any locking themselves.

Qt also offers some even lower-level classes, such as `QAtomicInt` and `QAtomic-Pointer`. These classes are ideal for creating thread-safe data structures and other low-level threaded components, but are beyond the scope of this book. (See *The Art of Multiprocessor Programming*—listed in the bibliography—for ideas about using them; ➤ 495.)

Qt's threading API also includes `QSemaphore`, `QThreadStorage`, and `QWaitCondition`. These classes are most often used in conjunction with `QThread` subclasses, although this chapter and the next don't happen to use them, relying instead on other classes and techniques, for example, using `volatile bool`. (See *C++ GUI Programming with Qt 4*—listed in the bibliography—for examples that show the use of the `QSemaphore`, `QThreadStorage`, and `QWaitCondition` classes.)

The `volatile` keyword is used to mark a variable as one that might change behind the program's back—this means that it will never be optimized away (or cached!) by the compiler. This is useful for situations where a variable is at a memory address that can be changed from outside the program—for example, at a hardware port. But in addition, `volatile bool` can be useful in threaded programs, where such a variable's value might be changed by one thread and read by another. It is important to note that although volatile is not suitable for threaded use with other datatypes (not even with ints) because of the possibility of two separate bytes being updated by separate threads, it is safe to use with bools.* In addition to volatile bool, the book's threading examples use QMutex, QMutexLocker, QReadWriteLock, QReadLocker, and QWriteLocker, and in the case of the QtConcurrent namespace's functions, QFuture and QFutureWatcher.

In general threading pays back best when the cost of setting up and running separate threads is outweighed by the benefits of spreading the work over multiple cores or processors. So apart from the obvious use in implementing parallel algorithms, threading is most effectively applied where we have at least one—and potentially many—relatively expensive bits of processing to do that can be done wholly or mostly independently.

There is one other important use case for threading in a GUI context. If we have expensive processing to perform and want to avoid tying up the user interface we might choose to solve the problem by creating a secondary thread that handles the processing. For networking this isn't necessary since Qt already handles network access asynchronously, but for our own processing, using one or more secondary threads can sometimes be very useful. A lighter-weight alternative that is viable in some cases is to use a local event loop as we saw in Chapter 2 (74 ◄).

Executing Functions in Threads

In cases where the number of items to process is quite small, but the processing of each is expensive, it is often convenient to do the processing in a separate thread of execution to keep the user interface responsive. Similarly, if there are lots of items to process, but they can be grouped together (or put on a work queue), then spreading the processing over just a few separate threads might make sense.

There are four main ways that processing can be spread over a few threads of execution or over a few processes: we can execute separate processes using the QProcess class (e.g., running multiple copies of a self-contained "worker" program); we can use QtConcurrent::run() to run functions or methods in secondary threads from Qt's global thread pool; we can create QRunnable objects and run them in secondary threads from Qt's global thread pool; or we can create QThread objects and execute them as secondary threads. In this section we will see how to use QtConcurrent::run() and QRunnable, and in the next chapter we will use QThread.

---

*See, for example, "volatile—Multithreaded Programmer's Best Friend" by Andrei Alexandrescu, www.ddj.com/cpp/184403766.

Using the QtConcurrent::run() function is straightforward: we create a function or method that does the processing we want and pass it to the QtConcurrent::run() function to execute. We can pass the same function (normally with different arguments) multiple times if we want to use multiple secondary threads. Using a QRunnable is quite similar. We create a QRunnable subclass and put all our processing inside our reimplementation of the pure virtual run() method, and pass as many instances as we want secondary threads to the QThreadPool::start() method.

Doing processing in secondary threads using QtConcurrent::run() or QRunnable has two potential drawbacks compared with using QThread. First, there is no support for signals and slots, so no communication facility (e.g., to indicate progress) is built in. Second, we are not notified when processing is finished, so if we need to know this, we must find out for ourselves. It is quite straightforward to overcome both of these drawbacks—and to provide support for stopping—as we will see later on in this section.

In this section we will create the Image2Image application (image2image), a program that searches a specified directory for image files and for each one creates a copy of the image using the specified format (such as .bmp, .tiff, and so on). The application is shown in Figure 7.1.*

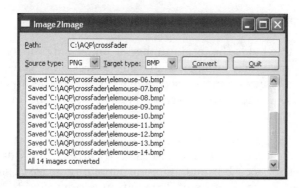

Figure 7.1 *The Image2Image application*

Converting an image involves reading it into memory in its original format and then saving it out again in a new format—a mixture of disk I/O and processing. For this application we have chosen to do the work in one or more secondary threads, with each thread being given its own unique list of files to convert. Since each thread has its own private work to do and there is no need for communication between the secondary threads, no locking is necessary. Of course, we will want to notify the main (GUI) thread about progress, but we'll

---

*Incidentally, the line edit used to enter the path uses a QCompleter which pops up a list of valid directories to minimize how much the user must type—this is covered in Chapter 9; ➤ 320.

do that by using techniques that leave Qt to take care of any locking that may be needed.

We have written the application so that it can use either QtConcurrent::run() or QRunnable, depending on a #define. In the following subsection we will see how to use QtConcurrent::run(), and in the subsection after that we will see how to use QRunnable. In both subsections we will cover the bare minimum of the user interface-related code, focusing instead on the threading aspects.

Although we use the same main window infrastructure and cancelation control for both, we use different means to communicate progress for each of them. For QtConcurrent::run() we communicate by using a custom event. For QRunnable we communicate by invoking a slot—and since QRunnable is not a QObject subclass, the slot must be called without using emit (i.e., without sending a signal in the normal Qt way). The use of these two approaches is purely to show the different techniques; we could just as easily have used custom events for both or invoked slots for both.

Apart from its methods and widgets, the main window class has three items of private data:

```
int total;
int done;
volatile bool stopped;
```

The total variable holds the total number of images to process, the done variable holds the number of images that were successfully converted, and the stopped Boolean is used to notify secondary threads if the user has canceled. Note that we use a single button (convertOrCancelButton) for initiating the conversions and for canceling.

Once the user has chosen a directory and their source and target formats, they can then click the Convert button to initiate the conversions. Once pressed this button becomes a Cancel button (simply by changing its text), so the user can stop the conversions at any time. This button is connected to the convertOrCancel() slot.

```
void MainWindow::convertOrCancel()
{
    stopped = true;
    if (QThreadPool::globalInstance()->activeThreadCount())
        QThreadPool::globalInstance()->waitForDone();
    if (convertOrCancelButton->text() == tr("&Cancel")) {
        updateUi();
        return;
    }

    QString sourceType = sourceTypeComboBox->currentText();
```

```
            QStringList sourceFiles;
            QDirIterator i(directoryEdit->text(), QDir::Files|QDir::Readable);
            while (i.hasNext()) {
                const QString &filenameAndPath = i.next();
                if (i.fileInfo().suffix().toUpper() == sourceType)
                    sourceFiles << filenameAndPath;
            }
            if (sourceFiles.isEmpty())
                AQP::warning(this, tr("No Images Error"),
                            tr("No matching files found"));
            else {
                logEdit->clear();
                convertFiles(sourceFiles);
            }
        }
```

This slot starts by setting the `stopped` variable to `true` to notify any running secondary threads that they must stop. Then it checks to see if there are any secondary threads still running in Qt's global thread queue, and if there are it waits (blocks) until they are all done.

The `QThreadPool::globalInstance()` method returns a pointer to Qt's global `QThreadPool` object, and `QThreadPool::activeThreadCount()` returns the number of threads in the thread pool that are actively working—this could be 0, of course. The `QThreadPool::waitForDone()` method waits for *all* the threads in the thread pool to finish, so it could potentially block the user interface for a long time. To avoid this problem we must ensure that we tell all the threads to finish before waiting for them, and in this application, we achieve this by setting the `stopped` variable to `true`.

If the user has canceled, we simply call the `updateUi()` method (not shown) to change the Cancel button's text to Convert and return, since we have stopped all the secondary threads.

If the user has clicked Convert we create a list of files in the chosen directory that have a suffix that matches the chosen source type. If the list is empty, we notify the user and return. If the list is nonempty we clear the log (a read-only `QPlainTextEdit`), and call `convertFiles()` with the list of files to actually perform the conversions.

We have two implementations of `convertFiles()`, one using `QtConcurrent::run()` which is shown in the following subsection, and another that uses `QRunnable` which is shown in the second subsection. In both cases we will show the `convertFiles()` method and the supporting infrastructure methods.

Using QtConcurrent::run()

The QtConcurrent::run() function takes a function, and optionally one or more arguments to pass to the function, and executes the function in a secondary thread from Qt's global thread pool. Its signature is

```
QFuture<T> run(Function, ...)
```

The Function must be a pointer to a function (or functor) that returns an object of type T. The ellipsis (...) indicates a variable argument list (i.e., zero or more additional arguments). If present, these arguments are passed to the Function when it is called by QtConcurrent, so if any of these arguments are passed, they must match the Function's signature.

Now we'll return to the image2image application and see an example of how QtConcurrent::run() is called in practice.

```
void MainWindow::convertFiles(const QStringList &sourceFiles)
{
    stopped = false;
    updateUi();
    total = sourceFiles.count();
    done = 0;
    const QVector<int> sizes = AQP::chunkSizes(sourceFiles.count(),
            QThread::idealThreadCount());

    int offset = 0;
    foreach (const int chunkSize, sizes) {
        QtConcurrent::run(convertImages, this, &stopped,
                sourceFiles.mid(offset, chunkSize),
                targetTypeComboBox->currentText());
        offset += chunkSize;
    }
    checkIfDone();
}
```

We begin by setting the stopped variable to false and then calling the update-Ui() method (not shown) to change the Convert button to a Cancel button by changing its text. We then set the total variable to the number of files in the list, and the done variable to 0, since none have been converted yet.

We could create a function to convert a single image file and call QtConcurrent::run() with the function and a filename once for each file we have to process, potentially creating as many secondary threads as there are files in the list. For a few very large files such an approach might make sense, but for lots of files no matter what their sizes, the setup costs of creating so many threads (especially on Windows) are likely to be out of all proportion to the potential savings of spreading the work over secondary threads.

Fortunately, the number of secondary threads that is best for the machine the program is running on—taking account of the operating system and the number of processors and cores the machine has—is provided by the QThread:: idealThreadCount() method. This might return a value of 1 for a single processor, single core machine, and higher numbers for machines with more processors and cores. The number is unlikely to exactly match the number of files we have to process, so we need to divide up the work so that each secondary thread (assuming more than one is used) gets as equal a number of files to process as possible. (Of course, dividing the work by the number of files may not be the best approach in all cases—for example, if we had a list of twenty files where the first ten files were very large and the last ten files were very small.)

To spread the load over the most appropriate number of secondary threads we begin by calling the custom AQP::chunkSizes() function (not shown, but included in the book's source code in the aqp.{hpp,cpp} module) which given the number of items in a container (here, the number of files), and the number of chunks we want (here, the ideal number of secondary threads), returns a vector of chunk sizes that sum to the number of items and that have the most equal numbers possible. For example, given a list of 97 items, with a number of chunks of 1 (one secondary thread) we would get the vector [97]; with a number of chunks of 2 we would get the vector [49, 48]; with 3 we'd get [33, 32, 32]; and so on.

Once we have the vector of chunk sizes, we iterate over it (just once if the ideal thread count is 1 since then there will be only one chunk size), and for each one we call QtConcurrent::run(). We pass five arguments: the convertImages() function (this is the function that will be run), and four other arguments that will be passed to convertImages() when it is called. These remaining arguments are a pointer to the main window (this) which we need for communicating progress, a pointer to the volatile stopped Boolean so that we can see if processing has been canceled, a unique list of files taken from the full list, and the target file type's suffix. Each call to QtConcurrent::run() is non-blocking, and once made, the convertImages() function is called in a secondary thread with the arguments intended for it.★

The QStringList::mid() method (actually, QList<T>::mid()) takes an *offset* and optionally a *count* and returns a sublist of *count* items from the *offset*—or of all items from the *offset* if *offset* + *count* is greater than the number of items, or if *count* isn't specified.

Once all the secondary threads have been started up, we call the checkIfDone() slot (which we will review shortly), which polls to see if processing has fin-

---

★As we noted earlier (247 ◄), using volatile bool is safe across threads, but this technique does *not* work with other datatypes.

ished. The `QtConcurrent::run()` function returns a `QFuture<T>` which if given to a `QFutureWatcher<T>` can be used to detect when the secondary thread has finished. We'll see how to handle `QFuture<T>`s returned by `QtConcurrent` functions in the next section, but here we prefer to ignore `QtConcurrent::run()`'s return value and poll, purely to show an example that uses polling.

```cpp
void convertImages(QObject *receiver, volatile bool *stopped,
        const QStringList &sourceFiles, const QString &targetType)
{
    foreach (const QString &source, sourceFiles) {
        if (*stopped)
            return;
        QImage image(source);
        QString target(source);
        target.chop(QFileInfo(source).suffix().length());
        target += targetType.toLower();
        if (*stopped)
            return;
        bool saved = image.save(target);

        QString message = saved
                ? QObject::tr("Saved '%1'")
                            .arg(QDir::toNativeSeparators(target))
                : QObject::tr("Failed to convert '%1'")
                            .arg(QDir::toNativeSeparators(source));
        QApplication::postEvent(receiver,
                            new ProgressEvent(saved, message));
    }
}
```

This function is called in one or more secondary threads, each time with its own unique list of files to process. Just before each expensive operation (loading and saving an image file), it checks to see if the user has canceled—if they have, the function returns and the thread it is executing in becomes inactive.

The processing itself is straightforward: for each image file in the list, we create a `QImage` object (the constructor reads in the given image file), then create a suitable name for the target image, and then save the image using the target's name. The `QImage::save()` method returns a simple success/failure Boolean flag.

The `QDir::toNativeSeparators()` static method takes a path or path and filename string and returns a string with directories separated by `QDir::separator()` (e.g., "\" on Windows and "/" on Unix-like systems). In source code, it is usually more convenient to use "/"s since these don't need to be escaped in strings and Qt understands them no matter what the underlying platform. But when we want to show paths to the user, it is best to present them in the form that is correct for the platform the application is running on.

We want to notify the user of progress for each file that is processed. The easiest and best way to do this is to invoke a slot in the calling widget—something we will see in the next subsection. But here we use the slightly less convenient approach of posting a custom event, just to show how it is done.

We begin by creating a message string, and then we post it, along with the success flag, inside a custom event to the receiver object (in this case the main window). The QApplication::postEvent() method takes ownership of the event, so we don't have to worry about deleting it.

In fact, there are two methods that can be used for sending events: QApplication::sendEvent() and QApplication::postEvent().

The sendEvent() method dispatches the event immediately—but it should be used sparingly, if at all. For example, in threaded programs sendEvent() makes the event handling occur in the sender's thread rather than in the receiver's thread. Also, no event compression or reordering can be done—for example, multiple paint events cannot be compressed into one. And sendEvent() doesn't delete the event, so the practice is to create events for sendEvent() on the stack.

The postEvent() method adds the event—which should be created on the heap using new—to the receiver's event queue so that it gets processed as part of the receiver's event loop processing. This is the technique that should normally be used, since it cooperates nicely with Qt's event processing.

In either case, we don't have to concern ourselves with the fact that the event goes from one thread to another—Qt seamlessly handles that for us.

```
struct ProgressEvent : public QEvent
{
    enum {EventId = QEvent::User};

    explicit ProgressEvent(bool saved_, const QString &message_)
        : QEvent(static_cast<Type>(EventId)),
          saved(saved_), message(message_) {}

    const bool saved;
    const QString message;
};
```

Here is the complete definition of the custom ProgressEvent. It is important to give every custom event a unique ID (QEvent::User, QEvent::User + 1, etc.) of type QEvent::Type, to avoid one event being mistaken for another. We have made the event a struct and left the Boolean saved flag and the message text publicly accessible.

```
bool MainWindow::event(QEvent *event)
{
    if (!stopped && event->type() ==
            static_cast<QEvent::Type>(ProgressEvent::EventId)) {
        ProgressEvent *progressEvent =
                static_cast<ProgressEvent*>(event);
        Q_ASSERT(progressEvent);
        logEdit->appendPlainText(progressEvent->message);
        if (progressEvent->saved)
            ++done;
        return true;
    }
    return QMainWindow::event(event);
}
```

We must reimplement QWidget::event() if we want to be able to detect and
process custom events in a particular widget. Here, if processing is ongoing
(i.e., hasn't been canceled), and we get a custom ProgressEvent, we append the
event's message text to the QPlainTextEdit log, and if the save was successful,
increment the count of files that have been done. We also return true to indicate that we have handled the event so that Qt will delete the event rather
than looking for another event handler to process it. But if the processing has
stopped, and for any other events, we pass the work on to the base class event
handler.

```
const int PollTimeout = 100;

void MainWindow::checkIfDone()
{
    if (QThreadPool::globalInstance()->activeThreadCount())
        QTimer::singleShot(PollTimeout, this, SLOT(checkIfDone()));
    else {
        QString message;
        if (done == total)
            message = tr("All %n image(s) converted", "", done);
        else
            message = tr("Converted %n/%1 image(s)", "", done)
                        .arg(total);
        logEdit->appendPlainText(message);
        stopped = true;
        updateUi();
    }
}
```

This slot is called at the end of the convertFiles() slot to initiate polling. (The
QObject::tr() usage is discussed later in the "Using the Three-Argument Form

of tr()" sidebar; ➤ 276.) We could have used a custom event or invoked a signal whenever a convertImages() function finished, but we would still have to check the active thread count to see if they had all finished, so there would be no real advantage over polling. An alternative approach is to keep the QFuture<T>s returned by the QtConcurrent::run() calls, and use QFutureWatcher<T>s to notify us when each secondary thread has finished—we will see how to use this approach in this chapter's second section.

Here, we begin by seeing if any of the secondary threads are running. If any are, we create a single shot timer and call this slot in 100 milliseconds time. Otherwise, they have all finished, so we append a suitable message to the log, reset the stopped variable (which will already be true if they finished due to the user canceling), and update the user interface (i.e., change the Cancel button's text to Convert).

```
void MainWindow::closeEvent(QCloseEvent *event)
{
    stopped = true;
    if (QThreadPool::globalInstance()->activeThreadCount())
        QThreadPool::globalInstance()->waitForDone();
    event->accept();
}
```

To achieve a safe cleanup, for multithreaded programs it is best to stop all secondary threads before terminating the application. We have done this by reimplementing the application's closeEvent(), and making sure that any active threads have finished before allowing the termination to proceed.

Using QRunnable

An alternative to using QtConcurrent::run() is to create a QRunnable subclass and execute it in a thread from Qt's global thread pool. In this subsection we will look at an alternative implementation of the previous subsection's convertFiles() method, along with the necessary supporting methods, to see how this is done.

```
void MainWindow::convertFiles(const QStringList &sourceFiles)
{
    stopped = false;
    updateUi();
    total = sourceFiles.count();
    done = 0;
    const QVector<int> sizes = AQP::chunkSizes(sourceFiles.count(),
            QThread::idealThreadCount());

    int offset = 0;
```

```
    foreach (const int chunkSize, sizes) {
        ConvertImageTask *convertImageTask = new ConvertImageTask(
                this, &stopped, sourceFiles.mid(offset, chunkSize),
                targetTypeComboBox->currentText());
        QThreadPool::globalInstance()->start(convertImageTask);
        offset += chunkSize;
    }
    checkIfDone();
}
```

This version of the convertFiles() method is structurally identical to the one
we saw earlier (252 ◄). The key difference is that for each chunk of files we
want to process we create a ConvertImageTask object (a QRunnable subclass) to
do the processing. (And we give the object exactly the same arguments as we
gave QtConcurrent::run() to pass on to the convertImages() function.) Once the
runnable is created we call QThreadPool::start() on it—this gives ownership of
the runnable to Qt's global thread pool and starts it running.

The thread pool will delete the runnable when it has finished, which is what
we want here. We can prevent this behavior by calling QRunnable::setAuto-
Delete(false), in which case we must take responsibility for deleting the
runnable ourselves.

```
class ConvertImageTask : public QRunnable
{
public:
    explicit ConvertImageTask(QObject *receiver,
            volatile bool *stopped, const QStringList &sourceFiles,
            const QString &targetType)
        : m_receiver(receiver), m_stopped(stopped),
          m_sourceFiles(sourceFiles),
          m_targetType(targetType.toLower()) {}

private:
    void run();
    ...
}
```

Here is the ConvertImageTask's definition, apart from the private member data
which we've omitted. By making its run() method private, we prevent the class
from being subclassed, but also prevent run() from being called on instances
(since run() should be called only by QThreadPool::start()).

```
void ConvertImageTask::run()
{
    foreach (const QString &source, m_sourceFiles) {
        if (*m_stopped)
            return;
```

```
            QImage image(source);
            QString target(source);
            target.chop(QFileInfo(source).suffix().length());
            target += m_targetType;
            if (*m_stopped)
                return;
            bool saved = image.save(target);

            QString message = saved
                    ? QObject::tr("Saved '%1'")
                                  .arg(QDir::toNativeSeparators(target))
                    : QObject::tr("Failed to convert '%1'")
                                  .arg(QDir::toNativeSeparators(source));
            QMetaObject::invokeMethod(m_receiver, "announceProgress",
                    Qt::QueuedConnection, Q_ARG(bool, saved),
                    Q_ARG(QString, message));
        }
    }
```

This method is structurally identical to the convertImages() function we saw earlier (253 ◄). The only difference is that instead of communicating progress using a custom event, we do so by invoking a slot in the main window (Main-Window::announceProgress()).

Since QRunnable is not a QObject subclass, it has no built-in support for signals and slots. One solution would be to multiply inherit both QObject and QRunnable, but if we wanted to do that we would be better off simply creating a QThread subclass since that is a QObject subclass and has several useful built-in signals and slots as standard. Another solution is to use custom events as we did in the previous subsection.

Here we have chosen to simply invoke a slot using the QMetaObject::invoke-Method() method. This method takes a receiver, the name of a slot to call, the type of connection (Qt::QueuedConnection is best for secondary threads since it uses the event queue just like QApplication::postEvent()), and the arguments to send. Each argument must be specified using Qt's Q_ARG macro which takes a type and a value. The QMetaObject::invokeMethod() method can pass up to nine arguments, and can also specify a return value, although using the return value only makes sense if the Qt::DirectConnection connection is used.

Since the slot invocation is put on the main (GUI) event queue, the slot execution takes place in the GUI thread, not in the secondary thread that called QMetaObject::invokeMethod(). This is also true of signals that are emitted in a secondary thread since behind the scenes Qt turns signals from secondary threads into events.

Some programmers consider using QMetaObject::invokeMethod() to be better style than sending a custom event since it works seamlessly with Qt's signals and slots mechanism and doesn't require the creation of a custom QEvent subclass or the reimplementation of QWidget::event() in the widgets the event will be sent to. Under the hood, signals and slots that cross threads are actually implemented using Qt's event mechanism, but we don't have to know or care about that to use QMetaObject::invokeMethod() and to enjoy the convenience of invoking methods rather than creating custom events.

```
void MainWindow::announceProgress(bool saved, const QString &message)
{
    if (stopped)
        return;
    logEdit->appendPlainText(message);
    if (saved)
        ++done;
}
```

This method appends the given message to the log and updates the number of files that have been done if the save was successful—or does nothing if the processing has stopped.

The rest of the infrastructure needed to support the ConvertImageTask QRunnable is the same as was needed for QtConcurrent::run(): polling to see if all the processing has finished using the checkIfDone() slot (256 ◄), and making sure that all the secondary threads are finished when the user terminates the application by reimplementing the closeEvent() (257 ◄).

Although we used custom events for communicating progress in the Qt-Concurrent::run() version and slot invocation in the QRunnable version, we could have used custom events for both, or slot invocation for both. In general, it is best to use slot invocation since it is more convenient and requires less code. For QRunnables we can monitor progress using polling as we have done here, but for QtConcurrent::run() we can either use polling or a QFutureWatcher<T> (QFuture<T> and QFutureWatcher<T> are covered in the next section).

The key difference between QtConcurrent::run() and QRunnable is that Qt-Concurrent::run() returns a QFuture<T>—this provides a means of keeping track of (and controlling) the processing's progress, and is something we will cover in the next section when we look at other QtConcurrent functions that return QFuture<T>s. Compare this with a QRunnable, where we must build in the functionality for monitoring and controlling progress ourselves.

Using QtConcurrent::run() or QRunnable is particularly useful when we have a lot of secondary processing to do, such as the need to process a few large items or, as here, the need to process lots of items, but doing so in chunks. Sometimes, though, we have to process lots of items where it isn't convenient to handle them in chunks. For such situations, Qt provides other QtConcurrent functions, as we will see in the next section.

Filtering and Mapping in Threads

The functions in the QtConcurrent namespace are ideal for situations where we have lots of data items that we want to process in the same way. For small numbers of items (say, fewer than five per core) we could create a function for QtConcurrent::run(), or a QRunnable, or a QThread to process each one. But when we have lots of items—perhaps even hundreds or thousands of items or more—then creating a thread for each one would probably involve such a massive overhead as to make processing the data sequentially much faster. As we saw in the previous section, one solution is to create just a few secondary threads and have each one process a group of items. But in some cases we really want each item to be processed individually, and QtConcurrent has functions to support this.

The functions offered by the *QtConcurrent* module are of four kinds: filters, mappers, reducers—all of which we cover in this section—and a run function that we covered in the previous section. The use case for filters, mappers, and reducers is to give them a collection of items to process—and to leave it up to Qt to distribute the work and perform the processing in its global thread pool's secondary threads.

The filtering and mapping concepts come from functional programming. In that context a filter is a higher-order function (i.e., a function that takes a function as one of its arguments) that given a sequence and a filter function returns a new sequence of those items for which the filter function returned true. And a mapper is a function that takes a sequence and a map function and returns a new sequence where each of the new items is produced by applying the map function to the corresponding item in the input sequence.

The QtConcurrent filters and mappers closely follow the functional programming approach. So, in QtConcurrent, filters take a sequence of items and a filter function and produce a new sequence that contains only those items from the original sequence that the filter function returns true for. This means that the resultant sequence could have no items, just some of the original items, or all of the original items. Conceptually a filter works like this:

```
QList<Item> filter(QList<Item> items, FilterFunction isOK)
{
    QList<Item> results;
    foreach (Item item, items)
        if (isOK(item))
            results << item;
    return results;
}
```

Although we have used a QList, any sequential container—or part of a container specified by using begin and end iterators—can be used for the items to be filtered, and any sequential container can be used for the results.

Mappers (not to be confused with the QMap container class!) take a sequence of items and a map function and produce a new sequence with exactly the same number of items (possibly of a different type from the original items) where each item in the original sequence has had the map function applied to it to produce an item in the result sequence. Conceptually a mapper works like this:

```
QList<Type2> mapper(QList<Type1> items, MapFunction map)
{
    QList<Type2> results;
    foreach (Type1 item, items)
        results << map(item);
    return results;
}
```

Here Type1 and Type2 could be the same type or different types—all that matters is that the map function accepts an item of type Type1 and returns an item of type Type2.

Reducers take a sequence of items and reduce them to a single item. For example, we might have a sequence of numbers and want to compute their sum or mean (average). The QtConcurrent namespace has functions that combine filtering with reducing and mapping with reducing. Conceptually, they work like this:

```
// Filter-Reduce                      // Map-Reduce
ResultType result;                    ResultType result;
foreach (Item item, items)            foreach (Item item, items)
    if (isOK(item))                       result.merge(map(item));
        result.merge(item);
```

Here we've used isOK() as a filter function and map() as a map function. The result object's merge() method takes in each item (or processed item, in the case of map–reduce), and somehow incorporates it into itself. For example:

```
struct ResultType
{
    ResultType() : sum(0) {}
    void merge(int item) { sum += item; }
    int sum;
};
```

If this ResultType were used with a sequence of numbers, after map–reducing (and assuming that the processing function was the identity function, int identity(int x) { return x; }), the sum would be available as result.sum.

Of course, what makes the QtConcurrent functions much more than simple for loops is that rather than process each item sequentially as shown here, they perform their processing in one or more secondary threads so that multiple items can be processed concurrently. What should also be clear is that for lightweight processing the overhead is probably not worthwhile, but for heavy processing, the QtConcurrent functions can improve throughput.

The QtConcurrent namespace provides both blocking and non-blocking (threading) versions of the filtering, mapping, and reducing functions. The blocking versions are suitable for use inside existing secondary threads (i.e., in QRunnable or QThread subclasses), or where we simply want the function's behavior and don't care about blocking. It is the non-blocking versions that we will consider in this chapter.

At the time of this writing, Qt's documentation indicates that no locking is required when using the QtConcurrent functions. This is true when processing independent data items that don't affect anything else. But what we cannot do is process the items in a model or a graphics scene, because Qt does not provide a means of locking models, scenes, or the items they contain. This can be solved by serially creating our own surrogate items, concurrently processing them, and then serially updating the model or scene—providing, of course, that the overhead is outweighed by the advantage of processing the items in parallel.

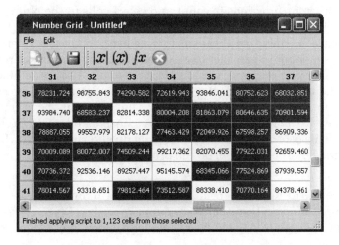

Figure 7.2 *The Number Grid application*

In this section we will review the Number Grid example (numbergrid). This program presents a grid of numbers, and is shown in Figure 7.2. We can generate an initial set of predefined or random numbers, and we can dynamically populate or change the grid's contents by creating a JavaScript script and executing it. (The script we create is called once for every cell and has predefined variables for the cell's value, row, and column.)

We have decided to perform all the number grid processing in secondary threads. To do this, whenever we want to process items, we must serially create a surrogate item for each model item we want to process, then give the surrogate items to a QtConcurrent function to process concurrently, and finally, serially iterate over the resultant surrogate items updating the model items as we go. By using independent surrogate items we avoid any requirement to lock the model, the view, or the model's items (none of which are possible anyway).

When it comes to applying a user-defined JavaScript script to items, although the steps are the same as those just described, we also want to keep track of how many errors occurred and also of the (unique) error messages. This requires that all the secondary threads be able to update the count and the error messages, and so for this aspect, we will need to use locking. As we will see, we will abstract all the locking details away in a small class, so that the client code can access the count and error messages without having to do any explicit locking itself.

The Number Grid uses QtConcurrent namespace functions to filter, filter and reduce, and to map. In particular, it uses filtering to select all the cells in the grid that meet certain criteria; filtering and reducing to count the number of cells that meet certain criteria; and mapping to apply a JavaScript script to every cell (or every selected cell) in the grid.

Using QtConcurrent functions to count and select cells in the Number Grid example is probably slower than counting and selecting them directly, since these operations are so cheap, so these particular uses should be taken merely as illustrations of how to use the QtConcurrent filtering and filter–reduce functions. However, the mapping usage where we apply a script to all or just the selected cells may well run faster using QtConcurrent than if we applied the script sequentially to each relevant cell. The potential speed improvement is more likely if the per-cell processing is expensive and a lot of cells must be processed. This is because the cost of setting up and running the threads may be outweighed by the ability to do the processing for two or more cells concurrently.

The Number Grid application is a conventional main-window-style C++/Qt application. It offers a traditional File menu with New, Open..., Save, Save As..., and Quit options. We won't look at any of these, since they are all standard.

The Edit menu has the options Count..., Select..., Apply Script, and Stop, all of which make use of QtConcurrent functions. If the user chooses to count or select, a dialog is popped up through which they can set the criteria to apply. For counting the user can specify a numeric relational operator ("<", "<=", "=>", ">", and

"~="—approximately equal), and a numerical amount, and whether to count all the cells that the criteria are true of or just count among those cells that are selected. For selecting, the user can specify a numeric relational operator and an amount, and these criteria are applied to all of the grid's cells. For applying a script the user is given a dialog where they can enter an arbitrary JavaScript script, and where the global variables cellValue, cellRow, and cellColumn are predefined. They can then choose whether to apply the script to all of the grid's cells, or to only those cells that are selected.

The slots called to perform the edit actions are editCount(), editSelect(), and editApplyScript(). We will review each of these in turn, followed by those classes, methods, or functions the slots make use of, so that we can build up a complete picture of how to use the QtConcurrent functions. Although the data processed by QtConcurrent functions should all be independent, in one case we do in fact use a QMutex to allow us to access some shared data. Before we look at the slots themselves, here is an extract from the main window's definition in the header file, showing some of its private data:

```
QStandardItemModel *model;
QFutureWatcher<SurrogateItem> selectWatcher;
QFutureWatcher<Results> countWatcher;
QFutureWatcher<SurrogateItem> applyScriptWatcher;
MatchCriteria countCriteria;
bool applyToAll;
mutable bool cacheIsDirty;
QString script;
ThreadSafeErrorInfo errorInfo;
```

We assume that the QStandardItemModel is familiar—this is used as a tabular model to hold all of the grid's numbers in a QStandardItem subclass which stores them as doubles in the Qt::EditRole. (Qt's table models were covered in Chapter 3.)

As we will see further on, when a non-blocking (threaded) QtConcurrent function is called, it immediately returns a QFuture<T> which represents the result of the computation. However, the returned QFuture<T> is not normally of any use—at least not straightaway—because the computation has only just been started. In fact, if we attempt to access a QFuture<T> before the computation is finished, the access will block until the computation has completed, which isn't normally what we want to happen. Once the computation is finished, the QFuture<T> will hold the expected result (in the case of reducing) or results (in the case of filtering and mapping).

The normal pattern of use with the non-blocking QtConcurrent functions is to give the returned QFuture<T> to a QFutureWatcher<T>. A future watcher keeps track of the QtConcurrent function's progress and emits signals indicating which result or results are ready (in the case of filtering and mapping which produce a sequence of results), and when the computation has finished (or been paused, resumed, or canceled). Future watchers also provide an API through which we can control the behavior of the QtConcurrent function—for example, using pause(), resume(), and cancel().

Notice that although filtering and mapping produce sequences of results, the type T used in QFuture<T> is always the type of a single result item, and the type T used in QFutureWatcher<T> must always be the same as the one used by the future being watched.

Here we have one future watcher for each QtConcurrent operation the application supports. For selecting cells and applying a script to cells in the grid we have a QFutureWatcher<SurrogateItem>—recall that we cannot concurrently process items in a model directly since we cannot lock a model or its items, so we must use surrogates instead, as we will see further on. For counting we have a QFutureWatcher<Results>; Results is a simple struct that is used to hold a count and a total value, as we will see later.

For both counting and selecting we let the user set criteria to specify which cells should be counted or selected. Here is the definition of the MatchCriteria structure and the enum it uses:

```
enum ComparisonType {LessThan, LessThanOrEqual, GreaterThan,
                     GreaterThanOrEqual, ApproximatelyEqual};

struct MatchCriteria
{
    ComparisonType comparisonType;
    double value;
    bool applyToAll;
};
```

The private member data declares countCriteria of type MatchCriteria to hold the criteria used for counting. For selecting and applying a script the criteria are held inside the SurrogateItems, as we will see later. When selecting, the applyToAll Boolean is ignored.

There is also a MainWindow::applyToAll Boolean member variable; if true then the counting or applying of a script is applied to all of the grid's cells, otherwise to only those cells that are selected.

The cacheIsDirty Boolean is used to keep track of whether the grid's data has changed. It is mutable so that we can use it inside const methods. We will see it in use later on.

The script string holds the JavaScript that will be executed on every cell (or every selected cell) if the user chooses the Apply Script... option. When executing the script, it is possible that an error will occur. We don't want to pop up a warning message box for every single error, because we could be processing hundreds or thousands of cells with an error occurring for each one. So instead, we simply keep a count of the number of errors that have occurred and a list of the unique error messages. Since the error count and error messages must be updatable from any of the threads that the QtConcurrent functions use, we need to provide a locking mechanism to serialize access to them, to ensure that only one thread is allowed to update the error count and error messages at any one time.

One approach to serializing access to the error information would be to create three variables, say, int *errorCount*, QStringList *errorMessages*, and QMutex *errorMutex*. Then, whenever we needed to access the error information we would have to lock the mutex. Such an approach means that we must do all the bookkeeping ourselves. We have chosen a different approach and created a ThreadSafeErrorInfo class. This class provides methods for reading the error information and for updating it, and internally has its own mutex and does its own locking. This means that users of the class's instances don't have to worry about locking, since that is handled automatically. Here is an extract from the ThreadSafeErrorInfo's definition:

```
class ThreadSafeErrorInfo
{
public:
    explicit ThreadSafeErrorInfo() : m_count(0) {}
    ...
private:
    mutable QMutex mutex;
    int m_count;
    QSet<QString> m_errors;
};
```

Superficially, the class is little more than a struct holding the two items of data we are interested in plus a mutex. We'll look at a few of its methods to see how the mutex is used.

```
QStringList errors() const
{
    QMutexLocker locker(&mutex);
    return QStringList::fromSet(m_errors);
}
```

The QMutexLocker takes a pointer to a mutex and blocks until it can lock the mutex. It releases the lock when it goes out of scope. The QList<T>::fromSet() static method produces a list from a set.

The ThreadSafeErrorInfo class also has a count() method that returns the number of error messages that occurred (including duplicates) and an isEmpty() method that returns true if the error count is 0: both these have exactly the same structure as the errors() method (and so are not shown).

```
void add(const QString &error)
{
    QMutexLocker locker(&mutex);
    ++m_count;
    m_errors << error;
}
```

This method increments the count of error messages and adds the new message to the set of messages. Since the messages are held in a set, if we try to add a duplicate message, it is silently discarded.

An alternative approach would be to store the messages in a QStringList and inside the errors() method, copy the list, call QStringList::removeDuplicates() on the copy, and then return the copy. However, this would mean that we might end up holding thousands or tens of thousands of duplicate error messages in memory, rather than just the unique ones held by the m_errors set.

```
void clear()
{
    QMutexLocker locker(&mutex);
    m_count = 0;
    m_errors.clear();
}
```

This method is used to clear the data, for example, ready for a new QtConcurrent function to be called.

Using a QMutex works fine for the ThreadSafeErrorInfo class—but is it the most efficient locking class to use in this situation? When we lock a mutex, we prevent *any* other access, including read-only access. In the ThreadSafeErrorInfo class we have some methods that need only read access, and others that need write access, so potentially, if no thread was writing, we could allow several threads to use the read access methods concurrently without any problem.

To distinguish between read and write accesses we would need to replace the QMutex with a QReadWriteLock. Then, in the read access methods (count(), errors(), and isEmpty()), we would use a QReadLocker, and in the write access methods (add() and clear()), we would use a QWriteLocker. We'll see an example of using a QReadWriteLock later on (➤ 304). So, although in this particular example, if only one secondary thread is used (e.g., on a single processor, single core machine), using a QMutex rather than a QReadWriteLock doesn't make any difference, on a machine with an ideal thread count greater than one, using a QReadWriteLock should improve performance—at least, in theory.

A class whose instances provide their own locking mechanism such as Thread-SafeErrorInfo and ThreadSafeHash (a class we'll see later on) is called a *monitor*. To avoid deadlock, a monitor method whose code is within the scope of a lock should not call another one of its methods that locks. And, of course, every lock that is applied in a monitor method must be unlocked before the method returns—a condition that is easy to achieve using Qt's QMutexLocker (or QRead-Locker or QWriteLocker).*

Now that we've had a brief introduction to the private member data, we will turn our attention to the general usage pattern for the QtConcurrent functions. We begin by calling a QtConcurrent function (e.g., filtered(), mapped(), filtered-Reduced(), or mappedReduced()), and store the returned QFuture<T> in a variable. Next, we call QFutureWatcher<T>::setFuture(), passing it the QFuture<T> as its argument. We can keep track of progress by connecting to the future watcher's signals, but at the least, we should connect to the finished() signal so that we know when processing is complete so that we can then access the results. This pattern is illustrated in Figure 7.3.

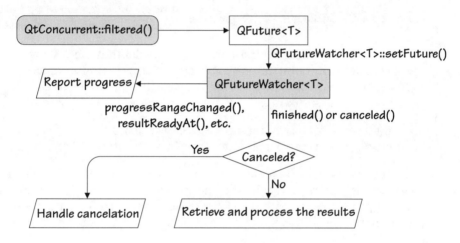

Figure 7.3 *Using QFutureWatcher*

The three future watchers used by the Number Grid application are all private member variables, and for all of them we initially create two signal–slot connections.

```
connect(editStopAction, SIGNAL(triggered()),
        &selectWatcher, SLOT(cancel()));
connect(&selectWatcher, SIGNAL(finished()),
        this, SLOT(finishedSelecting()));
```

Here are the initial connections for the selectWatcher—the same connections are used for the countWatcher and for the applyScriptWatcher, except that for them their finished() signals are connected to the finishedCounting() and finishedApplyingScript() slots.

---

* For a more detailed introduction to creating monitors, see the two-part *Qt Quarterly* article "Monitors and Wait Conditions in Qt" (qt.nokia.com/doc/qq/qq21-monitors.html).

The user interface provides a Stop menu option and toolbar button, so the user can cancel a long-running operation if they want to. To cater for this we connect the stop action to the future watcher's cancel() slot. Whether a concurrent computation finishes normally or as the result of being canceled, the finished() signal is always emitted.

We will see shortly that we also make additional connections whenever the future watcher is given a future to watch, so that we can show progress to the user using a progress bar that is superimposed on the status bar during processing.

In the following subsections we will look at how to filter, reduce, and map, using QtConcurrent functions, focusing mostly on the QtConcurrent-related code.

Using QtConcurrent to Filter

One way of processing all those items in a model that meet some criteria set programmatically or by the user is to use a QtConcurrent filter function. Several filter functions are provided, but the one we will use is QtConcurrent::filtered() which has these signatures:

```
QFuture<T> filtered(Sequence, FilterFunction)
QFuture<T> filtered(ConstIterator, ConstIterator, FilterFunction)
```

The Sequence is an iterable collection of items such as a QList<T> or a QVector<T>. The ConstIterators are begin and end iterators that identify a start point and an end point in a Sequence. The FilterFunction is used to identify which items to put in the result and which to drop. It must have the following signature:

```
bool filterFunction(const T&)
```

The type T must be the same type of item that is stored in the Sequence (and the same type that is used for the QFuture<T>). This function must return true for items that should be put in the results and false for those that should be dropped.

Since we cannot apply a QtConcurrent function directly to the items in a model, we must use the three-step process described earlier: first, create a sequence of surrogate items, each one corresponding to an item in the model; second, apply the QtConcurrent filter function, giving it the criteria, to the sequence of surrogate items—this produces a new sequence of those surrogate items that meet the criteria; and third, iterate over the result sequence of surrogate items, and for each one update the equivalent model item accordingly.

In the case of the Number Grid, we want to use filtering to select all those items in the model that match the user's criteria—for example, to select all the cells that have a value less than 3 250. To do this we need surrogate items—here is the complete SurrogateItem class:

```
struct SurrogateItem
{
    explicit SurrogateItem(int row_=0, int column_=0,
                           double value_=0.0)
        : row(row_), column(column_), value(value_) {}

    int row;
    int column;
    double value;
};
```

The class is trivial, but nonetheless essential. We will now look at how the three steps described above are done in practice, starting with the editSelect() slot that is invoked when the user chooses the Select... option.

```
void MainWindow::editSelect()
{
    MatchForm matchForm(MatchForm::Select, this);
    if (matchForm.exec()) {
        MatchCriteria matchCriteria = matchForm.result();
        stop();
        view->setEditTriggers(QAbstractItemView::NoEditTriggers);
        QList<SurrogateItem> items = allSurrogateItems();
        QFuture<SurrogateItem> future = QtConcurrent::filtered(items,
                SurrogateItemMatcher(matchCriteria));
        selectWatcher.setFuture(future);
        setUpProgressBar(selectWatcher);
        editStopAction->setEnabled(true);
    }
}
```

First we pop up a MatchForm dialog (not shown) to get the user's match criteria, that is, which comparison operator and numeric value they want to use. If they click OK we retrieve the match criteria and start off the selection process (we saw the MatchCriteria class earlier; 266 ◄). We begin by stopping any selection, count, or script applying that is in progress. Then we make the view read-only since we don't want the user to change any values during processing because that could invalidate the computation. Next we retrieve a list of surrogate items, one for each cell in the grid.

Once we have the surrogate items ready for processing we call the QtConcurrent function, in this case the non-blocking QtConcurrent::filtered() function, passing it the sequence of items to process and a filter function. The filter function is actually a functor (an instance of a class that implements operator()(), which we will review shortly). The filter function (or functor's operator()()) is called once for every item and must return true for those items that should go in the results, and false for those items that should be discarded.

The QtConcurrent::filtered() function immediately returns a QFuture<T>, and begins to perform its processing in one or more secondary threads, leaving the method it was called from to continue processing. We set the returned QFuture<SurrogateItem> as the future for the selectWatcher (of type QFuture-Watcher<SurrogateItem>); this will report progress and also provide a means of interacting with the processing—for example, to pause, resume, or stop it.

At the end we set up a progress bar to show the progress of the processing, and enable a Stop action (which has a corresponding menu option and toolbar button), so that the user can stop the processing at any time. In this case we have not provided the ability to pause and resume, but doing so is conceptually no different from providing the ability to stop the processing.

```
void MainWindow::stop()
{
    editStopAction->setEnabled(false);
    if (selectWatcher.isRunning())
        selectWatcher.cancel();
    ...
    if (selectWatcher.isRunning())
        selectWatcher.waitForFinished();
    ...
    editStopAction->setEnabled(false);
}
```

If the user invokes the Stop action this method is called. We have shown the code applicable in all cases (the first and last lines), but only the parts relevant to the selectWatcher regarding the future watchers since the same code is also present for the countWatcher and for the applyScriptWatcher. We begin by disabling the Stop action to give the user immediate feedback that we are stopping. Stopping is a two-step process: first we cancel the processing; and second we call QFutureWatcher<T>::waitForFinished() (which blocks) to make sure that the processing really has stopped before we continue.

The approach used here, that is, telling each secondary thread in turn to stop, and then waiting on each one in turn, works perfectly well in this case because we know that only one secondary thread (selecting, counting, or script applying) is ever active at a time. But in situations where two or more secondary threads could be executing, this approach means that we wait for the sum of the stopping times (since we wait for each one in turn linearly). Later on we will see how to stop multiple secondary threads with a stopping time pretty close to that of the slowest stopping thread (➤ 293).

```
const QList<SurrogateItem> MainWindow::allSurrogateItems() const
{
    static QList<SurrogateItem> items;
    if (cacheIsDirty) {
        items.clear();
        for (int row = 0; row < model->rowCount(); ++row) {
            for (int column = 0; column < model->columnCount();
                 ++column) {
                double value = model->item(row, column)->
                        data(Qt::EditRole).toDouble();
                items << SurrogateItem(row, column, value);
            }
        }
        cacheIsDirty = false;
    }
    return items;
}
```

This method is used to create a list of surrogate items, one for each cell in the grid. Although the list we return could have tens of thousands of items, thanks to Qt's widespread use of copy-on-write, only a pointer or so's worth of data is actually returned from the method.

We further improve the method's performance by making the list static to cache the items between calls—at some cost in memory—and only updating the list if the grid has changed. (The cacheIsDirty Boolean is set to true whenever the model emits a dataChanged() signal thanks to a signal–slot connection that isn't shown.)

```
void MainWindow::setUpProgressBar(QFutureWatcher<T> &futureWatcher)
{
    progressBar->setRange(futureWatcher.progressMinimum(),
                          futureWatcher.progressMaximum());
    connect(&futureWatcher, SIGNAL(progressRangeChanged(int,int)),
            progressBar, SLOT(setRange(int,int)));
    connect(&futureWatcher, SIGNAL(progressValueChanged(int)),
            progressBar, SLOT(setValue(int)));
    progressBar->show();
}
```

When processing is started we call this function, and pass it the associated future watcher. The progress bar was created in the constructor, hidden, and added to the status bar. Here we set the progress bar's range to that provided by the future watcher and create a couple of signal–slot connections to ensure that the progress bar's range and value are kept up to date. We must of course show the widget to make it visible—this will cause it to be superimposed over the status bar. We will see when the progress bar is hidden again when we look at the finishedSelecting() method.

Here is the entire SurrogateItemMatcher class:

```
class SurrogateItemMatcher
{
public:
    explicit SurrogateItemMatcher(MatchCriteria matchCriteria_)
        : matchCriteria(matchCriteria_) {}

    typedef bool result_type;

    bool operator()(const SurrogateItem &item)
    {
        switch (matchCriteria.comparisonType) {
            case LessThan:
                return item.value < matchCriteria.value;
            case LessThanOrEqual:
                return item.value <= matchCriteria.value;
            case GreaterThanOrEqual:
                return item.value >= matchCriteria.value;
            case GreaterThan:
                return item.value > matchCriteria.value;
            case ApproximatelyEqual:
                return qFuzzyCompare(item.value, matchCriteria.value);
        }
        Q_ASSERT(false);
        return false;
    }

private:
    MatchCriteria matchCriteria;
};
```

The SurrogateItemMatcher is a class whose instances are functors. To have functor instances, a class must implement the operator()() method. And for a functor to be suitable for use as the "function" passed to a QtConcurrent filter function, it *must* have a public result_type typedef that specifies the result type of the operator()() method.

When we create the functor instance we pass the match criteria to use (which contain the comparison operator and the numeric value) to the constructor.

Whenever an item is filtered, the QtConcurrent::filtered() function calls the functor's operator()() method and passes it the item to be considered. The operator()() method returns a bool depending on whether the item meets the criteria.

For the ApproximatelyEqual (~=) comparison, we use Qt's global qFuzzyCompare() function. This function can compare two floats or doubles for approximate equality (which is the best that can be achieved using standard floating-point representations).

Of course, it is perfectly possible to pass a normal function as a filter function—such a function must accept a const T& (i.e., an item) and must return a bool.

```cpp
void MainWindow::finishedSelecting()
{
    editStopAction->setEnabled(false);
    progressBar->hide();
    if (!selectWatcher.isCanceled()) {
        view->clearSelection();
        QItemSelectionModel *selectionModel = view->selectionModel();
        const QList<SurrogateItem> items = selectWatcher.future()
                                                         .results();
        QListIterator<SurrogateItem> i(items);
        while (i.hasNext()) {
            const SurrogateItem &item = i.next();
            selectionModel->select(
                    model->index(item.row, item.column),
                    QItemSelectionModel::Select);
        }
        statusBar()->showMessage(
                tr("Selected %Ln cell(s)", "", items.count()),
                StatusTimeout);
    }
    view->setEditTriggers(editTriggers);
}
```

When the future watchers were created, each had its finished() signal connected to a corresponding slot, in the case of the selectWatcher to this finished-Selecting() method. So when the filtering process stops—whether because it completed, or was stopped by the user invoking the Stop action—this slot is called.

We begin by disabling the Stop action, since that no longer makes sense, and we hide the progress bar since processing has finished. If the processing was not canceled, we start by clearing any existing selection. Then we iterate over all the surrogate items that were not filtered away (i.e., all those that met the user's selection criteria), and for each one, we select the corresponding item—whose model index is retrieved from the model—in the view, using the view's selection model.

The QObject::tr() call we have used for the status bar message is unusual. Normally, we just use the single argument form. The second argument is a

Using the Three-Argument Form of tr()

The most common uses of QObject::tr() are with one argument—the text to translate—or with two arguments, where the second argument is a string used to disambiguate when the text to translate is the same in two or more places but must be translated differently depending on context.

The three-argument form was introduced in Qt 4.2 and is used when dealing with numbers, and where the third argument is an integer count. When this form is used, the text for translation should contain %n which will be replaced by the count (or %Ln for a localized version of the count, e.g., with grouping commas in the U.S.). For English, it is also useful to add (s) at the end of the word that must be made singular or plural. Without translation, the text will appear pretty well as is, for example, "Selected 1 cell(s)" for a count of 1, which is readable if rather amateur-looking. But if a translation is used, then we can use our own choice of texts for the singular and plural cases.

Qt's translation tools are smart enough to be able to offer translators the opportunity to provide simple singular and plural forms for languages that pluralize like English (such as Dutch, Greek, Hebrew, and Zulu), and more options for those that don't (such as Arabic, Czech, French, Irish, Maori, Polish, and Russian).★

For applications developed in English it may seem strange to have an English translation file but it can often be useful. In the first place almost none of the words need be translated since Qt will default to the original English text if no translation is provided, so we only need to translate the three-argument QObject::tr() calls and can safely leave the rest untranslated. And in addition, if we find typos or other problems with some of our user-visible strings after the application has been deployed, if it has a stand alone .qm file, the erroneous texts can be "translated", in effect replaced, by correct texts simply by sending users a new .qm file.

In the case of the numbergrid application, out of a total of over sixty user-visible strings, we only needed to provide translations for four of them. For example, the text Selected %Ln cell(s) was translated as Selected one cell (singular) and Selected %Ln cells (plural).

string for disambiguation and is not needed here. The third argument is a numeric count, and is discussed in the "Using the Three-Argument Form of tr()" sidebar.

At the end we restore the edit triggers so that the user can once again interact with the cells in the grid. (The edit triggers are of type QAbstractItemView::

★For complete details see the *Qt Quarterly* article "Plural Form(s) in Translation(s)", qt.nokia.com/doc/qq/qq19-plurals.html.

EditTriggers; they were retrieved from the view when it was created, and are held in a member variable.)

We have now seen how to use QtConcurrent::filtered() with a sequence of items and a filter function (in our case a filter functor) to produce a filtered sequence in one or more secondary threads. In the next subsection we will look at how to perform a filter and reduce, and in the subsection after that, at how to map.

Using QtConcurrent to Filter and Reduce

There are several QtConcurrent functions for reducing, including QtConcurrent::mappedReduced(), and the QtConcurrent::filteredReduced() function that we will use in this subsection, and whose signatures are

```
QFuture<T> filteredReduced(Sequence, FilterFunction,
        ReduceFunction, QtConcurrent::ReduceOptions)
QFuture<T> filteredReduced(ConstIterator, ConstIterator,
        FilterFunction, ReduceFunction, QtConcurrent::ReduceOptions)
```

Just as for the QtConcurrent::filtered() function, the Sequence is an iterable collection of items such as a QList<T> or a QVector<T>, and the ConstIterators are begin and end iterators that identify a start point and an end point in a Sequence. Similarly, the FilterFunction is used to identify which items to put in the result and which to drop (we saw its signature earlier; 270 ◄). The ReduceFunction must have the following signature:

```
void reduceFunction(R&, const T&)
```

Strictly speaking the return type doesn't have to be void since it is ignored. The non-const R type is used to accumulate the results; the T type is the same type as the items in the Sequence and in the QFuture<T>.

The QtConcurrent::ReduceOptions is an enum type and in both overloads it has a default value of UnorderedReduce|SequentialReduce, so this argument is optional. The UnorderedReduce part says that items will be processed in whatever order QtConcurrent sees fit—we can force the Sequence's natural order to be respected by using OrderedReduce instead. The SequentialReduce part says that only one thread will enter the ReduceFunction at a time. This means that the reduce function need not be reentrant or thread-safe. (At the time of this writing there is no alternative to this option, although some future version of Qt might support a parallel reduce option which presumably will require a reduce function that is reentrant or thread-safe.)

Filtering and reducing is similar to filtering in that we must pass a Qt-Concurrent function a sequence of items and a function or functor that decides whether an item should be counted. But in addition we must pass a function that can be used as a results accumulator—this could perform some kind of merge of some aspect of each acceptable item, or it could be a simple counter; here we will do both.

Structurally the code for filtering and reducing is just like that for plain filtering: a slot to initiate the process (here, editCount()), and a slot that is called when the processing is finished or canceled (here, finishedCounting()), both of which we will now review, along with their supporting code.

```cpp
void MainWindow::editCount()
{
    MatchForm matchForm(MatchForm::Count, this);
    if (matchForm.exec()) {
        countCriteria = matchForm.result();
        stop();
        view->setEditTriggers(QAbstractItemView::NoEditTriggers);
        applyToAll = countCriteria.applyToAll;
        QList<SurrogateItem> items = applyToAll ? allSurrogateItems()
                                                : selectedSurrogateItems();
        QFuture<Results> future = QtConcurrent::filteredReduced(
                items, SurrogateItemMatcher(countCriteria),
                itemAccumulator);
        countWatcher.setFuture(future);
        setUpProgressBar(countWatcher);
        editStopAction->setEnabled(true);
    }
}
```

When passed a MatchForm::Count argument, the match form allows the user to choose a comparison operator, a value, and also whether the count should be applied to all the items, or only the selected items. If the user clicks OK in the dialog, we retrieve the match criteria (of type MatchCriteria; 266 ◄). Then, just as for the editSelect() slot we saw in the previous subsection, we stop any processing that might still be in progress and make the view read-only.

We note whether the processing should apply to all the items or just to the selected ones in the applyToAll member variable since we will need to know which was chosen when the processing is finished so that we can present an appropriate message. If the user wants to count all the items we retrieve the sequence of surrogate items from the allSurrogateItems() method (272 ◄); otherwise we use the very similar selectedSurrogateItems() method that we will see in a moment. The surrogate items are the same as the ones used before (271◄).

The QtConcurrent::filteredReduced() function takes a sequence of items, a filter function or functor (here again we have used a SurrogateItemMatcher functor; 274 ◄), and an accumulator function, itemAccumulator() (which we will

return to shortly). The call returns immediately with a QFuture<Results>; Results is a custom struct we have created for use by the accumulator function—
we will look at it when we review the accumulator.

The last few lines are almost the same as for the editSelect() slot: we pass the
future to a future watcher, set up the progress bar (273 ◄), and enable the Stop
action so that the user can cancel if they want to.

```cpp
QList<SurrogateItem> MainWindow::selectedSurrogateItems() const
{
    QList<SurrogateItem> items;
    QItemSelectionModel *selectionModel = view->selectionModel();
    for (int row = 0; row < model->rowCount(); ++row) {
        for (int column = 0; column < model->columnCount();
                ++column) {
            QStandardItem *item = model->item(row, column);
            if (selectionModel->isSelected(item->index())) {
                double value = item->data(Qt::EditRole).toDouble();
                items << SurrogateItem(row, column, value);
            }
        }
    }
    return items;
}
```

This method is structurally similar to the allSurrogateItems() method (272 ◄).
The only real differences are that instead of adding a surrogate for every item,
we only add a surrogate for those items that are selected, and we don't cache
the items.

Here, caching would cost us memory with no benefit in speed, since which
items go in the list depends on the selection model's items which are quite
likely to change from one call to the next.

```cpp
struct Results
{
    explicit Results() : count(0), sum(0.0) {}

    int count;
    long double sum;
};
```

This struct is in the main window's header file—it must go (or be included)
there because we use it in the declaration of the count future watcher: QFuture-
Watcher<Results> countWatcher;. The count member is used to keep a count of
the matching items and the sum member is used to accumulate the total value
of the matching items.

```
void itemAccumulator(Results &results, const SurrogateItem &item)
{
    ++results.count;
    results.sum += item.value;
}
```

This function is passed as the penultimate argument to the `QtConcurrent::`
`filteredReduced()` function; we saw its signature earlier (277 ◄). This function
is called for only those items that have been accepted by the filter function or
functor. Here we simply increment the count of items and the sum of their
values. Note that the initial results object (of type `Results` in this example)
is created by Qt, so it is important that we provide a default constructor that
correctly initializes the `struct`'s values.

Accumulating the sum of large numbers of floating-point numbers by adding
them one at a time is simple—and naïve. The potential problem is that sum-
ming two floating-point numbers that have very different magnitudes can lead
to loss of accuracy; that is, if we add a small enough number to a big enough
number the big number will be unchanged and the addition "lost". This can
happen even if all the numbers we start out with are small—if there are
enough of them—since eventually the sum we are accumulating might become
so big that adding more small numbers to it has no effect. There are solutions
to this problem, for example, the Kahan summation algorithm (en.wikipedia.
org/wiki/Kahan_summation_algorithm).

```
void MainWindow::finishedCounting()
{
    editStopAction->setEnabled(false);
    progressBar->hide();
    if (!countWatcher.isCanceled()) {
        Results results = countWatcher.result();
        QString selected(applyToAll ? QString()
                                    : tr(" from those selected"));
        AQP::information(this, tr("Count"),
                tr("A total of %Ln cell(s)%2 are %3 %4.\n"
                    "Their total value is %L5.", "", results.count)
                .arg(selected)
                .arg(comparisonName(countCriteria.comparisonType))
                .arg(countCriteria.value)
                .arg(stringForLongDouble(results.sum)));
    }
    view->setEditTriggers(editTriggers);
}
```

This function is structurally the same as the `finishedSelecting()` method we
saw earlier (275 ◄). The key difference is that instead of retrieving a sequence

of results we retrieve a single result object—this was created for us by Qt and was updated through calls to the accumulator function, one for each item that was accepted by the filter.

The `comparisonName()` function (not shown) simply returns a QString for a given comparison type—for example, given `LessThan`, it returns `"<"`.

Unfortunately, at the time of this writing, there is no `QString::arg()` method that accepts a `long double`, so we have had to create our own function to produce a QString for a given `long double`.

```
QString stringForLongDouble(const long double &x)
{
    const int BUFFER_SIZE = 20;
    char longDouble[BUFFER_SIZE + 1];
    int i = snprintf(longDouble, BUFFER_SIZE, "%.3Lf", x);
    if (i < 0 || i >= BUFFER_SIZE) // Error or truncation
        return QString("#####");
    return QString(longDouble);
}
```

This function uses the `snprintf()` function from the `<cstdio>` module. Rather than raising an exception or returning an error code we have chosen to return a spreadsheet-style error string in the case of a conversion error or truncation.

We have now seen how to filter and how to filter and reduce. In the next subsection we will see how to map. We don't explicitly cover mapping and reducing because it works the same way as filtering and reducing, the only difference being that all (processed) items are passed to the accumulator rather than only those that are accepted by a filter function.

Using QtConcurrent to Map

Mapping is a process whereby each item in a sequence of items is passed to a map function which in turn returns an item (perhaps of a different type) for each item it receives. There are several `QtConcurrent` mapping functions; the one we will use here has the following signatures:

```
QFuture<T> mapped(Sequence, MapFunction)
QFuture<T> mapped(ConstIterator, ConstIterator, MapFunction)
```

Just as for the filter and reduce functions we have already seen, the `Sequence` is an iterable collection of items such as a `QList<T>` or a `QVector<T>`, and the `ConstIterators` are begin and end iterators that identify a start point and an end point in a `Sequence`. The `MapFunction` must have the following signature:

```
U mapFunction(const T&)
```

The T type is the same type as the items in the Sequence and in the QFuture<T>. The U type is the type of the result produced by processing each T type item—and it can be type T if we want to produce a sequence of modified Ts.

In this subsection we will see how to process all the items in a table model. As with filtering, we cannot work directly on the items in the model because there is no way to lock them. So instead we create a sequence of surrogate items, pass each one to a map function, and then iterate over the resultant sequence, updating the model as we go.

In this particular example we will apply a user-created JavaScript script to each value in the grid.

```
void MainWindow::editApplyScript()
{
    ScriptForm scriptForm(script, this);
    if (scriptForm.exec()) {
        script = scriptForm.script();
        stop();
        view->setEditTriggers(QAbstractItemView::NoEditTriggers);
        errorInfo.clear();
        applyToAll = scriptForm.applyToAll();
        QList<SurrogateItem> items = applyToAll ? allSurrogateItems()
                                    : selectedSurrogateItems();
        QFuture<SurrogateItem> future = QtConcurrent::mapped(items,
                SurrogateItemApplier(script, &errorInfo));
        applyScriptWatcher.setFuture(future);
        setUpProgressBar(applyScriptWatcher);
        editStopAction->setEnabled(true);
    }
}
```

The script form is a simple dialog (not shown) that allows the user to enter some JavaScript code. In addition to the standard JavaScript functions and variables, we will provide three global variables, cellValue, cellRow, and cell-Column, that the user can make use of in their script. We have not provided access to the values of arbitrary cells in the grid—to do this would add a fair amount of complexity and would take us too far from this chapter's threading topic. (This constraint is why the program is merely a number grid and not a spreadsheet.)

If the user clicks OK we retrieve the script they want to apply. The ScriptForm:: accept() method uses the QScriptEngine::checkSyntax() method introduced in Qt 4.5, and only allows the user to leave the script form with a syntactically valid script—or by clicking Cancel.

As usual we stop any processing that is still ongoing, and make the view read-only. We also clear the error count and the script error messages using the errorInfo member variable of type ThreadSafeErrorInfo that we discussed earlier (267 ◄). We retrieve either all the items or just the selected items, depending on what the user requested. The QtConcurrent::mapped() function takes a sequence of items and a map function or functor—in this case we have used a functor, a SurrogateItemApplier instance.

The map function returns immediately and we set its future to the corresponding future watcher. Then we update the status bar and enable the Stop action.

Here is the complete definition of the SurrogateItemApplier class:

```
class SurrogateItemApplier
{
public:
    explicit SurrogateItemApplier(const QString &script_,
            ThreadSafeErrorInfo *errorInfo_)
        : script(script_), errorInfo(errorInfo_) {}

    typedef SurrogateItem result_type;

    SurrogateItem operator()(const SurrogateItem &item)
    {
        QScriptEngine javaScriptParser;
        javaScriptParser.globalObject().setProperty("cellRow",
                                                    item.row);
        javaScriptParser.globalObject().setProperty("cellColumn",
                                                    item.column);
        javaScriptParser.globalObject().setProperty("cellValue",
                                                    item.value);
        QScriptValue result = javaScriptParser.evaluate(script);
        if (javaScriptParser.hasUncaughtException()) {
            QString error = javaScriptParser.uncaughtException()
                            .toString();
            errorInfo->add(error);
            return item;
        }
        return SurrogateItem(item.row, item.column,
                             result.toNumber());
    }

private:
    QString script;
    ThreadSafeErrorInfo *errorInfo;
};
```

The class *must* provide a result_type typedef so that its instances can be passed to QtConcurrent functions. Other than that we simply keep the script, and a pointer to the ThreadSafeErrorInfo object that was passed to the constructor.

The `operator()()` method is called for each of the items in the sequence of items passed to the `QtConcurrent::mapped()` function. In this case we have chosen to return an object of the same type, `SurrogateItem`, but there is no requirement to do so—we can return any type we like so long as we specify it using the `result_type` typedef.

We begin by creating a JavaScript parser and setting three global values: the item's row, column, and value. We then evaluate the JavaScript script and retrieve the return value (the value of the last expression in the script). Here is a simple JavaScript example:

```
var result = cellValue;                                                      Java-
if (cellRow < 10 && cellColumn < 10)                                        Script
    result *= 2;
result;
```

Clearly this script simply doubles the values of the upper-left-most 100 cells.

If the script has an error and produces an unhandled exception, we add the error message to the `errorInfo` object. We don't have to worry about locking even though more than one secondary thread might be processing items, since the `ThreadSafeErrorInfo` class takes care of that for us (267 ◀).

At the end we return the original item unchanged (if an unhandled exception occurred), or a new item with the same row and column numbers as the original item, but with its numeric value set to the result returned by the evaluated script.

Although the `finishedApplyingScript()` slot is structurally similar to `finished-Selecting()` (275 ◀) and `finishedCounting()` (280 ◀), we will still review it so that we can see how script errors are handled.

```cpp
void MainWindow::finishedApplyingScript()
{
    editStopAction->setEnabled(false);
    progressBar->hide();
    if (!applyScriptWatcher.isCanceled() &&
        (errorInfo.isEmpty() || applyDespiteErrors())) {
        const QList<SurrogateItem> items = applyScriptWatcher.future()
                                                        .results();
        QListIterator<SurrogateItem> i(items);
        while (i.hasNext()) {
            const SurrogateItem &item = i.next();
            model->item(item.row, item.column)->setData(item.value,
                                                    Qt::EditRole);
        }
        QString selected(applyToAll ? QString()
                                    : tr(" from those selected"));
```

```
            statusBar()->showMessage(tr("Finished applying script "
                    "to %Ln cell(s)%1", "", items.count())
                    .arg(selected), StatusTimeout);
        }
        view->setEditTriggers(editTriggers);
    }
```

If the processing completed (i.e., if it wasn't canceled), and if there were no
errors or the user wants to apply the script despite errors, we begin by retrieving the processed items. (At this stage the model's data is unchanged; all the
results are in the surrogate items.) We then iterate over every result item and
set each corresponding item in the model to its newly computed value. We then
output a status message to tell the user how many cells were affected. And at
the end we restore the edit triggers so that the user can once more interact with
the grid's values.

```
    bool MainWindow::applyDespiteErrors()
    {
        const int MaxErrorStrings = 15;

        QStringList errors = errorInfo.errors();
        if (errors.count() > MaxErrorStrings) {
            errors = errors.mid(0, MaxErrorStrings);
            errors.append(tr("(and %L1 others...)")
                            .arg(errorInfo.count() - MaxErrorStrings));
        }
        return AQP::question(this, tr("Apply Script Error"),
                tr("%Ln error(s) occurred:\n%1", "", errorInfo.count())
                    .arg(errors.join("\n")),
                "", tr("&Apply Anyway"), tr("&Don't Apply"));
    }
```

If one or more errors occurred, this method is called. It pops up a dialog
showing at most 15 error messages (and indicates how many others there are
if there are more than 15). The reason for our caution about how many error
messages we show is that since the grid might have thousands of cells it is
possible that we will get thousands of error messages, far more than it could
ever be useful to show in a dialog.

We discussed the QStringList::mid() method earlier (253 ◄). The AQP::ques-
tion() function is like the similar functions we have seen earlier (e.g., AQP::ok-
ToDelete(); 101◄).

We have now completed our review of the QtConcurrent functions. We have
seen how to do filtering, filtering and reducing, mapping, and in the previous
section, running functions. We have not shown mapping and reducing, but the

technique is the same as we used for filtering and reducing, only we use a map function (or functor) instead of a filter function (or functor).

Using the non-blocking QtConcurrent functions involves some overhead in setting up the secondary threads, and in the case of model or graphics scene data, the creation of surrogate items. This overhead should be offset if the processing of each item is sufficiently expensive, especially if there are large numbers of items to process.

While QtConcurrent is ideal for performing costly computations on large numbers of items, there are cases where we have one or very few items that have expensive processing that we want to perform without making the user interface unresponsive. One solution is to use the QtConcurrent::run() function or a QRunnable as we saw in the previous section. But if we want to exercise fine control and have the convenience of Qt's signals and slots mechanism, then using QThread might be the best solution.

We have now completed our review of Qt's high-level threading classes. These provide the easiest route to enjoy the benefits of threading and at the same time minimize the risks. But in some situations we want to exercise finer control, and are prepared to take more responsibility for locking and for avoiding deadlocks. In such cases, we can use the lower-level QThread class—the subject of the next chapter.

Threading with QThread

This chapter covers the QThread class which provides fine control over threading, and support for Qt's signals and slots mechanism. Like the previous chapter it assumes prior knowledge of threading in general and the basics of Qt threading in particular. The chapter also assumes that you have at least read the beginning of the previous chapter.

If we have a small number of items (or a small number of groups of items) to process in the background, and we want to keep track of progress and completion, then often the best solution is to create a QThread subclass. Qt's QThread class (and also QRunnable) was modeled on Java's Thread class and so has a similar overall design—for example, requiring subclasses to reimplement the run() method, and starting thread execution by calling the start() method.

A key difference between QThread and QRunnable is that QThread is a QObject subclass, so we can use signals and slots to monitor progress—and in fact QThread provides some useful signals and slots that we can connect to.

Figure 8.1 provides a schematic illustration of how multiple QThread subclass instances are created and used.

In this chapter we will look at two different applications that use QThread, one that uses secondary threads to process independent items, and so requires no locking, and one that populates a shared data structure and needs to use locking to ensure safe access.

Processing Independent Items

In this section we will review the Cross Fader application (crossfader) shown in Figure 8.2. This application lets the user choose two images and creates a user-specified number of intermediate images to produce a sequence of crossfaded images. For example, if the user chose to create three crossfaded

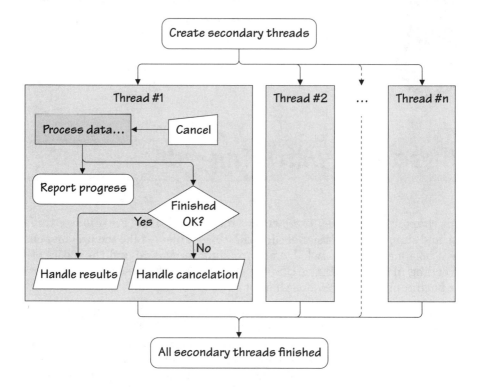

Figure 8.1 *Using QThread to process data*

images, they would end up with a sequence of five images with proportions
(first image:second image) as follows: first image (100:0), crossfaded image #1
(75:25), crossfaded image #2 (50:50), crossfaded image #3 (25:75), second image (0:100).

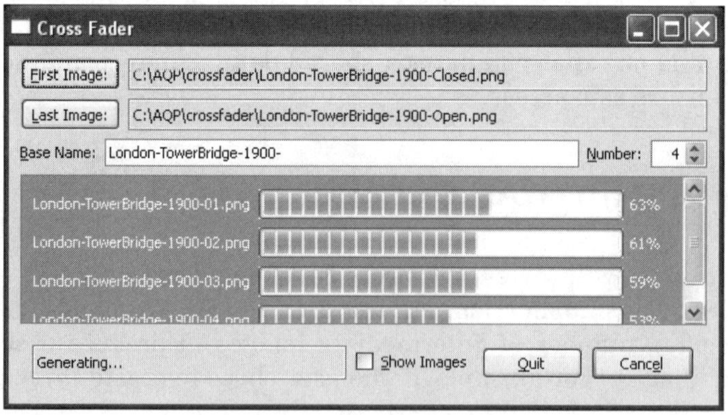

Figure 8.2 *The Cross Fader application*

Figure 8.3 *Six images—four crossfaded*

The effect of crossfading using four intermediate images is illustrated in the screenshot in Figure 8.2 and in the resulting images shown in Figure 8.3 which shows the first and last images and four crossfaded images in between, with proportions (100:0), (80:20), (60:40), (40:60), (20:80), (0:100).

The Cross Fader application uses a separate QThread subclass instance to create each crossfaded image. This is a reasonable choice since we limit the number of intermediate images that can be created. Also, since all the processing is done independently, no locks are required. If we wanted to allow a large number of images to be created concurrently, we might be better off using just a few worker threads and a shared work queue, an approach we will use in the application shown in the next section.

The application also creates a QLabel and a QProgressBar for each crossfaded image so that the user can monitor the application's progress. And since the user could choose to create any number of crossfaded images (actually, we have set the spinbox to allow a maximum of fourteen), we create as many threads, labels, and progress bars as the number they choose. In view of the fact that the number of labels and progress bars is variable, we lay them out inside a QScrollArea so that if there isn't enough room to show them all, a vertical scrollbar will automatically be provided.

We have opted to use a single button for generating and for canceling, so we set its text to Generate or Cancel depending on the circumstances. Also, if the user checks the Show Images checkbox, we open a platform-specific image viewer (if there is one available) to show the crossfaded images once all the images have been created.

Just as we did in the previous chapter, we will begin by showing the basic infrastructure to provide some context, and then we will look at the threading-related code, in this case the CrossFader QThread subclass that is used to create each image.

We will start by looking at an enum and a few of the private members of the application's MainWindow class.

```
enum StopState {Stopping, Terminating};

QWidget *progressWidget;

QMap<QString, QPointer<QProgressBar> > progressBarForFilename;
QList<QPointer<QLabel> > progressLabels;
QList<QPointer<CrossFader> > crossFaders;
bool canceled;
```

The StopState is used to distinguish between stopping because the user canceled and stopping because the user has quit; we'll see why this matters when we look at the cleanUp() method.

The progressWidget is put inside a QScrollArea and contains a QGridLayout. When the user starts generating images we will create a fresh set of labels and progress bars and lay them out inside this widget. We keep pointers to the progress bars in a QMap; each key is the filename of the image that the progress bar is showing progress for.

Rather than storing the widgets using plain pointers we have used QPointers—these are guarded pointers, that is, pointers that are automatically set to null if the object they point to is deleted. Like all kinds of smart pointers, QPointer is more expensive than a plain pointer—it uses slightly more memory and may be slightly slower to access—but the convenience of being able to check a QPointer before using it is really valuable in situations where we want to access an object *if* it hasn't been deleted. (Qt's other smart pointers were described earlier, in the "Qt's Smart Pointers" sidebar; 62 ◄.)

The QWeakPointer class introduced in Qt 4.6 can be used as a general weak pointer, or, for QObject subclasses, as a more efficient replacement for QPointer. However, QWeakPointer's API is different from—and slightly less convenient than—QPointer's, so we prefer to use QPointer here because its relative inefficiency is completely overshadowed by the expense of the processing (so doesn't matter). Using QPointer also means that our code compiles unchanged with Qt 4.5 and Qt 4.6.

The list of crossfaders is used to make it easy to perform actions on all the running secondary threads—for example, stopping them all if the user cancels. We will see why we hold the crossfaders using QPointers when we review the cleanUp() method. The canceled Boolean is used purely by the user interface; it is not used by the secondary threads (so it doesn't need to be volatile).

As soon as the user has chosen two images, the Generate button becomes enabled (due to some signal–slot connections not shown). If the user clicks this button, the generateOrCancelImages() slot is called and processing begins.

```
void MainWindow::generateOrCancelImages()
{
    if (generateOrCancelButton->text() == tr("G&enerate")) {
        generateOrCancelButton->setEnabled(false);
        statusBar->showMessage(tr("Generating..."));
        canceled = false;
        cleanUp();
        QImage firstImage(firstLabel->text());
        QImage lastImage(lastLabel->text());
        for (int i = 0; i < numberSpinBox->value(); ++i)
            createAndRunACrossFader(i, firstImage, lastImage);
        generateOrCancelButton->setText(tr("Canc&el"));
    }
    else {
        canceled = true;
        cleanUp();
        generateOrCancelButton->setText(tr("G&enerate"));
    }
    updateUi();
}
```

This slot is called when the generateOrCancelButton is clicked, but its behavior depends on whether the button is being used to initiate the generation of images or to cancel.

If the user has clicked Generate, we do some user interface-related things such as updating the status bar and setting canceled to false. We also call cleanUp() to make sure that no secondary threads are running and that any labels and progress bars laid out in the progress widget are deleted ready for a fresh start.

We then create one crossfader for each crossfaded image the user wants, and change the generateOrCancelButton into a Cancel button.

On the other hand, if the user has clicked Cancel, we set canceled to true so that other main window methods know that the generation has been canceled. Then we clean up, and turn the button back into a Generate button.

In either case, at the end we call the updateUi() method (not shown); this method simply enables or disables the Generate button depending on whether the user has chosen two filenames.

As usual, the keyboard accelerators are set automatically, in this case by calling AQP::accelerateWidget(this); in the constructor, after the widgets are created. But the generateOrCancelImages() method relies on knowing the text used by the Generate/Cancel button, and we cannot be certain where AQP::accelerate-Widget() will put the ampersand. One solution would be to compare the button text after stripping out the ampersand, for example, generateOrCancelButton->

text().replace("&", "") == tr("Generate"). But we chose to put the ampersands in the two texts this button uses ourselves, so as to ensure that the button always has the same accelerator (Alt+E), whether it shows Generate or Cancel. The accelerate*() functions honor any manually set accelerators. (For more about the alt_key.{hpp,cpp} module that provides the accelerate*() functions, see the "Keyboard Accelerators" sidebar; 15 ◄.)

It is now time to review the cleanUp() method. This method is called before a new set of images is generated, or when the generation is canceled, or when the program is terminated. We will review the method in two short parts for ease of explanation. In fact we will begin by showing a naïve implementation of the first part, then we'll discuss a problem that this approach has, and then we will review an implementation that avoids the problem. And after that we will look at the second part, which is the same for both first parts.

The first part of the cleanUp() method is concerned with stopping any running crossfader threads. We'll start by looking at the naïve version.

```
void MainWindow::cleanUp(StopState stopState)
{
    foreach (CrossFader *crossFader, crossFaders) { // Naive!
        crossFader->stop();
        crossFader->wait();
        crossFader->deleteLater();
    }
    crossFaders.clear();
```

This is the simplest possible approach. We iterate over all the crossfaders and call Crossfader::stop() on each one. This takes almost no time since all the method does is set a bool to true. Next we call QThread::wait()—the crossfader knows that it must stop so it will finish as soon as it reaches an if (m_stopped) statement. Once the QThread::wait() call returns we know that the thread has finished so we tell it to delete itself. And at the end we clear the crossFaders list since it now just contains dangling pointers.

This approach is simple, and we don't even need to use QPointers for our Cross-Faders, since plain pointers are sufficient. But there is one potentially important drawback: we wait for each thread to stop in turn, so overall it takes as long to stop as the sum of the threads' stopping times. If we are prepared to use a more complex algorithm, we can avoid this problem and reduce the stopping time to close to that of the slowest stopping thread.

Of course, there is no harm in using this simple approach and only switching to the more complex approach if it measurably outperforms the simpler one in realistic tests. However, if we do use the simple approach it would probably be better to use two separate loops, one for stopping and one for the waiting and deleting, as we'll see when we discuss the more complex approach.

The Cross Fader source code includes both implementations, with the one actually compiled dependent on a #define. Here's the first part of the implementation that is used by default:

```
const int StopWait = 100;

void MainWindow::cleanUp(StopState stopState)
{
    foreach (CrossFader *crossFader, crossFaders)
        crossFader->stop();
    while (crossFaders.count()) {
        QMutableListIterator<QPointer<CrossFader> > i(crossFaders);
        while (i.hasNext()) {
            CrossFader *crossFader = i.next();
            if (crossFader) {
                if (crossFader->wait(StopWait)) {
                    delete crossFader;
                    i.remove();
                }
            }
            else
                i.remove();
        }
    }
}
```

The first thing the method does is to tell each crossfader to stop. And as we noted earlier, the calls to CrossFader::stop() are fast since each call merely involves setting a bool to true. So, at the end of this loop every crossfader knows that it must stop.

The next loop is to wait for the crossfaders to actually stop so that we can delete them. Why use two loops? Because if we called stop() and then wait() (which blocks), each crossfader would be stopped serially rather than concurrently, so the total stopping time would be the sum of the stopping times. What we want to achieve is a total stopping time as close to that of the stopping time of the thread that's slowest to stop. For this reason, we tell the threads to stop in one loop, and then wait for them to stop in another.

The algorithm we have used to stop the threads is to continually iterate over all the crossfaders, retrieving each one in turn. If the crossfader has been deleted, thanks to the QPointer, it will be null, so we can simply remove it from the list of crossfaders (as we do in the else clause). If the crossfader still exists we call QThread::wait() on it. Normally this method waits "forever", but here we only wait for 100 milliseconds. If the thread has finished, wait() will return true, and in this case we delete the thread and remove it from the list. Otherwise, we do nothing, and on the next pass through the loop we try again.

This approach effectively gives each thread as many 100 millisecond time-slices as it needs in which to stop. It also means that if a thread is taking a long time to stop, it doesn't delay us from stopping the other threads because once the timeout has expired we try the next thread. This makes the overall stopping time much closer to that of the slowest stopping thread than to the sum of the threads' stopping times.

In the case of the Cross Fader application, the more complex algorithm provides little advantage over the simpler approach. This is because the QImage::save() method blocks and is slow (in terms of disk access compared with processing), so any thread that is saving its image to disk must wait for the save to complete even if we have told it to stop. So, here, the time-slicing isn't as beneficial as we might have expected.

The second part of the cleanUp() method is the same no matter which algorithm we use for stopping the threads; we'll review this part now.

```
    if (stopState == Terminating)
        return;
    foreach (QProgressBar *progressBar, progressBarForFilename)
        if (progressBar)
            progressBar->deleteLater();
    progressBarForFilename.clear();
    foreach (QLabel *progressLabel, progressLabels)
        if (progressLabel)
            progressLabel->deleteLater();
    progressLabels.clear();
}
```

Once all the threads have been stopped, if the application is terminating, we have done all that is necessary and can return. But if the cleanup is to prepare for another image generation, or is the result of generation being canceled, we also need to get rid of any labels and progress bars that were used to show progress from the previous generation (if any).

The deletion is straightforward: we iterate over all the progress bars and labels, and for those that still exist, we schedule them to delete themselves when the event loop has time, and then clear the container that held them. We don't have to bother doing this if the application is terminating because all the labels and progress bars are in a layout—this means that they all have parents, and so they will be deleted by Qt in the normal way when their parent widget (the progress widget) is deleted.

Deleting the label and progress bar widgets and then creating fresh ones as needed is clearly less efficient than reusing them. But reuse would require more code—for example, to hide those that have been created but are no longer needed (due to generating fewer images than last time), or to create extra ones (due to generating more images than last time). And also, if the user goes from wanting fourteen images to wanting five, it would mean that we kept nine unneeded labels and progress bars. By deleting and creating we minimize memory use at the expense of processing time. This seems a sensible trade-off since the time needed to create even one crossfaded image is likely to dominate the time needed to delete and create the labels and progress bars.

Each crossfader thread is created and started in the generateOrCancelImages() method by calls to the createAndRunACrossFader() method—we will review this now, in two short parts.

```
void MainWindow::createAndRunACrossFader(int number,
        const QImage &firstImage, const QImage &lastImage)
{
    QString filename = QString("%1%2.png").arg(baseNameEdit->text())
                        .arg(number + 1, 2, 10, QChar('0'));
    QLabel *progressLabel = new QLabel(filename);
    progressLabels << progressLabel;
    QProgressBar *progressBar = new QProgressBar;
    progressBar->setRange(0, 100);
    progressBarForFilename[filename] = progressBar;
    QGridLayout *layout = qobject_cast<QGridLayout*>(
            progressWidget->layout());
    Q_ASSERT(layout);
    layout->addWidget(progressLabel, number, 0);
    layout->addWidget(progressBar, number, 1);
```

The number passed in is the 0-based number of the crossfaded image to be created. We begin by creating a suitable name for the image (Image-01.png, Image-02.png, and so on), using 1-based two-digit base-10 numbers, padded with a leading 0 if necessary. Then we create a new label which we add to the list of labels, and a new progress bar which we add to the map of progress bars, using the filename as its key. We then retrieve the progress widget's grid layout—which thanks to the earlier cleanUp() call will be empty—and add both the label and the progress bar to the layout in the row corresponding to the image's number.

```
    double firstWeight = (number + 1) /
            static_cast<double>(numberSpinBox->value() + 1);
    double secondWeight = 1.0 - firstWeight;
    CrossFader *crossFader = new CrossFader(filename, firstImage,
            firstWeight, lastImage, secondWeight, this);
    crossFaders << crossFader;

    connect(crossFader, SIGNAL(progress(int)),
            progressBar, SLOT(setValue(int)));
    connect(crossFader, SIGNAL(saving(const QString&)),
            this, SLOT(saving(const QString&)));
```

```
    connect(crossFader, SIGNAL(saved(bool, const QString&)),
            this, SLOT(saved(bool, const QString&))));
    connect(crossFader, SIGNAL(finished()),
            this, SLOT(finished())));
    crossFader->start();
}
```

With the user interface set up we next turn to creating and starting the thread
that will create the crossfaded image. First we compute the "weights" to use—
for example, if the image was to be created with the proportions (60:40), the
weights would be 0.6 and 0.4. When the CrossFader object is created we give it
the filename to save to, and the images and weights to use. We then add the
crossfader to the crossfader list for ease of cleanup.

Since CrossFader is a QThread subclass (itself a QObject subclass), we can take
advantage of its signals and slots, and don't need to create custom events or
manually invoke slots as we did in the previous chapter's examples.

Here, we connect the crossfader's custom progress() signal directly to the
progress bar, and connect the other custom signals, and also the QThread::
finished() signal, to the corresponding main window slots. And at the end we
call QThread::start() to start the thread running.

```
const int StatusTimeout = AQP::MSecPerSecond * 10;

void MainWindow::saving(const QString &filename)
{
    statusBar->showMessage(tr("Saving '%1'").arg(filename),
                           StatusTimeout);
    if (QProgressBar *progressBar = progressBarForFilename[filename])
        progressBar->setRange(0, 0);
}
```

Whenever a crossfader finishes creating an image, just before it starts to save
the image it emits a custom saving() signal which results in this slot being
called. The slot informs the user via the status bar. And it also sets the corresponding progress bar's range to (0, 0), a special setting that tells the progress
bar to show a "busy" indicator rather than a percentage, which makes sense
since we don't know how long the save will take.

```
void MainWindow::saved(bool saved, const QString &filename)
{
    const QString message = saved ? tr("Saved '%1'")
                                  : tr("Failed to save '%1'");
    statusBar->showMessage(message.arg(filename), StatusTimeout);
    if (QProgressBar *progressBar =
            progressBarForFilename[filename]) {
        progressBar->setRange(0, 1);
```

```
                progressBar->setValue(saved ? 1 : 0);
                progressBar->setEnabled(false);
        }
    }
```

Whenever a crossfader finishes saving an image, it emits a custom `saved()` signal which results in this slot being called. The Boolean is the one returned by `QImage::save()` and indicates whether the save was successful. Just like the `saving()` method, this method informs the user via the status bar. It then updates the corresponding progress bar giving it an arbitrary range (but where the maximum is greater than the minimum), and setting its value to the maximum if the image was saved (this makes the progress bar show 100%) or to the minimum otherwise (which makes the progress bar show 0%). And the progress bar is also disabled to complete the effect of showing that work on the image has finished.

```
    void MainWindow::finished()
    {
        foreach (CrossFader *crossFader, crossFaders)
            if (crossFader && !crossFader->isFinished())
                return;
        generateOrCancelButton->setText(tr("G&enerate"));
        if (canceled)
            statusBar->showMessage(tr("Canceled"), StatusTimeout);
        else {
            statusBar->showMessage(tr("Finished"));
            if (statusBar->checkBox()->isChecked())
                QDesktopServices::openUrl(QUrl::fromLocalFile(
                        firstLabel->text())));
        }
    }
```

As with the `saving()` and `saved()` signals and slots, whenever a crossfader finishes, it emits a `finished()` signal which results in this slot being called. This slot iterates over all the crossfaders and if it finds one that hasn't finished it returns and does nothing, since work is still going on.

If all the crossfaders are finished the Generate button's text is changed back from Cancel and the user is informed via the status bar. If the generation finished rather than being canceled and if the Show Images checkbox is checked, the `QDesktopServices::openUrl()` method is called with the first image file's filename passed as a file:// protocol URL using the static `QUrl::fromLocalFile()` method.* If the `openUrl()` method is given an http:// protocol URL it tries to

---

*Qt 4.6 has an additional static method, `QUrl::fromUserInput()`, that takes a string and returns a QUrl which could use the file://, ftp://, or http:// protocol, depending on the input string.

start the system's web browser (or to open a new tab if a browser is already running) at the given URL. But if the openUrl() method is given a file:// protocol URL, it starts the platform-dependent application that is associated with the file's suffix, if such an association exists. So in this case, if the computer has a suitable image viewer, it will be launched and given the first image's filename.

Some image viewers will show the given image and also show thumbnails of any other images in the same directory, making it easy to navigate between them. Of course, it would be straightforward to add an image viewing facility to the Cross Fader application; this is left as an exercise.

The call to statusBar->checkBox() is slightly surprising. Rather than using a QStatusBar we have created a custom StatusButtonBar (not shown) that has a QLabel, a QCheckBox, and a QDialogButtonBox laid out in a QHBoxLayout, which is why all three are in the same "line" rather than having the status bar on the line below. This is illustrated by the screenshot in Figure 8.2 (288 ◄).

We have now completed our review of the application's user interface infrastructure, so we can now turn our attention to the CrossFader QThread subclass where all the work is done. We will begin by looking at some of the class's definition in the header file to provide some context.

```
class CrossFader : public QThread
{
    Q_OBJECT

public:
    explicit CrossFader(const QString &filename, const QImage &first,
                const double &firstWeight, const QImage &last,
                const double &lastWeight, QObject *parent=0);

public slots:
    void stop() { m_stopped = true; }

signals:
    void progress(int);
    void saving(const QString&);
    void saved(bool, const QString&);

private:
    void run();
    ...
    volatile bool m_stopped;
```

The volatile m_stopped variable is used to notify the thread that it should stop. (We discussed volatile bools in the previous chapter; 247 ◄.) We have just seen the slots the three custom signals are connected to; the finished() signal is inherited from QThread. We have not shown the private members that hold the variables passed in to the constructor (m_filename, m_first, and so on).

```
CrossFader::CrossFader(const QString &filename, const QImage &first,
        const double &firstWeight, const QImage &last,
        const double &lastWeight, QObject *parent)
    : QThread(parent),
      m_filename(filename), m_firstWeight(firstWeight),
      m_lastWeight(lastWeight), m_stopped(false)
{
    QSize size = first.size().boundedTo(last.size());
    m_first = first.scaled(size, Qt::IgnoreAspectRatio,
                            Qt::SmoothTransformation);
    m_last = last.scaled(size, Qt::IgnoreAspectRatio,
                            Qt::SmoothTransformation);
}
```

When a crossfader is created we start by finding out the size of the smaller of the two images—or the size of both images if they are the same size. (Correspondingly, the QSize::expandedTo() method returns the larger size of the QSize it is called on and the QSize it is passed.) We then scale both images to this minimum size so that both the images we work on, and the resultant crossfaded images, will be the same size.

When QImage::scaled() is called Qt checks the image's size against the requested size and if they're the same, it simply returns the original image. And returning the original image is cheap because Qt uses copy-on-write under the hood so all that's really passed is a pointer or so's worth of data.

For ease of explanation, we will review the run() method in two parts. And we will show two versions of the first part: one that is easy to understand but slow, and another that is slightly trickier but very fast.

```
void CrossFader::run()
{
    QImage image(m_first.width(), m_first.height(),
                QImage::Format_RGB32);
    emit progress(0);

    const float onePercent = image.width() / 100.0;
    for (int x = 0; x < image.width(); ++x) { // Naive and slow!
        for (int y = 0; y < image.height(); ++y) {
            QRgb firstPixel = m_first.pixel(x, y);
            QRgb lastPixel = m_last.pixel(x, y);
            int red = qRound((qRed(firstPixel) * m_firstWeight) +
                        (qRed(lastPixel) * m_lastWeight));
            int green = qRound((qGreen(firstPixel) * m_firstWeight) +
                        (qGreen(lastPixel) * m_lastWeight));
            int blue = qRound((qBlue(firstPixel) * m_firstWeight) +
                        (qBlue(lastPixel) * m_lastWeight));
```

```
                image.setPixel(x, y, qRgb(red, green, blue));
                if ((y % 64) == 0 && m_stopped)
                    return;
            }
            if (m_stopped)
                return;
            emit progress(qRound(x / onePercent));
        }
```

This method is where all the work is done. We begin by creating a new QImage of the right size and using 32-bit RGB (red, green, blue) colors. (We could easily have accounted for an alpha channel—transparency—but this would just make the code longer without changing its essential structure, so is left as an exercise.) Once the image is created we emit an initial progress() signal. The slot that this signal is connected to is in a different thread—the main (GUI) thread. Qt handles cross-thread signals by turning them into events that are added to the main thread's event queue. When the main thread reaches the event it responds by calling the slot the signal was connected to (passing any arguments that the signal may have had), so the slot is executed in the main thread, not the secondary thread from which the signal was emitted.

The crossfading is done by reading the first and last images' RGB values for all of their pixels, and for each one creating a new RGB value that is the rounded sum of the first and last images' weighted RGB values. For example, if the first image had a red value of 240 and a weighting of 0.6 and the second image had a red value of 120 and a weighting of 0.4, the crossfaded pixel would have a red value of 192: $(240 \times 0.6) + (120 \times 0.4) = 144 + 48 = 192$.

The QImage::pixel() method returns unsigned integers; QRgb is simply a typedef that makes their meaning clearer. The qRed(), qGreen(), and qBlue() functions, given a QRgb, return an integer—the appropriate red, green, or blue component. There is also a QRgba typedef that includes an alpha (transparency) component, and a qAlpha() function, as well as a qGray() function that produces a gray value given a QRgb (or given three integers for red, green, and blue).

The outer loop works by x-coordinates (columns) and the inner loop works by y-coordinates (rows). To make the thread sensitive to cancelation, every 64th pixel we check to see if the thread has been stopped. We also check after each column is completed, and emit a progress() signal with the column we have reached.

Unfortunately using QImage::pixel() and QImage::setPixel() is quite slow. There are two alternatives, both based on the knowledge that internally QImage stores its pixel data as a single contiguous array of values. One approach is to work in terms of horizontal scan lines (y-coordinates). The QImage::scanLine() method returns a pointer to a single "row" of pixel data. We can then work on this data directly rather than getting and setting pixels, and doing so provides a significant speedup. (Source code that shows this approach is included in the example's source code but not shown here.) Another approach is to work in terms of the raw array of values. This is accessed by the `QImage::bits()` method and produces the fastest possible access. Here's the same code as before but this time using `QImage::bits()`:

```cpp
void CrossFader::run()
{
    QImage image(m_first.width(), m_first.height(),
                QImage::Format_RGB32);
    emit progress(0);

    const int onePercent = qRound(image.width() * image.height() /
                                  100.0);
    QRgb *firstPixels = reinterpret_cast<QRgb*>(m_first.bits());
    QRgb *lastPixels = reinterpret_cast<QRgb*>(m_last.bits());
    QRgb *pixels = reinterpret_cast<QRgb*>(image.bits()); // Fastest
    for (int i = 0; i < image.width() * image.height(); ++i) {
        QRgb firstPixel = firstPixels[i];
        QRgb lastPixel = lastPixels[i];
        int red = qRound((qRed(firstPixel) * m_firstWeight) +
                         (qRed(lastPixel) * m_lastWeight));
        int green = qRound((qGreen(firstPixel) * m_firstWeight) +
                           (qGreen(lastPixel) * m_lastWeight));
        int blue = qRound((qBlue(firstPixel) * m_firstWeight) +
                          (qBlue(lastPixel) * m_lastWeight));
        pixels[i] = qRgb(red, green, blue);
        if ((i % onePercent) == 0) {
            if (m_stopped)
                return;
            emit progress(i / onePercent);
        }
    }
}
```

We use three calls to `QImage::bits()` to give us read-write access to all three images. Then, instead of iterating by *x*- or *y*-coordinates, we simply iterate over every bit in one fast linear sweep. (The source code has #defines that can be used to switch between the different approaches—they are worth experimenting with to see just how much faster using `QImage::bits()` is.) The only thing that slows down this implementation is the `if` statement—without that the code would run even faster, but at the price of being harder for the user to stop and with a much coarser indication of progress.

```cpp
    emit progress(image.width());

    if (m_stopped)
        return;
```

```
    emit saving(m_filename);

    if (m_stopped)
        return;
    emit saved(image.save(m_filename), m_filename);
}
```

Once the new image has been completed we emit a last progress() signal, and if the user has not canceled we then emit a saving() signal. Finally, we try to save the image, and emit a saved() signal with the result of the QImage::save() call. We do not explicitly emit a finished() signal; the base class will do that for us automatically once the run() method has finished.

Using QThread for this application was not difficult because no locking was required, and we could make full use of Qt's signals and slots mechanism. But if the number of images we wanted to concurrently create was potentially large, using a shared work queue and just a few threads—an approach we will look at in the next section—would provide a more scalable solution.

Processing Shared Items

If we have a large number of items to process and due to varying item sizes we don't know how to distribute them fairly among threads to get the maximum throughput, we may be better off using a shared work queue. In some scenarios involving shared work queues we can start putting work onto the queue and then start up a fixed number of secondary threads that can begin processing, adding work as we go. If we make the work queue thread-safe (i.e., if we build in locking), then each secondary thread that accesses the queue can treat it like any other data structure.

The scenario we will use in this section is slightly different since we use the secondary threads to populate a shared data structure (a hash) in the first place, and once the hash is populated the application then populates a model that reflects the hash's data into a view.

In this section we will develop the Find Duplicates application (findduplicates) shown in Figure 8.4. This application searches the user-specified directory and all its subdirectories to find duplicate files.* Duplication is determined by considering each file's size and *MD5* signature. MD5 (Message-Digest algorithm 5) is a cryptography function that given a chunk of data—for example, a file—provides a 128-bit (16 bytes) hash value. If two files have the same length and the same MD5, then they are very likely to have the same contents.

---

*Incidentally, just as with the Image2Image program discussed in the previous chapter, the line edit used to enter the user's choice of root directory uses a QCompleter which pops up a list of valid directories to minimize how much the user must type—this is covered in Chapter 9; ➤ 320.

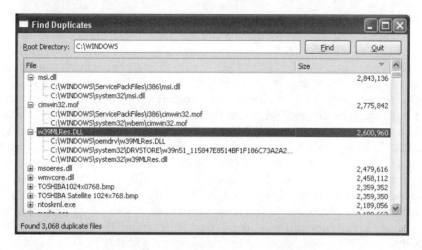

Figure 8.4 *The Find Duplicates application*

The application iterates over all the directories and populates a QHash<QPair<
QByteArray, qint64>, QStringList>. The hash's keys are made up of a QByteArray
to hold an MD5 and a qint64 to hold a file size; the value is a QStringList of
filenames (including full paths) of those files that have the corresponding MD5
and size. Once the hash is populated we can iterate over it knowing that any
items whose value contains more than one filename contains a list of duplicate
files. One advantage of using this approach is that we find duplicate files even
where their filenames differ. (See, for example, the w39MLRes.DLL entry shown
in Figure 8.4.)

Computing a file's MD5 is potentially expensive (proportional to the file's
size), so we want to distribute the work over one or more secondary threads
(the precise number being the ideal thread count that Qt reports). But why
bother going to the expense of computing MD5s when we could simply store
the files' contents in the QByteArray part of the hash keys, especially since we
have to read the file anyway to compute the MD5? If we did this we would end
up with a hash whose keys would consume as much memory as the directory's
contents (perhaps tens or hundreds of megabytes or more), whereas every MD5
QByteArray is a mere 16 bytes, no matter how large the file it represents.

The application needs to know which files it must process (i.e., which files to calculate the MD5 for and that should be added to the shared hash). The approach
we have taken is to create a list of the subdirectories in the user's chosen directory and divide this list as evenly as possible among the secondary threads.
Each secondary thread is then expected to add entries to the hash for every file
in every directory it processes, and for every file in every directory's subdirectories, and so on. This does not guarantee a fair distribution of work—for example, one secondary thread could end up with directories containing tiny icon
files and another with directories containing large music or DVD files.

If we wanted to guarantee a fair distribution of work, one approach would be to create a single data structure containing all the files—for example, a `QMap<qint64, QString>` with file size keys and filename values intrinsically ordered by size. Then we would have to allocate filenames to the threads according to file size. For example, if we had three secondary threads and twenty files to process we'd have to allocate the work (using index positions into the map—although in practice we'd simply use an iterator) as follows: thread #1 [0, 3, 6, 9, 12, 15, 18]; thread #2 [1, 4, 7, 10, 13, 16, 19]; thread #3 [2, 5, 8, 11, 14, 17]. This would add only a little more complexity to the program, but the real issue is that using this approach might take longer overall than the potentially unfair approach that we have used, and will certainly consume much more memory. This is because of the overhead involved in creating the list of all the files to be processed in the first place (even if we spread this work over one or more secondary threads), compared with simply giving each secondary thread a directory to work on, and not needing a possibly huge list of files. It might be interesting to compare the two approaches in practice; creating a truly fair version and comparing performance is left as an exercise.

Clearly, the key to this application is having a shared hash that all the secondary threads can update. Making a complete thread-safe hash is non-trivial, so what we have done is created a cut-down hash that provides the functionality that the program needs, and leaves out a lot of useful but unnecessary features.

We will start our coverage by looking at the application's bare bones Thread-SafeHash class. Then we will look at some of the infrastructure in the main window, and finally we will look at the QThread subclass where the processing takes place.

Here is the definition of the ThreadSafeHash class; we will look at some of its methods in a moment.

```
template<typename Key, typename Value>
class ThreadSafeHash
{
public:
    explicit ThreadSafeHash() {}
    ...
private:
    mutable QReadWriteLock lock;
    QMultiHash<Key, Value> hash;
};
```

The difference between a `QMultiHash` and a `QHash` (and similarly between a `QMultiMap` and a `QMap`) is that multiple values can be inserted for a given key. So, in effect, each key has a list of values. This leads to subtly different semantics compared with the single valued hash and map, so we must be careful to keep in mind the differences when using a QMultiHash or a QMultiMap. (In fact, both QHash and QMap have insertMulti() methods that allow for multiple values to be stored for the same key, but if that's our requirement, using QMultiHash and QMultiMap is likely to be more convenient.)

We have used a QReadWriteLock so that we can minimize locking times—for example, if no write lock is active, any number of threads can obtain read locks. The lock must be mutable since it will be used in some const methods.

```
QList<Value> values(const Key &key) const
{
    QReadLocker locker(&lock);
    return hash.values(key);
}
```

This method returns the values corresponding to the given key, or an empty list of values if the hash doesn't have an item with the given key.

A QReadLocker blocks until it gets a read lock on the QReadWriteLock it is passed as argument. When the QReadLocker is destroyed, its destructor releases the lock. This ensures that the lock is always released—whether the function or method containing the read locker returns normally, or is exited due to an unhandled exception.

For the Find Duplicates program the keys are of type QPair<QByteArray, qint64>, and the values are of type QString, so the value returned from this method will be a (possibly empty) QList<QString>.

A QList<QString> is compatible with QStringList—which inherits QList—but doesn't provide some of the QStringList convenience methods. If necessary we can easily convert a QList<QString> into a QStringList to get the extra methods since QStringList has a constructor that accepts a QList<QString>.

The ThreadSafeHash has several other methods with the same structure as this one—that is, they use a QReadLocker and return the result of a call on the aggregated hash. These include contains(), count(), and isEmpty() (none of which are shown).

```
void insert(const Key &key, const Value &value)
{
    QWriteLocker locker(&lock);
    hash.insert(key, value);
}
```

This method is used to insert a single value into the hash under the given key. If two or more values are inserted with the same key, they are all kept (in insertion order). If the key is not in the hash a new item is created with the given key and value.

A QWriteLocker blocks until it gets a write lock on the QReadWriteLock it is passed as argument. When the QWriteLocker is destroyed, its destructor releases the lock—exactly the same as for a QReadLocker.

```
const QList<Value> takeOne(bool *more)
{
    Q_ASSERT(more);
    QWriteLocker locker(&lock);
    typename QMultiHash<Key, Value>::const_iterator i =
            hash.constBegin();
    if (i == hash.constEnd()) {
        *more = false;
        return QList<Value>();
    }
    *more = true;
    const QList<Value> values = hash.values(i.key());
    hash.remove(i.key());
    return values;
}
```

Providing a thread-safe iteration mechanism is non-trivial, so we have chosen instead to implement a method that destructively removes arbitrary items from the hash, since this is sufficient for the Find Duplicates application's needs.

We begin by acquiring a write lock since we plan to change the hash. Since we don't have a particular key in mind (we just want to take any key), we must somehow access an item. Here, we have simply retrieved a const iterator to the "first" item in the hash. (We say "first" in quotes because unlike a QMap, a QHash or QMultiHash has no intrinsic order.) Unfortunately, the iterator declaration confuses some compilers so we have been forced to use typename to make the meaning clear.

If the iterator points past the end of the hash we know that the hash is empty. In this case, we set the Boolean more pointer's value to false and return an empty list of values.

If the hash is nonempty, we set more's value to true, and retrieve the list of values for the item pointed to by the iterator's key. (We can't use i.value() because that will return a single value, i.e., just the first value in the item's list of values.) Once we have a copy of the values we remove the item from the hash, and then return the values. We will see further on that the Find Duplicates application uses this method to populate a model once all the secondary threads have finished populating the thread-safe hash.

We have now finished reviewing all the relevant parts of the ThreadSafeHash. This data structure means that the threads used in the rest of the program can effectively treat the ThreadSafeHash as a normal data structure without us having to worry about locking.

We can now turn our attention to the application's main window infrastructure, starting with its data members (but excluding the model and the widgets which are all standard).

```
volatile bool stopped;
QList<QPointer<GetMD5sThread> > threads;
FilesForMD5 filesForMD5;
```

The stopped variable is used to tell the threads that the user has canceled. Keeping a list of the secondary threads is convenient as we will see when we review the processDirectories(), finished(), and stopThreads() methods further on. We will review the GetMD5sThread QThread subclass toward the end of this section. The filesForMD5 variable is the shared thread-safe hash that the secondary threads populate.

```
typedef ThreadSafeHash<QPair<QByteArray, qint64>,
                       QString> FilesForMD5;
```

We have created this typedef as a convenience so that we can avoid typing the rather unwieldy name for the hash in all the places it is needed.* The QPair is used as the hash's key, and the QString is the type of the values stored in each item's list of values.

```
void MainWindow::find()
{
    stopThreads();

    rootDirectoryEdit->setEnabled(false);
    view->setSortingEnabled(false);
    model->clear();
    model->setColumnCount(2);
    model->setHorizontalHeaderLabels(QStringList() << tr("File")
                                                   << tr("Size"));
    findButton->hide();
    cancelButton->show();
    cancelButton->setEnabled(true);
    cancelButton->setFocus();

    stopped = false;
    prepareToProcess();
}
```

---

*The use of a typedef here is quite a rare occurrence in this book. In fact, we avoid the use of typedefs as much as possible—purely to save readers from having to remember or look back every time they encounter one. However, we certainly advocate their use in production code.

This method is called when the user clicks the Find button. It begins by stopping any running secondary threads, and then updates the user interface and clears the model so that no duplicates are shown. It is best to switch off view sorting before making big changes to a model since this improves performance. And since clearing a model also sets its row and column counts to 0 and wipes out its headers, we must restore these ready for when the model is repopulated. At the end the method sets the stopped variable to false since the user has not canceled, and calls prepareToProcess() to get the list of directories to process.

Incidentally, rather than using a single button for Find and Cancel and changing its text, we have used two separate buttons, added one after the other in a QHBoxLayout. At any one time only one of the buttons is visible. This means that we can have the convenience of never having to change the buttons' texts and of having two separate slots, find() and cancel(), instead of a single *findOrCancel()* slot.

```
const int StopWait = 100;

void MainWindow::stopThreads()
{
    stopped = true;
    while (threads.count()) {
        QMutableListIterator<QPointer<GetMD5sThread> > i(threads);
        while (i.hasNext()) {
            QPointer<GetMD5sThread> thread = i.next();
            if (thread) {
                if (thread->wait(StopWait)) {
                    delete thread;
                    i.remove();
                }
            }
            else
                i.remove();
        }
    }
    Q_ASSERT(threads.isEmpty());
}
```

This method uses the same algorithm as we used in the Cross Fader example's cleanUp() method (293 ◀), and is designed to make the overall stopping time as close to that of the slowest stopping thread as possible.

```
void MainWindow::prepareToProcess()
{
    statusBar()->showMessage(tr("Reading files..."));
    QStringList directories;
    directories << rootDirectoryEdit->text();
```

```
        QDirIterator i(directories.first());
        while (!stopped && i.hasNext()) {
            const QString &pathAndFilename = i.next();
            const QFileInfo &info = i.fileInfo();
            if (info.isDir() && !info.isSymLink() &&
                i.fileName() != "." && i.fileName() != "..")
                directories << pathAndFilename;
        }
        if (stopped)
            return;
        processDirectories(directories);
    }
```

This method is used to create a list of directories to process. The first item in
the list is the directory entered by the user (the "root"), and the others (if any)
are the root's subdirectories. Even on a large directory, creating this list should
be very fast and not consume too much memory since we only go one level deep.
Once the list is complete we call processDirectories() to get the work done.

If the directory could be very large, then it might be worth putting the if
(stopped) check inside the loop, so that at least the user could cancel if they
changed their minds. Or we could even process it using multiple threads.

```
    void MainWindow::processDirectories(const QStringList &directories)
    {
        const QVector<int> sizes = AQP::chunkSizes(directories.count(),
                QThread::idealThreadCount());
        int offset = 0;
        foreach (const int chunkSize, sizes) {
            QPointer<GetMD5sThread> thread = QPointer<GetMD5sThread>(
                    new GetMD5sThread(&stopped, directories.first(),
                            directories.mid(offset, chunkSize),
                            &filesForMD5));
            threads << thread;
            connect(thread, SIGNAL(readOneFile()),
                    this, SLOT(readOneFile()));
            connect(thread, SIGNAL(finished()), this, SLOT(finished()));
            thread->start();
            offset += chunkSize;
        }
    }
```

This method uses the same algorithm for distributing the work as we used
in the previous chapter's convertFiles() methods (252 ◄). Each GetMD5sThread
object is created with a pointer to the stopped variable (so that it can detect if

the user canceled), the root directory (since this one shouldn't be recursed into), the directories to process, and the hash that the thread is to update.

Once a `GetMD5sThread` is created we add it to the list of threads. Then we connect the thread's custom `readOneFile()` signal and inherited `finished()` signal to corresponding slots in the main window, and start the thread processing.

```
void MainWindow::readOneFile()
{
    statusBar()->showMessage(tr("Read %Ln file(s)", "",
                                filesForMD5.count())));
}
```

Whenever a `GetMD5sThread` adds a filename to the hash it emits a `readOneFile()` signal which in turn calls this slot. Since the `FilesForMD5` hash is thread-safe we don't have to worry about locking to access its count; and, of course, the count is the total for all the secondary threads since they all share the same hash.

Strictly speaking the count is wrong, since it measures the number of unique (MD5, size) pairs rather than the actual number of files processed—a number that could be larger depending on how many duplicates there are. Nonetheless, the count is sufficiently close to being correct for indicating progress. This illustrates a trade-off that is sometimes made between accuracy and efficiency. Here, we don't need accuracy—the number shown will keep changing anyway, and is good enough to let the user know that the processing is taking place—so we don't waste CPU cycles or memory trying to compute a truly accurate result.

```
void MainWindow::finished()
{
    foreach (QPointer<GetMD5sThread> thread, threads)
        if (thread && thread->isRunning())
            return;
    processResults();
}
```

Whenever a `GetMD5sThread` finishes it emits a `finished()` signal (a behavior it inherits from its `QThread` base class). Since we might have more than one secondary thread we check them all to see if any are still running—if any are, we return and do nothing. And if there are no secondary threads running we know that this slot was called by the last one to finish, so we are able to call `processResults()`.

```
void MainWindow::processResults()
{
    stopThreads();

    qint64 maximumSize;
```

```
        forever {
            bool more;
            QStringList files = filesForMD5.takeOne(&more);
            if (!more)
                break;
            if (files.count() < 2)
                continue;
            addOneResult(files, &maximumSize);
        }
        updateView(maximumSize);
        statusBar()->showMessage(tr("Found %Ln duplicate file(s)", "",
                                    model->rowCount()));
        completed();
    }
```

This method is used to present the results to the user. It begins with a call to stopThreads() which deletes all the secondary threads since they are no longer needed.

We keep track of the largest-sized file since we will use this to determine how wide to make the view's Size column. The bare bones ThreadSafeHash doesn't provide an iterator or any way to index items except by their keys (and provides no means of supplying the keys); all it has is the destructive takeOne() method—but this is sufficient for our needs. We start an infinite loop using Qt's forever macro (essentially the same as while(1)), and try to retrieve a list of filenames. (The ThreadSafeHash::takeOne() method returns a QList<QString>; we rely on the non-explicit QStringList(QList<QString>&) constructor to perform the conversion.) If more is set to false the hash is empty and we break out of the loop. Otherwise, providing the list of filenames has at least two items (i.e., at least one duplicate), we call addOneResult() to populate the model with this information.

At the end we update the view—sorting it and setting its column widths—tell the user how many files are duplicated, and call completed() to prepare the user interface for another search.

```
    void MainWindow::addOneResult(const QStringList &files,
                                  qint64 *maximumSize)
    {
        QFileInfo info(files.first());
        if (info.size() > *maximumSize)
            *maximumSize = info.size();
        QStandardItem *parentItem = model->invisibleRootItem();
        QStandardItem *treeItem = new QStandardItem(info.fileName());
        QStandardItem *sizeItem = new QStandardItem(
                QString("%L1").arg(info.size(), 20, 10, QChar(' ')));
        sizeItem->setTextAlignment(Qt::AlignVCenter|Qt::AlignRight);
```

```
            parentItem->appendRow(QList<QStandardItem*>() << treeItem
                                                          << sizeItem);
        foreach (const QString &filename, files)
            treeItem->appendRow(new QStandardItem(
                    QDir::toNativeSeparators(filename)));
    }
```

This method creates a new top-level row based on the first filename in the list of filenames. The row's first item (i.e., its first column) is given the filename (stripped of its path), and the row's second item (i.e., its second column) is given the file's size (as a string). The method then adds one child row for every filename in the list, creating a single item for each one to hold the filename (including its path). This means there will always be at least two child rows for each top-level row. Note also that child items might not have the same filename as the top-level row's first item, since Find Duplicates finds duplicate files irrespective of their actual filenames.

The file size is displayed as a localized string but padded with leading whitespace so that if the user sorts the size column (by clicking the Size column header), the default alphabetical sorting will sort the numerical values correctly. And, of course, we use the static QDir::toNativeSeparators() method to make sure that path separators are shown correctly for the platform.

```
void MainWindow::updateView(qint64 maximumSize)
{
    if (model->rowCount()) {
        model->sort(0, Qt::AscendingOrder);
        view->expand(model->invisibleRootItem()->child(0)->index());
        QFontMetrics fm(font());
        int sizeWidth = fm.width(QString("W%L1W").arg(maximumSize));
        view->setColumnWidth(1, sizeWidth);
        sizeWidth += fm.width("W");
        view->setColumnWidth(0, view->width() - (sizeWidth +
                view->verticalScrollBar()->sizeHint().width()));
    }
}
```

This method is called once the model has been populated with duplicate files. It sorts the model by top-level filename and expands the first item to show its duplicates. It then computes a suitable width for the size column, using the localized maximum size and two "W"s to provide some horizontal margin. It then sets the width of the filename column to be whatever is left over, including accounting for the width of the vertical scrollbar plus some extra margin.

```
void MainWindow::completed()
{
    view->setSortingEnabled(true);
```

```
        cancelButton->setEnabled(false);
        cancelButton->hide();
        findButton->show();
        findButton->setEnabled(true);
        findButton->setFocus();
        rootDirectoryEdit->setEnabled(true);
}
```

Once the search is completed (or canceled), this method is called to prepare the user interface for another search. It also re-enables sorting (since all changes to the model have now been done), so that the user can sort by clicking the column headers.

```
    void MainWindow::cancel()
    {
        stopThreads();
        completed();
        statusBar()->showMessage(tr("Canceled"), StatusTimeout);
    }
```

If the user cancels, this slot is called. It stops the threads, prepares the user interface for another search, and confirms the cancelation. What it does *not* do is clear the model, so any duplicates found so far are shown. This is easy to change, of course.

```
    void MainWindow::closeEvent(QCloseEvent *event)
    {
        stopThreads();
        event->accept();
    }
```

If the user tries to terminate the application, we first make sure that any running secondary threads are finished, and then we allow the termination to proceed.

We have now reviewed enough of the application's infrastructure to see how the threads are created, connected to, and used. We will now review the—surprisingly straightforward—GetMD5sThread class. We will begin by looking at an extract from its definition, and then we will look at its run() method.

```
    class GetMD5sThread : public QThread
    {
        Q_OBJECT

    public:
        explicit GetMD5sThread(volatile bool *stopped,
                const QString &root, const QStringList &directories,
                FilesForMD5 *filesForMD5)
```

```
            : m_stopped(stopped), m_root(root),
              m_directories(directories), m_filesForMD5(filesForMD5) {}

    signals:
        void readOneFile();

    private:
        void run();
        ...
    };
```

The constructor takes the parameters needed to define the work that the thread must perform and stores them in member variables. Only one signal is declared since the finished() signal is inherited from QThread. By making its run() method private, we prevent the class from being subclassed, but also prevent run() being called on instances (since run() should be called only by QThread::start()).

```
    void GetMD5sThread::run()
    {
        foreach (const QString &directory, m_directories) {
            QDirIterator::IteratorFlag flag = directory == m_root
                    ? QDirIterator::NoIteratorFlags
                    : QDirIterator::Subdirectories;
            QDirIterator i(directory, flag);
            while (i.hasNext()) {
                const QString &filename = i.next();
                const QFileInfo &info = i.fileInfo();
                if (!info.isFile() || info.isSymLink() ||
                    info.size() == 0)
                    continue;
                if (*m_stopped)
                    return;
                QFile file(filename);
                if (!file.open(QIODevice::ReadOnly))
                    continue;
                QByteArray md5 = QCryptographicHash::hash(file.readAll(),
                        QCryptographicHash::Md5);
                if (*m_stopped)
                    return;
                m_filesForMD5->insert(qMakePair(md5, info.size()),
                                      filename);
                emit readOneFile();
            }
        }
    }
```

This method is at the heart of the application, and is where all the work is done. The thread iterates over the list of directories it has been given, and for each one creates a QDirIterator with which to iterate over the files that are to be processed. The original directory list was populated with the user-chosen directory (the "root") and that directory's immediate subdirectories. This means that the first thread's first directory will be the root whose directories are already in the list for processing, so if the directory to process is the root directory, we must not recurse into its subdirectories—something we account for by setting the QDirIterator flag.

We ignore anything that isn't a file, and also ignore zero-length files (even though, logically, these are all duplicates of each other). For those files we want to handle, we open them for reading in binary mode, and if the QFile::open() call succeeds, we pass their entire contents to the QCryptographicHash::hash() function to compute their MD5 using QFile::readAll(). Then we update the hash data structure, creating (or accessing) the item whose key has the MD5 and file size of the file we are working on, and appending the filename to its list of string values. Qt's global qMakePair() function is used to create QPair objects—in this case a (QByteArray, qint64) key. And, of course, we don't have to worry about locking since the ThreadSafeHash takes care of it for us.

At the end we emit a signal indicating that a file has been read. Since QThread is a QObject subclass we can use Qt's signals and slots mechanism normally—we don't have to resort to custom events or to invoking slots directly. (Behind the scenes, Qt uses its event processing mechanism to handle cross-thread signal–slot connections, but this is all done transparently, so we do not have to know or care about how it works.)

Notice that in a couple of places we check to see if the user has canceled, and immediately finish if they have.

Qt's QCryptographicHash class was introduced with Qt 4.3. It can provide a cryptographic hash using any of the MD5, MD4, or SHA1 algorithms. The static QCryptographicHash::hash() method we have used here takes a QByteArray (which is what QFile::readAll() returns), and the algorithm to use, and returns the cryptographic hash as a QByteArray. It is also possible to create a QCryptographicHash object and add data to it using one of its addData() methods (taking a char* and a length or taking a QByteArray), and calling QCryptographicHash::result() for the hash at the end.

We have now completed our review of the Find Duplicates application. This application demonstrates how to use QThread in conjunction with a thread-safe data structure. A slightly more useful variant might have a third column showing the number of duplicates of each file so that users could sort by this column to see which files had the most duplicates irrespective of their names or sizes. Another improvement would be the ability to delete files, and for Unix-like operating systems, the ability to link files (i.e., delete a duplicate and then create a soft link from one version to the now deleted duplicate). Adding all this functionality is left as an exercise.

We have now completed our review of Qt's high-level threading classes (in the previous chapter), and of QThread. Qt's support for threading is excellent, but there is no avoiding the fact that writing—and especially maintaining— threaded programs is potentially much more demanding than for single threaded programs. For this reason, threading should be used only when necessary, and with great care. We can minimize the risks and maximize the benefits that threading can provide by avoiding the need for locking at all (by processing items independently), or where locking is required, encapsulating it in a class so that the class's clients don't have to take on any locking responsibilities themselves. Using Qt's QtConcurrent functions and the QRunnable class makes the processing of independent items quite straightforward—and we can still use locking if necessary (for example, the ThreadSafeErrorInfo class we created in the previous chapter's second section). Even using QThread classes need not be too demanding, particularly if we use thread-safe data structures, although writing these can be quite a challenge if we want them to be both efficient and fully functional.

- Introducing QTextDocument
- Creating Custom Text Editors
- A Rich Text Single Line Editor
- Multi-line Rich Text Editing

Creating Rich Text Editors

Qt provides a rich text engine that can format and display text, lists, tables, and images.★ The heart of this text formatting engine is QTextDocument—this class can hold a single piece of text, a line, or an entire multi-page document, and fully supports text formatting (e.g., bold, italic, color, subscript), right down to the level of individual characters.

One of QTextDocument's great conveniences is that it can be given HTML, which makes it easy to include rich text in applications. And just like a web browser, QTextDocument can accept a CSS (Cascading Style Sheet) to provide globally consistent styling of the text it contains. Another feature QTextDocument has in common with web browsers is that it safely ignores markup it doesn't understand. The HTML tags and the CSS properties that Qt's rich text engine support are listed at qt.nokia.com/doc/richtext-html-subset.html.

In this chapter we will focus on creating rich text editors, including completion and syntax highlighting. And in the next chapter we will focus on outputting rich text, both by exporting to files—for example, in .odt (Open Document Text Format) and .pdf (Portable Document Format)—and by printing.

In the chapter's first section we will begin with an overview of the QText-Document class which provides in-memory storage of rich text documents. This overview is relevant to this chapter and to the next one. Then, in the second section we will show how to provide completion for a line editor, and then we will create a custom multi-line XML editor that provides both completion and syntax highlighting. In the third section we will show how to create a single line rich text editor. And in the fourth section we will show how to create a multi-line rich text editor—this allows us to provide more features than the

---

★Qt's rich text format is an in-memory data format that should not be confused with Microsoft's .rtf (rich text format) document interchange format, or with *enriched text* (RFC 1896) or with the text/richtext MIME type (RFCs 1341 and 1521), all of which are completely different.

317

single line editor, such as text alignment and indicating the character and paragraph formatting attributes that are in force at the cursor position.

Introducing QTextDocument

In this section we will briefly describe the structure of QTextDocuments. In this chapter we will use QTextDocuments to hold the rich text of custom editors, and in this chapter and the next we will use QTextCursors to programmatically edit and populate QTextDocuments.

It might appear that storing rich text is quite straightforward, but a glimpse of the 700-page Open Document Format specification (or Microsoft's 6 000-page OOXML specification) suggests that things aren't quite as simple as we might suppose. Fortunately, Qt rich text supports only a carefully chosen range of features, so it is not too difficult to learn, and at the same time is sufficient for most everyday needs.

Internally, QTextDocument stores its documents using a recursive structure that consists of a root frame that contains one (possibly empty) text block, followed by a sequence of zero or more frames, text blocks, or tables. Each frame under the root itself contains one (possibly empty) text block, again followed by a sequence of zero or more frames, text blocks, and tables. And this pattern repeats for frames within frames. Qt always puts a text block (even if empty) as a separator between each frame or table.

Figure 9.1 illustrates the structure of a QTextDocument with a schematic representation of a sample document's first page. The second page is also inside the root frame, and simply follows the last text block shown in the figure. Both pages' contents consist of a text block (holding a title), a text table (holding cells, each of which contains a text block containing a caption), and another text block (holding a paragraph at the end, and for all except the last page a page break indicator).

A QTextBlock can represent either a paragraph or a list, and nested lists are fully supported. If a text block represents a list, the QTextBlock::textList() method returns a pointer to a QTextList; otherwise (if it is just a paragraph of text) it returns 0. A QTextList consists of one or more QTextBlocks whose attributes (bullet or numbering style and indent) are stored in a single QTextList-Format.

A QTextBlock's paragraph formatting is stored in a QTextBlockFormat—this stores attributes such as the paragraph's alignment, margins, indents, and so on. A text block is composed of zero or more QTextFragments, each one of which holds a piece of text whose attributes (font, underlining, and so on) are stored in a single QTextCharFormat. The text could be as little as a single character (such as an underlined letter), or as much as a paragraph's worth of text. A

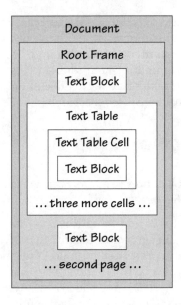

Figure 9.1 *A schematic representation of a sample document's first page*

nonempty text block whose text is all of the same format will usually contain a single text fragment.

The QTextFragment class should not be confused with the QTextDocumentFragment class. A QTextBlock is made up of one or more QTextFragments, while a QText-DocumentFragment is used to hold an arbitrary piece of a QTextDocument, and could contain paragraphs, tables, or even an entire QTextDocument. When the user makes a selection we can retrieve what they have selected using the QText-Cursor::selection() method—which returns a QTextDocumentFragment.

Images are represented by using a placeholder character (Unicode character U+FFFC) which is contained in a QTextFragment. This character has a QTextImage-Format (a QTextCharFormat subclass) that holds the size and name of the image. The name is the name of an image in the application's resources.

Tables are represented by the QTextTable class whose attributes (alignment, cell padding, cell spacing, number of columns, and so on) are stored in a single QTextTableFormat. Table cells are represented by the QTextTableCell class and can contain text blocks—or frames; so complex nesting is possible. Cells know the position they occupy in the table (their column and row), and have column and row span attributes and a QTextCharFormat.

Tables and frames are treated similarly in the document structure since the QTextTable class is a subclass of QTextFrame, the class used to represent frames. Each frame's attributes (border, margins, padding, width, and so on) are stored in a single QTextFrameFormat.

Qt has many more rich text-related classes, although several of the others are concerned with laying out the text rather than with the storing of document elements. One very important class in relation to QTextDocument is QTextCursor which provides a programmatic means of editing QTextDocuments. In this chapter we use QTextCursors to edit existing documents and in the next chapter we use them to create documents from scratch.

Creating Custom Text Editors

In this section we will look at how to make a line edit and a plain text multi-line editor more convenient for users.

The first convenience we will add to both is *completion*. Completion is where as the user types text (or, in some implementations, when they type a particular key sequence), they are presented with possible choices of text to complete what they're typing—typically in the form of a list. The user can navigate through the list to choose a text using the arrow keys and then press Enter—or they can just click the one they want. Or they can ignore the list—by continuing to type or by pressing Esc, or by clicking outside the list.*

The other conveniences we will add—to the multi-line editor—are highlighting of the current line and color syntax highlighting. Current line highlighting makes it easier for users to see where they are, and syntax highlighting helps reveal the structure of the text (for texts that use a particular syntax, in our example, XML), as well as making it easier for users to spot syntax errors.

Completion for Line Edits and Comboboxes

In both the Image2Image program (Chapter 7; 248 ◄) and the Find Duplicates program (Chapter 8; 302 ◄) we used a QCompleter in conjunction with a QLineEdit to provide users with completion when entering paths. In these programs we used a popup list of completions, although QCompleter can also perform in-line completion; both kinds are shown in Figure 9.2.

The QCompleter class takes a QAbstractItemModel (which should either have a list or tree of items), and uses the model's items as the completion candidates. The model used by the QCompleter may have its items sorted (case-insensitively or case-sensitively), or unsorted.

---

*A concept that is closely related to completion is *input methods*—these are means by which users can enter text. An everyday example is pressing the digit buttons on a cell phone to enter a text message. A desktop computing example is where, say, a Japanese user types sequences of Latin characters which are received by the program they're using as Japanese characters; see the QInputContext class's documentation for details.

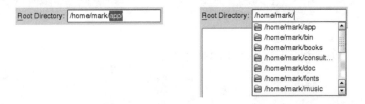

Figure 9.2 *Inline and popup completions*

Here is the start of the Find Duplicates program's `MainWindow::createWidgets()` method, where the line edit and its completer are created:

```
void MainWindow::createWidgets()
{
    rootDirectoryLabel = new QLabel(tr("Root Directory:"));
    rootDirectoryEdit = new QLineEdit(QDir::toNativeSeparators(
                                      QDir::homePath()));
    rootDirectoryLabel->setBuddy(rootDirectoryEdit);
    QCompleter *directoryCompleter = new QCompleter(this);
    directoryCompleter->setCaseSensitivity(Qt::CaseInsensitive);
    directoryCompleter->setModel(new DirModel(directoryCompleter));
    rootDirectoryEdit->setCompleter(directoryCompleter);
```

This is all that is necessary to provide completion—create a completer, give it a model, and set it on the editor widget—since Qt automatically handles the keyboard interaction and the popup list once everything is set up.

In this particular case, rather than using a `QDirModel` as is, we have created a custom subclass based on it.* This is purely so that we can show the correct path separators on all platforms. For completeness, here is the code for the custom model (it is almost identical to the one in Qt's `examples/tools/completer` example):

```
class DirModel : public QDirModel
{
public:
    explicit DirModel(QObject *parent=0) : QDirModel(parent) {}

    QVariant data(const QModelIndex &index,
                  int role=Qt::DisplayRole) const
    {
        if (role == Qt::DisplayRole && index.column() == 0) {
            QString path = QDir::toNativeSeparators(filePath(index));
            if (path.endsWith(QDir::separator()))
```

---

*From Qt 4.7, `QDirModel` is likely to be superceded by a new asynchronous `QFileSystemModel` class.

```
            path.chop(1);
        return path;
    }
    return QDirModel::data(index, role);
}
};
```

This model subclass simply replaces the `QAbstractItemModel::data()` method for the `Qt::DisplayRole` and ensures that the path shown to the user uses native separators and doesn't end with a path separator.

Clearly, it is easy to set up a completer for a `QLineEdit`—or for a `QComboBox` which also has a `setCompleter()` method that works the same way. And the setup is even easier if we have a static list of strings, since in such cases we can pass the strings to the `QCompleter` constructor and do not need to explicitly set a model at all.

Creating a completer for a multi-line text editor is somewhat more challenging since we must provide some means of invoking it (e.g., a particular key sequence), and we must populate it and position it correctly. We'll see how all this is done in the next subsection.

Completion and Syntax Highlighting for Text Editors

In this subsection we will develop a basic text editor widget for XML. In addition to all the functionality that we get for free from `QPlainTextEdit` and `QText-Edit` (such as copy and paste, undo/redo, and zooming), the two key features that we will add are completion and syntax highlighting.

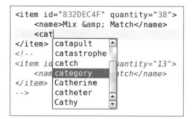

Figure 9.3 *XmlEdit's one word and multiple choice completions*

Figure 9.3 shows the `XmlEdit` widget (`xmledit`) we will cover in this subsection. The left-hand image shows when a user has entered des and then Ctrl+M (which is the keyboard shortcut we've used to invoke completion), and where there is only one word beginning with "des" in the completion model. In such cases the editor immediately inserts the missing portion of the one matching word and selects the inserted text. The user can accept the insertion by pressing Enter (in which case the inserted text is deselected and the cursor is moved to the end of the word), or they can reject it by pressing Esc (or by pressing Del, or simply by typing more characters). The right-hand image shows when a user has entered cat and then Ctrl+M, and where there are several words beginning with "cat". In these cases the editor pops up a list of words for the user to choose from. The user can choose a word from the list by clicking it, or by navigating to it using the up and down arrow keys and pressing Enter on the highlighted word. Or they can cancel, by pressing Esc, or by clicking somewhere other than the list, or simply by continuing to type.*

The XML shown in the images also gives an impression of the color syntax highlighting. We have chosen to color tags dark blue, attribute names blue, attribute values dark yellow, entities dark red, and comments green with an italic font. Notice also that both images show the background of the line the user is on highlighted. (For the screenshots we used a darker highlight than is in the source code; build and run the program to see the colors actually used.)

If we wanted to go a little further, it would be straightforward to add line numbering, although we leave this as an exercise—see Qt's examples/widgets/ codeeditor example to see how it is done. But if we want a full-blown feature-rich Qt plain text editor with syntax highlighting support for multiple languages and a whole host of power features, we would probably be best off using QScintilla (www.riverbankcomputing.co.uk/software/qscintilla), a Qt port of the C++ Scintilla editor component (www.scintilla.org).

Completion for Multi-line Editors

For the XmlEdit widget we will provide two kinds of completion. If the user invokes completion and there is a single candidate word, the rest of that word will be inserted immediately, and the inserted text will be selected. At this point, if the user presses Esc or Del, or types anything other than Enter (which accepts the insertion), the selected text will be removed, and in the case of the user typing a character, the character will be inserted as normal. If the user invokes completion and there are multiple candidates, a popup list of words to choose from will be presented, and the user can either choose from or cancel the popup.

We have chosen to subclass QPlainTextEdit rather than QTextEdit as the basis of the XmlEdit class. The QPlainTextEdit class has a slightly misleading name—it should perhaps have been called *QBasicTextEdit*—since it fully supports character formatting, such as bold, italic, and color, and even provides the QPlain-TextEdit::appendHtml() method! The QPlainTextEdit is very similar to QTextEdit and supports much of the same functionality, including the ability to utilize a

---

*On most platforms there is no standardized key press for completion, so, for example, different applications on Linux and Windows use their own unique ones. However, on Mac OS X, Esc is the standard key press for completion; if we want to honor that standard we could use an #ifdef Q_WS_MAC to set Esc as the completion key press on Mac OS X.

QSyntaxHighlighter, as we will see in the next subsubsection. The key differences are that QPlainTextEdit does not support frames or tables, and it uses a much simpler algorithm for laying out the text. This means that QPlainTextEdit is much faster than QTextEdit when it comes to handling large documents, which makes it an ideal class to use as a log viewer and as the basis for creating custom plain text editors.

In support of completion the XmlEdit class has three private member variables: completedAndSelected of type bool, completer of type QCompleter*, and model of type QStringListModel*. In addition to the constructor and methods to create the widget's child widgets and set up its connections, we must reimplement two event handlers and provide three slots and six (small) supporting methods to complete the implementation. We will start with the constructor to provide context.

```
XmlEdit::XmlEdit(QWidget *parent)
    : QPlainTextEdit(parent), completedAndSelected(false)
{
    createWidgets();
    createConnections();
    highlightCurrentLine();
}
```

The constructor is quite conventional. We will cover the highlightCurrentLine() method when we look at syntax highlighting in the next subsubsection.

```
void XmlEdit::createWidgets()
{
    (void) new XmlHighlighter(document());

    model = new QStringListModel(this);
    completer = new QCompleter(this);
    completer->setWidget(this);
    completer->setCompletionMode(QCompleter::PopupCompletion);
    completer->setModel(model);
    completer->setModelSorting(
            QCompleter::CaseInsensitivelySortedModel);
    completer->setCaseSensitivity(Qt::CaseInsensitive);
    completer->setWrapAround(true);
}
```

The first call creates a custom syntax highlighter and applies it to the QTextDocument (from the base class) that holds the XmlEdit's text and formatting data.

The rest of the method is concerned with completion. We begin by creating a model/view model for the completer to use, and then create a completer. We have chosen to use the popup completion mode, but we could have used QCompleter::InlineCompletion or QCompleter::UnfilteredPopupCompletion instead.

The call to QCompleter::setModelSorting() tells the completer how the model is sorted—it does *not* cause any sorting to be done! Here we have said that the model is using case-insensitive sorting; other options are QCompleter::CaseSensitivelySortedModel and QCompleter::UnsortedModel. If the completion model's completion role's data for its completion column is sorted, we should tell the completer that the model is sorted (as we have done here). If the completer knows that it has a sorted completion model it will use a fast binary search rather than a slow linear search when looking for completions—this can produce considerable performance improvements for large completion models.

The call to QCompleter::setCaseSensitivity() tells the completer whether it should be case-sensitive or not—if not, then it will show and insert completions regardless of case; otherwise it will show and insert only those completions that match the case of the text being completed. The last call, QCompleter::setWrapAround(), is used to determine what happens if the user navigates to the bottom or top of the completion list—for example, if set to true, then going "above" the top (first) item takes them to the bottom (last) item.

```
void XmlEdit::createConnections()
{
    connect(this, SIGNAL(cursorPositionChanged()),
            this, SLOT(highlightCurrentLine()));
    connect(completer, SIGNAL(activated(const QString&)),
            this, SLOT(insertCompletion(const QString&)));
    (void) new QShortcut(QKeySequence(tr("Ctrl+M", "Complete")),
                         this, SLOT(performCompletion()));
}
```

Three signal–slot connections are required, the second two used for completion. The first connection is used to ensure that whenever the cursor is moved (by the user typing, or navigating—for example, with the arrow keys, or by clicking), the current line is highlighted. We will discuss this in the next subsubsection.

The completer emits the activated() signal when the user chooses an item from the completion list; we connect to this signal so that we can insert the appropriate completion when this occurs.

The third connection is made as part of creating a new QShortcut, and is used to ensure that when the user presses Ctrl+M the performCompletion() slot is called.

```
void XmlEdit::performCompletion()
{
    QTextCursor cursor = textCursor();
    cursor.select(QTextCursor::WordUnderCursor);
```

```
        const QString completionPrefix = cursor.selectedText();
        if (!completionPrefix.isEmpty() &&
                completionPrefix.at(completionPrefix.length() - 1)
                                .isLetter())
            performCompletion(completionPrefix);
    }
```

When the user types Ctrl+M to invoke completion, we only want to set the completion process in motion if there is actually some text to complete. This slot starts by obtaining a cursor into the underlying QTextDocument, and then selects and retrieves the word (which could be a single character) the cursor is inside or that is immediately before the cursor (with no intervening whitespace). If the cursor is not inside a word or immediately following a word, an empty string is obtained.

If the word (i.e., the completion prefix) isn't empty and if it ends with a letter, we call the private overloaded performCompletion() method with the prefix.

Notice that we did not call QPlainTextEdit::setTextCursor() with the modified cursor. This means that the change we did (i.e., selecting a word) is not applied to the document, which is exactly what we want in this case.

As well as the ability to select individual words, the QTextCursor::select() method can be used to select the current line (QTextCursor::LineUnderCursor), the current paragraph (QTextCursor::BlockUnderCursor), or even the entire document (QTextCursor::Document). The QTextCursor API is shown in Tables 9.1, 9.2, and 9.3 (➤ 328–330).

```
    void XmlEdit::performCompletion(const QString &completionPrefix)
    {
        populateModel(completionPrefix);

        if (completionPrefix != completer->completionPrefix()) {
            completer->setCompletionPrefix(completionPrefix);
            completer->popup()->setCurrentIndex(
                    completer->completionModel()->index(0, 0));
        }

        if (completer->completionCount() == 1)
            insertCompletion(completer->currentCompletion(), true);
        else {
            QRect rect = cursorRect();
            rect.setWidth(completer->popup()->sizeHintForColumn(0) +
                    completer->popup()->verticalScrollBar()->
                    sizeHint().width());
            completer->complete(rect);
        }
    }
```

This method begins by populating the model used by the completer. It then makes sure that the completion prefix used by the completer matches the actual completion prefix, and selects the first item in the list of completions.

If there is only a single completion, we insert it immediately, passing `true` as the second argument to `insertCompletion()` to indicate this. Otherwise we call `QCompleter::complete()` to pop up the list of completions—the list will have the width and be at the position specified by the `QRect` we pass in. The `QPlainTextEdit::cursorRect()` method returns the text cursor's rectangle, but this is clearly much too narrow (a few pixels) to use for the popup list's width. So we set the rectangle's width to be wide enough for the popup's first (and normally, only) column, also allowing for the width of a vertical scrollbar.

Thanks to a signal–slot connection we made earlier (325 ◀), if the user chooses a completion from the popup list, the `insertCompletion()` slot will be called (with a default second argument of `false`, meaning a completion from a list of words, rather than from a single word).

```
void XmlEdit::populateModel(const QString &completionPrefix)
{
    QStringList strings = toPlainText().split(QRegExp("\\W+"));
    strings.removeAll(completionPrefix);
    strings.removeDuplicates();
    qSort(strings.begin(), strings.end(), caseInsensitiveLessThan);
    model->setStringList(strings);
}
```

This method is called every time a completion is invoked. It dynamically populates the completion model with words from the current document. This is done by extracting the document's entire text and splitting it into a list of words. Then we remove the completion prefix (if present), and any duplicate words, and then we sort the words and replace the model's existing strings with the new ones.

Creating a fresh list of completion words like this is fine for small documents, but may be computationally expensive for large documents. Also, for an empty document there will be no completions at all. One alternative would be to read in a list of words from a dictionary at application startup and populate the model just once. Another alternative would be to use an initial dictionary as just described, and to add any new unique words to it that the user enters as they type into the document. With either of these alternatives the model would be set once and never repopulated (although in the second alternative it would be updated).

Performing the sort is essential—the earlier call to `QCompleter::setModelSorting(QCompleter::CaseInsensitivelySortedModel)` told the completer how (or if) the model is sorted. So we must now honor that by ensuring that the model is sorted how we said it would be.

Table 9.1 *The QTextCursor API #1*

Method	Description
anchor()	Returns the anchor position; see also position()
atBlockEnd()	Returns true if the cursor is at the end of a block
atBlockStart()	Returns true if the cursor is at the start of a block
atEnd()	Returns true if the cursor is at the end of the document
atStart()	Returns true if the cursor is at the start of the document
beginEdit-Block()	Notifies the cursor that the editing actions to follow should be treated as a single action from an undo/redo perspective; see endEditBlock()
block()	Returns the QTextBlock that contains the cursor
blockChar-Format()	Returns the QTextCharFormat for the block containing the cursor; see also charFormat()
blockFormat()	Returns the QTextBlockFormat for the block containing the cursor
blockNumber()	Returns the line number for the cursor position in documents that don't have tables or frames (other than the root frame), such as QPlainTextEdit's QTextDocument
charFormat()	Returns the QTextCharFormat for the character immediately preceding the cursor position
clear-Selection()	Moves the anchor to the cursor position so that nothing is selected; see also removeSelectedText()
columnNumber()	Returns the position of the cursor in the line
createList(QTextList-Format)	Inserts and returns a QTextList using the given format (or given a QTextListFormat::Style) and with the current paragraph as the list's first item; see also insertList()
currentFrame()	Returns the current frame as a QTextFrame*
currentList()	Returns the current list as a QTextList* or 0 if the cursor position isn't in a list
currentTable()	Returns the current table as a QTextTable* or 0 if the cursor position isn't in a table
deleteChar()	If there is selected text, deletes it; otherwise deletes the character at the cursor position
deletePrevious-Char()	If there is selected text, deletes it; otherwise deletes the character before the cursor position
document()	Returns the cursor's document as a QTextDocument*

Table 9.2 *The QTextCursor API #2*

Method	Description
endEditBlock()	Notifies the cursor that the sequence of editing actions initiated by beginEditBlock() has finished
hasComplexSelection()	Returns true if the selection isn't a simple span of text, such as two or more cells in a table
hasSelection()	Returns true if there is a selection of any kind
insertBlock(QTextBlockFormat, QTextCharFormat)	Inserts a new empty block at the cursor position; there are two other overloads, one just taking a block format and the other taking no arguments
insertFragment(QText- DocumentFragment)	Inserts the given document fragment at the cursor position
insertFrame(QText- FrameFormat)	Inserts a QTextFrame with the given format at the cursor position, and moves the position (and any selection) into the frame
insertHtml(QString)	Inserts the HTML string at the cursor position
insertImage(...)	Inserts an image at the cursor position. There are overloads that accept a QTextImageFormat (optionally with a QTextFrameFormat::Position), a QString (filename), and a QImage
insertList(QText- ListFormat)	Inserts a new block at the cursor position and makes it the first item of a new QTextList using the given format (or given QTextListFormat::Style), and returns the list; see also createList()
insertTable(int, int, QTextTableFormat)	Inserts and returns a new QTextTable with the given number of rows and columns and with the (optional) format; see the text
insertText(QString, QTextCharFormat)	Inserts the text at the cursor position using the (optional) format
isCopyOf(QTextCursor)	Returns true if the given cursor is a copy of this cursor
isNull()	Returns true if this cursor is null (i.e., constructed without a QTextDocument)
joinPreviousEdit- Block()	Effectively "deletes" the last endEditBlock(), thus extending the scope of the previous beginEditBlock()
mergeBlockCharFormat(QTextCharFormat)	Merges the given format with the current block's (or selection's) character format
mergeBlockFormat(QTextBlockFormat)	Merges the given format with the current block's (or selection's) format

Table 9.3 *The QTextCursor API #3*

Method	Description
mergeCharFormat(QTextCharFormat)	Merges the given format with the format of the character (or selection) at the cursor position
movePosition(MoveOperation, MoveMode, int)	Moves the cursor position by the (optional) count times using the given operation. If the (optional) mode is KeepAnchor the anchor stays, thus creating a selection; the default mode is MoveAnchor (the move operations are listed in Table 9.4; ➤ 334).
position()	Returns the cursor's position; see setPosition()
removeSelectedText()	Deletes whatever is selected
select(SelectionType)	Selects text according to the type (Document, BlockUnderCursor, LineUnderCursor, WordUnderCursor)
selectedTableCells(int*, int*, int*, int*)	Populates the pointed-to ints with the first row and row count, and first column and column count, that identify the selected table cells
selectedText()	Returns the selection's text as plain text
selection()	Returns the selection as a QTextDocumentFragment
selectionEnd()	Returns the position of the end of the selection
selectionStart()	Returns the position of the start of the selection
setBlockCharFormat(QTextCharFormat)	Sets the character format for the current block (or for the current selection); see also mergeBlockCharFormat()
setBlockFormat(QTextBlockFormat)	Sets the block format for the current block (or for the current selection); see also mergeBlockFormat()
setCharFormat(QTextCharFormat)	Sets the format for the current character; see also mergeCharFormat()
setPosition(int, MoveMode)	Moves the cursor to the given position; if the move mode is KeepAnchor the anchor stays, thus creating a selection; see movePosition()
setVisual‐ Navigation(bool)	If set to true, hidden paragraphs are skipped when moving; the default is false
visualNavigation()	Returns the visual navigation setting as a bool

The global qSort() function can be called with a sequence such as QList<T>, QStringList, or QVector<T>, or with begin and end iterators if we want to sort just a portion of the sequence, or—as here—if we want to also provide a comparison function or functor. The sequences used by the qSort() function must provide an operator<() method, but the default < for QStrings performs a case-sensitive comparison, so here we have supplied our own tiny comparison function.

Qt also provides qStableSort() functions with the same APIs as the qSort() functions. Stable sorts have the same time complexity as standard sorts, but preserve the relative order of items where two or more items compare as equal.

```
bool caseInsensitiveLessThan(const QString &a, const QString &b)
{
    return a.compare(b, Qt::CaseInsensitive) < 0;
}
```

The QString::compare() methods are not locale-aware beyond the ability to do simple case folding if we pass Qt::CaseInsensitive as we do here.

We would have preferred to use a QString::localeAwareCompare() method, since these are specifically designed for sorting lists of user-visible strings. However, since at the time of this writing, the documentation is silent regarding the sorting understood by QCompleter, we have stuck with the simpler and faster QString::compare() method.

```
void XmlEdit::insertCompletion(const QString &completion,
                               bool singleWord)
{
    QTextCursor cursor = textCursor();
    int numberOfCharsToComplete = completion.length() -
            completer->completionPrefix().length();
    int insertionPosition = cursor.position();
    cursor.insertText(completion.right(numberOfCharsToComplete));
    if (singleWord) {
        cursor.setPosition(insertionPosition);
        cursor.movePosition(QTextCursor::EndOfWord,
                            QTextCursor::KeepAnchor);
        completedAndSelected = true;
    }
    setTextCursor(cursor);
}
```

This method inserts the characters needed to perform the completion. It begins by getting a cursor into the document. It then calculates how many characters need to be inserted—the completion list shows whole words but we only want to insert those characters necessary to complete the word the user has started to enter. Next we record the cursor's position (i.e., the position where the completion characters will be inserted) and then insert the portion of the completion string necessary to complete the word.

If `singleWord` is `true` it means that a single word completion has occurred and we must select the inserted characters so that the user can see them and easily be able to get rid of them if they're unwanted. In this case we put the cursor back to where the insertion was made and then use the `QTextCursor::movePosition()` method to move the cursor to the end of the completed word. This has the effect of selecting the inserted characters (as we'll discuss in a moment). We also set `completedAndSelected` to `true` since we need to treat the next key press (or mouse click) specially so that the user can easily accept or reject the single word completion.

At the end we set the document's cursor to the modified cursor to make our changes (insertion, and possibly selection) take effect.

The `QTextCursor::movePosition()` method mimics the user navigating in the document, and has `enums` for all the standard movements—these are listed in Table 9.4.

The `QTextCursor` maintains two positions, `QTextCursor::position()` (the current cursor position), and `QTextCursor::anchor()` (some other cursor position). Usually the position and anchor are the same, but if they are different, then everything between them is selected. That is, `QTextCursor` defines a selection in terms of the anchor and the position—and if they are the same then nothing is selected.

The position can be set directly using `QTextCursor::setPosition()`, but the anchor can only be set indirectly. The `QTextCursor::movePosition()` method has two modes of operation (passed as the second argument), `QTextCursor::MoveAnchor` (the default) and `QTextCursor::KeepAnchor`. If we choose the `KeepAnchor` mode, the anchor position will be where the position was before the move and the position will be the position after the move.

Note that our implementation has a weakness—in some use cases—in that it does not fix the case of the entered text to match that of the completion text. For example, if the user typed "ali" and the chosen completion word was "AlignLeft", the result would be "alignLeft". Modifying this method to match the case of completions is left as an exercise.

```
void XmlEdit::keyPressEvent(QKeyEvent *event)
{
    if (completedAndSelected && handledCompletedAndSelected(event))
        return;
    completedAndSelected = false;

    if (completer->popup()->isVisible()) {
        switch (event->key()) {
            case Qt::Key_Up:      // Fallthrough
            case Qt::Key_Down:    // Fallthrough
            case Qt::Key_Enter:   // Fallthrough
```

```
                case Qt::Key_Return:  // Fallthrough
                case Qt::Key_Escape: event->ignore(); return;
                default: completer->popup()->hide(); break;
            }
        }

        QPlainTextEdit::keyPressEvent(event);
    }
```

This event handler is called whenever the user presses a key in the XmlEdit widget. We have reimplemented it to handle two specific situations. First, if the user has done a single word completion, the *following* key press (or mouse click) they make determines whether the completion is accepted or rejected. And second, we want to ignore any key presses handled by the completion popup if the popup is active.

If completedAndSelected is true then we know that a single word completion has just been made, and so this key press is the following one. In this case we call the handledCompletedAndSelected() method which returns a Boolean to indicate whether it handled the key press, in which case we can return, or if we should continue with the event handler.

If the completer's popup is visible, we ignore the key press if it is one that the completer handles (i.e., the up and down arrow keys to choose a completion, Esc to cancel, and Enter to accept). For any other key press we cancel the completion by hiding the completer, and pass the event to the base class's keyPressEvent() handler to process in the normal way.

Note also that in all cases, completedAndSelected is set to false—it is only ever true *immediately* after a single word completion has occurred, and must always be made false on the next key press or mouse click.

```
    bool XmlEdit::handledCompletedAndSelected(QKeyEvent *event)
    {
        completedAndSelected = false;
        QTextCursor cursor = textCursor();
        switch (event->key()) {
            case Qt::Key_Enter:  // Fallthrough
            case Qt::Key_Return: cursor.clearSelection(); break;
            case Qt::Key_Escape: cursor.removeSelectedText(); break;
            default: return false;
        }
        setTextCursor(cursor);
        event->accept();
        return true;
    }
```

Table 9.4 *The QTextCursor::MoveOperation enum*

Enum	Description
Down	Moves the cursor down one line
End	Moves the cursor to the end of the document
EndOfBlock	Moves the cursor to the end of the current block
EndOfLine	Moves the cursor to the end of the current line
EndOfWord	Moves the cursor to the end of the current word
Left	Moves the cursor left one character
NextBlock	Moves the cursor to the start of the next block
NextCell	Moves the cursor to the table's next cell
NextCharacter	Moves the cursor to the next character
NextRow	Moves the cursor to the first cell of the table's next row
NextWord	Moves the cursor to the start of the next word
NoMove	Does not move the cursor position
PreviousBlock	Moves the cursor to the start of the previous block
PreviousCell	Moves the cursor to the table's previous cell
PreviousCharacter	Moves the cursor to the previous character
PreviousRow	Moves the cursor to the last cell of the table's previous row
PreviousWord	Moves the cursor to the start of the previous word
Right	Moves the cursor right one character
Start	Moves the cursor to the start of the document
StartOfBlock	Moves the cursor to the start of the current block
StartOfLine	Moves the cursor to the start of the current line
StartOfWord	Moves the cursor to the start of the current word
Up	Moves the cursor up one line
WordLeft	Moves the cursor left one word
WordRight	Moves the cursor right one word

The QTextCursor class is used to programmatically create and edit QTextDocuments. A suitable cursor can be obtained by calling QPlainTextEdit::textCursor(); this is effectively the same as calling QTextCursor(document()) since the QPlainTextEdit::document() method returns a pointer to the QTextDocument that holds its text and formatting. (All this is also true of QTextEdit, as is everything else we cover here.)

A QTextCursor allows us to mimic a user's actions—navigating through the document, inserting, deleting, and selecting text, and so on—through the API that it provides. We will see a lot more of this class in the next chapter when we use it to programmatically create QTextDocuments. The pattern of use for QTextCursor with QPlainTextEdit and QTextEdit is quite simple: obtain a cursor into the document, perform editing actions using the QTextCursor API, and then set the modified cursor as the document's cursor to make the changes take effect.

The handledCompletedAndSelected() method is called when the user presses a key immediately after a single word completion has been made. If they pressed Enter (or Return) to accept the completion, we clear the selection (since for single word completions the inserted text is selected, as we saw earlier; 331 ◄). If they pressed Esc to reject the completion, we delete the selected text. In either of these cases we call accept() on the event to tell Qt that we have handled it and return true to signify to our reimplemented keyPressEvent() method that there is no more to do.

If the user typed something else we return false so that what they typed can be handled. For example, if they typed a letter, the base class's key press event handler will delete the selected text and insert the letter that was typed. For almost every editing widget (and not just those provided by Qt) this is the default behavior when typing over selected text. This means that the user can reject a single word completion simply by continuing to type.

```
void XmlEdit::mousePressEvent(QMouseEvent *event)
{
    if (completedAndSelected) {
        completedAndSelected = false;
        QTextCursor cursor = textCursor();
        cursor.removeSelectedText();
        setTextCursor(cursor);
    }
    QPlainTextEdit::mousePressEvent(event);
}
```

If a single word completion has just taken place, completedAndSelected is true, and the user can accept or reject the completion using the keyboard as we have just seen. And for consistency with the completion popup, they can also reject the completion simply by clicking the mouse somewhere in the document. The code for removing the completion text is the same as that used in the handledCompletedAndSelected() method we saw earlier.

No matter whether a single word completion is accepted or rejected, as soon as the user has pressed a key or clicked the mouse, completedAndSelected must be set to false so that subsequent key presses are handled correctly.

We have now completed our review of completion. As we saw earlier, setting up completion for QLineEdits and QComboBoxes is easily done by calling their setCompleter() method. But for multi-line widgets such as QPlainTextEdit or QTextEdit, there is rather more work to do. In contrast, setting up current line highlighting and syntax highlighting is much more straightforward, although for the latter a good knowledge of regular expressions is very helpful, as we will see in the next subsubsection.

Syntax Highlighting

In this subsubsection we will focus primarily on syntax highlighting, but we will begin with a brief diversion to see how to highlight the current line. In the previous subsubsection we saw a signal–slot connection from the QPlainText-Edit's cursorPositionChanged() signal to a custom highlightCurrentLine() slot (325 ◄). This connection ensures that whenever the cursor is moved (whether by keyboard or mouse), the slot is called.

```
void XmlEdit::highlightCurrentLine()
{
    QList<QTextEdit::ExtraSelection> extraSelections;
    QTextEdit::ExtraSelection selection;
    QBrush highlightColor = palette().alternateBase();
    selection.format.setBackground(highlightColor);
    selection.format.setProperty(QTextFormat::FullWidthSelection,
                                 true);
    selection.cursor = textCursor();
    selection.cursor.clearSelection();
    extraSelections.append(selection);
    setExtraSelections(extraSelections);
}
```

Since Qt 4.2, the QPlainTextEdit and QTextEdit classes have supported the ability to programmatically add extra selections. The main use of these is to provide additional highlighting, such as here where we highlight the current line, or to highlight lines that have breakpoints, and so on.

The method begins by creating a list of selections (to which we will just add one). It then sets the selection's QTextCharFormat's background color and also one of its properties. The QTextFormat class (QTextCharFormat's base class) provides a property mechanism to make it easy to add more properties without breaking binary compatibility in future Qt releases. Some of the properties are for paragraphs (i.e., for QTextBlockFormat), others for characters, and some for either. Here we have said that the selection's formatting should apply to the selection's full width.

With the selection's format set up we retrieve the document's cursor and clear any existing selection—this moves the anchor to the current cursor position. We then set the extra selections—which includes the selection we have just created. After this we would not normally expect to see any selection at all— the anchor and position are at the same place, so there is nothing to select between them. However, by turning on the QTextFormat::FullWidthSelection property we have ensured that the selection is effectively extended over the full width of the line the cursor is in, regardless of the anchor.

The signal–slot connection and the highlightCurrentLine() method are all we need to provide current line highlighting. In contrast, to provide syntax high-lighting, we just need to create an instance of a QSyntaxHighlighter subclass with a pointer to our QTextDocument—and, of course, we must create the sub-class. (We saw the instance created earlier; 324 ◄.)

The Qt examples and source code include some ready-made QSyntaxHighlight-er subclasses. In the examples/richtext/syntaxhighlighter example, there is a syntax highlighter for C++/Qt code. And all the examples/xmlpatterns ex-amples have an XML syntax highlighter that is a bit shorter and simpler than the one we will review here. In addition, the *Qt Designer* source code, tools/designer/src/lib/shared, contains three syntax highlighters, csshigh-lighter.cpp for CSS (Cascading Style Sheets), htmlhighlighter.cpp for HTML, and qscripthighlighter.cpp for JavaScript. None of these are part of Qt's pub-lic API, but they might serve as useful starting points. Something else to con-sider is the GNU Source-Highlight library (www.gnu.org/software/src-highlite). This library provides syntax highlighting for a wide range of languages and formats, and the Source-Highlight Qt library (srchiliteqt.sourceforge.net) provides a QSyntaxHighlighter wrapper for it.

One of the most convenient ways of doing syntax highlighting is to use regular expressions (regexes), and that is one of the approaches we take here, so we assume a basic knowledge of regexes.* Using regexes can result in poor performance on large documents (which may be why the htmlhighlighter.cpp mentioned earlier doesn't use them).

A QSyntaxHighlighter subclass must provide an implementation of the high-lightBlock() method. This method is called to provide the highlighting for a single line of text and is called automatically whenever necessary. For syntaxes that span multiple lines (such as multi-line comments) it is often necessary to maintain some state to determine whether a given line is inside some multiple-line-spanning construct. To support this, we can associate an integer (i.e., a

---

* The QRegExp documentation at qt.nokia.com/doc/qregexp.html provides a very brief overview of regexes. A good book on regular expressions is *Mastering Regular Expressions* by Jeffrey E. F. Friedl, ISBN 0596528124—it does not explicitly cover QRegExp, but it does cover Perl regexes which are similar (although with many more features).

state ID) to each line using the `setCurrentBlockState()` method, and we can find out the state of the preceding line with the `previousBlockState()` method.

For the XmlEdit's `XmlHighlighter` class we support two states, four types of syntactic elements, and highlight using five different character formats. Here are the states, types, and formats we use—they are all private data in `xmlhighlighter.hpp`:

```
enum State {Normal=0x01, InComment=0x02};
enum Type {Tag, Attribute, Entity, Comment};

QTextCharFormat tagFormat;
QTextCharFormat attributeNameFormat;
QTextCharFormat attributeValueFormat;
QTextCharFormat entityFormat;
QTextCharFormat commentFormat;
QMultiHash<Type, QRegExp> regexForType;
```

We have used a `QMultiHash` to associate one or more regexes with each element type. Wherever one of the regexes matches, we will apply the formatting appropriate for its corresponding type. (We introduced `QMultiHash` in the previous chapter; 304 ◄.)

We will now review the constructor, the `highlightBlock()` method, and all their supporting methods to see how the syntax highlighting is achieved.

```
XmlHighlighter::XmlHighlighter(QTextDocument *parent)
    : QSyntaxHighlighter(parent)
{
    tagFormat.setForeground(Qt::darkBlue);
    attributeNameFormat.setForeground(Qt::blue);
    attributeValueFormat.setForeground(Qt::darkYellow);
    entityFormat.setForeground(Qt::darkRed);
    commentFormat.setForeground(Qt::darkGreen);
    commentFormat.setFontItalic(true);

    addRegex(Tag, "<[!?]?\\w+(?:/>)?", false);
    addRegex(Tag, "(?:</\\w+)?[?]?>");
    addRegex(Attribute, "(\\w+(?::\\w+)?)=(\"[^\"]+\"|'[^']+')");
    addRegex(Entity, "&(:?#\\d+|\\w+);");
    addRegex(Comment, "<!--.*-->");
}
```

In the constructor we pass to the base class the `QTextDocument` that the highlighting should be applied to. We also set up the `QTextCharFormat`s—in most cases just setting a foreground text color, but for comments we also make the font italic. Naturally, we could apply any other formatting that `QTextCharFormat` supports.

For each XML element we want to syntax highlight we add a regex to the QMultiHash using a custom addRegex() helper method. The helper's third argument defaults to true (which means use minimal, i.e., non-greedy, matching).

The first regex is used to match the opening part of a tag, or tags that are complete in themselves—for example, <*tag*, <!*tag*, <?*tag*, or <*tag*/>. The second regex is used to match a closing tag or the closing part of a tag—for example, </*tag*>, ?>, or >. The third regex matches a *key=value* attribute, such as *key*="*value*". Strictly speaking, attributes should only be highlighted if they occur inside a tag, but here we have taken a more simplistic approach and highlight any *key=value* we encounter. The fourth regex is used to match entities—for example, é or é. The last regex is used to match comments that occur within a single line—we will see how to match multi-line-spanning comments shortly. Apart from the first, all the regexes use minimal matching.

```
void XmlHighlighter::addRegex(Type type, const QString &pattern,
                              bool minimal)
{
    QRegExp regex(pattern);
    regex.setPatternSyntax(QRegExp::RegExp2);
    regex.setMinimal(minimal);
    regexForType.insert(type, regex);
}
```

This helper method creates a QRegExp, and inserts it into the QMultiHash with the type as its key.

Whenever we use capturing parentheses, we always call QRegExp::setPatternSyntax(QRegExp::RegExp2). This ensures that when we use non-minimal (i.e., greedy) matching, the behavior is like that of most other regex engines (in particular, Perl's) rather than QRegExp's own rather idiosyncratic behavior. (The more Perl-like behavior is expected to be the default in Qt 5.)

```
void XmlHighlighter::highlightBlock(const QString &text)
{
    setCurrentBlockState(Normal);

    highlightPatterns(text);
    highlightComments(text);
}
```

By default we assume that the current line's state is Normal (although we may change it). We have factored out the two approaches we use for syntax highlighting into two separate methods. The highlightPatterns() method uses regexes that work within the context of a single line, and the highlightComments() method uses string searching and handles multiple-line-spanning comments. We must call highlightComments() second because we want the highlighting for commented-out XML to override any other highlighting.

```
void XmlHighlighter::highlightPatterns(const QString &text)
{
    QHashIterator<Type, QRegExp> i(regexForType);
    while (i.hasNext()) {
        i.next();
        Type type = i.key();
        const QRegExp &regex = i.value();
        int index = regex.indexIn(text);
        while (index > -1) {
            int length = regex.matchedLength();
            if (type == Tag)
                setFormat(index, length, tagFormat);
            else if (type == Attribute) {
                setFormat(index, regex.pos(2) - index - 1,
                          attributeNameFormat);
                setFormat(regex.pos(2) + 1, regex.cap(2).length() - 2,
                          attributeValueFormat);
            }
            else if (type == Entity)
                setFormat(index, length, entityFormat);
            else if (type == Comment)
                setFormat(index, length, commentFormat);
            index = regex.indexIn(text, index + length);
        }
    }
}
```

This method is conceptually simple: we iterate over every regex in the QMulti-Hash, apply the regex to the current line (in text), and if we get a match, we apply the highlighting that is appropriate for the Type the regex is associated with.

It doesn't matter that some keys have more than one value; the iterator will return as many key–value pairs as there are values in the hash. Every time a regex matches, for most elements we apply the corresponding QTextCharFormat for the length of the match. The exception is for attributes where we format the key and value parts separately. Notice that although the first call to QRegExp::indexIn() starts from the beginning of the text (since no offset is given), the subsequent calls that occur inside the while loop are offset past the end of the last match.

One of the regex patterns matched comments that begin and end in the same line. The highlightComments() method is used to provide highlighting for comments that span multiple lines.

```
void XmlHighlighter::highlightComments(const QString &text)
{
```

```
        const QString StartOfComment("<!--");
        const QString EndOfComment("-->");

        if (previousBlockState() > -1 &&
            (previousBlockState() & InComment) == InComment) {
            int end = text.indexOf(EndOfComment);
            if (end == -1) {
                setFormat(0, text.length(), commentFormat);
                setCurrentBlockState(currentBlockState() | InComment);
                return;
            }
            else
                setFormat(0, end + EndOfComment.length(), commentFormat);
        }

        int start = text.lastIndexOf(StartOfComment);
        if (start != -1) {
            int end = text.lastIndexOf(EndOfComment);
            if (end < start) {
                setFormat(start, text.length(), commentFormat);
                setCurrentBlockState(currentBlockState() | InComment);
            }
        }
    }
```

The default block "state" value is −1, so we always use positive integers for our custom block states, in this case using 0x01 and 0x02 for the Normal and InComment states. We have chosen to specify the values in hexadecimal to make it more obvious that we want to be able to use bitwise operators on them. This isn't really necessary in this example, but for more complex highlighters, we might have more states (0x04, 0x08, 0x10, etc.) and might want to be able to combine states (say, 0x01 | 0x04, to produce a value of 0x05 which contains states 1 and 4).

The cases that this method must consider are:

1. We are already in a multi-line comment and the comment does or does not end in this line.

2. A multi-line comment begins in this line.

3. Neither of the above.

If we are already in a multi-line comment then the QSyntaxHighlighter::previousBlockState() will contain the InComment state. Since we want to support the ability to combine states, instead of comparing the previous block state directly with InComment, we mask the previous block state with InComment and then do the comparison. This approach allows us to detect the state we are interested in even if two or more states are combined. If we are inside a multi-line comment we check to see if the comment ends in this line. If the comment does not end here, we apply the comment format to this entire line and combine the InComment state with the current block's existing state (which we had set to Normal earlier; 339 ◄), and then return, since there is no more to do. But if the comment ends in this line, we apply comment formatting up to the end of the comment, and then continue with the method since a new multi-line comment might begin further on in the line.

If we are not in a multi-line comment, or if such a comment has ended in the current line, we look to see if a new multi-line comment begins in this line. If we find the start of a comment, we look for the comment's end. We must make sure that we ignore comments that both start and end in the line since we already format those elsewhere, and we must be careful that if we find an end comment element it occurs *before* the start comment element (i.e., any end comment element found is associated with a previous comment and is not the end of the multi-line comment starting in this line). And if a multi-line comment does begin on this line, we apply comment formatting from the comment's start to the end of the line, and combine the InComment state with the current state.

In any other case we do nothing since either there is no formatting to do at all, or the formatting has already been handled by the highlightPatterns() method.

This completes our review of the XmlHighlighter class and of syntax highlighting. We used regexes for some of our highlighting, and simple string searches for some of it. Another approach is to implement a parser and to read the text character by character. And if a state integer or bit-pattern isn't sufficient, we can supplement it by associating custom data with each line (using QSyntax-Highlighter::setCurrentBlockUserData()).

Of course, sometimes, it isn't highlighting that we want, but rather to give the user the ability to enter text with the colors, fonts, and font attributes of their choice. In the following sections we will see how this can be achieved, both for a single line editor, and for a multi-line editor.

A Rich Text Single Line Editor

Qt already provides a widget that can be used for editing rich text—QText-Edit—but it is designed for editing multiple lines of text rather than just the single line that is often what we need. Nonetheless, by subclassing QTextEdit we can take advantage of all the editing and rendering features it offers, and at the same time only allow a single line to be displayed and edited. We could, of course, subclass QPlainTextEdit, but using QTextEdit is more convenient since it provides many useful slots—such as QTextEdit::setFontItalic()—that are not provided by QPlainTextEdit.

Figure 9.4 *The RichTextLineEdit's tooltip and context menu*

In this section we will create a `RichTextLineEdit` widget that can be used to edit a single line of text and that allows the user to apply text effects to individual characters and words in the text, such as bold, italic, or setting the color. The `RichTextLineEdit` is used by the Timelog applications' `RichTextDelegate` that we saw in Chapter 5 (193 ◄). Figure 9.4 shows the tooltip and context menu that we will provide for the `RichTextLineEdit`.

We'll start by looking at an extract from the class's definition, but we won't show most of the private slots, methods, or data (although we will cover them all as we review the public and protected methods and slots).

```
class RichTextLineEdit : public QTextEdit
{
    Q_OBJECT

public:
    explicit RichTextLineEdit(QWidget *parent=0);

    QString toSimpleHtml() const;

    QSize sizeHint() const;
    QSize minimumSizeHint() const;

public slots:
    void toggleItalic() { setFontItalic(!fontItalic()); }
    void toggleBold() { setFontWeight(fontWeight() > QFont::Normal
                        ? QFont::Normal : QFont::Bold); }

signals:
    void returnPressed();

protected:
    void keyPressEvent(QKeyEvent *event);
    ...

private:
    enum Style {Bold, Italic, StrikeOut, NoSuperOrSubscript,
                Subscript, Superscript};
    ...
};
```

The setFontItalic() and setFontWeight() methods are inherited from QTextEdit, and although Qt can handle several different font weights, we have reduced the choice to a simple on/off for bold.

The returnPressed() signal is designed to make the RichTextLineEdit more like QLineEdit and helps the delegate (or any other object that connects to it) to know that the user has finished and confirmed their editing. The reimplementation of the keyPressEvent() is where we detect Enter and Return and emit the signal.

Since we have subclassed QTextEdit, we don't have to do any painting ourselves, and much of the standard behavior (such as copy and paste and undo/redo) is inherited. This means that the only work we must do is ensure that the RichTextLineEdit is fixed to show only one line, and to provide the additional custom behaviors we want. We will start our review, as usual, with the constructor.

```
RichTextLineEdit::RichTextLineEdit(QWidget *parent)
    : QTextEdit(parent)
{
    setLineWrapMode(QTextEdit::NoWrap);
    setWordWrapMode(QTextOption::NoWrap);
    setAcceptRichText(true);
    setTabChangesFocus(true);
    setVerticalScrollBarPolicy(Qt::ScrollBarAlwaysOff);
    setHorizontalScrollBarPolicy(Qt::ScrollBarAlwaysOff);
    createShortcuts();
    createActions();
    setContextMenuPolicy(Qt::CustomContextMenu);
    connect(this, SIGNAL(customContextMenuRequested(const QPoint&)),
            this, SLOT(customContextMenuRequested(const QPoint&)));
}
```

We use the constructor to do all the obvious changes that we need to make: we switch off line and word wrapping, ensure that if HTML is pasted from the clipboard it is accepted as rich text, make the Tab key move the focus rather than insert a tab character, and switch off the scrollbars.

The easiest way to provide a context menu is to add QActions to a widget and to set a context menu policy of Qt::ActionsContextMenu, and leave Qt to take care of it. For this particular widget, though, this is not a suitable solution since we want to update the checked state of the actions whenever the context menu is invoked. So the approach we have taken for the RichTextLineEdit is to set a context menu policy of Qt::CustomContextMenu, and to connect the customContextMenuRequested() signal that is emitted when a context menu is invoked when this policy is in force to a custom slot of the same name where we will set up and show the context menu ourselves.

```
void RichTextLineEdit::createShortcuts()
{
    QShortcut *boldShortcut = new QShortcut(QKeySequence::Bold,
            this, SLOT(toggleBold()));
    QShortcut *italicShortcut = new QShortcut(QKeySequence::Italic,
            this, SLOT(toggleItalic()));

    setToolTip(tr("<p>Use %1 to toggle bold, %2 to toggle italic, "
                  "and the context menu for color and other effects.")
              .arg(boldShortcut->key().toString(
                  QKeySequence::NativeText))
              .arg(italicShortcut->key().toString(
                  QKeySequence::NativeText)));
}
```

We provide keyboard shortcuts for bold and italic by creating suitable QShortcuts and using standard QKeySequences. On Linux and Windows the bold action's shortcut will be Ctrl+B, but on Mac OS X it will be ⌘+B.*

Once we have the shortcuts, we create a tooltip that shows them—converting them into string forms so that they appear correctly for the platform that the program is being run on.

```
void RichTextLineEdit::createActions()
{
    boldAction = createAction(tr("Bold"), Bold);
    ...
    colorAction = new QAction(tr("Color"), this);
    colorAction->setMenu(createColorMenu());

    addActions(QList<QAction*>() << boldAction << italicAction
            << strikeOutAction << noSubOrSuperScriptAction
            << superScriptAction << subScriptAction << colorAction);
    AQP::accelerateActions(actions());
}
```

This method is used to create the actions—most of which we've omitted since all but the last are created in the same way. The createAction() method, which we will look at in a moment, takes two arguments: the text to appear in the menu and an item of data—in this case one of the enums.

---

*Many standard keyboard shortcuts that use the Ctrl key on Windows and Linux (such as Ctrl+C to copy) use the ⌘ key on Mac OS X (e.g., ⌘+C). In view of this, when Qt was first ported to Mac OS X, to simplify cross-platform development, Qt simply "swapped" the Ctrl and ⌘ keys—which is why pressing, say, ⌘+X on Mac OS X is the same as pressing Ctrl+X on other platforms. With the benefit of hindsight this may not seem like such a wise decision, and from Qt 4.6 it is possible to prevent the key swap being done by calling QApplication::setAttribute(Qt::AA_MacDontSwapCtrlAndMeta).

Figure 9.5 *The RichTextLineEdit's color submenu*

The color action is unusual in that we don't connect it to anything, but instead we give it a menu.

Toward the end we add all the actions to the RichTextLineEdit; we could just as easily have held them in a private QList<QAction*>. And at the end we give them keyboard accelerators.

```
QAction *RichTextLineEdit::createAction(const QString &text,
                                        const QVariant &data)
{
    QAction *action = new QAction(text, this);
    action->setData(data);
    action->setCheckable(true);
    action->setChecked(false);
    connect(action, SIGNAL(triggered()), SLOT(applyTextEffect()));
    return action;
}
```

This is a convenience method that creates the actions we need, making them all checkable and initially unchecked. Each of these actions is connected to the applyTextEffect() method.

```
QMenu *RichTextLineEdit::createColorMenu()
{
    QMenu *colorMenu = new QMenu(this);
    QPixmap pixmap(22, 22);
    typedef QPair<QColor, QString> ColorPair;
    foreach (const ColorPair &pair, QList<ColorPair>()
            << qMakePair(QColor(Qt::black), tr("Black"))
            ...
            << qMakePair(QColor(Qt::darkRed), tr("Dark Red"))) {
        pixmap.fill(pair.first);
        QAction *action = colorMenu->addAction(pixmap, pair.second);
        action->setData(pair.first);
```

```
    }
    connect(colorMenu, SIGNAL(triggered(QAction*)),
            this, SLOT(applyColor(QAction*)));
    AQP::accelerateMenu(colorMenu);
    return colorMenu;
}
```

This method is used to create the color menu used by the color action; the menu is shown in Figure 9.5. We begin by creating a new QMenu on the heap and then we create a list of pairs—QColors and their names—that we immediately iterate over. For each pair, we create an action with a pixmap of the corresponding color, and with the name of the color, and set the action's data to the QColor value. (Qt's QPixmaps work like value classes since they use copy-on-write, so each action gets its own unique pixmap. In Chapter 12 we will see how to create nicer color swatches than the plain square ones we have used here.)

We connect the menu's triggered() action to the applyColor() slot—the QAction* that is passed is the one corresponding to the menu option chosen by the user. Finally, we create keyboard accelerators for the menu items and return the menu to the caller.

The use of the typedef is necessary because Qt's foreach macro has the syntax foreach (*item*, *sequence*). The comma is part of the syntax and used to distinguish between the item and the sequence. (It doesn't matter if the sequence has commas; only the first comma is important.) So, for item pairs, we must either use a typedef, or we must create the list and item in advance; for example:

```
QList<QPair<QColor, QString> > pairList;
pairList << qMakePair(QColor(Qt::black), tr("Black"))
    ...
         << qMakePair(QColor(Qt::darkRed), tr("Dark Red"));
QPair<QColor, QString> pair;
foreach (pair, pairList)
    ...
```

Using this approach requires slightly more code, but is obviously more convenient if we want to create the pairs separately—for example, to reuse them later—rather than at the point of use.

```
void RichTextLineEdit::applyColor(QAction *action)
{
    Q_ASSERT(action);
    setTextColor(action->data().value<QColor>());
}
```

This slot is called whenever the user chooses a color from the context menu's color submenu. It simply calls the base class's setTextColor() method to set the chosen color.

For classes in the *QtCore* library, QVariant provides getter methods—for example, QVariant::toDate(), QVariant::toPoint(), QVariant::toString(), and so on. But for classes in other Qt libraries (such as *QtGui*), we must use the QVariant::value<T>() getter, with T being the type we want to retrieve.

```cpp
void RichTextLineEdit::applyTextEffect()
{
    if (QAction *action = qobject_cast<QAction*>(sender())) {
        Style style = static_cast<Style>(action->data().toInt());
        QTextCharFormat format = currentCharFormat();
        switch (style) {
            case Bold: toggleBold(); return;
            case Italic: toggleItalic(); return;
            case StrikeOut:
                format.setFontStrikeOut(!format.fontStrikeOut());
                break;
            case NoSuperOrSubscript:
                format.setVerticalAlignment(
                        QTextCharFormat::AlignNormal);
                break;
            case Superscript:
                format.setVerticalAlignment(
                        QTextCharFormat::AlignSuperScript);
                break;
            case Subscript:
                format.setVerticalAlignment(
                        QTextCharFormat::AlignSubScript);
                break;
        }
        mergeCurrentCharFormat(format);
    }
}
```

If the user invokes any of the actions from the context menu (apart from the colors in the color submenu), then this slot is called. First we cast the invoking object to a QAction pointer (which should always work), then we extract the action's data—in this case the value of the RichTextLineEdit class's private Style enum. We then use this value to decide what formatting to apply. In the case of bold and italic, we just toggle the current setting and return. But for setting the strikeout state or the vertical alignment, we must update the copy of the current QTextCharFormat, and then merge this copy with the current format to make the change take effect.

The QObject::sender() method returns the QObject that invoked the slot (or 0 if the slot was called as a method). In this case the slot is only ever called by QActions. We could just as easily have used dynamic_cast<>() rather than qobject_cast<>(), but we prefer to always use qobject_cast<>() for QObjects, since it works even without RTTI (Run Time Type Information) support, and it works across dynamic library boundaries. An alternative to using sender() is to use a QSignalMapper; that would provide better encapsulation, at the cost of slightly increasing the size of the code. Or, of course, we could create a separate slot for every action.

```
void RichTextLineEdit::keyPressEvent(QKeyEvent *event)
{
    if (event->key() == Qt::Key_Enter ||
        event->key() == Qt::Key_Return) {
        emit returnPressed();
        event->accept();
    }
    else
        QTextEdit::keyPressEvent(event);
}
```

This handler is reimplemented purely to provide the returnPressed() signal, and to otherwise ignore Enter or Return key presses. All other key presses are passed on to the base class.

```
void RichTextLineEdit::customContextMenuRequested(const QPoint &pos)
{
    updateContextMenuActions();

    QMenu menu(this);
    menu.addActions(actions());
    menu.exec(mapToGlobal(pos));
}
```

When the user invokes the context menu (by right-clicking or by using a platform-specific key sequence), as a result of a signal–slot connection made in the constructor, this slot is called. We begin by calling updateContextMenu-Actions() to set each action's checked state appropriately. Then we create a menu and add to it the widget's actions (which we created earlier). At the end we pop up the menu, having converted the widget-relative position into the screen-relative (i.e., global) position, used by QMenu::exec().

If the user chooses a color from the color submenu, the applyColor() method we saw earlier will be called. Similarly, if any other option is chosen, the applyTextEffect() method is called.

```
void RichTextLineEdit::updateContextMenuActions()
{
    boldAction->setChecked(fontWeight() > QFont::Normal);
    italicAction->setChecked(fontItalic());
    const QTextCharFormat &format = currentCharFormat();
    strikeOutAction->setChecked(format.fontStrikeOut());
    noSubOrSuperScriptAction->setChecked(format.verticalAlignment() ==
            QTextCharFormat::AlignNormal);
    superScriptAction->setChecked(format.verticalAlignment() ==
                                  QTextCharFormat::AlignSuperScript);
    subScriptAction->setChecked(format.verticalAlignment() ==
                                QTextCharFormat::AlignSubScript);
}
```

This method is used to update the context menu's actions so that they reflect
the state of the text at the cursor's position. For all its long lines, the code is
very simple, checking or unchecking each action depending on the state of the
text's format at the current cursor position.

```
QSize RichTextLineEdit::sizeHint() const
{
    QFontMetrics fm(font());
    return QSize(document()->idealWidth() + fm.width("W"),
                 fm.height() + 5);
}
```

The size hint should be the ideal size the widget would like to be. We have created a size that is in effect based on the plain text content (since the non-dis-
played HTML markup would distort the calculation as we discussed when we
reviewed the RichTextDelegate::sizeHint() method; 198 ◄), and we have added
the width of one "W" character to allow a bit of horizontal margin. Similarly,
we give a height that is the actual height needed plus 5 pixels to give some vertical margin.

```
QSize RichTextLineEdit::minimumSizeHint() const
{
    QFontMetrics fm(font());
    return QSize(fm.width("WWWW"), fm.height() + 5);
}
```

The minimum size hint is actually the smallest size that Qt will ever shrink
the widget to. Here we have set it to be the width of four "W" characters, and
with the same height we used for the sizeHint().

We have now covered all the methods that the RichTextLineEdit really needs.
However, we added one additional custom method which we will now discuss.

The QTextEdit base class has a toHtml() method that returns the text in HTML format. We have chosen to ignore this and provide our own toSimpleHtml() method since we only need a very small subset of the HTML that QTextEdit can handle, and by restricting ourselves in this way we can produce the most compact HTML possible. To put this in perspective, if we have the HTML text The bold <font color='#0000ff'>blue</font> bear, the QTextEdit::toHtml() method will return the following HTML (with some spaces replaced with newlines to make it fit on the page):

```
<!DOCTYPE HTML PUBLIC "-//W3C//DTD HTML 4.0//EN"
"http://www.w3.org/TR/REC-html40/strict.dtd">
<html><head><meta name="qrichtext" content="1" />
<style type="text/css">p, li { white-space: pre-wrap; }</style>
</head><body style=" font-family:'Nimbus Sans L';
font-size:12pt; font-weight:400; font-style:normal;">
<p style=" margin-top:0px; margin-bottom:0px; margin-left:0px;
margin-right:0px; -qt-block-indent:0; text-indent:0px;">The
<span style=" font-weight:600;">bold</span>
<span style=" color:#0000ff;">blue</span> bear</p>
</body></html>
```

The actual output has 545 characters, although in practice this will vary slightly since the default font (here, Nimbus Sans L) will probably be different on other machines. Also, the output may differ between Qt versions. Compare this with the HTML produced by toSimpleHtml():

```
The <b>bold</b> <font color="#0000ff">blue</font> bear
```

This is just 54 characters. (Strictly speaking, this output isn't valid HTML; to be valid it would at the least need a DOCTYPE declaration and <html>, <head>, and <body> tags.) Of course, the toSimpleHtml() method is very limited and the toHtml() method is much more powerful, but for single lines of simple HTML, using a more compact format is clearly desirable.

```
QString RichTextLineEdit::toSimpleHtml() const
{
    QString html;
    for (QTextBlock block = document()->begin(); block.isValid();
         block = block.next()) {
        for (QTextBlock::iterator i = block.begin(); !i.atEnd();
             ++i) {
            QTextFragment fragment = i.fragment();
            if (fragment.isValid()) {
                QTextCharFormat format = fragment.charFormat();
                QColor color = format.foreground().color();
                QString text = Qt::escape(fragment.text());
```

```
            QStringList tags;
            if (format.verticalAlignment() ==
                QTextCharFormat::AlignSubScript)
                tags << "sub";
            else if (format.verticalAlignment() ==
                    QTextCharFormat::AlignSuperScript)
                tags << "sup";
            if (format.fontItalic())
                tags << "i";
            if (format.fontWeight() > QFont::Normal)
                tags << "b";
            if (format.fontStrikeOut())
                tags << "s";
            while (!tags.isEmpty())
                text = QString("<%1>%2</%1>")
                                .arg(tags.takeFirst()).arg(text);
            if (color != QColor(Qt::black))
                text = QString("<font color=\"%1\">%2</font>")
                                .arg(color.name()).arg(text);
            html += text;
        }
    }
  }
  return html;
}
```

We need to iterate over all the text held in the base class's internal QText-
Document and output the corresponding HTML while accounting for each piece
of text's format attributes. The QTextDocument class uses a tree-like hierarchy
that consists of a "root frame" which holds a sequence of QTextBlocks and QText-
Frames. Frames can contain blocks (and other things, such as lists and tables).
Each block consists of one or more fragments of text where each fragment has
its own uniform formatting. (The QTextDocument structure was discussed in the
chapter's first section; see also Figure 9.1; 319 ◀.)

Since we are concerned only with text, and in fact, with only one block since
the RichTextLineEdit holds only one line, we can iterate over the QTextDocument's
text blocks, and ignore frames—and in any case, there shouldn't be any frames
apart from the root frame. (In this particular case, we could even drop the outer
loop and just work on the first text block, since there will be only one, but we
prefer to use a more generic approach.)

Once we have a valid text block (i.e., line in this case), we must iterate over each
of its text fragments. In fact, if the line's text is all formatted the same, then
there will normally be just one fragment with one format. In our "bear" example the line has several different formats (e.g., some bold text and some colored

text), so we would expect to have a single text block with five fragments: "The " (including a following space), "bold" (in bold), " " (a space), "blue" (colored blue), and " bear" (including a preceding space).

For each fragment we retrieve its format (held in a `QTextCharFormat` object), its color, and its text. We HTML-escape the text, that is, we convert "&", "<", and ">" to their HTML equivalents (`&amp;`, `&lt;`, and `&gt;`). Then we build up a string list of HTML formatting tags based on the fragment's format. We need to use a list because multiple formatting attributes could be set—for example, bold *and* italic. Once we have the list of tags we wrap each one as a pair of start–end tags around the text (and around any previous pairs of tags), and then, if the text's color isn't black, we wrap the text in a pair of `<font>` tags to set the color. We then add the text, which now has all the necessary HTML formatting, to the `html` string we are building up, which the method returns at the end.

We have now completed our review of the `RichTextLineEdit` class. Using this class, or one inspired by it, we can give users the means to enter single lines of rich text, and we can store their text in the most compact HTML format possible. And, of course, out of the box, Qt already supports multi-line rich text editing with the `QTextEdit` class. But to make `QTextEdit` really useful to end users, we need to provide some means of applying font effects and so forth, as we did for the `RichTextLineEdit`. We'll see how to do this in the next section.

Multi-line Rich Text Editing

Qt's `QTextEdit` class provides so much functionality that we don't have to do much work to extend it into being a useful rich text editor. In this section we will create the `TextEdit` class shown in Figure 9.6. This class combines a couple of toolbars with a `QTextEdit` and makes it possible for the user to toggle bold and italic, set a text color, font, and font size, and to align the text. This by no means exhausts the character and paragraph formatting possibilities that we could support, but is sufficient to show the principles and practices involved. The Text Edit example (textedit) provides a means of testing and experimenting with the `TextEdit` class; and Chapter 12's Page Designer application (➤ 447) makes use of a `TextEdit`, but with the alignment functionality switched off.

There are basically two things that the `TextEdit` class must achieve. First, it must provide a means by which the user can apply the formatting they want. And second, it must show the formatting that is in force at the cursor's position.

Most of the work involved in creating the `TextEdit` is conventional: we create and set up the widgets, create actions, lay out the widgets, and create connections. Here are all the widgets' private member variables (taken from `textedit.hpp`), to provide some context:

```
QToolBar *fontToolBar;
QAction *boldAction;
QAction *italicAction;
QAction *colorAction;
QColorDialog *colorDialog;
QFontComboBox *fontComboBox;
QDoubleSpinBox *fontSizeSpinBox;
QToolBar *alignmentToolBar;
QAction *alignLeftAction;
QAction *alignCenterAction;
QAction *alignJustifyAction;
QAction *alignRightAction;
QTextEdit *textEdit;
```

The alignment actions are put in an action group in the createWidgets() method
(not shown). Simply doing this ensures that only one alignment is checked at
a time, since by default action groups treat their actions as exclusive.

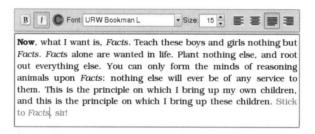

Figure 9.6 *The TextEdit component*

Most of the widget's behaviors can be implemented by calling the aggregated
textEdit using simple adaptor methods. Here are some examples, again taken
from the header:

```
QString toHtml() const { return textEdit->toHtml(); }
void setHtml(const QString &html) { textEdit->setHtml(html); }
void setBold(bool on)
    { textEdit->setFontWeight(on ? QFont::Bold : QFont::Normal); }
void setFontPointSize(double points)
    { textEdit->setFontPointSize(static_cast<qreal>(points)); }
void setFontFamily(const QFont &font)
    { textEdit->setFontFamily(font.family()); }
void alignLeft() { textEdit->setAlignment(Qt::AlignLeft); }
```

In addition to these, there are other adaptor methods that also pass on the
work to the aggregated QTextEdit—for example, toPlainText(), alignCenter(),
and so on. We haven't shown them since they are so similar to those shown.

Some actions, such as toggling italic, can be implemented purely by signal and slot connections, while others require an adaptor or a custom method. We will review some of the signal–slot connections and the custom methods, but we will skip the constructor, and the createWidgets() and createLayout() methods, since they are all conventional.

```
void TextEdit::createConnections()
{
    connect(fontComboBox, SIGNAL(currentFontChanged(const QFont&)),
            this, SLOT(setFontFamily(const QFont&)));
    connect(fontSizeSpinBox, SIGNAL(valueChanged(double)),
            this, SLOT(setFontPointSize(double)));
    connect(boldAction, SIGNAL(toggled(bool)),
            this, SLOT(setBold(bool)));
    connect(italicAction, SIGNAL(toggled(bool)),
            textEdit, SLOT(setFontItalic(bool)));
    connect(colorAction, SIGNAL(triggered()), this, SLOT(setColor()));
    connect(alignLeftAction, SIGNAL(triggered()),
            this, SLOT(alignLeft()));
    ...
    connect(textEdit, SIGNAL(currentCharFormatChanged(
                            const QTextCharFormat&)),
            this, SLOT(currentCharFormatChanged(
                        const QTextCharFormat&)));
    connect(textEdit, SIGNAL(cursorPositionChanged()),
            this, SLOT(cursorPositionChanged()));
    connect(textEdit, SIGNAL(textChanged()),
            this, SIGNAL(textChanged()));
}
```

The first five connections shown here are concerned with changing character attributes, and the sixth with changing a paragraph attribute. We use the QFontComboBox's currentFontChanged() signal purely to change the font family. The font's size is changed by a connection from the fontSizeSpinBox. The bold and italic actions are both toggle (checkable) actions used to toggle the corresponding font attributes. The color action is used to pop up a color chooser dialog. In addition to the connection for the align left toggle action, there are also equivalent connections for the other alignments (center, justify, right) that are not shown.

Notice that we are able to connect the italic action directly to the aggregated QTextEdit, whereas with the exception of the color action, all the others are connected to tiny adaptor methods implemented in the header (shown earlier) that in turn call the appropriate QTextEdit method.

The two penultimate connections are used to ensure that the toolbar's widgets correctly reflect the character and paragraph state at the cursor's position.

The state might change due to navigation (the user clicks somewhere else in the text or uses the arrow or other keys to move somewhere else), or due to changing the state at the current position—for example, the user clicks the bold toolbar button. The last connection (a signal–signal connection) is used to provide the TextEdit with a signal to match that of the aggregated QTextEdit.

We will look at both of the methods used to keep the toolbar buttons' state up to date in a moment, but first we will look at the setColor() method and its helper slot since it is the only state changing method that isn't implemented using an adaptor in the header.

```
void TextEdit::setColor()
{
    if (!colorDialog) {
        colorDialog = new QColorDialog(this);
        connect(colorDialog, SIGNAL(colorSelected(const QColor&)),
                this, SLOT(updateColor(const QColor&)));
    }
    colorDialog->setCurrentColor(textEdit->textColor());
    colorDialog->open();
}
```

This method pops up a platform-specific window-modal color chooser dialog with its initial color set to the current text color.* If the user clicks OK, the colorSelected() signal is emitted. We have connected this to a custom update-Color() slot.

```
void TextEdit::updateColor(const QColor &color)
{
    textEdit->setTextColor(color);
    updateColorSwatch();
}
```

This slot is used to set the current text color to the given color and to update the color swatch used in the toolbar. The toolbar's color action uses an icon that shows a bold "C" on a background that is the current text's foreground color. Whenever the color is changed, the icon must be updated, and this is done by the updateColorSwatch() method.

```
void TextEdit::updateColorSwatch()
{
    colorAction->setIcon(colorSwatch(textEdit->textColor(),
```

---

* Unfortunately, this approach does not work well on Mac OS X using Qt 4.6. On the author's MacBook running Leopard (10.5.8), with Qt 4.6.0 the program segfaults, and with Qt 4.6.1 and Qt 4.6.2, setting a color once works fine, but attempting to set it a second time freezes the program. The example contains #ifs so that the static QColorDialog::getColor() method is used on Mac OS X with Qt 4.6.

```
                              QSize(48, 48)));
    }
```

This method calls a custom global colorSwatch() function that takes a color and a size and returns an icon of the requested size and color. The colorSwatch() function and some others (brushSwatch(), penStyleSwatch(), penCapSwatch(), and penJoinSwatch()) are used by Chapter 12's Page Designer application (colorSwatch(); ➤ 442).

Although the code is only one line, we prefer to put it in a method of its own since its functionality is needed in more than one place.

```
void TextEdit::currentCharFormatChanged(
        const QTextCharFormat &format)
{
    fontComboBox->setCurrentFont(format.font());
    fontSizeSpinBox->setValue(format.fontPointSize());
    boldAction->setChecked(format.fontWeight() == QFont::Bold);
    italicAction->setChecked(format.fontItalic());
    updateColorSwatch();
}
```

This slot is called whenever the current *character* format changes—it is not called for paragraph-level changes such as changed alignment. It simply updates the toolbars' widgets to reflect the character format. The format could change as the result of a state change (such as the user changing the color), or as a result of navigation (the user moves onto a character that has a different format from the previous character the cursor was on).

```
void TextEdit::cursorPositionChanged()
{
    QTextCursor cursor = textEdit->textCursor();
    QTextBlockFormat format = cursor.blockFormat();
    switch (format.alignment()) {
        case Qt::AlignLeft:
            alignLeftAction->setChecked(true); break;
        case Qt::AlignCenter:
            alignCenterAction->setChecked(true); break;
        case Qt::AlignJustify:
            alignJustifyAction->setChecked(true); break;
        case Qt::AlignRight:
            alignRightAction->setChecked(true); break;
    }
}
```

This slot is only needed if we want to keep track of *paragraph* format changes. Whenever the cursor position changes it could mean that the cursor is now in a different paragraph. Since we only allow the user to change the paragraph's alignment, that is the only part of the format we need to keep track of. Here, we simply check whichever alignment action matches the paragraph's alignment, relying on the exclusive action group to uncheck all the others for us.

For the TextEdit we chose a subset of the most common character formatting and simple alignment for paragraph formatting, to show how to provide the user with the means to change these, and how to reflect their current states in the user interface. There are many other attributes that we could provide the means for the user to control and that we could track. For example, QText-CharFormat has methods for controlling overlining, strike-out, and underlining (including the line's color and style), as well as for setting a URL and a tooltip. And as we saw earlier when discussing the rich text single line editor, vertical positioning to produce subscripts and superscripts is also supported (342 ◄). There are also many other attributes we can expose for paragraphs. For example, QTextBlockFormat has methods for setting a paragraph's first line indent and its overall indent, and for setting margins and tab positions.

If we were more ambitious, we could provide the means for users to create lists and tables, and to insert hyperlinks and images. In fact, providing basic support for bulleted lists is extremely easy: we just call QTextEdit::setAutoFor-matting(QTextEdit::AutoBulletList), and the user can start a bulleted list by inserting an "*" (asterisk) in the left margin. However, it takes more work to provide a means of indenting and unindenting (to achieve nested lists), and for inserting and editing tables, and so on. All of these things are left as an exercise for those who want to dig more deeply into Qt's rich text engine.

We have now completed our review of the creation of rich text editors, including coverage of how to provide completion and syntax highlighting. But what if we want to create rich text documents programmatically—for example, to produce payslips or end of month customer bills. And how do we print such documents or export them into standard document formats? We will address these questions in the next chapter, as well as seeing how we can simply paint what we want without creating a QTextDocument at all.

10

- Exported QTextDocument File Quality
- Creating QTextDocuments
- Exporting and Printing Documents
- Painting Pages

Creating Rich Text Documents

In this chapter we will review three different approaches to creating rich text documents, and we will see how to export such documents in a variety of standard formats and also how to print them.★ This chapter assumes a basic familiarity with QTextDocument, as covered in the first section of the previous chapter (318 ◄). The three approaches we will use are, first, populating a QTextDocument with raw HTML, second, populating a QTextDocument using a QTextCursor, and third, painting a document with QPainter, in this last case purely for exporting and printing, with no in-memory representation.

Unfortunately, this can be a frustrating area of Qt programming, particularly for those wanting cross-platform solutions. This is because Qt's behavior regarding the export and printing of rich text documents can vary considerably across platforms and across Qt versions. In view of this, we will present a summary covering specific Qt versions, Qt 4.5.2 and Qt 4.6.1, on Mac OS X, Linux, and Windows, to make it easy to pick the approach that is likely to work best for your circumstances. Note, however, that the sample document we will work on is fairly complex—it involves a table, embedded SVG images, and rich text—so it may be the case that for other documents the quality of the results may be slightly, or even radically, different.

The two-page sample document we will produce is shown in Figure 10.1. The figure is a screenshot of a PDF file that has been exported from a QTextDocument that was created from raw HTML on Linux using Qt 4.5.2.

In this chapter we will begin by comparing the quality and sizes of exported files that represent the sample document in various formats. We will follow this by showing QTextDocument in use, in the second section populating it both

---

★As we noted in the previous chapter, Qt's rich text format is an in-memory data format that should not be confused with other "rich text" formats.

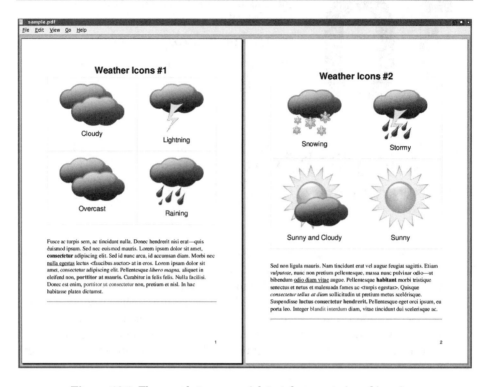

Figure 10.1 *The sample two-page rich text document viewed in evince*

from raw HTML and using a `QTextCursor`. In the third section we will see how to export a `QTextDocument` in a variety of formats, and also how to print `QTextDocuments`. And in the chapter's last section we will see how to create the same document purely by painting it, and how to export or print the results.

Before we dive into the chapter's sections, we will quickly review the data structures from which the sample document's page data originates, since this is common to all the approaches we cover.

```
struct OnePage
{
    QString title;
    QStringList filenames;
    QStringList captions;
    QString descriptionHtml;
};
```

The `title` holds a plain text page title. The two string lists hold parallel sets of image filenames and plain text caption texts. The `descriptionHtml` holds the paragraph that follows the table and uses HTML markup for text effects (such as color, bold, etc.).

The data for the document is held in a custom PageData object which holds a private variable, pages, of type QList<OnePage>. We will not cover the driver classes, or even most of the PageData class; instead we will focus on just those methods that are necessary to show how to populate a QTextDocument and how to export and print documents.

Exported QTextDocument File Quality

In this section we will compare the quality and file sizes that result from exporting (and painting) the sample document in many of the standard formats that Qt supports.

Figure 10.2 *The Output Sampler program*

The following figures are designed to give some hints as to what can be expected from each approach.° But in view of the variation across formats, platforms, Qt versions, and documents, we recommend being skeptical of the results presented here, and to do your own testing. All the output shown in this chapter was produced by the Output Sampler example (outputsampler) shown in Figure 10.2. It should be straightforward to adapt this example to output your own documents for testing purposes.

Platform/ Qt version	PDF Output Technique (Quality Bytes)		
	QTextDocument/ HTML	QTextDocument/ QTextCursor	QPainter
Linux/4.5.2	★★★★★ 136 251	★★★★★ 136 216	★★★★☆ 5 956 141
Linux/4.6.1	★★★★★ 143 985	★★★★★ 136 302	★★★☆☆ 6 669 547
Mac/4.5.2	★★★☆☆ 135 407	★★★★☆ 135 316	★★★★☆ 5 991 845
Mac/4.6.1	★★★★☆ 135 890	★★★★★ 135 481	★★★☆☆ 6 687 444
Windows/4.5.2	★★★★★ 147 838	★★★★★ 150 680	★★★★★ 5 998 190
Windows/4.6.1	★★★★★ 148 045	★★★★★ 150 881	★★★★☆ 6 689 564

Figure 10.3 *Comparison of PDF output quality and size*

°The "quality" stars reflect the author's subjective opinion and will vary for different documents. The sizes in bytes will also vary—they are included purely as a guide to *relative* file sizes.

Figure 10.3 compares PDF outputs produced by exporting using a QPrinter and outputting to file. PDF files can also be created by printing a document via the print dialog, and choosing the "print to file" option—this usually results in a different PDF output which may be slightly better or worse than is produced when using the exporting approach.[°] Another point to note is that QText-Document puts the page number in the bottom-right corner of each page whether we want this or not, and with no control over the page number's formatting. For documents produced with QPainter we paint everything ourselves of course.

The file sizes shown in the figure reveal that PDFs that are output using QPainter with embedded SVG images are very large. If we were to output pixmaps instead (which can be done by undefining EMBED_SVG in the .pro file), the QPainter-produced PDFs would shrink in size to around 100KB.

The outputsampler program can also export the document in PostScript (.ps) format. In our tests—using Qt 4.6.1 on Linux—we found that Qt's PostScript output of the sample document varied considerably in size depending on whether it was produced using a QTextDocument (~7MB with embedded SVG images and ~170KB with embedded .png images) or a QPainter (~16MB regardless of the embedded images' format). Also, we found that the sample document's PostScript files could not be viewed using the evince viewer (projects. gnome.org/evince), but worked fine in the more basic gv viewer (www.gnu.org/ software/gv). However, we won't present a comparison table, since for most purposes PDF format has superceded PostScript.

Platform/ Qt version	ODT Output Technique (Quality Bytes)	
	QTextDocument/ HTML	QTextDocument/ QTextCursor
Linux/Qt 4.5.2	★★☆☆☆ 135 432	☆☆☆☆☆ *invalid*
Linux/Qt 4.6.1	★★☆☆☆ 135 437	★★☆☆☆ 135 438
Mac/Qt 4.5.2	★★☆☆☆ 135 441	☆☆☆☆☆ *invalid*
Mac/Qt 4.6.1	★★☆☆☆ 135 444	★★☆☆☆ 135 443
Windows/Qt 4.5.2	★★☆☆☆ 135 407	☆☆☆☆☆ *invalid*
Windows/Qt 4.6.1	★★☆☆☆ 135 413	★★☆☆☆ 135 409

Figure 10.4 *Comparison of Open Document Format output quality and size*

Figure 10.4 shows the results of exporting the sample document as an Open Document Format (.odt) file. These can only be produced using a QTextDocument;

[°]On Windows, "print to file" will only produce PDF output if there is a PDF writer printer driver installed. Without this, the only way to output PDF on Windows is by exporting.

they cannot be painted with a `QPainter`. We tested the exported `.odt` files using OpenOffice.org 3 (`www.openoffice.org`).° The figure clearly indicates that Qt's support for this format is somewhat rudimentary, but also that it is improving.

Despite Qt's poor showing in our tests, it would be unwise to dismiss Qt's ability to output good `.odt` files. The sample document we have used, although short, is quite complex, and it may well be the case that other documents are output to a higher standard. And, of course, Qt's ability to export in `.odt` format is bound to improve in future versions.

Platform/ Qt version	HTML Output Technique (Quality Bytes)			
	QTextDocument/ HTML		QTextDocument/ QTextCursor	
Linux/Qt 4.5.2	★★★★☆	8 355	★★★★☆	6 795
Linux/Qt 4.6.1	★★★★☆	8 346	★★★★☆	6 795
Mac/Qt 4.5.2	★★★★★	8 363	★★★★★	6 803
Mac/Qt 4.6.1	★★★★★	8 363	★★★★★	6 803
Windows/Qt 4.5.2	★★★★☆	8 106	★★★★☆	6 539
Windows/Qt 4.6.1	★★★★☆	8 106	★★★★☆	6 539

Figure 10.5 *Comparison of HTML output quality and size*

Figure 10.5 shows a comparison of HTML format exports. HTML is such a ubiquitous format that being able to output HTML is essential for many applications. Qt's XML classes make this easy to do—for example, using `QXml-StreamWriter`—but often we want to have a single in-memory document (e.g., a `QTextDocument`) from which we can produce a variety of outputs, one of which is HTML. Just like Open Document Format, HTML cannot be painted with `QPainter`.

On Mac OS X we tested using the Safari web browser—this rendered the HTML pages extremely well, including the embedded SVG images. On Linux and Windows we used Firefox, and this did not show the SVG images at all.

Figure 10.6 shows a comparison of Scalable Vector Graphics (`.svg`) format outputs—and for this example, we only output the first page of the sample document. SVG supports what its name suggests—scalability without degrading quality.

°The generic term is "Open Document Format", and this includes formats for rich text documents (`.odt`), spreadsheets (`.ods`), and other document types. The use of the file suffix `.odt` (Open Document Text) is *essential* for correct interpretation by OpenOffice.org.

Platform/ Qt version	SVG Output Technique (Quality Bytes)		
	QTextDocument/ HTML	QTextDocument/ QTextCursor	QPainter
Linux/Qt 4.5.2	★★★☆☆ 94 535	★★★☆☆ 94 560	★★★★★ 94 156
Linux/Qt 4.6.1	★★★★☆ 91 756	★★★★☆ 91 436	★★★★☆ 102 061
Mac/Qt 4.5.2	★★★☆☆ 91 203	★★★☆☆ 91 195	★★★★☆ 94 124
Mac/Qt 4.6.1	★★★★☆ 92 905	★★★☆☆ 91 804	★★★★☆ 99 360
Windows/Qt 4.5.2	★★★☆☆ 92 066	★★★☆☆ 92 087	★★★★★ 95 338
Windows/Qt 4.6.1	★★★☆☆ 92 597	★★★☆☆ 92 663	★★★★☆ 100 544

Figure 10.6 *Comparison of SVG output quality and size*

Documents can also be output using pixmap formats such as .png (Portable
Network Graphics) or .bmp (Windows Bitmap). These formats do not scale
well—this is an intrinsic limitation of their design that has nothing to do with
Qt—so these formats are ideal for images that will not be scaled. We haven't
provided a figure comparing them since they are output with excellent fidelity
using all of the platforms, Qt versions, and techniques that we have used for
all the other formats.

Creating QTextDocuments

There are two techniques that can be used to populate a QTextDocument: give
it a QString of HTML-formatted text, or use a QTextCursor. We will show both
approaches in this section, starting with the use of HTML.

Of course, in some cases, we don't need a document at all, but simply want to
render our data into a file in a standard format or to print our data. In such
cases—and providing we don't need HTML or ODF output—we can avoid
using a QTextDocument at all and simply use a QPainter; this is covered in this
chapter's last section (➤ 379).

Creating QTextDocuments with HTML

Populating a QTextDocument using HTML is very convenient if we have a decent
knowledge of HTML, and probably requires the least code of all the techniques
considered in this chapter.

In the outputsampler example, to populate a QTextDocument using HTML, we
begin by creating an empty QTextDocument, and then pass a pointer to the

document to the `PageData::populateDocumentUsingHtml()` method, which itself has two helper methods.

```cpp
void PageData::populateDocumentUsingHtml(QTextDocument *document)
{
    QString html("<html>\n<body>\n");
    for (int page = 0; page < pages.count(); ++page) {
        html += pageAsHtml(page, false);
        if (page + 1 < pages.count())
            html += "<br style='page-break-after:always;'/>\n";
    }
    html += "</body>\n</html>\n";
    document->setHtml(html);
}
```

This method creates a `QString` of HTML that it then sets on the `QTextDocument` it is passed. It begins by adding a standard HTML `<html>` tag, omits a `<head>` tag, and begins the document proper with a `<body>` tag. Then, for each page in the list of `OnePages` it adds the HTML for the page, and for all except the last page adds a tag with the Qt-specific `page-break-after` style attribute to force a page break. And at the end, the opening tags are closed.

Notice that we have chosen to include newlines (\n) in our HTML; this is not necessary, but is sometimes convenient for debugging, and makes the HTML more human readable.

```cpp
QString PageData::pageAsHtml(int page, bool selfContained)
{
    const OnePage &thePage = pages.at(page);

    QString html;
    if (selfContained)
        html += "<html>\n<body>\n";
    html += QString("<h1 align='center'>%1</h1>\n")
                    .arg(Qt::escape(thePage.title));
    html += "<p>";
    html += itemsAsHtmlTable(thePage);
    html += "</p>\n";
    html += QString("<p style='font-size:15pt;font-family:times'>"
                    "%1</p><hr>\n").arg(thePage.descriptionHtml);
    if (selfContained)
        html += "</body>\n</html>\n";
    return html;
}
```

This method can be used to produce a simple self-contained HTML page if the second argument is true; the populateDocumentUsingHtml() method always calls it with this argument set to false.

The method begins by getting a reference to the page data that is to be converted to HTML. It creates an <h1> tag for the title, and is careful to use Qt's Qt::escape() function to convert any "&", "<", and ">" characters that might be in the title to HTML-escaped versions—&, <, and >.*

The HTML table used for the images and their captions is handled by a separate method that we will look at next. The descriptionHtml text is added at the end unescaped—since it is already in HTML format—but we precede it with a paragraph tag with a style attribute that provides a suitable font family and size. We also add a horizontal rule after the text.

The page number shown in the screenshot in Figure 10.1 (360 ◀) is added by Qt and we have no control over it.

```
QString PageData::itemsAsHtmlTable(const OnePage &thePage)
{
    QString html("<table border='1' cellpadding='20' width='100%'>");
    for (int i = 0; i < thePage.filenames.count(); ++i) {
        if (i % 2 == 0)
            html += "<tr>\n";
        html += QString("<td align='center'><img src='%1'/>"
                        "<p style='font-size:18pt'>%2</p></td>\n")
                    .arg(thePage.filenames.at(i))
                    .arg(Qt::escape(thePage.captions.at(i)));
        if (i % 2 != 0)
            html += "</tr>\n";
    }
    if (!html.endsWith("</tr>\n"))
        html += "</tr>\n";
    html += "</table>\n";
    return html;
}
```

This method creates an HTML table with four cells (2 × 2). Each cell contains an <img> tag whose src attribute is the image filename and a paragraph tag with a large font size to show the corresponding HTML-escaped plain text caption. (By default the outputsampler program uses SVG images, but it can be made to use PNG images by commenting out the EMBED_SVG symbol defined in the .pro file.)

---

*In Qt 4.5, Qt::escape() is not suitable for escaping text for HTML attribute values since it does not escape quotes. From Qt 4.6, Qt::escape() does escape double quotes.

These three methods are sufficient to create a long QString containing the HTML text to represent the document. Populating the QTextDocument with the string of HTML is a matter of a single method call: QTextDocument::setHtml(). And although we didn't use CSS (Cascading Style Sheets) for this particular example, as we mentioned in the last chapter, Qt does support them; see qt.nokia.com/doc/richtext-html-subset.html.

Creating QTextDocuments with QTextCursor

The QTextCursor class allows us to programmatically navigate and edit a QText-Document without needing to know any HTML. The QTextCursor class was introduced in the previous chapter where it was used for editing documents; in this subsection we will use it to create QTextDocuments from scratch. The QTextCursor API is shown in the previous chapter (328–330 ◄). The QTextCursor::movePosition() method was also discussed in the previous chapter (332 ◄), along with the QTextCursor::MoveOperation enum (334 ◄).

One unusual aspect of the QTextCursor API is that there are two different methods for inserting lists: createList() and insertList(). The former creates and inserts a list into the document with the current paragraph as its first item. The latter creates and inserts a list into the document and creates a new paragraph which becomes its first item.

The code that we have used to populate a QTextDocument using a QTextCursor is structurally very similar to that used for creating an HTML string, but requires the use of more helper methods. As with the HTML version, we begin by creating an empty QTextDocument and pass a pointer to it to a method that will populate the document.

```
void PageData::populateDocumentUsingQTextCursor(
        QTextDocument *document)
{
    document->setDefaultFont(QFont("Times", 15));
    QTextCursor cursor(document);
    for (int page = 0; page < pages.count(); ++page) {
        addPageToDocument(&cursor, page);
        if (page + 1 < pages.count()) {
            QTextBlockFormat blockFormat;
            blockFormat.setPageBreakPolicy(
                    QTextFormat::PageBreak_AlwaysAfter);
            cursor.mergeBlockFormat(blockFormat);
        }
    }
}
```

We begin by giving the document a default font—slightly larger than would normally be used but intended to be at least vaguely readable in the screenshot in Figure 10.1 (360 ◀).

We create a QTextCursor for the QTextDocument, and pass the cursor rather than the document to the helper methods. Just as we did for the HTML version, we add each page to the document in turn.

And for all pages except the last one, we put in a page break at the end. This is done by creating a new QTextBlockFormat (i.e., a paragraph format), and setting its page break policy to PageBreak_AlwaysAfter; two other policies are available—PageBreak_Auto which leaves Qt to figure out page breaks for us, and PageBreak_AlwaysBefore which forces a page break before the paragraph with this set for its block format. Once we have created the format, we *merge* it into the cursor's current block format (i.e., the format of the last paragraph that the cursor has inserted). The QTextCursor::mergeBlockFormat() method overrides the current block format's settings with any non-default settings from the format it is passed. There is a similar QTextCursor::mergeCharFormat() method for merging character format settings.

```
void PageData::addPageToDocument(QTextCursor *cursor, int page)
{
    const OnePage &thePage = pages.at(page);

    addTitleToDocument(cursor, thePage.title);
    addItemsToDocument(cursor, thePage);
    cursor->insertHtml(thePage.descriptionHtml);
    addRuleToDocument(cursor);
}
```

This method passes most of its work on to helper methods. The exception is the call to QTextCursor::insertHtml() which can be used to insert an arbitrary piece of HTML text into a QTextDocument at the cursor position.

```
void PageData::addTitleToDocument(QTextCursor *cursor,
                                  const QString &title)
{
    QTextBlockFormat blockFormat;
    blockFormat.setAlignment(Qt::AlignHCenter);
    blockFormat.setTopMargin(0);
    cursor->insertBlock(blockFormat);
    QTextCharFormat charFormat;
    charFormat.setFont(QFont("Helvetica", 24, QFont::Bold));
    cursor->insertText(title, charFormat);
}
```

We want the document's title to be horizontally centered and to use a big font. We also want the title to appear at the top of the page (i.e., immediately below the top margin). To achieve this we create a new text block format to provide the paragraph-level settings—alignment and the top margin—and insert a new block (i.e., an empty paragraph with the specified formatting) into the document with this format. We then create a text character format with the big font we want and insert the title text into the current paragraph using the character format we just created.

There is also a QTextCursor::insertText() method that takes only a QString argument, and therefore uses whatever formatting is already in force. And there is an overloaded QTextCursor::insertBlock() method that accepts both a text block format and a character text format. We almost always prefer to use the insertBlock() method which just accepts a text block format and to insert text using the insertText() methods, using the two-argument form where a character format is specified as we have done here, when that suits our needs.

```
void PageData::addItemsToDocument(QTextCursor *cursor,
                                  const OnePage &thePage)
{
    QTextDocument tableDocument;
    QTextCursor tableCursor(&tableDocument);
    QTextTable *table = tableCursor.insertTable(2, 2, tableFormat());
    for (int i = 0; i < thePage.filenames.count(); ++i)
        populateTableCell(table->cellAt(i / 2, i % 2), thePage, i);
    cursor->insertFragment(QTextDocumentFragment(&tableDocument));
}
```

Programmatically adding a table to a QTextDocument using a QTextCursor is slightly long-winded, although none of the steps are difficult.

If we try inserting a QTextTable directly into a QTextDocument using the QTextCursor::insertTable() method, it is very easy to get into a mess! This is because we must be sure to remember that once we have populated the table we must move the cursor to the position immediately following the table, before populating the rest of the document. This arises because when we insert the last item into the last cell in the table, the cursor is positioned immediately after this item—but is still *inside* the table's last cell.

Fortunately, there is a nice generic solution to this problem: we can create a stand-alone QTextDocument that only contains the table, and then we can insert this document as a document fragment into the document we are populating. This leaves the cursor neatly positioned after the fragment (i.e., immediately after the table), so we can then continue populating the document without having to worry about explicitly moving the cursor out of the table.

So, in this method, we create a new QTextDocument, the tableDocument, and create a new text cursor which we use to populate it. We start by calling QTextCursor::insertTable(), giving it the number of rows and columns, and the QTextTableFormat to use. (We will look at the tableFormat() method next.)

Once we have the QTextTable, we populate each of its QTextTableCells—retrieved using the QTextTable::cellAt() method—using a helper method.

And at the end, we insert the table document as a QTextDocumentFragment into the document we are populating. At this point the cursor will be positioned (as usual after a cursor insertion) immediately after the last thing we inserted. This means that the cursor will be positioned exactly where we want it: immediately after the table.

```
QTextTableFormat PageData::tableFormat()
{
    QTextTableFormat tableFormat;
    tableFormat.setAlignment(Qt::AlignCenter);
    tableFormat.setCellPadding(10);
    tableFormat.setTopMargin(10);
    tableFormat.setBottomMargin(10);
    QVector<QTextLength> widths;
    widths << QTextLength(QTextLength::PercentageLength, 50)
           << QTextLength(QTextLength::PercentageLength, 50);
    tableFormat.setColumnWidthConstraints(widths);
    return tableFormat;
}
```

We create the QTextTableFormat in this method, setting its alignment, padding, and two of its margins. (For the left and right margins we use the defaults since we don't specifically set them.) Rather than setting explicit widths for the two columns, we set each one to be 50% of the table's overall width. This leaves Qt to do the detailed calculations and ensures that the columns have the same width.

The QTextLength class can accept two other enum values, VariableLength and FixedLength; naturally we can use any combination of lengths for the columns of a table. Each FixedLength's value is a floating-point (qreal) number of pixels. To create a QTextLength representing a variable size use the default (no argument) constructor.

```
void PageData::populateTableCell(QTextTableCell tableCell,
                                 const OnePage &thePage, int index)
{
    QTextBlockFormat blockFormat;
    blockFormat.setAlignment(Qt::AlignHCenter);
    QTextCursor cursor = tableCell.firstCursorPosition();
    cursor.insertBlock(blockFormat);
    cursor.insertImage(thePage.filenames.at(index));
    blockFormat.setTopMargin(30);
    cursor.insertBlock(blockFormat);
    QTextCharFormat charFormat;
```

```
        charFormat.setFont(QFont("Helvetica", 18));
        cursor.insertText(thePage.captions.at(index), charFormat);
    }
```

This method is used to insert an image and a caption into each `QTextTableCell` it is passed. Since we want both the image and the caption to be horizontally centered, we begin by creating a text block format and setting its alignment accordingly. We then retrieve a cursor into the cell using the `QTextTableCell::firstCursorPosition()` method, and use this cursor to insert an empty paragraph with the block format we created. We then insert the image into this paragraph using the `QTextCursor::insertImage()` method.

The `QTextCursor::insertImage()` method has various overloads; the one we have used here takes a filename, but there is also one that accepts a `QImage`.

To ensure a bit of vertical spacing between the bottom of the image and the top of the caption we next set the block format's top margin—this will only affect future uses of the format. We then insert an empty paragraph, again using the block format. Then we create a character format and set a large font, and insert the caption using the character format.

```
    void PageData::addRuleToDocument(QTextCursor *cursor)
    {
        QTextBlockFormat blockFormat;
        blockFormat.setProperty(
                QTextFormat::BlockTrailingHorizontalRulerWidth, 1);
        cursor->insertBlock(blockFormat);
    }
```

At the end of each page we want to draw a horizontal rule. This is easily achieved by creating a text block format, setting its `BlockTrailingHorizontalRulerWidth` property to 1, and inserting the block. (In fact, in our tests, setting the property to any value at all was sufficient to get the rule.)

The `QTextFormat` class (`QTextBlockFormat`'s base class) supports over seventy properties (many of which can be accessed more conventionally using property-specific methods). However, the existence of `QTextFormat::setProperty()` and various getter methods (e.g., `QTextFormat::intProperty()`) means that the number of properties can be increased at any time (even for minor and patch releases), without affecting binary compatibility.

Exporting and Printing Documents

A `QTextDocument` can be output in a variety of standard formats, including Open Document Format and HTML. Such documents can also be output in vector formats (such as PDF, PostScript, or SVG), and in any of the pixmap formats that Qt supports (such as .png or .bmp). Documents can also be printed. We will cover all of these possibilities in this section.

Exporting QTextDocuments

In this subsection we will see how to export the fully formatted contents of a QTextDocument, including rich text and embedded images. For the image formats (SVG and pixmap formats), we will look at how to export a single image of a single page, and for all the other formats we will look at how to export an entire multi-page document.

In all cases we begin by creating an empty QTextDocument, and for the single page SVG and pixmap exports we explicitly set the page size and margins. Qt's documentation doesn't usually specify units, but in general units are pixels except for printing, where they are normally points ($\frac{1}{72}$").

```
QTextDocument document;
document.setPageSize(printer.pageRect().size());
document.setDocumentMargin(25);
```

For single page documents we set a default font, and create a QTextCursor, passing the QTextDocument as argument. Then we use the PageData::addPageToDocument() method we saw earlier to add just one page to the document (368 ◄).

For multi-page documents we call a populateDocument() method that takes a pointer to the empty QTextDocument as argument. We have seen two versions of this method: PageData::populateDocumentUsingHtml() (365 ◄) and PageData:: populateDocumentUsingQTextCursor() (367 ◄). In theory, it shouldn't make any difference which of these two methods we use, but in our experiments we found that the results usually differ, so we recommend performing your own tests on the documents, platforms, and formats that are of interest.

Exporting in PDF and PostScript Format

To export a document in PDF or PostScript format is very easy, given a filename and a QTextDocument. The method that we show here assumes that the filename it receives ends with .pdf or .ps.

```
bool MainWindow::exportPdfOrPs(const QString &filename,
                               QTextDocument *document)
{
    Q_ASSERT(filename.endsWith(".ps") || filename.endsWith(".pdf"));
    QPrinter printer(QPrinter::HighResolution);
    printer.setOutputFileName(filename);
    printer.setOutputFormat(filename.endsWith(".pdf")
```

```
                    ? QPrinter::PdfFormat : QPrinter::PostScriptFormat);
        document->print(&printer);
        return true;
    }
```

To export in PDF or PostScript we use a QPrinter, but instead of printing paper pages we use it to "print to file".* (We can also paint PDF and PostScript documents to a QPrinter using a QPainter, as we will see further on; ➤ 387.)

In most applications we would have a QPrinter as a private member variable in the main window. The advantage of doing this is that once the user has set up the printer any further uses of it start with the settings the user chose last time. But for the outputsampler application we have chosen to create a fresh QPrinter for those documents that we output without user intervention—such as when we export the sample document.

Apart from a little bit of setup for the QPrinter, the actual export is simply a matter of calling QTextDocument::print() and giving it a pointer to the QPrinter we want it to print on. By default, the print() method paginates using the printer's QPrinter::paperRect() as its printing area, but with a 20mm margin.

Exporting in Open Document Format

Exporting a QTextDocument in Open Document Format is even easier than exporting to PDF or PostScript, thanks to the QTextDocumentWriter class.

```
    bool MainWindow::exportOdf(const QString &filename,
                               QTextDocument *document)
    {
        Q_ASSERT(filename.endsWith(".odt"));
        QTextDocumentWriter writer(filename);
        return writer.write(document);
    }
```

Again, we pass a filename (this time assumed to have a file suffix of .odt), and a QTextDocument. In fact, the QTextDocumentWriter::write() method returns a Boolean success flag that we return to the caller. A QTextDocumentWriter can also be used to export in other formats by calling the QTextDocumentWriter::set-Format() method with a QByteArray argument of plaintext or html. The default format is "odf", but as we noted earlier, for the document to be recognized by OpenOffice.org, the file suffix must be .odt. The complete list of formats (which will always include at least these three) is returned by QTextDocument-Writer::supportedFormats().

---

* On Mac OS X if we use an output format of QPrinter::NativeFormat, the result will be PDF rendered using Apple's Quartz 2D drawing engine. For the sample file this doubled the size of the PDF and produced a very slight improvement in quality.

Unfortunately, as Figure 10.4 (362 ◀) indicates, Qt's Open Document Format output—at the time of this writing—is rather weak. Our experiments have shown that outputting Open Document Format can be very sensitive both to the document's contents, and sometimes even to how the document was populated. In view of this we recommend testing the output quality of your own documents using your target Qt versions and platforms to ensure that the output is satisfactory.

Exporting in HTML Format

To export in HTML format, we must create a string containing the HTML and then write the string to file. This is all standard C++/Qt, although we'll mention one subtle point after seeing the code.

```cpp
bool MainWindow::exportHtml(const QString &filename,
                           QTextDocument *document)
{
    Q_ASSERT(filename.endsWith(".htm") || filename.endsWith(".html"));
    QFile file(filename);
    if (!file.open(QIODevice::WriteOnly|QIODevice::Text)) {
        AQP::warning(this, tr("Error"),
                tr("Failed to export %1: %2").arg(filename)
                .arg(file.errorString()));
        return false;
    }
    QTextStream out(&file);
    out.setCodec("utf-8");
    out << document->toHtml("utf-8");
    file.close();
    return true;
}
```

Qt's QTextStream::setCodec() method is quite liberal about the encoding names that it will accept. Here, for example, we could have used "utf8". But the QText-Document::toHtml() method requires us to use an encoding name (if we specify an encoding at all) that is W3C (World Wide Web Consortium) compliant.* If no encoding is specified then the HTML's meta-data will not include a charset attribute; we recommend always using the UTF-8 encoding for HTML files.

If we only need to create HTML files, we can do so directly in code using QString —as we did when we populated a QTextDocument from HTML earlier in the chapter—or we can use Qt's QXmlStreamWriter which makes it easy to ensure that attributes and text are correctly escaped (since it is done for us).

---

* See www.w3.org/TR/2006/REC-xml11-20060816/#NT-EncodingDecl and www.iana.org/assignments/char-acter-sets for information about XML encodings.

Exporting in SVG Format

For our example of exporting in SVG format, for simplicity's sake, we have only populated the QTextDocument with a single page. The code to perform the export isn't difficult, but does have some important details that we'll discuss. Note that to use Qt's SVG support we must add the line QT += svg to the program's .pro file.

```
bool MainWindow::exportSvg(const QString &filename,
                           QTextDocument *document)
{
    Q_ASSERT(filename.endsWith(".svg"));
    QSvgGenerator svg;
    svg.setFileName(filename);
    QRect rect = printer.pageRect().adjusted(25, 25, -25, 25);
    svg.setSize(rect.size());
    QPainter painter(&svg);
    painter.setViewport(rect);
    document->drawContents(&painter);
    return true;
}
```

An SVG image is created by painting to a QSvgGenerator. Here we have used a QPrinter member variable, and we match the SVG image's size to that of the printer's page size, allowing for some margin. Having set up the SVG generator, we create a QPainter to paint on it, and set the painter's viewport (i.e., the area that will actually get painted on) to the SVG image's rectangle. The QTextDocument::drawContents() method is similar to QTextDocument::print(), except that it draws on a painter rather than on a printer, and accepts an optional clipping rectangle.

Here we have painted an SVG image using a QTextDocument convenience method. However, we can just as easily create SVG images using the QPainter API to draw shapes, images, and text, just as with any other paint device we care to draw on, as we will see further on when we look at the paintSvg() method (➤ 387).

Exporting in Pixmap Formats

Qt supports a lot of pixmap image formats out of the box. These normally include at least .bmp (Windows Bitmap), .jpg and .jpeg (Joint Photographic Experts Group), .png (Portable Network Graphics), .ppm (Portable Pixmap), .tiff (Tagged Image File Format), and .xpm (X11 Pixmap), but may include others. The precise list is reported by QImageWriter::supportedImageFormats(). (Note that the formats that Qt can write are usually fewer than those that it can read; the latter are returned by QImageReader::supportedImageFormats(). Also, the range of formats can be increased by the use of format-specific plugins.)

```
bool MainWindow::exportImage(const QString &filename,
                            QTextDocument *document)
{
    QImage image(printer.paperRect().size(), QImage::Format_ARGB32);
    QPainter painter(&image);
    painter.setRenderHints(QPainter::Antialiasing|
                           QPainter::TextAntialiasing);
    painter.fillRect(painter.viewport(), Qt::white);
    painter.setViewport(printer.paperRect());
    document->drawContents(&painter);
    return image.save(filename);
}
```

This method will export the given QTextDocument to the given file using whatever file format the filename's suffix indicates, providing the suffix is in the list of supported image formats for image writing.

Structurally, the code is fairly similar to that used for exporting an SVG image, only here we begin by creating a QImage rather than a QSvgGenerator. And the code is virtually identical to that used for painting a pixmap image to file, as we will see when we look at the paintImage() method further on (➤ 388).

We create a painter to draw the image, set up antialiasing, and give the image a white background. (We could just as easily have used Qt::transparent for the background instead.) As a rule of thumb we use antialiasing when producing on-screen and pixmap images (such as .bmp or .png), but not when printing or producing vector images (such as .svg). We set the painter's viewport to match the printer's paper rectangle—with no margins this time—and draw the document's contents. At the end we call QImage::save() (which returns a Boolean success flag) to save the image to the file in the requested format.

Printing and Previewing QTextDocuments

Printing a QTextDocument is very similar to exporting it, although normally we would give the user the option of setting up the printer and possibly doing a page preview before actually printing it.

For the outputsampler program we have chosen to have a QPageSetupDialog pointer as a main window member variable, and to create the dialog only if it is needed. This makes it simple to provide the user with page setup, and consumes almost no memory unless the dialog is actually used.

```
void MainWindow::pageSetup()
{
```

```
            if (!pageSetupDialog)
                pageSetupDialog = new QPageSetupDialog(&printer, this);
            pageSetupDialog->open();
        }
```

If we didn't offer page preview we might pass parameters to the QPageSetup-Dialog::open() call, for example, pageSetupDialog->open(this, SLOT(print())); this will result in the print() slot being called if the user accepts the setup dialog. The use of open() rather than exec() is so that the dialog appears as a sheet on Mac OS X; on other platforms it appears as a modal dialog as usual. (We touched on this issue earlier—for example, Chapter 2; 61◄, and Chapter 3; 102◄.)

For print preview we have opted to create a QPrintPreviewDialog on demand—and to do so every time one is required. This seems to be necessary because the preview dialog appears to cache its results. This is inconvenient for the outputsampler program since it can change how the pages are generated depending on which radio button is checked, so we need to force a fresh preview each time. In most other applications this shouldn't be necessary.

```
        void MainWindow::printPreview()
        {
            if (printPreviewDialog)
                delete printPreviewDialog;
            printPreviewDialog = new QPrintPreviewDialog(&printer, this);
            QSize size = qApp->desktop()->availableGeometry().size();
            size.rwidth() /= 2;
            printPreviewDialog->resize(size);
            if (painterRadioButton->isChecked())
                connect(printPreviewDialog, SIGNAL(paintRequested(QPrinter*)),
                        &pageData, SLOT(paintPages(QPrinter*)));
            else
                connect(printPreviewDialog, SIGNAL(paintRequested(QPrinter*)),
                        this, SLOT(printDocument(QPrinter*)));
            printPreviewDialog->open();
        }
```

We want the dialog to occupy the entire height of the user's screen so that they can see as much as possible. The QDesktopWidget returned by QApplication::desktop() can provide us with the actual screen geometry (screenGeometry()), or, as we have used here, the available geometry which excludes taskbars, and on Mac OS X excludes the menu bar and the dock. Both these methods accept an optional screen number for multi-head systems, and QDesktopWidget::screen-Count() returns the number of screens that are present. Since most modern desktop screens are much wider than they are tall, we have set the width to be half that of the screen.

For print preview to work we must supply a connection to the print preview dialog's `paintRequested()` signal. For the `outputsampler` example we have provided for two possibilities, although normally there would just be one. The second connection is to a `printDocument()` slot which we'll look at now, while we will cover the `PageData::paintPages()` slot in the next section.

Just like the `QPageSetupDialog`'s `open()` method, the `QPrintPreviewDialog::open()` method can be given a receiving object and a print slot to call if the user accepts the dialog.

Platform/ Qt version	Print Preview Output Technique		
	QTextDocument/ HTML	QTextDocument/ QTextCursor	QPainter
Linux/4.5.2	✔	✔	✔
Linux/4.6.1	✔	✔	✔
Mac/4.5.2	✘	✘	✓
Mac/4.6.1	✘	✘	✓
Windows/4.5.2	✔	✔	✔
Windows/4.6.1	✔	✔	✔

Figure 10.7 *Comparison of print previews*

Figure 10.7 shows the results of our print preview tests. Unfortunately, we observed problems on Mac OS X: print preview of `QTextDocuments` did not work at all, and print preview of painted documents rendered the preview on pages that were too narrow.

```
void MainWindow::printDocument(QPrinter *printer)
{
    QTextDocument document;
    populateDocument(&document);
    document.print(printer);
}
```

This method creates an empty `QTextDocument`, populates it using `PageData::populateDocumentUsingHtml()` (365 ◄) or `PageData::populateDocumentUsingQTextCursor()` (367 ◄), and then tells the document to print itself on the given printer.

```
void MainWindow::populateDocument(QTextDocument *document)
{
    Q_ASSERT(!painterRadioButton->isChecked());
    if (htmlRadioButton->isChecked())
        pageData.populateDocumentUsingHtml(document);
```

```
            else if (cursorRadioButton->isChecked())
                pageData.populateDocumentUsingQTextCursor(document);
    }
```

We show this method for completeness. It simply chooses which populate document method to use depending on the user's choice.

Painting Pages

We paint single page documents (such as SVG and pixmap files) by creating a QPainter and using the PageData::paintPage() method. And for multi-page documents we do almost the same thing, only we use the PageData::paintPages() method. In this section we will review the PageData methods used to paint pages, and then in the section's subsections we'll see how the paintPage() and paintPages() methods are used to paint PDF, PostScript, SVG, and pixmap files. For print preview, we have already seen that the page preview dialog calls the PageData::paintPages() method. There is no difference between exporting and printing when it comes to producing output using a QPainter.

Using QPainter places the burden of calculation on us rather than on, say, QTextDocument, but the payback we get is complete control over what is painted and where.

```
    void PageData::paintPages(QPrinter *printer, bool noUserInteraction)
    {
        if (noUserInteraction)
            printer->setPageMargins(25, 25, 25, 25, QPrinter::Millimeter);
        QPainter painter(printer);
        for (int page = 0; page < pages.count(); ++page) {
            paintPage(&painter, page);
            if (page + 1 < pages.count())
                printer->newPage();
        }
    }
```

This method has the same essential structure as the PageData::populateDocumentUsingHtml() (365 ◄) and PageData::populateDocumentUsingQTextCursor() (367 ◄) methods that we reviewed earlier.

If the pages are being output without user interaction, we set some page margins, otherwise we use the user's settings. Then we create a QPainter, and paint each individual page. We haven't switched on antialiasing since we consider painting to a printer to be like painting to a vector format file (such as an SVG file). After every page except for the last we call QPrinter::newPage(); this ejects the page that's just been printed and loads a fresh page ready to be printed. The `newPage()` method returns a Boolean success flag, although we have chosen to ignore it.

```
void PageData::paintPage(QPainter *painter, int page)
{
    const OnePage &thePage = pages.at(page);

    int y = paintTitle(painter, thePage.title);
    y = paintItems(painter, y, thePage);
    paintHtmlParagraph(painter, y, thePage.descriptionHtml);
    paintFooter(painter, tr("- %1 -").arg(page + 1));
}
```

Again, this method is structurally similar to one we have seen before (e.g., `PageData::addPageToDocument()`; 368 ◀), passing on the work for each part of the page to helper methods. One important difference with the helpers used here, though, is that each one except the last returns a y-coordinate. The coordinate is the furthest down the page that the helper has printed—so that the following method can continue printing down the page without overprinting what has gone before. (Although the `paintHtmlParagraph()` method returns the y-coordinate for the line after the paragraph, we ignore it because the `paintFooter()` method computes its y-coordinate based on the viewport's height and the footer's height, regardless of what has already been painted.)

If this method is used to paint a page onto a pixmap image, the caller that created the painter is expected to have switched on antialiasing.

```
int PageData::paintTitle(QPainter *painter, const QString &title)
{
    painter->setFont(QFont("Helvetica", 24, QFont::Bold));
    QRect rect(0, 0, painter->viewport().width(),
               painter->fontMetrics().height());
    painter->drawText(rect, title, QTextOption(Qt::AlignCenter));
    return qRound(painter->fontMetrics().lineSpacing() * 1.5);
}
```

This method prints the title in a very large font, horizontally centered. The rectangle's y-coordinate is 0 which is where the top margin lies, and is also used by the painter as the font's top position. In other words, the bottom of the text is at y + `painter->fontMetrics().height()`.

Once the text is drawn we return a y-coordinate for the next thing to be drawn, with a bit of vertical space in between. This is computed by using a y-coordinate that is one and a half lines down, which in effect creates a gap half a line high.

```
int PageData::paintItems(QPainter *painter, int y,
                         const OnePage &thePage)
```

```
    {
        const int ItemHeight = painter->viewport().height() / 3;
        const int ItemWidth = painter->viewport().width() / 2;

        paintItem(painter, QRect(0, y, ItemWidth, ItemHeight),
                thePage.filenames.at(0), thePage.captions.at(0));
        paintItem(painter, QRect(ItemWidth, y, ItemWidth, ItemHeight),
                thePage.filenames.at(1), thePage.captions.at(1));
        y += ItemHeight;
        paintItem(painter, QRect(0, y, ItemWidth, ItemHeight),
                thePage.filenames.at(2), thePage.captions.at(2));
        paintItem(painter, QRect(ItemWidth, y, ItemWidth, ItemHeight),
                thePage.filenames.at(3), thePage.captions.at(3));
        return y + ItemHeight + painter->fontMetrics().height();
    }
```

In the case of the `outputsampler` program we want to draw a 2×2 table of "items"—images and accompanying captions. This method is used to compute the rectangle that each item will occupy, and passes on the actual drawing to the `paintItem()` helper method.

The painter's viewport already accounts for the page's margins, so we can do calculations using the viewport directly. Here we have said that each item should be one-third of the page high and half of the page wide.

At the end we return a *y*-coordinate that is the height of two items plus `QPainter::fontMetrics().height()` which is the character height for the current font. An alternative would have been to use the current font's line height (`QFontMetrics::lineSpacing()`).

```
    void PageData::paintItem(QPainter *painter, const QRect &rect,
            const QString &filename, const QString &caption)
    {
        painter->drawRect(rect);

        const int Margin = 20;
        painter->setFont(QFont("Helvetica", 18));
        const int LineHeight = painter->fontMetrics().lineSpacing();

        QRect imageRect(rect);
        imageRect.adjust(Margin, Margin, -Margin, -(Margin + LineHeight));
        QSvgRenderer svg(filename);
        QSize size(svg.defaultSize());
        size.scale(imageRect.size(), Qt::KeepAspectRatio);
        imageRect.setSize(size);
        const int Xoffset = (imageRect.width() - size.width()) / 2;
        imageRect.moveTo(imageRect.x() + Xoffset, imageRect.y());
        svg.render(painter, imageRect);
```

```
        int y = rect.y() + rect.height() - LineHeight;
        QRect captionRect(rect.x(), y, rect.width(), LineHeight);
        painter->drawText(captionRect, caption,
                          QTextOption(Qt::AlignCenter));
    }
```

We draw each item in three parts: a rectangle outline, an image, and a caption. The rectangle is easy since it is passed as a parameter. We want the image to fit neatly inside the rectangle, and not to collide with the caption, so we begin by setting a margin and the caption's font. Once we have set the font we can use the painter's font metrics to compute a line height for the text.

We prefer to use SVG images since they can be scaled without degrading quality. We begin by creating a rectangle for the image based on the item's rectangle, but then reduce the image rectangle's size by the margin size, except for its height (actually its bottom y-coordinate), which we reduce by the margin plus the height of the caption line.

We use a QSvgRenderer to load and draw the SVG image on the painter. Once it is loaded, we retrieve the SVG image's default ("natural") size, and then scale this size to fit within the image rectangle, while preserving the aspect ratio. Using Qt::KeepAspectRatio reduces the size to fit. The other valid enums are Qt::IgnoreAspectRatio and Qt::KeepAspectRatioByExpanding; the expanding one causes the image to be expanded until one of its dimensions (width or height) matches the width or height that has been specified, with the other dimension expanded beyond its given dimension if necessary to preserve the aspect ratio.

Since we want the image to be horizontally centered, we compute a suitable x-offset. Then we set the image rectangle's size to the scaled size and move the rectangle so that it is horizontally centered. And then we call the QSvgRenderer::render() method to draw the SVG image on the painter using the image rectangle.

If we were using pixmap images rather than SVG images, the code for painting the image would be almost identical:

```
        QImage image(filename);
        QSize size(image.size());
        size.scale(imageRect.size(), Qt::KeepAspectRatio);
        imageRect.setSize(size);
        const int Xoffset = (imageRect.width() - size.width()) / 2;
        imageRect.moveTo(imageRect.x() + Xoffset, imageRect.y());
        painter->drawImage(imageRect, image);
```

The only difference is that we use QImage rather than QSvgRenderer to load the image and obtain its size, and that we use QPainter::drawImage() rather than QSvgRenderer::render() to draw the image. One improvement that we could consider would be to only scale the pixmap image's rectangle (and therefore the drawn pixmap) if the image's size is larger than the image rectangle's size. (Note that in the source code we use a #define to switch between using embedded SVG and embedded pixmap images, with the default being to use SVG images.)

Once the image has been drawn, we must draw the caption. We find the necessary y-coordinate by taking the y-coordinate of the rectangle passed in, plus its height to give the coordinate of the bottom of the rectangle, and then reduce this (i.e., move back up) by one line. We then create a suitable rectangle for the caption and draw it centered (both horizontally and vertically) within the rectangle. This ensures that the caption is drawn at the bottom of the rectangle, with a gap (the size of the margin) between the top of the caption and the bottom of the image. This does mean that descenders from the caption will reach the bottom of the rectangle (and so come very close to the rectangle outline drawn at the beginning); we leave the adding of some margin below the text as an exercise.

When it comes to painting paragraphs of HTML text we can give the HTML to a QTextDocument. This then gives us two choices about how we render the document's contents. The easier approach is to get the QTextDocument to render the HTML directly on the painter; the harder approach is to treat the QTextDocument as a container of rich text fragments and to iterate over these fragments ourselves, painting each one as we go. We will show both approaches, beginning with the code that creates the QTextDocument and that is common to both. (The source code covers both approaches, using a #define to switch between them at compile time.)

```
int PageData::paintHtmlParagraph(QPainter *painter, int y,
                                 const QString &html)
{
    const QFont ParagraphFont("Times", 15);
    painter->setFont(ParagraphFont);
    QTextDocument document;
    document.setHtml(html);
```

We begin by setting a default paragraph font; as we noted earlier, this is larger than would normally be used but is intended to be more legible in the screenshot (360 ◀). We set the font on the painter so that we can use the painter's font metrics. Then we create a QTextDocument and populate it with the paragraph of HTML that has been passed in.

```
    document.setDefaultFont(ParagraphFont);
    document.setUseDesignMetrics(true);
    document.setTextWidth(painter->viewport().width());
    QRect rect(0, y, painter->viewport().width(),
               painter->viewport().height());
```

```
        painter->save();
        painter->setViewport(rect);
        document.drawContents(painter);
        painter->restore();
        return y + document.documentLayout()->documentSize().height() +
                painter->fontMetrics().lineSpacing();
    }
```

We begin by giving the QTextDocument the same default font as the painter.
We tell the document to use design metrics since this should produce higher-
quality results. We also limit the document's width to the width of the
viewport—this is crucial to get the layout to work well (although if we were
not constrained by the physical page size we could use QTextDocument::ideal-
Width()). The QTextDocument::drawContents() method can accept a second argument of a clipping rectangle, but we don't need it here. We want the text
drawn about two-thirds of the way down the page, but there is no way to tell the
QTextDocument to do this. So instead, we save the painter's state and change its
viewport to be a rectangle starting at the y-coordinate we want and having the
width and height of the page. We then tell the document to draw its contents on
the painter (which will occur within the painter's new viewport, exactly where
we want it), and then we restore the painter's original viewport.

At the end we compute the y-coordinate for whatever follows the paragraph
(such as another paragraph), by adding the height of the document (which is
now known since to draw its contents the document had to lay itself out), plus
one line's spacing.

The second possibility for painting an HTML paragraph using a QTextDocument
is to paint the text ourselves. If this is the case, we are in effect using QText-
Document as an HTML parser which converts HTML into an internal document
structure that we then iterate over, painting each individual word as we go. We
will see how this is done by looking at another version of the second part of the
paintHtmlParagraph() method.

```
        QTextBlock block = document.begin();
        Q_ASSERT(block.isValid());
        int x = 0;
        for (QTextBlock::iterator i = block.begin(); !i.atEnd(); ++i) {
            QTextFragment fragment = i.fragment();
            if (fragment.isValid()) {
                QTextCharFormat format = fragment.charFormat();
                foreach (QString word,
                        fragment.text().split(QRegExp("\\s+"))) {
                    int width = painter->fontMetrics().width(word);
                    if (x + width > painter->viewport().width()) {
                        x = 0;
                        y += painter->fontMetrics().lineSpacing();
```

```
                    }
                    else if (x != 0)
                        word.prepend(" ");
                    x += paintWord(painter, x, y, word, ParagraphFont,
                                   format);
                }
            }
        }
        return y + painter->fontMetrics().lineSpacing();
    }
```

A paragraph is held in a single `QTextBlock`, and the block contains one or more `QTextFragment`s, each with its own `QTextCharFormat`. We iterate over the fragments (or *the* fragment, if the paragraph's text all has the same character format), and for each fragment we extract its format and iterate over the words it contains. The regex we use for breaking the fragment's text into words splits on "one or more whitespaces", so in effect we are treating any sequence of one or more whitespaces as a single whitespace. This makes sense since the source of the text was HTML which uses exactly this logic regarding whitespace. (Incidentally, creating the regex inside the loop isn't as expensive as it looks: `QRegExp` is smart enough to remember the most recently used regexes, so the regex will be compiled into the internal regex format the first time it is constructed, and on subsequent iterations the already compiled format will be used.)

Once we have a word we ask the painter's font metrics to tell us how wide it is. If the word will not fit on the current line we reset the x-coordinate to 0 and increment the y-coordinate by one line; otherwise we prepend a space to the word (to separate it horizontally from the previous word on the line), and leave the coordinates unchanged. Then we call our `paintWord()` helper method, and increment the x-coordinate by the offset the method returns.

And at the end, we return the y-coordinate plus one line's height so that the next thing that gets painted will be on the line below the paragraph.

```
    int PageData::paintWord(QPainter *painter, int x, int y,
            const QString &word, const QFont &paragraphFont,
            const QTextCharFormat &format)
    {
        QFont font(format.font());
        font.setFamily(paragraphFont.family());
        font.setPointSize(paragraphFont.pointSize());
        painter->setFont(font);
        painter->setPen(format.foreground().color());
        painter->drawText(x, y, word);
        return painter->fontMetrics().width(word);
    }
```

For each word that we paint (which is either a word or a space followed by a word), we begin by creating a font based on the character format's font, but then overriding the family and point size by the paragraph font's family and size. We then set this font on the painter, and set the painter's pen to be the format's foreground color, so that we honor colored text. We then draw the text at the given *x*- and *y*-coordinates. And finally, we return the width of the word we have just drawn so that the caller can increment its *x*-coordinate's position.

```
void PageData::paintFooter(QPainter *painter, const QString &footer)
{
    painter->setFont(QFont("Helvetica", 11));
    painter->setPen(Qt::black);
    const int LineHeight = painter->fontMetrics().lineSpacing();
    int y = painter->viewport().height() - LineHeight;
    painter->drawLine(0, y, painter->viewport().width(), y);

    y += LineHeight / 10;
    painter->drawText(
            QRect(0, y, painter->viewport().width(), LineHeight),
            footer, QTextOption(Qt::AlignCenter));
}
```

We set a different font for the footer and set the pen to the default color. We draw a horizontal rule across the page at a position one line above the bottom margin. And then we draw the footer (plain) text centered just below the rule.

We have now completed our review of the code for painting a document rather than using a QTextDocument. If we were to count lines of code we would probably find that for the sample document, using a QTextDocument with raw HTML required the least code and painting required the most; but this may well be different for different documents, so we recommend using whichever approach best suits the circumstances rather than whichever is likely to need the fewest lines.

The methods we have seen are all called from PageData::paintPages() (which takes a QPrinter argument), which in turn calls PageData::paintPage() (which takes a QPainter argument). This means that these methods can be used to paint the sample document on any printer or other paint device, as we will see in the following short subsections.

Painting PDF or PostScript   III

We can paint a PDF or PostScript document directly; all we need is a filename ending with .pdf or .ps.

```
bool MainWindow::paintPdfOrPs(const QString &filename)
{
    Q_ASSERT(filename.endsWith(".ps") || filename.endsWith(".pdf"));
    QPrinter printer(QPrinter::HighResolution);
    printer.setOutputFileName(filename);
    printer.setOutputFormat(filename.endsWith(".pdf")
            ? QPrinter::PdfFormat : QPrinter::PostScriptFormat);
    pageData.paintPages(&printer);
    return true;
}
```

We begin by creating a QPrinter, but instead of using the printer to print paper pages, we set it to "print to file", giving it the filename to print to and the format to use. (Structurally, this code is just the same as the exportPdfOrPs() method we saw earlier; 372 ◄.)

Painting SVG   III

SVG files can be painted using a QSvgGenerator, given a filename to write the SVG to, and a page size. (Even though SVG images are scalable it is conventional to provide a default or "natural" size for them.) For SVG files we have opted to create a single SVG image for a single page rather than using the entire multi-page document.

```
bool MainWindow::paintSvg(const QString &filename)
{
    Q_ASSERT(filename.endsWith(".svg"));
    QSvgGenerator svg;
    svg.setFileName(filename);
    QRect rect = printer.pageRect().adjusted(25, 25, -25, 25);
    svg.setSize(rect.size());
    QPainter painter(&svg);
    painter.setViewport(rect);
    pageData.paintPage(&painter, 0);
    return true;
}
```

The painting is very simple: we create a QPainter, and paint a page (page 0). Here we have chosen to offset the image to provide some margin. (Structurally, this code is the same as in the exportSvg() method we saw before; 375 ◄.)

Painting Pixmaps

A QPainter paints images which can be rendered as pixmaps or as vectors. So, a QPainter can paint to a QImage and a QImage can be saved in any pixmap format that Qt supports. (The list of formats is returned by the static QImageWriter::supportedImageFormats() method.)

```
bool MainWindow::paintImage(const QString &filename)
{
    QImage image(printer.paperRect().size(), QImage::Format_ARGB32);
    QPainter painter(&image);
    painter.setRenderHints(QPainter::Antialiasing|
                           QPainter::TextAntialiasing);
    painter.fillRect(painter.viewport(), Qt::white);
    painter.setViewport(printer.pageRect());
    pageData.paintPage(&painter, 0);
    return image.save(filename);
}
```

Here we create a QImage of the size we need, set up antialiasing, fill the background with white to clear it—we could just as easily have used Qt::transparent—and then we paint one page (page 0). Just as for painting SVG images we have opted to create a single image for a single page. (Structurally, this method is identical to the exportImage() method we saw earlier; 375 ◄.)

We have now seen how to print and export documents that include rich text, images, and complex formatting (e.g., tables). We have seen how to print and export a single page of a QTextDocument as an SVG image and in any of the standard pixmap formats that Qt supports, and how to achieve the same thing directly using a QPainter. We have also seen how to print and export entire multi-page QTextDocument documents in PDF, PostScript, Open Document Format, and HTML, and how to paint documents directly using a QPainter to produce PDF and PostScript.

In this chapter we made extensive use of QPainter to paint documents, and as we know from previous chapters, QPainter is also used to paint custom widgets and graphics. But Qt offers a powerful alternative to QPainter for sophisticated graphics: the graphics/view architecture, which is the subject of the next two chapters.

11

- The Graphics/View Architecture
- Graphics/View Widgets and Layouts
- Introducing Graphics Items

Creating Graphics/View Windows

By reimplementing a custom QWidget subclass's paintEvent() and using a QPainter, we can draw anything we want. This is ideal for custom widgets, but is not at all convenient if we want to draw lots of individual items, especially if we want to provide the user with the ability to interact with the items. For example, in the past some users have created graphical applications using literally thousands of custom widgets to stand as graphical items, and although widget painting is very fast, handling a single mouse click in such situations could easily consume almost the whole CPU's processing capability. Fortunately, Qt 4.2 introduced the graphics/view architecture which perfectly fulfills the need for high-performance item-based drawing and interaction.

Although originally designed as a superior replacement for Qt 3's QCanvas class, Qt 4's graphics/view architecture has gone far beyond the canvas's functionality. In fact, some applications now use a QGraphicsView as their main window's central widget and place all the widgets used to provide the user interface inside the view as graphics items in their own right.

In this chapter's first section we begin with a brief overview of the graphics/view architecture, including a sidebar on some significant changes introduced in Qt 4.6. Then, in the second section, we will review an application whose main window's central widget is a QGraphicsView and which has both widget items and conventional graphics items. And finally, in the chapter's third section, we will look at a simple QGraphicsItem subclass and the QGraphicsItem API.

In the next chapter we will look at a more conventional graphics/view application—a basic drawing program—and there we will look more closely at most of the graphics/view classes, and will present more examples of how to create custom graphics items. Incidentally, we will revisit the examples presented in

389

this chapter and the next in Chapter 13 where we create modified versions of them that make use of some Qt 4.6-specific features.

The Graphics/View Architecture

Rather like Qt's model/view architecture, the graphics/view architecture has a non-visual class for holding the item data as a model (QGraphicsScene), and a class for visualizing the data (QGraphicsView). We can visualize the same scene in many different views if that is required. A graphics scene contains items that are derived from the abstract QGraphicsItem class.

Since its original introduction, Qt's graphics/view architecture has benefited from a great deal of development effort to improve both its speed and its capabilities. Scenes can be scaled, rotated, and printed, and rendering can be done using Qt's rendering engine or using OpenGL. The architecture also supports animation and drag and drop. Graphics scenes can be used to present anything from just a few items up to tens of thousands of items or more.

Qt provides many predefined graphics item types that can be used out of the box; they are shown in Figure 11.1. Most of the class names are self-explanatory, but we will mention a few that may not be so obvious. A QGraphicsPathItem represents a QPainterPath—essentially an arbitrary shape that is composed of all the fundamental things that Qt can draw, including, arcs, Bézier curves, chords, ellipses, lines, rectangles, and text. A QGraphicsSimpleTextItem represents a piece of plain text and a QGraphicsTextItem represents a piece of Qt rich text (which can be specified using HTML; we discussed rich text in the previous two chapters). The QGraphicsWidget class is provided as a base class for the creation of custom widgets that are designed to live in graphics scenes. It is also possible to embed standard QWidget-derived widgets in scenes—this is done by adding the widget to a QGraphicsProxyWidget and putting the proxy widget into the scene. Using proxy widgets (or QWidgets directly) is "slow"—but whether this is noticeable will depend on the application.* The QGraphicsWebView class was introduced in Qt 4.6 and provides a graphics item version of the QWebView class we discussed in Chapter 1, for presenting web content in a scene.

For scenes that have small numbers of items we can use the QGraphicsObjects introduced in Qt 4.6—or for Qt 4.5 and earlier, we can derive from both QObject and QGraphicsItem—as the basis for our own custom items. This increases each item's overhead (e.g., items consume more memory), but provides the convenience of support for signals and slots and for Qt's property system. For scenes that have lots and lots of items it is usually best to use the lightweight QGraphicsItem class as the basis for the custom items that will appear in large

---

*For a discussion of the performance issues of using QWidgets and proxies in scenes, see labs.qt. nokia.com/blogs/2010/01/11/qt-graphics-and-performance-the-cost-of-convenience.

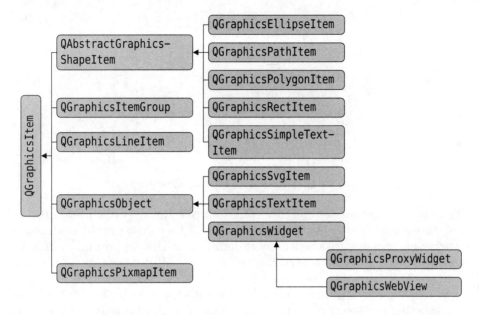

Figure 11.1 *Qt's QGraphicsItem hierarchy*

numbers, and only use QGraphicsObjects for items that will appear in small numbers.

The graphics view classes are essentially two-dimensional, although every item has a z value, with higher z-valued items being drawn in front of those with lower z values. Collision detection is based on item (x, y) positions. In addition to information about collisions, the scene can tell us which items contain a particular point or are in a particular region, and which are selected. Scenes also have a foreground layer which is useful, for example, to draw a grid that overlays all the items in the scene; they also have a background layer that is drawn underneath all the items, useful for providing a background image or color.

Items are either children of the scene, or a child of another item, rather like Qt's normal parent–child widget relationships. When transformations are applied to an item, they are automatically applied to all the item's children, recursively to the greatest descendant. This means that if an item is moved—for example, dragged by the user—all of its children (and their children, and so on) will be dragged with it. It is possible to make a child item ignore its parent's transformations by calling QGraphicsItem::setFlag(QGraphicsItem:: ItemIgnoresTransformations). Other, more commonly used flags include ones for making an item movable, selectable, and focusable by the user. (All the flags are listed in Tables 11.6 and 11.7; ➤ 406–407.) Items can also be grouped by making them children of a QGraphicsItemGroup; this is useful for creating ad hoc collections of items.

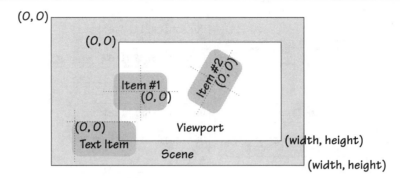

Figure 11.2 *Graphics items use local logical coordinates*

The graphics view classes use three different coordinate systems, although in practice we usually care about only two of them. Views use the physical coordinate system. Scenes use a logical coordinate system that we normally define by passing a QRectF to their constructor. Qt automatically maps scene coordinates to view coordinates. In essence, scenes use "window" (logical) coordinates and views use "viewport" (physical) coordinates. So, when we are positioning items we place them in terms of scene coordinates. The third coordinate system is the one used by items. This is particularly convenient because it is a logical coordinate system centered on point (0, 0). Each item's (0, 0) is actually at the item's center position in the scene (apart from text items where it is the item's top-left corner). This means that in practice, we can always draw items in terms of their own center point—and we do not have to care about any transformations that have been applied to them by parent items, since the scene will automatically take care of these for us. Note also that in Qt, *y*-coordinates increase downward—for example, point (5, 8) is 6 pixels *above* point (5, 14). Figure 11.2 illustrates the relationship between scene and item coordinates.

Certain aspects of Qt's graphics/view architecture's behavior have changed between Qt 4.5 and Qt 4.6; these are summarized in the "Qt 4.6 Graphics/View Behavior Changes" sidebar (➤ 393).

Graphics/View Widgets and Layouts

In this section we will review the Petri Dish application (petridish1) shown in Figure 11.3. The application has a MainWindow class that inherits QMainWindow and uses a QGraphicsView as its central widget. Petri Dish is a dialog-style simulation application that simulates "cells" that grow if they aren't too crowded, but shrink if they are too isolated, too crowded, or too big, and where small cells randomly "die". We won't say much more about the simulation itself, or about the application's logic, since the focus of this chapter is Qt's graphics/view architecture.

Qt 4.6 Graphics/View Behavior Changes

The graphics/view classes underwent considerable development between Qt 4.5 and Qt 4.6, resulting in greatly improved performance. One consequence of these under the hood changes is that certain user-visible behavior changes were necessary to allow for the best possible optimizations to be achieved. The key behavior changes are as follows:

- QStyleOptionGraphicsItem's public variable, exposedRect of type QRectF, holds the item's exposed rectangle in item coordinates. However, this variable is only ever set for graphics items that have the ItemUsesExtendedStyleOption flag set.

- QStyleOptionGraphicsItem's levelOfDetail and matrix variables are both obsolete. The correct Qt 4.6 way to get the level of detail is to use the static QStyleOptionGraphicsItem::levelOfDetailFromTransform() method.

- QGraphicsView no longer calls QGraphicsView::drawItems() or QGraphicsView::drawItem()—unless you set the QGraphicsView::IndirectPainting "optimization" flag (which is not recommended).

- QGraphicsItem no longer calls itemChange() for position and transformation changes. To be notified of these changes, set the QGraphicsItem:: ItemSendsGeometryChanges flag. (This flag is already set by default for QGraphicsWidgets and for QGraphicsProxyWidgets.)

  Even with the ItemSendsGeometryChanges flag set, when transformations are made, itemChange() is only called if setTransform() is used. From Qt 4.7 it is expected that if the flag is set, itemChange() will also be called if setRotation(), setScale(), or setTransformOriginPoint() (all introduced in Qt 4.6) are called.

How much—or even whether—these changes will affect any particular application depends on what graphics/view features the application uses. In the case of the examples presented in this book, the next chapter's Page Designer application was affected by the last behavior change listed above.

Here we will review the relevant main window methods (or extracts from these methods) to show how to create a main window based on a graphics scene. And in the next section we will look at the Cell items (derived from QGraphicsItem), focusing on the basics of creating a custom graphics item and introducing the QGraphicsItem API without looking at the irrelevant simulation logic. (The source code is in the petridish1 subdirectory.)

The application has start, pause/resume, stop, and quit buttons to control the simulation, and the user can set an initial cell count and whether to show cell IDs—which is useful for cells that are otherwise too small to see. (The initial cell count is disabled during a simulation run, as the screenshot illustrates.)

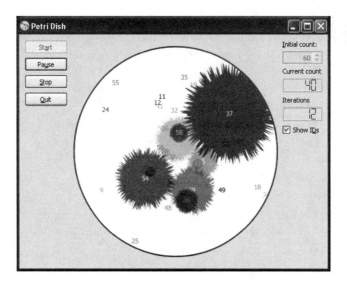

Figure 11.3 *The Petri Dish application*

The user interface uses a couple of QLCDNumbers to show how many cells are left and how many iterations the simulation has run for.

We will begin by looking at the main window's constructor, and then at some of the helper methods that are relevant to the graphics/view programming we are concerned with here.

```
MainWindow::MainWindow(QWidget *parent)
    : QMainWindow(parent), simulationState(Stopped), iterations(0)
{
    scene = new QGraphicsScene(this);
    scene->setItemIndexMethod(QGraphicsScene::NoIndex);

    createWidgets();
    createProxyWidgets();
    createLayout();
    createCentralWidget();
    createConnections();

    startButton->setFocus();
    setWindowTitle(QApplication::applicationName());
}
```

The creation of the QGraphicsScene is slightly unusual since we have not specified the scene's dimensions. Although we know the height we need (high enough for the petri dish plus some margin), the width depends on how wide the widgets are, so we will set the dimensions once the widgets have been created and laid out.

When items are added, moved, or removed from a scene, location computations are required. For example, if an item is added in a visible portion of the scene it must be drawn, or if a visible item is moved or removed, whatever it had covered and is now revealed must be drawn. For scenes with lots of static items these computations can be considerably speeded up by using an index method of QGraphicsScene::BspTreeIndex (Binary Space Partitioning); but for highly dynamic scenes with lots of items added, moved, or removed, it is better to switch off indexing (as we do here), since the overhead of using it outweighs the savings it delivers.

In common with our coding style throughout the book, we call helper methods in the constructor to perform most of the widget's initialization. Since we are using a graphics scene for the main window's central widget, all of the helpers are relevant, so we will show and discuss them all (but omitting repetitive code where possible).

```
void MainWindow::createWidgets()
{
    startButton = new QPushButton(tr("St&art"));
    pauseOrResumeButton = new QPushButton(tr("Pa&use"));
    pauseOrResumeButton->setEnabled(false);
    stopButton = new QPushButton(tr("Stop"));
    quitButton = new QPushButton(tr("Quit"));

    QString styleSheet("background-color: bisque;");
    initialCountLabel = new QLabel(tr("Initial count:"));
    initialCountLabel->setStyleSheet(styleSheet);
    ...
    AQP::accelerateWidgets(QList<QWidget*>() << startButton
            << stopButton << quitButton << initialCountLabel
            << showIdsCheckBox);
}
```

The application uses standard QWidgets, and their creation holds no surprises. The only slightly unusual thing we have done is to provide the widgets (not including the push buttons) with a style sheet that provides a uniform background color. The push buttons are not given style sheets because we prefer them to retain their platform- and theme-specific look.

```
void MainWindow::createProxyWidgets()
{
    proxyForName["startButton"] = scene->addWidget(startButton);
    proxyForName["pauseOrResumeButton"] = scene->addWidget(
            pauseOrResumeButton);
    ...
}
```

All the widgets must be added to the scene since the scene's view is the main window's central widget. We could easily have adopted a different approach—for example, using a plain QWidget as the central widget, and giving the widget a QHBoxLayout, with this layout having a QVBoxLayout holding the buttons, then the QGraphicsView, and then another QVBoxLayout holding the other widgets. But just to show that it can be done, we have chosen to use the QGraphicsView itself as the central widget and to put all the other widgets, as well as the graphics items, inside it.

The way to add standard QWidgets to a scene is to create a QGraphicsProxyWidget for each QWidget, and add the proxy to the scene. In this method we use the QGraphicsScene::addWidget() method which creates a QGraphicsProxyWidget that represents the widget it is passed as argument, and returns a pointer to the proxy widget as its result. For convenience, we keep a hash whose keys are widget names and whose values are proxy widget pointers, and add each proxy we create to the hash. (The hash is declared in the header file as QHash<QString, QGraphicsProxyWidget*> proxyForName;.)

Once the widgets and their proxies have been created we can lay them out. This works in a similar way to using Qt's standard layouts, except that we must use graphics-scene-specific layout classes. We will look at the createLayout() method in two parts, first looking at the creation of the layouts, and second looking at the setting of the scene's dimensions.

```
const int DishSize = 350;
const int Margin = 20;

void MainWindow::createLayout()
{
    QGraphicsLinearLayout *leftLayout = new QGraphicsLinearLayout(
            Qt::Vertical);
    leftLayout->addItem(proxyForName["startButton"]);
    leftLayout->addItem(proxyForName["pauseOrResumeButton"]);
    leftLayout->addItem(proxyForName["stopButton"]);
    leftLayout->addItem(proxyForName["quitButton"]);

    QGraphicsLinearLayout *rightLayout = new QGraphicsLinearLayout(
            Qt::Vertical);
    foreach (const QString &name, QStringList()
            << "initialCountLabel" << "initialCountSpinBox"
            << "currentCountLabel" << "currentCountLCD"
            << "iterationsLabel" << "iterationsLCD"
            << "showIdsCheckBox")
        rightLayout->addItem(proxyForName[name]);

    QGraphicsLinearLayout *layout = new QGraphicsLinearLayout;
    layout->addItem(leftLayout);
    layout->setItemSpacing(0, DishSize + Margin);
```

```
layout->addItem(rightLayout);

QGraphicsWidget *widget = new QGraphicsWidget;
widget->setLayout(layout);
scene->addItem(widget);
```

The `QGraphicsLinearLayout` class is a graphics/view layout class that corresponds to the `QBoxLayout` class from which the `QHBoxLayout` and `QVBoxLayout` classes are derived. The APIs are very similar, except that instead of adding widgets using `QBoxLayout::addWidget()`, we use `QGraphicsLinearLayout::addItem()`. This method adds a `QGraphicsLayoutItem` (which is one of `QGraphicsWidget`'s—and therefore `QGraphicsProxyWidget`'s—base classes) to the layout. There is also a `QGraphicsGridLayout` class that corresponds to the `QGridLayout` class. And Qt 4.6 introduced the `QGraphicsAnchorLayout` class which implements a novel approach to layouts not seen in Qt before, based on positioning widgets relative to each other, and to the edges and corners of the rectangle the layout occupies.

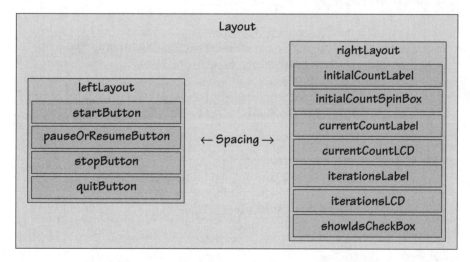

Figure 11.4 *The Petri Dish's main window layout*

In this method we create three `QGraphicsLinearLayouts`. The first layout is used to provide a vertical column of the buttons' proxy widgets on the left, and the second is used to provide a vertical column of proxy widgets on the right. The third is used to provide an overall horizontal layout which contains the left layout, a spacer (to provide room for the petri dish itself), and the right layout. The layout is shown schematically in Figure 11.4.

Once we have created the layouts, we create a new "blank" `QGraphicsWidget`. This class has no visual representation of itself and is specifically designed both to serve as a base class for custom graphics/view widgets and for the purpose we put it to here—to contain one or more child widgets organized into a layout. After creating the widget, we set the overall layout on it, and add the widget to the scene. As a result, all the layouts and proxy widgets are reparented—for example, the proxy widgets as children of the scene. (The widgets are reparented to their proxies during the QGraphicsScene::addWidget() calls.)

```
int width = qRound(layout->preferredWidth());
int height = DishSize + (2 * Margin);
setMinimumSize(width, height);
scene->setSceneRect(0, 0, width, height);
}
```

We set the scene to be wide enough to show the layout at its preferred width, and tall enough to display the petri dish with some vertical margin. We also set the main window's minimum size so that it can never be shrunk too small to properly show the petri dish and the widgets.

```
void MainWindow::createCentralWidget()
{
    dishItem = new QGraphicsEllipseItem;
    dishItem->setFlags(QGraphicsItem::ItemClipsChildrenToShape);
    dishItem->setPen(QPen(QColor("brown"), 2.5));
    dishItem->setBrush(Qt::white);
    dishItem->setRect(pauseOrResumeButton->width() + Margin,
            Margin, DishSize, DishSize);

    scene->addItem(dishItem);

    view = new QGraphicsView(scene);
    view->setRenderHints(QPainter::Antialiasing|
                        QPainter::TextAntialiasing);
    view->setBackgroundBrush(QColor("bisque"));
    setCentralWidget(view);
}
```

Once we have created the scene and populated it with widgets (or rather, with widget proxies), this method is called to create the petri dish and the view to complete the setting up of the application's appearance.

We begin by creating a new graphics ellipse item—although in this case it will be a circle since we make its width and height the same. We set the item to clip its children. All the simulated cells are created as children of the petri dish, so this ensures that any cells that are outside the petri dish's area are not shown, and that any cells that straddle the dish's border only have that portion of themselves that is within the border drawn. We set the petri dish's rectangle to have an x-coordinate that is the width of one of the buttons in the left-hand layout plus some margin, and its y-coordinate to allow a little margin above it. Once the dish item has been created, we add it to the scene.

We create a standard `QGraphicsView` with antialiasing switched on and using the same background color as we set in the style sheet for some of the widgets. We then make the view the main window's central widget, and the application's appearance is complete.

Structurally, using the graphics/view architecture to provide a main window's widgets is not so very different from the more conventional approach. The only significant differences are that we must create and add proxy widgets for the actual widgets, and that we must use graphics/view-specific layouts rather than the standard layout classes. Of course, if we wanted to use `QGraphicsWidget` subclasses there would be no need to create proxies for them, since we can add these directly into a scene. (At the time of this writing the only `QGraphicsWidget` subclass besides `QGraphicsProxyWidget` is `QGraphicsWebView`, although we can freely create our own `QGraphicsWidget` subclasses if we wish.)

```
void MainWindow::createConnections()
{
    connect(startButton, SIGNAL(clicked()), this, SLOT(start()));
    connect(pauseOrResumeButton, SIGNAL(clicked()),
            this, SLOT(pauseOrResume()));
    connect(stopButton, SIGNAL(clicked()), this, SLOT(stop()));
    connect(quitButton, SIGNAL(clicked()), this, SLOT(close()));
    connect(showIdsCheckBox, SIGNAL(toggled(bool)),
            this, SLOT(showIds(bool)));
}
```

This method is just like those we have seen many times in earlier chapters, with connections being made from the (actual) widgets' `clicked()` signals to corresponding slots. It isn't relevant to graphics/view programming as such, but is presented here to provide a contrast with the Qt 4.6 version of the example shown in Chapter 13 which uses a `QStateMachine` to control the application's behavior, and as a result has fewer slots and simpler logic.

Introducing Graphics Items

The `QGraphicsItem` class is the base class for all graphics items. Although the class provides a prodigious number of methods—over two hundred in Qt 4.6—it cannot be instantiated because it has two pure virtual methods: `bounding-Rect()` and `paint()`. The `paint()` method corresponds to `QWidget::paintEvent()`, and must be reimplemented to paint the item. The `boundingRect()` method gives the graphics/view architecture a bounding rectangle for the item—this is used for collision detection and to ensure that the item is only repainted if it is visible in a `QGraphicsView`'s viewport.

If we are creating non-rectangular custom graphics items, it is best to also reimplement the shape() method. This method returns a QPainterPath that precisely describes the item's outline. This is useful for accurate collision and mouse click detection.

There are many virtual methods that can be reimplemented, including advance(), boundingRect(), collidesWithItem(), collidesWithPath(), contains(), isObscuredBy(), opaqueArea(), paint(), shape(), and type(). All the protected methods (except for prepareGeometryChange()) are also virtual, so all the graphics item event handlers (including contextMenuEvent(), keyPressEvent, and the mouse events) can be reimplemented. All these are very briefly described in Tables 11.1 through 11.4 (➤ 403–406).

If we want a custom shape it is easiest to use one of the standard QGraphicsItem subclasses, such as QGraphicsPathItem or QGraphicsPolygonItem. And if we also want the shape to have custom behavior, we can subclass the item and reimplement some of the protected event handlers such as keyPressEvent() and mousePressEvent(). If we simply prefer to do our own painting, we can subclass QGraphicsItem directly and reimplement the boundingRect(), paint(), and shape() methods, plus any event handlers needed to provide the behaviors we want. And for all QGraphicsItem subclasses it is best to provide a Type enum and reimplement the type() method as we will discuss in a moment.

Here we will briefly review the pure graphics/view aspects of the Petri Dish application's Cell class, a direct QGraphicsItem subclass. We will start with the definition in the header file, but omit the private section.

```
class Cell : public QGraphicsItem
{
public:
    enum {Type = UserType + 1};

    explicit Cell(int id, QGraphicsItem *parent=0);

    QRectF boundingRect() const { return m_path.boundingRect(); }
    QPainterPath shape() const { return m_path; }
    void paint(QPainter *painter,
            const QStyleOptionGraphicsItem *option, QWidget *widget);
    int type() const { return Type; }
    ...
};
```

Although it is not mandatory to reimplement the type() method or to provide a Type enum, we recommend supplying both for every custom graphics item subclass. This makes it easy to uniquely identify each of our custom graphics items' types, and also means that they will work with qgraphicsitem_cast<>()— which casts QGraphicsItem pointers to the correct QGraphicsItem subclass. (The qgraphicsitem_cast<>() function only supports casts from QGraphicsItem pointers to subclasses, not from subclasses back to QGraphicsItem pointers. For casts back to QGraphicsItem pointers we must use other techniques. We will discuss graphics item casts further in the next chapter; ➤ 423.)

In this particular example, we have a private member variable, m_path of type QPainterPath (which changes shape dynamically as the simulation progresses). Since we have this path, we are able to use it to supply both the item's bounding rectangle and its shape. Note, though, that computing a bounding rectangle from a painter path is not particularly fast, although it is quick enough for the Petri Dish application. Other applications that use a painter path in this way might benefit from caching the path's bounding rectangle.

The shape() method is trivial to implement since, as we will see in a moment, the path is painted with no pen, only a brush. If we were painting a path with a pen—say a doughnut-shaped item produced by using a path that was an ellipse and using a big pen—then the returned shape would not be accurate since it would not account for the thickness of the outline. This means that the user might click the outline to no effect because it is "outside" the ellipse. In such cases we could create a QPainterPathStroker, set its pen-related methods (setWidth(), setJoinStyle(), etc.), and then call QPainterPathStroker::create-Stroke(), giving it the painter path as argument. The createStroke() method's return value is a new painter path that is an outline of the original path but using the pen-related settings we set.

For the Cell, all the constructor (not shown) does, is to set a brush and an initial size and to call a private method (also not shown) to create the initial shape. This makes the paint() method much simpler than it would otherwise be, since it only has to paint the path—and optionally an item ID.

```
void Cell::paint(QPainter *painter,
                 const QStyleOptionGraphicsItem *option, QWidget*)
{
    painter->setPen(Qt::NoPen);
    painter->setBrush(m_brush);
    painter->drawPath(m_path);
    if (s_showIds) {
        QPointF center = m_path.boundingRect().center();
        QString id = QString::number(m_id);
        center.setX(center.x() - (option->fontMetrics.width(id) / 2));
        center.setY(center.y() + (option->fontMetrics.height() / 4));
        painter->setPen(QPen());
        painter->drawText(center, id);
    }
}
```

We begin by setting up the painter's pen (Qt::NoPen means no outline will be drawn), and its brush, and then we draw the cell's path. (The Cell class also has a Boolean static variable, s_showIds, with some static accessors, and an ID member variable—m_id of type int—none of which are shown.) If the item's ID is to be shown we find the center of the path and draw the ID horizontally centered and vertically a quarter of the way down from the top using a QPen(). The default QPen constructor produces a *cosmetic* pen with a black solid line that is 1 pixel wide. A pen is described as cosmetic if it ignores transformations.

The QStyleOptionGraphicsItem* parameter holds, for example, the item's exposed rectangle, font metrics—which is what we have used it for here—and palette. The QWidget* parameter is rarely used.

The paint() method's implementation is fast enough for the Petri Dish application, but it is far from optimal. It probably isn't worth caching the path's bounding rectangle in this case because Cells shrink or grow at every iteration of the simulation. But cell IDs never change, so we could trade a tiny bit of memory for speed and keep a private member variable, m_idString of type QString, that we would create in the constructor—this will avoid using QString::number() in the paint() method which allocates memory every time it is called. Computing the font metrics width and height is also slow; we could easily calculate these in the constructor and cache the results. As a rule of thumb it is probably best to just get the painting working, and then, if it turns out to be too slow, start finding things that can be cached. Naturally, it is best to benchmark any changes, just to be sure that the hoped-for benefits really are achieved.

The Cell class does not reimplement any event handlers, nor does it set any flags (such as ItemIsMovable or ItemIsSelectable), so it is not possible for users to interact directly with Cell items. We will see examples where these flags are set and where event handlers are implemented in the following chapter. The end of this chapter is devoted to tables summarizing the QGraphicsItem API. Tables 11.1 through 11.4 (➤ 403–406) summarize the QGraphicsItem class's methods, and Tables 11.5 through 11.7 (➤ 406–407) summarize the most important enums used by the methods.

We have now finished our review of the Petri Dish application, and of the QGraphicsItem API. There are a few details of minor interest in the example's source code that we haven't covered. For example, after each iteration we use a single shot timer to initiate the next iteration—we can't use a QTimer with a fixed time interval since the time it takes to perform the computations in each iteration varies. Also, we make the entire window slightly transparent when the application is paused, an effect that seems to work best on Windows.

In the next chapter we will look at an application that makes more conventional use of the graphics/view architecture, and see more examples of how to create custom graphics items, as well as covering how to save and load scenes to and from files, and how to manipulate items in scenes—for example, transforming them, and copying, cutting, and pasting them.

Table 11.1 *The QGraphicsItem API (Selected Methods) #1*

Method	Description
advance()	Reimplement to do animations; other approaches can also be used (see, for example, Chapters 12 and 13)
boundingRect()	Reimplement to return the item's bounding rectangle in item coordinates; see sceneBoundingRect() and shape()
childItems()	Returns a list of the item's immediate children (Qt 4.4)
collidesWithItem(QGraphicsItem*, Qt::ItemSelectionMode)	Returns true if this item collides with the given item according to the mode; see the Qt::ItemSelectionMode enum (➤ 406)
collidesWithPath(QPainterPath, Qt::ItemSelectionMode)	Returns true if this item collides with the given path according to the mode
collidingItems(Qt::ItemSelectionMode)	Returns a list of all the items this item collides with according to the mode
contains(QPointF)	Returns true if the point is within this item
ensureVisible()	Forces any QGraphicsViews associated with the scene containing this item to scroll if necessary to show this item
group()	Returns the QGraphicsItemGroup this item belongs to or 0 if it doesn't belong to one
hide()	Hides this item; see show() and setVisible()
isObscuredBy(QGraphicsItem*)	Returns true if this item's bounding rectangle is completely obscured by the shape of the given non-transparent item
isSelected()	Returns true if this item is selected; see setSelected()
isVisible()	Returns true if this item is *logically* visible (even if it is fully obscured or is outside the view's viewport)
keyPressEvent(QKeyEvent*)	Reimplement this to handle key presses on the item—it will only be called if the ItemIsFocusable flag is set
mouseDoubleClickEvent(QGraphicsSceneMouseEvent*)	Reimplement this to handle double clicks

Table 11.2 *The QGraphicsItem API (Selected Methods) #2*

Method	Description
mouseMoveEvent(QGraphicsSceneMouseEvent*)	Reimplement this to handle mouse moves
mousePressEvent(QGraphicsSceneMouseEvent*)	Reimplement this to handle mouse presses
moveBy(qreal, qreal)	Moves the item by the given amounts horizontally and vertically
opaqueArea()	Reimplement this to return a painter path that shows where the item is opaque, as used by isObscuredBy()
paint(QPainter*, QStyleOptionGraphicsItem*, QWidget*)	Reimplement this to paint the item; see also boundingRect() and shape()
parentItem()	Returns the item's parent item or 0
pos()	Returns the item's position in its parent's coordinates—or in scene coordinates if it has no parent; see scenePos()
prepareGeometryChange()	This method *must* be called before changing an item's bounding rectangle; it will automatically call update()
resetTransform()	Resets the item's transformation matrix to the identity matrix, thus eliminating any rotation, scaling, or shearing
rotation()	Returns the item's rotation in degrees (-360.0°, 360.0°); the default is 0.0° (Qt 4.6)
scale()	Returns the item's scale factor; the default is 1.0, that is, unscaled (Qt 4.6)
scene()	Returns the scene that the item belongs to or 0 if it hasn't been added to a scene
sceneBoundingRect()	Returns the item's bounding rectangle in scene coordinates; see boundingRect()
scenePos()	Returns the item's position in scene coordinates—this is the same as pos() for items with no parent
setFlag(GraphicsItemFlag, bool)	Sets the flag on or off according to the Boolean (default on)
setFlags(GraphicsItemFlags)	Sets the OR-ed flags on; see the QGraphicsItem::GraphicsItemFlag enum (➤ 406)

Table 11.3 *The QGraphicsItem API (Selected Methods) #3*

Method	Description
setGraphicsEffect(QGraphicsEffect*)	Sets the given graphics effect on the item (deleting any previous one); these include QGraphicsBlurEffect, QGraphicsDropShadowEffect, and QGraphicsOpacityEffect (Qt 4.6)
setGroup(QGraphicsItemGroup*)	Adds this item to the given group
setParentItem(QGraphicsItem*)	Sets (or changes) the item's parent to the given item
setPos(QPointF)	Sets the item's position in parent coordinates; there is also an overload that takes two qreals
setRotation(qreal)	Sets the item's rotation to the given number of degrees (-360.0°, 360.0°) (Qt 4.6)
setScale(qreal)	Scales the item; 1.0 means unscaled (Qt 4.6)
setSelected(bool)	Selects or deselects the item depending on the Boolean
setToolTip(QString)	Sets a tooltip for the item
setTransform(QTransform, bool)	Sets the item's transformation matrix to the given one; or combines it with the given one if the Boolean is true (Qt 4.3); there is also a rather different setTransformations() method
setVisible(bool)	Hides or shows the item depending on the given Boolean
setX(qreal)	Sets the item's x position in its parent's coordinates (Qt 4.6)
setY(qreal)	Sets the item's y position in its parent's coordinates (Qt 4.6)
setZValue(qreal)	Sets the item's z value
shape()	Reimplement this to return a painter path describing the exact shape of the item; see boundingRect() and paint()
show()	Shows the item; see hide() and setVisible()
toolTip()	Returns the item's tooltip
transform()	Returns the item's transformation matrix; there is also a transformations() method
type()	Returns the item's QGraphicsItem::Type as an int; custom QGraphicsItem subclasses should normally reimplement this and provide a Type enum

Table 11.4 *The QGraphicsItem API (Selected Methods) #4*

Method	Description
update()	Schedules a paint event for the item
x()	Returns the item's x position in its parent's coordinates
y()	Returns the item's y position in its parent's coordinates
zValue()	Returns the item's z value

Table 11.5 *The Qt::ItemSelectionMode enum*

enum	Description
Qt::ContainsItemShape	Select items whose shape is completely within the selection area
Qt::IntersectsItemShape	Select items whose shape is within or intersects the selection area
Qt::ContainsItemBoundingRect	Select items whose bounding rectangle is completely within the selection area
Qt::IntersectsItemBoundingRect	Select items whose bounding rectangle is within or intersects the selection area

Table 11.6 *The QGraphicsItem::GraphicsItemFlag enum #1*

enum	Description
QGraphicsItem:: ItemAcceptsInputMethod	The item supports input methods (Qt 4.6)
QGraphicsItem:: ItemClipsChildrenToShape	The item clips all its children (recursively) to its own shape (Qt 4.3)
QGraphicsItem:: ItemClipsToShape	The item is clipped to its own shape regardless of how it is painted; nor can it receive events (e.g., mouse clicks) outside of its shape (Qt 4.3)
QGraphicsItem:: ItemDoesntPropagate- OpacityToChildren	The item does not propagate its opacity to its children (Qt 4.5)
QGraphicsItem:: ItemHasNoContents	The item does not paint anything (Qt 4.6)
QGraphicsItem:: ItemIgnoresParent- Opacity	The item's opacity is whatever it has been set to rather than combined with that of its parent (Qt 4.5)

Table 11.7 *The QGraphicsItem::GraphicsItemFlag enum #2*

enum	Description
QGraphicsItem:: ItemIgnores– Transformations	The item ignores transformations applied to its parent (although its position is still tied to its parent); useful for items that are used as text labels (Qt 4.3)
QGraphicsItem:: ItemIsFocusable	The item accepts key presses
QGraphicsItem:: ItemIsMovable	The item (and its children, recursively) can be moved by being clicked and dragged
QGraphicsItem:: ItemIsPanel	The item is a panel (Qt 4.6); see the online documentation for more about panels
QGraphicsItem:: ItemIsSelectable	The item can be selected by clicking, by rubber band dragging, or if it is in the region affected by a QGraphicsScene::setSelectionArea() call
QGraphicsItem:: ItemNegativeZ– StacksBehindParent	The item automatically stacks behind its parent if its z value is negative
QGraphicsItem:: ItemSends– GeometryChanges	The item calls itemChange() for changes of position and for transformations (Qt 4.6); see also the "Qt 4.6 Graphics/View Behavior Changes" sidebar (393 ◀)
QGraphicsItem:: ItemSendsScene– PositionChanges	The item calls itemChange() for position changes (Qt 4.6)
QGraphicsItem:: ItemStacks– BehindParent	The item is stacked behind its parent rather than in front (which is the default); useful for creating drop shadows
QGraphicsItem:: ItemUsesExtended– StyleOption	This gives the item access to additional QStyleOptionGraphicsItem attributes

12

- Scenes, Items, and Actions
- Enhancing QGraphicsView
- Creating a Dock Widget Toolbox
- Creating Custom Graphics Items

Creating Graphics/View Scenes

In this chapter we will look at a conventional application that makes use of Qt's graphics/view architecture. The program is a basic drawing application that shows how to create various kinds of custom items and how to save and load graphics items using a custom file format. The application's implementation also shows how to provide the user with the means to add items to a scene, change their properties (including those of groups of selected items), and remove items. Considered together, this example and the one shown in the previous chapter cover a lot of the features and functionality provided by the graphics/view architecture—although by no means all of it. Nonetheless, this chapter and the previous one should provide a solid foundation for learning more and for developing your own graphics/view applications. Incidentally, as we mentioned in the previous chapter, we will revisit both these examples in Chapter 13 where we create modified versions of them that make use of some Qt 4.6-specific features.

In this chapter we will review the Page Designer application (pagedesigner1). This is by far the largest and most "complete" example presented in the book, weighing in at nearly 3 300 lines of code. Even so, Page Designer is still only a bare bones application and lacks many useful features. However, it is more than adequate to serve its primary purpose of showing key graphics/view features. The application is shown in action in Figure 12.1.

Page Designer is a standard main window-style application, and uses dock widgets to present three "toolboxes", one for transformations, one for setting the brush (fill), and one for setting the pen (outline). The application has all the standard File menu options: New, Open..., Save, Save As..., Export... (in pixmap or SVG formats), Print..., and Quit. And particularly relevant to graphics/view programming, the application has an Edit menu that offers Edit Selected Item... (which will call an item's custom edit() slot if it has one, e.g., to pop up an item-specific context menu or dialog), Add Text... (for adding a rich text item), Add Box

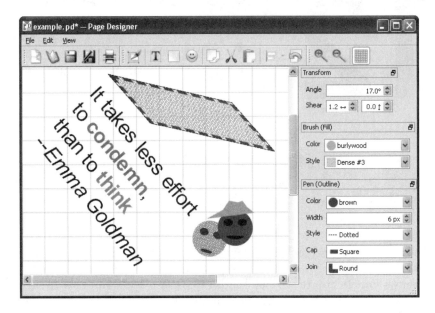

Figure 12.1 *The Page Designer application*

(for adding a resizable rectangle), and Add Smiley (for adding an application-specific custom item with a non-rectangular shape). In addition, the Edit menu offers the usual Cut, Copy, and Paste options, and also an Alignment submenu (for lining up two or more selected items in relation to each other), and a convenient Clear Transformations option to reset the selected items' rotation and shears to 0. The application also has a View menu through which the user can zoom in or out and show or hide the guideline grid. Most of the menu options are also accessible via toolbar buttons.

Although the application provides only three kinds of graphics items (text, box, and smiley), between them, these represent all the kinds of graphics items that are needed in a drawing program. For example, the code relating to box items can serve as an example for adding any other standard shaped items, and the smiley-related code can serve for adding any other custom shaped items.

When an individual item is selected (e.g., by clicking it), the toolboxes are updated to reflect the item's angle, shears, brush, and pen settings. Page Designer also supports some operations on groups of selected items. (The QGraphicsView class supports the selection of items by Ctrl+Clicking them, or ⌘+Clicking on Mac OS X. It is also possible—as we will see later—to switch on rubber band selection where everything in or touching the rubber band's rectangle is selected.) For example, all the selected items can be cut, copied, deleted, or aligned in relation to each other. Similarly, clearing or setting transformations, and setting the brush and pen, are applied to the selected item or items.

In this chapter's sections we will look at the application's overall infrastructure to give an overview of how it works—including saving and loading scenes—and then we will look at various graphics/view-related aspects in more detail. First, we will begin with the application's main window.

Scenes, Items, and Actions

The application's main window has a private slot for each of the File, Edit, and View menus' actions. It also has many private helper methods. Here we will begin by looking at the main window's private data (but excluding the QActions) to provide some context.

```
    private:
        ...
        TransformWidget *transformWidget;
        BrushWidget *brushWidget;
        PenWidget *penWidget;

        QPrinter *printer;
        QGraphicsScene *scene;
        GraphicsView *view;
        QGraphicsItemGroup *gridGroup;
        QPoint previousPoint;
        int addOffset;
        int pasteOffset;
    };
```

The three custom widgets are the toolboxes held in the application's dock widgets. We keep pointers to them because whenever a new item is added to the scene we connect it to the relevant toolboxes so that when an item is selected, its properties (such as its brush and pen) are reflected into the toolboxes. We will review one of these widgets in a later section (➤ 440).

We keep a pointer to a QPrinter so that each time the user prints, the settings from the previous printing are retained for the user's convenience. When a QPrinter is constructed, it starts with sensible defaults—for example, using U.S. Letter size in the U.S. or A4 size in Europe.

Rather than setting the guideline grid as a background we have chosen to create it out of graphics items. This is really just to show how to use a QGraphics-ItemGroup and how to be selective in what items we save, print, and export.

We will discuss the previousPoint and the addOffset and pasteOffset when we cover the code that uses them.

There is no filename string—instead we store the filename using setWindow-FilePath(). This method puts the filename in the window's title bar (so long as we don't use setWindowTitle()), in a platform-appropriate way—for example, showing just the name and not the path—along with the application's name. For this method to be used sensibly we must have called QApplication::set-ApplicationName(), typically in main(). Whenever we need the filename, we can retrieve it using windowFilePath()—for new files we will get back "Unnamed", assuming we set this string in the fileNew() method.

For the rest of the main window, we will look at the (interesting) code in the following subsections, starting with the main window's constructor and some of its helper methods.

Creating the Main Window

As with most small to medium-sized Qt applications, the main window is at the heart of things. And as usual, the main window's constructor is where the user interface is created—both in terms of its appearance, and in terms of its behaviors.

```
const int OffsetIncrement = 5;
const QString ShowGrid("ShowGrid");
const QString MostRecentFile("MostRecentFile");

MainWindow::MainWindow(QWidget *parent)
    : QMainWindow(parent), gridGroup(0), addOffset(OffsetIncrement),
      pasteOffset(OffsetIncrement)
{
    printer = new QPrinter(QPrinter::HighResolution);

    createSceneAndView();
    createActions();
    createMenusAndToolBars();
    createDockWidgets();
    createConnections();

    QSettings settings;
    viewShowGridAction->setChecked(
            settings.value(ShowGrid, true).toBool());
    QString filename = settings.value(MostRecentFile).toString();
    if (filename.isEmpty() || filename == tr("Unnamed"))
        QTimer::singleShot(0, this, SLOT(fileNew()));
    else {
        setWindowFilePath(filename);
        QTimer::singleShot(0, this, SLOT(loadFile()));
    }
}
```

The constructor begins by setting some variables that we will discuss when we make use of them later on. It then creates a printer—the printer's page size is used as the basis for the main window's initial size in the reimplemented size-Hint() method (not shown). The rest of the user interface setup is offloaded onto various helper methods, in a style that should be very familiar by now. The createActions(), createMenusAndToolBars(), and createConnections() methods all follow the same patterns that we have seen many times before, so we won't quote them here. (As always, the source code is available in the book's examples, in this case in the pagedesigner1 subdirectory.)

We start with the guideline grid shown or hidden depending on how it was set the last time the application was run—defaulting to shown if this is the very first run. We will cover the private custom viewShowGrid() slot that is connected to the viewShowGridAction's triggered() signal later on (➤ 435).

At the end of the constructor we retrieve the name of the file that the application was editing the last time it was run. If this is empty (because the application is being run for the first time) or is "Unnamed" (because the last edited page design was never saved), we invoke the fileNew() slot (not shown), so that the user can start drawing immediately. Otherwise, we load the file. As usual, we use single shot timers so that fileNew() or loadFile() is called after construction is complete.

Both the ShowGrid and MostRecentFile settings are saved in the reimplemented closeEvent() (not shown).

```
void MainWindow::createSceneAndView()
{
    view = new GraphicsView;
    scene = new QGraphicsScene(this);
    QSize pageSize = printer->paperSize(QPrinter::Point).toSize();
    scene->setSceneRect(0, 0, pageSize.width(), pageSize.height());
    view->setScene(scene);
    setCentralWidget(view);
}
```

The creating and the setting up of the view, the scene, and the application's central widget are all straightforward. We make the scene's size proportional to the paper size, effectively mapping points ($\frac{1}{72}$") to pixels. (The paperSize() method returns a QSizeF which we convert to a QSize using the QSizeF::toSize() method.) The only notable aspect is that we have used a custom GraphicsView class (a QGraphicsView subclass) which provides zooming and mouse wheel support. We will review this tiny subclass later on (➤ 439).

```
void MainWindow::createDockWidgets()
{
    setDockOptions(QMainWindow::AnimatedDocks);
```

```
QDockWidget::DockWidgetFeatures features =
        QDockWidget::DockWidgetMovable|
        QDockWidget::DockWidgetFloatable;

transformWidget = new TransformWidget;
QDockWidget *transformDockWidget = new QDockWidget(
        tr("Transform"), this);
transformDockWidget->setFeatures(features);
transformDockWidget->setWidget(transformWidget);
addDockWidget(Qt::RightDockWidgetArea, transformDockWidget);
...
}
```

This method is where the three toolbox widgets are created and added to dock widgets. We have only shown the first one since the code for all of them is identical apart from the particular toolbox widget added to each one.

We begin by setting the dock options. The QMainWindow::AnimatedDocks option means that when the user drags a dock widget over a dock area, the dock area creates a gap showing where the dock widget will go if dropped, moving other dock widgets out of the way if necessary. This makes it much easier for users to see what is happening.

The default dock options are QMainWindow::AnimatedDocks|QMainWindow::Allow-TabbedDocks, so by setting only the former, we disallow the latter. When tabbed docks are allowed, the user can drop a dock widget *between* other dock widgets (the usual behavior), or *on* another dock widget, in which case Qt puts the dropped dock widget and the dock widget it was dropped on into a tab widget with only the dropped dock visible. The user can then click the tabs to switch between the widgets. By default, the tabs appear at the bottom of the dock widget, but this can be changed by using QMainWindow::setTabPosition(). Clearly, this is a useful option when the number of dock widgets is large—or when individual dock widgets occupy a lot of space.

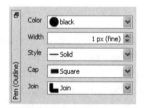 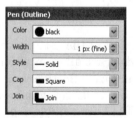

Figure 12.2 *The Page Designer pen dock widget with vertical title bar and free-standing*

There are two other dock options that can be used (and that are mutually exclusive). One is QMainWindow::ForceTabbedDocks; this forces all dock widgets to be tabbed, but has the disadvantage that at most only one dock widget will be visible in each dock area. The other is QMainWindow::AllowNestedDocks; if this is set, each dock area can be split to create more than one row (or column) of dock widgets in the area. This has the disadvantage of making the user interface more difficult for the user to manipulate. Both of these options are best avoided where possible.

For each of the dock widgets, we set two features: `QDockWidget::DockWidget-Movable`, which means that users can drag dock widgets from one dock area to another; and `QDockWidget::DockWidgetFloatable`, which means that users can drag dock widgets out of their dock area and have them float as free-standing windows in their own right. If we wanted the user to have the option of closing (i.e., hiding) dock widgets we could set `QDockWidget::DockWidgetClosable`. One other feature is supported: `QDockWidget::DockWidgetVerticalTitleBar`. This feature can reduce the amount of vertical space occupied by dock widgets, which is especially useful for dock widgets in the left and right dock areas. Figure 12.2 shows a dock widget with a vertical title bar and a dock widget that has been dragged out of its dock area and that is floating free-standing as a window in its own right.

We didn't show the code for the creation of the main window's actions, menus, and toolbars, since the code is standard, but in the following subsection's subsections, we will look at the methods that implement the application's high-level graphics/view-related behaviors, starting with saving and loading scenes.

Saving, Loading, Printing, and Exporting Scenes

The Page Designer application has the usual Save, Open, Print..., and Export... actions and corresponding `fileSave()`, `fileOpen()`, `filePrint()`, and `fileExport()` slots. We'll skip the file saving and loading infrastructure (it is very similar to what we have used in earlier examples), and focus purely on the graphics/view-relevant methods and their helpers.

Saving Scenes

Inside the `fileSave()` slot, the application opens a `QFile` object in binary mode, and opens a `QDataStream` to write to the file. The Page Designer magic number and file format version numbers (both integers) are written to the data stream, and then the stream's version is set—in this case to Qt 4.5. This means that the application cannot be compiled with any earlier Qt version, and ensures that the data will be readable no matter what Qt 4.x version (where $x \geq 5$) is used. Next, the `MainWindow::writeItems()` method is called with two arguments—the data stream, and a list of all the scene's items.

The `QGraphicsScene::items()` method that we use to provide the second-argument returns a list of all the scene's graphics items. There are several `items()`

overloads, including one that accepts a sort order, one that returns the items that intersect a particular point, and ones that are within or intersect a particular rectangle, polygon, or painter path. In this example, the items include the items used for the guideline grid which we don't need or want to save, but this isn't a problem as we will see in a moment.

```
void MainWindow::writeItems(QDataStream &out,
                           const QList<QGraphicsItem*> &items)
{
    foreach (QGraphicsItem *item, items) {
        if (item == gridGroup || item->group() == gridGroup)
            continue;
        qint32 type = static_cast<qint32>(item->type());
        out << type;
        switch (type) {
            case BoxItemType:
                    out << *static_cast<BoxItem*>(item); break;
            case SmileyItemType:
                    out << *static_cast<SmileyItem*>(item); break;
            case TextItemType:
                    out << *static_cast<TextItem*>(item); break;
            default: Q_ASSERT(false);
        }
    }
}
```

This method iterates over the list of graphics items it is passed. For each one it first checks to see if the item is or belongs to the gridGroup (of type QGraphics-ItemGroup*) that the guideline items belong to, and if it is or does, the item is skipped since we don't want to save the guidelines. For the other items, the method then writes each one's QGraphicsItem::Type (a unique constant integer identifying each type of graphics item and returned by a reimplementation of the QGraphicsItem::type() method), and then the graphics item itself. The main window's writeItems() method does not know how to save the graphics items, instead relying on them to provide an operator<<() method that operates on a QDataStream (which they all do, of course, as we will see when we cover the graphics items themselves).

An additional benefit of factoring the writeItems() method out of the fileSave() method is that we can reuse this method when we want to cut or copy items—something we will cover in a later subsubsection (➤ 427).

Using the writeItems() method we have saved the scene in the easiest possible way, simply as a sequence of graphics items. A more sophisticated application would probably save some meta-data as well as the items themselves. Now that we have seen how a scene is saved, we will see how it is loaded, and then we will see how to print and export the scene in standard pixmap and vector formats.

Loading Scenes

Inside the fileOpen() slot, the application prompts the user to provide a file-name, and if one is chosen a QFile is created for the file. Then, a QDataStream is created to read the file's contents, and the magic number and file format version number are read. If any problem occurs, a warning message box is popped up to inform the user. Otherwise, the data stream is set to Qt 4.5 to match the version used for saving, then the existing scene's items are cleared, and the items stored in the file are read in to repopulate the scene.

It is slightly regrettable that the readItems() method (like the writeItems() method we have just seen and the editAddItem() method covered further on) must operate in terms of specific known types, since this means that if we add new item types these three methods must be modified to account for each new type that is added. However, there doesn't seem to be any really nice solution to this issue. On a more positive note, all the other methods use Qt's property system (since all our custom item types inherit QObject), which means that they will work unchanged—and correctly—even if we add new item types, providing, of course, that the new item types also inherit QObject.

```
void MainWindow::clear()
{
    scene->clear();
    gridGroup = 0;
    viewShowGrid(viewShowGridAction->isChecked());
}
```

The QGraphicsScene::clear() method removes every graphics item—including those used for the guideline grid, so we must be sure to set the gridGroup to null since it has been deleted. Of course, the need for a grid group wouldn't arise if the guideline grid was produced by using a background brush or painted by reimplementing QGraphicsView::drawBackground()—one of which is what we would do in practice. (For the Page Designer application, we use a QGraphics-ItemGroup for the background purely to show how to use the class and to show how to distinguish between sets of items.) We then call viewShowGrid() (➤ 435) to create a new set of guidelines, which are set to be visible or hidden depending on the state of the viewShowGridAction.

```
void MainWindow::readItems(QDataStream &in, int offset, bool select)
{
    QSet<QGraphicsItem*> items;
    qint32 itemType;
    QGraphicsItem *item = 0;
```

```
    while (!in.atEnd()) {
        in >> itemType;
        switch (itemType) {
            case BoxItemType: {
                BoxItem *boxItem = new BoxItem(QRect(), scene);
                in >> *boxItem;
                connectItem(boxItem);
                item = boxItem;
                break;
            }
            ...
        }
        if (item) {
            item->moveBy(offset, offset);
            if (select)
                items << item;
            item = 0;
        }
    }
    if (select)
        selectItems(items);
    else
        selectionChanged();
}
```

This method is used to read a scene's items from a QDataStream opened on a file. And it is also used to paste copied or cut items back into the scene, in which case the reading is from a data stream opened on a QByteArray retrieved from the clipboard rather than from a file. The offset (which has a default of 0) and the select (which has a default of false) are used only when pasting.

This method reads the data stream until it reaches the end. It reads each item in two parts, first the item's QGraphicsItem::Type, and then the item itself. The code for reading smiley and text items has been elided since it is almost identical to that shown for box items, the difference being that for the smiley and text items the first argument passed to their constructors is QPoint() rather than QRect(). All items need to be connected to the relevant toolbox widgets, and this is done by the connectItem() method that we will review next. Similarly to the writeItems() method, the readItems() method does not know how to read our custom item types, instead relying on them to provide suitable operator>>() methods that operate on a QDataStream (as, of course, they do).

If the items are being pasted, the offset will be nonzero and select will be true, in which case the item is moved relative to its current position and added to a set of items. At the end, if select is true, all the items in the set are selected; otherwise we call selectionChanged() to ensure that the toolbox widgets reflect the properties of the selected item since the last item read will select itself in its constructor, as we will see further on (➤ 449).

```
void MainWindow::connectItem(QObject *item)
{
    connect(item, SIGNAL(dirty()), this, SLOT(setDirty()));
    const QMetaObject *metaObject = item->metaObject();
    if (metaObject->indexOfProperty("brush") > -1)
        connect(brushWidget, SIGNAL(brushChanged(const QBrush&)),
                item, SLOT(setBrush(const QBrush&)));
    if (metaObject->indexOfProperty("pen") > -1)
        connect(penWidget, SIGNAL(penChanged(const QPen&)),
                item, SLOT(setPen(const QPen&)));
    if (metaObject->indexOfProperty("angle") > -1) {
        connect(transformWidget, SIGNAL(angleChanged(double)),
                item, SLOT(setAngle(double)));
        connect(transformWidget, SIGNAL(shearChanged(double, double)),
                item, SLOT(setShear(double, double)));
    }
}
```

This method is called by the readItems() method (i.e., when a new item is read from a scene file, and when a new item is pasted into a scene), and when a new item is added to a scene. It relies on items being QObject subclasses so that we can use Qt's property system to determine which signal–slot connections to make. The disadvantage of this approach is that all of our custom item types must inherit QObject, but the advantage is that we don't have to know which specific item type is being connected—and this makes the method much more scalable, since no matter how many new item types we add, the method does not have to be changed at all.

We have adopted the convention that for the Page Designer application, all items—apart from the guideline grid items—are QObjects and emit a custom dirty() signal if they experience a significant change of state.

For each property we are interested in, we ask the item's meta-object if the item (or more specifically, if an item of the QObject class the meta-object is for) has the property. (A property index of -1 signifies that there is no such property.)

Box items have brush, pen, angle (of rotation), and horizontal and vertical shear properties, so for them, all of the connections are made. We have adopted the convention for the Page Designer application that if an item has an angle property, then it can also be sheared. We could easily separate these if preferred, just as we could choose to assume that items with a pen property also have a brush property rather than checking for them individually.

The connections ensure that if the user changes one of these properties in one of the toolbox widgets—for example, if they change the brush—this box item (and indeed, all the items that are connected to the `BrushWidget`'s `brushChanged()` signal) will be notified of the change. And as we will see when we review the box item, the notification is only acted upon by those items that are selected.

The connections could have been made inside the `readItems()` method, but we have factored them out because we also need to make them when the user adds a new item to the scene.

At the end of the `readItems()` method we saw earlier, if the items read are to be selected (which they will be if they have been pasted rather than read from file), the `selectItems()` method is called to do the selecting.

```
void MainWindow::selectItems(const QSet<QGraphicsItem*> &items)
{
    scene->clearSelection();
    foreach (QGraphicsItem *item, items)
        item->setSelected(true);
    selectionChanged();
}
```

This method deselects all the scene's items and then iterates over all the items that need to be selected and selects each one of them. Then it calls the `selectionChanged()` method (covered later; ➤ 433), so that the toolbox widgets are updated to reflect the properties of one of the selected items.

Printing and Exporting Scenes

In addition to saving and loading scenes, we can also print them, and export them, both in vector (SVG) format, and in any of the pixmap formats that Qt supports. Printing is easily achieved using the `filePrint()` method. To print or export a scene we must create a suitable `QPainter`, get rid of the guideline grid, and render the scene to the painter.

```
const int StatusTimeout = AQP::MSecPerSecond * 30;

void MainWindow::filePrint()
{
    QPrintDialog dialog(printer);
    if (dialog.exec()) {
        {
            QPainter painter(printer);
            paintScene(&painter);
        }
        statusBar()->showMessage(tr("Printed %1")
                .arg(windowFilePath()), StatusTimeout);
    }
}
```

The print dialog gives the user the opportunity to change various printing-related settings before printing, and because we pass it a QPrinter pointer, it starts out with the QPrinter's settings as its defaults. By this means settings are preserved between printings. If the user accepts the dialog we create a painter to paint on the printer (i.e., on the printer's page), and paint the scene using the custom paintScene() method.

One slightly unusual aspect of this method and the other methods that call paintScene() is that we create the painter and paint the scene inside a scope (i.e., inside a separate braces-delimited block). This is simply a convenience that ensures that the painter is destroyed when we have finished with it, since it releases any resources it uses in its destructor. An alternative that doesn't require the use of a scope is to call QPainter::end() once the painting is finished.

The string returned by windowFilePath() is the filename (including path) we set with setWindowFilePath()—this could be "Unnamed", in the case of a new file that hasn't been saved, assuming that we set this as the window file path in the fileNew() method (which we do, of course).

```
void MainWindow::paintScene(QPainter *painter)
{
    bool showGrid = viewShowGridAction->isChecked();
    if (showGrid)
        viewShowGrid(false);
    QList<QGraphicsItem*> items = scene->selectedItems();
    scene->clearSelection();

    scene->render(painter);

    if (showGrid)
        viewShowGrid(true);
    foreach (QGraphicsItem *item, items)
        item->setSelected(true);
    selectionChanged();
}
```

When rendering the scene we want to avoid painting the guideline grid or selection rectangles. We do this by hiding all the guidelines (using viewShowGrid(), a method we will review later on; ➤ 435), and by saving a list of the selected items and then clearing the selection.

Once the preparations are complete we render the scene to the painter. The QGraphicsScene::render() method can optionally be passed both a target rectangle (useful for rendering onto part of an existing image), and a source rectangle (for rendering just a particular portion of a scene). And if both target and source rectangles are supplied, another optional argument—of type Qt::

AspectRatioMode—can be given, which is useful if the dimensions of the target and source rectangles are different.

Once the painting is done we show the guideline grid if it was previously visible, and re-select any items that were selected before, so that the scene is restored to the state it had prior to the export. We also call selectionChanged() to make the toolbox widgets reflect one of the selected items' properties.

When it comes to exporting a scene, setting up the painter is very similar to what we did in Chapter 10 when we exported QTextDocuments (379 ◀). For completeness, we will show both export methods, both of which rely on the custom paintScene() method that we have just seen. There is a single fileExport() slot that pops up a file save dialog and that chooses the export method to call based on the file suffix of the filename that the user entered.

```
void MainWindow::exportSvg(const QString &filename)
{
    QSvgGenerator svg;
    svg.setFileName(filename);
    svg.setSize(printer->paperSize(QPrinter::Point).toSize());
    {
        QPainter painter(&svg);
        paintScene(&painter);
    }
    statusBar()->showMessage(tr("Exported %1").arg(filename),
                             StatusTimeout);
}
```

To make use of Qt's SVG functionality we must put QT += svg in the application's .pro file. We begin by creating an SVG generator object and giving it the filename of the file to write to. We set its page size to the Page Designer's page size, create a painter to paint on the SVG generator, and then call the paintScene() helper method to do the work. We could use a very similar approach to render the scene to a PDF file by using a QPrinter as the paint device, as we saw in Chapter 10; we leave this as an exercise.

```
void MainWindow::exportImage(const QString &filename)
{
    QImage image(printer->paperSize(QPrinter::Point).toSize(),
                 QImage::Format_ARGB32);
    {
        QPainter painter(&image);
        painter.setRenderHints(QPainter::Antialiasing|
                               QPainter::TextAntialiasing);
        paintScene(&painter);
    }
    if (image.save(filename))
```

```
            statusBar()->showMessage(tr("Exported %1").arg(filename),
                                     StatusTimeout);
    else
        AQP::warning(this, tr("Error"), tr("Failed to export: %1")
                                     .arg(filename));
}
```

Exporting a pixmap image works in a very similar way to exporting an SVG image, except that we turn on antialiasing (since our rule of thumb is to use antialiasing for on-screen and pixmap images but not for printing or vector images). Also, since `QImage::save()` returns a Boolean success indicator, we have made use of it.

Now that we have seen how to save, load, print, and export scenes, we are ready to see how individual items are added to a scene, and how items are manipulated—for example, copied or cut and pasted, and aligned.

Manipulating Graphics Items

Page Designer supports adding items, manipulating individual items (i.e., the one selected item), and for some operations, manipulating all the selected items. For example, if the user invokes the Edit Selected Item... action, the corresponding slot is called.

```
    void MainWindow::editSelectedItem()
    {
        QList<QGraphicsItem*> items = scene->selectedItems();
        if (items.count() != 1)
            return;
        if (QObject *item = dynamic_cast<QObject*>(items.at(0))) {
            const QMetaObject *metaObject = item->metaObject();
            metaObject->invokeMethod(item, "edit", Qt::DirectConnection);
        }
    }
```

We allow only one item to be edited at a time, so we begin by seeing if there is exactly one selected item. If there is, we retrieve the meta-object associated with the item, and attempt to call the item's `edit()` slot. The `QMetaObject::in-vokeMethod()` method returns `true` if the named slot exists and can be invoked; otherwise it safely does nothing and returns `false`. The `Qt::DirectConnection` argument tells Qt to call the slot immediately rather than scheduling it to be called when the event loop has time. We discussed `invokeMethod()` in an earlier chapter (134 ◀). This means that the `editSelectedItem()` method does not need to know anything about the selected item's type, and so will work correctly even if new item types are added and regardless of whether they have an `edit()` slot—always providing that they inherit `QObject`.

In the case of the Page Designer application, our BoxItems don't have an edit() slot, so for them this method harmlessly does nothing. But both SmileyItems and TextItems have edit() slots, which for smileys pops up a context menu and for text items pops up an editor dialog. So, if we were to allow edit() to be called on every selected item rather than only one, we might have dozens or even hundreds of menus and dialogs pop up.

The use of dynamic_cast<>() here (and elsewhere) means that Page Designer is dependent on RTTI (Run Time Type Information). Most modern compilers for desktop systems support this and have it switched on by default. But RTTI may not be switched on—or even available—for compilers targeting embedded devices. An alternative is to use qobject_cast<>() which doesn't depend on RTTI, but unfortunately it won't work in this case because it doesn't accept QGraphicsItem pointers. However, it is possible to get qobject_cast<>() to work. It would mean that all of our graphics items would have to be derived from QGraphicsObject, in which case the cast would be written as QObject *object = qobject_cast<QObject*>(item->toGraphicsObject()), at least for Qt 4.6, which introduced the QGraphicsItem::toGraphicsObject() method. In Page Designer's case, this would work for smiley and text items, both of which derive from QGraphicsObject, but not for box items which don't, although we can work around this as we will see in a moment.

A solution that avoids dynamic_cast<>(), and that also avoids using Qt's meta-object system—perhaps because we don't want all of our custom item types to be QObject subclasses—is to use qgraphicsitem_cast<>(). The disadvantage of doing this is that we must hard-code the specific item types, but of course we must do that anyway when writing, reading, or adding items. To use qgraphicsitem_cast<>() we must replace the editSelectedItem() method's second if statement and associated block with these lines:

```
QGraphicsItem *item = items.at(0);
if (TextItem *textItem = qgraphicsitem_cast<TextItem*>(item))
    textItem->edit();
else if (SmileyItem *smileyItem =
            qgraphicsitem_cast<SmileyItem*>(item))
    smileyItem->edit();
```

Here we retrieve the selected item as a QGraphicsItem pointer rather than as a QObject pointer. Notice also that we make no mention of BoxItems since they don't have an edit() slot, and so are safely ignored. If we added a BoxItem:: edit() slot, we would have to add another else if to the code shown here—although in the version of the code that uses Qt's meta-object system, no changes to this method would be required at all.

For the pagedesigner2 version (which requires Qt 4.6, and which we discuss in Chapter 13), we do not use dynamic_cast<>() at all. Instead, we have a single function, qObjectFrom(), which returns a QObject pointer given a QGraphicsItem pointer.

```
QObject *qObjectFrom(QGraphicsItem *item)
{
    if (!item)
        return 0;
    // Types not inheriting QGraphicsObject must be handled explicitly
    if (item->type() == BoxItemType)
        return qobject_cast<QObject*>(static_cast<BoxItem*>(item));
    // Types inheriting QGraphicsObject can be handled generically
    return item->toGraphicsObject();
}
```

For those items that are not derived from QGraphicsObject, we must cast them to their actual QGraphicsItem class (which must also inherit QObject), and then cast this to a QObject. But for all types that inherit QGraphicsObject, we can simply use QGraphicsItem::toGraphicsObject() to give us the QObject pointer we need.

With this function in place, the Qt 4.6 version of Page Designer (using an #ifdef) replaces every use of dynamic_cast<QObject*>(item) with qObjectFrom(item). The downside of this approach is that if we add new (QObject-derived) item types, we must edit qObjectFrom() to explicitly add any new types that are not QGraphicsObject subclasses, whereas if we use dynamic_cast<>(), no changes to our code would be required.

Adding Items

The application's user interface provides separate actions for adding each type of item that is supported. Each of these actions has the relevant item Type as user data and all of them are connected to the same editAddItem() slot.

```
void MainWindow::editAddItem()
{
    QAction *action = qobject_cast<QAction*>(sender());
    if (!action)
        return;
    QObject *item = 0;
    int type = action->data().toInt();
    if (type == BoxItemType)
        item = new BoxItem(QRect(position(), QSize(90, 30)), scene);
    else if (type == SmileyItemType)
        item = new SmileyItem(position(), scene);
    else if (type == TextItemType) {
        TextItemDialog dialog(0, position(), scene, this);
```

```
            if (dialog.exec())
                item = dialog.textItem();
        }
        if (item) {
            connectItem(item);
            setDirty(true);
        }
    }
```

This slot is invoked if the user asks to add any kind of item. (We discussed using QObject::sender() and alternatives earlier; 349 ◀.) If a box has been requested it is given a default size and a position returned by the position() method that we will look at shortly. For a text item, instead of simply creating a default item as we do for boxes and smileys, we have chosen to pop up a dialog so that the user can set the text item's text to what they want in the first place. The TextItemDialog (code not shown, but pictured in Figure 12.3; ▶ 450) is a typical add/edit dialog where the first argument is an item to edit (when invoked by a call to the item's edit() slot) or 0 (as here), with 0 meaning that a new item must be created (if the user clicks OK in the dialog). If the dialog is accepted, we retrieve a newly created TextItem using the custom TextItemDialog::textItem() method.

Once we have created the requested item, we connect it to the appropriate toolbox widgets so that the user can change the item's properties—in the case of a box item, for example, its brush, pen, and transformations. We covered the connectItem() method earlier (419 ◀). And, of course, we must call setDirty() (▶ 437) since adding a new item changes the scene significantly.

```
    const int OffsetIncrement = 5;

    QPoint MainWindow::position()
    {
        QPoint point = mapFromGlobal(QCursor::pos());
        if (!view->geometry().contains(point)) {
            point = previousPoint.isNull()
                    ? view->pos() + QPoint(10, 10) : previousPoint;
        }
        if (!previousPoint.isNull() && point == previousPoint) {
            point += QPoint(addOffset, addOffset);
            addOffset += OffsetIncrement;
        }
        else {
            addOffset = OffsetIncrement;
            previousPoint = point;
        }
        return view->mapToScene(point - view->pos()).toPoint();
    }
```

This method is used to provide a suitable position for newly added items. We start by creating a QPoint at the mouse position. If this is not within the view we set the point to be just inside the view—or to the previous point where an item was added if there is one. Then, if the point is the same as the previous one at which an item was added, we add an offset to move the point slightly right and down, and also increase the add offset increment. Otherwise—if the new point isn't in the same place as the previous one—we reset the increment to its original amount and set the previous point to this point. And at the end we return the point offset into the scene and in scene coordinates. This ensures that if items are repeatedly added, each one is added offset slightly right and below the previous one rather than all added on top of one another, to make them more visible to the user.

Now that we have seen how individual items have their edit() method called (if they have one), and how they are added by the user, we will look at how Page Designer provides support for copy, cut, and paste.

Copying, Cutting, and Pasting Items

To support copying, cutting, and pasting, we use the system's clipboard. This has the advantages that other applications can access our copied or cut items (assuming that they can understand our data format), and Page Designer can paste items put on the clipboard by other applications (providing we can understand their data format). The one disadvantage of using the clipboard to hold our copied or cut items (rather than, say, a private QByteArray member variable) is that if the user context switches to another application and does a copy or cut, our items are deleted from the clipboard. The solution, of course, is to provide undo/redo support, something we don't cover, but will mention again at the end of the chapter.

In addition to using the clipboard we also maintain a private member variable, pasteOffset (of type int), which is used to ensure that when items are pasted they are offset slightly from their original positions so that the user can more clearly see that the paste has taken place.

```
void MainWindow::editCopy()
{
    QList<QGraphicsItem*> items = scene->selectedItems();
    if (items.isEmpty())
        return;
    pasteOffset = OffsetIncrement;
    copyItems(items);
    updateUi();
}
```

When the user invokes the Copy action, this slot retrieves the list of selected items, resets the paste offset to its initial setting (5 pixels), and calls the `copyItems()` helper method to copy the selected items to the clipboard. These items can then be pasted back; but they will be lost (overwritten or deleted) if another copy (or cut) is done—in this application or by another application—or if the user quits the application, before a paste occurs. And at the end, we call `updateUi()` (➤ 437) to make sure that the Paste action is enabled.

```
const QString MimeType = "application/vnd.qtrac.pagedesigner";

void MainWindow::copyItems(const QList<QGraphicsItem*> &items)
{
    QByteArray copiedItems;
    QDataStream out(&copiedItems, QIODevice::WriteOnly);
    writeItems(out, items);
    QMimeData *mimeData = new QMimeData;
    mimeData->setData(MimeType, copiedItems);
    QClipboard *clipboard = QApplication::clipboard();
    clipboard->setMimeData(mimeData);
}
```

This method creates an empty `QByteArray` and then uses the `writeItems()` method that we saw earlier (416 ◄) to populate it with the items to be copied. It then creates a new `QMimeData` object on the heap and gives it the byte array specifying our custom MIME type to identify the data's format. We then get a pointer to the system's clipboard and give the MIME data to the clipboard—which also takes ownership of the data, so we don't have responsibility for deleting it.

```
void MainWindow::editCut()
{
    QList<QGraphicsItem*> items = scene->selectedItems();
    if (items.isEmpty())
        return;
    copyItems(items);
    QListIterator<QGraphicsItem*> i(items);
    while (i.hasNext()) {
        QScopedPointer<QGraphicsItem> item(i.next());
        scene->removeItem(item.data());
    }
    setDirty(true);
}
```

Cutting items from a scene is slightly more involved than copying since they must be both copied and removed. This method starts out the same as the `editCopy()` method, but having done the copy it then goes on to remove—and delete—each copied item from the scene.

The `QGraphicsScene::removeItem()` method removes the item it is given (and the item's children, recursively) from the scene, and passes ownership of the item to the caller. Here, we immediately delete removed items (and their children, recursively), to avoid memory leaks, as soon as the scoped pointer goes out of scope, that is, at the end of each iteration through the loop.★ And at the end we call `setDirty()` since cutting items (unlike merely copying them) changes the scene. (The `setDirty()` slot calls the `updateUi()` slot, so after a cut, the Paste action will be enabled; ➤ 436.)

```cpp
void MainWindow::editPaste()
{
    QClipboard *clipboard = QApplication::clipboard();
    const QMimeData *mimeData = clipboard->mimeData();
    if (!mimeData)
        return;

    if (mimeData->hasFormat(MimeType)) {
        QByteArray copiedItems = mimeData->data(MimeType);
        QDataStream in(&copiedItems, QIODevice::ReadOnly);
        readItems(in, pasteOffset, true);
        pasteOffset += OffsetIncrement;
    }
    else if (mimeData->hasHtml() || mimeData->hasText()) {
        TextItem *textItem = new TextItem(position(), scene);
        connectItem(textItem);
        if (mimeData->hasHtml())
            textItem->setHtml(mimeData->html());
        else
            textItem->setPlainText(mimeData->text());
    }
    else
        return;
    setDirty(true);
}
```

If the user has copied or cut items they can paste the items back into the scene using this method. Also, we have added the ability to paste HTML and plain text copied from other applications.

We begin by getting a pointer to the system's clipboard and retrieving a QMime-Data object that holds the clipboard's data—if it has any. Next we check to see if the MIME data has data in Page Designer's custom format. If it has, we retrieve the data as a QByteArray and use the readItems() method we reviewed earlier (417 ◄) to populate the scene with the items. Unlike when reading items

---

★In the source code we have an `#if QT_VERSION` so that the code will compile with Qt 4.5 and where we use a plain `QGraphicsItem*` and call `delete` on each item that has been removed from the scene.

from a file, here we provide an offset to ensure that pasted items are not pasted exactly on top of the original items (since the user might not even see them if we did so), and the items are also selected so that they can be manipulated—for example, moved or deleted—as a group. Afterwards we increment the paste offset; this ensures that if the user pastes the same items repeatedly, each paste is offset from the last, again to help make them visible to the user.

If the MIME data doesn't offer our custom Page Designer format, we check to see if it offers HTML or plain text. In either of these cases we create a new TextItem at a suitable place in the scene using the position() method (426 ◄), and connect it to the toolbox widgets. Then we insert the HTML or plain text into the text item using the appropriate methods. (Note that we should always check MIME formats in our order of preference, i.e., most preferred first. For example, if we have HTML text in the clipboard both QMimeData::hasText() and QMimeData::hasHtml() are likely to return true, since many applications will copy text in multiple formats to the clipboard and will probably offer both text/html *and* text/plain formats.)

At the end, if we added items by reading them or created a new text item, we call setDirty() since a pasting significantly changes the scene.

Manipulating Selected Items

In this subsubsection we will review the editAlign() slot and its helper method to see a typical example of how a method that is used to manipulate two or more selected items is implemented. And we will also look at what happens when the selection changes.

The user interface allows the user to align multiple items in either of two ways: they can invoke a specific alignment action (such as Align Top) using the menu or the Align toolbar button's menu; or they can click the Align toolbar button in which case the last alignment that was used is applied—or the default alignment if this is the first alignment applied since the application started.

To provide some context, here is how the alignment actions are set up (quoted from the main window's createMenusAndToolBars() method):

```
QMenu *alignmentMenu = new QMenu(tr("Align"), this);
foreach (QAction *action, QList<QAction*>()
        << editAlignLeftAction << editAlignRightAction
        << editAlignTopAction << editAlignBottomAction)
    alignmentMenu->addAction(action);
editAlignmentAction->setMenu(alignmentMenu);
```

Further on, the edit alignment action is added to the edit menu and to the edit toolbar. When using the menu, the user can only select one of the specific alignment actions, but when using the toolbar the user can either click the toolbar button itself (thus invoking the edit alignment action), or its menu, in which case they can click one of the specific alignment actions. In view of this our code must account for the possibility that either a specific alignment action, or the edit alignment action itself, is invoked. Note also that the updateUi() slot (➤ 437) enables the alignment action only if there are at least two selected items, since alignment doesn't make sense if one or no item is selected.

We will look at the slot in three parts for ease of explanation.

```cpp
void MainWindow::editAlign()
{
    QAction *action = qobject_cast<QAction*>(sender());
    if (!action)
        return;

    Qt::Alignment alignment = static_cast<Qt::Alignment>(
            action->data().toInt());
    if (action != editAlignmentAction) {
        editAlignmentAction->setData(action->data());
        editAlignmentAction->setIcon(action->icon());
    }
```

We begin by finding out which action invoked the slot. The required alignment is stored in the action's data, so we retrieve it for use further on. If the action is not the edit alignment action itself, we set the edit alignment action's data to be the chosen specific alignment, and its icon to match this alignment. This ensures that if the edit alignment action is invoked rather than a specific alignment, it will use the last specific alignment that was set.

```cpp
    QList<QGraphicsItem*> items = scene->selectedItems();
    QVector<double> coordinates;
    populateCoordinates(alignment, &coordinates, items);
    double offset;
    if (alignment == Qt::AlignLeft || alignment == Qt::AlignTop)
        offset = *std::min_element(coordinates.constBegin(),
                                   coordinates.constEnd());
    else
        offset = *std::max_element(coordinates.constBegin(),
                                   coordinates.constEnd());
```

The algorithm we use to do the alignment is quite simple. We create a vector of all the items' edge coordinates for the required alignment, for example, their x-coordinates if we are aligning left, or their y-coordinates plus their heights if we are aligning bottom. We then compute an offset which is the minimum coordinate (for left or top alignment) or maximum (for right or bottom), and move every item by the difference between the offset and its actual coordinate.

The std::min_element() and std::max_element() functions are provided by the STL (Standard Template Library) in the <algorithm> header. These functions accept a start and end iterator and return an iterator that points to the minimum (or maximum) element in the sequence the iterators refer to. So, here, we immediately extract the value from the iterator using operator*(). (If we wanted to avoid the STL we could write our own template min() and max() functions that take a sequence argument, or we could write, say, qSort(coordinates); offset = coordinates.first(); for the minimum and use coordinates.last() for the maximum.)

```
    if (alignment == Qt::AlignLeft || alignment == Qt::AlignRight) {
        for (int i = 0; i < items.count(); ++i)
            items.at(i)->moveBy(offset - coordinates.at(i), 0);
    }
    else {
        for (int i = 0; i < items.count(); ++i)
            items.at(i)->moveBy(0, offset - coordinates.at(i));
    }
    setDirty(true);
}
```

Here is where we iterate over every item, moving it horizontally or vertically by the amount necessary to line it up with the left-most (or right-most, and so on) item. And once all the items have been moved, we call setDirty(), since the scene has been changed significantly.

From the user's point of view, as soon as they invoke an alignment action the selected items immediately snap into their new positions. In Chapter 13 we will revisit this method and see how to animate the alignment to make it more obvious to the user which items were moved, and at the same time make the moving more visually elegant.

```
    void MainWindow::populateCoordinates(const Qt::Alignment &alignment,
            QVector<double> *coordinates,
            const QList<QGraphicsItem*> &items)
    {
        QListIterator<QGraphicsItem*> i(items);
        while (i.hasNext()) {
            QRectF rect = i.next()->sceneBoundingRect();
            switch (alignment) {
                case Qt::AlignLeft:
                    coordinates->append(rect.x()); break;
                case Qt::AlignRight:
                    coordinates->append(rect.x() + rect.width()); break;
                case Qt::AlignTop:
                    coordinates->append(rect.y()); break;
                case Qt::AlignBottom:
```

```
                    coordinates->append(rect.y() + rect.height()); break;
            }
        }
    }
```

This method iterates over the list of items it is given and populates the vector of doubles it is given with the corresponding *x*- or *y*-coordinates. The QGraphics-Item::sceneBoundingRect() method returns the item's bounding rectangle in scene coordinates. It is much more common to use QGraphicsItem::bounding-Rect() which returns the item's bounding rectangle in item coordinates, but here we need scene coordinates because we plan to move items within the scene (i.e., to line them up). Selected methods from the QGraphicsItem API, as well as key enums used by the API, were presented earlier in Tables 11.1 to 11.7 (403–407 ◄).

Another common requirement for drawing programs is to be able to distribute items vertically or horizontally. This means, given three or more items, while keeping the two end items in place, moving the item or items in between such that the gap between each item is the same. Since implementing this would not teach anything more about the graphics/view architecture than is already covered, we leave adding such functionality to Page Designer as an exercise.

Before leaving this subsubsection on manipulating graphics items we will review one more slot.

```
    void MainWindow::selectionChanged()
    {
        QList<QGraphicsItem*> items = scene->selectedItems();
        if (items.count() == 1) {
            if (QObject *item = dynamic_cast<QObject*>(items.at(0))) {
                if (item->property("brush").isValid())
                    brushWidget->setBrush(
                            item->property("brush").value<QBrush>());
                if (item->property("pen").isValid())
                    penWidget->setPen(
                            item->property("pen").value<QPen>());
                if (item->property("angle").isValid()) {
                    transformWidget->setAngle(
                            item->property("angle").toDouble());
                    transformWidget->setShear(
                            item->property("shearHorizontal").toDouble(),
                            item->property("shearVertical").toDouble());
                }
            }
        }
        updateUi();
    }
```

This slot is connected to the `QGraphicsScene::selectionChanged()` signal, and we use it to make sure that the toolbox widgets reflect the properties of the selected item. (As noted earlier, the use of `dynamic_cast<>()` makes the application dependent on the availability of RTTI—Run Time Type Information—although there are various ways to avoid this; 424 ◄.)

Here we are concerned with the case where the selection has changed such that a single item only is selected. If two or more items are selected we would not know which one's brush, pen, or transformation properties to show, so in such cases we leave the toolboxes unchanged. We cannot disable the toolboxes when two or more items are selected, though, because the user might want to apply a change to multiple items in one go—for example, to rotate all the selected items, or to change their brushes.

Once again we have used Qt's meta-object system to make the method as generic as possible, so that it will not need to be changed even if new custom item types are added. (And as already noted, we could use `qgraphics-item_cast<>()` instead if we didn't want our custom item types to be QObjects.) Earlier, in the `connectItem()` method (419 ◄), we used the item's (class's) meta-object and the `QMetaObject::indexOfProperty()` method to see if a particular item had a particular property. Here, we have taken a more direct—yet more ambiguous—approach, and used the `QObject::property()` method. This method takes a property name and returns a `QVariant`—an invalid `QVariant` if the object does not have a property with the given name.*

How many items are selected (none, one, two or more) profoundly affects the user interface. If no items are selected, then the toolbox widgets ought to be disabled because they can have no effect; if exactly one item is selected the Edit Selected Item... action should be enabled; and if two or more items are selected the alignment actions should be enabled. All of this, and more, is handled by the `updateUi()` slot which we will review shortly (➤ 436).

As Page Designer stands, the `BrushWidget` and `PenWidget` will show the selected item's brush and pen if the item is a box or smiley, and the `TransformWidget` will show the item's rotation and shears. (We will review the `BrushWidget` later on; ➤ 440.) Recall that if the user changes the properties in a toolbox widget—for example, the brush—*every* item that has a brush property is notified; but only the selected item or items update their brushes in response, as we will see when we cover the custom graphics items further on (➤ 447).

---

*The `QObject::property()` method will return an invalid `QVariant` if there is no property of the given name—or if the property's value is an invalid `QVariant`. So if we really need to know whether an object has a particular property, we must use the `QMetaObject::indexOfProperty()` approach.

Showing and Hiding the Guideline Grid

It is probably easiest and best to show a guideline grid by setting the scene's background to a suitable brush using QGraphicsScene::setBackgroundBrush(), or by reimplementing the QGraphicsScene::drawBackground() method. We chose to use neither of these approaches purely to show how to use QGraphicsItemGroup, and how to be selective regarding the items we save or manipulate.

In the Page Designer application we have a viewShowGridAction toggle action that is connected to the viewShowGrid() slot that creates and shows or hides the guideline grid.

```
void MainWindow::viewShowGrid(bool on)
{
    if (!gridGroup) {
        const int GridSize = 40;
        QPen pen(QColor(175, 175, 175, 127));
        gridGroup = new QGraphicsItemGroup;
        const int MaxX = static_cast<int>(std::ceil(scene->width())
                / GridSize) * GridSize;
        const int MaxY = static_cast<int>(std::ceil(scene->height())
                / GridSize) * GridSize;
        for (int x = 0; x <= MaxX; x += GridSize) {
            QGraphicsLineItem *item = new QGraphicsLineItem(x, 0, x,
                                                            MaxY);
            item->setPen(pen);
            item->setZValue(std::numeric_limits<int>::min());
            gridGroup->addToGroup(item);
        }
        ...
        scene->addItem(gridGroup);
    }
    gridGroup->setVisible(on);
}
```

When this method is called, we create the guidelines' grid group if it doesn't exist—for example, because the application has just started or because we have cleared the scene. We set the pen that draws the guidelines to be a semi-transparent light gray. And since we haven't specified a pen width it will default to 0, which means a cosmetic pen, 1 pixel wide. Cosmetic pens (whatever their width) are always painted at their specified width, no matter what transformations are in force (except for width 0, which is treated as 1). Contrast this with non-cosmetic pens whose width is scaled in proportion to whatever scaling is in force.

We create a new QGraphicsItemGroup and compute the furthest x- and y-coordinates in the scene. We then iterate in GridSize increments from an x-coordinate of 0 to MaxX, and in each iteration we create a standard QGraphicsLineItem passing it $(x1, y1, x2, y2)$ coordinates. And since we give it two identical x-coordinates and different y-coordinates, we get a vertical line. Once we have the line we set its pen to the one we created earlier, and give it a large negative z value to make sure that it is always underneath any other items, and then add it to the grid group. There is an analogous loop for drawing the horizontal lines that has been elided since it is structurally the same as the one shown.

When a QGraphicsItem is created, all the graphics item flags are disabled, so, for example, by default a graphics item cannot be moved or selected by the user. This behavior is exactly what we want for the guidelines.

Once all the line items have been created and added to the group, the group is added to the scene. And at the end, we show or hide the group (and therefore all the line items it contains) depending on the on Boolean passed as the slot's parameter by the corresponding action's toggled(bool) signal.

Incidentally, the std::ceil() function (from <cmath>) returns the smallest integer that is greater than or equal to its argument, and the std::numeric_limits< int>::min() function (from <limits>) returns the smallest (i.e., most negative) integer.

One method that we haven't covered here is editClearTransforms(); we will cover this later, at the end of the "Graphics Item Transformations" subsubsection (➤ 453).

Keeping the User Interface Up to Date

A lazy way to reflect application state changes into the user interface is not to reflect them at all. With this approach, the user can invoke any action at any time, and each action is responsible for checking that it makes sense, and doing nothing if it doesn't. For example, we could leave the Paste action permanently enabled, even if there is nothing to paste, and similarly leave the Copy action enabled, even if no item or items are selected (and thus there is nothing to copy).

Unfortunately, leaving every action enabled can confuse users. For example, they might invoke the Paste action and then wonder why nothing has appeared. So, insofar as possible, we prefer to enable and disable actions and the widgets inside dock widgets depending on the application's state. This isn't always easy. For example, if the user has selected a box item, a smiley item, and a text item, which toolbox widgets should we enable? We could just enable the toolbox or toolboxes that are applicable to all the selected items, so in this case we would only enable the transformations toolbox. For Page Designer, we decided that this would be inconvenient for users, so instead we enable every toolbox that applies to at least one of the selected items. So, in this case we enable the transformations, pen, and brush toolboxes, even though text items don't have pen or brush properties. This works well since if we change, say, the brush, the change will be safely ignored by text items but will correctly be applied to any selected box and smiley items.

In Page Designer, whenever a significant change takes place, the setDirty() slot is called. In the case of the Save action, it is called with a false argument, since after saving the scene isn't dirty. But for most other changes it is called with true (which is its argument's default value).

```
void MainWindow::setDirty(bool on)
{
    setWindowModified(on);
    updateUi();
}
```

Rather than maintain our own Boolean dirty member variable we make use of the main window's windowModified property. And whenever a change in the dirty state occurs we call updateUi() (which is also called from elsewhere—for example, in editCopy() and selectionChanged()), to appropriately enable or disable the application's actions and toolbox widgets.

```
void MainWindow::updateUi()
{
    fileSaveAction->setEnabled(isWindowModified());
    bool hasItems = sceneHasItems();
    fileSaveAsAction->setEnabled(hasItems);
    fileExportAction->setEnabled(hasItems);
    filePrintAction->setEnabled(hasItems);
    int selected = scene->selectedItems().count();
    editSelectedItemAction->setEnabled(selected == 1);
    editCopyAction->setEnabled(selected >= 1);
    editCutAction->setEnabled(selected >= 1);
    QClipboard *clipboard = QApplication::clipboard();
    const QMimeData *mimeData = clipboard->mimeData();
    editPasteAction->setEnabled(mimeData &&
            (mimeData->hasFormat(MimeType) || mimeData->hasHtml() ||
            mimeData->hasText())));
    editAlignmentAction->setEnabled(selected >= 2);
    editClearTransformsAction->setEnabled(selected >= 1);
    transformWidget->setEnabled(selected >= 1);
    bool hasBrushProperty;
    bool hasPenProperty;
    getSelectionProperties(&hasBrushProperty, &hasPenProperty);
    brushWidget->setEnabled(hasBrushProperty);
    penWidget->setEnabled(hasPenProperty);
}
```

The Save action is enabled if there are unsaved changes. The Save As, Export, and Print actions are enabled if the scene has at least one item. The Edit Selected Item… action is enabled if there is exactly one selected item, and the Copy and Cut actions are enabled if there is at least one selected item. The Paste action is enabled if the system clipboard has data in Page Designer's own MIME format, or has HTML or plain text; we discussed the clipboard handling earlier (427 ◄). The Align action (and therefore the Align Left, Align Right, and so on, actions) is enabled if at least two items are selected. And the Clear Transformations action is enabled if at least one item is selected. Strictly speaking, we should only enable the Clear Transformations action if the selected item (or at least one of the selected items) has a nonzero rotation or shear; checking for this isn't difficult, but we leave this refinement as an exercise.

We enable the transformation toolbox widget if at least one item is selected since all of Page Designer's custom items support transformations. But we only enable the brush and pen toolbox widgets if the selected item (or at least one of the selected items) has a brush or pen property.

For completeness, we will very briefly review the updateUi() slot's two helper methods.

```
bool MainWindow::sceneHasItems() const
{
    foreach (QGraphicsItem *item, scene->items())
        if (item != gridGroup && item->group() != gridGroup)
            return true;
    return false;
}
```

This method returns true if the scene has at least one item (not including the guideline grid).

```
void MainWindow::getSelectionProperties(bool *hasBrushProperty,
                                        bool *hasPenProperty) const
{
    Q_ASSERT(hasBrushProperty && hasPenProperty);
    *hasBrushProperty = false;
    *hasPenProperty = false;
    foreach (QGraphicsItem *item, scene->selectedItems()) {
        if (QObject *object = dynamic_cast<QObject*>(item)) {
            const QMetaObject *metaObject = object->metaObject();
            if (metaObject->indexOfProperty("brush") > -1)
                *hasBrushProperty = true;
            if (metaObject->indexOfProperty("pen") > -1)
                *hasPenProperty = true;
            if (*hasBrushProperty && *hasPenProperty)
                break;
```

```
        }
    }
}
```

This method iterates over every selected item, checking to see if it has a brush or pen property. We have included a tiny efficiency shortcut in that if the brush and pen properties are both true we know that we can return immediately. (As noted earlier, the use of dynamic_cast<>() makes the application dependent on the availability of RTTI, although this can be avoided; 424 ◄.)

Enhancing QGraphicsView

The QGraphicsView class does not support zooming out of the box, so we have created a tiny subclass (all implemented in a header file) that provides the necessary functionality, and also taken the opportunity to switch on antialiasing and support for rubber band selections. Here is the complete definition of the GraphicsView class:

```
class GraphicsView : public QGraphicsView
{
    Q_OBJECT

public:
    explicit GraphicsView(QWidget *parent=0) : QGraphicsView(parent)
    {
        setDragMode(RubberBandDrag);
        setRenderHints(QPainter::Antialiasing|
                       QPainter::TextAntialiasing);
    }

public slots:
    void zoomIn() { scaleBy(1.1); }
    void zoomOut() { scaleBy(1.0 / 1.1); }

protected:
    void wheelEvent(QWheelEvent *event)
        { scaleBy(std::pow(4.0 / 3.0, (-event->delta() / 240.0))); }

private:
    void scaleBy(double factor) { scale(factor, factor); }
};
```

In the constructor we begin by switching on rubber band drag mode. This means that if the user clicks and drags, a rubber band (i.e., a rectangle, filled with a semi-transparent color on some platforms) is stretched out, and every item in or touching the rectangle is selected. The default drag mode is QGraphicsView::NoDrag which does nothing. One other drag mode is supported:

QGraphicsView::ScrollHandDrag; when this is set, clicking and dragging scrolls the view.

To support zooming we have provided two slots, both of which scale the view. And we have also reimplemented the mouse wheel event handler, to scale in proportion to how far the wheel has been rotated—zooming out for forward movement and zooming in for backward movement. The QWheelEvent::delta() value reports how far the wheel has been rotated in "steps" (where each step usually corresponds to a wheel rotation of 15°), with positive values indicating forward movement and negative values indicating backward movement. The std::pow() function (from the <cmath> header) raises its first argument to the power specified by its second argument. In essence, what we do here is increase or decrease the scale by a factor of $1\frac{1}{3}$ for every mouse wheel step.

All the scaling is done by the private scaleBy() method that simply calls the QGraphicsView::scale() method and uses the single scale factor as the amount to scale both horizontally and vertically to maintain the view's aspect ratio.

By default, a QGraphicsView uses wheel events for scrolling, so by reimplementing the wheelEvent() event handler, we have effectively disabled this behavior. This means that users can only use the mouse wheel for scrolling if the mouse is actually over a scrollbar.

Creating a Dock Widget Toolbox

The Page Designer's main window has three dock widgets, one for transformations (rotation and shears), one for the brush, and one for the pen. Structurally all three widgets are similar, and logically they are all used for the same two purposes: to reflect the relevant properties of the single selected widget—for example, to show its brush color and style—and to change the relevant properties of the selected item or items when the user manipulates the dock widget's editing widgets.

All of Page Designer's dock widgets are similar in structure and function, so we will review only one of them—the BrushWidget. The code for others is, of course, in the application's source code. All three dock widgets can be seen in Figure 12.1 (410 ◀).

As we often do, we will begin by looking at the class's definition in the header file, but eliding the private slots and methods, all of which we will cover as needed when we review the public slots and methods.

```
class BrushWidget : public QWidget
{
    Q_OBJECT

public:
```

```
    explicit BrushWidget(QWidget *parent=0);

    QBrush brush() const { return m_brush; }
public slots:
    void setBrush(const QBrush &brush);
signals:
    void brushChanged(const QBrush &brush);
    ...
};
```

The widget has one item of private member data, m_brush of type QBrush. The class provides a suitable getter, and a slot as a setter so that the brush can be set as the result of the activating of a signal–slot connection. If the brush is changed—for example, if the user changes the color or style—the brushChanged() signal is emitted. We saw earlier that every item that has a brush property, that is, box and smiley items, connects to this signal. (We will see how they respond to the signal when we cover the custom items' implementations later on; ➤ 447.)

```
BrushWidget::BrushWidget(QWidget *parent)
    : QWidget(parent)
{
    createWidgets();
    setBrush(QBrush());
    createLayout();
    createConnections();
    setFixedSize(minimumSizeHint());
}
```

The constructor passes most of its work on to private helper methods. It sets an initial black brush with a style of Qt::NoBrush (so the brush won't actually have any effect). Once the child widgets have been created and laid out we set the brush widget to have a fixed size of its minimum size hint since there doesn't seem to be much point in letting the user resize it. (For the curious it might be worth commenting out the setFixedSize() calls in all three toolbox widgets and seeing what effect this has.)

```
void BrushWidget::createWidgets()
{
    colorComboBox = new QComboBox;
    foreach (const QString &name, QColor::colorNames()) {
        QColor color(name);
        colorComboBox->addItem(colorSwatch(color), name, color);
    }

    styleComboBox = new QComboBox;
```

```
typedef QPair<QString, Qt::BrushStyle> BrushPair;
foreach (const BrushPair &pair, QList<BrushPair>()
        << qMakePair(tr("No Brush"), Qt::NoBrush)
        << qMakePair(tr("Solid"), Qt::SolidPattern)
        ...
        << qMakePair(tr("Diagonal Cross"), Qt::DiagCrossPattern))
    styleComboBox->addItem(brushSwatch(pair.second), pair.first,
                            pair.second);
}
```

The widget contains four child widgets—two labels and two comboboxes. To help the user choose the brush color or brush style, rather than simply list their names we provide swatches (little pixmaps) to illustrate the values. For each color we use a circular pixmap filled with the associated color, and for each brush style we use a square pixmap filled with the current color (which is initially black), using the corresponding brush style.

For each color, we add a combobox item that has a color swatch, the name of the color (in the form of a QString using HTML color syntax, e.g., "#FF0000" for red), and a data QVariant holding the QColor itself. The static QColor::colorNames() method returns a sorted QStringList of human-readable color names (such as "palegreen", "red", and so on).* We take the same approach for brush styles, giving each combobox item a swatch illustrating the brush style, the style's name, and a data QVariant holding the style's enum value—and, of course, we have elided most of the brush pairs from the code shown above since they all follow the same pattern.

As we noted in Chapter 9 (347 ◄), inside Qt's foreach construct the first comma encountered is used to separate the item from the sequence, so we cannot use items that contain a comma. We have solved the problem here using our usual practice of creating a typedef.

One other aspect to notice is that we create only the comboboxes, not the labels. We will get the layout class to create the labels for us, as we will see shortly.

The application has five swatch functions: colorSwatch(), brushSwatch(), penStyleSwatch(), penCapSwatch(), and penJoinSwatch(). We will review only the simplest of them—brushSwatch()—as representative. (The others are more complicated, but not in particularly interesting ways—for example, the color swatch can add a "C" character in a contrasting color, and the pen join swatch paints a polyline of two lines that meet so as to show the join style.)

---

*At the time of this writing, the documentation doesn't explicitly say that the color names are sorted, so it would be more defensive to retrieve the names into a variable and call QStringList::sort() before adding them, or to just call QComboBox::model()->sort(0), to sort the first (and only) column in ascending order, after populating the combobox.

```
QPixmap brushSwatch(const Qt::BrushStyle style, const QColor &color,
                    const QSize &size)
{
    QString key = QString("BRUSHSTYLESWATCH:%1:%2:%3x%4")
        .arg(static_cast<int>(style)).arg(color.name())
        .arg(size.width()).arg(size.height());
    QPixmap pixmap(size);
    if (!QPixmapCache::find(key, &pixmap)) {
        pixmap.fill(Qt::transparent);
        QPainter painter(&pixmap);
        painter.setRenderHint(QPainter::Antialiasing);
        painter.setPen(Qt::NoPen);
        painter.setBrush(QBrush(color, style));
        painter.drawRect(0, 0, size.width(), size.height());
        painter.end();
        QPixmapCache::insert(key, pixmap);
    }
    return pixmap;
}
```

This function takes a brush style, an optional color (which defaults to black), and an optional size (which defaults to 24 × 24 pixels) and returns a square pixmap drawn using a brush of the specified style, color, and size.

Rather than creating a fresh pixmap every time the function is called we cache pixmaps—up to 10MB worth by default, and changeable using QPixmap-Cache::setCacheLimit(). To use the cache we must uniquely identify each pixmap we cache with a key. Here we use a string that identifies the pixmap as a brush swatch (in contrast to a color swatch, pen style swatch, and so on), and that is followed by information that identifies the swatch, in this case the brush style (as an int), the color (as an HTML color string), and the pixmap's width and height. For example, a solid brown 24 × 24 brush would have a key of "BRUSHSTYLESWATCH:1:#a52a2a:24x24".

Once we have created the key we create a pixmap of the right size. The QPix-mapCache::find() method is used to retrieve a pixmap from the cache with the given key. The method returns true and populates the QPixmap it is passed by pointer—or by non-const reference (i.e., no &) for Qt 4.5 and earlier—if the key is found; otherwise it returns false. So, the first time we request a particular pixmap its key is not found and we fill the pixmap ourselves. We begin by filling it with transparent color, and then we create a QPainter to paint a rectangle over the entire pixmap using the specified brush. Although we paint the whole pixmap, we must still fill it with transparent or some other color in the first place, since most brush styles aren't solid and leave some background showing through. Once created, we insert the pixmap into the cache using the key. And at the end we return the pixmap we retrieved or created.

Structurally, all the other swatch methods are the same as this one—they differ only in that they use different keys and draw different things on the pixmap. Note that the keys we use must never begin with the string "$qt" since Qt uses the QPixmapCache itself with this as the prefix for all of its own keys.

```
void BrushWidget::createLayout()
{
    QFormLayout *layout = new QFormLayout;
    layout->addRow(tr("Color"), colorComboBox);
    layout->addRow(tr("Style"), styleComboBox);
    setLayout(layout);
}
```

We have chosen to show the createLayout() method since it uses the QFormLayout class introduced in Qt 4.4, and creates two of the labels for us. One nice feature of creating labels in this way is that Qt automatically makes them buddies of the widget that is added, which means that if the keyboard focus goes to one of the labels it is immediately passed on to its buddy.

```
void BrushWidget::createConnections()
{
    connect(colorComboBox, SIGNAL(currentIndexChanged(int)),
            this, SLOT(updateColor(int)));
    connect(styleComboBox, SIGNAL(currentIndexChanged(int)),
            this, SLOT(updateStyle(int)));
}
```

This method is shown for completeness. If the user changes the color or the brush style, a corresponding slot is called so that any connected widgets can be notified, and in the case of color changes so that we can update the brush swatches to use the newly set color.

We have now finished looking at the constructor and its private helper methods. Next we will look at the public setBrush() slot, and then at the private slots and a private helper method.

```
void BrushWidget::setBrush(const QBrush &brush)
{
    if (m_brush != brush) {
        m_brush = brush;
        colorComboBox->setCurrentIndex(
                colorComboBox->findData(m_brush.color()));
        styleComboBox->setCurrentIndex(
                styleComboBox->findData(
                        static_cast<int>(m_brush.style())));
    }
}
```

This slot is called when exactly one item is selected in the view—providing that item has a brush property, as box and smiley items do. In response this slot sets the private brush to the one passed in and sets the two comboboxes' current items to match the color and style of the new brush.

The QComboBox::findData() method takes a QVariant and returns the index of the first matching item (or -1). We can use QColors directly, but for enums we must cast them to ints since that is how they are stored in QVariants.

```
void BrushWidget::updateColor(int index)
{
    m_brush.setColor(colorComboBox->itemData(index).value<QColor>());
    updateSwatches();
    emit brushChanged(m_brush);
}
```

Whenever the brush color changes—either as a result of the user manipulating the colorComboBox or due to an item being selected and calling the setBrush() slot—this method is called.

The QComboBox::itemData() method returns the QVariant of data associated with the item with the given index. (By default this is an invalid QVariant.) And since QVariant only provides conversion methods for *QtCore* types (QVariant::toInt(), QVariant::toSize(), and so on), for other types we must use the QVariant::value<T>() template method, specifying the type of the value we want it to return.

Once we have updated the private brush to use the new color, we call the private updateSwatches() method to make sure that the brush style swatches are shown using the new color. And at the end we emit the brushChanged() signal to notify any connected QObjects of the new brush.

```
void BrushWidget::updateStyle(int index)
{
    m_brush.setStyle(static_cast<Qt::BrushStyle>(
                     styleComboBox->itemData(index).toInt()));
    emit brushChanged(m_brush);
}
```

This method is the brush style equivalent of the updateColor() method. The brush style is specified using an enum, so we begin by retrieving the data QVariant for the given item as an int, and then we cast this to the appropriate enum type before updating the private brush. And at the end we emit the brushChanged() signal with the updated brush.

There is no need to call updateSwatches() from this method, since all the swatches in the combobox are updated whenever the color is changed, so when the brush style combobox is manipulated by the user or has its index changed programmatically, it already has swatches that use the correct color.

```
void BrushWidget::updateSwatches()
{
    QColor color = colorComboBox->itemData(
            colorComboBox->currentIndex()).value<QColor>();
    for (int i = 0; i < styleComboBox->count(); ++i)
        styleComboBox->setItemIcon(i, brushSwatch(
                static_cast<Qt::BrushStyle>(
                    styleComboBox->itemData(i).toInt()), color));
}
```

To make it as easy as possible for users to see the effects of changing brush colors, whenever the brush color is changed we update the brush style swatches in the styleComboBox so that they use the same color. The effect can easily be seen by running Page Designer, clicking the brush style combobox, and choosing any style except NoBrush, then clicking the brush color combobox and using the up and down arrow keys to change the color—while watching the swatch shown in the brush style combobox as it changes to match the chosen color. (On some platforms it is necessary to click Esc after first clicking the color combobox so that when the arrow keys are used the brush combobox is visible.) And the same effect can be achieved with the pen toolbox by using the up and down arrows on the pen color combobox and watching the pen style, cap, and join swatches change color.

The method begins by retrieving the current color. Then we iterate over every item in the brush style combobox, and for each one we change the icon it uses (and relying on a non-explicit QIcon constructor that takes a QPixmap argument) to one returned by a call to the brushSwatch() function. For the first argument to the brushSwatch() function we pass the brush style by retrieving the data QVariant's value as an int and then casting it to the appropriate enum type. And instead of using the default black color, we pass the color combobox's current color as second argument.

The TransformWidget and PenWidget (neither of which is shown) are structurally and logically very similar to the BrushWidget we have reviewed here.

We have now reviewed all of the Page Designer application's infrastructure, including how to save, load, and export scenes, how to add and manipulate individual items, and how to manipulate groups of selected items. The only things left to cover are the implementations of the custom graphics items themselves, which is the subject of the next section.

Creating Custom Graphics Items

All graphics/view items have QGraphicsItem as their direct or indirect base class. Most of the QGraphicsItem convenience subclasses were introduced with the graphics/view architecture in Qt 4.2, with QGraphicsProxyWidget and QGraphics-Widget being added in Qt 4.4, and QGraphicsObject and QGraphicsWebView in Qt 4.6. (Qt 4.7 may add QGraphicsVideoItem for showing videos in scenes which makes use of Qt's low-level *QtMultimedia* module.) The class hierarchy was shown earlier (391◄), as were selected QGraphicsItem methods and enums (in Tables 11.1 to 11.7; 403–407 ◄).

Having so many graphics item classes means that in most cases we do not need to create subclasses purely to paint custom shapes. After all, practically anything can be drawn using QGraphicsEllipseItem, QGraphicsLineItem, QGraphics-PathItem, QGraphicsPolygonItem, and QGraphicsRectItem. So the main purpose of subclassing graphics items is to provide custom behavior.

In this section we will review three different custom graphics item types to show a variety of approaches. The first subclass we will look at is a QGraphics-TextItem subclass which merely adds some simple behavior, leaving all the painting to Qt. The second we will look at is a QObject and QGraphicsRectItem subclass which adds more sophisticated behaviors, including key press and mouse interactions. The third is a QGraphicsObject subclass (or QObject and QGraphicsItem subclass for Qt 4.5 and earlier) that implements custom behavior and also paints itself—as well as providing implementations of boundingRect() and shape(). In fact, this last class could have avoided doing its own painting had it been a QGraphicsPathItem subclass—something that is true of most shapes—but we wanted to show an example where both behavior and appearance are implemented.

For convenience we have defined the custom item type numbers in a separate header file:

```
const int BoxItemType = QGraphicsItem::UserType + 1;
const int SmileyItemType = QGraphicsItem::UserType + 2;
const int TextItemType = QGraphicsItem::UserType + 3;
```

Hopefully, this will help us to avoid accidentally giving two custom items the same type numbers.

Enhancing QGraphicsTextItem

The QGraphicsTextItem class—which inherits both QObject and QGraphicsItem—is used to show Qt rich text in a scene. (If plain text is sufficient, that is, text that has a single font and color, we can use QGraphicsSimpleTextItems instead.)

We need to subclass QGraphicsTextItem because we want to provide it with custom behavior. In particular, we want the user to be able to rotate and shear it
through the user interface, and to be able to edit the text it shows. We also want
the subclass to announce changes via a custom dirty() signal, and to be able to
write and read itself to and from a QDataStream. The painting, and the computation of the bounding rectangle and the shape, are left to the base class.

We will start by looking at the definition of the custom TextItem class in the
header file, but omitting the private section.

```
class TextItem : public QGraphicsTextItem
{
    Q_OBJECT
    Q_PROPERTY(double angle READ angle WRITE setAngle)
    Q_PROPERTY(double shearHorizontal READ shearHorizontal
               WRITE setShearHorizontal)
    Q_PROPERTY(double shearVertical READ shearVertical
               WRITE setShearVertical)

public:
    enum {Type = TextItemType};

    explicit TextItem(const QPoint &position, QGraphicsScene *scene);
    int type() const { return Type; }

    double angle() const { return m_angle; }
    double shearHorizontal() const { return m_shearHorizontal; }
    double shearVertical() const { return m_shearVertical; }

public slots:
    void setAngle(double angle);
    void setShearHorizontal(double shearHorizontal)
        { setShear(shearHorizontal, m_shearVertical); }
    void setShearVertical(double shearVertical)
        { setShear(m_shearHorizontal, shearVertical); }
    void setShear(double shearHorizontal, double shearVertical);
    void edit();

signals:
    void dirty();

protected:
    QVariant itemChange(GraphicsItemChange change,
                        const QVariant &value);
    void mouseDoubleClickEvent(QGraphicsSceneMouseEvent*) { edit(); }
    ...
};
```

As we mentioned in the previous chapter, it is good practice to provide a Type enum and to reimplement the type() method to support the use of qgraphics-item_cast<>() which is used to cast QGraphicsItem pointers to the correct QGraphicsItem subclass.

We have made the item's angle of rotation and shears into properties so that we can query and set them via Qt's property system—for example, querying them in the selectionChanged() method (433 ◄), and setting them in the editClearTransforms() method (► 454). And we have made them doubles rather than qreals to ensure that they are saved and loaded correctly. (We discussed the fact that qreals should never be used with QDataStreams in Chapter 3; 104 ◄.)

The first two slots are used to make the item able to respond to changes in the TransformWidget toolbox. The itemChange() method is used to emit the dirty() signal if the change matters—for example, if the item's position or transformation is changed, but not if the item becomes selected or deselected.

The provision of an edit() slot is a convention we have adopted for the Page Designer application, so that we can have an Edit Selected Item... action that will invoke edit() to provide item-specific editing. (The editSelectedItem() slot was covered earlier; 423 ◄.) In addition, we reimplement the mouse double-click event handler to provide another means of invoking edit().

In addition to the class definition, the header also includes two other declarations:

```
QDataStream &operator<<(QDataStream &out, const TextItem &textItem);
QDataStream &operator>>(QDataStream &in, TextItem &textItem);
```

These operators are used by the readItems() and writeItems() methods we discussed earlier (417 ◄ and 416 ◄).

We will now review all the methods that are not implemented in the header file as well as the global stream operators, beginning with the constructor.

```
TextItem::TextItem(const QPoint &position, QGraphicsScene *scene)
    : QGraphicsTextItem(), m_angle(0.0), m_shearHorizontal(0.0),
      m_shearVertical(0.0)
{
    setFont(QFont("Helvetica", 11));
    setFlags(QGraphicsItem::ItemIsSelectable|
             QGraphicsItem::ItemSendsGeometryChanges|
             QGraphicsItem::ItemIsMovable);
    setPos(position);
    scene->clearSelection();
    scene->addItem(this);
    setSelected(true);
}
```

When a `TextItem` is constructed we set its angle and shears to 0.0 and then we give it an initial position (in scene coordinates) and the scene it belongs to.

We want the user to be able to select and move the item, so we set the appropriate flags to permit this. In Qt 4.5 and earlier, when an item's geometry changes (e.g., when it is resized), `itemChange()` is called; but from Qt 4.6, for performance reasons, this no longer happens unless we explicitly request it by setting the `ItemSendsGeometryChanges` flag as we do here. (We discussed this issue in the previous chapter in the "Qt 4.6 Graphics/View Behavior Changes" sidebar; 393 ◄.) Next, we set the item's position, clear any existing selection, and add the item to the scene. And at the end, we select the item—so that the user can immediately delete it or edit it.

```
void TextItem::edit()
{
    QWidget *window = 0;
    QList<QGraphicsView*> views = scene()->views();
    if (!views.isEmpty())
        window = views.at(0)->window();
    TextItemDialog dialog(this, QPoint(), scene(), window);
    if (dialog.exec())
        emit dirty();
}
```

This slot is called when a single `TextItem` is selected and the user invokes the Edit Selected Item... action (via the menu or toolbar), or when the user double-clicks a `TextItem`.

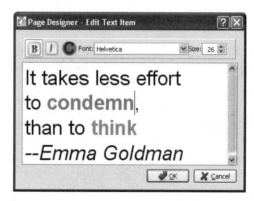

Figure 12.3 *The Page Designer application's TextItemDialog in edit mode*

The custom `TextItemDialog` (code not shown, but pictured in Figure 12.3) is an add/edit-style dialog that provides the user with the means of editing the item's text, including using different fonts and colors. We want to make sure that the dialog pops up in the right place and does not produce an additional entry in the taskbar, both easily achieved by giving it a top-level window as its parent. However, we don't have a pointer to a top-level window handy. One solution would be to call `QApplication::topLevelWidgets()`, and to use the first one from that list that isn't hidden. But while that will get a top-level window, it might not be the most appropriate one. So instead, we retrieve the list of views associated with the item's scene—of which in this application there is just one—and then call `QWidget::window()` to get the view's top-level window (or the view itself, it if was being used as a top-level window in its own right).

Internally, the `TextItemDialog` uses the `TextEdit` class we reviewed in Chapter 9 (353 ◄), but without the text alignment functionality. The dialog is *smart* (i.e., the dialog has application knowledge, and can operate almost independently), so if the user clicks OK, it updates the `TextItem` and schedules it for a repaint, so all we have to do is emit `dirty()` if the dialog is accepted.

```
QVariant TextItem::itemChange(GraphicsItemChange change,
                              const QVariant &value)
{
    if (isDirtyChange(change))
        emit dirty();
    return QGraphicsTextItem::itemChange(change, value);
}
```

This method is called by Qt whenever the item experiences a change of state. However, as we have noted, from Qt 4.6, for certain changes (e.g., those affecting its position and transformation), Qt will only call this method if we have explicitly asked it to by setting an appropriate `QGraphicsItem::GraphicsItemChange` flag, that is, `QGraphicsItem::ItemSendsGeometryChanges`. (Recall also that even with the flag set, the only transformation changes that result in `itemChange()` being called are those made by `setTransform()`. Qt 4.7 is due to extend this to cover the `setRotation()`, `setScale()`, and `setTransformOriginPoint()` methods that were introduced in Qt 4.6.)

We only want to emit the `dirty()` signal for those changes that affect the scene in terms of saving and loading it. For example, we do not keep track of selected items in scene files, so changes to an item's selected state do not make the scene dirty.

Since all our custom graphics items reimplement the `itemChange()` method we have factored out the determination of whether a change makes the scene dirty into the global `isDirtyChange()` function.

```
bool isDirtyChange(QGraphicsItem::GraphicsItemChange change)
{
    return (change == QGraphicsItem::ItemPositionChange ||
            change == QGraphicsItem::ItemPositionHasChanged ||
            change == QGraphicsItem::ItemTransformChange ||
```

```
        change == QGraphicsItem::ItemTransformHasChanged);
    }
```

This function returns true if the item's position or transformation has changed; for any other change it returns false.

We will look at the last TextItem methods, setAngle() and setShear(), in a separate subsubsection shortly, when we discuss graphics item transformations. First, though, we will look at the global QDataStream operators through which TextItems are written to and read from data streams.

```
    QDataStream &operator<<(QDataStream &out, const TextItem &textItem)
    {
        out << textItem.pos() << textItem.angle()
            << textItem.shearHorizontal() << textItem.shearVertical()
            << textItem.zValue() << textItem.toHtml();
        return out;
    }
```

For all the custom item operator<<()s, we write out the item's position (in scene coordinates), its angle, its shears, and its z value. (Page Designer does not provide any means of changing z values; adding such functionality is left as an exercise.) Next we write the item-specific data, in this case simply the item's text in HTML format (to preserve the fonts, colors, and other formatting).

As we saw earlier, this operator is used both to write TextItems to files, and also into a QByteArray when they are copied or cut to the clipboard (416 ◀; 427 ◀).

```
    QDataStream &operator>>(QDataStream &in, TextItem &textItem)
    {
        QPointF position;
        double angle;
        double shearHorizontal;
        double shearVertical;
        double z;
        QString html;
        in >> position >> angle >> shearHorizontal >> shearVertical >> z
            >> html;
        textItem.setPos(position);
        textItem.setAngle(angle);
        textItem.setShear(shearHorizontal, shearVertical);
        textItem.setZValue(z);
        textItem.setHtml(html);
        return in;
    }
```

This get from operator is used to read in the items written by the put to operator. As always with QDataStream, it is essential that we read back the same types in the same order as they were written. And just as with the put to operator, this operator is used for two purposes—to read files, and to paste the items from a QByteArray held in the system's clipboard into the scene (417 ◀; 427 ◀).

Graphics Item Transformations

If an item is rotated (with no shearing or scaling), it can be restored to its original position by changing its rotation back to its original angle (e.g., 0°). Similarly, if an item is sheared horizontally (with no rotation, no scaling, and no vertical shear), it can be restored by setting its horizontal shear back to its original value (e.g., 0.0). And the same applies for a vertical shear. But if any of these are combined (rotation with shearing, or vertical shearing with horizontal shearing, or rotation with scaling, and so on), restoring the angle to 0°, the shears to 0.0, and the scaling to 1.0 will *not* restore the original image. In fact, we can't generally undo transformations simply by reversing the actions (i.e., by applying "opposite" transformations) that we took to apply them. (This is because transformations are normally—and in Qt—represented as matrices, and not all matrices are invertible.)

For the Page Designer application, we have solved this problem by never applying transformations to transformations. Instead we always create and set fresh transformations, and this entirely avoids the undo problem. The way we achieve this is by maintaining private member variables in each item that hold the angle of rotation and the shears. This means that whenever the user changes the angle or shears, we create and set a new QTransform for the item.

We have not provided control over horizontal and vertical scaling because the code and logic would be almost the same as for shearing, and so would not teach anything beyond what we already cover. So, we leave adding support for scaling as an exercise.

To provide transformation support we need one method for each kind of transformation to set the relevant transformation component (angle, shears, etc.), and a private updateTransform() method to create and set a suitable QTransform. We'll start by looking at the setAngle() and setShear() slots, and then we will look at the updateTransform() method.

```
void TextItem::setAngle(double angle)
{
    if (isSelected() && !qFuzzyCompare(m_angle, angle)) {
        m_angle = angle;
        updateTransform();
    }
}
```

This method is called if the item is rotated, that is, if the user has changed the angle in the `TransformWidget`'s angle spinbox. Since *every* item is connected to the angle spinbox's `valueChanged()` signal, we must be careful to apply the change only to the item or items that are selected. In addition, we have used `qFuzzyCompare()` as an optimization that ensures that we apply the transformation only if the new angle is different enough from the old angle to matter.

```
void TextItem::setShear(double shearHorizontal, double shearVertical)
{
    if (isSelected() &&
        (!qFuzzyCompare(m_shearHorizontal, shearHorizontal) ||
         !qFuzzyCompare(m_shearVertical, shearVertical))) {
        m_shearHorizontal = shearHorizontal;
        m_shearVertical = shearVertical;
        updateTransform();
    }
}
```

As with the `setAngle()` method, we only change this item's shear if the item is selected and if at least one of the new shears is different enough from the old.

```
void TextItem::updateTransform()
{
    QTransform transform;
    transform.shear(m_shearHorizontal, m_shearVertical);
    transform.rotate(m_angle);
    setTransform(transform);
}
```

This private method is used to apply a transformation to the item. We begin by creating a fresh `QTransform` (which holds an identity matrix, i.e., it has no rotation, scaling, or shearing). Then we apply the shears and the angle of rotation, and at the end we set the item's transformation to the one we have created.

Notice that we do not explicitly emit the `dirty()` signal; thanks to setting the `ItemSendsGeometryChanges` flag, the `itemChange()` method is called, and that is where `dirty()` is emitted.

We mentioned earlier that the main window provides a Clear Transformations action. To round off this subsubsection on transformations, we will review the main window slot that is called when that action is invoked.

```
void MainWindow::editClearTransforms()
{
    QList<QGraphicsItem*> items = scene->selectedItems();
    Q_ASSERT(!items.isEmpty());
    QListIterator<QGraphicsItem*> i(items);
```

```
        while (i.hasNext()) {
            if (QObject *item = dynamic_cast<QObject*>(i.next())) {
                if (item->property("angle").isValid()) {
                    item->setProperty("angle", 0.0);
                    item->setProperty("shearHorizontal", 0.0);
                    item->setProperty("shearVertical", 0.0);
                }
            }
        }
    }
    transformWidget->setAngle(0.0);
    transformWidget->setShear(0.0, 0.0);
    setDirty(true);
}
```

This method clears transformations from the selected items, by setting their rotation angles to 0.0° and setting their shears to 0.0. Then we update the TransformWidget so that it correctly reflects the transformation state of the selected item or items by setting its angle to 0.0° and its shears to 0.0. And at the end, we call setDirty() since the changes are significant. (The use of dynamic_cast<>() requires the use of RTTI, although it is possible to avoid it; 424 ◄.)

We use an assertion to check that the list isn't empty—after all, we only enable the Clear Transformations action if there is at least one selected item—so if the list is empty our program has a bug.

Strictly speaking this method isn't necessary since users can achieve the same thing by selecting the relevant items and changing the angle and shears in the TransformWidget to 0.0. But having the method is convenient—merely requiring the user to click a toolbar button, rather than to set three spinboxes to 0.0. And if support for scaling were added to the application, this method would be even more convenient, because without it the user would have to set up to five spinboxes to 0.0.

Enhancing an Existing Graphics Item

In this subsection we will look at the BoxItem subclass which multiply inherits QObject and QGraphicsRectItem. This class has more custom behavior than the previous subsection's TextItem class. In particular, the user can move a box item by dragging it or by pressing an arrow key with the Ctrl key held down (⌘ key on Mac OS X), and they can resize the box by Shift+Clicking a corner and then dragging or by pressing an arrow key with the Shift key held down.

```
class BoxItem : public QObject, public QGraphicsRectItem
{
    Q_OBJECT
```

```
    Q_PROPERTY(QBrush brush READ brush WRITE setBrush)
    Q_PROPERTY(QPen pen READ pen WRITE setPen)
    ...
public:
    enum {Type = BoxItemType};

    explicit BoxItem(const QRect &rect, QGraphicsScene *scene);
    int type() const { return Type; }
    ...
signals:
    void dirty();

public slots:
    void setPen(const QPen &pen);
    void setBrush(const QBrush &brush);
    ...
protected:
    QVariant itemChange(GraphicsItemChange change,
                        const QVariant &value);
    void keyPressEvent(QKeyEvent *event);
    void mousePressEvent(QGraphicsSceneMouseEvent *event);
    void mouseMoveEvent(QGraphicsSceneMouseEvent *event);
    void mouseReleaseEvent(QGraphicsSceneMouseEvent *event);
    ...
};
```

We have elided the angle and shear properties, accessors, and slots, since they are the same as for the TextItem we saw in the previous subsection.

The constructor's implementation (not shown) is very similar to the TextItem constructor we saw in the previous subsection, only for BoxItems we set an additional flag (QGraphicsItem::ItemIsFocusable) so that they can receive keyboard events, and of course we set the QGraphicsRectItem's base class's rectangle to that passed to the constructor. The BoxItem also has a private m_resizing variable of type bool, in addition to the same private angle and shear doubles as TextItems.

The BoxItem has public slots for setting its pen, brush, angle, and shears, and reimplements the protected itemChange(), keyPressEvent(), mousePressEvent(), mouseMoveEvent(), and mouseReleaseEvent() event handlers. We will review all the event handlers except for itemChange() which is the same as for the TextItem. Of the slots, we will review only setBrush() since the setPen() slot is structurally identical, and the setAngle() and setShear() slots are the same as those in the TextItem that we have already seen. We will start with the setBrush() slot.

```
void BoxItem::setBrush(const QBrush &brush_)
{
    if (isSelected() && brush_ != brush()) {
        QGraphicsRectItem::setBrush(brush_);
```

```
            emit dirty();
        }
    }
```

Since all items that have a brush property are connected to the BrushWidget, we only apply a brush change to an item if it is selected—and then only if the new brush is different from the old one. If a new brush is set we emit dirty() to notify any interested objects.

```
void BoxItem::keyPressEvent(QKeyEvent *event)
{
    if (event->modifiers() & Qt::ShiftModifier ||
        event->modifiers() & Qt::ControlModifier) {
        bool move = event->modifiers() & Qt::ControlModifier;
        bool changed = true;
        double dx1 = 0.0;
        double dy1 = 0.0;
        double dx2 = 0.0;
        double dy2 = 0.0;
        switch (event->key()) {
            case Qt::Key_Left:
                if (move)
                    dx1 = -1.0;
                dx2 = -1.0;
                break;
                ...
            default:
                changed = false;
        }
        if (changed) {
            setRect(rect().adjusted(dx1, dy1, dx2, dy2));
            event->accept();
            emit dirty();
            return;
        }
    }
    QGraphicsRectItem::keyPressEvent(event);
}
```

We have provided keyboard support for moving items (Ctrl+*arrow* or ⌘+*arrow* on Mac OS X), and for resizing items (Shift+*arrow*). (In QGraphicsViews, using the arrow keys without using a keyboard modifier scrolls the view.) In both cases we compute *x*- and *y*-coordinate differences depending on which arrow key was pressed and then reset the box's rectangle to a new rectangle based on the current one but adjusted by the computed coordinate differences. If we have handled the key press, we accept the event (so that Qt can forget about it), emit dirty() since a move or resizing is a significant change, and return; otherwise we pass on the key processing to the base class to handle (which in this case means the key press will be ignored).

```
void BoxItem::mousePressEvent(QGraphicsSceneMouseEvent *event)
{
    if (event->modifiers() & Qt::ShiftModifier) {
        m_resizing = true;
        setCursor(Qt::SizeAllCursor);
    }
    else
        QGraphicsRectItem::mousePressEvent(event);
}
```

Since we set the QGraphicsItem::ItemIsMovable flag, the user can move box items simply by clicking and dragging. We have extended the box's behavior by providing support for resizing, both using the keyboard as we have just seen, and also by Shift+Clicking and then dragging.

If the user clicks with the Shift key held down, we initiate resizing by setting m_resizing to true and changing the mouse cursor.

```
void BoxItem::mouseMoveEvent(QGraphicsSceneMouseEvent *event)
{
    if (m_resizing) {
        QRectF rectangle = rect();
        if (event->pos().x() < rectangle.x())
            rectangle.setBottomLeft(event->pos());
        else
            rectangle.setBottomRight(event->pos());
        setRect(rectangle);
    }
    else
        QGraphicsRectItem::mouseMoveEvent(event);
}
```

If resizing is in progress we simply update the box's rectangle's bottom left or right corner to match the current mouse position. A more sophisticated algorithm would handle the x- and y-coordinates separately, but what we have here is sufficient to illustrate the idea.

```
void BoxItem::mouseReleaseEvent(QGraphicsSceneMouseEvent *event)
{
    if (m_resizing) {
        m_resizing = false;
        setCursor(Qt::ArrowCursor);
        emit dirty();
    }
```

```
        else
            QGraphicsRectItem::mouseReleaseEvent(event);
    }
```

Once the user releases the mouse during resizing, we switch off resizing and restore the mouse cursor. We also emit dirty() because resizing an item is a significant change.

We have now covered almost all of the BoxItem class. We won't show the streaming operators since they are very similar to those used for TextItems, only instead of writing and reading a string of HTML, we write and read the box's rectangle, pen, and brush instead.

Creating a Custom Graphics Item from Scratch

In this subsection we will review the SmileyItem class, a QGraphicsItem subclass that provides code for both its appearance and its behavior. For Qt 4.5 and earlier we must inherit both QObject and QGraphicsItem, but for Qt 4.6 and later we only need to inherit QGraphicsObject. Since the definition in the header file is rather long we have elided the properties and their accessors and slots (which are all the same as those for BoxItems), as well as the private parts.

```
class SmileyItem : public QGraphicsObject
{
    ...
public:
    enum Face {Happy, Sad, Neutral};
    enum {Type = SmileyItemType};

    explicit SmileyItem(const QPoint &position,
                        QGraphicsScene *scene);
    int type() const { return Type; }
    ...
    Face face() const { return m_face; }
    bool isShowingHat() const { return m_showHat; }

    void paint(QPainter *painter,
            const QStyleOptionGraphicsItem *option, QWidget *widget);
    QRectF boundingRect() const;
    QPainterPath shape() const;
signals:
    void dirty();

public slots:
    ...
    void setFace(Face face);
    void setShowHat(bool on);
```

```
        void edit();

protected:
        QVariant itemChange(GraphicsItemChange change,
                            const QVariant &value);
        void mouseDoubleClickEvent(QGraphicsSceneMouseEvent*) { edit(); }
        void contextMenuEvent(QGraphicsSceneContextMenuEvent*) { edit(); }
        ...
};
```

In addition to the standard Type enum we have also provided a class-specific enum to indicate which kind of face the item is to have. And since we are handling the item's appearance ourselves, we must also provide reimplementations of the paint(), boundingRect(), and shape() methods.

To provide the item's behavior we have provided various public slots (only a few of which are shown) to set the item's properties, and also a dirty() signal and an edit() slot to fit in with the conventions we have adopted for the Page Designer application.

As usual, we have reimplemented itemChange() so that we can emit the dirty() signal when appropriate. We have also provided two means of invoking the item's edit() slot—mouse double click, which is a Page Designer convention, and context menu invocation, since for this item the edit action is to pop up a menu.

The private data (not shown) is used to keep track of the pen, brush, face, whether the hat is to be shown, and the angle and shears. We also keep two painter paths—the face path is simply an ellipse, while the hat path is a more complex eight-point polygon.

The constructor (not shown) is similar to the one used for TextItems, only we set initial values for the private data (happy face, no pen, yellow brush, not showing hat, angle of 0.0°, and shears of 0.0), and call the createPaths() helper method to create the face and hat paths.

```
const int SmileySize = 60;
...
void SmileyItem::createPaths()
{
    m_facePath.addEllipse(-SmileyHalfSize, -SmileyHalfSize,
                          SmileySize, SmileySize);

    const int LeftX = -(SmileyHalfSize + (SmileyMargin / 2));
    const int RightX = SmileyHalfSize - (SmileyMargin / 2);
    const int Y = -SmileyHalfSize + (SmileyMargin / 2);
    QPolygonF polygon;
    polygon << QPointF(LeftX * 1.4, Y + SmileyMargin)
            ...
            << QPointF(LeftX * 1.4, Y + SmileyMargin);
```

```
        m_hatPath.addPolygon(polygon);
    }
```

We have elided most of the points used for the hat's polygon, and also most
of the constants. The hat's shape can be seen in the smiley item shown in
Figure 12.4.

```
void SmileyItem::setFace(Face face)
{
    if (m_face != face) {
        m_face = face;
        update();
        emit dirty();
    }
}
```

This method is used to change the face. If the new face setting is different from
the current one the private variable is updated, `update()` is called to schedule a
repaint, and `dirty()` is emitted, since a change of face is a significant change.

We won't show the `setPen()`, `setBrush()`, `setAngle()`, `setShear()`, or `itemChange()`
methods, since all of them have the same code as we have seen in the previous
two subsections.

```
void SmileyItem::setShowHat(bool on)
{
    if (m_showHat != on) {
        prepareGeometryChange();
        m_showHat = on;
        emit dirty();
    }
}
```

This slot is used to show or hide the hat. Clearly, the bounding box and shape
of the item will be different depending on whether the hat is shown, so we *must*
notify the graphics/view architecture that the item's geometry is changing.
This is easily done by calling `QGraphicsItem::prepareGeometryChange()`—which
in turn calls `update()` which is why we don't need to call it ourselves.

```
void SmileyItem::edit()
{
    QMenu menu;
    QAction *showHatAction = createMenuAction(&menu, QIcon(),
            tr("Show Hat"), m_showHat);
    connect(showHatAction, SIGNAL(triggered(bool)),
            this, SLOT(setShowHat(bool)));
    menu.addSeparator();
```

```
QActionGroup *group = new QActionGroup(this);
createMenuAction(&menu, QIcon(":/smileysmile.png"),
        tr("Happy"), m_face == Happy, group, Happy);
...
AQP::accelerateMenu(&menu);
QAction *chosen = menu.exec(QCursor::pos());
if (chosen && chosen != showHatAction)
    setFace(static_cast<Face>(chosen->data().toInt()));
}
```

For this item type we have set its edit action to pop up a context menu. The menu offers the ability to show or hide the hat and to choose the face; it is shown in Figure 12.4.

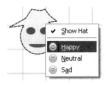

Figure 12.4 *The Page Designer application's smiley context menu*

We've elided the creation of the neutral and sad face actions since the code is structurally the same as for the happy face—and in all three cases we pass on most of the work to a helper method. For the showHatAction, we make a direct signal–slot connection to the item's setShowHat() slot, so that action takes care of itself. But for the face choosing actions we haven't made any connections at all. Instead, if the user chooses an action—they don't have to; they could click Esc to cancel the menu—we check to see what action they have chosen, and if they chose one at all and it isn't the showHatAction, then it must be one of the face choosing actions, so we call setFace(). In the createMenuAction() method, we associate the appropriate Face enum value with each action, so we can extract and use it to choose the face the user specified.

```
QAction *SmileyItem::createMenuAction(QMenu *menu, const QIcon &icon,
        const QString &text, bool checked, QActionGroup *group,
        const QVariant &data)
{
    QAction *action = menu->addAction(icon, text);
    action->setCheckable(true);
    action->setChecked(checked);
    if (group)
        group->addAction(action);
    action->setData(data);
    return action;
}
```

This small convenience helper method saves us a few lines of code in the edit()
slot. The action group ensures that only one of the items in the group is ever
checked at any one time.

We have now covered the methods and slots that provide the item's behavior
(apart from those shown in earlier subsections). The streaming operators are
much the same as for TextItems, only instead of writing and reading an HTML
string we write and read the item's face (converting the enum to and from a
qint16), pen, brush, and whether the hat is showing. So now we can finish off by
covering the painting and the shape() and boundingRect() reimplementations.

```
void SmileyItem::paint(QPainter *painter,
        const QStyleOptionGraphicsItem*, QWidget*)
{
    paintFace(painter);
    if (m_showHat)
        paintHat(painter);
    if (isSelected())
        paintSelectionOutline(painter);
}
```

We've refactored this method so that it shows the high-level logic without
getting bogged down with any of the details. In all cases we paint the face, then
we paint the hat if that's required, and finally we paint the selection indicating
outline if the item is selected.

```
void SmileyItem::paintFace(QPainter *painter)
{
    painter->setPen(m_pen);
    painter->setBrush(m_brush);
    painter->drawPath(m_facePath);
    int leftX = -SmileyHalfSize + SmileyMargin;
    int rightX = SmileyHalfSize - SmileyEyeWidth - SmileyMargin;
    paintEyes(painter, leftX, rightX);
    paintMouth(painter, leftX, rightX);
}
```

To paint the face we draw the face path (an ellipse), and then draw the eyes and
mouth on top of it.

```
void SmileyItem::paintEyes(QPainter *painter, int leftX, int rightX)
{
    int y = -SmileyHalfSize + qRound(SmileyMargin * 1.5);
    painter->setBrush(m_brush.color().darker());
    painter->drawEllipse(leftX, y, SmileyEyeWidth, SmileyEyeHeight);
    painter->drawEllipse(rightX, y, SmileyEyeWidth, SmileyEyeHeight);
}
```

Using Off-Screen Rendering

The performance of graphics/view-based applications depends on what is rendered and how it is rendered. If our custom item needs to draw complex shapes, text, or gradients, or to apply complex clipping, our application's performance may suffer.

If slow and complex rendering is required, one solution is to create an image of the item using an image editing application, and in our QGraphicsItem::paint() reimplementation, load the image into a QPixmap and draw the pixmap. In most cases, drawing a single pixmap will outperform classic piece-by-piece rendering. Unfortunately, this approach has many limitations, the most obvious being that the pixmap cannot visually react to state changes (e.g., if the item changes color), and any transformations—such as scaling—are likely to make the pixmap look pixelated and fuzzy.

A more versatile solution is to make use of the off-screen cache that QGraphicsItems provide. By default the CacheMode is QGraphicsItem::NoCache, but if we enable caching by calling QGraphicsItem::setCacheMode(), the cached item will render itself into a pixmap. We can manually set the size of the pixmap by passing a QSize as a second argument to setCacheMode(); otherwise the size will be calculated for us based on the item's boundingRect(). This pixmap is then reused for subsequent exposures of the same item, completely eliminating calls to QGraphicsItem::paint(). The cache operates transparently, so whenever we call update(), the pixmap will be updated before the item is rendered.

We can, of course, enable caching for existing items, such as QGraphicsTextItem, to speed up rendering when this makes sense. Be aware, however, that extensive use of caching may exhaust the machine's graphics memory.

The cache has two operating modes that determine which coordinate system is used. If we use the ItemCoordinateCache mode, the item will be rendered in local coordinates. This mode converts the item's logical units into pixels, which means that the visual result will degrade if we scale or zoom the item or the view—for example, if we zoom in, the item will look pixelated and fuzzy. In this mode the cache persists when the item is transformed. This makes the mode ideal for items that use animated transformations such as being rotated—for example, in OpenGL applications that have lots of transformations.

The second cache mode, DeviceCoordinateCache, renders the item in device coordinates. This mode ensures a pixel-perfect visual result, with transformations of the item resulting in the cache being regenerated to keep the visual result correct. In fact, the cache remains valid as long as we only move the item or scroll the view, so it is only regenerated if, say, the item is rotated. This makes the mode very fast—for example, much faster than painting when items are moved—and convenient, since it always renders perfectly.

The eyes are just two ellipses painted with a slightly darker brush than we use for the face itself.

```
void SmileyItem::paintMouth(QPainter *painter, int leftX, int rightX)
{
    int y = SmileyHalfSize - qRound(SmileyMargin * 1.1);
    int offset = 0;
    if (m_face == Neutral)
        offset = SmileyMargin;
    else {
        offset = SmileyMargin / 2;
        if (m_face == Happy)
            y -= SmileyMargin;
        else if (m_face == Sad)
            y -= SmileyMargin / 2;
    }
    QPointF leftPoint(leftX + offset, y);
    QPointF rightPoint(rightX + SmileyEyeWidth - offset, y);
    QRectF mouthRect(leftPoint, rightPoint);
    mouthRect.setHeight(m_face == Neutral ? SmileyMargin / 2
                                          : SmileyMargin);
    if (m_face == Neutral)
        painter->drawRoundedRect(mouthRect, 5, 5);
    else if (m_face == Happy)
        painter->drawChord(mouthRect, 170 * 16, 200 * 16);
    else
        painter->drawChord(mouthRect, 30 * 16, 120 * 16);
}
```

This is the most complicated part that must be drawn. For a neutral face's mouth we draw a rounded rectangle, but for happy and sad faces we draw the mouth as a chord, with the ends pointing up or down accordingly. The QPainter::drawRoundedRect() method takes a rectangle and the radii of the ellipses used to define the rounded corners, while the QPainter::drawChord() method takes a rectangle, a start position angle, and a span angle—with both angles specified in $\frac{1}{16}$ of a degree.

```
void SmileyItem::paintHat(QPainter *painter)
{
    QPen pen(m_pen);
    if (pen.style() != Qt::NoPen)
        pen.setColor(pen.color().lighter());
    painter->setPen(pen);
    QBrush brush(m_brush);
    if (brush.style() != Qt::NoBrush)
        brush.setColor(brush.color().lighter());
```

```
        painter->setBrush(brush);
        painter->drawPath(m_hatPath);
    }
```

If the hat is to be painted we use a slightly lighter pen (or no pen) and a slightly
lighter brush (or no brush), and then simply draw the hat painter path.

```
    void SmileyItem::paintSelectionOutline(QPainter *painter)
    {
        QPen pen(Qt::DashLine);
        pen.setColor(Qt::black);
        painter->setPen(pen);
        painter->setBrush(Qt::NoBrush);
        painter->drawPath(m_showHat ? m_facePath.united(m_hatPath)
                                    : m_facePath);
    }
```

To paint a selection outline we have chosen to use a dashed black 1 pixel wide
cosmetic (i.e., unscaled) pen, and no brush. We draw the outline by drawing
the face path, or the face path united with the hat path if the hat is showing.

```
    QRectF SmileyItem::boundingRect() const
    {
        QRectF rect(-SmileyHalfSize, -SmileyHalfSize, SmileySize,
                    SmileySize);
        if (m_showHat)
            rect = rect.united(m_hatPath.boundingRect());
        return rect;
    }
```

For the bounding rectangle, we could have used the statement QRectF rect(
m_facePath.boundingRect()); but we have opted to do a simpler and faster
computation instead based on the item's size. However, if the hat is showing,
we extend the rectangle to incorporate the hat's bounding rectangle.

```
    QPainterPath SmileyItem::shape() const
    {
        QPainterPath path;
        path.addPath(m_facePath);
        if (m_showHat)
            path.addPath(m_hatPath);
        return path;
    }
```

The item's shape is easy to calculate since it is either the face's path, or the
face's path combined with the hat's path.

We have now completed our review of the Page Designer application, including its graphics items. There are many improvements that could be made to the application, the most obvious being the addition of new shapes. This should be easy to do since every new shape could follow the pattern of the box, smiley, or text items that are already supported. It would also be a good idea to get rid of the guideline items and provide the guideline grid using a background brush or by reimplementing QGraphicsView::drawBackground(). And, of course, we have already mentioned some other features that could be added such as distributing items. Adding drag and drop support would be nice too, that is, allowing the user to drag from a shape toolbar button such as the smiley, and drop it onto the page. Of course, just clicking the toolbar button is easier, but with drag and drop the user can drop the item exactly where they want it to be. A much larger and more complex improvement would be to make use of Qt's undo/redo architecture so that users could undo and redo all their actions.* We leave all these as an exercise.

This also brings us to the end of our coverage of Qt's graphics/view architecture. Our examples have taken the classic Qt approach where the behavior and appearance of widgets (or graphics items) are provided by those widgets (or items) themselves. But when we have scenes containing thousands or tens of thousands of items we may prefer to use a different approach. Instead of making each item a QObject subclass, we might rely instead on the facilities offered by QGraphicsScene and QGraphicsView to provide item-specific behaviors. For example, we could create a scene or view subclass, reimplement its key press and mouse event handlers, and use the various items() methods to see which item was interacted with, and apply changes to it accordingly. The graphics/view architecture is very rich, and has improved in speed and quality with each new Qt release. It is well worth learning about and experimenting with, and the demos and examples that Qt provides are interesting to study.

---

*Qt provides two graphics/view examples that show undo/redo—examples/tools/undoframework for the basics, and demos/undo for more advanced features. Qt's documentation provides an overview of the undo/redo framework, and there is also an article by this author introducing it—using PyQt4—at www.informit.com/articles/article.aspx?p=1187104.

13

- Introducing the Animation Framework
- Introducing the State Machine Framework
- Combining Animations and State Machines

The Animation and State Machine Frameworks

Qt 4.6 introduced many new features, including two major frameworks: the animation framework (part of the "Kinetic" project), and the state machine framework. In this chapter we will briefly introduce both of these frameworks.* Doing animations in Qt has always been possible using timers, and this was made a great deal easier when Qt 4.2 introduced the QTimeLine class. (We very briefly mentioned this class in an earlier chapter; 133 ◄.) The new animation framework in Qt 4.6 provides a higher-level, more flexible, and more sophisticated approach to animations.

In the chapter's first section we will introduce the animation framework and present a small modification to Chapter 12's Page Designer application (pagedesigner2) to animate the alignment of graphics items rather than having them jump immediately into position. In the chapter's second section we will introduce the state machine framework and present a modified version of Chapter 11's Petri Dish application (petridish2), showing how to implement the application's logic using a state machine rather than managing it all ourselves. And in the final section we will present a small dialog that makes use of both the animation and state machine frameworks to show how they can be used together, and where the animation is of standard widgets rather than of the graphics items shown in this chapter's first section.

Introducing the Animation Framework

Qt's animation framework is quite sophisticated, but the fundamental concepts are easy to understand. The underlying theory is based on David Harel's fi-

---

*Unlike all the previous chapters' examples, the examples presented in this chapter use Qt 4.6-specific features and will not compile with Qt 4.5.

nite Statecharts, with the semantics of the state machine's execution based on SCXML (State Chart XML). In practical terms, the framework is based on QObjects and Qt's property system. The simplest approach is to create a QPropertyAnimation for each property of each QObject we want to animate, and to give the property animation a duration, an initial value, and a final value.

All property animations operate on QVariants, and the properties concerned must be writable (i.e., they must have a setter). For Qt 4.6 the QVariant types that can be animated—that is, those types that Qt can interpolate values for—are int, float, double, QColor, QLine, QLineF, QPoint, QPointF, QRect, QRectF, QSize, and QSizeF.

For example, we might give a duration of 5000 milliseconds and initial and final geometries specified as QRects. Once the animation is started the object will immediately be set to the initial geometry, and then its geometry will be changed over a 5 second period to reach the final geometry, with Qt setting the intermediate geometry values using linear interpolation. So, if the initial width was 100 pixels and the final width 400 pixels, the width would be 160 pixels after 1 second, 220 pixels after 2 seconds, 280 pixels after 3 seconds, 340 pixels after 4 seconds, and finally, 400 pixels after 5 seconds. (In this case the increment is 60 pixels per second calculated from the difference between the final and initial widths divided by the duration, i.e., $\frac{400-100}{5} = 60$. Of course, Qt will use a much finer time granularity than seconds, so the actual change of width might be from 100 pixels to 103 pixels to 106 pixels and so on.)

Although the animation framework is simple to use for simple cases, we can easily achieve more advanced effects. For one thing, we are not limited to linear interpolation—Qt provides the QEasingCurve class which offers over forty different interpolation graphs. Also, animations can be grouped and executed either sequentially or in parallel. The animation framework can be used with the graphics/view architecture—but only with items that are QObjects—or with ordinary QWidgets.

In this section we will show a very short and simple example that adds animation to the manipulation of some graphics items; in the chapter's last section we will look at a more complex animation that involves widgets.

The Page Designer application has alignment actions that allow the user to line up two or more selected graphics items to the left-most (or right-most, or top-most, or bottom-most) item. The alignment occurs immediately, with the items jumping into their new positions too fast for the eye to see. It would be nice to provide some visual feedback to the user to show them which items are being aligned and for them to see the alignment actually take place. We must, of course, be careful not to make the alignment too slow since that would be irritating.

The code for doing the alignment is in the editAlign() slot that we discussed in Chapter 12's "Manipulating Selected Items" subsubsection (430 ◄). We originally reviewed the slot in three parts, with the alignment being performed in the last part. Here is a new version of that last part, only this time instead of calling QGraphicsItem::moveBy() on each item in the loops, we merely record what the new position should be.

```
QList<QPointF> positions;
if (alignment == Qt::AlignLeft || alignment == Qt::AlignRight) {
    for (int i = 0; i < items.count(); ++i)
        positions << items.at(i)->pos() +
                     QPointF(offset - coordinates.at(i), 0);
}
else {
    for (int i = 0; i < items.count(); ++i)
        positions << items.at(i)->pos() +
                     QPointF(0, offset - coordinates.at(i));
}

animateAlignment(items, positions);
setDirty(true);
```

At the end of whichever loop is executed we know the new position that each item should occupy. We call the custom animateAlignment() method to perform the moves, passing it the list of items and a parallel list of the new positions.

```
void MainWindow::animateAlignment(const QList<QGraphicsItem*> &items,
                                  const QList<QPointF> &positions)
{
    int duration = ((qApp->keyboardModifiers() & Qt::ShiftModifier)
                    != Qt::ShiftModifier) ? 1000 : 5000;
    for (int i = 0; i < items.count(); ++i) {
        QObject *object = dynamic_cast<QObject*>(items.at(i));
        if (!object)
            continue;
        QPropertyAnimation *animation = new QPropertyAnimation(
                object, "pos", this);
        animation->setDuration(duration);
        animation->setEasingCurve(QEasingCurve::InOutBack);
        animation->setKeyValueAt(0.0, items.at(i)->pos());
        animation->setKeyValueAt(1.0, positions.at(i));
        animation->start(QAbstractAnimation::DeleteWhenStopped);
    }
}
```

We have set a duration of 1 second—or 5 seconds if the Shift key is held down. One second is long enough for normal use, but if we want to see the effect of the animation more slowly to show it off, or to help us see how it works during development, then we can press Shift to make it take a more leisurely 5 seconds. (Note that the `QApplication::keyboardModifiers()` method returns the modifiers that were in force at the last key press event. There is also a similar `QApplication::mouseButtons()` method.)

We iterate over every item that is to be aligned. For each one we create a new `QPropertyAnimation`, giving it the `QObject` it is to operate on (recall that all of the graphics items apart from the guideline grid items in the Page Designer application are `QObjects`), the name of the property to animate, and a parent. (As noted in Chapter 12, the use of `dynamic_cast<>()` makes the application dependent on the availability of RTTI—Run Time Type Information—although there are various ways to avoid this; 424 ◄.)

You might remember that when we reviewed the Page Designer's custom items and saw their properties none of them had a `pos` property. In fact, we didn't show that property because it wasn't relevant at the time, but every one has the following property declaration:

```
Q_PROPERTY(QPointF pos READ pos WRITE setPos)
```

This is in addition to the other property declarations that we saw. The getter and setter are provided by the `QGraphicsItem` base class, so nothing more is needed to get a `pos` property.

Once the property animation has been created we set its duration, its easing curve (which is optional and defaults to `QEasingCurve::Linear`), and its initial and final property values. The `QPropertyAnimation::setKeyValueAt()` method is used to set a property value for a particular point in the animation, where 0.0 is the start and 1.0 is the end. Here, we have set the start value of the `pos` property to be the item's current position, and the end value of the `pos` property to be the item's aligned position. We can set intermediate values too, for example, at 0.5, or at 0.3 and 0.6, and so on. If we have only a start and an end value, as here, we could instead use `QPropertyAnimation::setStartValue()` and `QPropertyAnimation::setEndValue()` which both take a single `QVariant`; but we preferred to show `setKeyValueAt()` since it is more versatile.

With the animation set up we call `QPropertyAnimation::start()` to start it executing. By default, property animations remain in memory until their parent is deleted, but we don't need the animations after we have finished with them, so we pass a deletion policy to the `start()` method which ensures that the animation will delete itself once it has completed.

The easing curve we chose to use, `QEasingCurve::InOutBack`, provides quite an amusing effect. For example, if the user selects some items and chooses Align Left, what will happen is that the items will all move *right* (the wrong way!), but only a little bit. Then they will bounce back to the left, but instead of stopping at the left-most position they will overshoot. And finally they'll bounce back to be left-aligned with whichever one of them was left-most in the first place.

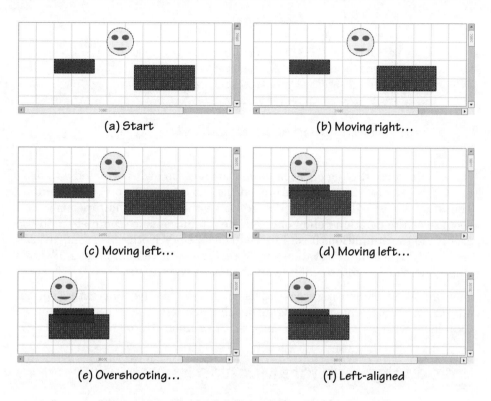

(a) Start   (b) Moving right...

(c) Moving left...   (d) Moving left...

(e) Overshooting...   (f) Left-aligned

Figure 13.1 *Aligning left with an InOutBack easing curve*

And thanks to the interpolations that Qt applies, all of these movements are completely smooth. A left alignment is illustrated in Figure 13.1.

One other point to note is that the animations were started off sequentially. This isn't a problem here in practice since the start() calls return almost immediately. However, if we wanted to be sure that the animations occur in parallel we could achieve this using a QParallelAnimationGroup as the following animateAlignment() implementation shows.

```cpp
void MainWindow::animateAlignment(const QList<QGraphicsItem*> &items,
                                  const QList<QPointF> &positions)
{
    int duration = ((qApp->keyboardModifiers() & Qt::ShiftModifier)
                    != Qt::ShiftModifier) ? 1000 : 5000;
    QParallelAnimationGroup *group = new QParallelAnimationGroup;
    for (int i = 0; i < items.count(); ++i) {
        QObject *object = dynamic_cast<QObject*>(items.at(i));
        if (!object)
            continue;
        QPropertyAnimation *animation = new QPropertyAnimation(
```

```
                        object, "pos", this);
            animation->setDuration(duration);
            animation->setEasingCurve(QEasingCurve::InOutBack);
            animation->setStartValue(items.at(i)->pos());
            animation->setEndValue(positions.at(i));
            group->addAnimation(animation);
        }
        group->start(QAbstractAnimation::DeleteWhenStopped);
    }
```

Here, instead of starting off each animation as soon as it is created we add it to a QParallelAnimationGroup, and only at the end do we start off the animation. The start() call will start all the group's animations simultaneously, and because of the deletion policy, once all the animations are complete both the group and the animations it contains will be deleted. Notice also that we used setStartValue() and setEndValue(), which are more convenient in cases like this where there are no intermediate values that we want to use.

Qt's animation framework is easy to use and very effective for creating special effects. We'll make use of it again in this chapter's last section when we combine it with a state machine and use it to animate standard QWidgets.

Introducing the State Machine Framework

The state machine framework provides a means of maintaining state in complex applications. For simple dialogs and main windows the framework offers no real benefits—in fact, it can require much more code. However, as complexity increases, the state machine framework becomes more and more attractive, since it scales very well and makes managing complex states much easier than doing everything by hand.

The user interfaces for some kinds of applications—such as calculators and media players—are intrinsically stateful. Keeping track of the state (such as degrees/radians, playing/paused, and so on) can be quite tricky using variables, especially if there are nested states. In these cases, using a state machine can be very advantageous, with the state machine diagram serving as useful documentation, and with maintenance often a matter of simply adding or removing transitions.

Using Qt's state machine framework is quite straightforward and only involves understanding a few basic concepts. And like the animation framework, it is heavily dependent on QObjects and Qt's property system. To set up a state machine we begin by creating a QStateMachine. Then we create the states we need (these are instances of QState or QFinalState), and for each state we specify triples of (QObject, property, value), so that the state machine knows that in the given state the object's property must be set to the given value. Once the states have been set up we then create the transitions—these specify how the state machine goes from one state to another. For example, clicking a particular button in a particular state might switch the state machine into another state.

Whenever a change of state occurs the state that has been left emits an exited() signal, and the state that has been entered emits an entered() signal. When (and if) the state machine finishes, it emits a finished() signal.

Once everything is set up we tell the state machine which state to use as its initial state and then call QStateMachine::start() to start things off.

Even as described here, the state machine framework is very powerful and flexible, but it has far more functionality than we have mentioned so far. For example, states can be grouped, state histories can be tracked so that states can be saved and restored, parallel states can be set up, and much more besides. Nor is the framework confined to graphics—it could just as easily be applied to modeling a network communications protocol.

In this section we will show how to use the state machine in practice by creating a new version of the Petri Dish application (in the petridish2 examples directory and shown in Figure 11.3; 394 ◄). Recall that the application has four buttons, Start, Pause/Resume, Stop, and Quit, an Initial count spinbox, and a Show IDs checkbox. The simulation might be running, paused, or stopped, and in each case we must make sure that the correct widgets are enabled or disabled and that in the case of the Pause/Resume button it shows the correct text. In the original version (petridish1), we achieved this by having a SimulationState enum and start(), pauseOrResume(), and stop() slots which not only effected the appropriate simulation behavior but also enabled/disabled the widgets and set the Pause/Resume button's text.

For the state machine Petri Dish, we don't need the enum, the start() slot is concerned purely with setting up the simulation, the thirteen line pauseOrResume() slot is replaced with a two line pause() slot, and the six line stop() slot has been eliminated altogether. Nonetheless, the state machine version's mainwindow.cpp file is about forty lines longer than the original. This is because there is more setup code for the state machine. However, if the complexity of the states were to increase, or if more states were added, at some point the state machine version would almost certainly have fewer lines of code since it will scale better.

Before diving into the code it is best to make a plan identifying the states that are required and how we are going to transition between them. There are three obvious states that will be needed: stopped, running, and paused. But in addition, we will create an initial state where we can do any setup that's necessary at application startup, and a final state which we can use to do any cleanup and to stop the application. And since we want the user to be able to quit the application at any time we will create the "normal" state which will serve as a parent state for the stopped, paused, and running states, so that no

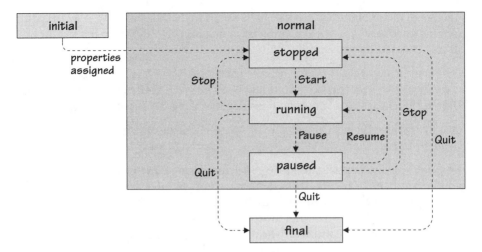

Figure 13.2 *The Petri Dish state transitions*

matter which of these states is active, the normal state is also active and can be used to transition to the final state.

As soon as the initial state's properties have been set we can transition into the stopped state. If the user clicks the Start button we will transition into the running state. In the running state the user could click the Stop button in which case we must transition back to the stopped state, or the Pause/Resume button in which case we must transition to the paused state. In the paused state the user could click the Stop button in which case we must transition back to the stopped state, or the Pause/Resume button in which case we must transition to the running state. Since the stopped, running, and paused states are all children of the normal state, after the initial state has been left, the state machine is always in the normal state (and some child state, such as running). If the user clicks the Quit button we must transition from the normal state (no matter what the current child state) to the final state. The transitions are illustrated in Figure 13.2.

Now that we have an overview of what needs to be done we will look at the code. We'll start with some extracts from the header file.

```
    Q_PROPERTY(bool running READ running WRITE setRunning)
    ...
private:
    ...
    bool running() const { return m_running; }
    void setRunning(bool running) { m_running = running; }
    ...
    QStateMachine stateMachine;
    QState *initialState;
    QState *normalState;
```

```
QState *stoppedState;
QState *runningState;
QState *pausedState;
QFinalState *finalState;

bool m_running;
```

We use the running property to keep track of whether the simulation is currently running. We have a state machine and one QState for each state plus a QFinalState for the final state.* We also have the private m_running Boolean to store the running property's value.

```
MainWindow::MainWindow(QWidget *parent)
    : QMainWindow(parent), iterations(0), m_running(false)
{
    scene = new QGraphicsScene(this);
    scene->setItemIndexMethod(QGraphicsScene::NoIndex);

    createWidgets();
    createProxyWidgets();
    createLayout();
    createCentralWidget();

    createStates();
    createTransitions();
    createConnections();

    setWindowTitle(tr("%1 (State Machine)")
                    .arg(QApplication::applicationName()));

    stateMachine.setInitialState(initialState);
    QTimer::singleShot(0, &stateMachine, SLOT(start()));
}
```

The constructor is very similar to the original version, only this time we create the states and transitions, set up some signal–slot connections (different from and fewer than before), give the state machine its initial state, and start it off. As usual, we use a single shot timer to ensure that the window is fully constructed before we start processing. Now we will review the createStates(), createTransitions(), and createConnections() methods. For ease of explanation we will review the createStates() method in four short parts.

```
void MainWindow::createStates()
{
    initialState = new QState(&stateMachine);
```

---

*Due to a subtle bug known to affect Qt 4.6.0–4.6.2 on Windows and Mac OS X, for this particular example, we had to change the QStates and the QFinalState member variables into module variables in the .cpp file using #if statements, to prevent the application from crashing at startup.

```
initialState->assignProperty(showIdsCheckBox, "checked", true);
initialState->assignProperty(initialCountSpinBox, "minimum", 1);
initialState->assignProperty(initialCountSpinBox, "maximum", 100);
initialState->assignProperty(initialCountSpinBox, "value", 60);
```

We begin by creating our first state as a child of the state machine, and set some property triples using the QState::assignProperty() method. These calls do *not* set the given objects' properties to the given values! Instead, they record that if and when this state is entered, the given objects must have these properties set to the specified values.

```
normalState = new QState(&stateMachine);

runningState = new QState(normalState);
runningState->assignProperty(startButton, "enabled", false);
runningState->assignProperty(initialCountSpinBox, "enabled",
                             false);
runningState->assignProperty(stopButton, "enabled", true);
runningState->assignProperty(pauseOrResumeButton, "enabled",
                             true);
runningState->assignProperty(pauseOrResumeButton, "text",
                             tr("Pa&use"));
runningState->assignProperty(this, "running", true);
```

The initial state was created as a child of the state machine itself, and so is the normal state. The normal state exists purely to group states inside it (running, paused, stopped), so that we can have transitions that apply no matter which of the normal state's child states is active. To make this work we must give the child states the normal state as their parent rather than using the state machine.

For the running state we ensure that the Start button and Initial count spinbox are disabled, the Stop and Pause/Resume buttons are enabled, and the latter has the correct text. We also set the main window's running property to true. As noted before, none of these settings is applied at the time of the assignProperty() calls —they only occur when (and if) the state is entered.

```
pausedState = new QState(normalState);
pausedState->assignProperty(pauseOrResumeButton, "text",
                            tr("Res&ume"));
pausedState->assignProperty(this, "running", false);
```

In the paused state we set the Pause/Resume button's text and set the main window's running property to false. In this state the Start button should be disabled, but we don't have to set this explicitly (although it is harmless to do so), because the button is disabled when we enter the running state and the

paused state can only be transitioned to from the running state, so we know
that the Start button is already correctly disabled.

```
        stoppedState = new QState(normalState);
        stoppedState->assignProperty(startButton, "enabled", true);
        stoppedState->assignProperty(initialCountSpinBox, "enabled",
                                     true);
        stoppedState->assignProperty(pauseOrResumeButton, "enabled",
                                     false);
        stoppedState->assignProperty(pauseOrResumeButton, "text",
                                     tr("Pa&use"));
        stoppedState->assignProperty(stopButton, "enabled", false);
        stoppedState->assignProperty(this, "running", false);

        finalState = new QFinalState(&stateMachine);
    }
```

In the stopped state we enable the Start button and the Initial count spinbox,
disable the Pause/Resume button (and set its text), and disable the Stop button.
We also set the running property to false.

We have created the final state purely to provide a state to transition to (from
the normal state) when the user quits, since this saves us from having to create
individual transitions from each of the stopped, paused, and running states.

```
    void MainWindow::createTransitions()
    {
        initialState->addTransition(initialState,
                SIGNAL(propertiesAssigned()), stoppedState);
        stoppedState->addTransition(startButton, SIGNAL(clicked()),
                                     runningState);
        runningState->addTransition(pauseOrResumeButton,
                                     SIGNAL(clicked()), pausedState);
        runningState->addTransition(stopButton, SIGNAL(clicked()),
                                     stoppedState);
        pausedState->addTransition(pauseOrResumeButton,
                                     SIGNAL(clicked()), runningState);
        pausedState->addTransition(stopButton,
                                     SIGNAL(clicked()), stoppedState);
        normalState->addTransition(quitButton, SIGNAL(clicked()),
                                     finalState);
    }
```

The first transition we create is from the initial state to the stopped state. This
transition occurs as soon as the initial state's properties have been assigned.
From the user's point of view this transition happens as soon as the application
starts up (actually when the QStateMachine::start() slot is called once the

window's construction is complete), so the initial state is only entered once, briefly, and from then on the application is in the normal state plus one of its child states (stopped, paused, or running).

For the stopped state we create a transition to the running state. And for the running state we create two transitions, one to the paused state and another to the stopped state. Similarly, for the paused state we create transitions to the running state and to the stopped state. We also create a transition from the normal state (which includes all of its child states) to the final state.

Notice that there are two different transitions that can occur when the Pause/ Resume button is pressed. If we are in the running state, pressing the button causes a transition to the paused state, and if we are in the paused state, pressing the button causes a transition to the running state. This ability to interpret the same button click in two completely different ways is a very powerful feature of the state machine framework. (In the original Petri Dish application we had to create a pauseOrResume() slot that was connected to the button's clicked() signal and that used the button's text to decide whether the user was pausing or resuming; the state machine approach used here is much cleaner and simpler.)

```
void MainWindow::createConnections()
{
    connect(showIdsCheckBox, SIGNAL(toggled(bool)),
            this, SLOT(showIds(bool)));

    connect(runningState, SIGNAL(entered()), this, SLOT(start()));
    connect(pausedState, SIGNAL(entered()),
            this, SLOT(pause()));
    connect(&stateMachine, SIGNAL(finished()), this, SLOT(close()));
}
```

The first connection is quite conventional and is used to update the simulation to show or hide cell IDs.

The other three connections are all state machine related. The connection from the running state's entered() signal means that in addition to the properties being set appropriately when the running state is entered, we also call the start() slot which is used to set up the simulation and to start it running. Similarly, when the paused state is entered, in addition to properties being set we call the pause() slot (which is used purely to make the window slightly transparent, an effect most noticeable on Windows and very subtle on Mac OS X). The last connection is activated when the state machine finishes (i.e., when the final state is entered); here we just use it to close the application.

Qt's state machine framework has a lot more facilities than we made use of in this example. Nonetheless, we have covered the key concepts that the framework uses and seen it in practical use. In the next section we will use a couple of state machines and combine one with the animation framework we covered in the chapter's first section to show more complex effects.

Combining Animations and State Machines

In this section we will review the Find Dialog example (finddialog), a typical example of a dialog used for performing search operations. The dialog uses two independent state machines, one to enable/disable the Find button depending on whether the user has entered any search text, and another that works in conjunction with the animation framework to show or hide extra widgets depending on the state of the More toggle button.

When the dialog first appears the More button is in the "up" position (i.e., unchecked) and the extra widgets are not visible. If the user clicks the More button it goes into the "down" position (i.e., checked), and at the same time the dialog increases in size to allow for the extra widgets. Once the dialog has enlarged, the extra widgets emerge from beneath the More button, initially tiny in size, with a very small font size, and transparent. They grow, increase their font size, and become more opaque, as they slide left and down toward their final positions. By the time the extra widgets have reached their correct positions they are of the right size, have the correct font size, and are completely opaque. This process is illustrated in Figure 13.3. If the user clicks the More button again, it returns to the "up" position, and the extra widgets slide back under the More button, shrinking, decreasing their font size, and becoming transparent as they go. And at the end, the dialog itself shrinks to fit around the visible widgets.

We will start with a brief extract from the dialog's header file to see some of its private member data.

```
QCheckBox *wholeWordsCheckBox;
QLabel *syntaxLabel;
QComboBox *syntaxComboBox;
QList<QWidget*> extraWidgets;

QStateMachine *findStateMachine;
QState *nothingToFindState;
QState *somethingToFindState;

QStateMachine *extraStateMachine;
QState *showExtraWidgetsState;
QState *hideExtraWidgetsState;
```

We have omitted the widgets that are always visible (the line edit, the Find button, and so on), but have shown the extra widgets that are shown or hidden depending on the state of the More button. We also keep a list of the extra widgets so that we can process them all together.

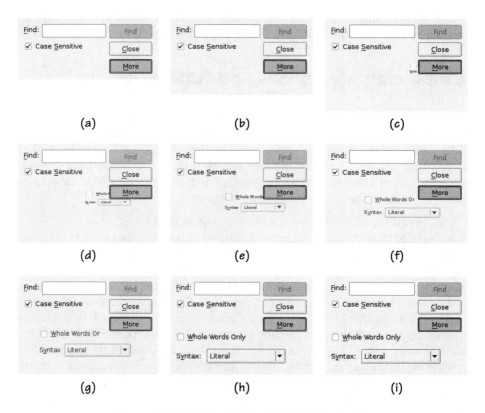

Figure 13.3 *Clicking the FindDialog's More button*

Both state machines have only two states each, and their names should make
their meanings clear.

The constructor (not shown) follows a familiar pattern, creating the widgets,
layout, and connections, and then creating the state machines and transitions.
Here is an extract from the createWidgets() method that shows the creation
and setup of the extra widgets:

```
wholeWordsCheckBox = new QCheckBox(tr("Whole Words Only"), this);
wholeWordsCheckBox->setChecked(false);

syntaxLabel = new QLabel(tr("Syntax:"), this);

syntaxComboBox = new QComboBox(this);
syntaxLabel->setBuddy(syntaxComboBox);
syntaxComboBox->addItem(tr("Literal"), QRegExp::FixedString);
syntaxComboBox->addItem(tr("Regex"), QRegExp::RegExp2);
syntaxComboBox->addItem(tr("Wildcard"), QRegExp::Wildcard);
syntaxComboBox->setCurrentIndex(0);
```

```
        extraWidgets << wholeWordsCheckBox << syntaxLabel
                    << syntaxComboBox;

    foreach (QWidget *widget, extraWidgets) {
        QGraphicsOpacityEffect *effect = new QGraphicsOpacityEffect;
        effect->setOpacity(1.0);
        widget->setGraphicsEffect(effect);
    }
```

The QGraphicsEffect class and its subclasses, QGraphicsBlurEffect, QGraphicsCol-
orizeEffect, QGraphicsDropShadowEffect, and QGraphicsOpacityEffect, were introduced in Qt 4.6. They can be used with the QGraphicsItems in a QGraphicsScene,
or, as here, with ordinary QWidgets. We have added an opacity effect to each of
the extra widgets, setting the initial opacity to 1.0 (fully opaque).

```
    void FindDialog::createStateMachines()
    {
        findStateMachine = new QStateMachine(this);
        createFindStates();
        createFindTransitions();
        findStateMachine->setInitialState(nothingToFindState);
        findStateMachine->start();

        extraStateMachine = new QStateMachine(this);
        createShowExtraWidgetsState();
        createHideExtraWidgetsState();
        createShowExtraWidgetsTransitions();
        createHideExtraWidgetsTransitions();
        extraStateMachine->setInitialState(hideExtraWidgetsState);
        extraStateMachine->start();
    }
```

This method is used to create, set up, and start the two state machines. For
the extra state machine we set up the show and hide states and transitions in
separate helper methods to keep each method a manageable size.

```
    void FindDialog::createFindStates()
    {
        nothingToFindState = new QState(findStateMachine);
        nothingToFindState->assignProperty(findButton, "enabled", false);

        somethingToFindState = new QState(findStateMachine);
        somethingToFindState->assignProperty(findButton, "enabled", true);
    }
```

The find states are very simple: the Find button is enabled or it is disabled.

```
void FindDialog::createFindTransitions()
{
    nothingToFindState->addTransition(this,
            SIGNAL(findTextIsNonEmpty()), somethingToFindState);
    somethingToFindState->addTransition(this,
            SIGNAL(findTextIsEmpty()), nothingToFindState);
}
```

The find state transitions are made depending on whether the find text is empty or not, and like the find states are very simple.

We could have implemented control over the Find button's enabled property using an updateUi() slot as we have done in many earlier examples—and doing so would involve much less code than we have used here. However, using the state machine approach gives us a clean separation of logic into individual states, and should make maintenance and the addition of more functionality much easier and less error-prone than relying on an increasing spaghetti of signal–slot connections.

```
void FindDialog::createConnections()
{
    connect(findTextLineEdit, SIGNAL(textEdited(const QString&)),
            this, SLOT(findTextChanged(const QString&)));
    connect(moreButton, SIGNAL(toggled(bool)),
            this, SLOT(showOrHideExtra(bool)));
    connect(buttonBox, SIGNAL(rejected()), this, SLOT(close()));
}
```

We need to emit a findTextIsEmpty() signal or a findTextIsNonEmpty() signal whenever the find text changes. To do this we connect the find text line edit's textEdited() signal to a custom findTextChanged() slot which emits the signal we need depending on the find text.

Buttons don't have "checked" and "unchecked" signals, only clicked(bool) and toggled(bool), but we need to emit showExtra() and hideExtra() signals, depending on whether the More button is up or down. So, we connect the More button's toggled() signal to a custom showOrHideExtra() slot that emits the correct signal depending on the button's toggled state.

The third signal is used to close the dialog.

```
void FindDialog::findTextChanged(const QString &text)
{
    if (text.isEmpty())
        emit findTextIsEmpty();
    else
        emit findTextIsNonEmpty();
}
```

This slot in effect converts the `QLineEdit::textEdited()` signal into either a `findTextIsEmpty()` signal or a `findTextIsNonEmpty()` signal, and these are used by the find state machine to transition between the nothing to find state and the something to find state.

```
void FindDialog::showOrHideExtra(bool on)
{
    if (on)
        emit showExtra();
    else
        emit hideExtra();
}
```

In effect, this slot is used to convert the `QPushButton::toggled()` signal into either a `showExtra()` signal or a `hideExtra()` signal depending on the More button's toggled state. We will see how these signals are used further on when we look at the extra state machine's transitions, but first we will look at the setting up of the extra state machine's states.

```
void FindDialog::createShowExtraWidgetsState()
{
    QSize size = extraSize();
    size.rheight() += minimumSizeHint().height();
    size.setWidth(qMax(size.width(), minimumSizeHint().width()));

    QList<QRectF> rects;
    int y = sizeHint().height() - margin;
    rects << QRectF(margin, y, wholeWordsCheckBox->sizeHint().width(),
                    wholeWordsCheckBox->sizeHint().height());
    y += wholeWordsCheckBox->sizeHint().height() + margin;
    int height = qMax(syntaxLabel->sizeHint().height(),
                      syntaxComboBox->sizeHint().height());
    int width = syntaxLabel->sizeHint().width();
    rects << QRectF(margin, y, width, height);
    int x = margin + syntaxLabel->sizeHint().width() + margin;
    width = qMin(sizeHint().width(), size.width()) - (x + margin);
    rects << QRectF(x, y, width, height);

    showExtraWidgetsState = new QState(extraStateMachine);
    foreach (QWidget *widget, extraWidgets) {
        showExtraWidgetsState->assignProperty(
                widget, "geometry", rects.takeFirst());
        showExtraWidgetsState->assignProperty(
                widget, "font", font());
        showExtraWidgetsState->assignProperty(
                widget->graphicsEffect(), "opacity", 1.0);
    }
```

```
    showExtraWidgetsState->assignProperty(this, "minimumSize", size);
}
```

For the show extra widgets state we need to provide a geometry (position and size) and a font for each of the extra widgets, and to set their opacity effects to 1.0 (fully opaque). And we also need to set the dialog's minimum size to be large enough to accommodate the extra widgets. All this is achieved in this method.

We begin by computing the additional width and height needed to show the extra widgets and create a size object of type QSize that accounts for this and represents the minimum size the dialog should be. We then create a list of QRectFs holding the geometries of each of the extra widgets. Once we have completed the calculations we create the show extra widgets state. Then, for each extra widget in this state, we assign to the widget's geometry property the corresponding computed rectangle, and to the widget's font property the dialog's font. We also set every extra widget's opacity effect's opacity property to 1.0. (As always, no properties are set at this time; they are only set when and if the relevant state is entered.) Finally, we set the dialog's minimum size to the size we calculated was necessary to show the dialog with all the extra widgets.

```
QSize FindDialog::extraSize() const
{
    const int Width = syntaxLabel->sizeHint().width() +
            syntaxComboBox->sizeHint().width() + (2 * margin);
    const int Height = wholeWordsCheckBox->sizeHint().height() +
            qMax(syntaxLabel->sizeHint().height(),
                syntaxComboBox->sizeHint().height()) + (2 * margin);
    return QSize(Width, Height);
}
```

This helper method calculates the extra width necessary by using the sum of the widths of the syntax label and syntax combobox plus some margin, and the extra height by using the sum of the whole words checkbox, and the tallest of the syntax label and syntax combobox, again plus some margin.

```
void FindDialog::createHideExtraWidgetsState()
{
    QRectF rect = QRectF(buttonBox->x() + (moreButton->width() / 2),
            buttonBox->height() - (moreButton->height() / 2), 1, 1);
    QFont smallFont(font());
    smallFont.setPointSizeF(1.0);

    hideExtraWidgetsState = new QState(extraStateMachine);
    foreach (QWidget *widget, extraWidgets) {
        hideExtraWidgetsState->assignProperty(
                widget, "geometry", rect);
```

```
            hideExtraWidgetsState->assignProperty(
                    widget, "font", smallFont);
            hideExtraWidgetsState->assignProperty(
                    widget->graphicsEffect(), "opacity", 0.0);
    }
    hideExtraWidgetsState->assignProperty(
            this, "minimumSize", minimumSizeHint());
}
```

The hide extra widgets state is a bit simpler than the show extra widgets state since every extra widget gets the same property values. We set each extra widget's geometry property to a 1 × 1 rectangle positioned in the middle of the More button, the font property to a small font, and the graphics effect's opacity property to 0.0 (fully transparent). And finally, we set the dialog's minimum size property to its minimum size hint (which correctly does not account for the extra widgets).

```
const int Duration = 1500;

void FindDialog::createShowExtraWidgetsTransitions()
{
    QSignalTransition *transition =
            hideExtraWidgetsState->addTransition(this,
                    SIGNAL(showExtra()), showExtraWidgetsState);

    createCommonTransitions(transition);

    QPropertyAnimation *animation;
    animation = new QPropertyAnimation(this, "minimumSize");
    animation->setDuration(Duration / 3);
    transition->addAnimation(animation);

    animation = new QPropertyAnimation(this, "size");
    animation->setDuration(Duration / 3);
    QSize size = extraSize();
    size = QSize(qMax(size.width(), width()),
                    sizeHint().height() + size.height());
    animation->setEndValue(size);
    transition->addAnimation(animation);
}
```

We create a transition from the hide extra widgets state to the show extra widgets state that is triggered by the showExtra() signal. We also keep a pointer to the transition so that we can use it to add animations.

For this transition we want to control five properties: the dialog's minimum size and size, and each extra widget's geometry, font, and opacity effect's opacity.

For the extra widgets we have pushed the work onto a helper method since the same property animations are used for showing and hiding the extra widgets.

For the dialog's minimum size and size properties we set up property animations that will take one-third of the time we use to do the widget property animations (i.e., it will happen faster). For the size property we set an end value size that is large enough to accommodate the extra widgets.

```
void FindDialog::createCommonTransitions(
        QSignalTransition *transition)
{
    QPropertyAnimation *animation;
    foreach (QWidget *widget, extraWidgets) {
        animation = new QPropertyAnimation(widget, "geometry");
        animation->setDuration(Duration);
        transition->addAnimation(animation);
        animation = new QPropertyAnimation(widget, "font");
        animation->setDuration(Duration);
        transition->addAnimation(animation);
        if (QGraphicsOpacityEffect *effect =
                static_cast<QGraphicsOpacityEffect*>(
                        widget->graphicsEffect())) {
            animation = new QPropertyAnimation(effect, "opacity");
            animation->setDuration(Duration);
            animation->setEasingCurve(QEasingCurve::OutInCirc);
            transition->addAnimation(animation);
        }
    }
}
```

Whether we are showing or hiding the extra widgets we use the same property animations. For the geometry and font properties (and for the dialog property animations) we use a linear easing curve (since we don't explicitly set an easing curve and linear is the default), but for the opacity we use QEasingCurve::InOutCirc which changes slowly at first, then changes rapidly, and then changes slowly at the end.

All the property animations we have set up change the property from its start state to its end state. Yet here we use the same animations for transitioning from the hide extra widgets state to the show extra widgets state and from the show extra widgets state back to the hide extra widgets state. This works because for both states we have defined property values—for example, in the hide extra widgets state we have set the opacity effect's opacity property to 0.0, and in the show extra widgets state the opacity property is 1.0. So, when the animation takes place it either goes from 0.0 to 1.0 or from 1.0 to 0.0 depending on which transition is taking place, and therefore the animation uses 0.0 (or 1.0) as the start value and 1.0 (or 0.0) as the end value.

```
void FindDialog::createHideExtraWidgetsTransitions()
{
    QSignalTransition *transition =
            showExtraWidgetsState->addTransition(this,
                    SIGNAL(hideExtra()), hideExtraWidgetsState);

    createCommonTransitions(transition);

    QPropertyAnimation *animation = new QPropertyAnimation(this,
                                                    "size");
    animation->setDuration(Duration);
    animation->setEndValue(sizeHint());
    transition->addAnimation(animation);
}
```

The transition from the show extra widgets state to the hide extra widgets state uses the same animations as the transition that goes the opposite way. And in addition, we animate the dialog's size property—this time taking as much time as the widget transitions so that the size doesn't reduce more quickly than the time it takes for the extra widgets to shrink and hide.

As we noted earlier, all property animations operate on QVariants, and the properties concerned must be writable. It is also possible to provide custom interpolators for those QVariant types for which no animation support is currently provided. One approach is to subclass QVariantAnimation (QPropertyAnimation's base class) and reimplement the interpolated() method. Another approach is to implement an interpolation function that takes start and end values of the type we want to interpolate and a qreal progress value, and returns the interpolated value as a QVariant. This function must then be registered using the global qRegisterAnimationInterpolator<>() function.

You might have noticed that Qt does not support interpolation for QFonts, yet we successfully interpolated the extra widgets' font property from one point to the default font size. This was achieved by putting a fontInterpolator() function in the finddialog.cpp file, and registering the function in the FindDialog's constructor.

```
QVariant fontInterpolator(const QFont &start, const QFont &end,
                          qreal progress)
{
    qreal startSize = start.pointSizeF();
    qreal endSize = end.pointSizeF();
    qreal newSize = startSize + ((endSize - startSize) *
                            qBound(0.0, progress, 1.0));
    QFont font(start);
    font.setPointSizeF(newSize);
    return font;
}
```

This interpolator function returns a font whose size ranges from the size of the start font to the size of the end font. The progress value normally ranges from 0.0 to 1.0, but for some easing curves it may have negative values or values greater than 1.0, so we must account for this. Here, we have simply clamped the progress value since negative font sizes don't make sense; we could, however, have used qMax(0.0, progress) to ensure that the font size is always greater than or equal to 0.0 but could be greater than 1.0 times the end font size.

The interpolator function must be registered for it to have any effect. Here's the line that we used in the FindDialog constructor:

```
qRegisterAnimationInterpolator<QFont>(fontInterpolator);
```

The template argument tells Qt that the given function should be used as the interpolation function for objects of the specified type—in this case for QFonts.

We have now completed our review of the Find Dialog. It would be easy to add an effect to the Find button—for example, a blur effect that is animated to turn on when the button is disabled and off when it is enabled. The extra widgets' moving, resizing, and opacity animations work well, but they have one limitation: the widgets retain their essentially rectangular shapes during the transitions. It would have been a lot more attractive if the widgets had deformed—for example, as they went away, having their right-hand ends shrink faster than their left-hand ends to make them funnel shaped during the transitions—a "genie" transition.*

We have now seen how to use the state machine framework for controlling widget states, and how to use it in conjunction with the animation framework to produce smooth visual transitions from one state to another. Using animation effects requires more code (thus introducing more scope for bugs), and consumes more CPU cycles than if they were not used. However, just as modern GUI applications usually feature lots of icons (e.g., in menus and toolbars), more and more applications are using animation effects. And, of course, animations have some very concrete benefits: they can be used to make it much more obvious to users what has happened (e.g., when we animated the alignment of graphics items in the previous section), whereas the user might not even notice an instant change and may try to repeat the operation not realizing that it has already been completed.

---

*For more about genie transitions see labs.qt.nokia.com/blogs/2008/12/15/genie-fx.

Epilogue

This book has presented a broad range of approaches and techniques for Qt programming, although it has concentrated on key areas of Qt's functionality. All of the book's examples—the .hpp and .cpp code files, the .qrc resource files, and the Qt .pro project files—were created and edited using a plain text editor, and *Qt Designer* wasn't used at all. Nowadays, Qt development need not be quite so austere. For those who prefer to design their windows visually, the *Qt Designer* tool is available, and for those who want a complete IDE (Integrated Development Environment), the *Qt Creator* tool (which integrates *Qt Designer*) can be used. For the libraries and basic tools get a standard Qt distribution; for everything—including *Qt Creator*—get the Qt SDK distribution.

Qt contains an enormous amount of functionality, but nonetheless, additional components are available. Some are available from Qt Development Frameworks—for example, the Qt Solutions, many of which are now LGPL licensed. These provide many additional widgets and various utility classes; see qt.nokia.com/products/appdev/add-on-products/catalog/4. There are also third-party component providers. The Qwt library (qwt.sourceforge.net) provides widgets and utility classes of particular use in scientific and engineering applications. The LibQxt library (www.libqxt.org) provides a lot of utility modules and classes including bindings to the Berkeley DB library, and a wide variety of additional widgets. The qt-apps.org web site provides a repository for third-party Qt add-ons, and includes a large collection of components and widgets.

To learn more about Qt, naturally it is worth looking at the wide variety of Qt books now available—Qt Development Frameworks maintains a list of them at qt.nokia.com/developer/books. In addition, ICS (Integrated Computer Solutions, Inc.; www.ics.com/learning/icsnetwork) regularly provides free online video webcasts that explain Qt technologies and provide summaries of what's new in new Qt releases. Most of the talks given at the Qt Development Frameworks annual Qt Developer Days are filmed and viewable online, with the keynotes and technical sessions being particularly interesting (qt.nokia.com/developer/learning/online/talks). Another useful source of Qt information is *Qt Quarterly*, a free online magazine that provides short timely articles on Qt programming (qt.nokia.com/doc/qq/index.html), although for more up to the minute information there is the corporate Qt blog, blog.qt.nokia.com, and even better, the Qt developers' Qt Labs blog, labs.qt.nokia.com/blogs. Questions can be asked on the qt-interest mailing list—this is a very high-traffic list, but it has some really excellent posters—just be sure to check with Google and the documentation first, to avoid being flamed!

Qt Development Frameworks provides a roadmap (qt.nokia.com/developer/ qt-roadmap) that describes where Qt is heading. As might be expected from a Nokia-owned company, the roadmap includes new APIs supporting touch screens and mobile phone-related APIs for messaging and mobile services. But there is also lots of interest for desktop developers.

The biggest new feature, scheduled for release in Qt 4.7, is Qt Quick (Qt User Interface Creation Kit). This will introduce a completely new paradigm for creating user interfaces. Qt Quick uses a JavaScript-based declarative language, QML—Qt Meta-Object Language—that makes full use of the animation and state machine frameworks to provide very slick and easy-to-create user interfaces. Using Qt Quick is much more flexible than the conventional widgets and layouts approach, and makes it really easy to apply animated transformations to widgets. Qt Quick is best for situations where an application needs different user interfaces for different devices and form factors. The traditional QWidgets approach is best for when we want a single user interface design to be used on all targets and that has excellent integration with the platform's native look and feel. So, overall, Qt Quick is ideal for consumer electronics and embedded devices, whereas QWidgets are ideal for desktop applications.

In the medium to long term, there is also a huge amount of work going on in the field of graphics. Considerable efforts are being made to provide a simpler and more Qt-like 3D API as a layer above the OpenGL APIs (which will remain fully accessible), so as to abstract away as much of the complexity and platform specificity of the OpenGL APIs as possible.

Here are a few things that aren't on the roadmap, that perhaps should be. The undo/redo framework ought to be fully integrated with the model/view architecture. At present it isn't easy to provide undo/redo for models and even when it is achieved, we must be careful to use our own methods for certain operations rather than the usual ones, to keep the undo/redo working correctly. Another thing that would be nice to see is improved database support. At present no Qt widget understands NULL values, and the database support feels like it has been rather awkwardly squeezed to fit the model/view architecture. Also, database behavior, particularly regarding SQLite, seems to change in subtle ways even between minor releases. Let's hope that future Qt versions improve in this area. On a more positive note, the Item Views NG (Next Generation) project seems to be making steady progress, and is on its way to being more powerful, more flexible, and yet easier to use than the current model/view architecture—and by the time you read this, it might be ready for prime time.

A few more "blue sky"—and personal—wishes for a future Qt would be the addition of a PDF API that supports the reading, editing, and writing of PDF files, and that covers every PDF feature. It would also be nice if Qt provided a similar API for reading and editing Open Document Format files, as well as improving the writing of files in this format. Support for reading and writing the most common archive formats would be useful—especially .tar files (including those compressed with `gzip` or `bzip2`), and `.zip` files (for which Qt already has internal APIs, at least for writing). It would also be nice to see Qt increasing its support of larger environments—for example, with high-level APIs to support client–server programming. And, of course, more widgets would be welcome, particularly 2D and 3D graph widgets that would make Qt more convenient for scientific and engineering users out of the box. For Qt 5, it would be nice to see the Meta-Object Compiler being dropped. The Boost libraries have already shown that it is possible to implement a signals and slots mechanism and a property system using standard C++, but whether it is possible to implement all of (or enough of) Qt's object model remains an open question.

Of course, it is no longer necessary to wait for the Qt developers to add the features that we want. Qt is now developed in a more open way than ever before, so if there is a feature you would like added, you can implement it yourself and try to get it merged into the official version of Qt: see `qt.gitorious.org` for details.

Qt is a superb software development framework that has seen a huge investment by Nokia to improve and extend the functionality it offers. Qt can be used for non-GUI programming, including servers, web backends, and command line tools; and for GUI programming, supporting applications that have sophisticated, attractive, and highly dynamic user interfaces. Qt can be used on embedded devices—anything from toasters to mobile phones and PDAs—through to desktop systems and way beyond.

Qt's huge size can be daunting, but once the fundamentals are learned, Qt's API consistency makes it straightforward to learn whatever other classes and modules are relevant to your needs. The excellent documentation, Qt's examples' and demos' source code, books such as this, the online resources mentioned above, training courses, and, of course, Qt's own source code should be sufficient for anyone's learning needs. And unlike some platform-specific libraries we could mention, Qt makes programming a pleasure, allowing us to develop on the platform of our choice, and to deploy on the platforms our users prefer.

Selected Bibliography

The Art of Multiprocessor Programming

Maurice Herlihy and Nir Shavit (Morgan Kaufmann, 2008, ISBN 978-0123705914)

This book provides a thorough introduction to multithreaded programming, including small but complete working examples (in Java) that demonstrate all the key techniques. The last chapter provides a brief introduction to transactional memory, one of the hopes for a higher-level approach to threading that doesn't burden programmers with all the petty bookkeeping details that conventional techniques demand.

C++ GUI Programming with Qt 4, Second Edition

Jasmin Blanchette and Mark Summerfield (Prentice Hall, 2008, ISBN 0132354160)

This is the ideal introduction to C++/Qt programming, and a perfect complement to the Qt documentation. The book teaches C++ programmers how to make the best use of Qt's classes and modules to create complete applications. This is the official Qt textbook.

C++ in a Nutshell

Ray Lischner (O'Reilly, 2003, ISBN 059600298X)

This very useful book provides a solid, compact, and comprehensive reference to the C++ language and its standard libraries (including the C libraries that are part of the C++ standard).

The C++ Programming Language, Third Edition

Bjarne Stroustrup (Addison-Wesley, 2000, ISBN 0201889544)

This is the standard C++ text written by the creator of C++. It serves as a useful reference.

Clean Code

Robert C. Martin (Prentice Hall, 2009, ISBN 0132350882)

This book addresses many of the "tactical" issues in programming: good naming, function design, refactoring, and similar. The book has many interesting and useful ideas that should help any programmer improve their coding style and make their programs more maintainable. (The book's examples are in Java.)

Code Complete: A Practical Handbook of Software Construction, Second Edition
Steve McConnell (Microsoft Press, 2004, ISBN 0735619670)
This book shows how to build solid software, going beyond the language specifics into the realms of ideas, principles, and practices. The book is packed with ideas that will make any programmer think more deeply about their programming.

Design Patterns
Erich Gamma, Richard Helm, Ralph Johnson, and John Vlissides (Addison-Wesley, 1998, ISBN 0201633612)
One of the most influential programming books of modern times, even if it isn't always easy to read. The design patterns are fascinating and of great practical use in everyday programming.

Domain-Driven Design
Eric Evans (Addison-Wesley, 2004, ISBN 0321125215)
A very interesting book on software design, particularly useful for large multi-person projects. At heart it is about creating and refining domain models that represent what the system is designed to do, and about creating a ubiquitous language through which all those involved with the system—not just software engineers—can communicate their ideas.

Effective C++, Third Edition
Scott Meyers (Addison-Wesley, 2005, ISBN 0321334876)
This book is essential reading for any C++ programmer. It describes many subtle pitfalls and explains lots of good practices.

GUI Bloopers 2.0
Jeff Johnson (Morgan Kaufmann, 2008, ISBN 9780123706430)
Don't be put off by the slightly whimsical title; this is a serious book that every GUI programmer should read. You won't agree with every single suggestion, but you will think more carefully and with more insight about user interface design after reading this book.

JavaScript: The Definitive Guide, Fifth Edition
David Flanagan (O'Reilly, 2006, ISBN 9780596101992)
This is an ideal tutorial and reference for JavaScript/ECMAScript, and is deservedly the book that the Qt documentation recommends for learning QtScript. It will also be of use to those learning the Qt Quick QML language that will be introduced in Qt 4.7.

The Little Manual of API Design
Jasmin Blanchette (Trolltech/Nokia, 2009)
This very short document (www4.in.tum.de/~blanchet/api-design.pdf) provides ideas and insight into the design of APIs, and draws most of its examples from Qt.

Mastering Regular Expressions, Third Edition
> Jeffrey E. F. Friedl (O'Reilly, 2006, ISBN 0596528124)
> This is the standard text on regular expressions—a very interesting and useful book.

Rapid GUI Programming with Python and Qt
> Mark Summerfield (Prentice Hall, 2007, ISBN 0132354187)
> This book teaches PyQt4 programing, probably the easiest route into Qt programming generally. PyQt can be used to create applications in their own right, and can also be used as a prototyping tool for C++/Qt programs.

Index

All non-global functions and methods are listed under their class (or their class's base class—which could be QWidget *or* QObject*), and as top-level terms in their own right. Where a method or function name is close enough to a concept, the concept is not usually listed. For example, there is no entry for "joining a string list", but there are entries for the* QString::join() *method. Note also that many references are purely to quoted code (i.e., to show examples of use).*

Symbols

A

long double, converting to string, 281

M

Mac OS X
    platform differences, 26, 61, 211, 378
    sheets, 61
magic numbers, 72, 106
main window; *see* QMainWindow
main window startup policy, 133
mainFrame() (QWebPage), 39, 41
mapFromGlobal() (QWidget), 427
mapped() (QtConcurrent), 281, 282
mappers, 262, 281–286
mapToGlobal() (QWidget), 349
mapToScene() (QGraphicsView), 427
matchedLength() (QRegExp), 340
Matrix Quiz example, 44–52
max_element() (std), 431, 432
MD5 (Message-Digest algorithm 5), 302
media data sources, devices, and nodes, 63
    see also audio and video
media path, 64
menus
    creating context, 12, 344, 349
    creating popup, 29
mergeBlockCharFormat() (QTextCursor), 329
mergeBlockFormat() (QTextCursor), 329, 368
mergeCharFormat() (QTextCursor), 330, 368
mergeCurrentCharFormat() (QTextEdit), 348
meta-data, audio, 71
metaObject() (QObject), 419, 423, 439
method invocation, 134
method pointer, 137
mid()
    QList, 150, 183, 252, 253, 258, 285, 309

mid() *(cont.)*
    QString, 13
MIME types, 71, 72, 159, 169, 428
    see also QMimeData
mimeData()
    QAbstractItemModel, 159, 169
    QClipboard, 429, 438
mimeTypes() (QAbstractItemModel), 159, 169
min_element() (std), 431, 432
minimumSizeHint() (QWidget), 232, 236, 350, 441, 486, 487
.mng (files), 53
modal (window-modal) dialogs, 356
modal dialogs, 61
model index; *see* QModelIndex
modeless dialogs, 102
models
    class hierarchy, 89
    creation policy, 112
    custom vs. QStandardItemModel, 112
    deleting rows, 99–100
    filtering, 99
    for combobox, 93
    for views, 95
    kinds of, 89
    mapping selection model indexes, 100
    non-string data, 99, 106, 186
    proxy, 92, 93
    proxy source model, 94
    resizable, 116, 123, 125, 158
    selecting items in, 97
    sorting, 111, 312
    see also QAbstractItemModel, QItemSelectionModel, and QSortFilterProxyModel
ModelTest, 114–115, 135
model/view classes; *see* QAbstractItemModel and QAbstractItemView
modules
    Phonon, 60, 72, 85
    QtCore, 20, 348

About the Author

Mark Summerfield

Mark is a computer science graduate with many years of experience working in the software industry, primarily as a programmer. He also spent almost three years as Trolltech's documentation manager during which he founded and edited Trolltech's technical journal, *Qt Quarterly*. (Trolltech is now Nokia's Qt Development Frameworks.) Mark is the coauthor of *C++ GUI Programming with Qt 4* (with Jasmin Blanchette), and author of *Rapid GUI Programming with Python and Qt: The Definitive Guide to PyQt Programming*, and *Programming in Python 3: A Complete Introduction to the Python Language*. Mark owns Qtrac Ltd., www.qtrac.eu, where he works as an independent consultant, programmer, author, editor, and trainer, specializing in C++, Qt, Python, and PyQt.

Production

The text was written using the gvim text editor and marked up with the Lout typesetting language. All the diagrams were produced using Lout. The index was compiled by the author. All of the code snippets were automatically extracted directly from the example programs and from test programs. The text and source code were version-controlled using Bazaar. The monospaced font used for code is derived from a condensed version of DejaVu Mono and was modified using FontForge. Some of the images are from the Open Clip Art Library and some are from Wikimedia Commons; most of the icons used are those that come with Qt or are from KDE. The marked-up text was previewed using gv, and especially evince, and converted to PostScript by Lout, then to PDF by Ghostscript. The cover was provided by the publisher.

All the editing and processing were done on Ubuntu and Fedora systems. All the example programs have been tested on Windows, Linux, and Mac OS X using Qt 4.6 and where possible Qt 4.5 (e.g., using #if QT_VERSION).

4.6.1

More from
Mark Summerfield

Rapid GUI Programming with Python and Qt

Mark Summerfield | ISBN-13: 978-0-13-235418-9

The Insider's Best-Practice Guide to
Rapid PyQt 4 GUI Development

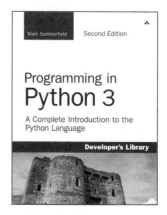

Programming in Python 3, Second Edition

Mark Summerfield | ISBN-13: 978-0-321-68056-3

A Fully Revised Edition Featuring New Material
on Coroutines, Debugging, Testing, Parsing,
String Formatting, and More

C++ GUI Programming with Qt 4, Second Edition

Jasmin Blanchette, Mark Summerfield | ISBN-13: 978-0-13-235416-5

The Only Official, Best-Practice Guide to
Qt 4.3 Programming

These titles are available in both print and electronic formats.

For more information and to read sample material, please visit informit.com.

Titles are also available at safari.informit.com.